School and Society

Historical and Contemporary Perspectives

School and Society

Historical and Contemporary Perspectives

Seventh Edition

Steven E. Tozer
University of Illinois, Chicago

Guy Senese
Northern Arizona University

Paul C. Violas
Late of University of Illinois,
Urbana-Champaign

The McGraw-Hill Companies

Connect
Learn
Succeed™

SCHOOL AND SOCIETY: HISTORICAL AND CONTEMPORARY PERSPECTIVES, SEVENTH EDITION

Published by McGraw-Hill, a business unit of The McGraw-Hill Companies, Inc., 1221 Avenue of the Americas, New York, NY, 10020. Copyright © 2013 by The McGraw-Hill Companies, Inc. All rights reserved. Printed in the United States of America. Previous editions © 2009, 2006, and 2002. No part of this publication may be reproduced or distributed in any form or by any means, or stored in a database or retrieval system, without the prior written consent of The McGraw-Hill Companies, Inc., including, but not limited to, in any network or other electronic storage or transmission, or broadcast for distance learning.

Some ancillaries, including electronic and print components, may not be available to customers outside the United States.

This book is printed on acid-free paper.

1 2 3 4 5 6 7 8 9 0 QVR/QVR 1 0 9 8 7 6 5 4 3 2

ISBN: 978-0-07-802440-5
MHID: 0-07-802440-4

Senior Vice President, Products & Markets: *Kurt L. Strand*
Vice President, General Manager, Products & Markets: *Michael Ryan*
Director: *Michael Sugarman*
Brand Manager: *Allison McNamara*
Executive Director of Development: *Lisa Pinto*
Managing Development Editor: *Penina Braffman*
Editorial Coordinator: *Adina Lonn*
Marketing Specialist: *Alexandra Schultz*
Senior Project Manager: *Lisa A. Bruflodt*
Buyer: *Laura Fuller*
Cover Designer: *Studio Montage, St. Louis, MO*
Cover Image: *Library of Congress Prints and Photographs Division [LC-USZ62-90603]; Ron Nickel/Design Pics/Getty Images*
Media Project Manager: *Sridevi Palani*
Typeface: *10.5/12 Garamond*
Compositor: *Laserwords Private Limited*
Printer: *Quad/Graphics*

All credits appearing on page or at the end of the book are considered to be an extension of the copyright page.

Library of Congress Cataloging-in-Publication Data

Tozer, Steven.
School and society : historical and contemporary perspectives / Steven E. Tozer, Guy Senese, Paul C. Violas.—7th ed.
    p. cm.
ISBN: 978-0-07-802440-5 (alk. paper)
1. Educational sociology—United States. 2. Education—United States—History. I. Senese, Guy B. II. Violas, Paul C. III. Title.
LC191.4.T69 2012
306.43'20973—dc23

2012026260

The Internet addresses listed in the text were accurate at the time of publication. The inclusion of a website does not indicate an endorsement by the authors or McGraw-Hill, and McGraw-Hill does not guarantee the accuracy of the information presented at these sites.

www.mhhe.com

We dedicate this book to two historians of education who have influenced us and countless others

Clarence J. Karier and Paul C. Violas

About the Authors

Steven E. Tozer is Professor of Education in the College of Education at the University of Illinois, Chicago, where for 10 years he has taught preservice and graduate-level courses in Social Foundations of Education and Education Leadership. He formerly taught at the University of Illinois, Urbana-Champaign, for 12 years, serving as the Head of the Department of Curriculum and Instruction from 1990 to 1994. He taught the preservice course in Social Foundations for eight years, receiving the college and campus awards for Excellence in Undergraduate Instruction.

Professor Tozer has been Chair of the Committee on Academic Standards and Accreditation for the American Education Studies Association and President of the Council for Social Foundations of Education. He also served on the Board of Examiners for the National Council for Accreditation of Teacher Education. He has written for such journals as *Education Theory, Education Studies, Educational Foundations,* and *Teachers College Record* and is coeditor of two books in social foundations.

Professor Tozer completed his A.B. in German at Dartmouth College, his M.Ed. in Elementary and Early Childhood Education at Loyola University of Chicago, and his Ph.D. in Philosophy of Education at the University of Illinois, Urbana-Champaign. He has taught at the early childhood, elementary, and secondary levels.

Guy Senese is Professor of Foundations and Educational Leadership in the College of Education at Northern Arizona University, Flagstaff. He taught for 11 years in Social Foundations and Philosophy of Education at Northern Illinois University. He received his Ph.D. in Educational Policy Studies and his M.A. in Social Studies Education at the University of Illinois, Urbana-Champaign (UIUC). He received a baccalaureate in Philosophy at Northern Illinois University. He taught high school at the Rough Rock Demonstration School on the Navajo reservation in Arizona. He also served as Title One program specialist for the Illinois State Board of Education. He has written in the fields of social philosophy and multicultural curriculum, Native American education, critical theory, and cultural studies in education. Professor Senese is a coauthor of *Simulation, Spectacle and the Ironies of Education Reform* and author of *Self-Determination and the Social Education of Native Americans* and *Throwing Voices: Five Autoethnographies on Postradical Education and the Fine Art of Misdirection.* He has also published in *Educational Theory, Journal of Thought, Educational Foundations,* and *Harvard Educational Review.* He is past president of the Midwest History of Education Society.

Until his death in 1999, **Paul C. Violas** was Professor of History of Education in the College of Education at the University of Illinois, Urbana-Champaign. During his last decade as a teacher, he received the College of Education Award for Excellence in Undergraduate Teaching, the College Career Teaching Award, and the University's Luckman Award for Undergraduate Teaching. During the 1970s, with the aid of his graduate students, he designed the social foundations of education course on which this text is based. More than 40 of his former advisees and graduate assistants have gone on to teach at colleges and universities in the United States and Europe.

Professor Violas received his baccalaureate and master's degrees in history at the University of Rochester, where he later received his Ed.D. degree. He taught secondary school social studies for six years before embarking on his career in higher education. In addition to teaching and lecturing assignments in England and Greece, he served for six years as Associate Dean of Graduate and Undergraduate programs at the College of Education, University of Illinois, Urbana-Champaign. He was a regular contributor to such journals as *Education Theory, Teachers College Record, Harvard Education Review,* and *The History Teacher.* He was also the coauthor of *Roots of Crisis* and the author of *The Training of the Urban Working Class.*

Brief Contents

Contents

Chapter 4
Social Diversity and Differentiated Schooling: The Progressive Era   82

Chapter 5
Diversity and Equity: Schooling Girls and Women   124

Chapter 6
Diversity and Equity: Schooling and African Americans   156

Part Two
Educational Aims in Contemporary Society   251

Chapter 9
Liberty and Literacy Today: Contemporary Perspectives   252

Primary Source Reading

Chapter 10
Teaching in a Public Institution: The Professionalization Movement   288

Primary Source Reading

Chapter 11
Differentiated Schooling, Labor Market Preparation, and Contemporary School Reform: The Post–Cold War Era   324

Preface

School and Society: Historical and Contemporary Perspectives, seventh edition, is designed for courses in teacher education and school leadership commonly labeled School and Society, Social Foundations of Education, History and Philosophy of Education, or simply Foundations of Education. Such courses may be offered at the introductory or at more advanced levels in professional preparation programs, at undergraduate or graduate levels. Their purpose is to help prepare educators who are able to reflect critically on their teaching practices in social and institutional contexts. With this in mind, we built the following features into our text.

Historical-Contemporary Analysis

Understanding contemporary educational ideas and processes, we believe, requires an understanding of their historical origins: how and why they first arose and then developed into their present forms. For this reason history plays a central role throughout this work. In Part 1 we analyze the relationships among the political economy, the prevailing ideology, and the educational practices of each major period in the development of American public education. For each period we show how the intersection of these forces influenced one or more perennial issues in education that still confront us early in the 21st century.

While Part 1 examines perennial school-society issues in terms of their historical origins in American history, Part 2 provides a contemporary analysis of the same issues by discussing such questions as, What is the relationship between liberty and literacy? What are the purposes of public education in a democratic society? To what degree can schools promote social equality? Who decides what the school's curriculum should be—teachers, administrators, or someone else? Thus, each enduring issue receives a two-part historical-contemporary examination. The result is a highly integrated text, in which each chapter in Part 1 has a corresponding chapter or chapters in Part 2.

Diversity-Equity Focus

Today's educators must confront the still-unresolved question of how to provide an increasingly diverse school population with an education that is of equitably high quality. Consequently, we have made this issue a major focus of our text. In Part 1, we examine the histories of four educationally underserved groups in this country: the working class, women, African Americans, and Native Americans. Then, in Part 2, we analyze the educational status of these and other underserved groups in contemporary America. The related themes of diversity and equity (racial, ethnic, cultural, language, gender, and ability) constitute possibly the most important tension facing schools in the 21st century. Consequently, we have given it heavy emphasis, from the Chapter 1 introduction to Athenian ideals of democracy to the last chapter on contemporary cultural influences on children and youth.

Critical Thinking Skills and Primary Sources

Since good teachers must be able to think critically in and about their practice, we wanted to produce a text that actively promotes critical thinking skills. This text does so by (1) providing the basic conceptual tools needed for analytical inquiry, (2) demonstrating their use throughout the text, and (3) providing readers with opportunities to practice critical analysis as they read primary sources for themselves.

Consequently, we have structured our text as follows. First, Chapter 1 presents six analytic concepts (social theory, political economy, schooling, training, education, and ideology) that we have found to be especially useful in understanding American public education. Next, we have systematically demonstrated their usefulness by organizing chapter narratives around them. Both the historical chapters in Part 1 and the contemporary chapters in Part 2 utilize these concepts.

Finally, at the end of each chapter, we have provided primary source readings that students are asked to critically evaluate. In short, each chapter models the analytical use of these terms, while end-of-chapter readings and questions provide an opportunity for their use. *In fact, it is our hope that reflective readers will use their own experiences and viewpoints to challenge the authors' analyses whenever there seems cause to do so.* In the seventh edition we have again included questions for critical thinking in each chapter.

In each edition we seek to improve the quality of the primary source readings. The few changes we have made in this edition are designed to fulfill an important function that is lost when primary source readings are overlooked by students or instructors: These original selections provide students with a chance to exercise their interpretive and critical abilities in a way that they would not be able to do without having read the chapter. Thus, the primary source readings become a unique interactive opportunity for applying and testing new understanding and developing new critical insights that go well beyond the authors' analysis. By focusing students' attention on the original voices of historical and contemporary educators, including teachers, this volume gives students a chance not only to think critically about those educators' views but to apply the same critical skills to their reading of the authors' voices in the 14 chapters of the textbook.

Text Integration

Rather than producing a text of independent chapters on discrete topics in education, we have produced one that is highly integrated. We have already described two of the primary mechanisms used to accomplish this: (1) the use of persistently bedeviling educational problems as a device for integrating the book's historical and contemporary parts and (2) the use of end-of-chapter readings as vehicles for applying (and thereby mastering) the analytic terms. In addition, the analytic framework used throughout the text, especially the political–economic and ideological discussions, provides integrative threads rarely found in foundations texts. We have strengthened the application of the analytic framework throughout the text, as described below.

Text Features

- **Building a Philosophy of Education feature.** Beginning in Chapter 1 with an examination of Aristotle on education and concluding in Chapter 14 with an examination of contemporary influences on youth, readers are helped to develop their own philosophies of education. Each chapter concludes with a section that highlights chapter content germane to educational philosophy. This section challenges educators to shape their educational goals and methods, and their justifications for both, in today's cultural context.

- **The analytic framework model** helps students understand and integrate the relationships among ideology, political economy, and schooling in each chapter. This feature appears at the beginning of each chapter to help students organize their reading and analysis.

- **A historical timeline** in each chapter allows students to see at a glance some of the major cultural events that provide context for the educational issues under discussion. All timelines for the seventh edition have been made more concise and more closely tied to chapter content. Students are asked to examine the timelines interpretively, critically examining how various historical events relate to education and schooling.

- **Thinking Critically about the Issues** boxes, distributed throughout the text, are designed to stimulate students' interpretive, critical thought about what they are reading.

- **Developing Your Professional Vocabulary** boxes present new terms from the field of social foundations of education, accompanied by a glossary of professional terms at the back of the book.

Supplements

- **Online Learning Center.** The Online Learning Center, at www.mhhe.com/tozer7e, includes a study guide (with quizzes), Web links, and extending resources.

- **Instructor's Online Learning Center.** Located at www.mhhe.com/tozer7e, the Instructor's Online Learning Center contains teaching resources including Instructor's Manual, Test Bank, and computerized test bank.

- *Only* **a Teacher Video Series.** *School and Society* is accompanied by the *Only* **a Teacher Video** series, produced and directed by Claudia Levin, as shown on PBS. *Only* **a Teacher** is the first documentary to explore the diverse faces and many roles of the American teacher from the 1820s to the present day. The program takes the form of a dialogue between past and present, as contemporary teachers reflect on many of the issues that have confronted their predecessors over the past 180 years. The series combines thoughtful commentary, teacher interviews, and classroom footage with archival materials to convey teachers' experiences and attitudes about their work.

  The series contains three one-hour segments:

- Episode One, **A Teacher Affects Eternity,** begins during the Common-School Era (1830s–1880s), as free public schooling spread across the expanding nation and women began to fill out the ranks of teachers. This program explores the ongoing importance of teachers in the lives of their students, emphasizing their crucial influence as role models and upholders of society's norms.

- Episode Two, **Those Who Can . . . Teach,** considers teachers in their profession, tracing the early development of school bureaucracies and the attendant rise of teachers' unions. This episode also looks at teacher training, salaries, and working conditions, and exposes America's ambivalence toward a profession practiced mostly by women.

- Episode Three, **Educating to End Inequity,** delves into teachers' efforts to level the educational—and social—playing field for their students.

For more information on this series, please visit www.pbs.org/onlyateacher.

Acknowledgments

This book originated in Educational Policy Studies 201, a required undergraduate course in social foundations of education at the University of Illinois in Urbana-Champaign. The course was originally designed by Paul Violas and his graduate students in 1975 and was subsequently modified by Steve Tozer and his graduate teaching assistants from 1982 to 1990. Consequently, a great many doctoral students have contributed over the years to developing that course and the early editions of this text.

Our most important partners in this effort have been those who wrote chapters for our first edition in their areas of expertise: James Anderson, Chapter 7; Steve Preskill, Chapter 5; Kal Alston, Chapter 10; and Robert Carson, Chapter 13. These faculty members, all of whom once taught or currently are teaching at the University of Illinois at Urbana-Champaign, drafted a third of the original volume and gave it a depth of insight it would not otherwise have had. Steve Preskill revised Chapter 5 for the fifth edition. Finally, we are grateful for the patient and persistent help provided by our colleagues at McGraw-Hill, including Sarah Kiefer, Amanda Peabody, and Allison McNamara.

Steven E. Tozer
Guy Senese

Part One

Educational Aims
in Historical Perspective

Introduction Understanding School and Society

Chapter Overview

Chapter 1 introduces students to the basic analytic vocabulary, or "tools of inquiry," used throughout *School and Society,* emphasizing why *social context* is important to consider if we want to understand schooling. The chapter challenges the common view that *theory* and *practice* are opposites, arguing instead that good social theory seeks to describe and explain the real world, including the world of practice. It also presents the three-part *analytic framework,* or organizing ideas, used throughout the book, in which the terms "political economy," "ideology," and "schooling" are understood as social phenomena that influence one another. To illustrate how the analytic framework can be used to interpret the way school and society relate to each other, a brief sketch of classical Athens is presented. This example raises the question of *why* teachers need to study the history, philosophy, and social context of education—and how such study applies to teaching practices. Finally, the special relationship between democratic values and educational practice is introduced— a relationship that will be explored throughout the volume.

In classical Athens, education was the birthright of the citizen, to be pursued throughout life.

Chapter Objectives

Among the objectives that Chapter 1 seeks to achieve are these:

1. Readers should become acquainted with the basic conceptual tools used throughout the book, especially political economy, ideology, and schooling. They should begin to understand how they influence one another, although that influence is not of equal proportion and varies from situation to situation.

2. By entertaining the view that good theorizing explains practical phenomena and therefore can guide practice, readers should begin to question the idea that theory and practice are opposed to one another, or the idea that if something is theoretical, it probably is not practical.

3. This chapter presents basic distinctions among schooling, training, and education. Readers should recognize that *education* is a value-laden ideal that allows one to evaluate schooling and training practices for their *educational* worth.

4. The classical Athenian period presents the opportunity for interpreting relationships among political economy, ideology, and schooling practices. The chapter illustrates how these basic tools of inquiry operate in historical cultural contexts different from ours.

5. Readers should begin considering the meanings and limitations of the concept of democracy in cultural context. The chapter invites readers to notice the egalitarian impulses of an Athenian society that selected legislators by lottery and to reflect critically on how a "democratic" culture can exclude most of its residents from political participation.

6. Readers are invited to begin thinking about the idea of a philosophy of education and the extent to which they already are developing such a philosophy.

7. Finally, a major purpose of this chapter is to equip each reader with "new eyes" with which to read and critically interpret the Primary Source Reading from Aristotle's *Politics*.

Introduction: Conducting Inquiry into School and Society

The public schools are perhaps the most familiar but least understood institutions in our society. Most Americans spend over 12 years attending public schools and later, as adults, confront a wide array of school-related issues. School board elections, school tax referendums, PTA meetings, and their children's school experiences all require immediate personal attention.

Individuals and the mass media often express concern about the overall quality of the public school system. Is it equipping the young to support themselves in a changing economy? Is it promoting an equitable society by educating all our students? Is it equipping them with the skills and attitudes needed to live in a society that is increasingly diverse and pluralistic? Is it teaching them to respect and protect an increasingly endangered environment? In short, how well does our nation's public school system serve the major needs of our society?

These are complicated questions open to competing interpretations, and not just any interpretation will do. Schools are complex institutions with varied and intricate relationships to their surrounding communities, and a great deal of scholarship has been conducted in an effort to understand these relationships. Explaining why children from some social and economic groups tend to perform better than others in schools, for example, may need to rely on a variety of historical, sociological, and theoretical arguments that most editorial writers and newspaper readers don't have at hand. Such explanations are not a part of commonsense knowledge, but they can and should be a part of a teacher's professional expertise.

The development of such professional levels of interpretation and understanding is a major purpose of this text. Achieving such understanding, however, requires that students engage not in "learning the text" but in actively inquiring into important questions about the purposes and consequences of education and schooling.

The Place of Social Foundations in Teacher Education

You may well think, "That's all very interesting, but how is it going to make me a better teacher? Wouldn't it be better to spend this time studying methods that are successful in today's classrooms?"

While study and practice of teaching methods are a central part of teacher preparation, methods make sense only in particular social contexts and to achieve specific goals. These goals, for students and for the wider society, are not always agreed upon. In the last analysis, teachers must make decisions about goals and methods for themselves. How to educate teachers to make the best decisions on these matters has long been a topic of debate.

In the 1930s, for example, teacher educators at Teachers College, Columbia University, began developing a new program of study for school teachers and administrators called "social foundations of education." Rather than have teachers and administrators study such fields as philosophy of education, history of education, and sociology of education in isolation from one another, the scholars at Teachers College believed that school practitioners would benefit most if they integrated the study of all these fields around perennial school–society issues. Who should be educated? What knowledge and values should be taught? Who should control the curriculum and for what purposes? When, where, and how should education be delivered? To study such issues, they believed, required historical perspective, philosophical insights, and sociological knowledge. The problems to be understood, they reasoned, were multidimensional and did not fit neatly into any one of those disciplines. To study schooling required studying the social underpinnings (social foundations) of education, and they believed that the better teachers understood the larger society in which schools are embedded, the better they would understand the particular school problems they faced. The schools, in their view, were an important *expression* of the surrounding society—expressing its political and economic systems as well as its ideological commitments.[1]

The authors of this text share this view. It is our conviction that teachers should have the best possible understanding of the relations between their schools and the larger society in which those schools are embedded. We think teachers need more than *training* in how to deliver a set curriculum or technique, though such training (like medical or music training for doctors and musicians) is necessary and valuable. Teachers also need to be *educated* as critical thinkers who have the ability to diagnose unique and complicated situations and create original solutions to these problems (more on training versus education shortly). Such professional education should take place in all components of a teacher education program.

We believe that one central purpose of studying social foundations of education is to equip teachers to make sense of classroom situations by understanding the larger social context that surrounds and shapes what goes on in classrooms. Another central purpose, therefore, is to think critically about the multiple purposes and values that schools and teachers serve in society, and how teachers can make ethical choices about whose interests their work will serve.

Study in the social foundations of education, then, provides background information about school–society relationships that helps teachers contextualize classroom events and thereby enables them better to understand and adjust their teaching practices. For example, unless you understand the effects that school culture can have on students from minority cultures in the United States, you may not be able to discriminate between a child with a learning disability and a child whose home culture differs so markedly from that of the school that he or she encounters academic and social adjustment problems. When is it fair to have different educational goals for different students, and when might different goals categorize students and lead to discriminatory practices on the part of teachers or other students?

The purpose of this book is, in part, to give you practice in thinking through issues such as these. By reflectively engaging such social and educational issues (including their historical origins), you will be developing as an educational thinker and decision maker whose ability to define and solve school problems is more highly developed than that of the everyday citizen who has not received such specialized education. Two examples will illustrate these points.

The Meaning of Democracy in Educational Practice

One illustration of how teachers can apply social foundations knowledge to their teaching practice concerns the aims of teaching. Teachers typically accept the notion that a major goal of teaching is to prepare citizens for life in a democratic society, and most teachers believe that their teaching contributes to achieving this goal. Yet college students preparing to teach are rarely given an opportunity to engage in a sustained study of what life in a democratic society really means or how to go about educating students for participation in such a society. To understand the meaning of democracy and to fit students for life in a democratic society require careful analysis. It is obvious, for example, that school systems

in all cultures seek to fit people to their surrounding societies. It is not so obvious, however, that in a democratic society this process should involve equipping people to think critically about the degree to which their society is in fact democratic and to participate effectively in overcoming its undemocratic aspects. Thus, to prepare students for participation in a democratic society, a teacher may have to consider how well his or her choice of teaching and management strategies fosters critical thinking and active political participation.

Similarly, the classical notion that the moral basis of democracy is not only fairness or even equality but human development through participation in decision making needs to be explored. Consideration of this point might lead a democratically oriented teacher toward a policy of greater student participation in problem solving and classroom decision making, in which students are encouraged to learn from their mistakes. Whether a classroom is more student-centered or teacher-centered often stems from the teacher's belief concerning this basic issue.

Such sustained inquiry into democratic ideals might well lead prospective teachers to modify their teaching goals and then identify classroom problems differently than before. For example, whereas an obedient and unquestioning classroom might have seemed desirable at one time, that orderliness might seem alarming in a classroom focused on student development through shared decision making. One important goal of this book is to provide you with the opportunity to rethink what democracy means in practice and then reevaluate your teaching goals and methods accordingly.

Education of Diverse Students

A second illustration concerns problems confronting teachers in multicultural classrooms. Teachers are increasingly called upon to teach students who are racially or ethnically different from themselves and to recognize that students of all races have the same academic potential. Yet new teachers' experiences seem at first to tell them otherwise. How can they avoid stereotyping certain groups as more or less academically able when they see significant differences in academic performance and attitudes toward school?

To understand and nurture the learning potential of *all* students, teachers need to understand the influences that culture and social class exert on both students and schools. The differences in the performance of various ethnic groups in this nation's schools have historical and sociolinguistic dimensions. In the case of African American students, for example, teachers need to understand how schools have systematically discriminated against African American children and realize that Black English vernacular is not indicative of impaired intellectual ability to learn standard English. They also need to understand that students from lower socioeconomic classes and lower-achieving ethnic groups tend to engage in resistant behaviors as they encounter a school environment that they sometimes experience as hostile. Well-informed teachers could then respond to those resistance strategies not as behavior problems but as intelligent yet counterproductive responses to school culture. Teachers who have studied the social contexts of schooling are able to view old school problems with new eyes and, as a result, approach those problems with fresh ideas and open minds.

To summarize, prospective teachers need to recognize that problems in classroom learning are inevitably embedded in the broader social and cultural contexts that surround their schools and classrooms. Perceptions of gender differences, racial and ethnic attitudes, school organization and culture, social class differences, and prevailing ideologies are only some of the factors teachers need to study to understand their workplace. Failure to understand these factors inevitably impairs their ability to interpret school and classroom events and consequently to construct meaningful solutions to perennial problems.

Tools of Inquiry

This text uses six main tools of inquiry to assist students in developing critical understandings of school and society: social theory, schooling, training, education, political economy, and ideology. Each will be examined, and then the three most fundamental ideas will be arranged into an analytic framework. Later in the Chapter we discuss the important case of education in Classical Athens, as both an illustration of early democratic theory, practice and for its importance as a classic model of education which influenced our current school forms and education theory. The following chapters will use this analytic framework to examine the evolution of American public schools (Part 1 of this textbook) and some of the most significant contemporary issues facing the public school system (Part 2).

Social Theory

The term "theory" is often scorned by critics of higher education, as if college education were "too theoretical." Frequently, educators in public schools and colleges of education proclaim that they are interested in "practice," not "theory." Such announcements should make us pause to consider what the term "theory" means. It does not have a complex meaning. Very simply, a theory is an interpretation and explanation of phenomena. A social theory is an attempt to make sense of and explain social phenomena. A theory attempts to answer the questions how and why. It is not something separate from "reality" and "practice"; rather, it attempts to explain reality and practice. Thus, to say that we are not interested in theory is to say that we are not interested in knowing how or why something occurs.

We might be interested, for example, in the rise in public school attendance during the past century. Why did increasing percentages of American children attend school for increasing lengths of time? One explanation (i.e., theory) is that the increase reflected the rise in democratic sentiment and greater potential for social mobility in the United States. An alternative theory emphasizes economic factors, such as the decreased dependence on child labor on farms and in factories, accompanied by the need for adult workers with specialized skills (e.g., clerical training) and workforce behaviors (e.g., punctuality).

These potentially conflicting theories raise an important question: How do we judge theories? Is it simply a matter of opinion or personal taste? If there were not adequate ways to evaluate theories, those who assert that they are not interested in theory might be on sounder ground. Fortunately, there are criteria and procedures we can use to intelligently accept or reject a theory. First, we ask whether the theory is internally consistent. That is, are there contradictions within the theory? If so, the explanatory power of the theory is weakened. Second, how well does the theory account for the data (i.e., information) we have amassed about what we are trying to understand? Few theories, if any, will be able to account for all the data; nevertheless, the more data it can account for, the better the theory. Third, how well does a theory agree with other theories we have accepted that relate to what we are trying to understand? A theory that conflicts less with other theories is generally judged as more satisfactory.

A cautionary note to students: When we have subjected our theories to these evaluative procedures, we should not believe that we have achieved something called Truth. The notion that humans can achieve absolute, eternal truth is an ambitious goal that Western civilization has long cherished. It found expression in 5th-century Athens with Plato, in the early Christian era with Augustine of Hippo, and in the 18th century with the Enlightenment philosophers. The evolution of 20th-century science has made us less optimistic about discovering absolute truth, especially in the human sciences. When we argue that it is possible to judge theories, we are simply asserting that some theories explain social phenomena better than others do, not that the ones we judge as better are absolutely true. Social theories will always need further refinement. We seek the best available explanations on which to base our understanding and our most enlightened choices for social action.

Our theory-based explanations are not infallible, but neither are they "just an interpretation," if by that we mean that they are no better or worse than any other explanation. Our explanations may be strong or weak, more valid or less valid, depending on how well they stand up to critical investigation, that is, how thoroughly and consistently they explain the phenomena we are trying to understand. *Throughout this book, it is important to remember that you are reading neither "the absolute truth" nor "just another interpretation."* Instead, you are reading the best efforts of scholars who are trying to understand both the historical and the contemporary relationships between schooling and society. You should read these theoretical explanations critically, asking yourself if they do in fact help you better understand your experience with schools and the wider culture.

Schooling

Schooling is also a relatively simple concept but one that is often confused with education. Schooling simply refers to the totality of experiences that occur within the institution called school, not all of which are educational. Schooling includes all the activities that take place within the curriculum of a school—that is, within courses and programs of study. It also includes the activities called "extracurricular," such as sports, clubs, school newspapers, and other activities not included in the formal curriculum. In addition, schooling involves teaching and learning not included in either curricular or extracurricular activities. This type of learning occurs in the school's "hidden curriculum" and is generally not spoken of as curriculum by school authorities. Such learning often occurs because of the way schools are structured: their organization, architecture, time management, teaching methods, and authority structures. In the hidden curriculum, students learn powerful

"lessons," for example, about punctuality, respect for and even fear of authority, time organization, and competition for limited rewards.[2]

Focusing on schooling as opposed to focusing more broadly on education can reveal the relation of the state to schooling. State governments provide for school buildings and establish length of school terms and teachers' qualifications. Those of us who have always believed that there was a special connection between public (i.e., state) schools and democracy should remember that for most of Western history this was not the case. Democratic Athens and republican Rome did not have state schools. For most of Western history, state schooling supported nondemocratic governments. The state schools of Sparta, the Roman Empire, the German states during the Reformation, and until recently 20th-century Soviet Russia all utilized state schooling for nondemocratic ends. All these state schools sacrificed individualism, creativity, and independent judgment in the interest of "citizenship."

Training

Training, like schooling, is often confused with education. Training may be described as a set of experiences provided to some organism (human or not) in an attempt to render its responses predictable according to the goals of the trainer. After the development of behavioral psychology in the 20th century, training techniques became more sophisticated and took on the aura of science. The increased efficiency of training techniques has led many astute social observers to become pessimistic about the future of creative individualism. This pessimism can perhaps best be seen in the "anti-utopia" novels of that century, such as Aldous Huxley's *Brave New World* and George Orwell's *1984*. What these anti-utopian writers fear is the vast potential for social control and manipulation inherent in training techniques. The potential for indoctrination certainly should be of concern for all educators. However, this does not mean that all training is to be shunned. For example, when approaching a busy intersection, most motorists hope that all other drivers approaching that intersection have been trained to automatically use their brakes when they see a red or yellow traffic light. We all want that response to be predictable. Other examples of the value of training include memorizing multiplication tables and irregular verbs in Spanish. At a more ambitious level, we might refer to a musician's training in classical piano or a doctor's medical training, both of

Learning to use a computer in school is an example of schooling that can support a good education as well as a specific program of training.

which indicate preparation for specific roles. Training, then, has an important but specifically limited value in both schooling and education.

Education

Education is related to training but is more difficult to explain. The educational reformer Abraham Flexner tried this explanation in 1927:

> Between education and training there exists a vast distinction. Education is an intellectual and spiritual process. It has to do with opening the windows of the human mind and the human soul. It involves the effort to understand, to comprehend, to be sensitive to ideas, aspirations, and interests to which the individual might otherwise be indifferent. Not so with training. Training connotes improved ability to do something, without deepened understanding, widened sympathy, or heightened aspirations. One can train a brick layer to lay three hundred bricks instead of one hundred and fifty. One

can train a stenographer to increase her speed and skill. . . . But one educates in the realm of thought, feeling, and intelligence. Occasionally, to be sure, training must precede education. One must be trained to read before one can become educated in literature; one must be trained to add and multiply before one can be educated in the higher mathematics; one must be trained to use a fever thermometer, before one can be educated as a physician. But always training concerns itself with tools and devices, while education concerns itself with something that has intellectual or spiritual content and motive. Training is means; education is end.[3]

Although Flexner's explanation could be more thorough (one can certainly construe medical training to mean medical education, for example), he does identify significant differences between education and training. Education certainly involves some training. Moreover, it involves some of the processes that make communal living possible. But it is more. Education involves reason, the intellect, intuition, creativity. It is a process or set of experiences that allows humans to "create" themselves. The educated person's responses to a problematic situation are based on trying to understand and make calculations about that situation, hypothesizing possible outcomes, and choosing among possible courses of action. Education builds on the successes and failures of ancestors, whereas training tends to reproduce the response(s) of the trainer. Education produces responses that the educator may not have contemplated.

Because of these differences between training and education, we typically think of training as preparing a person for a specific social or economic role, while education seeks to prepare an individual for a wide range of roles. For example, we typically speak of a nurse's training or a boxer's or a musician's training, emphasizing by this term the skills and understandings needed for each specific role. To be educated, however, is to develop a wide range of human capacities that equip one to fill a variety of roles in one's culture: as a worker, a citizen, a parent, a person who relates ethically to others, a person who uses leisure in productive ways, and so on. Think about it: would you rather be trained or educated—or both?

Thinking Critically about the Issues   #1

Identify one schooling experience you can recall from your elementary or secondary education and indicate whether that experience primarily reflected a context of schooling, training, or education or a combination of these. Explain your assessment.

Political Economy

Political economy is a durable, flexible concept that includes the social, cultural, economic, political, and demographic dimensions of a society. To study the political economy of a particular society is to examine how that society is organized—how its structures, processes, and physical and mental resources give it its character and distinctiveness. The school, like the family, the police force, and the banking industry, is one of the institutions that make up the political economy of American society. This book will focus on analyzing those aspects of the political economy that are of special relevance to American public schools. Crucial to the method of analysis is the assumption that when any part of the political economy experiences significant change, other parts of it are likely to be affected.

Thinking Critically about the Issues   #2

Identify a prominent schooling practice—curricular or extracurricular—that most American students have experienced and explain how that practice prepares students for the political economy of the United States. In your view, how educationally beneficial to the student is this practice? Explain.

Ideology

Ideology, like education, is a frequently used concept that is difficult to define. If "political economy" refers to the *material* components of a culture, "ideology" refers to its *ideas*. Every society explains and justifies its social, political, and economic arrangements and its relations to the outside world in terms of what its members understand and value about the world. Members of one society might explain and justify their "free enterprise" system on the basis of beliefs in the importance of private property and individual freedom. Members of another society might justify their military dictatorship on the grounds that social order and control are more fundamental to human well-being than is equality or civil rights. In each case, those who are doing the explaining and justifying are revealing the underlying values that support their respective ideologies.

It may be useful to think of an ideology as an interpretive lens through which a society looks to organize its experiences. Although the notion of a "system of ideas"

is no doubt too simplistic and neat, it holds some value for understanding the term.

Ideology does not refer primarily to how individuals think; rather, it refers to the beliefs, value systems, and understandings of social groups. In this book, the term "ideology" refers to the beliefs, values, and ways of understanding that guide policy formation in any society and that are *intended* to explain and justify the society's institutions and social arrangements—intended, because the ideas and values that explain and justify major social institutions may not be satisfactory to all members of society. The ideology that becomes dominant in a society is almost always articulated by those who derive the most power, goods, and prestige from the existing social organization. Generally, those who benefit most from the social arrangement are more satisfied with the "dominant" ideology than are group members who benefit less. Those who wield less power or are oppressed by society understandably are less satisfied by justifications of existing social arrangements. In many cases, such groups may embrace conflicting ideologies or variants of the dominant ideology. The result can be social unrest and even revolution. Colonial Americans of Benjamin Franklin's persuasion, for example, shared the same society, but not the same ideology, as loyalists to the king. Similarly, slaves and masters in the pre–Civil War South shared the same society but usually not the same ideology.

Even in relatively stable societies in which social unrest does not approach revolution, it should not be assumed that the dominant ideology is fully endorsed by all social groups and economic classes. It is safe to assume that a society's dominant economic class can explain and justify the prevailing social arrangements according to the dominant ideology, but such explanations may not accurately reflect the views of people from less privileged economic classes. The police force in U.S. society, for example, may be understood by middle and upper classes as an institution that benevolently enforces the law and protects the rights and well-being of all members of society. People from less-privileged economic classes, however, may have experienced the police as an organization that uses its special powers to harass and interfere with their lives in order to protect the advantages of wealth.

This does not mean that various segments of society necessarily develop entirely different ideologies; often they share important parts of the dominant ideology.

It does suggest, however, that all classes do not necessarily accept all parts of the ideology that the dominant class most fully articulates.

The history of the term "ideology" is marked by many different uses, but all fall more or less into two main categories: (1) ideology as "false belief" and (2) ideology as a universal condition that underlies all social understanding. Ideology as false belief is illustrated by the statement "Of course they don't understand freedom; they're blinded by their ideology." The underlying assumption here is that ideology is something that distorts "their" vision and prohibits understanding. Central to this notion is that ideology is something that "others," especially our opponents, have, while we are free of ideology and consequently can see things clearly. However, this is not the view of ideology used in this text.

The view employed here is that ideologies are embedded in all societies, that they facilitate the organization of a society's perceptions and understandings, and that it is important to recognize ideologies, both our own and others'. To argue that ideologies are embedded in all societies is not to say that we cannot make judgments about ideologies or that the values of a given ideology are as "good" or as true as those of any other. We can, for example, use our own ideology to judge the dominant ideology of Nazi Germany as being morally corrupt. We need not hesitate to make moral judgments just because we recognize they are grounded in our own ideological framework. Without the values and beliefs that our cultural history provides us, we would not be able to make moral judgments at all. Nevertheless, the beliefs and values of any culture should be critically examined for their internal consistency and their consequences in practice.

Thinking Critically about the Issues   #3

Identify a practice in school that you think reflects some component of the prevailing belief system, or ideology, of the contemporary culture and show how the prevailing ideology might be used both to explain and to justify that schooling practice. In your view, is that justification adequate? Explain your position.

HW vs. Students

Schooling plays an important role in teaching and legitimating a society's ideology. The ideology served by the public school is almost inevitably the dominant ideology of the larger society. This suggests both potential strengths and weaknesses in schooling. Whereas schooling may help people share in the life of their society, it may also help blind them to problems within it. Schooling prepares people to participate in a society's political economy and share its dominant ideology, but by doing so, it may further disadvantage those from the less-advantaged groups while contributing to the already privileged position of the more powerful.

This ideological sharing need not be done in a mindless and uncritical manner that "indoctrinates" students into beliefs and values that might better be questioned. However, the danger is always there. At the heart of the democratic ideal is the belief that children will be afforded the opportunity to mature into independently thinking adults who can analyze and criticize their society and its dominant ideology, who can recognize where its ways of thinking and ways of life are inadequate and in need of improvement. One of the aims of this book is to employ these analytic concepts to help students develop that kind of critical understanding.

Analytic Framework

The relationship between American society and its public schools can best be understood by examining the relationship between three of the six analytic terms: political economy, ideology, and schooling. The relationship is pictured schematically in Exhibit 1.1.

A basic premise of this analytic framework is that an ecological relationship exists among the three components. Any significant change or disturbance in one of them will set off a ripple effect through the others until a new state of equilibrium is achieved. Put another way, this framework shows how political economy (social conditions) and ideology influence each other and how both influence educational practice. It also shows how educational practice in turn influences a society's ideology and political economy. This is not to claim that each of these elements is equally powerful in bringing about change in the others. It seems clear, for example, that changes in the political economy are more influential in causing changes in the schools than vice versa. The important point here is that any one of these elements can be influenced by any one of the others.

The interactive relationship among political economy, ideology, and schooling becomes clearer when they are examined in different historical circumstances.

Exhibit 1.1   Analytic Framework

The analytic framework illustrated here appears in every chapter, but it will be different every time. This is because each chapter looks at a different era of schooling or, in Part 2 of the book, a different feature of schooling in the contemporary era. The framework in each chapter won't mean as much to you as it will when you have finished the chapter. Later, the framework will serve as a good organizer that summarizes a great deal of information about how schools in Jefferson's era, or in the progressive era, or in our own era are closely related to the political economy and ideology of that time. The authors selected certain elements of each era to represent the political economy, and other elements to represent the ideology and features of schools at that time. You should be able to see relationships among them. *You might also have chosen differently.* That is, there may be different elements of schooling, or political economy, or ideology that you believe are just as important as those the authors have selected. If you can support your choices with evidence and reasoning, you are demonstrating a good understanding of this material.

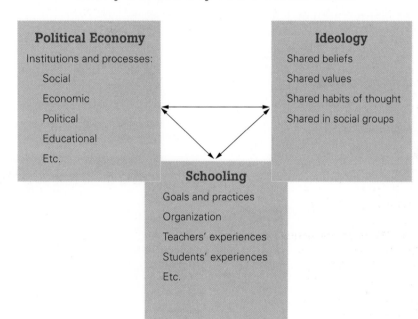

Analytic Framework
Liberty and Literacy in the United States

Political Economy

Institutions and processes:

   Social

   Economic

   Political

   Educational

   Etc.

Ideology

Shared beliefs

Shared values

Shared habits of thought

Shared in social groups

Schooling

Goals and practices

Organization

Teachers' experiences

Students' experiences

Etc.

Part 1 of this text will apply the same analytic framework to each of the major historical periods of American education. Part 2 will apply it to some of the most perplexing issues facing today's schools.

Applying the Terms of Inquiry: An Illustration from History

Schooling and Culture in Classical Greece

To a great extent, contemporary educational debates can be profitably viewed through the Greek conceptions of reason, freedom, and citizenship and especially through the Greek contribution to the modern conception of democracy. Classical Greece, particularly as expressed in the life of Athens, was a potent symbol for those who participated in the democratic revolutions of the 17th and 18th centuries. A central ideal was the notion that the pursuit of the Good Life may be shared by more than a hereditary minority, served by the vast majority. This central ideal is crucial to progress away from imposed unnatural limits to opportunity and human thriving. However, the Athenian example also demonstrates the powerful lesson that forms of socially, not naturally, constructed status conditions life chances, despite appeals to democracy and fairness. Pluralistic democracy today continues to struggle with the status of groups who, because of class, gender, race, and ethnic prejudice, are systematically excluded from decision-making processes, just as similar groups were excluded from Athenian democracy. However, an understanding of Greek ideals in education first requires an understanding of the historical setting—the political economy and ideology—in which those ideals made sense.

The historical context from which classical educational ideals emerged is perhaps best illustrated by Athens. Although Athens was only one of many Greek city-states, it was the intellectual and creative heart of classical Greece, the home of both Plato and his teacher Socrates, and the adopted home of Plato's student Aristotle, all of whose ideas have influenced Western educational thought.

Athenian Political Economy

Athens was first of all a city-state: a political and geographical unit that included a central city and the surrounding villages and lands under its protection. During the 5th-century Golden Age of Athens, its population was 350,000 to 400,000 people, including citizens, slaves, metics (neither citizens nor slaves), and children. The foundation of the economy was agriculture, although there was some limited trade, substantial handcrafting of goods for sale, and significant wealth achieved through victory in war. Most of the productive labor was done not by citizens but by metics and slaves.[4]

The most prominent Athenian social category was that of citizen. There were perhaps 50,000 to 70,000 citizens in Athens, less than one-fifth of the population, but they constituted the governing membership of the city-state. Citizens came from several social classes, ranging from the old Athenian aristocracy to peasants in remote Athenian villages. What these citizens had in common is that they were male, adult, and (with few exceptions) born in Athens. Unless they were very wealthy, they were expected to serve in the military, which the very wealthy supported through taxes rather than combat.

Some citizens farmed, a few did craft work, and a very few pursued commerce, which was considered unseemly. All citizens owned property, sometimes in very small plots, sometimes in great tracts. The wealthiest did not labor on the land, but had their slaves do the work. Leisure was considered very desirable since it brought an opportunity to cultivate the mind and character and to participate in the city's governance. Consequently, citizens avoided labor if they could afford to.

The most distinctive feature of citizenship was the opportunity to be a voting member of the Athenian general assembly and to serve on the legislative council. It was the business of the council—formally called the Council of Five Hundred because of the number of citizens who served on its various committees—to propose legislation to the assembly, which consisted of all citizens who wished to attend its meetings. Typically, about one citizen in eight attended the meetings of the assembly, at which time they could approve or reject the proposals of the Council of Five Hundred.

Membership on the council lasted only one year, and only two consecutive terms were permitted. Any citizen could run for council membership, but since the work and time required were considerable, the poorer citizens and those who lived far from the center of the city-state were not likely to serve. After candidates were identified, they were chosen by lottery rather than by election. Athenians considered it an important mark of their democratic way that they could trust any citizen, chosen by the luck of the draw, to serve in their legislative council.

Plato taught at the school he founded, the Academy, with the aim of developing an ideal balance of reasoning powers, emotional moderation, and physical fitness.

It is probable that selection by lot came to an end shortly after Aristotle's death in 322 B.C., as the classical period drew to a close. During the time of his teacher, Plato, oligarchy (government by the privileged few) had ruled briefly from 404 to 403 B.C. Therefore, it should not be assumed that the stable democratic processes that prevailed at the time of Plato's birth (429 B.C.) continued unbroken throughout the Golden Age. Plato's career was a time of tension between the established aristocratic families of Athens and others who sought democracy. Although Aristotle's life spanned a more stable period of Greek democracy than Plato's, the rift between the wealthy few and the poorer common citizen remained.

Despite the achievements of the Athenians in establishing a more democratic way of life, the overwhelming majority of inhabitants were systematically excluded from citizenship. Among these were Athenian women, slaves, children, and metics. Women were not allowed to participate in public life either socially or politically. The "proper" place for the wife of a citizen was in the household, where she could supervise domestic slaves, do household chores, and teach her daughters how to weave, garden, and so on. Women who were not wives or daughters of citizens were slaves or metics.

Despite major differences, the institution of slavery in Athens bears some similarity to the historical institution of slavery in the United States. Athenian slavery, like that in the southern United States, was chattel slavery, in which slaves were private property. This was not the case in Sparta, where slaves were state-owned. Also like U.S. slavery 2,000 years later, slavery in Athens was fundamental to the life of leisure that the upper-class citizen could expect to pursue. Without slavery, the economic and class systems could not have been what they were. This does not mean that only the wealthy owned slaves. As was later true of southern white farmers in the United States, poorer Athenians could sometimes afford one or two slaves, who might be required to labor in the house, the field, the shop, or all three. Some slaves also managed farms and shops for their owners. One of the things that connects the development of the American and Athenian democratic progressions is the following paradox. Both histories show that as democracy developed, characterized by citizen and not monarchial rule, so did slavery develop.

As was later true in the United States, the Greeks justified the institution of slavery on racist grounds. Non-Greeks were judged fit only to be slaves based on

Historical Context

Classical Athens

The few selected events in this table help situate the discussion of education in Athens among cultural events that may already be familiar to you. Each of these events provides a clue about the cultural practices and institutions (political economy) and/or the beliefs and values (ideology) of classical Athens. As this chapter shows, education in Athens would reflect the culture's practices, beliefs, and values.

Before the Classical Athenian Era

800 B.C.	Homer writes the first epic poems, including the *Iliad* and the *Odyssey*
800	Sparta and other Greek city-states established
776	Olympic games begin
750	Greeks adapt alphabet for writing
594	Solon establishes government reforms that lay basis for Athenian democracy by property owners; serfdom is abolished

Classical Athens

508	Athenian democracy extended to all Athenian freemen rather than only landed aristocrats
496	The playwright Sophocles is born
484	The historian Herodotus is born
469	Socrates, philosopher and teacher of Plato, is born
450	The age of Pericles begins and will last until 429 B.C.
450	The Greek war against Persia ends
447	The Parthenon and other buildings are erected on the Acropolis
428	Plato, student of Socrates and founder of European philosophy, is born
411	An oligarchic regime briefly rules Athens, followed by Spartan rule
403	Athenian democracy is restored
387	Plato founds Academy at Athens
384	Plato's student Aristotle is born
~335	Lyceum, Aristotle's school, is opened
334–324	Aristotle's student Alexander the Great conquers vast empire, including parts of Asia and Africa

Thinking Analytically about the Timeline

As an exercise in analytic thought, identify one example where democratic ideology interacts with the dimension of Athenian political economy.

the view that the Greeks were a separate and superior race of people. When Athenians defeated other Greeks in battle, men from opposing city-states were rarely made slaves, although women and children might be enslaved. Most slaves, however, came to Athens through a vigorous trade with eastern slave dealers.

Metics were a class of Athenian residents who were neither slaves nor citizens. They came freely to Athens from other lands and were allowed to pursue their lives, but were not granted the voting rights of citizenship. Some farmed, some became successful traders and bankers—occupations that were considered beneath the dignity of a citizen—and many became craftsmen. Some were allowed the privilege of going to battle for Athens if they were able to purchase armor, for each soldier supplied his own.

Metics worked side by side with slaves and citizens in a variety of occupations. Except for slaves, workers controlled the conditions of their labor, owning their tools, setting their own schedules, and setting the prices on finished products. Even massive projects, such as the building of the Parthenon, were contracted in small portions to individual teams of workers—citizens, slaves, and metics together—each man taking responsibility for his own piecework. On such civic projects, these craftsmen contracted individually with the city for their services, and were not employed by a large, wage-paying construction contractor, as is typically the case today. For one citizen to hire out his labor to another was, for an Athenian, a violation of his status as a free person.

The military, for which all male citizens were trained, was a significant feature of the political economy. First, of course, it protected the city-state against aggressive neighbors, such as Sparta. Second, it helped shape the classical conception of citizenship by replacing the great warrior hero of Homer's time with multitudes of common men who could win honor for themselves and their city. The army was supported by taxes paid by the wealthy as well as by the soldiers, whose honor it was to defend Athens.

Athenian Ideology To classical Athenians, the ideal life was one led in accord with Reason and Virtue. Through reason humans could perceive the true realities of the universe, and through virtue they could live in harmony with that universe. Athenians viewed the world not as a random tangle of hostile mysteries beyond human understanding but as an orderly system governed by principles of nature that are discoverable through observation and logical reflection. They believed that humankind, particularly male Athenians, who held citizenship, was distinctively equipped with powers of reason that revealed the workings of the natural world. It was this rationality, they believed, that equipped common citizens to govern and be governed by turn in the Athenian democracy. Our own conception of public education is in line with the Athenian notion that human reason is real, is not restricted to nobility, and needs to be grown and developed. This provided an ideal, a guideline for including ordinary persons in the process of education. Later in this book you will see how democracy itself becomes a promise that reason and education will work toward its perfection. However, it is important to begin understanding also the paradox involved in this extension of promise. To be worthy of education is, for the Greeks, to be human.

Humanity is an endowment, however, that is socially constructed under conditions of privilege and property rights. The history of democracy becomes the history of social struggles by groups excluded from the full rights expected by "humanity." Opportunity for those rights has historically been the exclusive property of those in greater control of power and property, and thus the material conditions required for the exercise of freedom.

Thus, women, slaves, immigrant workers without property, and so on are deprived of full education, or simply trained for service, as a coincidence of their distance from the centers of power. "Humanity" thus conceived is only incompletely "natural." One's social status and property condition the degree of access to education.

To live in accord with reason and with the virtues of Athenian culture, rather than according to arbitrary authority or in accord with momentary desires or inclinations, was, in the Athenian view, to live freely. Political democracy was important so that each citizen might live as reason and virtue dictated—to live as one chose and to choose wisely. Women, metics, and slaves were believed to be inferior in rational capacity, and thus their relative lack of freedom and political participation was justified by the dominant ideology.

Athenians believed that the road to virtue as well as to freedom was paved with reason. Virtue resided in acting justly, and justice was determined by reason. They believed that virtue resided in a harmony among the physical, emotional, and rational dimensions of each human being and that it was the rational dimension that must ultimately determine the proper harmony. Virtue also was to be found in moderation in all things, and the slogan "Nothing in excess" served as a guide for daily living.[5] Athenians sought virtue in balancing the needs of the individual with the needs of society, balancing work with leisure, balancing cultivation of the mind and the body, and so on. Essential to understanding this ideology, however, is its justification of humanity for some and a life in service for others. However, the inspiration for democracy is the growth of the notion that it is unnatural and thus unjust to exclude entire classes of persons from "humanity."

Athenian Schooling   The schools of classical Athens clearly reflected the political–economic and ideological traits of Athenian society. Schools were available to all young male Athenians, for as citizenship was their birthright, so was the education needed for enlightened citizenship. These schools were private, but quite inexpensive. Females and slaves did not attend schools, although they often received tutoring in order to conduct their affairs and to teach young males at home. Early schooling was not compulsory; it was assumed that all Athenian boys would attend in order to develop their minds and bodies for virtue and wisdom. Boys attended primary school from about age 6 to age 14, and the curriculum consisted of gymnastics, literature, and music. Musical training might include instrumental and vocal performance, but was never far from the stories and histories that were accompanied by voice and, often, lyre. Those who could afford further schooling from private teachers—and those lucky enough to find teachers like Plato, who taught free of charge—went to secondary school from age 14 to age 18. There they continued their work in gymnastics, literature, and music but studied dialectic and philosophy as well. From age 18 to age 20, military training was compulsory for all males. The city-state's security, after all, depended on its ability to defend itself against enemy states.

The curriculum of gymnastics combined with music and literature was grounded partly in the Athenian respect for a balance of healthy mind and healthy body. It was grounded also in the view that rigorous gymnastics, including boxing and wrestling, contributed to the preparation for military service. The attention to music and literature was preparation for a life of wisdom, virtue, citizenship, and appreciation of the arts of leisure, such as poetry and drama. The school curriculum did not directly or specifically prepare youths for vocations or occupations. Plato noted that "technical instruction and all instruction which aimed only at money-making was vulgar and did not deserve the name education. True education aimed solely at virtue, making the child yearn to be a good citizen, skilled to rule and obey."[6]

Such a position is understandable in light of the Athenian regard for the leisurely pursuits of contemplation, politics, and appreciation of the arts. These leisurely aspirations are in turn understandable within the context of a society in which a privileged minority of citizens was able to rely on a slave and noncitizen population to do the hard work of producing necessary goods. For Athenian citizens, the most important aspect of life was not material wealth but the development of wisdom and virtue. The school curriculum reflected these priorities in its concentration on activities of body and mind that would help develop the good man and citizen.

The case of classical Athens has been given extended treatment in order to introduce issues that will recur throughout the book. For example, the Athenian notion of democracy becomes subject to criticism when it is seen that the majority of Athenians were excluded from political decision making. This historical backdrop enables us to examine more clearly whether major segments of our society have been, and continue to be, similarly excluded.

Further, Aristotle's notion that a democratic society seeks to provide the same basic education to all its citizens, so that all may be prepared to exercise rational judgment in ruling and being ruled, raises questions about whether our society seeks to provide a similar education to all its citizens or whether, as in feudal Europe, different kinds of education are deemed suitable for different people according to their station in life. At issue too is the degree to which contemporary society embodies the Athenian faith that all citizens are endowed with sufficient rationality to be entrusted with public decision-making powers and whether the primary goals of schooling include the greatest possible development of those powers for all citizens.

Finally, the Athenian notion that individual freedom should include self-governance in the workplace, not just periodic civic participation, raises questions about our limited view of what freedom means in contemporary society. Many other points of contact between Athenian and contemporary social and educational ideals exist. Several will emerge in subsequent chapters.

BUILDING A PHILOSOPHY OF EDUCATION

The purpose of this brief section is to begin a process that to some degree you will have already begun on your own: shaping your own philosophy of education. Philosophy of education is on the one hand a formal field of scholarship, with roots in European culture that are traceable in Jewish, Christian, and

Islamic texts; in ancient and classical Greece; and elsewhere. Today's philosophy of education, as a field of academic study, also has roots in Eastern culture in religious texts and in the teachings of Confucius. And today there are numerous journals and books that focus on this academic field and are read by specialists in the philosophy of education.

But at the same time, many teachers and school administrators who are not specialists in philosophy of education can rightly be said to be guided by their own philosophies of education. Such educators are thoughtful and clear about their educational goals and about the best educational methods for achieving their goals. In addition, they can tell you why they prefer these goals and methods: they can provide justifications for them. It might be said that, at the very least, a coherent philosophy of education is explicit about educational goals, methods for attaining those goals, and the justifications for both. Those justifications will inevitably reflect the institutions and practices of our society (political economy) as well as the culture's beliefs and values (ideology). At the same time, teachers and administrators have to make choices about those parts of the social order and prevailing ideology they want their practices to serve: that the United States has one of the largest prison systems of any nation on earth, for example, does not lead teachers to set a goal that a similar percentage of their students should be prepared for imprisonment. And simply because racism continues to be a part of the belief system of many people in the culture does not mean that a percentage of children should be taught to embrace racist values. Educators need to make choices about what ideals they will serve, and how they will serve them. Those choices might be said to be based on the philosophies of education that guide teachers and school leaders.

Educational goals might have to do with overarching social goals (such as contributing to a more literate or a more democratic society), or they might address individual learning outcomes (such as, each child in my classes will be able to read at least at grade level by the end of the year). Educational goals can be ambitious and complex. For example, a teacher's goals should probably address what students should know (their knowledge), what they should be able to do (skills), and also what kinds of values, habits, and inclinations they should have (often referred to as dispositions). Attending to all of these different kinds of goals is important. Otherwise, for example, a teacher might successfully use the threat of severe punishment to make sure that every child learns certain mathematical skills. But if the cost were that some or all students hated learning mathematics as a result, it would be a case of serving some goals (knowledge and skills) at the expense of others (a disposition to want to learn more mathematics). It is doubtful that the teacher would desire such an outcome, or that he or she would want to justify it.

In the preceding section that describes education in classical Athens, one can find evidence of most of these elements of a philosophy of education. Athenian educators had certain goals they wanted to achieve in education, specific ways of achieving them, and justifications for their goals and methods. If philosophy is the discipline of thinking about thinking, it might be said that Aristotle demonstrated how an educator could become thoughtful, purposeful, and clear in his thinking about the ideas that guided his educational practice. When educators today articulate their goals, methods, and justifications in ways that are thoughtful, purposeful, and clear, it is fair to say they are articulating a philosophy of education. Different successful educators—teachers and school administrators alike—might well articulate different philosophies of education; it is doubtful that there is only one right way to educate or one right way to think about educating. In this volume, you will be given many opportunities to shape, revisit, and revise your own thinking about your philosophy of education; the knowledge, skills, and dispositions you most value, why you value them, and whether you value them for all people or just for some. Do you believe that all people should be prepared to go to college, for example, or just some people? The distinctions among schooling, training, and education might also be useful for your thinking. Should all members of society today be educated, or is it sufficient to educate some while offering only training for others? After all, how much education does it take to work in the fast-food industry? Or should educators make choices that are not defined simply by the limited demands of the workplace?

In the accompanying Primary Source Reading, you will notice that Aristotle begins right away with a question about Athenian education goals. He asks what kind of society his contemporaries are seeking through education: if a nondemocratic society, then certain implications follow for education. But if a democratic society is desired, then a different approach to education follows.

You will find it useful, after reading this chapter, if you take 15 minutes or so to record your thinking so that you have a sketch of your philosophy of education at this point in time: a sketch that you will have a chance to develop and revise for the remainder of this volume and for years to come. One way to frame this sketch is simply to respond to the following: What are your goals for your students; how will you achieve those goals; and what are your reasons for those goals and methods? You may, if you like, use the concepts of knowledge, skills, and dispositions as ways to help you think about your goals. Your justifications might address what you think is good for a person's happiness and fulfillment as an individual, and they might also address (like Aristotle) what kind of society you wish to contribute to with your education practice. In each chapter, there will be a section like this called "Building a Philosophy of Education" that will provide you an opportunity to become increasingly thoughtful, purposeful, and clear about your educational ideas. This is an example of where good theory can become very practical. If humans are beings whose actions are guided by their understandings and values, then what you understand and what you value is almost certain to affect your actions as a teacher. Developing a coherent educational philosophy will not only make your understanding and values clearer to you; that clarity will surely guide the day-by-day choices you make.

Primary Source Reading

According to translator Ernest Barker, Aristotle wrote *The Politics* over a period of several years before his death in 322 B.C. Thomas Jefferson, an architect of American democracy and, like Aristotle, an educator, philosopher, and slaveholder, was said to have been reading from *The Politics* when he died in 1826, more than 2,000 years later. The timeless issues Aristotle addresses in this brief section concern the purposes of public education. What's the point of education? Aristotle says we can't answer that question until we decide what kind of society we want. That is, certain kinds of education will support some kinds of beliefs and values and not others; and certain kinds of education will support some kinds of government and socioeconomic order and not others. When you know what kind of society you wish to have, says Aristotle, you can talk about how to educate people for that society. In other words, education is intimately linked to political economy and ideology.

Source: Excerpted from *The Politics of Aristotle* edited and translated by Ernest Barker by permission of Oxford University Press.

Barker's 1940s translation reads strangely to modern readers at first, so read carefully and thoughtfully. Take your time, and see if you can hear Aristotle's message. He begins with governors and governed, and he ends with the bodies, souls, and minds of children.

The Politics of Aristotle
Aristotle

As all political associations are composed of governors and governed, we have to consider whether the two should be distinguished for life, or merged together in a single body. The system of education will necessarily vary according to the answer we give. We may imagine one set of Circumstances in which it would be obviously better that a lasting distinction should once and for all be established between governors and governed. This would be if there were one class in the state surpassing all others as much as gods and heroes are supposed to surpass mankind—a class of men so outstanding, physically as well as mentally, that the superiority of the ruling stock was indisputably clear to their subjects. But that is a difficult assumption to make; and we have nothing in actual life like the gulf between kings and subjects which the writer Scylax describes as existing in India. We may therefore draw the conclusion, which can be defended on many grounds, that all should share alike in a system of government under which they rule and are ruled by turns. In a society of peers equality means that all should have the same rights: and a constitution can hardly survive if it is founded on injustice [i.e., if it gives *different* rights to men who are of the same quality]. The subject citizens will then be joined by all [the serfs] of the country-side in a common policy of revolution; and the civic body will be too small to cope successfully with all its enemies. On the other hand, it cannot be denied that there should be a difference between governors and governed. How they can differ, and yet share alike, is a dilemma which legislators have to solve. We have already touched on a possible solution in a previous chapter.

Nature, we have suggested, has provided us with the distinction we need. She has divided a body of citizens who are all generically the same into two different age-groups, a younger and an older, one of them meant to be governed and the other to act as the government. Youth never resents being governed, or thinks itself better than its governors; and it is all the less likely to do so if it knows that it will take over government on reaching a proper maturity. In one sense, therefore, it has to be that governors and governed are the same sort of persons; in another, that they are different. The same will be true of their education: from one point of view it must be the same, from another it has to be different, and, as the saying goes, "If you would learn to govern well, you must first learn how to obey." [We may first treat of learning how to obey.] Government, as has already been said in our first part, may be conducted in two different ways. One way is to govern in the interest of the governors: the other, to govern in the interest of the governed. The former way is what we call "despotic" [i.e., a government of slaves]; the latter is what we call "the government of freemen." [This is the sort of government which the young must begin by learning to obey; but they must also learn to obey some orders which may seem more appropriate to a government of slaves.] Some of the duties imposed [on the free] differ [from those of slaves] not in the work they involve, but in the object for which they are to be done. This means that a good deal of the work which is generally accounted menial may none the less be the sort of work

which young freemen can honourably do. It is not the inherent nature of actions, but the end or object for which they are done, which make one action differ from another in the way of honour or dishonour.

[We may now treat of learning, how to govern.] We have laid it down that the excellence of the full citizen who shares in the government is the same as that of the good man. We have also assumed that the man who begins by being a subject must ultimately share in the government [and will therefore require the same sort of excellence as the good man]. It follows on this that the legislator must labour to ensure that his citizens become good men. He must therefore know what institutions will produce this result, and what is the end or aim to which a good life is directed.

There are two different parts of the soul. One of these parts has a rational principle intrinsically and in its own nature. The other has not; but it has the capacity for obeying such a principle. When we speak of a man as being "good," we mean that he has the goodnesses of these two parts of the soul. But in which of the parts is the end of man's life more *particularly* to be found? The answer is one which admits of no doubt to those who accept the division just made. In the world of nature as well as of art the lower always exists for the sake of the higher. The part of the soul which has rational principle is the higher part. [It is therefore the part in which the end of man's life is more particularly to be found.] But this part may in turn be divided, on the scheme which we generally follow into two parts of its own. Rational principle, according to that scheme, is partly practical, partly speculative.

It is obvious, therefore, that the part of the soul which has the principle must fall into two corresponding parts. We may add that as the parts of the soul have their hierarchy, so, too, have the activities of those parts. It follows on this that those who can attain all the activities possible [i.e., rational activity of the speculative order, rational activity of the practical order, and the activity of obedience to rational principle], or *two* of those activities, will be bound to prefer the activity of the part which is in its nature the higher. All of us always prefer the highest we can attain.

Life as a whole is also divided into its different parts—action and leisure, war and peace; and in the sphere of action we further distinguish acts which are merely necessary, or merely simply useful, from acts which are good in themselves. The preferences which we give to the parts of life and their different activities will inevitably follow the same general line as those which we give to the parts of the soul and their different activities. War must therefore be regarded as only a means to peace; action as a means to leisure; and acts which are merely necessary, or merely and simply useful, as means to acts which are good in themselves. The legislation of the true statesman must be framed with a view to all of these factors. In the first place, it must cover the different parts of the soul and their different activities; and in this field it should be directed more to the higher than the lower, and rather to ends than means. In the second place it must also cover, and it must place in the same perspective, the different parts or ways of life and the different categories of acts. It is true that the citizens of our state must be able to lead a life of action and war; but they must be even more able to lead a life of leisure and peace. It is true, again, that they must be able to do necessary or useful acts; but they must be even more able to do good acts. These are the general aims which ought to be followed in the education of childhood and of the stages of adolescence which still require education.

The Greek states of our day which are counted as having the best constitutions [and therefore the best "ways of life"], and the legislators who framed their constitutional systems, have fallen short of this ideal. It is plain that their constitutions have not been made with a view to the higher ends of life, or their laws and systems of education directed to all the virtues. On the contrary, there has been a vulgar decline into the cultivation of qualities supposed to be useful and of a more profitable character. A similar spirit appears in some of our recent writers who have adopted this point of view. They laud the constitution of Sparta, and they admire the aim of the Spartan legislator in directing the whole of his legislation to the goal of conquest and war. This is a view which can be easily refuted by argument, and it has now been also refuted by the evidence of fact. Most men are believers in the cause of empire, on the ground that empire leads to a large accession of material prosperity. It is evidently in this spirit that Thibron, like all the other writers on the constitution of Sparta, lauds its legislator for having trained men to meet danger and so created an empire. To-day the Spartans have lost their empire; and we can all see for ourselves that they were not a happy community and their legislator was not right. It is indeed a strange result of his labours: here is a people which has stuck to his laws and never been hindered in carrying them out and yet it has lost all that makes life worth

living. In any case the partisans of Sparta are in error about the type of government for which the legislator should show a preference. [It is not, as they think, the "despotic" type]: the government of freemen is a finer government, and a government more connected with goodness, than any form of despotism. . . .

Excellence must not be sought by a training such as the Spartan. The Spartans are like the rest of the world in their view of the nature of life's highest goods [which they identify, like everybody else, with the external goods of fortune]: they only differ from others in thinking that the right way of getting them is to cultivate a single excellence [i.e., military courage]. Regarding external goods as higher than any others, and the enjoyment they give as greater than that derived from the general cultivation of excellence, [they cultivate only the single excellence which they consider useful as a means to securing those goods. But it is the *whole* of excellence which ought to be cultivated], and cultivated for its own sake, as our argument has already shown. That still leaves us, however, with the problem, "How, and by what means, is a general excellence to be achieved?"

Using the distinction already made in a previous chapter, we may say that the means required for achieving general excellence are natural endowment, habit, and rational principle. So far as the first of these is concerned, we have already determined [in c. VII] the character of the endowment with which our citizens should start. It remains to consider the other two means, and to determine whether training in habit or training in rational principle ought to come first. The two modes of training must be adjusted to one another as harmoniously as possible [which not only means starting first with the mode that ought to come first, but also directing both modes alike to the same sort of high purpose]; otherwise rational principle may fail to attain the highest ideal, and the training given through habit may show a similar defect. With a view to this result, we may assume two things as evident. First, in the sphere of man's life (as in all life generally), birth has a first beginning [i.e., the union of parents], but the end attained from such a beginning is only a step to some further end. The exercise of rational principle and thought is the ultimate end of man's nature. It is therefore with a view to the exercise of these faculties that we should regulate, from the first, the birth and the training in habits of our citizens. Secondly, as soul and body are two, so there are also two parts of the soul, the irrational and the rational; and there are also two corresponding states of these parts—the state of appetite, and the state of pure thought. In order of time and in date of birth, the body is prior to the soul, and the irrational part of the soul is prior to the rational. This is proved by the fact that all the signs of appetite—such as anger, self-will, and desire—are visible in children from their very birth; while reasoning and thought are faculties which only appear, as a rule, when they grow older. The conclusion which follows is obvious. Children's bodies should be given attention before their souls; and their appetites should be the next part of them to be regulated. But the regulation of their appetites should be intended for the benefit of their minds— just as the attention given to their bodies should be intended for the benefit of their souls.

Developing Your Professional Vocabulary

A good understanding of this chapter's content would include an understanding of why each of these terms is important to education.

Athenian citizenship

Athenian slavery

democracy

education through participation

ideology

political economy

schooling versus education

social foundations of education

social theory

training versus education

Questions for Discussion and Examination

1. Aristotle believed that in a democratic society all citizens ought to have the same basic education: one that would equip them to serve as legislators and obey laws intelligently. In a nondemocratic society, the basic education people received would be different for different people because some would be equipped to rule and others to follow. Judging from your experience in schools, which of Aristotle's models more resembles American schooling? Explain your position.

2. Aristotle argued that the primary purpose of education should be to develop human reason. In your view, how does this compare with the primary purpose(s) of education in U.S. schools today? Support your view with evidence from your experience.

3. Choose any single feature of schooling as you have experienced it—organization, rules, processes, subjects taught—and explain how that feature reflects elements of the ideology and political economy of the larger society.

OLC Online Resources

Go to the Online Learning Center at **www.mhhe.com/ tozer7e** to take chapter quizzes, practice with key terms, access study resources, and link to related websites. Also available on the Online Learning Center are PowerWeb articles and news feeds.

Liberty and Literacy The Jeffersonian Ideal

Chapter Overview

Chapter 2 treats political economy, ideology, and schooling in the 50 years after the American Revolution. Chief features of the political economy of the early republic include an agrarian economy, a decentralized republican government, relative homogeneity of local culture, and a social hierarchy defined by race and gender. Ideologically, the origins of democratic thought in early America can be understood in the context of the breakdown of feudalism in Europe and the rise of classical liberalism in Europe and the United States. Each of the following features of classical liberalism helps define the character of the ideology shared by Jefferson and his contemporaries: a commitment to human reason, a belief in a universe governed by natural law, a conception of human virtue shaped by sacred and secular influences, a belief in the inevitability of progress, a newfound sense of nascent nationalism, and a many-sided concept of freedom.

The classic liberal commitment to education—and, for Jefferson, free public education—can be understood in relationship to each of the components of classical liberalism previously identified. To examine Jefferson's beliefs about popular schooling requires an understanding of his views about the relationship between participatory democracy and education.

However, we must also seriously contend with the degree to which the development of reason for some was purchased at the price of freedom and access to reason for others. We must contend with the legacy that the foundations of reason and scientific knowledge grow dependent on human classifications that correspond to the animal classification. Ironically, these include a nascent scientific racism that excludes persons from full recognition of civil and educational rights. This is not an attempt to discredit Jefferson for his contribution to the language of freedom in our democratic life. It is an effort to try to understand this language and how it coexisted with the evils of exploitation and slavery.

One can rightly criticize Jefferson's racist and sexist assumptions, but in doing so, it is important to recognize that those assumptions were part and parcel of the limits of classical liberal commitments to such ideals as reason, freedom, and democracy. The limitations of the dominant ideology are identified not to excuse Jefferson from his biases but to show the extent to which the meanings of terms such as "equality," "freedom," "education," and "virtue" vary with historical context.

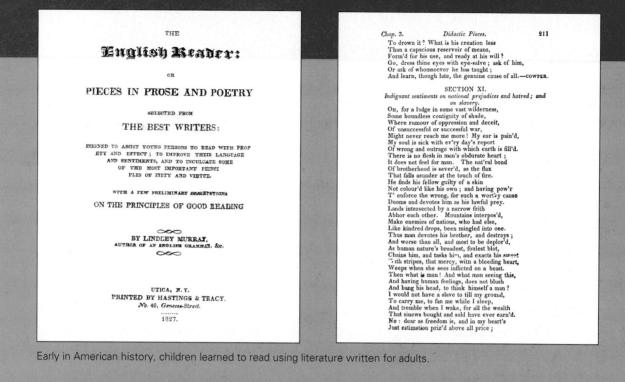

Early in American history, children learned to read using literature written for adults.

Chapter Objectives

Among the objectives that Chapter 2 seeks to achieve are these:

1. In this chapter readers should be able to talk and write about the relationships among various dimensions of political economy, ideology, and the nature of schooling in the early republic.

2. Readers should begin to critically evaluate the strengths and weaknesses of classical liberalism, noting its potential for realization of democratic ideals but noting its limitations on population groups excluded because of race, gender, and economic class.

3. Readers should be able to understand Jefferson's rationale for his educational proposals as it relates to the political economy and ideology of that time.

4. Readers should begin to entertain and evaluate alternative views of democracy: that it can be construed as a system of representative government but also as an ideal of human interaction in which all individuals are expected to share in making the decisions that affect their lives.

5. This chapter raises questions about whether there might be a potential for conflict between ideals of meritocracy and ideals of democracy, particularly if the definition of "merit" is derived from a segment of the population that is not representative of the entire population.

6. Readers should think critically and appreciatively about Jefferson's proposals for who should fund and control public schooling in Virginia, comparing those ideas with their knowledge of how schooling is funded and controlled today.

7. Finally, this chapter is intended to equip readers with increased ability to interpret the many issues presented in two Primary Source Readings: one by a prominent proponent of the American Revolution, Thomas Paine.

Analytic Framework
The Early American Period

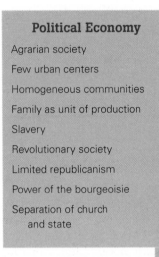
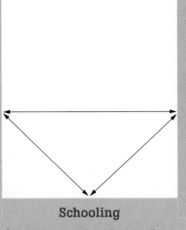

Political Economy

Agrarian society

Few urban centers

Homogeneous communities

Family as unit of production

Slavery

Revolutionary society

Limited republicanism

Power of the bourgeoisie

Separation of church
    and state

Ideology

Classical liberalism

Patriarchy

Progress via revolution

Reason

Republican virtue

Natural aristocracy

Capitalism/freedom

Laissez-faire

Faculty psychology

Schooling

Schools but no school "system"

Regional differences in schooling

Local financing and local control

Schooling primarily for white males

Religious and democratic purposes
    of schooling

Curriculum: rote learning of the
    3 Rs

Failure to create state-funded
    school system

Introduction: Why Jefferson?

Our examination of American education begins with one of this nation's most important and controversial figures, Thomas Jefferson. Of particular interest has been the controversy surrounding the argument that Jefferson fathered four children by a slave, Sally Hemmings. Thus we witness the apparent paradox of Jefferson as both slave owner and author of the "language of equal rights" in his Declaration of Independence.[1] Students who care to research the Web for "Thomas Jefferson" will discover ongoing dialogue today among his critics and defenders. Why do Jefferson's social and educational ideals continue to intrigue people today?

Jefferson was arguably the single most prominent American liberal during the era of the Revolution and the early republic. While his vocations were law and agriculture, he gained fame as a scientist, philosopher, and statesman, and as a revolutionary recognized throughout the Western world. At age 33, he authored the American Declaration of Independence. Subsequently, he served as governor of Virginia, U.S. ambassador to France, the first American secretary of state, vice president, and president of the United States for two terms. His retirement activities included agricultural experiments and the founding of the University of Virginia. During Jefferson's entire adult life, he wrote about and worked for education. His educational thought was not simply another aspect of his many talents; it was an integral part of all his other work.

Yet while his greatness is praised, serious questions continue to be raised about Jefferson's ideas and practices. What was his commitment to the "self-evident" truth, "that all men are created equal," which he proclaimed in the Declaration of Independence? Did he believe it applied to women, African Americans, and Native Americans? How far did he follow his stated belief in intellectual freedom? What level of trust did he have in the "common man"? To what extent did his belief in the "natural aristocracy" conflict with democratic ideals, especially in his educational proposals? Why does he appear to reject the vestige of feudalism represented by hereditary aristocracy and hereditary servitude, yet maintain crucial limits regarding the freedom of some groups of Americans? These kinds of questions should be kept in mind as we analyze Jefferson's ideas and work.

Jefferson's prominence as a spokesperson for the prevailing ideology of his time and his dedication to education make him useful in understanding the problems and educational ideals of early liberalism in the United States. By examining the revolutionary era through the lens of Jefferson's thought, one can see the strengths and limitations of the ideology, political economy, and educational arrangements of a formative period in the evolution of American schooling.

The study of Jefferson's legacy also brings us to a great paradox in American life, which also has its roots in classical thought: the exploitation of men and women on the basis of race, gender, ethnicity, and social class. The growth of a great democracy through education cannot be watered by the runoff of social exploitation and exclusion. Yet that is part of the legacy of classical Athens, which we saw in Chapter 1. The vestiges of exclusion continue to affect education, where educational privileges, from liberal education to university access, are connected inextricably to property ownership and private wealth. Access to knowledge in this period is freighted with the bitter legacy of slavery. Women's access to schooling is almost nonexistent, and predicated on role-playing, manners, and "civilized" refinements. Citizenship and the reason required to sustain the health of the commonwealth are in the reserved seats of the American dream.

Our study of Jefferson is an effort to confront directly this legacy, and to search for the roots of expanded educational rights in the work of a man who owned slaves and who would seek only the most menial training for them, who argued for women's public education at the most rudimentary level, and not at all for women's leadership potential. The burden of slavery and patriarchy lies heavily on the promise of democracy. In a recent book, Pulitzer Prize–winning historian Garry Wills argues that Jefferson's presidency itself was dependent on maintaining the three-fifths slave vote representation in the Constitution, votes that remanded directly to owners, in proportion to their slave numbers. In addition the Louisiana Purchase was pursued not for the grandeur and power it would bring to the Union, but primarily to include slave territories. Wills is a proven admirer of Jefferson, and author of two other prize-winning books on him. His account of Jefferson's blind spot on slavery is a reminder that with all that is admirable regarding his contribution comes a price that is etched in the political economy of American life. The growth of democracy where human reason is celebrated has been over an undertow of other arguments that some persons are not fully human, and thus do not merit full access to the life of the mind. This is a powerful legacy that has nation-state democracy replacing feudalism at a time when state powers thrive on the repression of colonized peoples.[2]

Jefferson and his contemporaries debated social and educational problems with clarity and articulated their conclusions with a force seldom rivaled thereafter. This chapter first discusses the political economy of the Jeffersonian era, examining the geography, population, work culture, family structure, and governmental arrangements of the time. In examining these aspects of the society separately, one must remember that they influence one another in complex ways—only a few of which will be captured in the following descriptions.

Political Economy of the Jeffersonian Era

Geography, Transportation, and Communication

Geographically, the new nation could be divided in several different ways. Most often it was thought to be separated into three regions: New England, the middle Atlantic states, and the southern states. New England was mountainous, with rocky and relatively unproductive soil and harsh winters but a rugged coast with fine harbors. As a result, New England became the center of fishing, shipping, and mercantile interests. During the three decades before the Civil War, it became the manufacturing center of the nation. The middle Atlantic states were characterized by rich farmland, navigable rivers, and excellent

Thomas Jefferson and many other colonial leaders felt that land ownership would encourage the attitude of independence and self-sufficiency needed in a democracy.

ports. New York City and Philadelphia soon became the leading ports and largest cities of the nation. The major exports from these states were grains and livestock. The southern states were rich agricultural areas known first for tobacco, rice, and indigo. After the invention of the cotton gin in 1793, cotton increased in importance, and so did the "peculiar institution" of slavery.

A second conception of regional differences was to divide the country into port areas served by the coast and navigable rivers versus the interior areas. The port-served areas had better and cheaper transportation and more rapid communication. They tended to be easier places to live, more cosmopolitan, and more urban. It was in those areas that commerce and trade thrived. Often the inhabitants of the interior areas considered themselves at the economic mercy of these commercial centers. These divisions between port-served areas and the interior areas continued well into the 20th century.

A third division, a concept that fired the imaginations of Americans in general and Jefferson in particular, was between the settled lands and the "frontier." This frontier was constantly moving west. First, the frontier was western Massachusetts; later, west of the Hudson River and the Appalachian Mountains; and finally, west of the Mississippi River. As settlers pushed westward, forcibly removing Native Americans from their ancestral lands, there was continuous conflict between the whites and the Native Americans, between the British settlers and the French, and finally, between the United States and whatever nation might stake a rival claim. The frontier played a significant role in the minds of Americans. What distinguished America from Europe in the imaginations of formerly land-starved Europeans was the magnificent promise of abundant land. The "West" would allow all ambitious Americans to be landowners. In reality, western lands were not that easy for the common person to acquire. Nevertheless, Jefferson and his contemporaries believed that land ownership meant independence and freedom. The man who owned and farmed his land, it was thought, depended on no one for the livelihood of his family. Thus, Jefferson argued, the West would enable Americans to escape the fate of Europe, with its remnants of feudal distinction. He based his vision of free, independent yeoman farmers as the backbone of the new republic in part on the availability and promise of land to the west. Jefferson's agrarianism was a family freehold farm, one of many in which the farmer was freed to pursue politics and ideas because his land was being worked by slaves, and his household managed by women.

Thinking Critically about the Issues   #1

Describe how your community members make their living, and how this differs from the period described in this chapter. Does it make a difference in the way education is conducted, public or otherwise?

Thomas Jefferson was born in 1743, the son of a relatively prosperous landowner and farmer in western Virginia. What was to become the United States of America at that time consisted of several British colonies nestled along the Atlantic coast stretching from Massachusetts to Georgia. The western boundary was a line along the Appalachian mountains. Most of the population lived along the coast or concentrated next to navigable rivers inland. When Jefferson became president in 1800, the total free population of the United States was less than six million. Only New York had more than 50,000 people, and only five other cities had over 10,000 people. About 94 percent of the population was classified as rural.[3] Over 90 percent of the working population was engaged in agriculture, with the remainder in shipping, commerce, and crafts. Except for some German and Dutch settlers in Pennsylvania and New York, the vast majority of the inhabitants were of British origin.

Any analysis of work at the beginning of the 19th century must center on farming as a way of life. When Jefferson became president in 1800, agriculture was the source of income for over 90 percent of the population: slaves, free men and women, and indentured servants. There were important regional differences in agriculture. In the south, especially along the tidewater and navigable rivers, farms tended to be large estates worked by slaves and indentured servants, though small farms were plentiful too. In New England and the interior regions of both the South and the West, farms were most often small. Family-worked subsistence farms rather than cash-crop farms were the norm, although indentured servitude was common here as well. Mechanized farming did not exist, and so humans and animals supplied the requisite energy.

From our late 20th-century perspective of rapid transportation and instantaneous communications, it is difficult to conceptualize transit and communications during the years of the Revolution and the early republic. To do so, we must imagine a society without television, telephones, computers, photocopiers, telegraph, radio, tape recorders, automobiles, trains, or airplanes. Communication was by word of mouth, letter, or newspaper. All travel was propelled by humans, animals, river currents, or the wind. For example, in 1791 it took Jefferson 19 days to travel the 920 miles of roads and trails from New York to his home in Virginia.[4] With the introduction of steam-powered boats in the second decade of the 19th century and the steam railroad in the third decade, travel time was greatly reduced. It was not until after the Civil War, however, that transportation and communication began to resemble those with which 20th-century Americans are familiar. The nature of transportation and communication in Jefferson's era ensured that speed, distance, and time were experienced in ways drastically different than they are today. Knowing this helps explain some of Jefferson's political and educational ideas, especially his democratic localism—the belief that local communities should be self-governing, ruled as little as possible by state and national governments.

Early American Governance

During Jefferson's time the *community*, through its mores together with court decisions and legislation, regulated and reinforced many of the activities of the family. Marriage was sanctioned by the community and was conceived as a contract designed to specify mutual responsibilities and rewards: regular and exclusive cohabitation; peaceful living; division of economic roles; and heterosexual, exclusive sexual relations. The community also monitored the family in its child-rearing practices. If an individual family failed in those responsibilities, the courts often intervened. When it was believed that many families were faltering, the colonial and, later, state legislatures intervened by introducing new institutions, such as town schools in colonial times and reform schools in the mid-19th century. Should such monitoring by the community and state be viewed as interference and an infringement on the rights and integrity of individuals, or was this community activity a legitimate reinforcement of familial values? The latter interpretation appears to have been accepted by most Americans of the revolutionary era. While not autonomous or completely independent, the family was the basic social and economic unit of early America. This view was well reflected in local laws in colonial and state governance.

Jefferson lived under three different kinds of government. At his birth, the lands that were to become the original 13 United States were separate colonies under the authority of the British crown. Each had a colonial legislature more or less representative of the colonists, a British-appointed governor who exercised veto power, and final authority resident in the British crown. From the Revolution until 1789, there was a Confederation of States. In this arrangement, most of the power was reserved to the states' governments, which consisted of selected legislatures and an elected governor. In 1789 the present Constitution, which greatly increased the authority of the national government, was adopted.

Although very dissimilar in particulars, there were certain important commonalities in all three forms of government. First and foremost, all three were based on the assumption of the historical "rights of English-men" to have representation in their government. Precisely what this representation meant and how it would be effected was a matter of serious and continuing debate, yet some groups, such as women, African Americans, and Native Americans, were consistently excluded from political influence. Second, each of these governmental arrangements assumed that male citizens' civil liberties could be infringed only for serious reasons of state. Again, the specifications of the liberties and definitions of serious reasons were hotly contested. Third, it was assumed that education was important for White men and that the colonial and state governments each had ultimate authority in this area. Under each of these governments during Jefferson's time, this educational authority was most often delegated to the parents and local communities.

For Jefferson and his political allies, the most profound political fact, however, was the Revolution. The prerevolutionary era was seen as harboring remnants of feudalism. Special rights reserved for the aristocracy, a close connection between church and state, the lack of intellectual freedom, restrictions on the civil and political rights of the common man and woman, and the belief that only the "well born" could benefit from education were among the remnants of feudalism which Jefferson challenged. The Revolution symbolized a break from the old world and old regime. It initiated a "noble experiment" in self-government. Much of Jefferson's philosophical, political, and educational thought was directed toward ensuring the success of this experiment.

Ideology of the Jeffersonian Era

The preceding sketch of the political economy of Jefferson's time provides one of the two major societal contexts within which early American education must be understood. The second context is the ideology of the era. The men of Jefferson's time were roughly divided into two worldviews, liberal and conservative, although those terms differ markedly from their meanings today. Jefferson and his allies were classical liberals, while his opponents were conservatives. The conservatives were thus named because they wished to hold on to, or conserve, an older and established set of ideas and values inherited from European traditions. This conservative ideology bore the strongest remnants of feudalism. The revolutionary generation was characterized by the struggle between two powerful post-feudal ideologies. In one influential debate, between Thomas Paine and Edmund Burke, we see Burke's effort to maintain the rights and power of those who hold hereditary property, and Paine's wish to challenge this with a vision of rights held by citizens, regardless of property or traditional privileges.[5]

The Breakdown of Feudalism

Feudalism was an economic, military, political, and religious system that developed in Europe during the centuries after the collapse of the Roman Empire. Although money was not absent, goods and services were generally bartered. A military class developed to provide protection in exchange for residence on the nobles' land and a portion of the peasant class's agricultural production. A religious class also developed that owned land through the church, provided spiritual solace, and exercised considerable political and economic power. Eventually these classes became somewhat fixed, and stations in life were assigned by heredity. The nobility and clergy were referred to as the "first estate" and the "second estate," respectively, and those who belonged to the land—the peasants—were the "third estate." To resist the feudal order was to resist God's will. This theory was provided and assented to by the learned men of the court, the universities, and the church.

Thinking Critically about the Issues   #2

List and discuss those rights you have as an "inheritance" from your family, and those you have as a citizen.

This feudal system slowly disintegrated until its collapse in the 16th and 17th centuries. It provided order and stability for a "closed" society. However, it could not easily accommodate new ideas, inventions, or trade. The beginning of the end came with the renaissances of the 12th and 14th centuries. Ideas from the Byzantine and Arab worlds stimulated European thinkers, who began to challenge the basic cosmology of the church. The ideas of men such as Galileo, Copernicus, Kepler, and Newton shook the foundations of feudal religious thought by challenging biblical and church accounts of the natural world with new scientific explanations. These challenges to church truths were grounded in a kind of authority new and different from religious revelation: scientific reason.

In addition to serving two terms as president, Thomas Jefferson was the colonial era's most eloquent spokesperson for education and was the founder of the University of Virginia.

Intercourse with the Middle East included goods as well as ideas. Commerce produced the need for money, merchants, banks, craftsmen, and, later, manufacturers. These people tended to congregate in trading centers, which became cities. The people who lived in the cities and made a handsome living from trade became known as the *bourgeoisie,* from the original term *bourg,* which was the fortress around which the cities developed.[6] They eventually developed into a very wealthy class, but with the same social and political status as the peasants—that is, they were members of the third estate. Additionally, the introduction of explosive powder from China paved the way for the invention of firearms and rendered the feudal warrior, with his long training, heavy armor, and prestige, scarcely equal to the peasant soldier with a rifle or a cannon.

When these seeds of the feudal system's destruction were first sown, they went almost unnoticed, except as minor irritants. By the 15th century, however, feudalism was entering its decline, in some ways a victim of its own successful establishment of the nation-state under the authority of a king who ruled by "divine right." As the British and French kings established national control, they required larger standing armies that, along with other governmental functions now required at court, necessitated increased taxes. Although the path took somewhat different routes and schedules, eventually England in the 17th century and France in the 18th both experienced rebellions. The American Revolution can be seen as an extension or continuation of the unfinished English revolutions of the 17th century. In all cases, it was necessary to justify the action of rebellion against "God's appointed" ruler. By what right could common people challenge the centuries-old authority of the church and the monarch? This justification was part of the development of "liberalism." Major contributors to the development of liberalism were Milton and Locke in England; Voltaire, Montesquieu, Condorcet, and Rousseau in France; and Franklin, Jefferson, and Madison in the United States.

The Classical Roots of Liberal Ideology

One inevitably oversimplifies when attempting to summarize the major ideas of an ideology, since individuals always subscribe to an ideology in different degrees and with various nuances. Nevertheless, it is helpful for the student of education in Jeffersonian America to have a summary of what has come to be called the "classical" liberalism of that era to distinguish it from the "modern" liberalism that descended from it in the 20th century. In addition, "classical" serves to associate this historical liberalism with the classical Athenian ideals on which liberal Enlightenment thought was based. One should remember, however, that the following ideas were not recited like a catechism, nor were they subjects of an oath of allegiance by classical liberals, who often conflicted with one another in how to apply these ideas in practice. Six ideas that were central or fundamental to classical liberalism will be examined: faith in reason, natural law, republican virtue, progress, nationalism, and freedom. Not only these ideas themselves but the relations *among* them are central to an understanding of the classical liberal worldview.

One shorthand way to think about the fundamental tenets of classical liberal ideology is to consider how the feudal commitment to hierarchy, in which one's worth was determined by one's place in society, was replaced by a commitment to individualism. Classical liberals embraced the right of individuals to control their economic destinies through merchant *capitalism*. Rejecting a state religion, liberals argued for the individual's right to freedom of worship and the legal separation of church and state. Denying the "divine right of kings," liberals believed in the right of individuals to govern themselves through representative government, or *republicanism*. To the revolutionary American, classical liberal ideology took the institutional forms of capitalism and republicanism. Exhibit 2.1 illustrates these major concepts.

Faith in Reason   These individualistic tendencies were justified in part by a fundamental tenet of liberalism, the belief in *reason*. The ruling classes of the feudal system had placed little faith in the human ability to reason. Jefferson said that "reason is the first born daughter of science." Jefferson's use of "daughter" here is ironic because classical liberals placed little faith in the ability of women to reason as men could, and this prejudice was reflected in the relative exclusion of women from political life and even from formal education above the elementary level.

Natural Law   If faith in human reason was the fundamental tenet of liberalism, its root metaphor was "the universe is a machine." The universe was often compared to a clock, at that time the perfect machine, with its many interrelated parts operating in precise harmony. This metaphor, of course, flowed from liberals' belief in natural law. Although Sir Isaac Newton had many distinguished predecessors, the publication of his *Mathematical Principles of Natural Philosophy* in 1687 signaled a revolution in the way the Western world viewed nature. No longer would nature be mysterious and governed by divine whims or heavenly intercessions. In England, poet Alexander Pope wrote:[7]

> Nature and Nature's laws
> Lay hid in night;
> God said, *Let* Newton *be!*
> And all was light.

Perhaps nature had been created by a divine intelligence, but this God created a perfect machine governed by precise mathematical laws. Similarly, it did not take liberals long to generalize from the idea of natural law in the physical realm to the belief in *natural law* in the social arena. With the advent of Newtonian physics, science began to replace theology as the reliable guide to action—and the authority of reason increasingly challenged the authority of the church and monarchy.

Republican Virtue   Classical liberals realized that human reason could be used for good or for ill, and they placed great store in another human capacity that was considered essential for the good life and the good society: *virtue* was an important part of their view of human nature. Historian John Miller has noted that during the revolutionary era "it was commonly believed that the republican form of government could not exist

Exhibit 2.1   Fundamental Dimensions of Classical Liberalism: A Schematic Representation

Emergence from Feudalism	
From Feudal Ideology	To Classical Liberal Ideology
State control of economy ⟶	Capitalism
State religion ⟶	Separation of church and state
Divine right of kings ⟶	Republicanism (representative government)

without 'virtue'—which signified, in the vocabulary of the eighteenth century Enlightenment, love of country, an austere style of living, probity, strict observance of the moral code and willingness to sacrifice private profit for the public good."[8] Classical liberals had great faith in the perfectibility of the individual, which was to be accomplished through virtue as well as reason. Virtue consisted largely in fulfilling one's duties to God and to nature. Meeting one's duties to God were understood as piety, which included worship, reading the Bible, and living a life of moral responsibility. The Protestant Reformation emphasized the duty to obey not the priesthood or an absolute king but the dictates of individual conscience in a right relationship with God.

While it might seem odd to us today that classical liberals were passionately committed to reason and natural law and at the same time emphasized virtue through piety and faith in God, there was no necessary contradiction in these commitments. Most classical liberals in the United States and England were Protestants. Not all Protestants, however, were classical liberals. Many of these liberals were deists, whose religious beliefs included the idea of God as the "first cause" in the universe but excluded most of the doctrine of Christianity.[9] Franklin, an ardent naturalist and scientist, spoke for many classical liberals when he said, "There is in all men something like a natural principle, which inclines them to *Devotion,* or the Worship of some unseen Power."[10] Knowledge of the world through science and of God through worship seemed to be part of the natural scheme of things.

Also regarded as part of that natural scheme was the view that the womanly and manly virtues differed. Men's virtues were to be found largely in the public spheres of commerce and politics, while women's virtues were exercised in the home and hearth—the "private sphere." Women were thought virtuous if they did not speak in public gatherings, did not question public authorities on religion or law, and fulfilled the duties of child rearing and caring for the home. The socially valued virtues of women in early America were piety, purity, submissiveness, and domesticity.[11] Given that their responsibilities were limited to the home and hearth, women were educated for the private, not the public, sphere.

Progress   The fourth fundamental idea of liberalism was belief in *progress.* Historian Russell Nye writes, "If a majority of eighteenth century Americans agreed on one idea, it was probably the perfectibility of man and the prospect of his future progress."[12] The belief in progress shows how interrelated these ideas were—free intellects developing their reason would continue to discover more about natural law and, with the resulting control over the physical universe and social relations, would constantly improve human life. Liberals assumed that men could discover what *ought* to be and would change the world accordingly. This was not only a justification but sometimes a demand for revolution.

In feudal times the perfect society was thought to be the one that followed tradition, including the tradition of inherited property and privilege, while classical liberals believed that society was progressive if it followed human reason, natural law, and the "natural rights" of individuals. When government violated those rights, wrote Jefferson, it was the duty of the people to overthrow it. Revolution, then, was an important classical liberal vehicle for progress. Embedded in this idea was a commitment to *social meliorism* (the amelioration, or improvement, of imperfect social conditions) and humanitarianism. The liberal's method of meliorism was usually through environmental control and manipulation of institutions. At times such social intervention conflicted with the liberal's ideal of freedom from governmental control. Because of the history of strong and often oppressive government under feudalism, liberals were fearful of a strong government. Jefferson often expressed his belief that the best government was "that which governed least."

Sir Isaac Newton (1642–1727): "God said, Let Newton be, and all was light."

Jefferson's belief in the inevitability of progress without a strong central government was partly grounded in a strong faith in the benefits of *education*. It was through education that individuals would develop their reason and virtue. Education would facilitate the development of all that liberals held important. Enlightenment of the population was seen as essential for self-government. In a 1786 letter to George Wythe, Jefferson urged the establishment of education in the new republic in these words: "I think by far the most important bill in our whole code is that for the diffusion of knowledge among the people. No other sure foundation can be devised for the preservation of freedom and happiness," and he admonished his friend, "Preach, my dear sir, a crusade against ignorance: establish and improve the law for educating the common people."[13] The antithesis of virtue for the liberals was ignorance rather than sin, and the cure for ignorance was education. No one argued this case with more power, clarity, and elegance than Jefferson. While Jefferson, as we shall see, differed from many of his contemporaries in his belief that the state had a responsibility to provide schools for educating the children of the common man and woman, even the opponents of state-supported schooling regarded education as essential to a life well lived. Whether the poor could afford it or not, their education was for classical liberals a concern of the state.

Nationalism   A fifth basic belief embedded in classical liberal ideology was the developing commitment to a nation-state. As European feudalism gave way to republican liberalism, a new spirit of national identity emerged in changing European societies. Similarly, in the colonies, Americans increasingly saw themselves less as "American subjects of the King," in Franklin's words, and more as a people with a national mission. Even before the Revolutionary War, Patrick Henry proclaimed that "the distinctions between Virginians . . . and New Englanders are no more. All America is thrown into one mass. I am not a Virginian, but an American."[14] The emotions of the Revolution, of course, heightened this nationalist allegiance, and citizens of the new nation began to forge a new identity. Americans saw themselves as blessed with unparalleled natural resources and a historical mission to differentiate themselves from the traditions and influences of the old country.

Classical liberals maintained an uneasy balance between these two liberal commitments to nationalism and freedom. It was a balance perhaps best captured by the concept of *federalism,* which seemed to respect the autonomy of individual states while affirming a new collective identity.

Freedom   The classical liberal conception of *freedom*— the sixth fundamental belief in the ideology—was primarily what a 20th-century British philosopher, Isaiah Berlin, has called "negative freedom," that is, freedom from restraint or interference.[15] Four types of freedom were considered the basic rights of White males: intellectual, political, civil, and economic. Intellectual freedom was the most fundamental. Liberals argued that the intellect must be free from the chains of the state and the tethers of the church if reason was to comprehend and control the physical and social worlds. By the 18th century, the history of science was replete with examples of church and state thwarting scientific discovery by forcing allegiance to dogma. (Galileo's persecution is perhaps the best-known illustration.)

Closely associated with intellectual and political freedom was the liberals' advocacy of civic freedom, a notion often embodied in the current term "civil liberties." The distinction between political and civic freedom is at least as old as Aristotle, who distinguished between the freedom to participate in making the laws (political freedom) and the freedom to "live as one pleases" (civic freedom). This advocacy was for guarantees against the transgression of the limits of power and authority by even representative government. It was usually manifested in demands for guarantees such as the American Bill of Rights, which protected citizens from government interference in their right to speak as they saw fit, assemble, bear arms, refuse the quartering of troops in their homes, and so on. The argument for economic freedom was informed by a long history of government control, appropriation, and taxation during the feudal era. The liberals tended to oppose most government action in the economic sphere. Their slogan, "Laissez-faire," literally "allow to act," was a demand for the protection of private property from government regulation. Embedded in this idea of economic freedom was the belief, most clearly articulated by Adam Smith in *The Wealth of Nations,* that if left alone, the marketplace would self-regulate for the good of society. Historically, this economic principle of laissez-faire has provided government support for "free" enterprise capitalism with little accompanying government control. Conversely, it inhibited liberals from developing government policy to aid the poor.

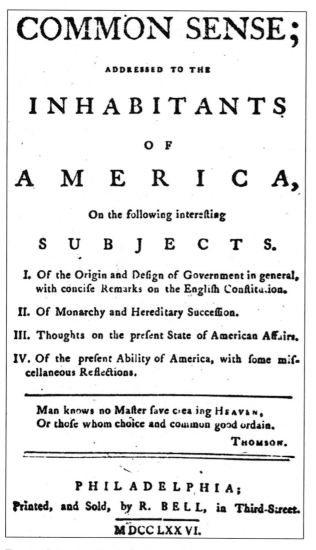

COMMON SENSE;

ADDRESSED TO THE

INHABITANTS

O F

AMERICA,

On the following interesting

S U B J E C T S.

I. Of the Origin and Defign of Government in general, with concife Remarks on the Englifh Conftitution.

II. Of Monarchy and Hereditary Succeffion.

III. Thoughts on the prefent State of American Affairs.

IV. Of the prefent Ability of America, with fome mifcellaneous Reflections.

Man knows no Mafter fave creaing HEAVEN,
Or thofe whom choice and common good ordain.
THOMSON.

PHILADELPHIA;
Printed, and Sold, by R. BELL, in Third-Street.
MDCCLXXVI.

Thomas Paine, like Thomas Jefferson and other classical liberals, believed that when government violates human reason, virtue, and the human rights granted by nature, revolution is justifiable.

Jefferson as Classical Liberal

This brief summary of classical liberal ideology suggests the lens through which Jefferson viewed the world and developed his ideas on education (see Exhibit 2.2). The Declaration of Independence, Jefferson's most famous written work, expressed the core of his ideology: "We hold these truths to be self-evident, that all men are created equal, that they are endowed by their Creator with certain unalienable Rights, that among these are Life, Liberty, and the Pursuit of Happiness." The effective establishment of life, liberty, and the pursuit of happiness was a moral end for Jefferson. Other issues, such as freedom of the press, ownership of property, and the form of government, were means to these ends.

Jefferson's substitution of "the Pursuit of Happiness" in the Declaration of Independence for John Locke's term "Property" in his *Second Treatise of Government* was deliberate. His attempt to correct Lafayette's draft of "rights" in the early stages of the French Revolution provides explicit evidence of this. Lafayette had written that every man was born with rights that included "property and the care of his honor." Jefferson objected to both terms. He argued that property, like government, was only a *means* to human happiness, not a natural and unalienable right.[16] Further, his objection to excessive concentration of wealth as a cause of poverty and resulting decrease of happiness for the masses indicated his belief that property was only a means to happiness.

Thinking Critically about the Issues	#3

Explain how Jefferson's educational proposals were related to both the political economy of postrevolutionary Virginia and classical liberalism.

The conception of happiness that was central to Jefferson's philosophy was drawn in part from a conception of human nature that followed Aristotle (with whose work Jefferson was familiar) in believing that happiness was obtainable only if the rational part of one's nature governed the appetites and passions. Jefferson employed this Aristotelian model of the division in human nature, for example, in explaining why African Americans and women, whom he understood to be governed more by appetites and passions than by reason, were less capable

Exhibit 2.2   Basic Tenets of Classical Liberalism

Reason	Progress
Natural Law	Nascent Nationalism
Virtue	Freedom
	Economic
	Civil
	Political
	Intellectual

of self-governance than White men—and thus should submit to the reason of White men if they were to find happiness. In many ways, this conception of happiness governed Jefferson's life.[17]

Jefferson and Intellectual Freedom

Instrumental to the pursuit of happiness, for Jefferson, was intellectual freedom. Tradition, dogma, and coercion were antithetical to intellectual freedom. Jefferson considered his successful campaign against the union of church and state as one of his major victories for intellectual freedom and therefore an important contribution to human happiness. At the time of the Revolution, most states had an established church, and these churches persisted until after the Civil War. The prohibition of established religion in the Bill of Rights was interpreted to apply only to the federal government, not to the state governments. As a result, state tax monies continued to be used to support the established church, and in some states nonmembers were barred from the exercise of certain civil rights, such as voting and holding public office. Moreover, the established church often had the authority to censor books and condemn individuals for heresy.

Jefferson responded to this condition by designing the famous American "wall of separation" between church and state. In 1779, he wrote the Bill for Establishing Religious Freedom for the Virginia legislature. It was passed in 1786 and became the model for several subsequent state disestablishment laws. The bill contended that a man's religious beliefs were his own private affair and in no way should be infringed on by the state. It severed the connection between church and state. In it, Jefferson asserted the now famous justification for intellectual freedom and the determination of truth through the free competition of ideas: that "truth is great and will prevail if left to herself; that she is proper and sufficient antagonist to error, and has nothing to fear from conflict unless by human interposition disarmed of her natural weapons, free argument and debate; errors ceasing to be dangerous when it is permitted freely to contradict them."[18] His *Notes on the State of Virginia* angrily asserted the right of religious nonconformity: "Millions of innocent men, women and children, since the introduction of Christianity, have been burnt, tortured, fined, imprisoned; yet we have not advanced one inch toward uniformity. What has been the effect of coercion? To make one half the world fools, and the other half hypocrites."[19] And if uniformity could somehow be

achieved, he believed, its results would stifle intellectual activity. Several years later, in 1815, Jefferson wrote to his friend P. H. Wendover: "Difference of opinion leads to inquiry, and inquiry to truth; and that, I am sure, is the ultimate and sincere object of us both."[20]

The issue that troubled Jefferson's conservative opponents was how to maintain social order. Like Jefferson, they sought a middle ground between the chaos of too little government and the tyranny of too much. Unlike Jefferson, however, their primary concern was anarchy and chaos. Jefferson replied—in theory, although not always in practice—by relying on the free play of the human intellect and open debate. He resoundingly rejected coercion and force. His noted affinity for a free press stemmed from the same faith in a free intellect as the means to truth and human happiness. In a 1787 letter to his friend Edward Carington, he wrote, "Were it left to me to decide whether we should have a government without newspapers or newspapers without a government, I would not hesitate for a moment to prefer the latter." He went on with this important qualification: "But I should mean that every man shall receive these papers and be capable of reading them."[21] Newspapers, he believed, would be the instructor of the masses and the vehicle for debate. His ardor for them cooled considerably during his second administration as president, when partisan newspapers printed volumes of political gossip, half-truths, and outright lies. He even privately encouraged his political allies in Connecticut to bring suits against enemy papers.[22] He complained, "Nothing can now be believed which is seen in a newspaper." He modified his support for a free press, arguing that newspapers should be free to print the "truth."[23] On this issue, it should be remembered that a free press was not an end for Jefferson; rather, it was the means to bring information to citizens so that they could exercise intellectual freedom and come to the truth as part of their pursuit of happiness. Newspapers stood as a symbol for information: when they printed lies, Jefferson believed, they lost their usefulness.

One is left to wonder, however, why Jefferson thought that truth had lost its strength. Had he lost some of his earlier faith in the common man to follow free argument and debate? What is the justification for debate if only "the truth" is allowed a hearing? Are there special qualifications to be met before one is eligible to engage in an open debate between truth and error?

An 1825 letter Jefferson wrote to his friend and fellow trustee of the University of Virginia adds sharpness to these questions. The letter was about Jefferson's plans for the upcoming meeting of the trustees. After stating the general principle that trustees should not interfere in the choice of texts by professors, Jefferson argued for an exception in regard to professors of government. He claimed that if the trustees were not watchful about what was taught in the subject of government, "heresies may be taught, of so interesting a character to our own state and to the United States, as to make it a duty in us to lay down the principles which are to be taught." He went on to assert that this was necessary because the trustees could not be certain of the political persuasion of future professors of government. Jefferson endorsed a resolution to this effect, which he intended to offer at the trustees' meeting. He then requested, "I wish it kept to ourselves, because I have always found that the less such things are spoken of beforehand, the less obstruction is contrived to be thrown in their way."[24] Here Jefferson is not simply arguing to protect the common man from errors contained in newspapers; rather, that professors, university students, and his fellow trustees should be insulated from potential error. If one were to argue for selective admission to open debate between truth and error, who would be eligible if not professors, university students, and university trustees? In light of these examples, what are we to make of Jefferson's arguments for intellectual freedom?

Moreover, Jefferson and his contemporary liberals believed that "truth" could be discovered by man through the free exercise of intellect and reason. This was basic to their view of natural law and underpinned by Newtonian physics. This "truth," Jefferson believed, would be acknowledged by all rational men. Like other classical liberals, Jefferson believed that truth was not *created* by human inquiry and therefore subject to revision by further inquiry but instead was a property of the natural world and therefore absolute and unchanging, waiting to be *discovered* by human inquiry. Once discovered, it followed for classical liberals, such truth should be taught—whether it was $2 + 2 = 4$ or that republican government was the surest route to social justice and human happiness. Modern science, as we will see in Chapter 4, has become much more tentative about the origins and permanence of truth.

Jefferson, Democracy, and Education

A second major concern for Jefferson, then, was the establishment of the kind of government most likely to promote human happiness. Again, the Declaration of Independence can serve to summarize Jefferson's thought: "That to secure these rights [life, liberty, and the pursuit of happiness], Governments are instituted among men, deriving their just powers from the consent of the governed." Eleven years later, in a letter to his closest political confidant, James Madison, he stated another of his political axioms: "I am not a friend of the very energetic government. It is always oppressive."[25] It is clear that Jefferson's political ideal would be a representative republic composed of educated, informed, and rational citizens. The government would have limited powers circumscribed by a constitution containing a declaration of rights reserved for the people. Daniel Boorstein has described Jefferson's aim as "a government too weak to aid the wolves yet strong enough to protect the sheep."[26]

Jefferson's arguments for a democratic republic as well as for education are based in his moral philosophy and are succinctly stated in a 1787 letter advising his young friend Peter Carr about his education. He noted that "man is destined for society." Therefore, the creator must have endowed us with a "moral sense of conscience" that "is as much a part of man as his leg or arm." Moral sense is innate in all humans, for Jefferson, "in a greater or less degree. It may be strengthened by exercise, as may any particular limb of the body."[27] This moral sense that equipped all men to participate in their own governance could be enhanced or debased according to environmental circumstances. Democracy was thus the most moral of governments for Jefferson not only because it protected "inalienable rights" but also because it provided for the moral development of individuals.

Referring to the situation in the United States in 1820, Jefferson wrote, "I know of no safe depository of the ultimate powers of society but the people themselves; and if we think them not enlightened enough to exercise their control with a wholesome discretion, the remedy is not to take it from them, but to inform their discretion by education."[28] Four years later he noted, "The qualifications for self-government are not innate. They are the result of habit and long training."[29] Jefferson remained remarkably constant in this belief. In a 1787 letter to James Madison, he had written, "above all things I hope the education of the common people will be attended to: convinced that on their good senses we may rely with the most security for the preservation of a due degree of liberty."[30]

This letter indicated that in addition to an innate moral sense, sufficiently educated, an effective citizenship required a particular kind of economic base. Then ambassador to France, Jefferson wrote, "I think our governments will remain virtuous for many centuries; as long as they are chiefly agricultural; and this will be as long as there shall be vacant lands in any part of America. When they get piled upon one another in large cities as in Europe they will become as corrupt as in Europe."[31] Agriculture was more to Jefferson than crops and income; it was a way of life that developed independence, perseverance, industry, self-sufficiency, and strength. These characteristics were essential to Jefferson for virtue and human happiness. In his *Notes on the State of Virginia*, he referred to farmers as "the chosen people of God," and the "mobs of the great cities" as cancers sapping the strength of democratic governments.[32] His desire to guarantee an adequate supply of "vacant" land for agriculture led him as president to purchase the vast Louisiana Territory even though this act expanded the power of the federal government—an expansion of power which Jefferson and other classical liberals generally opposed. The end he pursued in this act, however, was the pursuit of happiness, and thus to Jefferson more important, in principle, than keeping federal power limited.

Government by a "Natural Aristocracy"

Even in the "noble experiment" that American liberals considered the beacon for all humankind, Jefferson did not intend for all free men to participate on an entirely equal basis. For 14 years, until both died on Independence Day in 1826, Jefferson and John Adams, who had been bitter political enemies from the early 1790s, carried on an extended correspondence. One of Jefferson's most interesting letters was written in the fall of 1813 and portrays his conception of the proper political aristocracy. He contrasts this "natural aristocracy" with an "artificial" or "pseudo-aristocracy." The natural aristocracy that Jefferson believed should govern was based on "virtue and talent," while the artificial aristocracy was based on birth and wealth. The previous, artificial aristocracy had been the target of the Revolution. Because humans had been created for society, Jefferson explained to Adams, it naturally followed that God would also provide for "virtue and wisdom" to manage society. He argued, "that form of government is best, which provides the most effectively for a pure selection of these natural *aristoi* into the office of government," and the most effective procedure was "to leave to the citizens the free election and separation of the *aristoi* from the *pseudo-aristoi*, of the wheat from the chaff."[33]

Jefferson's Plan for Popular Education

Education was not only crucial in Jefferson's political theory, it was also an important means for the pursuit of happiness, for he understood happiness to include the pursuit of knowledge. It should not be surprising that education commanded Jefferson's attention throughout his life. His public statements on education began when, in Virginia, he wrote the Bill for the More General Diffusion of Knowledge,[34] the Bill for Amending the Constitution of the College of William and Mary, and Substituting More Certain Revenues for Its Support,[35] and the Bill for Establishing a Public Library.[36] These three legislative proposals contained the core of his educational thought. Their contents were elaborated in his subsequent *Notes on the State of Virginia* and numerous private letters. After his administration, he authored a Bill for the Establishment of a System of Public Education[37] and the Report of the Commission Appointed to Fix the Site of the University of Virginia. (It was referred to as the "Rockfish Gap Report" because it was at a tavern in Rockfish Gap, Virginia, on August 1, 1818, that the commissioners met to sign it.)[38]

Thinking Critically about the Issues   #4

Jefferson's Bill for the More General Diffusion of Knowledge tried to establish state funding for schooling in Virginia, but it also sought to protect local control of schools. To what degree is such a combination—state funding and local control of schools—consistent with various dimensions of the classical liberal conception of freedom? Is this still an issue today? How? What is your position on local control?

There were four interrelated parts or tiers in Jefferson's proposed educational structure: elementary schools, grammar schools, the university, and lifelong learning. Elementary and grammar school education were outlined in his 1776 Bill for the More General Diffusion of Knowledge, his *Notes,* and the 1817 Bill for the Establishment of a System of Public Education. The elementary school was to be the foundation of the entire educational structure. Although both bills were defeated in the Virginia legislature, they provide us with important insights into Jefferson's conception of education.

Historical Context

The Jeffersonian Era

The following events should help you situate the educational developments in this chapter in a broader historical context. Every chapter will have such a timeline. In each chapter, the events are illustrative—you might have chosen differently if you were constructing a timeline of your own. For any item, you should be able to consider, "What is its educational significance?" Some events are not mentioned in the text narrative and might lead you to further inquiry. Finally, you might find the Online Learning Center useful: www.mhhe.com/tozer7e.

The Breakdown of Feudalism in Europe

1452	Leonardo Da Vinci is born	1605	Shakespeare writes *Macbeth* and *King Lear*
1455	Gutenberg prints the first book	1687	Newton writes *Principia Mathematica*
1534	Martin Luther publishes German translation of the Bible	1689	*The Bill of Rights* and *The Act of Toleration* are declared in England
1543	Copernicus publishes *Revolutions of the Heavenly Bodies*	1690	John Locke writes *An Essay Concerning Human Understanding*

Prerevolutionary Period

1607	Jamestown is established by English settlers in Virginia	1693	College of William and Mary is founded in Virginia
1636	Harvard College is founded	1701	Yale University is founded in Connecticut
1647	Massachusetts law requires that every town of 50 families or more must hire a teacher to teach reading and writing	1734–1735	Freedom of press in American colonies is established
1690	*The New England Primer*, a widely used colonial textbook, is published		

Early National Period in United States

1776	Continental Congress adopts Declaration of Independence	1789	Power-driven textile machinery arrives in the United States
1779	Jefferson unsuccessfully proposes his Virginia Plan for public schools	1789–1797	George Washington serves as first president of United States
1783	Noah Webster's *American Spelling Book* is published	1793	Eli Whitney invents cotton gin
1789	Constitution is ratified by 11 of 13 states	1797–1801	John Adams serves as second president
1791	U.S. Bill of Rights is ratified		
		1800	First of a series of southern state laws barring Blacks from access to education is passed in South Carolina
		1826	On July 4, 50 years after the Declaration, Jefferson and John Adams die

Thinking Analytically about the Timeline

What items from the section on the breakdown of feudalism in Europe seem to have influenced events you can identify in the prerevolutionary and early national periods in the United States?

Elementary School Districts

Jefferson proposed to divide the state into small districts, or "wards," of five to six square miles. These districts would serve a dual purpose. First, they would become the local unit of government. As he explained in a letter to John Adams, "My proposition had, for a further object, to impart to these wards those portions of self-government for which they are best qualified, by confiding to them the care of their poor, the roads, police, elections, the nominations of jurors, administrations of justice in small cases, elementary exercise of the militia; in short, to have made them little republics, with a warden at the head of each, for all those concerns which, being under their eye, they would better manage than the larger republics of the county or the State."[39] Thus, Jefferson not only would have decentralized governmental authority to local districts, which be believed could most effectively exercise power, but would have provided a laboratory for self-government. Additionally, this effort at decentralization of both civil and educational governance must be understood within the limitations of transportation and communication then available.

Second, each of the districts would establish an elementary school where "all free children, male and female," would be entitled to attend without cost for three years, or longer at their private expense. An overseer, responsible for approximately 10 schools, would be appointed by the alderman elected in the districts. General governance of the elementary schools, including the hiring and dismissal of teachers, examination of students, and supervision of the curriculum, would have been in the care of the overseers.

The curriculum of Jefferson's elementary schools was uncluttered and wholly intellectual. "At every of these schools shall be taught reading, writing, and common arithmetic, and the books which shall be used therein for instructing the children to read shall be such as will at the same time make them acquainted with Graecian, Roman, English, and American history."[40] This three-year curriculum would provide the extent of schooling for the mass of the population, certainly for the females, who would not go on to secondary or higher education. Jefferson conceived these elementary years as an education for life, providing the requisite skills for the daily life of the yeoman farmer and for the wife and mother of the household in the early American republic.

Common arithmetic would enable them to do the calculations to purchase goods, sell their surplus production, figure their taxes, and in general understand the relatively simple agrarian economy within which they labored. Writing would empower them to communicate with those at a distance. Reading was necessary to comprehend distant communications, newspapers, government announcements, and laws and, most important, would enable graduates to continue their education throughout life through the medium of books. In *Notes on the State of Virginia,* Jefferson explained the emphasis on history in the three-year curriculum, which would have provided the entire formal schooling for the common people:

> History, by appraising them of the past, will enable them to judge the future; it will avail them of the experience of other times and other nations; it will qualify them as judges of the actions and designs of men. . . . Every government degenerates when trusted to the rulers of the people alone. The people themselves therefore are its only safe depositories. And to render even them sage, their minds must be improved to a certain degree. This indeed is not all that is necessary, though it be essentially necessary.[41]

History, then, would provide the masses with lessons to enable them to understand when their elected officials had mischief on their minds.

Each year the overseer of schools would choose from each elementary school "the boy of best genius in the school, of those whose parents are too poor to give them further education, and to send him forward to one of the grammar schools" at public expense.[42] After the first year at the grammar school, the scholarship boys would be examined and the bottom third dismissed. At the end of the second year, the best scholarship student in each grammar school would be chosen to continue and the remainder dismissed. As Jefferson put it in his *Notes on the State of Virginia,* "By this means twenty of the best geniuses will be raked annually from the rubbish, and instructed, at public expense, so far as the grammar schools go."[43]

In short, Jefferson had proposed three years of free elementary schooling, which he believed would function as a screen to identify future leaders from among the masses and equip the remainder to function effectively in the civic, economic, and private spheres of life. He expected this formal schooling to provide the basis for lifelong self-education among the population. Moreover, he understood that in America of the early 19th century, the school did not stand as the sole educating institution in society. Nevertheless, his goals were ambitious, so much so that the Virginia legislature did not approve the plan either in 1779 or in 1817 (see Exhibit 2.3). One may pause to wonder how Jefferson might appraise the present condition of his "noble experiment."

Thinking Critically about the Issues   #5

Jefferson believed that three years of literacy instruction in elementary school would be valuable in safeguarding the liberties of the population. Today this seems to be far too little schooling for so important a task. To what degree do the dimensions of political–economic life in Jefferson's time make his belief in the power of basic literacy plausible?

Grammar Schools

The second tier of schools in Jefferson's proposals were called "grammar schools" in his 1779 bill and "district schools or colleges" in his 1817 bill. These schools should

Exhibit 2.3   Objectives for Elementary and University Education in Summary of the 1818 Rockfish Gap Report

Elementary Education Is to Develop in Every Citizen	University Education Is to Develop
Information sufficient to transact business	Political leaders
Writing skills	Knowledge leading to political freedom
Calculation skills	Understanding to improve the economy
Reading skills	Reason, morals, virtue, and order
Improved morals	Understanding of science and math to promote the general health, security, and comfort
Understanding of duties	
Knowledge of rights	Habits of reflection and correct actions in students that render them
Ability to vote intelligently	examples of virtue to others and bring happiness to themselves
Ability to judge officeholders' conduct	
Ability to fulfill social relationships	

Source: Data from Roy Honeywell, *The Educational Work of Thomas Jefferson* (Cambridge, MA: Harvard University Press, 1931), p. 250.

not be confused with the present-day American high school, for they were more like the European lyceum. They were to be boarding schools. Approximately 20 were to be established throughout the state at various locations so that no scholar would be required to travel more than one day's journey from home to school. Except for the 1779 provision for one scholarship student from each elementary school, scholars would be required to pay tuition, room, board, and other necessary expenses. Of the 20 scholarship boys who finished the grammar schools, half were to be chosen to receive a further scholarship to complete the university courses at public expense.

The grammar schools were seen as "preparatory to the entrance of students into the university." Because Jefferson believed that between the ages of 10 and 15, students were best suited to learn languages, and because languages were "an instrument for the attainment of science," languages were the center of grammar school. Greek, Latin, and English grammar, along with advanced arithmetic, geometry, navigation, and geography, were to be the basic subjects in the six-year curriculum. Such a course of study, Jefferson asserted, would either fit the boy for entrance to the university or lay the foundation for the "various vocations of life needing more instruction than merely menial or praedial labor."[44]

It seems clear that Jefferson intended that local leaders would come from among those educated at the grammar school. Its graduates would provide leadership in business, transportation, surveying, the militia, and local government. He also expected that teachers for the elementary schools would be drawn from those who finished the grammar school curriculum, especially from among the scholarship boys not chosen for university attendance.

University Education

Jefferson's conception of university education is displayed in a wide range of private letters and summarized in his Report of the Commission Appointed to Fix the Site of the University of Virginia.[45] His view of higher education differed considerably from the fashion of the day. He explicitly contrasted his university proposals with the popular academies of the early 19th century, which he called "petty academies." These he condemned in a letter to John Adams: "They commit their pupils to the theater of the world, with just taste enough for learning to be alienated from industrious pursuits, and not enough to do service in the ranks of science."[46]

He also rejected the Harvard model of a prescribed course of study. In a letter to George Ticknor, he stated, "We shall, on the contrary, allow then the uncontrolled choice in the lectures they shall choose to attend, and require elementary qualifications on and sufficient age. . . . Our institution will proceed on the principle . . . of letting everyone come and listen to whatever he thinks may improve the condition of his mind."[47] Nevertheless, Jefferson modified free election somewhat in his Rockfish Gap Report. After stating that "every student shall be free to attend the schools of his choice, and not other than he chooses," the report added this qualification:

> But no diploma shall be given to anyone who has not passed an examination in the Latin language as shall have proved him able to read the highest classics in that language with ease, thorough understanding and just quality; and if he be also proficient in Greek, let that, too, be stated in his diploma.[48]

This idea of relatively free election was based on the premise that all students would enter the university with a common basic education acquired in the grammar schools.[49] The University of Virginia was thus conceived as a place of professional and advanced scientific education rather than simply as a collegiate institution of general liberal studies, which was the model in American higher education of Jefferson's time.

Jefferson was unrestrained in his goals for university education (see Exhibit 2.3) because he rejected "the discouraging persuasion that man is fixed, by the law of his nature, at a given point; that his improvement is a chimera, and the hope delusive of rendering ourselves wiser, happier or better than our forefathers were." On the contrary, he proclaimed that similar to the pruners' art of grafting, "Education in like manner, engrafts a new man on the native stock, and improves what in his nature was vicious and perverse into qualities of virtue and social worth."[50]

The university would provide the education for the natural *aristoi* for Jefferson's society. Its graduates would become the legislators, governors, and jurists who would provide governmental leadership. They would fill those vocations which would at a later time be called professions.

Jefferson's republic was to be based on what he called the natural aristocracy. Today we call such an arrangement a *meritocracy*: a social system in which positions of greatest influence and prestige are filled by those who "merit" them by demonstrated talent. He argued that education was a prerequisite for leadership. Is his argument convincing? Given that his proposals were defeated, it is worth speculating: *Would* his proposed educational system have provided the necessary education for leadership and for the masses? We might also ask whether in subsequent history the "people" have generally elected the "really good and wise." If not, is this because of a flaw in Jefferson's conception, or have we not fully developed his ideas? Perhaps most important, is the Jeffersonian meritocracy equivalent to democracy? If not, is it an adequate substitute for democracy? What kind of educational system would be necessary for a democracy?

Thinking Critically about the Issues   #6

Jefferson claimed that the Bill for the More General Diffusion of Knowledge would help locate the "natural aristocracy" of society: those with the virtue and talent to lead in a republican form of government. To what degree do you think his plan, if passed, would have adequately rewarded virtue and talent?

(1) What were the limitations of the plan in terms of social class, race, and gender?

(2) In your experience, are today's schools successful in locating students with the most "virtue and talent"? (3) Do they successfully locate a natural aristocracy in today's society, or (4) do "wealth, birth, or other accidental condition or circumstance," as Jefferson said, play a significant role? Explain.

Self-Education

The elementary school, the grammar school, and the university were the first three tiers of Jefferson's educational structure. They did not, however, outweigh the fourth tier—lifelong self-instruction. Indeed, in important ways, the first three were but preparations for the fourth. Jefferson's passionate commitment to lifelong self-education was expressed in many of his private letters, in the construction of his own library, in his enthusiasm for newspapers, and in the Bill for Establishing a Public Library. In that bill, Jefferson proposed in 1779 that Virginia build a public library in Richmond and provide an annual allotment for the purchase of books, paintings, and statues.[51] His commitment to lifelong self-education was grounded in his conviction that the development of reason, the expansion of intellect, and inquiry into the mysteries of the universe were indeed fundamental to human happiness. In 1817, as he was preparing the Rockfish Gap Report for the Virginia legislature, he expressed in a letter to George Ticknor his fear that the legislature might not understand the "important truths, that knowledge is power, that knowledge is safety, and that knowledge is happiness." Nevertheless, he contended that persistence was necessary, for if "we fail in doing all the good we wish, we will do at least all we can. This is the law of duty in every society of free agents, where everyone has equal right to judge for himself."[52]

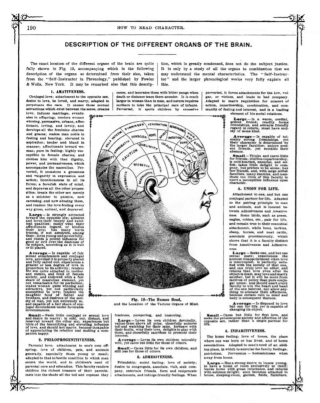

Faculty psychology was based on two metaphors that were useful in planning curriculum (mind as a muscle to be exercised and mind as a vessel to be filled)—and that emphasized mental "faculties" such as memory and attentiveness.

Most American educational theorists since Jefferson have agreed that a fundamental aim of all education is to prepare the student for lifelong learning. Again, a number of questions present themselves: To what extent has this goal been achieved? What are the factors that militate against its success? Why did Jefferson believe his proposed educational system would facilitate lifelong learning? What kind of lifelong learning would you expect from the graduates of each of Jefferson's three tiers of formal schooling? In each instance, would this learning be sufficient to enable the graduates to engage in Jefferson's ideal of the pursuit of happiness?

Jefferson, like most classical liberals, held to what would later be called faculty psychology, which contended that the mind was made up of distinct "faculties." For Jefferson, the faculties of the mind included memory, reason, and imagination.[53] Like muscles, these faculties had to be exercised for development. Moreover, he conceived the mind as an empty vessel to be "filled" with useful facts. Faculty psychology held that developed faculties, with minds appropriately exercised and filled, could "transfer" this training and understanding to any situation in life—that is, the student would be able to generalize from school experience to life experience.

Jefferson's Views on Slavery, Native Americans, and Women

Though classical liberals differed sharply on many issues—race, education, and voting rights, for example—Jefferson was America's outstanding spokesperson for the liberalism of his time and perhaps of all time. His Declaration of Independence proclamations on human rights and human equality were borrowed by Lincoln for the first sentence of the Gettysburg Address and a century later gave moral force to the civil rights and women's equality movements in this country. Freedom, liberty, the rule of reason in human affairs, the unfettered pursuit of truth, the stimulation of scientific investigation, and the creation of political and educational structures for the support of those goals were his life's work. Nevertheless, we have seen that there are reasons to question some of Jefferson's ideas in these areas. Moreover, a serious study of Jefferson forces one to consider at least three additional problem areas: his actions and views on slavery, Native Americans, and women.

Slavery   There can be little question that Jefferson's entire philosophy required the rejection of slavery. Indeed, Jefferson's first legislative act as a representative in the Virginia colonial assembly[54] was to offer a bill allowing the voluntary emancipation of slaves by their owners. In 1770, as a lawyer, he undertook the defense of a slave who sued for his freedom.[55] Most significantly, in his proposed draft of the Declaration of Independence Jefferson included the following statement about the British monarch:

He has waged cruel war against human nature itself, violating its most sacred rights of life and liberty in persons of a distant people who never offended him, capturing and carrying them into slavery in another hemisphere, or to incur miserable death in their transportation hither. This piratical warfare, the opprobrium of INFIDEL powers, is the warfare of the CHRISTIAN king of Great Britain. Determined to keep open a market where MEN should be bought and sold, he has prostituted his negative for suppressing every legislative attempt to prohibit or restrain this execrable commerce.[56]

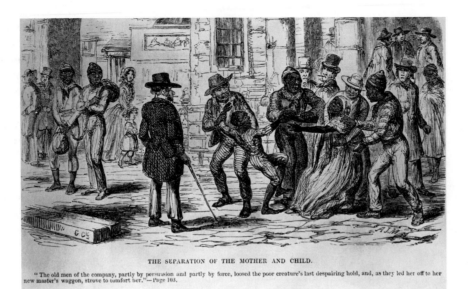

THE SEPARATION OF THE MOTHER AND CHILD.

" The old men of the company, partly by persuasion and partly by force, loosed the poor creature's last despairing hold, and, as they led her off to her new master's waggon, strove to comfort her."—Page 103.

Although this section was struck by the full assembly, its inclusion by Jefferson and his emphasis of the word "MEN" are significant when one attempts to comprehend how slavery fits with Jefferson's social philosophy. It seems to indicate that philosophically Jefferson included African Americans in the category of "men" and that they should be covered by all the provisions the Declaration makes for "men."

However, his writings about African Americans provide an ambiguous judgment of the race. At times he seems to see African Americans as inferior, at other times he calls them equal or superior to Whites in some attributes, and at still other times he argues that their inequalities are due to the degradation of slavery and are remediable if they are placed in more favorable circumstances.[57] As a representative to the national Congress, he unsuccessfully proposed that the Northwest Ordinance prohibit slavery after 1800 in any states or territories created from the Northwest Territory. From that time until his death, however, Jefferson was remarkably quiet in public about his opposition to slavery. In private, Jefferson often condemned slavery. For example, in August 1825, he wrote in a private correspondence, "The abolition of the evil [slavery] is not impossible. It ought never to be despaired of. Every plan should be adapted, every experiment tried, which may do something towards the ultimate object."[58]

During his two terms as president, however, Jefferson did not actively support the abolition of slavery. Moreover, in none of his major legislative proposals on education did he include the education of slaves. This is most surprising, since those weaknesses he attributed to Blacks were weaknesses that Jefferson believed could be improved through education. Jefferson's biographer Dumas Malone suggests that he may have remained silent on the slavery question while president because he considered it a state rather than a federal issue.[59] This explanation, however, is unconvincing, especially when one remembers Jefferson's willingness to expand federal power to purchase the Louisiana Territory. Such an expansion of power was justified by a higher end, he argued, and government was simply a means. Could the pursuit of open land for freehold farmers be more worthy than the elimination of human bondage? Was Jefferson practicing what he believed was political realism according to his own axiom: "No more good must be attempted than the nation can bear"?[60] If so, did this "realism" require that he continue to own slaves—at times as many as 200?[61] Is there a contradiction between "political realism" and moral leadership?

As historian Ronald Takaki points out, although Jefferson wrote in 1788 that "nobody [more] wishes to see an abolition of the [African slave] trade [and] of the condition of slavery; and certainly nobody will be more willing to encounter every sacrifice for that object," he continued to add slaves to his plantation while some 10,000 slaves were being freed by slave owners in Virginia alone in the 1780s.[62] Jefferson justified his slaveholding partly on economic grounds—he could not afford to free them until he paid off his debts (which he never succeeded in doing)—and partly on his belief that, unlike Native Americans, African Americans did not have the natural intellectual endowment necessary for self-governance. Jefferson wrote in 1781:

> In general, their existence appears to participate more of sensation than reflection. . . . Comparing them by their faculties of memory, reason, and imagination, it appears to me that in memory they are equal to whites: in reason much inferior, as I think one could scarcely be found capable of tracing and comprehending the investigations of Euclid; and that in imagination they are dull, tasteless, and anomalous.[63]

Jefferson's beliefs about the racial inferiority of African Americans led him to argue against intermarriage: Their "amalgamation with the other color produces a degradation to which no lover of his country, no lover of excellence in the human character can innocently consent." This is particularly ironic in light of continuing research on Jefferson's apparent sexual relationship with his slave, Sally Hemmings, with whom he is said to have fathered several children. Although DNA evidence supports this conclusion, according to the Thomas Jefferson Foundation, it remains disputed by the Thomas Jefferson Heritage Society. As legal scholar Annette Gordon-Reed writes, the Jefferson–Hemmings controversy mirrors a number of complicated issues in our national history and in our present-day thinking. Just as our founding fathers were conflicted about slavery, so does our society today continue to bear the fruits of those conflicts, which remain unresolved. As long as racism is a part of the fabric of our lives, historians will look to Jefferson, Washington, and other founding fathers to try to understand how we became what we are.[64]

Native Americans   As is often the case with racial and ethnic prejudice, Jefferson's racism regarding African Americans took a different form where Native Americans were concerned. He believed that intermarriage between White people and Native Americans was acceptable because Native Americans in his view were equal to Whites in natural endowment, although their culture was vastly inferior. He wrote in 1785, "I am safe in affirming that the proofs of genius given by the Indians of N. America, place them on a level with whites in the same uncultivated state. . . . I believe the Indian to be in body and mind equal to the white man. I have supposed the black man, in his present state, might not be so."[65] The consequence of this view for Jefferson was that Native Americans either had to be "civilized" into White culture or had to be driven west

of the Mississippi. His economic priorities, as Takaki points out, influenced his views of both races: what the Whites wanted from African Americans was their labor, while what Whites wanted from Native Americans was their land. If the latter agreed to cultivate the land as Whites did, however, they could stay—and Jefferson believed it was the province of Whites to instruct the Native Americans in acquiring the necessities of European culture while abandoning their own. While U.S. president, he told the Potawatomies:

> We shall . . . see your people become disposed to cultivate the earth, to raise herds of the useful animals, and to spin and weave, for their food and clothing. These resources are certain: they will never disappoint you: while those of hunting may fail, and expose your women and children to the miseries of hunger and cold. We will with pleasure furnish you with implements for the most necessary arts, and with persons who may instruct you how to make and use them.[66]

Jefferson's stance toward forcing the Native Americans away from their own culture into the ways of European Americans, as we shall see in Chapter 7, is one that would become formal government policy in the 20th century.

Women   If Jefferson was regrettably contradictory in his statements about African Americans and inconsistent in his actions toward slavery, his views regarding women were clear and consistent, but still regrettable from our contemporary vantage point. His conception of the female was as a wife, homemaker, bearer of children, and delight to her husband—period.[67] He was reportedly loving toward his wife and caring of his daughters, but he understood women to be the legal appendages to their husbands. When Jefferson stated, "All *men* are created equal" or made pronouncements regarding the rights and reason of man, his terms were always gender-specific.

In all his proposals for education, females were provided schooling only in the elementary school. The grammar schools and the university were exclusive male preserves. As important as he believed education was for the pursuit of happiness, and although he devoted the greater part of his adult life to thinking about the relationship between free men and education, in 1818, at age 75, Jefferson wrote, "A plan of female education has never been a subject of systematic contemplation with me. It has occupied my attention so far only as the education of my own daughters occasionally required." The education he provided for them was much as "might enable them, when they become mothers, to educate their own daughters, and even to direct the course for sons, should their fathers be lost, or incapable, or inattentive."[68] For Jefferson, the education of women should enable them to participate in such "amusements of life" as dancing, drawing, and music and to assume their role in the "household economy."[69] It seems that Jefferson reflected too much the sentiments of George Saville, Marquis of Halifax, whose *Advice to a Daughter* saw 15 editions between 1688 and 1765, and too little those of Abigail Adams and Mary Wollstonecraft, both staunch defenders of women's rights during Jefferson's time. Like most other classical liberals, and just as the Greeks had done in Aristotle's time, Jefferson uncritically accepted the placement of women into the private or domestic sphere of the household and perceived no need to educate women for public participation in a democratic society in which citizenship was a male privilege.

Are the issues of slavery, domination of Native Americans, and women's rights anomalies in Jefferson's philosophy flaws in his character, or do they represent a deeper flaw in liberalism? The posing of such questions imposes historical hindsight on both Jefferson and classical liberalism. Jefferson's thoughts and actions in these issues were indeed an advance over his conservative opponents. Is that sufficient for one who is thought to be committed to democracy? Privileged White males, that is, Jefferson's natural aristocracy, have always been a tiny minority in American history. Did classical liberalism adequately provide for women, African Americans, Native Americans, or nonprivileged White males—in other words, the non-*aristoi*? What becomes of Jefferson's democratic ideas if the large majority of the population is excluded from his most important goal, the pursuit of happiness? Are there possible corrections that could rescue Jefferson's philosophy? If not, what are our assessments of Jeffersonian democracy and of classical liberal ideology more generally?

 BUILDING A PHILOSOPHY OF EDUCATION

Chapter 2 makes clear how schools and other educational arrangements of the early American period reflected the ideology and political economy of that time, using Virginia, Jefferson's home state, as an illustration.

As you continue to develop your own philosophy of education, it is helpful to reflect on how many of these kinds of issues are alive today. Debates persist about whether the government should fund education in religious schools, for example, or how local communities should participate in governing its schools. And arguments continue about whether it is democratic to have, within the same state school system, districts that fund schools at very high levels (say, $15,000 per year per child) while other districts in the same state fund schools at a third of that level. Are the interests of democracy well served in such a system? How intrusive should government be in making funding more equal?

Also, as you develop your philosophy of education, it is useful to ask whether you are keeping all of your students, with all of their differences, in mind as you set your educational goals and decide on your approach to reaching those goals. Just as Jefferson scarcely considered African Americans, Native Americans, and females in his plans for a public school system, each teacher has to be careful about omitting important parts of the student body. Will your educational philosophy respond equally well to rich and poor, to students of all ethnic backgrounds and different sexual orientations, and to students with physical or cognitive or emotional disabilities? What in your philosophy of education explicitly includes those groups in your educational goals and methods, and how do you justify that? How high are the goals you set for these children? How can you develop a philosophy that will guide your action as an educator?

Finally, it is noteworthy that Jefferson intentionally had very little to say about the vocational goals of education. He wanted to develop students' human capacities for rationality, critical thinking, right action, and happiness. He also had social–political goals, for a republican democracy. Today, it might make sense to think about your educational goals as helping prepare people for three major dimensions of life: as individual persons, as citizens in a democracy, and as participants in economic life who must earn a living. Getting explicit about how your teaching will serve all of those goals is a step toward a more practical philosophy of education.

Primary Source Reading

The first Primary Source Reading is from Thomas Paine's 1791 work, *The Rights of Man*. Paine was part of the intellectual force that influenced the revolutionary spirit of Jefferson's contemporaries. In this work, Paine argues that our rights under government are given by nature and not man. If they were provided by government or any other social institution, they would be privileges, not rights. Thus human beings possess a suite of capacities that must be honored and be free to develop. Government institutions may be tested by judging the degree to which human "nature" is realized or limited by them. Paine believed that deliberation, protest, and reform were essential to this process and that continuing violation justifies revolution. Paine penetrates the illogic of relying on heredity to determine who will be the best author or artist. In the same way it would not just be unfair, but foolish to form governments based on heredity. Despite this ideal, Paine lives in a world, as we still do, where inherited access to social goods, including education, is influenced by the vestiges of the feudalism that the Enlightenment sought to overturn. Hereditary property and poverty both still powerfully condition fair access to life chances through public institutions like schools.

The second Primary Source Reading, an exchange between Thomas Jefferson and author/scientist/mathematician Benjamin Banneker, reveals much about its era and its protagonists. Banneker, a descendant of slaves, English servants, and freedmen, was dark skinned and referred to as an "Ethiopian" in one newspaper account of the time. Like Secretary of State Jefferson, he was highly accomplished in many different fields. In sending Jefferson the first edition of an Almanac he had authored in 1791, Banneker writes that he can't help but comment on the condition of slavery and Jefferson's own public position on that institution. His language is respectful, precise, and challenging to Jefferson. Jefferson responds to Banneker within two weeks, but in doing so seems not to want to address Banneker's central concerns. The language is polite but evasive. Positioned at the end of a chapter on liberty and literacy, it raises a number of issues that bear discussing in class. One of them is how each man treats issues of race, slavery, and liberty. Another is, how many students and teachers today can write at Banneker's level of precision and literary quality? Why is that?

Years later, Jefferson wrote to his friend Joel Barlow that he doubted that Banneker had done all the Almanac calculations himself, citing the long 1791 letter as evidence of average talents. Such is the power, one might say, of ideology to shape our perceptions of the world. Each man went on to great achievement after this exchange, and slavery continued to flourish after both had passed away.

From The Rights of Man

Thomas Paine

The representative system takes society and civilisation for its basis; nature, reason, and experience, for its guide.

Experience, in all ages, and in all countries, has demonstrated that it is impossible to control Nature in her distribution of mental powers. She gives them as she pleases. Whatever is the rule by which she, apparently to us, scatters them among mankind, that rule remains a secret to man. It would be as ridiculous to attempt to fix the hereditaryship of human beauty, as of wisdom. Whatever wisdom constituently is, it is like a seedless plant; it may be reared when it appears, but it cannot be voluntarily produced. There is always a sufficiency somewhere in the general mass of society for all purposes; but with respect to the parts of society, it is continually changing its place. It rises in one to-day, in another to-morrow, and has most probably visited in rotation every family of the earth, and again withdrawn.

As this is in the order of nature, the order of government must necessarily follow it, or government will, as we see it does, degenerate into ignorance. The hereditary system, therefore, is as repugnant to human wisdom as to human rights; and is as absurd as it is unjust.

As the republic of letters brings forward the best literary productions, by giving to genius a fair and universal chance; so the representative system of government is calculated to produce the wisest laws, by collecting wisdom from where it can be found. I smile to myself when I contemplate the ridiculous insignificance into which literature and all the sciences would sink, were they made hereditary; and I carry the same idea into governments. An hereditary governor is as inconsistent as an hereditary author. I know not whether Homer or Euclid had sons; but I will venture an opinion that if they had, and had left their works unfinished, those sons could not have completed them.

Do we need a stronger evidence of the absurdity of hereditary government than is seen in the descendants of those men, in any line of life, who once were famous?

Is there scarcely an instance in which there is not a total reverse of the character? It appears as if the tide of mental faculties flowed as far as it could in certain channels, and then forsook its course, and arose in others. How irrational then is the hereditary system, which establishes channels of power, in company with which wisdom refuses to flow! By continuing this absurdity, man is perpetually in contradiction with himself; he accepts, for a king, or a chief magistrate, or a legislator, a person whom he would not elect for a constable.

It appears to general observation, that revolutions create genius and talents; but those events do no more than bring them forward. There is existing in man, a mass of sense lying in a dormant state, and which, unless something excites it to action, will descend with him, in that condition, to the grave. As it is to the advantage of society that the whole of its faculties should be employed, the construction of government ought to be such as to bring forward, by a quiet and regular operation, all that extent of capacity which never fails to appear in revolutions.

This cannot take place in the insipid state of hereditary government, not only because it prevents, but because it operates to benumb. When the mind of a nation is bowed down by any political superstition in its government, such as hereditary succession is, it loses a considerable portion of its powers on all other subjects and objects. Hereditary succession requires the same obedience to ignorance, as to wisdom; and when once the mind can bring itself to pay this indiscriminate reverence, it descends below the stature of mental manhood. It is fit to be great only in little things. It acts a treachery upon itself, and suffocates the sensations that urge the detection.

Though the ancient governments present to us a miserable picture of the condition of man, there is one which above all others exempts itself from the general description. I mean the democracy of the Athenians. We see more to admire, and less to condemn, in that great, extraordinary people, than in anything which history affords.

What is called a republic is not any particular form of government. It is wholly characteristic of the purport, matter or object for which government ought to be instituted, and on which it is to be employed, RES-PUBLICA, the public affairs, or the public good; or, literally translated, the public thing. It is a word of a good original, referring to what ought to be the character and business of government; and in this sense it is

naturally opposed to the word monarchy, which has a base original signification. It means arbitrary power in an individual person; in the exercise of which, himself, and not the res-publica, is the object.

Every government that does not act on the principle of a Republic, or in other words, that does not make the res-publica its whole and sole object, is not a good government. Republican government is no other than government established and conducted for the interest of the public, as well individually as collectively. It is not necessarily connected with any particular form, but it most naturally associates with the representative form, as being best calculated to secure the end for which a nation is at the expense of supporting it.

War is the common harvest of all those who participate in the division and expenditure of public money, in all countries. It is the art of conquering at home; the object of it is an increase of revenue; and as revenue cannot be increased without taxes, a pretence must be made for expenditure. In reviewing the history of the English Government, its wars and its taxes, a bystander, not blinded by prejudice nor warped by interest, would declare that taxes were not raised to carry on wars, but that wars were raised to carry on taxes.

Thinking Critically about the Issues   #7

What is Paine's argument for natural aristocracy? If his ideal in *Rights of Man* were in force, describe how the schooling, in any community you are aware of, would change.

Primary Source Reading

Exchange between Benjamin Banneker and Thomas Jefferson

SIR,

I AM fully sensible of the greatness of that freedom, which I take with you on the present occasion; a liberty which seemed to me scarcely allowable, when I reflected on that distinguished and dignified station in which you stand, and the almost general prejudice and prepossession, which is so prevalent in the world against those of my complexion.

I suppose it is a truth too well attested to you, to need a proof here, that we are a race of beings, who have long labored under the abuse and censure of the world; that we have long been looked upon with an eye of contempt; and that we have long been considered rather as brutish than human, and scarcely capable of mental endowments.

Sir, I hope I may safely admit, in consequence of that report which hath reached me, that you are a man far less inflexible in sentiments of this nature, than many others; that you are measurably friendly, and well disposed towards us; and that you are willing and ready to lend your aid and assistance to our relief, from those many distresses, and numerous calamities, to which we are reduced. Now Sir, if this is founded in truth, I apprehend you will embrace every opportunity, to eradicate that train of absurd and false ideas and opinions, which so generally prevails with respect to us; and that your sentiments are concurrent with mine, which are, that one universal Father hath given being to us all; and that he hath not only made us all of one flesh, but that he hath also, without partiality, afforded us all the same sensations and endowed us all with the same faculties; and that however variable we may be in society or religion, however diversified in situation or color, we are all of the same family, and stand in the same relation to him.

Sir, if these are sentiments of which you are fully persuaded, I hope you cannot but acknowledge, that it is the indispensible duty of those, who maintain for themselves the rights of human nature, and who possess the obligations of Christianity, to extend their power and influence to the relief of every part of the human race, from whatever burden or oppression they may unjustly labor under; and this, I apprehend, a full conviction of the truth and obligation of these principles should lead all to. Sir, I have long been convinced, that if your love for yourselves, and for those inestimable laws, which preserved to you the rights of human nature, was founded on sincerity, you could not but be solicitous, that every individual, of whatever rank or distinction, might with you equally enjoy the blessings thereof; neither could you rest satisfied short of the most active effusion of your exertions, in order to secure their promotion from any state of degradation, to which the unjustifiable cruelty and barbarism of men may have reduced them.

Sir, I freely and cheerfully acknowledge, that I am of the African race, and in that color which is natural to them of the deepest dye; and it is under a sense of the most profound gratitude to the Supreme Ruler of the Universe, that I now confess to you, that I am not under that state of tyrannical thraldom, and inhuman captivity, to which too many of my brethren are doomed, but

that I have abundantly tasted of the fruition of those blessings, which proceed from that free and unequalled liberty with which you are favored; and which, I hope, you will willingly allow you have mercifully received, from the immediate hand of that Being, from whom proceedeth every good and perfect Gift.

Sir, suffer me to recal to your mind that time, in which the arms and tyranny of the British crown were exerted, with every powerful effort, in order to reduce you to a state of servitude: look back, I entreat you, on the variety of dangers to which you were exposed; reflect on that time, in which every human aid appeared unavailable, and in which even hope and fortitude wore the aspect of inability to the conflict, and you cannot but be led to a serious and grateful sense of your miraculous and providential preservation; you cannot but acknowledge, that the present freedom and tranquility which you enjoy you have mercifully received, and that it is the peculiar blessing of Heaven.

This, Sir, was a time when you clearly saw into the injustice of a state of slavery, and in which you had just apprehensions of the horrors of its condition. It was now that your abhorrence thereof was so excited, that you publicly held forth this true and invaluable doctrine, which is worthy to be recorded and remembered in all succeeding ages: "We hold these truths to be self-evident, that all men are created equal; that they are endowed by their Creator with certain unalienable rights, and that among these are, life, liberty, and the pursuit of happiness." Here was a time, in which your tender feelings for yourselves had engaged you thus to declare, you were then impressed with proper ideas of the great violation of liberty, and the free possession of those blessings, to which you were entitled by nature; but, Sir, how pitiable is it to reflect, that although you were so fully convinced of the benevolence of the Father of Mankind, and of his equal and impartial distribution of these rights and privileges, which he hath conferred upon them, that you should at the same time counteract his mercies, in detaining by fraud and violence so numerous a part of my brethren, under groaning captivity and cruel oppression, that you should at the same time be found guilty of that most criminal act, which you professedly detested in others, with respect to yourselves.

I suppose that your knowledge of the situation of my brethren, is too extensive to need a recital here; neither shall I presume to prescribe methods by which they may be relieved, otherwise than by recommending to you and all others, to wean yourselves from those narrow prejudices which you have imbibed with respect to them, and as Job proposed to his friends, "put your soul in their souls' stead;" thus shall your hearts be enlarged with kindness and benevolence towards them; and thus shall you need neither the direction of myself or others, in what manner to proceed herein. And now, Sir, although my sympathy and affection for my brethren hath caused my enlargement thus far, I ardently hope, that your candor and generosity will plead with you in my behalf, when I make known to you, that it was not originally my design; but having taken up my pen in order to direct to you, as a present, a copy of an Almanac, which I have calculated for the succeeding year, I was unexpectedly and unavoidably led thereto.

This calculation is the production of my arduous study, in this my advanced stage of life; for having long had unbounded desires to become acquainted with the secrets of nature, I have had to gratify my curiosity herein, through my own assiduous application to Astronomical Study, in which I need not recount to you the many difficulties and disadvantages, which I have had to encounter.

And although I had almost declined to make my calculation for the ensuing year, in consequence of that time which I had allotted therefor, being taken up at the Federal Territory, by the request of Mr. Andrew Ellicott, yet finding myself under several engagements to Printers of this state, to whom I had communicated my design, on my return to my place of residence, I industriously applied myself thereto, which I hope I have accomplished with correctness and accuracy; a copy of which I have taken the liberty to direct to you, and which I humbly request you will favorably receive; and although you may have the opportunity of perusing it after its publication, yet I choose to send it to you in manuscript previous thereto, that thereby you might not only have an earlier inspection, but that you might also view it in my own hand writing.

And now, Sir, I shall conclude, and subscribe myself, with the most profound respect,

Your most obedient humble servant,

BENJAMIN BANNEKER.

TO MR. BENJAMIN BANNEKER.
Philadelphia, August 30, 1791.

SIR,

I THANK you, sincerely, for your letter of the 19th instant, and for the Almanac it contained. No body wishes more than I do, to see such proofs as you exhibit, that nature has given to our black brethren talents equal to those of the other colors of men; and that the appearance of the want of them, is owing merely to the degraded condition of their existence, both in Africa and America. I can add with truth, that no body wishes more ardently to see a good system commenced, for raising the condition, both of their body and mind, to what it ought to be, as far as the imbecility of their present existence, and other circumstances, which cannot be neglected, will admit.

I have taken the liberty of sending your Almanac to Monsieur de Condozett, Secretary of the Academy of Sciences at Paris, and Member of the Philanthropic Society, because I considered it as a document, to which your whole color had a right for their justification, against the doubts which have been entertained of them.

I am with great esteem, Sir, Your most obedient Humble Servant,

THOMAS JEFFERSON.

Thinking Critically about the Issues   #8

What do you think are the specific messages that Banneker is trying to send Jefferson, beyond pointing out the inhumanity of slavery? What are the main messages Banneker likely received from Jefferson's reply? Support your interpretations with evidence from the letters.

Developing Your Professional Vocabulary

A good understanding of this chapter's content would include an understanding of why each of these terms is important to education.

Bill for the More General
  Diffusion of
  Knowledge

bourgeoisie

capitalism

civic freedom

classical liberal

conservative

democratic localism

"divine right" of the
  nobility

elementary schools

faculty psychology

faith in human reason

feudalism

freedom and "negative"
  freedom

grammar schools

happiness

intellectual freedom

nationalism

natural
  aristocracy/meritocracy

natural law

patriarchy

political freedom

progress

religious revelation

republicanism

scientific reason

social meliorism

virtue

Questions for Discussion and Examination

1. This chapter raises the following possibility: Jefferson's attitudes toward women, Native Americans, and African Americans tell us not just about his personal prejudices but also about the liberal ideology of his time. Which dimensions of classical liberalism seem to have justified to classical liberals the subordination of women, African Americans, and Native Americans?

2. Discuss the meritocratic aspects of Jefferson's educational proposals. In your essay, analyze which groups may have been disadvantaged by the proposal.

3. Until 1999, when scientists discovered Jefferson's DNA in African American citizens who had long claimed Jeffersonian ancestry, historians resisted that claim. Despite centuries-old evidence that Jefferson fathered children by the slave Sally Hemmings, nearly all prominent Jefferson historians had rejected that evidence before the DNA findings. To what degree does the concept of ideology help explain this recent change in historians' interpretation? Explain.

 ## Online Resources

Go to the Online Learning Center at **www.mhhe.com/tozer7e** to take chapter quizzes, practice with key terms, access study resources, and link to related websites. Also available on the Online Learning Center are PowerWeb articles and news feeds.

Chapter 3

School as a Public Institution The Common-School Era

Chapter Overview

An understanding of the beginning of common schooling in the United States requires attention to social changes such as urbanization, early industrialization, and patterns of immigration, all in the Northeast. Ideologically, the common-school era was rooted in classical liberalism, which had practical consequences in urban New England different from those in rural Jeffersonian Virginia. These variations were due to differences in regional political economy as well as shifts in religious thought. While Jefferson had encountered difficulty gaining a consensus for a *state-funded but locally controlled* school system, Horace Mann sought a *state-funded and state-controlled* school system. In part because of the contrasts in political economy between Massachusetts and Virginia and in part because of differences between the paternalistic Whig liberalism of urban Massachusetts and the more laissez-faire liberalism of agrarian Virginia, Mann succeeded in creating a school system in Massachusetts.

The interaction of political economy and ideology was illustrated by U.S. citizens' responses to Irish immigration. The moral and cultural judgments made by New Englanders about Irish Catholics, along with the way schooling was used as a solution to the "Irish problem," illustrate one way of responding to cultural diversity. The efforts of Mann and others to use the schools to shape the character of Massachusetts youth for moral uprightness as well as greater social stability are detailed in this chapter. Mann's effort to create a system of education through *common schools* as well as *normal schools* leads to a discussion of his conception of the occupation of teaching and how teachers should be educated.

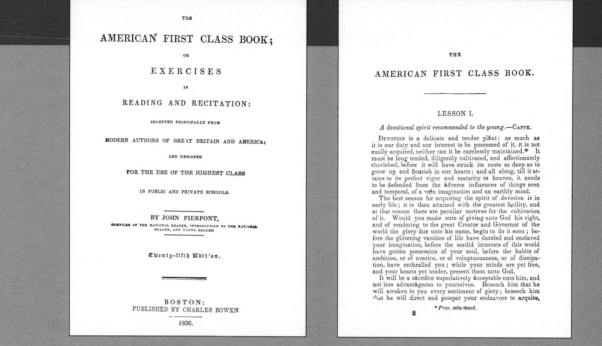

Reading instruction has long provided the opportunity to impart a society's dominant moral values.

Chapter Objectives

Among the objectives that Chapter 3 seeks to achieve are these:

1. Students should understand the distinctions between the political economy of Jefferson's agrarian Virginia and the urban centers in Massachusetts and how each created different conditions for the growth of common schools.

2. Students should understand how a wide range of components interacted in the political economy of Massachusetts during the common-school era. They also should understand that a combination of Irish immigration, the beginnings of industry, and the Jacksonian revolution, among other factors, created fertile ground for common-school legislation.

3. Students should seek to understand the ideological framework of religion, republicanism, and capitalism within which the school reformers operated.

4. Students should become acquainted as much as possible with the mind and career of Horace Mann to understand the dominant ideology of his historical setting. They should evaluate how Mann's ideological orientation, particularly toward democracy, was or was not consistent with Jefferson's democratic ideals.

5. Students should understand and *evaluate* how Mann and others thought the specific curriculum of the common schools would address the cultural needs of Massachusetts at that time.

6. Students should assess the degree to which Mann's conceptions of the teacher and teacher education were adequate for that time and for ours.

7. Finally, this chapter is designed to help students critically interpret the Primary Source Reading.

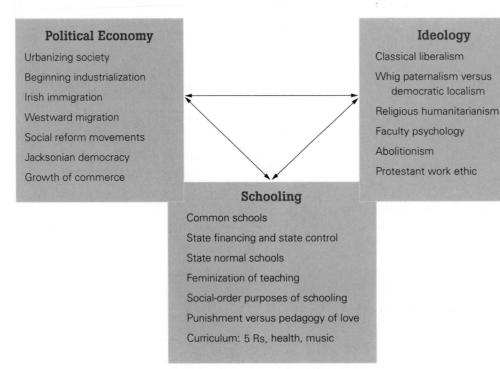

Analytic Framework
The Early Common-School Era

Political Economy

Urbanizing society

Beginning industrialization

Irish immigration

Westward migration

Social reform movements

Jacksonian democracy

Growth of commerce

Ideology

Classical liberalism

Whig paternalism versus
democratic localism

Religious humanitarianism

Faculty psychology

Abolitionism

Protestant work ethic

Schooling

Common schools

State financing and state control

State normal schools

Feminization of teaching

Social-order purposes of schooling

Punishment versus pedagogy of love

Curriculum: 5 Rs, health, music

Introduction: Schooling in New England

When Thomas Jefferson died on Independence Day in 1826, his dream of a state-supported system of education was still unrealized not only in Virginia but throughout the new nation. Nevertheless, the massive changes occurring in the political economy of New England would affect its educational efforts and provide the impetus for an educational system in Massachusetts that, by the Civil War, became the model for the nation.

From its founding, the Massachusetts Bay Colony had been known for its commitment to schooling. Its laws were driven, in part, by a religious as well as legal and economic view of the public good. Historian Ellwood Cubberley writes that in 1642, the first Massachusetts law relating to children stated:

> "In evry towne ye chosen men" shall see that parents and masters not only train their children in learning and labor, but also "to read & understand the principles of

religion & and the capital lawes of this country," with power to impose fines on such as refuse to render accounts concerning their children.[1]

Five years later, Massachusetts enacted the Old Deluder Satan Law, requiring any community with at least 50 households to establish and support schools, "It being the chief project of old deluder, Satan, to keep men from the knowledge of the Scriptures." The Massachusetts legislators believed specifically that literacy would combat Satan's designs on the uneducated.[2] Soon after the ratification of the U.S. Constitution in 1789, the state of Massachusetts renewed this commitment with the passage of a law requiring all towns with a population of 50 or more families to provide an elementary school for at least six months each year and those with more than 199 families to provide a grammar school to teach classical languages. This law probably had little direct impact, as many towns were already in accordance and those which failed to comply were rarely called to task. In any case, at the turn of the 19th century only a small percentage of school-age children attended schools, even in Boston.[3]

During the following three decades, education became a topic of increasing concern in Massachusetts as the number of elementary schools and school attendance both increased. By the 1830s most children in the state had access to elementary schooling. Locally controlled schools with voluntary attendance were almost universal. The conditions of those schools, however, were usually less than optimal. Most school buildings were poorly constructed and inadequately ventilated, and provided seats, desks, and lighting that were condemned by contemporary doctors. Moreover, schools were often located in the most undesirable sector of the town, in part because wealthier families hired private tutors for their children. Many of the teachers were barely literate; often they were hired because they would accept an inadequate salary. It was not unusual for a teacher to confront a large number of students ranging from 2 to 25 years of age, using whatever range of texts could be brought from home.[4] Educational historian Carl Kaestle's assessment of the state of American education at this time was especially applicable to Massachusetts: "America had schools, but, except in large cities, America did not have school systems."[5] It was within this educational context that the movement for educational reform began in the mid-1820s in Massachusetts. But the reform movement did not arise in a vacuum. Momentous economic, social, political, demographic, and intellectual developments impelled both the reformers and reform. These developments will be the focus of the first part of this chapter.

Political Economy of the Common-School Era

Demographic Changes

The first demographic change was the massive flow of settlers from the coastal states into the interior territories, initially into the Ohio and Mississippi river valleys and subsequently the trans-Mississippi Great Plains and the Pacific coast. The territories of Kentucky, Tennessee, Ohio, Indiana, Illinois, and Michigan, for example, collectively grew from about 110,000 inhabitants in 1790 to almost 950,000 in 1810.[6] As there were definite overland and water routes from the settled to the "new" areas, groups of settlers from New England tended to congregate in specific locales, as did pioneers from other

The unprecedented flow of immigrants with different ethnic and religious backgrounds helped turn 19th-century schools into socialization factories where, it was hoped, "American" values could be instilled into a diverse population.

sections. These settlers tended to bring and retain many of their social, political, and religious values. This, in part, helped account for the establishment of familiar institutions in the territories. While the struggle over slavery in the territories may appear as the most important effect of this migration, there were other subtle but significant effects as well.

One such effect was the impact of westward migration on American nationalism. This migration stretched the population over a much larger expanse of territory. Long distances and resulting travel times loosened old ties of kinship, community, and national loyalty. It is important to remember that American nationalism was still in its infancy and relatively weak compared with loyalty to the various states. Consequently, a major concern of postrevolutionary intellectual leaders such as Benjamin Rush and Noah Webster had been to forge a unique and widespread sense of American identity or nationalism. Moreover, the War of 1812 and the subsequent controversy over slavery created heated sectional conflict, which further eroded nationalism and increased alarm among American nationalists. In this context of concern about the potential weakening of nationalism, the westward migration generated a felt need for increased patriotic impulses.

As if in response to this need, the three decades before the Civil War witnessed the development of such national symbols as the flag, patriotic songs, and cartoons such as Uncle Sam. The glorification of national heroes like George Washington also occurred at this time. Such patriotism led many to view the school as an obvious means of building a nationalistic spirit in the next generation.[7]

A second demographic development was immigration, especially by the Irish, motivated by privation, starvation, and English crown civic oppression. Germans also came in large numbers, escaping widespread political upheaval. Beginning with a trickle in the early 1820s, immigration increased to a tidal wave by 1850. Most of the Irish immigrants settled in the Northeast, especially in New England cities. The Irish presented a series of problems for New Englanders. Many were uneducated and unskilled. What caused most concern, however, was their religion. Overwhelmingly, the Irish were Roman Catholic. To many native Protestants this was almost worse than atheism. Additionally, the Irish workers competed with native workers for jobs during times of economic distress, such as the recession of 1837. Thus the Irish were met with religious bigotry, economic and social prejudice, and occasionally mob violence.

As their numbers increased, they huddled in segregated sections of the cities and became integrated into the economic system—especially in jobs that natives rejected, such as working in factories, digging canals, building railroads, and constructing urban sewers. Many of the natives worried about how these newcomers could fit into the nation. Once again, schooling seemed an obvious answer.

Thinking Critically about the Issues   #1

Did your own ancestors play a role in response to or as a part of the 19th-century immigrant experience? What might have been their experience in work and in reaction to earlier immigrants' now ideologically dominant religion and customs? Research family history and discuss with groups in class, exploring differences and similarities.

A third demographic feature of the era was urbanization. Between 1790 and 1810, the percentage of the population living in urban areas increased from 5.1 to 7.3 percent. Significantly, however, most of this increase occurred in the port cities of Boston, Baltimore, New York, and Philadelphia. The reason for this growth was the rapidly expanding maritime trade. Until the mid-1820s commerce remained the primary economic activity of American cities.[8] As we shall later see, a commerce-driven economy carries certain educational prerequisites. From 1830 to 1850 the percentage of urban dwellers in the U.S. population grew from 10 to 20 percent. At that time, however, urban growth was stimulated by industrialization, especially in cotton textiles.[9] This urban expansion was accompanied by a marked and growing gap between rich and poor, increased crime, a rise in the consumption of alcoholic beverages, and what the intellectual and religious leaders perceived as a general and dangerous lowering of morality. Many hoped that these problems caused by industrialization could be ameliorated by schooling.

Political Developments

The second category of change that stimulated educational reforms was political. The first third of the 19th century witnessed a major expansion in suffrage for White males. When the new federal Constitution went into effect in 1789, fewer than one White male in seven was qualified to vote; by the election of Andrew

Jackson in 1828, four in seven were qualified. The major criterion for eligibility was property ownership. The expansion of the electorate gave increased power to the Jacksonian Democrats, who were the heirs to Jefferson's party. The New England upper classes, who had earlier supported the Federalist party, now supported the Whig party. They were generally alarmed at the political power of lower economic classes, whom they considered intellectually unready for the moral responsibilities of the vote. Further, the Irish Catholics were especially considered unready for representative government because of their perceived allegiance to the authority of a European pope rather than to independent self-government. One response by the largely urban, Protestant Whigs was to support education, which they believed would "inform" and thus "make safe" an otherwise ignorant electorate. The Whigs' conceptions of "inform" and "make safe" were, of course, grounded in their own view of what was right and good for society. "Right" and "good," as we shall see, were defined in accord with an ideology of Protestant, classical liberal values.

Thinking Critically about the Issues   #2

How does the idea of schooling to make society "safe" resonate with elements of the ideology of classical liberal educational theory and fit with and/or differ from the schools with which you are familiar today?

Economic Developments

Changes in demography and politics were significant factors in the school reform movement of the first half of the 19th century. Of equal, if not greater, importance were the changes in the economy of Massachusetts, where readily observable economic developments occurred in transportation. Through road building and improvement, then the digging of a vast system of canals, and finally the construction of a network of railroads, Massachusetts and the entire northeastern portion of the nation were soon connected by an impressive system for moving people, produce, and goods.

A perceptive observer would have seen another significant development during the first third of the century. This was the huge expansion of commerce centered in the great port cities, especially New York, Philadelphia, Boston, and Baltimore. Much of the rapid growth of these cities resulted from labor market demands as dockworkers, warehouse workers, teamsters, and a variety of clerks were needed by the expanding mercantile establishments.[10] The educational needs of clerks in particular exceeded the mere literacy demanded by New England Calvinists for religious reading. To a large degree these needs were met by academies, or private schools, and expanded public schooling in the urban areas. The growth of commerce also resulted in the amassing of large fortunes by some merchants and, at the other end of the economic scale, poverty for some workers, especially during slack seasons. Indeed, contemporary commentators noted with alarm the development of extremes of wealth and poverty.

The most complex and revolutionary economic change was the advent of industrialization. Initially subtle and almost unnoticed, industrial development did not begin in the cities but in the countryside as small-scale cottage industry in textiles and shoemaking. Generally, farmers and their wives practiced these crafts during slack times to supplement their farm livelihood. As demand for these products increased, the cottage industries underwent an evolution. Independent artisans producing and selling their goods directly to the public gradually lost their marketing freedom to enterprising merchants who not only organized the distribution of the finished good but also attempted to organize production through a "putting-out" system, which placed the raw materials with the home artisans. The artisans, however, continued to control the production process; that is, they set the time, the place, the pace, and the quality of work, thus controlling the most important conditions of their own labor. The merchants had an economic stake in the productive process not only because they needed the finished products to satisfy their markets but also because they had financed the raw materials. When the cottage artisans neglected shoemaking for financially more attractive pursuits, such as fishing and hunting, or were careless about the quality of their work, the merchants became convinced that the system of putting-out was inefficient and unsatisfactory. Eventually the production process was organized by manufacturers who concentrated production in a central location. Thus, we see the beginning of factories in New England.

This development is described by Paul Faler, who notes that the central factor in the evolution of industry was the need to control the quality and quantity of production.[11] Integral to this control was the development of a set of values, or an industrial morality, in the producers. Historians E. P. Thompson and Herbert

G. Gutman explained how the development of an industrial morality was in reality the displacement of a traditional culture with a modern culture.[12] In a preindustrial culture, values revolve around family, community, festivals, and seasons. Work, family life, and leisure are all integrated, and the transition from childhood to youth and, subsequently, to adulthood is blurred. In marked contrast, industrial morality or modern cultural commitments reflect a strict adherence to clock time and punctuality; continuous exclusive labor for a set number of hours in a setting sharply separated from family or leisure; enforced respect for rules, law, and authority; and a clear demarcation between childhood, youth, and adulthood.

Thinking Critically about the Issues   #3

How do the "reasoning" requirements appear to differ between cottage industry, home production, and factory production? What are the implications for the school curriculum? How does work today look from these different points of view?

Both the merchants who had organized the cottage industries and the entrepreneurs who developed factories felt the need to convert the workers from traditional to modern cultural commitments, that is, to instill an industrial morality. Economic rewards; reform movements such as temperance and religion; formal organizations such as the Society for the Promotion of Industry, Frugality, and Temperance; and eventually schools were some of the means used to instill this industrial morality.[13]

The evolution from cottage to factory industry took place in Massachusetts during the first third of the 19th century. As factories became common during the 1830s, manufacturing displaced commerce as the principal economic activity of the state's cities. Several features of these early factories should be kept in mind. First, it was initially difficult to lure adult males into the factories. Many of the early establishments, especially textile mills, were run with women, children, and inmates of charitable institutions as laborers. Later, as Irish immigration increased, the immigrants replaced native-born females as factory workers. The native adult males appeared to be incorrigibly committed to traditions of worker autonomy, and industrialists chose to focus their reform efforts on the next generation of workers. This focus ensured their attention to education and schooling. Second, as successive waves of immigrants came, it seemed necessary to enculturate them and their children in the appropriate values. This process continued well into the 20th century and was a factor in subsequent school reforms. Third, these early factories resembled post–Civil War factories primarily in employing workers for wages and requiring workers with an industrial morality. In terms of size, utilization of machine processes, and complexity of technology, however, they were qualitatively different.

In Massachusetts during the 1830s, all these political–economic factors provided the soil from which school reforms grew. Demographic factors such as urbanization, immigration, and westward migration raised problems which many believed could be addressed by education. Likewise, the successive rise of commerce and then industrialization presented needs that schooling might fulfill. None of these changes in demography, politics, or economics occurred without conflict. The immigration of the Irish engendered overt opposition and sometimes physical violence as some natives resented the Catholic religion of the Irish and others resented their competition for jobs at or near the bottom of the economic structure. Importantly, each of these conflicts provided a powerful stimulus for school reform, for the schools were coming to be viewed by the business classes and Protestant reformers alike as institutions where common values could be developed as a basis for individual moral growth and social stability.

But these "common values" were not easily agreed on. Shifts in Protestantism and in classical liberalism were sweeping Massachusetts, but they were vigorously resisted by Calvinists and Jeffersonian democrats. Political-economic changes were understood by leaders in Massachusetts within a shifting ideological framework, to which we now turn.

Ideology and Religion

Throughout the 17th and most of the 18th centuries, Puritanism, with its Calvinist doctrines, held sway in New England. The Puritan God was an angry God who demanded strict justice with harsh punishment for sinners. Puritans believed all human history had been foreordained at creation and that only a few had been elected by God for salvation. While they required all believers to read the Bible and expected that personal as well as collective behavior might be a sign of election, no one could earn salvation through doing good works. Salvation was a gift from God for the select few. In an important sense, this was a faith with an aristocracy of the elect. The Puritans' theology had extensive ramifications for their definitions of human nature, the good society, the appropriate relationship of the individual to the social order, and discipline—in the home, society, and school.[14]

The defining religious characteristic of 19th-century New England was the gradual but cumulative displacement of Puritanism by increasingly less harsh and more humane doctrines.[15] Immigration of non-Puritans helped dilute the strength of Puritan orthodoxy. More important was the impact of scientific discovery, which demythologized nature and replaced it with Enlightenment thought, which emphasized progress, human perfectibility, and reason. This change also occurred within Puritanism itself, as liberal ministers such as Charles Chauncy began chipping away at Calvinist dogma at the close of the 18th century. The center of gravity for religious thought in New England shifted from the Calvinist Congregational denomination to the more liberal Unitarian churches during the first three decades of the 19th century. Most influential in this shift was William Ellery Channing of Boston's Federal Street Congregation. Channing made a frontal assault on the basic dogma of Calvinism as he rejected the notion of human depravity and the absolute sovereignty of God. Instead, he proclaimed humans to be rational beings capable of understanding God's works, and asserted that God was a morally perfect being. From these positions Channing not only assailed Calvinism but built an alternative theology, a conception of human nature and of the good society that was both humane and in tune with Enlightenment thought. What Channing began was extended by other liberal ministers, such as Horace Bushnell, and the transcendentalists Ralph Waldo Emerson and Henry David Thoreau.

The result was a belief in a benevolent God who had created a rational universe and had endowed human nature with the rationality needed to develop an ever more perfect social order. The possibility of progress seemed to carry an injunction to New Englanders for reform. If God had given them the power for improvement, it seemed their duty to exercise it. The emphasis on the essential goodness of human nature and even the divinity of the human personality pushed the reform impulse in humanitarian directions.

> ### Thinking Critically about the Issues   #4
>
> How does this notion of reform instead of punishment fit with classical liberal ideology? How does each concept take a position in our current ideas about education and criminal rehabilitation?

The Calvinist position implied mass literacy because all believers were required to read the scriptures. The more liberal religious views of the 19th century, however, required more than mass literacy. The new views of human nature, progress, and a rational universe required mass education that would equip the young to understand the natural and social worlds in order to make rational responses to the challenges they would face in life. The safety, health, and progress of both individuals and society would depend, reformers believed, on the adequacy of these responses.

Consolidation of Classical Liberalism

During the common-school era the major development in ideology was the consolidation and spread of classical liberalism from intellectual leaders to the general public. Among the primary components of classical liberalism, as discussed in Chapter 2, were a basic faith in human reason, the enduring reality of Newton's conception of natural law, and continuing progress; belief in the importance of education; a commitment to nationalism; and a belief in the value of republican virtue and the centrality of freedom to the American condition. The principal vehicles for dissemination were politics, newspapers, and churches. By the mid-1830s these ideas were commonly accepted across the United States. While the spread of classical liberalism from the intellectuals to the commoners was the defining characteristic of ideology from the 1820s to the mid-1840s, not all was static within that ideology. Already by the 1830s the forces of economic change were beginning to gather momentum, especially with the birth of the factory system and the development of the railroads. Both would demand some degree of government assistance. Factory owners wanted protective tariffs; the railroads coveted financial aid and land grants. Moreover, the immigration of the Irish added a challenging dimension to the American social order. These developments would occasion some innovations in the prevailing ideology.

Subtle but significant ideological accommodations followed. The most important were in beliefs about the role of government. Complete laissez-faire would not meet the new economic requirements, and so government was asked to play a significant economic role. No longer was it sufficient for the government to stay out of economic affairs. At first the breach was slight, but it foreshadowed developments of the late 19th and early 20th centuries. Laissez-faire was amended to mean that government should stand on the sidelines *except* when necessary for it to assist economic development. Such assistance would include protective tariffs to keep out foreign competition and financial aid to industries such as the railroads. Between the mid-1830s and the end of the 19th century, the federal government gave the railroad companies land equal in area to the state of Texas. The seed of the 20th-century welfare state had been sown; its earliest germination was welfare for the industrial class. It was defended on the grounds that it would ultimately benefit all members of society.

Demands for an increasingly active government in the economic area were accompanied by an increased willingness to allow the general growth of government power and centralization of authority. Again, this began slowly but increased over the succeeding decades. The concentration of state power over education, in the form of state school boards, was only one example of the decline of local self-government. Another was the passage of a compulsory school attendance law by Massachusetts in 1852. In part, this acceptance of increased state authority may have been stimulated by the fear of social disintegration engendered by Irish immigration.

Closely associated with these ideological accommodations was a modification in the definition of freedom. Jefferson had argued for a "negative" freedom, that is, freedom from government interference in the individual's private life. However, leaders in the 1830s began to emphasize the responsibility of government to create the conditions for freedom through economic and educational intervention. This was a beginning step in the direction of the ideal of a "positive" freedom espoused in the 20th century by modern liberals, as we shall see in Chapter 4.

The third adjustment to classical liberal ideology occurred in the concept of rationality. Jefferson and other earlier classical liberals held that humans were capable of reason and should be approached on that basis. Horace Mann and other common-school reformers adopted the "new discipline" of love as a classroom methodology. This reflected a subtle but significant change in the idea of human rationality. The basis of the new discipline was manipulation of the child's nonrational psyche through the granting or withholding of affection. Rather than rely solely on a rational explanation of the rules and punishments for violation, Mann urged teachers to use affection to mold appropriate behaviors. This approach would later be amplified by modern liberals as they tried to shape children emotionally as well as rationally.

The debate between Mann and Orestes Brownson (see the Primary Source Reading) in large part concerned these redefinitions of classical liberalism. Brownson represented the older view, and Mann championed the modifications to that view. Brownson advocated local control of schools, attacked state normal schools, and attacked Mann's list of approved texts. All these moves reflected a Jeffersonian version of classical liberalism, while Mann's ideas signaled a newer view.

Horace Mann was perhaps the best example of a political leader whose policies and career embodied these ideological adjustments. He began his political career as a spokesperson for the industrial and railroad interests in the Massachusetts legislature. He also championed reforms such as temperance and the institutional care of the insane and juvenile delinquents. Each of these reforms augured increased power for government and a shrinking of private freedom. In totality, Mann was clearly a classical liberal. Nevertheless, he may be seen as a transitional figure bridging classical and new liberalism. Similarly, the era of the common school may be seen as an era of transition to modern schooling.

Horace Mann: An Exemplar of Reform

Early Life

Perhaps no individual more accurately represented through his family and personal biography the successive changes that altered the life and thought of Massachusetts than did Horace Mann. He was a direct descendant of William Mann, who came to the Bay Colony in 1633, and his paternal ancestors included a graduate of Harvard College who became a Puritan minister and another who was a member of the Committee of Correspondence during the Revolution. All had remained in Massachusetts, were Calvinists, and, with the exception of one minister, had been farmers. Horace, born in 1796 at Franklin, Massachusetts, was the last child of Thomas Mann and Rebecca Stanley Mann.[16]

Horace Mann (Detail), who was the first secretary to the Massachusetts State Board of Education from 1837 to 1848, is best remembered as the primary champion of America's new common-school movement.

Thomas Mann raised his family on a farm that had been in the Mann family since 1709, when his grandfather, also named Thomas, purchased it. Horace's childhood resembled that of past generations of New Englanders. Subsistence farming provided nearly all life's necessities. Horace learned not only farming but traditional values while helping with the daily farm chores. The family was also a primary setting for literacy and religious training, with older siblings often helping parents introduce younger children to reading, ciphering, and dogma. Later in his life, after he suggested that he had been largely self-taught, his sister Lydia reminded Horace, "Every day of your life when you were with your parents and sister you were at school and learning that which has been the foundation of your present learning."[17]

Between 1819 and 1822, Mann tutored at Brown and simultaneously studied law. After serving as an apprentice lawyer, he graduated from the Litchfield Law School and in 1823 was admitted to the Massachusetts bar in Dedham, where he began to practice law. During the next four years Mann firmly established his reputation as a lawyer and an orator.

Mann's Political Career

Mann's career in the Massachusetts legislature continued until 1837, during which time he continued to reflect the changes in his society. His first legislative speech came during a debate on a petition by the First Religious Society of Blandford for incorporation. Mann opposed granting this Congregationalist group perpetual control over its endowment, resting his argument on the principle of religious freedom. The defeat of the petition strengthened the Unitarians in their struggle with the Congregationalists.

As a legislator he supported a number of humanitarian reforms, such as the overturning of the state's debtor laws, humane treatment of the insane, and the temperance movement.

The two major humanitarian reform movements that did not find Horace Mann in their ranks during the early 1830s were public education and abolition. His position on the abolition of slavery displayed the conflict between his moral beliefs, his economic and political commitments, and his sense of political reality. Mann considered slavery to be a moral abomination that required eventual eradication. The abolitionists, however, with their demands for the immediate end of slavery, seemed to him to be threatening not only the political stability of the republic but the institution of private property. Moreover, he believed their demands and moral stridency only strengthened the slave states' resolve to defend their "peculiar" institution, thus delaying a peaceful resolution of the problem. The abolitionists' goals could be achieved, he felt, only by force of arms, and such a course would threaten the republic. Additionally, even if freedom could be peacefully won, it was not clear to Mann what could be done with the freed African Americans.

As Jefferson once wrote, Mann thought that the African American's future was not in America, but he was not sanguine about African recolonization. Interestingly, when it came to cases of individual African Americans, Mann was egalitarian and sympathetic, often at great personal cost. In 1844, for example, he canceled his scheduled speech before the New Bedford Lyceum when he learned that it restricted membership to Whites. Three years later, when a Black woman, Chloe Lee, was admitted to the State Normal School at West Newton and could not find accommodations among the townspeople, she was welcomed into the Mann home. It appears that especially during the years when he was secretary to the State Board of Education, his concern for preserving social harmony led him to silence his support for the abolitionist cause. Later, however, as a member of the U.S. House of Representatives, filling the seat of recently deceased John Quincy Adams, he delivered a memorable antislavery speech in opposition to the Compromise Bill of 1850, a speech that nearly cost him his House seat in the next election and was a major factor in his defeat in the subsequent one.

While the abolitionists and slavery caused Mann considerable concern during his legislative career, educational questions were not on his agenda. It was not until 1837 that his attention focused on public education. By then much of the groundwork for educational reform in Massachusetts had been already done by others. When Mann did enter the fray, however, he left a lasting mark on American education. The issue that directed Mann's interest to education was the dispersal of funds that had been allocated to the state by the federal government to compensate for the Massachusetts state militia's service during the War of 1812. Mann supported the use of these monies for the state's common schools. Although he lost the fiscal battle, the legislature created a state board of education authorized to collect and disseminate information about schools to the local districts and the public at large. Much to the surprise of his contemporaries, Mann accepted the appointment as secretary to the board, a position he occupied from 1837 to 1848.

Mann resigned from the secretary's post in 1848 and was elected in 1848 and 1850 to the U.S. House of Representatives from the Eighth Congressional District. During his four years in Congress, sectional issues surrounding the slavery question commanded most of his attention, and he gained national prominence for his antislavery position. His antislavery and temperance positions were the major factors in his defeat for reelection in 1852.

Soon after that electoral defeat, Mann accepted the presidency of the yet-to-be-established Antioch College in Ohio. In the last stage of his career he continued to reflect the mood of his times. He turned to higher education as the nation began to focus attention on that area. He moved west to Yellow Springs, Ohio, and thus became part of the great westward migration from the Northeast. One of Mann's prime presidential concerns was the higher education of women. Shortly after the women's suffrage movement was launched, in July 1848 at Seneca Falls, New York, he was attempting to provide women with the same collegiate education that male students received. To this end, he expanded the development begun earlier at Oberlin. Antioch College was open to men and women of all races, and no distinction was made for race or gender in curricular questions, although he was known to have some vocal reservations about absolute social equality among men and women. By the time he died in 1859 at Yellow Springs, his life reflected nearly all the important intellectual, social, political, and economic developments of his time.

Thinking Critically about the Issues   #5

Mann was involved in the following movements as either an activist or a debater: women's higher education, which he supported; state control of public education; crime prevention; and the slavery question. How might public schooling be regarded as another "humanitarian reform" in that historical context?

Mann and the Common Schools

Mann's most far-reaching contributions to education were made during the years he spent as secretary to the Massachusetts State Board of Education, 1837 to 1848. He had been at the pinnacle of his political career when he accepted Governor Everett's offer to quit the state senate and direct the state's efforts to reform public education. The importance he assigned to the task was evident when he wrote to a friend, "My lawbooks are for sale. My office is 'to let'! The bar is no longer my forum. My jurisdiction is changed. I have abandoned jurisprudence, and betaken myself to the larger sphere of mind and morals."[18] Although he had grown somewhat disillusioned with the possibility of voluntary reform in adults, his pessimism did not extend to the young. He explained his optimism by saying, "Having found the present generation composed of materials almost unmalleable, I am transferring my efforts to the next. Men are cast iron; but children are wax. Strength expended upon the latter may be effectual, which will make no impression on the former."[19]

The Massachusetts State Board of Education held its first meeting on June 29, 1837, and formally elected Mann as its secretary. The duties of the board were closely circumscribed by the law that had created it; two of its duties were to present to the legislature an annual abstract of the school reports received by its secretary and to report to the legislature all its activities, its reflections on the condition of education in the state, and any recommendations it might have for improvement of that condition.[20] The secretary's duties were similarly specifically prescribed: the secretary "shall, under the direction of the board, collect information of the actual conditions and efficiency of the common schools and other means of popular education; and diffuse as widely as possible throughout every part of the

Commonwealth, information of the most approved and successful methods of arranging the studies and conducting the education of the young, to the end that all children in this Commonwealth, who depend upon common schools for instruction, may have the best education which those schools can be made to impart."[21] While these duties were clearly prescribed, the means for effecting them were not. Moreover, the powers of the board and its secretary were limited to the collection and dissemination of information.

Regardless of their reform preferences, the only option open to Mann and the board was to seek voluntary cooperation from local districts. To effect educational reform, Mann proceeded to demonstrate the power of information when systematically disseminated through an official government office. Initially, Mann's most effective device for conveying information to the people of the state was the county educational convention. During the first year he held an advertised meeting in every county of the state where he presented educational questions to the local citizens. A wide range of educational topics was discussed, including teaching methods, the most appropriate location of schools, school apparatus, texts, discipline, the duties of local school board members, attendance problems, finance, and European educational innovations. Mann took particular pains to ensure the attendance of local dignitaries who were known friends of education.

A second method of disseminating information was through the annual reports of the board and the secretary, which were sent to all district school boards as well as to the state legislature and the governor. Educational officials throughout the nation obtained copies of these reports, thus adding to the national influence of school reforms in Massachusetts. In addition, Mann established the semimonthly *Common School Journal* in 1839, which published articles and news items about education and was available to most teachers in the state.[22]

Among the wide variety of educational topics addressed by Mann during his tenure as secretary, perhaps

the most significant were school buildings, moral values, the example of Prussian education, discipline, teachers, and the economic value of education. The question of curriculum subject matter was not one of the most important issues for Mann, perhaps because the curriculum was mandated by state legislation. He addressed this question only once, in his *Sixth Annual Report,* for the year 1842, where he noted that the law required instruction in "orthography, reading, writing, English grammar, geography and arithmetic." Mann further explained that these were "the minimum but not the maximum."[23] He then spent the remaining 110 pages presenting a detailed plan for studying physiology, a subject that he felt was wrongly neglected. Generally, however, when he dealt with curricular subjects, he approached the topic from the perspective of teaching methods rather than as subject matter. The six issues that the secretary seemed to find most central to his reform efforts will now be examined.

School Buildings

Under the general heading of school buildings, Mann included a variety of items that involved the physical setting of schooling. One of his less acclaimed accomplishments, from which generations of schoolchildren benefited, was the vastly improved physical setting of school life. The idyllic "little red schoolhouses" nestled under giant oak trees beside babbling brooks and surrounded with green meadows were usually fictional creations of writers who romanticized the American educational past. Such scenes definitely did not describe the reality of most district schools in the late 1830s. Most were poorly constructed, offering little protection from the cold winters. Few had adequate windows or artificial means to provide sufficient light. Rare was the school large enough to accommodate its students. Many provided only backless benches, which were not only uncomfortable but dangerous. Frequently, schools were without toilet facilities and water for drinking and washing. Many schools were located in unattractive, and sometimes unhealthful, sites apparently chosen because they were unsuitable for any other productive use.

The secretary marshaled the power of "information" to combat these conditions. In the *First Annual Report* the board, under the subject of important topics, listed "the proper and commodious construction of schoolhouses." In the secretary's section of the same report, he stated, "There are four cardinal topics. . . . First in order is the situation, construction and number of the

Thinking Critically about the Issues   #6

States go far beyond the collection and dissemination of information about education; they now require specific tests for prospective teachers and to assess student progress. What would Mann say? What do you think?

Horace Mann addressed the adequacy of Massachusetts school buildings in his *First Annual Report* to the State Board of Education in 1838.

school-houses."[24] The circular Mann sent to each county in 1837 to advertise his county educational conventions listed 11 questions "to direct attention to some leading considerations": the first was, "Is inconvenience or discomfort suffered from the construction or location of School Houses in your Town, and if so in what manner?"[25] The following year Mann praised the city of Salem's improvements in seating, ventilation, and reconstruction of its school as a carrot to tempt other districts to follow suit. Lest the recalcitrant miss the point, he warned,

> In many other places, improvements of the same kind have been made, though to a less extent, and in a part only of the houses. It would be a great mistake, however, to suppose, that nothing remains to be done in this important department of the system of public instruction. The cases mentioned are the slightest exceptions, compared with the generality of the neglect. . . . The children must continue to breathe poisonous air, and sit upon seats threatening structural derangement, until parents become satisfied, that a little money may well be expended to secure to their offspring, the blessings of sound health, a good conformation, and a strong, quick-working mind.[26]

In his report three years later, Mann returned again to the question of school buildings as he expressed guarded optimism and satisfaction with the general progress around the state. He included, in the appendix, designs and descriptions of the new buildings at Springfield, Lowell, and Salem. He suggested that other districts might "select any one of them as a model, or they may attempt a combination which will be an improvement

upon all. These and others erected during the past year, are ornaments to the respective places of their location, an honor to their inhabitants and a pledge of the elevated character of their posterity."[27] Moreover, the secretary's annual publication of each town's rank in school expenditures caused some towns, such as Palmer, "mortification" and others, such as Lowell, an occasion to boast.[28] It is not difficult to imagine the cumulative effect of this kind of publicized information.

Thinking Critically about the Issues   #7

Discuss the school buildings you are familiar with. How does the quality of the physical environment affect teaching and learning?

Moral Values

instill

At the core of Mann's effort to reform common schooling was his belief that the school must inculcate an appropriate set of moral values in the state's children. This belief was not entirely an innovation in Mann's time; schools in Massachusetts had traditionally been seen as institutions auxiliary to the home and the church in the inculcation of Puritan values in the young. What was new with Mann was the centrality of the school, the set of values to be inculcated, and the role of the state in determining and inculcating those values. Mann was

Urban centers in Massachusetts began building new schools during the common-school era.

particularly concerned with the apparent breakdown of moral consensus and the resulting conflict in his society. The religious struggle between the Calvinists and more liberal sects, the economic strife between rich and poor, the riots pitting Irish immigrants against native workers—all were evidence to Mann of a dangerous social disharmony that threatened the stability of society. The common school was to become the central institution to ameliorate this situation. It was necessary for all children to develop a commitment to a common core of values. But not just any core of values would suffice. The necessary values were those which later social scientists would call *modern* values—that is, values that would support and sustain industrial development.

Mann called these values the "common elements" of the common school. They would include the "great Christian truths," which he believed all rational men would agree on. In one sense they were values based in religious belief, and as such they represented a pan-Protestant perspective that reinforced the liberal wing of New England Protestantism in direct opposition to traditional Calvinism. This raised the opposition of a minority of Congregationalist ministers, who remained committed to Calvinist dogma. The issue became galvanized when the state board began the practice of recommending books that districts might purchase for school libraries. Led by Frederick Packard, the American Sunday School Union claimed, after some of its materials were rejected, that Mann was attempting to eliminate religion from the common schools.

It is significant that Mann received general support from Protestant ministers and even from an apparent majority of Congregationalist ministers.[29] Irish Catholics were later to object to the "common elements," especially when they were accompanied with the reading of the King James version of the Bible. They rightly saw the common school as positioned against Catholicism, and eventually they built a separate system of parochial schools. Thus, ironically, Mann's effort to unify society around commonly held values led to a competing private school system with potentially conflicting values. That the Catholic schools did not promote the divisive values Mann feared from sectarian schooling is another irony that cannot be explored here.[30]

The predominance of Christian religious sentiment in New England blinded Mann and the constituents to an important implication of the "common elements" he believed should be taught in the common schools. The issue was raised, however, by England's John Stuart Mill, one of the most prominent philosophers of the 19th century. In the late 1840s English public education was racked by religious conflict between Anglicans, various dissenting Protestant sects, and Catholics. In an attempt at compromise, educational reformers proposed a system of national education that would be "unsectarian" and would adopt a "common elements" approach similar to Mann's. In a speech prepared in 1849, Mill fired withering salvos at the basic principles of this proposal that were equally applicable to Mann's program. Mill correctly noted that it was indeed religion that would be taught in the proposed public schools. And no matter how the final compromise among the competing Christian sects was effected, he argued, the resulting religion of the public school would be some variant of Christianity. What would this result mean? Mill pointed out to the proponents, "If you could carry all the sects with you by your compromise you would have effected nothing more but a compact among the more powerful bodies to cease fighting among themselves and join in trampling the weaker. You would have contrived a national education not for all, but for the believers in the New Testament. The Jew and the unbeliever would be excluded from it though they would not the less be required to pay for it. . . . Religious exclusion and inequality are as odious when practiced against minorities as majorities." Mill's conclusion was unambiguously stated: "Education provided by the public must be education for all, and to be education for all it must be purely secular education."[31] Mill's logic escaped most New Englanders, but not all. (Orestes Brownson was an exception, as the Primary Source Reading at the end of this chapter shows.)

In a way, Frederick Packard's criticism of Mann's common elements was correct. When Packard argued that Mann wanted to take religion out of the common school, he understood religion to mean Calvinism. Indeed, that and more was what Mann had in mind. Henceforth the public school would not contribute to the creation of Congregationalists, Unitarians, Baptists, or Methodists. Instead, it would attempt to create citizens committed to a secular faith whose moral values would play much the same role that doctrine had played in sectarian faith. In a figurative sense, the school would become the temple, the teacher the minister, and the school boards the temple elders. American schoolchildren would be taught a pan-Protestant brand of citizenship that would wed religion and nationalism in "one nation under God," as the Pledge of Allegiance would later put it. God, of course, was presumed to be the God of Protestantism. The principle was not new, for this idea had energized earlier Puritan education. What was new was the systemic government-supported scope of this approach. It would take a series of painful U.S. Supreme Court decisions in the mid-20th century to eliminate religious references and rituals in schools, thus rectifying the Protestant precedent set by Mann in Massachusetts.

Lessons from the Prussian School System

Soon after he turned his attention to educational questions, Mann began to read available commentaries on education. He was first introduced to Prussian schools by French educator Victor Cousin's popular report of their successes.[32] The Prussian system had been organized in the 1820s along a model recommended by Johann Fichte, a German philosopher, during the Napoleonic occupation of Prussia. Fichte's proposals, in his *Addresses to the German Nation,* were designed to develop Prussian nationalism and a nation strong enough to unite the German states for world leadership. By the mid-1830s the Prussian experiment had excited educators in Western Europe and the United States.

The Prussians had developed a state-financed system that was free, universal, and compulsory through the elementary grades. The system was class-based and consisted of two separate tiers of schooling. The tier for the aristocratic class had three levels, beginning with the *vorschule.* This elementary school, responsible for preparing upper-class youth for the *gymnasium,* was academically oriented. The gymnasium provided a classical education closely akin to American and English collegiate educations. Graduates of the gymnasium might continue their higher education in either the military academies, designed to produce the future officers of the Prussian military, or the universities. The university, as envisioned by Fichte and developed in 19th-century Germany, was primarily a research institution whose dual functions were to produce new knowledge and to educate the next generation of civic and religious leaders.

The tier for the common people had two levels. The elementary *volkschule,* or people's school, was compulsory. Its goal was to develop patriotic citizens, and its motto was "God, Emperor, and Country." In addition to loyalty and obedience to authority, it taught basic literacy and numeracy. Most of the graduates of the volkschule went directly into the workforce. A few continued their training at the second level: either the technical schools, which produced technicians and middle-range managers for the Prussian economy, or the normal schools, which trained teachers for the volkschule. The curricular emphasis in the normal schools was on how to teach, that is, methods. It was deemed not only unnecessary but counterproductive for volkschule teachers to have knowledge or understanding much beyond that necessary for the volkschule. Loyalty and obedience, not initiative or critical thinking, were the goals for the training of the common people. As Fichte had written on the education of the German child, "If you want to influence him at all, you must do more than merely talk to him. You must fashion him, and fashion him in such a way that he cannot will otherwise than you wish him to will."[33]

During the spring and summer of 1843, at his own expense, Mann traveled to Europe to examine its educational systems firsthand. He was relatively unimpressed with the quality of education in England and

Exhibit 3.1   The Prussian School System in the Mid-19th Century

Popular Education	Aristocratic Education
Volkschule	**Vorschule**
1. Attendance was compulsory for all common children. 2. Curriculum: reading, writing, arithmetic, religion, and patriotism. 3. Objective: to develop students with literacy, loyalty, and obedience (motto: "God, Emperor, and Country"). 4. Teachers were normal-school graduates.	1. Students came from aristocratic families. 2. Curriculum: academic subjects. 3. Objective: to prepare students for the gymnasium. 4. Teachers were university or gymnasium graduates.
Technical Schools	**Gymnasiums**
1. Students were drawn from the top ranks of the volkschule. 2. Curricula: Various technological subjects (not science) designed to produce specialists in various specific technologies. 3. Objective: to produce midrank managers and technicians. They were to transmit, not originate, orders and provide stability for an in-place economic system. 4. Teachers were graduates of technical schools, generally after work experience.	1. Students came from the vorschule. 2. Curriculum: similar to a combination of grammar school and collegiate education in 19th-century America—i.e., a "classical curriculum" of Latin, literature, math, and some sciences. 3. Objective: to prepare students for universities, military academies, or upper levels of state and business bureaucracies. 4. Teachers were university graduates.
Normal Schools	**Universities**
1. Students were drawn from the top ranks of the volkschule. 2. Curriculum: heavily oriented toward methods courses and a few elementary content courses. How to teach was seen as more important than content. 3. Objective: to produce teachers for the volkschule who would develop loyal, patriotic, and efficient citizens. 4. Teachers were recruited from among graduates of normal schools after teaching experience.	1. Students came from the vorschule and the gymnasium. 2. Curricula: specialized research areas in the liberal arts, the sciences, math, engineering, and art. 3. Objective: to produce the intellectual leaders for the state and produce "new knowledge." 4. Teachers were from the universities.
	Military Academies
	1. Students came from the gymnasium. 2. Curricula: military strategy, tactics, and discipline. 3. Objective: to train future officers for the Prussian general staff. 4. Teachers were from the Prussian general staff.

Note: This representation is idealized. Not all volkschule teachers, for example, were trained in normal schools; not all technical school teachers had technical school degrees.

France. The Prussian schools, however, made a distinctly positive impression on him, and he devoted much of his 1843 *Annual Report* to enumerating their praises. Moreover, Mann continued to cite Prussian examples during the remainder of his tenure when he urged school reform. The secretary was not completely oblivious to the dangers inherent in using institutions designed for an authoritarian society as models for a democracy, but he quickly dismissed those dangers as inconsequential. He argued that education was a means which could be made to serve diametrically opposed ends. In summation, he said, "If Prussia can pervert the benign influences of education to the support of arbitrary power, we surely can use them for support and prepetuation of republican institutions."[34] (See Exhibit 3.1.)

The Prussian volkschule evoked Mann's most enthusiastic responses. The idea of a free, state-financed and state-controlled universal and compulsory school that would affect all of the young was its most obvious attraction. He seemed to ignore the class separation into volkschule and vorschule. This is surprising, since he waged unending war against private schools for the wealthy in Massachusetts. These schools, he argued, not only would encourage class distinctions and thus class hatred but would siphon off the interest and support of the best elements of society from the common schools to the private schools attended by their children.

His second observation about the volkschule was the joy of learning it engendered among the students. The secretary was fond of noting that during his extensive visits to the Prussian schools, he "never saw one child in tears."[35] This he claimed was due to the absence of corporal punishment and the superior methods of the teachers.

The superiority of Prussian teachers was not accidental, according to Mann. Rather, it was the direct result of their superior training. The Prussians had developed normal schools for the training of its volkschule teachers. In the normal schools the teachers were carefully schooled in pedagogy and the subjects taught in the volkschule. The apparent success of these institutions reinforced Mann's commitment to the state normal schools he had been struggling to secure in Massachusetts. While the Prussian model differentiated students socially and thus academically, it was also responsible for an increased level of literacy, and some have argued that this laid the foundation for later political agitation and revolutionary activity involving volkschule teachers.[36]

Thinking Critically about the Issues   #8

How does this system of volkschule, vorschule, and university research compare to teacher education as we know it today?

School Discipline and the Pedagogy of Love

The problems surrounding discipline in the schools concerned Mann throughout his tenure as secretary. His approach to discipline reveals much about his educational beliefs and their relation to his broader social and political philosophies. He discussed disciplinary issues in several of his *Annual Reports* and speeches. One

speech, "On School Punishments," first delivered in Boston in 1839, revised in 1845, and included in his *Lectures on Education* published in 1854, succinctly summarized his general position.

Mann began the speech with the assertion, "Punishment, when taken by itself, is always to be considered as an evil":[37] an evil, however, that may be used as a last resort, as a doctor uses poison to arrest a disease so that it may be treated. By punishment, Mann meant physical beatings or harsh words. Such treatment, he asserted, always caused fear in the child, "and fear is a most debasing, dementalizing passion."[38] He contended that fear corrupted not only the intellect but also the personality and morality of the child. Moreover, if the teacher is to control the moral, social, and intellectual development of the child, she must know the child, that is, have access to the child's inner self. But "the moment a child's mind is strongly affected by fear, it flies instinctively away and hides itself in the deepest recesses it can find. . . . Instead of exhibiting to you his whole consciousness, he conceals from you as much as he can. . . . Your communication with that child's heart is at an end."[39] In this discussion Mann exhibited insights into the nature of social psychology and the potential for manipulation of the psyche through affection, which was not generally understood until the end of his century. It would be left to the 20th-century progressive educational theorists (as discussed in Chapter 4) to further develop this approach to pedagogy—an approach that is both more humane and potentially more manipulative than a pedagogy of overt authoritarianism.

The common use of corporal punishment in New England had been inspired by Calvinist beliefs in the depravity of human nature, which led adults to think it necessary to "beat the devil out of children." In sharp contrast, Mann's conception of human nature was grounded in Enlightenment and Unitarian beliefs. He therefore saw the child as a rational being more appropriately approached through intelligence and love. The good teacher, "singularly gifted with talent and resources, and with the divine quality of love, . . . can win the affection, and, by controlling the heart, can control the conduct of children."[40] As a realist and a shrewd social observer, Mann understood that such an approach required two conditions: first, children who had been reared in homes where love, reason, and sound moral values predominated; and second, teachers who had been adequately prepared to understand the child, classroom management, and the subject matter. Neither of these conditions was universally present in Mann's Massachusetts. When teachers were

One of Mann's most enduring legacies was to help replace the Calvinist view that children, being naturally depraved at birth, must have the "devil beaten out of them."

not capable of more enlightened methods or students were incorrigible because of bad home conditions, Mann believed punishment was the only alternative in order to "save" young delinquents from a life of immorality, dissipation, or crime. The teacher or parent should always consider whether the evil to be cured was sufficiently greater than the evil of punishment. Mann went on to describe how and when, as a last resort, punishment should be used to prevent greater evils. He challenged teachers to constantly try to decrease their use of punishment, with the goal of eliminating it completely from the common school. Thus he effectively presented punishment as an acceptable alternative for teachers who were not *yet* fully adequate but who, as they became more proficient in their profession, would obviously resort less often to punishment. The good teacher would understand, according to the secretary, that "a child may surrender to fear, without surrendering to principle. But it is the surrender to principle only which has any permanent value."[41]

In his *Eighth Annual Report,* Mann clearly indicated the relation between his ideas on discipline and his sociopolitical ideals. In the 1840s the number of schools that were closed before the end of the term because teachers could not maintain the order necessary to conduct them was decreasing significantly, while the total number of schools was increasing. But this progress was not sufficient for Mann. He explained that one of the most important goals of schooling was "training our children in self-government." He proclaimed, "So tremendous, too, are the evils of anarchy and lawlessness, that a government by mere force,

however arbitrary and cruel, has been held preferable to no-government. But self-government, self-control, a voluntary compliance with the laws of reason and duty, have been justly considered as the highest point of excellence attainable by a human being." He went on to argue that self-government required rational understanding of the rules and laws. This understanding could not come through fear inspired by punishment. Mann informed teachers that it was a teacher's duty to prevent "violations" of moral law "by rectifying that state of mind out of which violations come. Nor is it enough that the law be obeyed. As far as possible, he is to see it is obeyed from right motives. As a moral act blind obedience is without value. As a moral act, also, obedience through fear is without value; not only so, but as soon as the fear is removed, the restrained impulses will break out and demand the arrears of indulgence as a long-delayed debt."[42] Mann left no room for doubt that he believed the implications of his notions of discipline and self-government extended beyond the school and childhood. He explicitly noted they have "extraordinary force, in view of our political institutions, founded as they are upon the great idea of the capacity of man for self-government."[43]

The Quality of Teachers

The importance of the teaching corps to Mann's educational reforms, while implicit in nearly all his work, was nowhere more explicit and obvious than in his discussions of school discipline. Both the board and the

with the writings of subsequent human capital theorists or educators for whom economic justifications for education are paramount. The first: "For the creation of wealth then—for the existence of a wealthy people and a wealthy nation—intelligence is the grand condition."[64] And the second: "The greatest of all arts in political economy is, to change a consumer into a producer; and the next greatest is, to increase the producer's producing power;—an end to be directly attained, by increasing his intelligence."[65] Subsequently Mann provided several pages of examples showing how increased intelligence in artisan workers might result in their developing more ingenious labor-saving techniques, thus increasing the productive capacity of all workers intelligent enough to use the innovations.

Somewhat contradictorily, Mann's businessperson supporters failed to link a common-school education with the application of creative intelligence in workers. As Maris A. Vinovskis has shown, "Although each of the respondents to Mann's survey mentioned the ability of educated workers to work more efficiently than others, none of them emphasized the importance of the 'inventiveness' which Mann stressed through the *Fifth Annual Report*. Instead, they tended to concentrate on the fact that these workers were able to follow directions better, were more punctual and reliable, and less likely to be unreasonable during periods of labor turmoil."[66] The traits emphasized by the industrialists were elements of what was then called "industrial morality" and is currently called "modern" (as opposed to "traditional") cultural commitments. While Mann was emphasizing the intellectual results of common schooling, his industrial supporters were emphasizing the enculturation of a value system amenable to industrialized factory life.

Opposition to Mann's Common-School Reforms

The secretary's attempts to reform the common schools of Massachusetts did not go unchallenged. The opposition, inspired by different issues, came from three groups. The first conflict centered on Mann's efforts to make the common schools nondenominational. As we have seen, the conservative Calvinists led by Frederick A. Packard lost this battle in the early 1840s. The second, more parochial conflict resulted from the offense taken by the Boston schoolmasters to Mann's *Seventh Annual Report*. They believed that Mann's criticism of teaching methods, especially recitation and corporal punishment, had been directed at them. In response, they published

Orestes Brownson

Remarks on the Seventh Annual Report of the Hon. Horace Mann,[67] which challenged his pedagogic positions. After a war of words, the Boston schoolmasters attempted to rally the state's teachers against Mann by founding a state teachers' association, which they hoped would condemn Mann's policies. This tactic was generally unsuccessful, as Mann's supporters soon gained control of the organization.[68]

The third group in opposition to Mann's reforms was more broadly based and was concerned with the ideological and political implications of his approach. Mann was a member of the Whig party, which had created the state school board and sponsored Mann's ideas in state government. The Democrats, led by Marcus Morton, had generally opposed his measures. A leading public spokesperson for the Democratic position was Orestes Brownson, who had undergone a religious transformation similar to Mann's. Brownson moved from the Calvinism of his youth to Presbyterianism and then to Unitarianism by the early 1830s. In 1838 he became editor of a leading Democratic publication, the *Boston Quarterly Review,* and in that journal he launched his attacks on Mann's reforms. In an 1839 article, "Education of the People," Brownson lashed out at the state board for proposing a system that would be used for political domination of the people. He singled out the establishment of normal schools as particularly offensive. "The most we can hope from them is some little aid to teachers in the methods of teaching."[69] But more importantly, he argued, they were potentially dangerous to a free society. Based on the Prussian model, these normal schools, he believed, would produce conservative teachers who would in turn impart Whig values to the children of the state. Moreover, Brownson asserted, the board was attempting to influence the books placed in school libraries. The result of teachers' imparting Whig philosophy and controlling schoolbooks would be "to give Whiggism a self-perpetuating power."[70]

Underlying Brownson's opposition was his commitment to *democratic localism*, a belief that most governing and decision-making powers should be kept at the local level, in the hands of the people. He saw the common-school reforms as centralizing power at the state level, thus taking decisions out of popular control.[71] Two years later Brownson elaborated his critique of state board–sanctioned books for school libraries: "We object also to the sanction of the Board, because it is an approach to a censorship of the press." Then, as if able to foresee the events of the 20th-century publishing world, he declared, "The publishers will not dare insert in their series a book not sanctioned by the Board, however valuable it may be in itself, or however acceptable it would be to a large number of school districts; and the author will not dare pour out his whole thought, but only such a portion of it as he has reason to believe the Board will not refuse to sanction."[72] Brownson's estimation of the board of education's goals for the common schools was summed up in the 1838 article when he claimed:

> In the view of this respectable Board, education is merely a branch of general police, the schoolmasters are only a better sort of constables. The Board would promote education, they would even make it universal, because they esteem it the most effectual means possible of checking pauperism and crime, and making the rich secure in their possessions. Education has, therefore, a certain utility which may be told in solid cash saved to the Commonwealth. This being the leading idea, the most comprehensive view which the Board seem to take of education, what more should be expected of their labors, than such modifications and improvements as will render it more efficient as an arm of general police?[73]

It is difficult to ascertain the effect Brownson's attack had on the general populace of Massachusetts, but in the elections of 1839 the Democratic candidate for governor, Marcus Morton, won the statehouse after 12 previous unsuccessful attempts. In the spring of

Historical Context

The Common-School Era

Pre-Common-School Era		1830s	
1808	Elizabeth Seton establishes a school for girls in Baltimore	1833	American Anti-Slavery Society is created
1821	The first public high school in the United States is established	1836	American Temperance Union is created
1826	The first public high schools for girls open in New York and Boston	1837	The Massachusetts State Board of Education is created; Horace Mann is its first executive secretary
1828	Work begins on the Baltimore and Ohio Railroad	1838	The first state normal school in the United States opens in Massachusetts
1828	The first western president, Andrew Jackson, is elected	1838	Mount Holyoke College, the first seminary for female teachers in the United States, is founded in South Hadley, MA, by Mary Lyon; it opens the following year with 87 students
1833	Oberlin College in Ohio is founded, the first coeducational college in the United States		

1840s		1850s	
~1840	Blackboards are introduced, prompting educators to predict a revolution in education	1852	Massachusetts is first U.S. state to mandate compulsory school attendance
1844	Horace Mann describes the Prussian school system in his *Seventh Annual Report*	1852	In North Carolina, the first state superintendent of schools is appointed in a southern state
1846	The "potato famine" begins in Ireland	1859	Horace Mann dies
1848	The first women's rights convention is held at Seneca Falls, New York	1859	John Brown attempts to start slave insurrection at Harper's Ferry, West Virginia

Thinking Analytically about the Timeline

In your opinion, which of the social reform movements taking place in this era would eventually prove to have the greatest impact on education in the United States?

Exhibit 3.2   Comparison between Horace Mann and Orestes Brownson

Issue	Horace Mann	Orestes Brownson
Control of schools	State	Parents in local district
Religion in schools	State-mandated	Local choice
Texts	From state-approved list	Local choice
Teacher training	State normal schools	Colleges and academies
Teacher certification	State	Local school boards
Purpose of certification	Moral, political, and economic	Moral and political
Agency to determine principles for schools to impart	State board of education	Local school boards
Political affiliation	Whig	Democrat

1840 the legislature narrowly defeated a report of the Democrat-controlled Education Committee that condemned both the state board of education and the new normal schools. The vote was 245 to 182.[74] Although this vote did not end the attacks on Mann's reform efforts, by the mid-1840s he had prevailed over all opposition, and his reforms were well on the way to becoming institutionalized (see Exhibit 3.2).

Accounting for the Success of the Common-School Reforms

Why were Mann's common-school reforms so successful? The answer is more complex than most historical accounts suggest. The first and perhaps most important reason was that the secretary was able to enlist the support of diverse elements in Massachusetts for his programs. One element of the supporting coalition was wealth. No reform movement in American history has had long-term success without forging an alliance with the money interests. Mann was successful, in part, because the mercantile, banking, and manufacturing interests were convinced that his common-school reforms would provide long-term benefits for them. Moreover, he seemed to convince many working people that the common school would provide better education than was previously available. Additionally, his suggestion that common-school education was the vehicle to upward economic mobility was attractive to some less-than-affluent parents. Secondly, he gained the support of most of the religious (Protestant) communities because his "common elements," while not all that each group desired, represented a compromise that was the most they could realistically expect. Finally, the common school and the slogans that carried its programs

into the public discussion embodied the controlling classical liberal ideology of the age and thus successfully captured the popular imagination.

Thinking Critically about the Issues   #10

How does the Kansas school board's 1999 decision to limit discussion of the theories of biological evolution (a decision it reversed in 2001) relate to the Brownson–Mann debate?

Lessons from Horace Mann's Common-School Reforms

It seems that every item of Horace Mann's common-school reforms, with the possible exception of his campaign to improve the physical conditions of schools and school equipment, can be viewed as containing both positive and negative elements. Any fair evaluation of his efforts as well as any attempt to draw lessons from them must address both aspects. His insistence on the teaching of the "common elements" of the great Christian truths to inculcate a common set of moral values not only helped stem the sectarian bickering among the major Protestant groups but provided society with a potentially unifying value system to replace the outworn Calvinist doctrine. Did this contribution, however, outweigh the potential loss of a truly pluralistic society where all individuals were more free to choose values compatible with their own cultural and class histories and characteristics? Did the Prussian model of universal state-supported and state-controlled education and improved pedagogical methods bring with it the antidemocratic impulses inherent in the despotic system of government it was designed to enhance? Mann's condemnation of punishment meant that the practitioners of child beating in schools would be on the defensive. But what would counter the potential dangers of psychological manipulation inherent in his "loving" pedagogy? Were Mann's contributions to the gains achieved by women in the teaching field adequate to offset the belief, made explicit in his arguments, that women are less rational than men? While the normal schools certainly represented a recognition that teachers needed education, was the pedagogically oriented education that they established as the norm for succeeding generations of teachers adequate? Mann's use of arguments asserting the economic value of schooling surely increased the popularity of schooling among nearly all segments of society, but should economic motives be the driving force behind education? Such questions require students of education to examine their own fundamental beliefs and values regarding human nature, the good society, and the appropriate relationship of the individual to that society—as well as their conception of the learning process and the teacher's role in that process. Such questions are inherent in all attempts to evaluate educational arguments, including those which dominated the common-school era of Horace Mann.

BUILDING A PHILOSOPHY OF EDUCATION

Chapter 3 has introduced some new issues and tensions relevant to building a philosophy of education. Whereas late-18th-century Virginia was fundamentally agrarian and excluded its minority population, slaves of African descent, from education, Massachusetts was beginning to feel the pressures of urbanization and industrialization, and its largest minority group was Irish Catholic, a challenge to the Whig Protestant conception of order and morality, but not excludable from education. As a prominent social reformer in Massachusetts, Horace Mann saw schools not primarily as a *private good* for those families who could afford them, but as a *public good* and a means of building support for republican and Protestant moral values in the population, including the Irish. Instead of

advocating Jefferson's dictum, "That government governs best which governs least," Mann saw the schools as an arm of government that could achieve social change. Instead of believing that a little disorder, even rebellion, was good for democracy, Mann believed that too much disorder already existed, and that a state-controlled school system could be used to help establish a more stable moral order. An example to be emulated, for Mann, was the Prussian school system, which contemporaries such as Orestes Brownson were quick to remind him was part of the foundation of a very antidemocratic society (see the Primary Source Reading). Would Mann have had a more democratic approach if he had followed Brownson's advice, providing state funding but allowing local control of schools so that Irish Catholics could take responsibility for deciding how their children would be educated? Or would such an approach violate the constitutional separation of church and state? Or was Brownson correct that this separation was being used to disguise the power of Whig Protestants over Irish Catholics, or what John Stuart Mill of England termed "the tyranny of the majority"?

For Massachusetts to attain both the standardization and professionalization needed for teachers to help establish the moral and educational consensus he sought, Mann established the state's first normal school for the training of teachers. His view of teaching as a loving, nurturing profession instead of a punitive one, together with his desire to save money for the state, led him to advocate increasing the proportion of women in the teaching profession. While he believed he was helping to establish religious and republican virtue through these measures, his critics accused him of substituting Whig paternalism for the kind of democratic local control that Jefferson advocated.

A number of these tensions remain alive for educators today. One of them has to do with the *public* mission of public schools. Who is the public whose beliefs and values should be represented in the schools? When teachers take a position in the schools, it is important for them to recognize that they are expected to serve the ideals of a democratic culture, which is supposed to respect difference, diversity, and pluralism of values among different social and ethnic groups. On the other hand, the schools inevitably privilege the teaching of the dominant language, values, and beliefs of the European American, English-speaking, capitalist social order that we have inherited from the colonial conflicts among such 16th- to 18th-century powers as England, Spain, France, and Native Americans. How does a teacher today help induct young people into full participation in the dominant culture while respecting the diverse origins, languages, and values of students of Native American, African American, Hispanic, Asian, and Middle Eastern cultures, and the many non-English-speaking groups who populate the schools of today, just as the Irish did in Massachusetts over 150 years ago? Can a classroom be an environment in which students of diverse origins feel their cultures are respected and honored, or does that undermine the mission to help students develop the knowledge, skills, and values they will need to achieve their aspirations in the dominant culture of the United States? How does a teacher serve the whole public, so that parents from every background feel privileged that their child has such a teacher? How can a teacher's philosophy of education sort out these issues in a way that communicates these ideas to others?

Your philosophy of education should make clear what *public* goals you think are appropriate for the public schools, and how you will help achieve these. To state that you wish to help children and youth read and write, for example, or think for themselves, is something the public will pay you to do only if you have a good idea of how the public good will be served by it. Horace Mann was able to convince the public that schools would serve the public good. It is important for you to be able to articulate what public goods you think your teaching will serve. For example, you might argue that the better educated people are, the less likely it is that they will commit crimes against person and property. Is that enough of an argument, or are there other public goods that your teaching will serve?

A related issue concerns the role of the schools in social change more generally. Mann wanted schools to help improve the social order. Again, the question arises: Whose vision of social change should direct the teacher's work? Moreover, *should* schools be significant agents of social change, or does a social change agenda, no matter whose agenda, risk making each child a means to accomplish someone's vision of the good society? How can a teaching philosophy balance the tension between teaching toward some vision of the good society and a vision of supporting each child's growth for its own sake? Is there a potential conflict, for example, between wanting children to develop a shared set of common values and wanting children to learn to think critically and independently? This issue will be revisited in some depth in Chapter 4, but it is useful to start exploring how you might address this tension in your own philosophy of education.

Finally, the development of the standardization and professionalization of teaching raises a related tension. How can a teacher exemplify the standards of the profession, which seek greater consistency among teachers to achieve greater consistency of student learning, without sacrificing the individuality, creativity, and autonomy that seem to be necessary to excellent performance in any profession, including teaching? Can a teacher or school leader be "standardized" through a professional preparation program and still be unique—and still nurture the special qualities and interests that make each child unique? How? And how can this be reflected in one's philosophy of education in a way that makes sense to oneself and to others?

Primary Source Reading

Orestes Brownson was introduced in this chapter as a member of the Democratic Party, a journalist, and a political and educational critic of Horace Mann. The following excerpt is a wide-ranging critique of Mann's political, religious, and educational aims for common schooling. Brownson further assails the wisdom of the normal-school effort Mann successfully began in Massachusetts.

Part of Brownson's critique is grounded in a view of the educated person similar to Aristotle's notion of "the cultivation of human excellence for its own sake," an ideal that Brownson believes Mann is abandoning in favor of education for instrumental social ends. In making this argument, Brownson distinguishes between "special" and "general" education, a distinction borrowed from the Greeks and still important today as we debate the balance of specialized versus general liberal studies in the school or college curriculum. In considering what it means to be educated as a human being, Brownson attacks Mann's common-schooling approach to religious education as an abandonment of what gives religion its essential value to human life, and he argues that Mann's academically narrow and standardized teacher education curriculum will only exacerbate this problem.

Brownson assails Mann's common-schooling ideas on other fronts as well, relying on Jeffersonian ideals of democratic localism in doing so.

Decentralization: Alternative to Bureaucracy?

Orestes Brownson

We can hardly be expected at this late day, in this ancient commonwealth especially, to go into any labored argument in favor of popular education, either as a matter of right or as the only firm foundation of a free government. For ourselves, we hold that every child born into a community is born with as good a natural right to the best education that community can furnish, as he is to a share of the common air of heaven or the common light of the sun. We hold also that the community, which

Source: From "Second Annual Report of the Board of Education, together with the Second Annual Report of the Secretary of the Board" (Boston, 1839), review in the *Boston Quarterly Review* 2 (October 1839), pp. 393–418.

neglects to provide the best education it can for all its children, whether male or female, black or white, rich or poor, bond or free, forfeits its right to punish the offender. We hold, moreover, that a popular government unsupported by popular education is a baseless fabric.

The real question for us to ask is not, Shall our children be educated? but, To what end shall they be educated, and by what means? What is the kind of education needed, and how shall it be furnished?

As an individual I am something more than the farmer, the shoemaker, the blacksmith, the lawyer, the physician, or the clergyman. Back of my professional character there lies the man, that which I possess in common with all my species and which is the universal and permanent ground of my being as a man. This education must reach, call forth, and direct as well as my professional pursuit. Individual education is divided then into general education and special—my education as a man and my education as a doctor, lawyer, minister, artisan, artist, agriculturalist, or merchant.

Special education appears to be that which we at present are most anxious to make provision for. Few people think of anything beyond it. The popular doctrine, we believe, is that we should be educated in special reference to what is to be our place in society and our pursuit in life. We think more of education as a means of fitting us for a livelihood than for anything else. The tendency has long been to sink the man in what are merely his accidents, to qualify him for a profession or pursuit, rather than to be a man. . . .

General education, which some may term the culture of the soul, which we choose to term the education of humanity, we regard as the first and most important branch of education. This is the education which fits us for our destiny, to attain our end as simple human beings. . . .

Man has a destiny, an end he should seek to gain, and religion is the answer to the question, What is this end, this destiny? According to the principles we have laid down then, education, to be complete, to be what it ought to be, must be religious. An education which is not religious is a solemn mockery. Those who would exclude religion from education are not yet in the condition to be teachers; long years yet do they need to remain in the primary school.

Man is also a social being and needs an education corresponding to his social nature. He is not a mere individual. He stands not alone . . . that deserves not the name of a social education which leaves untouched the problem of society, the destiny of the race. And the social education must needs vary precisely as vary our solutions of this problem. In Russia they solve this problem in their fashion. Society has there for its object the accomplishment of the will and the manifestation of the glory of the Autocrat. Hence, the Russian children are carefully taught, by authority, that they and all they may possess are his and that they must love him in their hearts and honor him as their God. In Austria the problem is solved much in the same way and so also in Prussia. Absolutism has its solution and educates accordingly. Liberalism has also its solution and its corresponding education. . . . If the aristocratic element be the true foundation of social order, then should our schools be under the control of the aristocracy, be aristocratic in their basis and superstructure, and be nurseries of the aristocratic principle. But, if the democratic element be the true basis of society, then should the social education give the democratic solution of the problem, create a love for democracy, and discountenance every aristocratic tendency. It should, also, not only accept the democratic element but disclose the means by which it may insure the victory and make all other social elements subordinate to itself. It must, then, touch the nature and organization of the state, determine the mission of government and the measures it must adopt in order to secure or advance the democracy. It rushes into the midst of politics, then, and decides on national banks and subtreasuries. An education which does not go thus far is incomplete and insufficient for our social wants.

Education, then, must be religious and social, or political. Neither religion nor politics can be excluded. Indeed, all education that is worth anything is either religious or political and fits us for discharging our duties either as simple human beings or as members of society. . . .

Assuming now the absolute necessity of religious and political education, and the worthlessness of every other kind of education, when taken alone, the great and the practical question becomes, How is this education to be provided? In what schools and under what schoolmasters?

We have looked into the reports before us, with the hope of finding an answer to this question, but here (as everywhere else in the world) we have been doomed to disappointment. . . . The normal schools, which the board proposes to establish, will do nothing to impart such an education as we contend for. The most we can hope from them is some little aid to

teachers in the methods of teaching. Beyond improving the mechanism of education, they will be powerless or mischievous.

Schools for teachers require in their turn teachers, as well as any other class of schools. Who, then, are to be the teachers in these normal schools? What is to be taught in them? Religion and politics? What religion, what politics? These teachers must either have some religious and political faith, or none. If they have none, they are mere negations and therefore unfit to be entrusted with education of the educators of our children. If they have a religious and a political faith, they will have one which only a part of the community hold to be true. If the teachers in these schools are Unitarians, will Trinitarians accept their scholars as educators? Suppose they are Calvinists, will Universalists, Methodists, Unitarians, and Quakers be content to install their pupils as instructors in common schools?

But the board assure us Christianity shall be insisted on so far, and only so far, as it is common to all sects. This, if it means anything, means nothing at all. All who attempt to proceed on the principle here laid down will find their Christianity ending in nothingness. Much may be taught in general, but nothing in particular. No sect will be satisfied; all sects will be dissatisfied. For it is not enough that my children are not educated in a belief contrary to my own; I would have them educated to believe what I hold to be important truth; and I always hold that to be important truth, wherein I differ from others. . . .

If we come into politics, we encounter the same difficulty. What doctrines on the destiny of society will these normal schools inculcate? If any, in this commonwealth, at present, they must be Whig doctrines, for none but Whigs can be professors in these schools. . . . Establish, then, your Whig board of education; place on it a single Democrat, to save appearances; enable this board to establish normal schools and through them to educate this board to establish normal schools and through them to educate all the children of the commonwealth, authorize them to publish common-school libraries, to select all the books used in schools, and thus to determine all the doctrines which our children shall imbibe, and what will be the result? We have then given to some half a dozen Whigs the responsible office of forming the political faith and conscience of the whole community. . . .

The truth is, we have, in the establishment of this board of education, undertaken to imitate despotic Prussia, without considering the immense distance between the two countries. . . .

Let it be borne in mind that in Prussia the whole business of education is lodged in the hands of government. The government establishes the schools in which it prepares the teachers; it determines both the methods of teaching and the matters taught. It commissions all teachers and suffers no one to engage in teaching without authority from itself. Who sees not then that all the teachers will be the pliant tools of the government and that the whole tendency of the education given will be to make the Prussians obedient subjects of Frederic the king? Who sees not that education in Prussia is supported merely as the most efficient arm of the police and fostered merely for the purpose of keeping out revolutionary or, what is the same thing, liberal ideas?

A government system of education in Prussia is not inconsistent with the theory of Prussian society, for there all wisdom is supposed to be lodged in the government. But the thing is wholly inadmissible here not because the government may be in the hands of Whigs or Democrats, but because, according to our theory, the people are supposed to be wiser than the government. Here the people do not look to the government for light, for instruction, but the government looks to the people. The people give the law to the government. To entrust, then, the government with the power of determining the education which our children shall receive is entrusting our servant with the power to be our master. This fundamental difference between the two countries, we apprehend, has been overlooked by the board of education and its supporters. In a free government, there can be no teaching by authority, and all attempts to teach by authority are so many blows struck at its freedom. We may as well have a religion established by law, as a system of education, and have the government educate and appoint the pastors of our churches, as well as the instructors of our children. . . .

Introduce now a system of normal schools under the supervision of a government board of education. These schools must be governed by popular men, men of reputation, not men who have the good of the people at heart and are known only by their infidelity to popular interests, but men who are generally regarded as safe, in whom the mass of the active members of the community have confidence. But on what condition does a man come into this category of popular men? Simply on the condition that he represent, to a certain extent, the opinions now dominant. . . .

In order to be popular, one must uphold things as they are, disturb the world with no new views, and alarm

no private interest by uttering the insurrectionary word, Reform. He must merely echo the sentiments and opinions he finds in vogue; and he who can echo these the loudest, the most distinctly, and in the most agreeable voice, is sure to be the most popular man—for a time. Men of this stamp do never trouble their age; they are never agitators, and there is no danger that they will stir up any popular commotion; they are the men to be on boards of education, professors in colleges, constables, mayors, members of legislative assemblies, presidents, and parish clerks. . . .

In consequence of this invariable law of Providence, the men who can be placed at the head of the normal schools, if established, will not be the men who represent the true idea of our institutions or who will prepare their pupils to come forth [as] educators of our children for the accomplishment of the real destiny of American society. They will teach them to respect and preserve what is, to caution them against the licentiousness of the people, the turbulence and brutality of the mob, the dangers of anarchy and even of liberty; but they will rarely seek to imbue them with a love of liberty, to admonish them to resist the first encroachments of tyranny, to stand fast in their freedom, and to feel always that it is nobler to die, nay, nobler to kill, than to live a slave. They will but echo the sentiments of that portion of the community on whom they are the more immediately dependent, and they will approve no reform, no step onward, till it has been already achieved in the soul of the community.

We confess, therefore, that we cannot look for much to meet the educational wants of the community, from the favorite measures of the Massachusetts Board of Education. In the view of this respectable board, education is merely a branch of general police, and schoolmasters are only a better sort of constables. The board would promote education, they would even make it universal, because they esteem it the most effectual means possible of checking pauperism and crime and making the rich secure in their possessions. Education has, therefore, a certain utility which may be told in solid cash saved to the commonwealth. This being the leading idea, the most comprehensive view which the board seem to take of education, what more should be expected from their labors except such modifications and improvements as will render it more efficient as an arm of general police? More, we confess, we do not look for from their exertions. The board is not composed of men likely to attempt more, and even if it were composed of other men, with far other and more elevated and comprehensive views, more could not be effected. Boards of trade may do something, but boards of education and boards of religion are worthy of our respect only in proportion to their imbecility. To educate a human being to be a man, to fulfill his destiny, to attain the end for which God made him, is not a matter which can, in the nature of things, come within the jurisdiction of a board, however judiciously it may be constituted.

Nevertheless, the board may, perhaps, do something. There is room to hope that it will do something to improve the construction of school-houses and to collect the material facts concerning the state of education as it now is; and, judging from the accompanying report of its accomplished secretary, it may also effect some progress in the methods of teaching our children to spell. This will be considerable and will deserve gratitude and reward. Nothing desirable in matters of education, beyond what relates to the finances of the schools, comes within the province of the legislature. More than this the legislature should not attempt; more than this the friends of education should not ask. Let the legislature provide ample funds for the support of as many schools as are needed for the best education possible of all the children of the community, and there let it stop. The selection of teachers, the choice of studies and of books to be read or studied, all that pertains to the methods of teaching and the matters to be taught or learned are best left to the school district. In these matters, the district should be paramount to the state. The evils we have alluded to are in some degree inseparable from all possible systems of education which are capable of being put into practice, but they will be best avoided by placing the individual school under the control of a community composed merely of the number of families having children to be educated in it.

Developing Your Professional Vocabulary

A good understanding of this chapter's content would include an understanding of why each of these terms is important to education.

character education

decentralization

discipline and a
  pedagogy of love

feminization of teaching

humanitarian reform

normal school

Prussian model

sectarianism

university

urbanization

Questions for Discussion and Examination

1. On the one hand, Mann's promotion of women into the teaching force might be regarded as a positive advance for women in the public sphere. On the other hand, it might be argued that Mann was reinforcing the subservience of women by limiting them to public-sphere nurturing roles in institutions controlled by governing boards composed entirely of men. In your view, was the feminization of teaching an advance for women or negative in its impact?

2. Discuss Mann's ideas for a new "pedagogy of love." In your essay explain why Mann wanted to change school discipline and the effect those changes would have on teachers and students. Analyze the appropriateness of this pedagogy of love for schools in a democratic society.

3. The idea of educating the "citizen" was central to Mann's educational ideals. Discuss Mann's concept of the citizen and show how it was reflected in his educational proposals.

 Online Resources

Go to the Online Learning Center at **www.mhhe.com/ tozer7e** to take chapter quizzes, practice with key terms, access study resources, and link to related websites. Also available on the Online Learning Center are PowerWeb articles and news feeds.

Social Diversity and Differentiated Schooling **The Progressive Era**

Chapter Overview

In a number of ways Chapter 4 is a pivotal chapter in this textbook. It examines perhaps the most dramatic changes in political economy, ideology, and schooling that have taken place in U.S. history. While the Jeffersonian chapter treated the first 50 years of the republic, and the common-schooling chapter treated the transitions in urban life and classical liberalism of the next 50 years, Chapter 4 unveils the modern era in American culture and schooling that emerged from the 1870s to the 1920s. Major political–economic changes included the emergence of a largely urban society, immigration from new sources in Asia and southern and eastern Europe, and far-reaching developments in industrialization and monopoly capitalism. Ideologically, classical liberalism was transformed by political, economic, and intellectual developments into a new form of liberalism termed "new," "modern," or "corporate" liberalism. This revised liberalism maintained commitments to scientific rationality, progress, and freedom but transformed those commitments to be consistent with the needs of the emerging leaders of government and business.

The chapter begins by using the Gary, Indiana, school system to illustrate how schools were transformed and how that transformation was publicly justified during the progressive era. School reform became a major priority on the national agenda for members of the business community, journalists, social reformers, educators, and educational psychologists, who began to explain human learning in decidedly new terms. As a result of these reform efforts, new objectives for schooling emerged, including training students with employable skills for the industrial workforce, enhancing social stability, providing a form of equal educational opportunity that assumed markedly different talents among students, and establishing a system of meritocracy that appeared to make different educational outcomes contingent only on the talent and effort of the students. To achieve those objectives, schools changed sharply in the progressive era in terms of who was required to attend, the different curricula offered to the students, the establishment of extracurricular activities for social and educational aims, and the shift in control of schools from local neighborhoods to centralized school boards comprised largely of businesses and professional class membership.

ANALYTICAL FOURTH READER.

EXAMPLES FOR ELOCUTIONARY DRILL

WE now wish to apply the principles and rules which we have been learning, and for that purpose the pupil is requested to study carefully the following pieces, and the explanations that are placed before them.

The first is the song of the Skaters. It is full of joy and spirit. In reading it, you are to imagine yourself on the ice with the laughing, shouting company. Say "Hurrah! Hurrah!" just as you would if you were throwing up your hat and shouting out of doors. You must use great force, high pitch, and rapid speed. Look back to the explanations and see what these things mean. Be careful, too, about the inflections and the emphases. Study what is said about them in the explanations, and then find out what words in the piece require emphasis, and what inflections the different sentences require.

With what inflection should you say "Hurrah"?

I.—THE SKATERS.

LUELLA CLARK.

1. Hurrah! Hurrah! Who cares for the cold?
   Winds are rough, but skaters are bold.
   Winds may blow, for skaters know,
   As over the ice so swift they go,
   Winds cannot worry them—let them blow.

Early school textbooks left little room for individual interpretation.

Chapter Objectives

Among the objectives that Chapter 4 seeks to achieve are these:

1. Students will understand and be able to evaluate the massive shifts in political economy, ideology, and schooling that took place at the beginning of the 20th century.

2. Students will also develop a deeper and broader base from which to evaluate the history of racial and ethnic prejudice in the United States. They should be able to compare progressive educational responses to ethnic differences with the responses to Irish Americans identified in Chapter 3 and later with the responses to African Americans identified in Chapter 6.

3. This chapter provides opportunity to assess the degree to which scientific management in the industrial workplace served the interests of workers and was or was not consistent with democratic ideals—including the role of women in society. Students will also be able to assess whether progressive social reform was consistent with democratic ideals.

4. The chapter also helps students evaluate the degree to which modern liberal ideology was consistent with specifically articulated conceptions of democracy, such as Jeffersonian participatory democracy and Dewey's developmental democracy.

5. Students will consider the degree to which domestic social order was achieved by the exercise of the force of arms and by political and economic control of schooling, thus calling into question a "consensus" theory of social order.

6. Students will be able to distinguish among different strands of progressive education and evaluate the interests served by those different camps.

7. Finally, the chapter enables students to consider the degree to which all population groups of students were or were not equally well served by the four progressive educational aims of social stability, employable skills, equal educational opportunity, and meritocracy.

The Political Economy of the Progressive Era

Urbanization

Shortly after the Civil War and through the end of the 19th century, the United States remained a predominantly agrarian society. In 1870, fewer than 10 million Americans, or only 26 percent of the population, lived in cities (communities of over 2,500 persons; see Exhibit 4.2). Not until about 1920 did over half the U.S. population live in cities. It was in this 50-year period, then, that the nation shifted demographically from being primarily rural to being primarily urban in character. Between 1870 and 1920, as Exhibit 4.2 illustrates, the number of cities with a population over half a million grew from 2 to 12.

The shift from rural to urban life, however, was not just a matter of numbers; it also involved matters of culture and the quality of life. As people came to the cities from rural areas in the United States and abroad, they encountered conditions few had ever imagined. Historians Dinnerstein and Reimers, in *Ethnic Americans,* provide some sense of the conditions under which urban dwellers lived in the larger cities at the turn of the century.

> Whole neighborhoods were filthy, foul-smelling, and overcrowded. In cities like Boston, New York, and Chicago houses adjoined stables, and offal, debris, and horse manure littered the streets. Piles of garbage in front of buildings or in narrow passageways between houses gave rise to stomach-turning odors and a large rat population. The population density was astronomical, some sections of Chicago, for example, having three times as many inhabitants as the most crowded portions of Tokyo and Calcutta. In 1901 a Polish neighborhood in the Windy City averaged 340 people per acre, and a three-block area housed 7,306 children! . . . One survey taker found that 1,231 Italians were living in 120 rooms in New York; another reporter could not find a single bathtub in a three-block area of tenements.[3]

The cities had other problems in addition to abject poverty, inadequate living quarters, and sanitation. As Jefferson had feared, urbanization brought an increase in crimes against persons and property, governmental corruption,[4] and, as we shall see, strife between laborers and employers. All of these, together with mistrust and misunderstanding of the burgeoning population of "new immigrants," did much to disrupt the American dream of peace, plenty, and harmony for all.

Immigration

The urbanization of late-19th-century America could not have happened nearly so rapidly or dramatically without massive immigration to swell the numbers of city dwellers. Just as significant as the great numbers of immigrants coming to the United States during this period were the national origins of those "new immigrants," as they were called by journalists of that time. Exhibit 4.3 illustrates a striking contrast in the "old" and "new" immigrants of the 19th century. In the five-year period from 1866 through 1870, 98 percent of the 1.3 million Europeans who immigrated to the United States came from northern and western Europe and Germany. Those settlers from England, Scotland, Wales, Ireland, Scandinavia, and Germany had left Europe largely during periods of economic depression and population growth in their homelands. European industrialization had decreased the number of people needed to work the farms at a time of economic boom in the United States.

Exhibit 4.2   The Nation Becomes Increasingly Urban

	1870	1880	1890	1900	1910	1920
Urban population (000s)	9,902	14,130	22,106	30,160	41,999	54,158
Rural population (000s)	28,656	36,026	40,841	45,835	49,973	51,553
Percentage of total U.S. population						
that is urban	26%	28%	35%	40%	46%	51%
Cities of over 500,000	2	4	4	6	8	12
Cities of 100,000–500,000	12	16	24	32	42	56
Cities of 25,000–100,000	38	57	96	122	178	219

Source: Historical Statistics of the U.S., Colonial Times to 1970, Bicentennial Edition (Washington, DC: U.S. Department of Commerce, Bureau of Census, 1975), pp. 11–12.

Exhibit 4.3   Changing Patterns in American Immigration, 1886–1920

Year	Total European Immigration to the U.S. (000s)	Percentage of Total European Immigration from Northwestern Europe and Germany	Number of Immigrants (000s)				
			Northwestern Europe* and Germany	Southern Europe†	Central Europe‡	Eastern Europe§	Asia
1866–1870	1,338	98%	1,314	14	7	3	40
1871–1875	1,462	94	1,368	37	33	24	66
1876–1880	813	87	704	40	40	29	58
1881–1885	2,508	86	2,154	121	149	84	60
1886–1890	2,231	73	1,625	212	205	189	8
1891–1895	2,073	55	1,143	314	277	339	24
1896–1900	1,477	34	501	390	315	271	52
1901–1905	3,646	26	939	1,051	944	712	116
1906–1910	4,493	22	973	1,260	1,201	1,059	128
1911–1915	3,801	21	790	1,138	890	983	124
1916–1920	581	36	207	323	12	39	69

*Primarily includes immigrants from Great Britain, Ireland, and the Scandinavian countries.

†The vast majority of immigrants from this region during this period came from Italy.

‡Primarily includes immigrants from Austria-Hungary.

§Primarily includes immigrants from Russia, Poland, and Russian-controlled territories.

Source: Derived from *Historical Statistics of the U.S., Colonial Times to 1970, Bicentennial Edition* (Washington, DC: U.S. Department of Commerce, Bureau of Census, 1975), pp. 105–9.

As the industrial and agricultural revolutions spread eastward from Great Britain through Germany and into southern and eastern Europe, the origins of immigrants shifted by the 1906–1910 period, nearly 4.5 million immigrants were leaving their overcrowded conditions of scarcity for the United States, where jobs and land were reputed to be plentiful. Not only had the number of European immigrants more than tripled, but now only 22 percent were the "old" immigrants; the remainder were new immigrants from southern and eastern Europe: Italy, Greece, Russia, Poland, Hungary, Bulgaria, Czechoslovakia, Lithuania, and other countries. Among these eastern Europeans were nearly two million Jews who fled persecution in Russia and elsewhere in hopes of finding religious, cultural, and economic freedom in the United States.

Open versus Restricted Immigration   The dreams of the Jews, however, like the dreams of the new immigrants in general, were only partially realized. There were greater opportunities in America than they had enjoyed in Europe, but they also encountered prejudice from the "old" immigrants, who were by then the established Americans of the dominant culture. Just as English-origin, Protestant Bostonians had discriminated against Irish Catholic immigrants early in the 19th century, the established Americans regarded the new immigrants with considerable disdain late in that century.

The United States had a traditional commitment to welcoming immigrants to the new world. In 1885, for example, a bill restricting the importation of contract laborers affirmed that tradition by noting, "this bill in no measure seeks to restrict free immigration; such a proposition would be odious, and justly so, to the American people."[5] But three years earlier, in response to pressure from West Coast residents, Congress had passed the Chinese Exclusion Act of 1882, setting a precedent for limiting immigration of people from targeted countries. The anti-Chinese sentiment was overtly racist, as illustrated in an 1876 California legislative committee report which stated that "the Chinese are inferior to any race God ever made. . . . [They] have no souls to save, and if they have, they are not worth saving."[6]

Philadelphia, 1897: horse-drawn wagons and carriages, an electric trolley car, and pedestrians congest a cobblestone street.

Yet in 1886, the Statue of Liberty was erected in New York Harbor as a symbol of freedom for immigrants, bearing an inscription that reads in part,

> Give me your tired, your poor,
> Your huddled masses yearning to breathe free,
> The wretched refuse of your teeming shore,
> Send these, the homeless, tempest-tost to me;
> I lift my lamp beside the golden door![7]

Despite such assurances, prejudice against the new immigrants was inflamed by a kind of pseudoscientific racism that interpreted national differences as racial differences. Slavs, Jews, and Italians, for example, were thought to be of different racial "stock" than the Nordic peoples, who were the established Americans. Since the publication of Charles Darwin's *On the Origin of Species* in 1859, there were some in the United States who created "scientific" arguments that certain racial groups were more evolved than others, and American nativists argued that the nation had to decide whether it would be "peopled by British, German, and Scandi-navian stock, historically free, energetic, progressive, or by Slav, Latin, and Asiatic races, historically downtrod-den, atavistic, and stagnant."[8] The Nordic stock was characterized as tall and fair, while the new arrivals, es-pecially those from Italy and Greece, were branded as short, dark, and low in intelligence. As early as 1894, the newly founded Immigration Restriction League led a campaign to restrict immigrants through the use of literacy tests, a device already found effective in limiting voter participation by African Americans in the American South. The Ku Klux Klan, noted for its virulent attacks on southern Black people, grew to a membership of over four million by the 1920s and worked to restrict the new immigration on the grounds of the immigrants' genetic inferiority.[9]

But it wasn't just crudely racist organizations such as the Klan that subscribed to eugenics theories and sought to control the gene pool of the American pop-ulation. Prominent educators such as psychologist Edward L. Thorndike and University of Wisconsin president Charles Van Hise, leading sociologists such as

Exhibit 4.4   Ethnic Diversity in Five Selected Cities

	Chicago	New York	Milwaukee	San Francisco	Atlanta
Total Population (000s)					
	2,185	4,767	374	417	155
Foreign-born White	781	1,928	111	131	4
Native White, foreign parentage	705	1,445	135	107	4
Native White, mixed parentage	208	375	47	46	3
Black	44	92	1	2	52
Asian	2	6	0.1	15	0.1
Percentage of Total Population					
At least one foreign-born parent (1910)	78%	79%	78%	68%	7%
Foreign-born White:					
1900	35	37	31	30	3
1910	36	40	30	31	3
1920	30	35	24	28	2
Black:					
1910	2	2	0.3	0.5	34
1920	4	3	0.4	0.5	31

Chicago		New York		Milwaukee		San Francisco		Atlanta
Major Immigrant Groups*								
Poland	(17)	Russia	(25)	Germany	(36)	Italy	(17)	None
Germany	(14)	Italy	(20)	Poland	(21)	Germany	(14)	
Russia	(13)	Ireland	(10)	Russia	(06)	Ireland	(13)	
Italy	(07)	Germany	(10)	Austria	(05)	England	(07)	
Sweden	(07)	Austria	(06)	Hungary	(05)	France	(05)	
Ireland	(07)	England	(04)			Canada	(05)	
Czechoslovakia	(07)	Hungary	(03)			Sweden	(04)	

*Percentage of total foreign-born population in 1920 in parentheses. Figures on major ethnic groups from 1920 rather than from 1910 were used because the 1920 census included separate figures for Polish, Czech, Slovak, and Hungarian immigrants, whereas the 1910 census included these figures in the figures for the nations that then controlled their homelands: Germany, Austria-Hungary, and Russia. The relative proportions of the various immigrant groups in 1920 are probably at least roughly comparable to those in 1910.

Sources: Fourteenth Census of the U.S. Taken in the Year 1920 (Washington, DC: Government Printing Office, 1922), vol. 3, pp. 109, 118, 222, 247, 261, 679, 691, 1,121, 1,131; Thirteenth Census of the U.S. Taken in the Year 1910 (Washington, DC: Government Printing Office, 1913), vol. 2, pp. 162, 180, 400, 482, 504, and vol. 3, pp. 216, 240, 1,078, 1,096.

E. A. Ross and Charles H. Cooley, and administrators of the Carnegie Institution of Washington (which took control of the independently established Eugenics Records Office in 1918) supported such efforts to "control the evolutionary progress of the race."[10] One popularizer of racist anthropology, Madison Grant, wrote in 1916 in his book *The Passing of the Great Race* that "the new immigration . . . contained a large number of the weak, the broken, and the mentally crippled of all races drawn from the lowest stratum of the Mediterranean basin and the Balkans, together with the hordes of the wretched, submerged populations of the Polish Ghettos."[11]

Such prejudice was exacerbated by public anxiety over the conditions of the cities in which the new immigrants lived, worries about the impact of immigrants on competition for jobs, and the hostility toward foreigners fueled by World War I. By 1921 this antagonism finally resulted in Congress's establishing immigration restrictions based on nationality. This initial act was reinforced with stronger national quotas in 1924 and 1929, and immigration from southern and eastern Europe was slashed dramatically after the 1920s. For many nationalities the annual quota was cut by 99 percent below the peak years of earlier immigration.[12]

Millions of new immigrants and their children were already part of the American social fabric, however, and the hostile and racist attitudes toward these new residents continued. In the large cities, a sizable majority of the population consisted of immigrants or children born of immigrant parents. As Exhibit 4.4 indicates, in

further, "This task specifies not only what is to be done but how it is to be done and the exact time allowed for doing it."[18]

To illustrate the value of his approach, Taylor offered the account of his supervision of a Dutch native named Schmidt at the Bethlehem Steel mill in Pennsylvania. Taylor wrote that under the old system of management, Schmidt earned only $1.15 per day for loading 12.5 tons of pig iron. With proper scientific management, however, Schmidt's output increased almost fourfold. In Taylor's words:

> Schmidt started to work and all day long, and at regular intervals, was told by the man who stood over him with a watch, "now pick up a pig and walk. Now sit down and rest. Now walk—now rest," etc. He worked when he was told to work, and rested when he was told to rest, and at half-past five in the afternoon had his 47½ tons loaded in the car.[19]

Taylor boasted that under scientific management, everyone benefits: goods can be produced more cheaply, workers receive higher wages, and total output increases. In Schmidt's case, noted Taylor, the laborer's wages rose from $1.15 daily to $1.85 daily, a 60 percent increase, while his production rose 400 percent.

Thinking Critically about the Issues   #1

Why might liberal education be incompatible with workplace requirements after Taylorization? Should workplace requirements limit what is taught in schools?

But despite the prospect of wage increases for common laborers, Taylor encountered resistance directly from the workers. As early as the 1880s, while working as a gang boss in a machine shop at Midvale Street, Taylor entered into a long battle with the machinists, who wanted to continue being paid by the piece rather than by the hour. Said Taylor,

> Now that was the beginning of a piecework fight that lasted for nearly three years, as I remember it—in which I was doing everything in my power to increase the output of the shop, while the men were absolutely determined that the output should not be increased. Anyone who has been through such a fight knows and dreads the meanness of it and the bitterness of it. I believe that if I had been an older man—a man of more experience—I should hardly

have gone into such a fight as this—deliberately attempting to force the men to do something they did not propose to do.[20]

As we shall soon see, worker dissatisfaction did not end with one three-year battle at one steel plant. It increased throughout the decades to follow, until the schools became one of the agencies to which anxious capitalists would turn in their battle for absolute control over the shop floor. But how could schools help address worker resistance to the scientific management of the workplace? Progressive education would help provide an answer.

Significance for Women and Office Work   Before further investigating worker responses to industrialism and to scientific management in particular, one other important development needs attention: the significance of scientific management for the employment of women. While there is much to be said about the participation of women in the industrial workplace, women in labor movements, and legislation protecting women from long hours and injurious labor conditions, the aspect of women's labor in the progressive era that is of most interest here has directly to do with the increases in office work that were stimulated by scientific management.

As urbanization and industrialization increased in the 19th century, and as people left the countryside for the city, the home became less a place of production and more a place of consumption only. That is, whereas women on the farm were expected to help produce goods such as food and clothing for the family and for sale, city dwelling offered little in terms of resources for production. To supplement family income some family women, immigrants and rural migrants alike, boarded single men who were working in mills, factories, and meatpacking plants, and other women took in seasonal piecework of various kinds. Also, single women worked outside the home in a few different job categories. In fact, by 1900, 90 percent of all women who worked outside the home were working in just four different areas: domestic service (39 percent); manufacturing, particularly in the textile, clothing, and tobacco industries (25 percent); agriculture, especially among Black women in the South (18 percent); and the professions, primarily teaching and nursing (8 percent).[21]

The rise of business and industry, and particularly the rise of scientific management, brought great changes to this pattern of women's work. While the percentage of women in manufacturing held steady (as the actual numbers of women in manufacturing grew rapidly) and the proportion of agricultural women declined, office work emerged as the number one employer of working women by 1920. Prior to 1900, approximately 76 percent of clerks and secretaries were male, but with the growth of scientific management, these secretarial and clerical jobs were increasingly filled by women. By 1920, the four major job categories employing women had changed: office work (25.6 percent), manufacturing (23.8 percent), domestic service (18.2 percent), and agriculture (12.8 percent). Office positions were attractive to young women because they did not require a great deal of training and were therefore relatively easy to leave and reenter, and they were considered more suitable for women than blue-collar industrial jobs. Further, these positions were considered dead-end jobs for men in that they did not lead to advancement and paid very little, while for women these positions were considered to be opportunities to earn income outside the home.[22]

Such positions multiplied rapidly with the growth of scientific management after the 1890s because of the rise of the bureaucracy in business and industry. If all decision making and planning were to be taken away from workers on the shop floor, elaborate systems of planning, monitoring, and reporting had to be established, systems that required a great deal of paperwork. Adding this layer of bureaucracy to the production process could be costly and inefficient unless it, too, was managed scientifically by having a low-paid, low-skilled corps of clerks who could follow directions and do the routine paperwork, such as record keeping, typing, and mailing, that would otherwise occupy their more highly paid decision-making superiors. Women were considered ideal candidates for such positions, in part because office employment would reduce the degree to which women competed with men for higher-paying industrial jobs.[23] The rise of women in office work, as will later be discussed, had a significant impact on the secondary school curriculum provided for working-class girls.

Worker Responses to Industrial Management

Workers (including women) tried to fight against the new scientific management by forming unions in various kinds of labor, including office work.[24] But union organization was only one of the ways workers sought

to protect their health, incomes, and, perhaps above all, right to make decisions about the conditions of their own labor. In the late 19th century, workers fought against the industrial order in ways that cost many of them their jobs and in some cases their lives. What is important to recognize, however, is that workers did not fight against industrialization itself but against the way in which the industrial workplace was organized and controlled by those who owned the factories.

John Morrison, a 23-year-old machinist testifying before Congress during this period, recognized the deskilling developments in his own trade and recognized as well the loss of worker autonomy and the subsequent effects on the workers:

> The trade has been subdivided and those subdivisions have been again subdivided, so that a man never learns the machinist's trade now. . . . There is no system of apprenticeship, I may say, in the business. You simply go in and learn whatever branch you are put at, and you stay at that unless you are changed to another. . . . It has a very demoralizing effect on the mind throughout. . . . [The machinist] knows that he cannot leave that particular branch and go to any other; he has got no chance whatever to learn anything else because he is kept steadily and constantly at that particular thing, and of course his intellect must be narrowed by it. . . . In fact he becomes almost a part of the machinery.[25]

While the reduction of workers to being "almost a part of the machinery" was an indictment of the workplace from the worker's point of view, it was good for profits from the capitalist's point of view. An observer described one female worker and her work: "One single precise motion each second, 3600 in one hour, and all exactly the same. The hands were swift, precise, intelligent. The face was stolid, vague and vacant." It is not surprising that her manager praised her as "one of the best workers we have. . . . She is a sure machine." Controlling people like machines instead of allowing them to make decisions like people led to widespread practices such as are reflected in this remark by a superintendent of Swift & Co.: "If you need to turn out a little more, you speed up the conveyor a little and the men speed up to keep pace."[26] Economist Robert Reich summarizes the experience of many workers:

> The organization was structured like the machine at its core, engineered to follow the sequence of steps specified by the settings on their controls. Scientific management made the large enterprise, and everyone who contributed to it, an extension of the high volume machine.[27]

One of the by-products of scientific management was bringing young women into office jobs previously occupied by men. Such jobs required little training, were relatively easy to leave and reenter, and were considered more suitable for women than were blue-collar industrial jobs.

The move to corporate capitalism was intended to provide greater market share, even market control, for the capitalists, thus increasing their profits. But the capitalists' allegiance to profit and to the stockholders led to ever more authoritarian control of the workers in the effort to increase efficiency of production. The management movement had begun in the 1870s and 1880s, before Taylor's scientific management refinements, and worker resistance was becoming strong by the 1880s. In the five-year period from 1893 to 1898 surrounding the 1895 publication of Taylor's first paper on scientific management, over 7,000 strikes were reported against American companies. In the next five years, that number more than doubled to 15,000.[28] But strikes were just one of the ways workers resisted the new industrial order of corporate capitalism.

Neither African Americans arriving from rural America nor immigrants from predominantly rural portions of Europe, nor skilled artisans, nor women working outside the home for the first time were accustomed to the managed regimen of the factory system. For a variety of reasons, including subdivision of skills, low earnings, the authoritarian nature of the shop floor, and the long hours and injurious practices, among other factors, workers resisted the new management system of corporate capitalism in organized ways. Some of these ways were initiated by workers themselves and challenged the very power of capital to determine and manage the organization of production: these organized forms of resistance included populism, socialism, and a militant trade unionism unfamiliar to most Americans today. Another form of resistance to the unbridled power of corporate capital, progressive reform, was not initiated by workers and did not fundamentally challenge the power of capital to control the production processes. Each of these merits a brief discussion.

Trade Unionism   One form of organized worker resistance to the new industrial order was unionism. Today we are accustomed to thinking of unions as organizations that represent workers in a specific trade or occupation—miners, machinists, truck drivers, office workers, air traffic controllers, teachers, and so on—and bargain on behalf of those people for higher wages, better benefits, and better working conditions—and conduct strikes if the bargaining process breaks down. This kind of union organization by specific trades, or *trade unionism,* had roots in trade organizations prior to the Civil War, although strikes before the war were few because most workers were self-employed. But unions late in the 19th century were not always organized by trades and did not necessarily accept wage bargaining as their

The dehumanizing effects of scientific management and corporate capitalism led to a series of strikes in the late 19th century.

primary task. Historian Norman Ware writes that "the reluctance of the labor movement to accept collective bargaining as its major function was due largely to the fact that this involved an acceptance of the wage system."[29] Again, it was not just low wages but the organization of industry to which workers objected.

After the Civil War, trade unions were extremely weak, especially when the nation was plunged into depression in the early 1870s. But the depression eventually led to a series of railroad workers' strikes that culminated in a great national railway strike in 1877. Crowds of angry strikers stopped the railroads, stopped factory production in some cities, and became violent when fired on by troops. In Pittsburgh, when the governor called in the militia to control the strikes, the militia joined the strikers. Six hundred more militia were called in, this time from Philadelphia, and they attempted to disperse the crowd by firing on them, resulting in the deaths of 26 people. The crowd then turned on the militia, trapping them in a railroad roundhouse, which was set afire before the militia escaped. The crowd also burned 104 locomotives, over 2,000 railroad cars, and every railroad building it could find while the militia escaped from the city.

The Railway Strike of 1877 was the most extensive labor conflict of the 19th century, and it refocused public attention on labor and unions. The strike stimulated greater union membership, especially for the fledgling Knights of Labor, which rejected the trade union concept in favor of an organization that would unite all wage laborers, "the draughtsman, the time keeper, the clerk, the school teacher, the civil engineer, the editor, the reporter, or the worst paid, most abused and illy appreciated of all toilers—women," in an effort "to abolish the wage system."[30] The Knights were one of those organizations that, like the Populists and Socialists, challenged the power relations of capitalism. Membership in the Knights of Labor fluctuated but by 1886 reached a peak of 729,000. In that year alone strikes were conducted, by the Knights and by other labor unions, against 10,000 different establishments involving a half-million workers. The "labor problem," as worker resistance to the organization of corporate capitalism was called, was widely regarded as the most pressing social problem of the era.

By 1892 the battle lines between labor and owner-ship were firmly drawn. Five years previously, in Chicago, the heart of the eight-hour-day movement, a bomb at Haymarket Square killed or injured scores of people at a late-night workers rally that had been peaceful until the police, against orders from the mayor, attempted to disperse the assembly.[31] That May 1 date is still commemorated by workers and nations throughout the world as an international labor day. At the steel plant in Homestead, Pennsylvania, the Carnegie Steel Corporation hired an army of Pinkerton guards to put down a steelworkers' strike against wage cuts and other grievances. The armed Pinkerton troops numbered 32,000, more than the standing U.S. Army at the time, and the armed battles that followed their arrival killed some 70 people in all.

At Homestead, the state militia was brought in, but the strike only spread to other steel plants. Carnegie and the state militia responded by bringing in strikebreakers to work in the plant and having the strike leaders arrested and charged with treason against the government. Although no strikers were found guilty, the tactic was successful at breaking the strike after several months' struggle. When the mill was reopened, hiring preference was given to the least-skilled workers, who would work for less and were more controllable than the more highly skilled craftspersons. As a result, from 1892 to 1907 "daily earnings of highly skilled mill workers at Homestead shrank by one fifth, while their hours increased from eight to twelve."[32]

In this and other incidents, the industrial owners demonstrated that they would go to any lengths to protect their control over the workplace and over the laborers. Since the railroad strikes of 1877, state governments had increased the size of their militias and had begun building armories in cities in large part to be able to control labor resistance. Ownership had the wealth and power to define the issue in the press (also a profit-making enterprise) as "the labor problem" and to enlist the forces of the police and government to restore order when the problem became otherwise unmanageable.

Populism   A second form of resistance to corporate capital industrialism had its roots in the ideology of agrarian localism that Jefferson considered to be the most fertile seedbed of democracy in America. *Populism* flourished in the 1890s primarily in the rural midwestern states, but it was not opposed to industrialism itself. Rather, it expressed opposition to the way in which industry was organized. Populists opposed the effects of industrial capitalism on costs of farm production, which were increasing, and on prices for farm products, which were declining. They opposed in particular the growing legislative financial assistance to big business and industry, such as the millions of dollars' worth of land granted by the government to the railroad industry. Finally, populists strongly opposed the effects of management on workers even before Taylor's scientific management movement matured. It was not just earnings but the power to decide on the industrial organization that populists most disputed. One Nebraska newspaper called for the elimination of "monopolistic privileges and power," and a journal, the *Farmers Alliance,* called for the establishment instead of "an *industrial democracy* in which each citizen shall have an equal interest" (emphasis added).[33] In a speech in 1894, Kansas populist Frank Doster clarified the idea of industrial democracy by arguing that "the industrial system of a nation, like its political system, should be a government of and for and by the people alone."[34] And a speaker at a meeting of the labor group Farmers Alliance in Nebraska proclaimed the populist position as follows: "Thus we see organized capital arrayed against the producers. . . . The irrepressible conflict between capital and labor is upon us."[35]

Space does not allow treatment of the complex economic and political issues attending the rise and fall of populism as an organized movement and political party. The point here is to illustrate that workers had ways of understanding corporate capitalism that were very different from the ways in which capitalists understood their own enterprise and that workers did seek to organize in the name of industrial democracy. In the 1892 election that brought Democrat Grover Cleveland to the White House, Populists peaked in their political power, winning six western states in the national elections, putting some 1,500 state legislators in office, and electing 15 U.S. senators and representatives, a remarkable feat by today's standards. Soon thereafter, however, populism began to weaken as a political force. The party was divided by inner conflicts, and its positions were seen as too conservative by Socialist party leaders who might otherwise have supported populism. Further, support lagged among urban workers who were unaccustomed to traditions of agrarian democracy. Also, Populist leaders believed that in the absence of an adequate base of support for their more radical positions, at least some of their aims could be achieved by the progressive elements within the Democratic party. As historian Norman Pollack notes, third parties have historically not done well in the United States, and the Populist thrust was by the late 1890s absorbed and blunted by the Democratic party.[36]

Socialism A third major worker response to the new industrial order was socialism. The Socialist Labor party was founded in 1877 and developed an agenda that was in some ways very similar to that of the Populists.[37] The Socialists, however, regarded the Populists as too conservative and inadequately industrial working class in their ideology and origins. Further, the Socialists' base was primarily urban, not rural, and there was a certain amount of competition between Socialists and Populists for worker support.

A split within the Socialist Labor party in 1899 led to the founding of the Socialist party in 1901, and that party remained very strong by today's standards until 1919. The party grew throughout the first two decades of the 20th century, depending on several different groups of workers for support. Among women, for example, a significant number of Protestants identified socialist values with Christian values because of their common concern for human equality, compassion for the poor, and sharing of goods, as opposed to the capitalist ethic of competition for limited wealth. Many feminists supported socialism because it stood for political and social equality for women, and immigrant women saw socialism as speaking for their interests against those of industrialists. Among African Americans, socialism found support in both the North and the South for its stand on racial and class equality, and they, like workers more generally, found hope in the social advocacy of "industrial democracy"—the belief that workers should have power to shape the decisions that affect their labor.

In 1912, charismatic candidate Eugene Debs captured a remarkable 6 percent of the American presidential vote, and Socialists elected 79 mayors in 24 states. In all, Socialists won 1,200 political offices coast to coast in the 1912 election. By 1916, however, despite some success in local elections and the election of one Socialist congressperson, the Socialist party had begun its decline. The Socialists could not find a compelling candidate to make up for the loss of the proven vote getter Eugene Debs, and just as had happened with the Populists, the Democratic party took votes away from the Socialists by appearing to champion the workers. Even if the progressive reforms of the Democratic platform were pale in contrast to the Socialist party platform, many Socialists supported Democratic candidates because the third party had little chance of major success

and the Democrats were regarded by Socialists as the lesser of two evils compared with the Republicans, who had come to be identified with the interests of big business by the end of the 1880s.

Perhaps the most significant factor in the decline of socialism in America was the action of the federal government during and immediately after World War I. Using the War Powers Act, the federal government arrested several leaders of the socialist movement, confiscated the presses of socialist newspapers, and prohibited the sending of socialist materials through the U.S. mail. In 1918 Attorney General Palmer, during the infamous "Red Scare," had hundreds of socialists arrested and deported. These actions struck a blow from which American socialism never recovered.

Progressivism Insofar as militant trade unionism struggled for "workplace democracy," it resembled populism and socialism in its effort to challenge corporate power. However, the corporations had on their side not only armed forces but also the support of the leadership of the two major political parties, which sought to address the labor problem *without* fundamentally challenging corporate power over production. As a response to industrialism, the *progressive* era (roughly the 1890s through the 1920s) saw government regulations over business and industry that sought to end the conflict between labor and ownership without altering the unequal power relations. As historian Gabriel Kolko has shown, it was this cooperation between business and government that lay at the heart of the progressive movement in the economy.[38] Kolko's important contribution to our understanding of the progressive era is captured in the title of his book, *The Triumph of Conservatism,* in which he argues that progressivism did not serve the interests of the laboring classes so much as it stabilized the economy and protected the power of ownership through government regulation.

History has tended to portray the progressive era as a triumph for the common person over the giant monopolies that emerged at the turn of the century. Kolko argues, however, that it was big business itself that ultimately succeeded in bringing about government regulation. It did this for several reasons. First, the "free market" system was so unstable that it led to countless business failures, severe economic depressions, and a seemingly unending string of worker revolts. Second, it made sense for business leaders to trust government officials to assist them because they shared the same social class backgrounds and the same worldviews about what was good for society and even shared close personal and professional ties. For example, Kolko cites President Grover Cleveland's past business partnership with financier J. P. Morgan's lawyer. Finally, the federal government had a good record of providing direct economic gain to big business in the form of land grants to the railroads, tariffs against imported goods, subsidies for corporations, and so on.

Further, contrary to the commonly held view that big monopolies were invincibly controlling the market, many if not most monopolies needed help desperately. As more and more businesses were bought and merged into giant corporations, these enormous firms weakened in competitive power. Fewer than half the mergers in the era made a profit, and 40 percent failed altogether. As rapidly as new inventions were patented, small businesses were able to introduce innovations in production and marketing, while the monopolies could not so quickly change their giant operations to incorporate innovations. With high overhead costs and persistent difficulties in managing laborers, the big corporations failed to control the market. Even U.S. Steel, which resulted from merging 138 smaller steel companies, controlled only 60 percent of the market, and its stock declined from $55 per share in 1901 to $9 a share in 1904. By 1907 steel industry leaders began meeting with the Department of Justice and the Department of Commerce to reduce competition and protect monopoly investments by regulating the steel market.[39]

Major government regulation of the economy had been established earlier in the progressive period, and the presidencies of Theodore Roosevelt and Woodrow Wilson were marked by a flurry of appointed regulatory commissions. Those commissions, which were established by such legislation as the Interstate Commerce Commission Act (1887), the Sherman Anti-Trust Act (1890), the Federal Reserve Act (1913), the establishment of the Federal Trade Commission, and the Clayton Anti-Trust Act (both 1914), all put considerable power in the hands of officials who were not elected by the people—and therefore not directly accountable to them—but appointed by the executive branch in consultation with Congress and big business. The establishment of these commissions meant the centralization of economic and political power in the hands of the federal government at a level that had never been seen before, and this centralized power is one of the hallmarks of progressive reform at the federal, state, and local levels. We will soon see a progressive defense of this centralization model as we examine modern liberal ideology.

Progressive reform at the state level tended in part to follow the federal model of establishing appointive regulatory bodies to oversee commerce, politics, and labor relations. A different example of centralization of power at the state level is compulsory schooling legislation. Well into the progressive era, schooling was still largely a voluntary enterprise, and classical liberal presumptions about the limited right of the state to constrain individual choice about such matters prevailed. But in an effort to respond to humanitarian concerns about abusive employment of youth in mines and factories, to provide education for all youth, to "Americanize" immigrant youth, and in general to socialize youth to new political–economic conditions, all state governments had passed and begun enforcing compulsory attendance laws by 1918.[40] More will be said about compulsory schooling later; it is mentioned here as an example of progressive centralization at the state level.

Progressive Urban Reform   Of greater interest than state government is centralization at the city level, where, in Robert Wiebe's words, "The heart of Progressivism was the ambition of the new middle class to fulfill its destiny through bureaucratic means."[41] In Wiebe's view, progressive reform of city government amounted essentially to scientific management of the cities in ways that might be considered analogous to the scientific management of the worker in industry. This analysis challenges the traditional historical view that progressive urban reform was a victory for democracy won by muckraking journalists, settlement-house social workers, educators, government officials, and other reformers who opposed harmful labor practices, slum conditions, and political corruption in city government.

The cities at the turn of the century were in many respects chaotic, particularly by the standards of the business and professional classes who lived there. Whether city life was more chaotic then than now might be a good question for historical debate, however, for the governmental corruption that the reformers despised was also a source of order and unity in the cities at the turn of the century. Journalists Lincoln Steffens and Lord James Bryce were among those who wrote articles attacking the "ward boss" system of machine politics.[42] The ward system promoted a kind of "you scratch my back and I'll scratch yours" morality between the alderman and their constituency, most of whom were newly immigrated ethnics. As even the progressive social reformer Jane Addams had to admit, if the aldermen brought business and city services to his ward; helped citizens who had problems with police and the courts; used his resources to distribute food during holidays, buy gifts at weddings and christenings, and outfit a local youth band; and paid for funerals for poor immigrants so that they didn't have to be buried by the county, his constituency would forgive his ill-gotten wealth and enthusiastically reelect him.[43] The ward system offered a way for immigrants to have a voice in the affairs of their neighborhood, even if that voice manipulated the law in doing so.

Not only did "honest graft" offend the moral sensibilities of the reformers, the system of ward politics preserved ethnic identity and made possible the strength of such independent movements as socialism—both of which offended the established American, middle-class capitalist ideology shared by reformers, journalists, and the business community. This would in part explain why progressive reform in the cities was a decidedly middle-class and upper-class effort. Even if the middle class, made up largely of businesspersons and professionals, was a small minority compared with the far greater numbers of blue-collar immigrants, it was a powerful minority. Historian Richard C. Wade characterizes progressive urban reform as "a movement of the periphery against the center," because the middle-class residential areas were located on the outer ring of the cities, while the source of the boss's strength was the inner city, where the new immigrants had settled.[44] Historian Samuel P. Hays expresses the source of the reform movement in stronger class terms, arguing that the reformers are more accurately described as upper-class than middle-class:

> The movement for reform in municipal government, therefore, constituted an attempt by upper-class, advanced professional and large business groups to take formal political power from the previously dominant lower and middle-class elements so that they might advance their own conceptions of desirable public policy. . . . Reformers, therefore, wished not simply to replace bad men with good; they proposed to change the occupational and class origins of decision-makers. Toward this end they sought innovations in the formal machinery of government which would concentrate political power by sharply centralizing the processes of decision-making.[45]

Centralization of Power and Expertise   One effective way of centralizing power was to eliminate the ward system of balloting, creating instead a system in which aldermen were elected at large from throughout the city. Candidates with the wealth and stature to run a citywide campaign were usually backed by business and professional classes, and the class composition of city councils changed dramatically with the reform movements of the progressive era. Reformers claimed that the new citywide system was more democratic because it discouraged local ward corruption by eliminating ward bosses. But immigrants, African Americans, blue-collar workers, and small businesspersons thereafter had a much-diminished voice in the affairs of the city government that ruled over their neighborhoods. The ideology of reform, together with the power of the professional classes to enact their agenda, resulted in a sweeping change in city governance in both large and small cities throughout the nation. Not until a landmark Supreme Court decision of 1986 did a neighborhood constituency—in this case, African American voters in Springfield, Illinois—successfully challenge the at-large election system as unconstitutionally depriving citizens of representation in city government. The impact of that court decision on other city governments remains to be seen.[46]

Urban school buildings in the late 19th and early 20th centuries looked less like a schoolhouse and more like a factory or a public building.

If Hays and others are correct in viewing progressive urban reform as a victory of the professional- and business-class interests over the interests of the blue-collar and ethnic majority, there is another dimension to that victory as well: the victory of "expert" decision making over processes of public debate. The centralization process increased city governments' dependency on professional planners and administrators. Those experts were hired by the cities to make decisions that would be scientifically planned for greater efficiency and reliability. In matters of urban planning, budgeting, and general administration, a cadre of accountants, engineers, administrative experts, and other professionals were called upon to make decisions that had formerly been made in heated council debates among council representatives. But those debates, it was charged, were often decided by corrupt politics, resulting in personal gain to the representatives, and the reliance on experts would do away with such corruption and the waste and inefficiency that attended it.

Perhaps more than any other historian, David Tyack has shown that progressive reform in urban school governance followed the same pattern that Hays described in city government.[47] Tyack argues that city school reformers successfully eliminated neighborhood control over schools by replacing ward school boards with one central school board per city. This was more efficient in the sense that it allowed for greater coordination of budgetary and curriculum matters for the entire city. It allowed what Tyack calls "administrative progressives" to make important decisions affecting standards for teachers and administrators and to conduct schools along bureaucratic and hierarchical lines that had proved effective in business administration. Again, however, such centralization had its price. In this case, local ethnic communities were no longer allowed to play a significant role in making decisions about their own children's schools. One result was that neighborhood schools that had conducted classes in both English and a neighborhood immigrant language, such as Polish or Lithuanian, were no longer allowed to do so. Another result was that school decisions were no longer made by people from the same classes as people in the neighborhoods but increasingly by members of the professional and business classes who now were elected to the central city school board. Finally, the voice of the common person was diminished in another way that was similar to what had happened to municipal government reform: decisions were made not through public debate but by administrative experts with formal training in areas of curriculum

and pedagogy. Their claim to scientific knowledge, or "depoliticized expertise," appeared to legitimize their decision making, even if democratic processes of decision making were sacrificed.

The liberal reformers believed that these developments in urban and school government constituted important progress toward a more moral, orderly, and democratic society. An alternative interpretation is that scientific management, which owners had imposed on workers in industry at the beginning of the progressive period, had by the end of the era been extended to city government and school reform as well—and that democracy had been sacrificed in the process.

New Liberal Ideology

If it is even partly correct that the progressive movement in industry; in national, state, and local government; and in school governance resulted in the imposition of the will of the wealthy and educated few over the less educated and less powerful majority, the question arises, How could the progressive reformers have believed they were acting in the name of liberal democracy? The answer to this question must include an understanding of how the middle and upper classes changed in their view of what democracy meant in a complex, urban, industrial society divided by racial, ethnic, class, and gender allegiances. The old classical liberal understandings gave way to newer liberal beliefs and values that intellectuals at the time recognized as "new" or "modern" liberalism. The fundamental commitments to such classical liberal tenets as natural law, rationality, and freedom remained, but they were greatly modified to respond to new social and political conditions as well as to new scientific understandings that followed Darwin's revolutionary contributions.

This chapter began with an excerpt from the Gary school report, which cautioned that in order to understand the progressive schools, one must take into account "modern psychology, ethics, and social philosophy" and their impact on educational thought. It is not just the changed political economy that must be understood, Flexner was saying in the Gary report, but the changes in liberal ideology as well.

Natural Law

One way to sketch very briefly the differences between the old Jeffersonian liberalism and the modern liberalism of the progressive era is to show how each of the components of classical liberalism was modified by new liberals. One can begin with the classical liberal belief that the world operated according to laws of nature and that these laws could be known through science. The belief in natural law that was founded on the discoveries of Newton, Bacon, and other scientists was modified by the discoveries of Darwin. With the publication in 1859 of *On the Origin of Species,* the universe was no longer seen as a fixed mechanism governed by the unchanging laws of nature. Rather, it was now understood as an organism, changing and evolving just as species of plants and animals in nature evolved. This in turn suggested that truth itself was not permanent and therefore could not be known with absolute certainty. What we believe to be true today, argued modern philosophers such as William James and John Dewey, might be shown false tomorrow, as our ways of arriving at scientific truth are improved by new instruments and new methods.[48] That is, any truth is only as good as our methods of arriving at it, and our methods might improve with time. Since we can never be absolutely sure of even scientific truth, they said, the best we can have is a temporary agreement about what is true, based on our methods for verifying our claims. Dewey said the best we can do is to provide evidence and arguments to support our *assertions,* and thus instead of truth, only "warranted assertibility" is possible.

Scientific Rationality

Such a view had great significance for the modern liberal conception of human reason. Unlike Jefferson's faith in the common person's ability to arrive at reasonable ideas in the free marketplace of public debate, the modern liberal conception of truth required *scientific methods* for arriving at the most reasonable conclusions. Further, Darwin's research suggested to many intellectuals that not all races of humans were as fully evolved as others, and consequently some races were more capable of reason than others. The free marketplace of ideas was thus an unreliable way to arrive at rational conclusions; a reliance on experts was needed. The modern liberals still believed in reason as a route to progress, but they began to emphasize the importance of expert knowledge and scientific method as the way to achieve reason. Dewey, for example, as committed to democratic processes as he was, believed that the scientific method was the "method of intelligence" itself. One effect of such thinking among many new liberals was to foster distrust of the thinking of the majority of common citizens in favor of reliance on experts as the arbiters of reason. Not all modern liberals were equally optimistic about the newly privileged position of experts in public affairs. Dewey, for example, argued that a society run by a class of experts would inevitably function to serve the interests of experts at the expense of the majority. The world had suffered more at the hands of experts, he wrote, than at the hands of the masses.[49]

From Virtue to Rational Ethics

The growing reliance on science as the embodiment of reason had great import for the modern conception of human morality. The classical liberal concept of "virtue," which was grounded in the absolute truth of religious teachings, gave way to a notion of civic morality that was more consistent with the nonpermanent truths of scientific rationality. That is, it was no longer taken for granted that what was moral and good was revealed for all time in religious texts. The Darwinian challenge to religious truth, together with the new faith in expert reason, suggested that the moral and the good had to be determined with respect to what was reasonable in the context of particular social conditions. If social conditions changed, what was moral might change also. Further, the best judges of what social conditions required of citizens, it was believed, were those experts who understood the situation best. Emphasis on the "virtuous person" was thus replaced by a view of the "good citizen" where what was "good" could be determined by debate among experts and might change over time. Further, if the social leadership could not trust the home, farm, and church to instill virtue in young people, the public schools were an obvious choice as the institution to instill the civic morality of the 20th century. Whereas religious leaders have criticized this view as "secular, relativist morality," modern liberals believed it was a rational way to solve the problem of preserving an allegiance to moral life when the religious bases of morality were being challenged by scientific findings.

Progress

The modern liberal faith in expert rationality and rationalist ethics provided the basis for modifying the classical liberal view of progress as well. For classical liberals, human progress was virtually inevitable and would eventually emerge from the temporary chaos of rebellions and revolutions. Jefferson, like others, believed that human reason would triumph over the basic tendencies of human nature and that rebellion against tyranny was sometimes the most rational way to achieve that progress. New liberals, however, influenced in part by Darwin's findings that species don't always survive and in part by the decline in public welfare brought about by urban crowding and poverty, industrial exploitation and strife, and other modern conditions that Jefferson had not foreseen, came to believe that progress was not necessarily inevitable. If progress was to be ensured, it would require human rationality of the scientific type. Thus, progressives relied heavily on expert planning for a better society, and this helps explain their reliance on administrative experts rather than on citizen decision making in city and school governance. Democracy, they believed, was too risky a proposition in chaotic and threatening times; scientifically trained

expertise was the most promising means to progress. In contrast to the classical liberalism that fueled the American and French revolutions, rebellion and revolution were considered by new liberals to be a failure of rational processes.

Nationalism

One other means to progress, for new liberals, was a greater emphasis on national identity. Classical liberals' allegiance to the nation had been tempered by the fear of a too-powerful national government (recall Jefferson's "That government governs best which governs least"). However, faced with worker alliances against ownership and immigrant allegiance to ethnic origins, modern liberals viewed nationalism as a potentially unifying influence. Economic, political, and educational reforms were increasingly justified "in the national interest," and it was taken for granted that some of the primary purposes of the school were national in scope.

Freedom

The growing emphasis on nationalism is particularly interesting in light of the classical Greek tradition, which held that a too-strong government was the greatest enemy to freedom. In the progressive era, the national government was increasingly regarded not as an enemy to freedom but as the only real route to freedom. The dominant conception of freedom in America's classical liberal era was earlier described as "negative freedom" to emphasize the idea that freedom was achieved through lack of interference from the government. Some have referred to the modern liberal conception of freedom as "positive freedom" to indicate the new liberal belief that the conditions for freedom require positive government action rather than a noninterventionist, laissez-faire government. New liberals pointed out that a laissez-faire approach to freedom allowed the most powerful elements of society—such as corporate owners—to prosper at the expense of the majority of citizens and that people living in squalor could not exercise any freedoms worth having. Through government intervention, they believed, the freedoms of the least powerful could be protected. These new liberals could point, for example, to the 19th-century need for government intervention on behalf of slaves: a truly laissez-faire approach would have prohibited government from interfering with the power of slaveholders to earn a profit by enslaving others. In other instances, however, the case for government intervention was

This reference to the Spanish-American War suggests the flavor of nationalism in the United States during the progressive era.

more difficult to support—as in government regulation to stabilize the economy and thus protect major corporations against the market forces that weakened them. Progressive-era conservatives such as sociologist William Graham Sumner argued that giving the government greater power to regulate society in the name of freedom achieved just the opposite, because a strong central government almost inevitably gave greater power to the wealthy to use the government to manipulate the populace.

Sumner and his contemporary conservatives are often referred to as *social Darwinists* because they wanted individuals and institutions to survive difficult times on the merits of their own "fitness" to survive rather than through government intervention to help them. The more dominant application of Darwin, however, held that society was one corporate organism and that the misfortunes of some members had an inevitable impact on all members, like diseased cells in a corporate body. This way of thinking was used to justify the right and responsibility of those in power to regulate society for the good of all.[50] Despite the arguments of Sumner and others, the progressive era saw greater and greater powers accrue to government in the name of a more free and democratic society. The days of laissez-faire, "negative" freedom were numbered.

Modern liberalism, then, was clearly an outgrowth of the classical liberalism of Jefferson's day, as Exhibit 4.6 suggests. The liberal democratic outlook continued, in altered form, to serve as a worldview that explained and justified the dominant political–economic institutions of the United States. As those institutions came under the pressures of urbanization, industrialization, and immigration, and as scientific knowledge changed with Darwin's findings, such classical liberal conceptions as absolute truth, human reason, progress, and even freedom underwent profound changes. These changes allowed modern liberals to justify, in the name of liberal democracy, centralization of power in the hands of governmental agencies and centralization of decision making in the hands of experts with professional training. Progress, they believed, demanded greater efficiency in public institutions, including the schools, and this greater efficiency could not be achieved through traditional policies of local governance. So powerful a hold did this revised liberal ideology have on the leadership of economic and political institutions that new liberalism became the central outlook of both major political parties—Democrats and Republicans. Within each party, those who sought to preserve classical liberal perspectives and social policies became known as "conservatives," while those who embraced a stronger role for government in economic and social affairs were identified as "liberals." But the opportunities for alternative ideological positions—such as socialism, populism, and a labor-party position—to marshal any political power became increasingly scarce as new liberalism became more dominant.

Exhibit 4.6   Comparison of Selected Components of Classical and Modern Liberalism

Basic Concept	Classical Liberals	Modern Liberals
Natural law	Newtonian mechanics Fixed truth	Darwinian biology Relative truth
Reason	Fundamental part of each human's nature	Defined by scientific method, experts, and organizations
Individualism	The rugged individual as the political ideal	The person only as a cell in social organism; the rugged individual seen as problematic
Progress	Inevitable: the result of natural law and reason	Possible: the result of scientific planning and management
Role of government	Laissez-faire as the route to individual freedom	Positive government: regulation to create conditions for freedom
Plasticity of human nature	Improvement of most people possible through education	Improvement limited by genetic endowment
Freedom	"Negative" freedom	"Positive" freedom

New Psychology   Before leaving the discussion of the new liberal ideology, which Flexner and Bachman alluded to in explaining the Gary schools in light of "modern ethics and social philosophy," it is important to try to understand what they meant by "modern psychology." Understanding any culture's approach to education requires understanding that culture's assumptions about the human mind and human learning, for there can be important relations between these ideas and schooling practices. If we assume that people learn best when they are under threat of physical punishment, for example, we may take a different approach to schooling than we will if we think people learn best when motivated by their interest in the subject matter. Similarly, while the educators of one era may assume that proficiency in Latin and Greek is indispensable to the educated mind, the educators of another era reject this assumption because of a sharp change in how human learning is understood.

Chapters 2 and 3 briefly discussed the view of the human mind that dominated educational thought prior to the late 19th century—a view that had come to be called "faculty psychology" but which, in its basic principles, extended at least as far back as Plato. This view, which influenced Thomas Jefferson, Horace Mann, and their contemporaries, portrayed the human mind as a collection of faculties that could be developed through rigorous exercise and could be informed by the best thought and achievement that human culture had to offer.

On the one hand, faculty psychology led to a somewhat fixed and rigid approach to education and schooling. Students exercised what was thought to be one of the most important faculties, memory, by hour upon hour of rote memorization of texts. The texts were those that were thought to be the highest achievements of Western culture: passages from Homer, Cicero, the Bible, and other "classics." And they were memorized in Latin and Greek as well as English—not because translations were not available but because the rigors of learning difficult languages would help strengthen the mind. Another reason was that students would develop a sense of style, rhythm, and grace by reading these works in the original, and these sensibilities would be applied by the students in other endeavors.

This notion of application, or "transfer" of learning from the classical curriculum to other learning, was central to faculty psychology. The classical curriculum was defended not primarily on the grounds that students would need such information in their daily lives but

because the strenuous rigors of studying traditional texts strengthened and informed the learner's mind for all of life's intellectual and ethical challenges. One learned, it was presumed, to develop one's ability to *think,* because the capacity for rationality set humans apart from all other creatures. This capacity for rationality was presumed to be essential to human freedom, for it was argued that one could be free only by obeying rationality, not by obeying the dictates of others or the impulses of emotion.

While faculty psychology often led to schooling practices that were inflexible and even punitive for those who didn't bow to the fixed curriculum, it had an optimistic dimension: a high regard for the distinctiveness of human rationality and the ability of each person to develop his or her rational capacities through intellectual exercise. In this regard, it might be argued that faculty psychology gave more credit to the power of reason than did the "modern psychology" that replaced it during the progressive era.

Educational historian Clarence Karier has pointed out that what was known as "modern psychology" or "new psychology" during the progressive era was no single psychological viewpoint but a revised view of human nature that was influenced by several new approaches to psychology.[51] What these very different approaches had in common was that each of them claimed to be scientific; they all worked together to replace the more "unscientific" faculty psychology as the dominant conception of human mind and learning, and together they emphasized *nonrational* origins of human learning and behavior. Finally, these new psychologies, which still influence our ways of talking about the human mind and learning, came to prominence during a critical period of change in schools and society, when together these new views would have a significant influence on the conduct of schooling.

Karier draws attention, for example, to the *psychoanalytic* approach of Sigmund Freud (1856–1939) as one which emphasized the unconscious, and emotional, wellsprings of human thought and behavior. With a very different approach, G. Stanley Hall (1844–1924), the first person in the United States to receive a Ph.D. in psychology and the founder of the American Psychological Association, also provided support for attention to the emotional origins of human learning with his *primitivist* psychology, emphasizing biological stages of human development. Educators' growing awareness of the physiological and emotional dimensions of learning was accompanied by the rise of *social psychology,* which was developed primarily by George Herbert Mead (1863–1949). Mead argued that human values, perception, identity, and behavior are all importantly shaped by social interactions, particularly those within the various groups of which a person is a member.

These various approaches to understanding the human mind did much to dispel the view that learning is exclusively, or even primarily, a rational and intellectual process. As they gained prominence, these views provided greater support for educating children and youth by emphasizing physiological, emotional, and social dimensions of schooling. "Learning by doing" in the school workshop and home economics kitchen, in extracurricular clubs and other organizations in which groups of young people could be supervised by school personnel, and in school assemblies emphasizing patriotism and unity—all these were progressive era innovations that helped dramatically change the small schoolhouse to a physical plant with workshops, gymnasium, auditorium, and playground.

Thinking Critically about the Issues   #2

If the "new psychology" has influenced 20th-century ideology, we should see evidence of these psychological concepts in how people think about the mind and learning today. Can you recognize the influence of new psychology in today's ways of looking at human nature?

Easily the best-known educational psychologist of this time, as Karier points out, was Edward L. Thorndike (1874–1949). At Teachers College, Columbia University, Thorndike contributed much to the new changes in schooling. His contribution to modern psychology, referred to as *connectionism* for its emphasis on physiological connections in the mind formed by stimulus- and-response processes, became the foundation of modern *behaviorism,* most associated in our time with B. F. Skinner (1904–1990). Thorndike based his theory of human learning on his studies of animal learning, challenging the old classical liberal view that the human mind is distinctively different from the animal mind. In fact, Thorndike specifically attacked faculty psychology and transfer-of-training assumptions, arguing that school subjects did not have general value for developing the mind but rather were valuable only for the specific information and skills they imparted. This argument proved influential in moving away from the classical curriculum of Latin and Greek toward a more "modern" curriculum of subjects directly applicable to the new industrial society. Thorndike's emphasis on learning as a physiological, stimulus-response process helped provide support for the "learning by doing" of the vocational education movement as well. Finally, Thorndike's view that intelligence was physiological and therefore quantifiable made him an apostle for the intelligence-testing movement, which helped educators classify students into "superior" and "inferior" categories. Such classification, argued Thorndike, was important for educational efficiency and social progress. He wrote:

> [I]n the long run, it has paid the "masses" to be ruled by intelligence. . . . What is true in science and government seems to hold good in general for manufacturing, trade, art, law, education, and religion. It seems entirely safe to predict that the world will get better treatment by trusting its fortunes to its 95- or 99-percentile intelligences than it would get by itself. The argument for democracy is not that it gives power to all men without distinction, but that it gives greater freedom for ability and character to attain power.[52]

For Thorndike, as for many other educators of his time, schools needed to be changed not only to reflect the changes in the population, the workplace, and social values but also to reflect changes in how psychologists understood human learning. The emphasis on human beings as distinctively rational, in the image of God, gave way rapidly to an emphasis on human beings as physiological, emotional, and social creatures who were not very different from animals. The education of the "whole child," which sought to recognize the complexity of the child and also categorized presumably different children for different kinds of learning, became a mixed legacy of the progressive era.

Progressive Education

Progressive education is a simple term applied to a set of phenomena so complex that scholars continue to debate exactly what progressive education was. There is general agreement that the progressive movement in education started just before 1900 and had established its central innovations by 1920, although the Progressive Education Association (PEA) was founded only in 1919 and continued until the 1950s. There is also general agreement that progressive education constituted a response to urbanization, industrialization, and immigration; that it was articulated in terms of the emergent ideology we have termed new liberalism; and that it was shaped by new psychological approaches that replaced faculty psychology. Finally, most writers would claim that progressive education rejected the traditional, classical curriculum and its methods of rote learning in favor of a child-centered curriculum that emphasized student interests and activities related to the larger society. But within those generalizations, progressive education varied greatly in conception and implementation, and it is not always clear today what is meant by the term.

Educational historian Patricia Albjerg Graham argues that there were two different phases of progressive education: one roughly before America's involvement in World War I from 1913 to 1917 and the other following the war. Graham argues that the popular conception many people today hold about progressive education—that it was a permissive, experimental approach to schooling primarily for the children of the privileged—stems from the post–World War I innovations of a few highly publicized "progressive" schools.[53] The much more extensive phenomenon, according to Graham, was progressive schooling prior to World War I, in which the "chief thrust of reforms was in the schools serving lower-class families" and in which "probably the most radical change . . . was the wide-scale introduction of vocational and technical courses."[54] Graham's division of progressive education into these two general periods, the first of which will be discussed in the next section, helps locate an interesting irony. By the time the PEA formed in 1919, the greatest work of the progressive movement had already been accomplished. After its formation, the PEA attended primarily to the "experimental school" kind of progressive education, the impact of which has been minimal compared to the pre-1920 innovations affecting the majority of American youth.

Two Strands of Progressivism: Developmental Democracy and Social Efficiency

The phase of progressive education to be examined here is the earliest and most important phase, that which dramatically transformed American schooling in less than three decades from the 1890s to the 1920s. As David Nasaw points out, beginning in the 1880s critics of the schools were already describing such problems as:[55]

- The failure of the traditional classical curriculum to interest and motivate students.

- High dropout rates at both elementary and secondary levels.

- Growing problems of juvenile delinquency and illiteracy among urban youth.

- Waste and inefficiency in school management practices in neighborhood-controlled (especially immigrant-controlled) schools.

- Irrelevance of the traditional curriculum to the "real" needs of modern industrial society.

Under pressures from a business community unhappy with labor unrest, muckraking journalists who wrote about waste and inefficiency in the schools, social reformers concerned about the plight of youth in the cities, and educators who argued that a new approach to educating "new students" was needed, a rough consensus emerged regarding the changes needed in schools. However, progressives differed sharply among themselves over the specifics of these changes. For example, progressive educators in general believed that it was important to replace the traditional classical curriculum with a "varied" curriculum that reflected the needs and interests of the children. But within that general agreement came a sharp split between those who interpreted "needs and interests" to mean the specific concerns and motivations of each child and those who interpreted this phrase to mean "in the best interests of the child." In the first interpretation, the curriculum should respond to what each student finds interesting, while in the second interpretation, each child should be placed in the academic or vocational "track" for which his or her abilities are deemed most suited. These two interpretations of "replace classical curriculum with a varied curriculum" are distinctly different, but both are part of our inheritance from progressive education.

Differing interpretations also surround the conception of "progress." One conception of progress might be termed the *developmental-democracy* conception, in which it was believed that direct participation by all citizens in the decision-making processes of political and economic life, once begun, would develop individual and social capacities for problem solving through rational means. In this developmental view, grounded in the views of Thomas Jefferson and held by 20th-century educators Francis Parker and John Dewey, among others, school life should be organized very much like a democratic community so that students could begin developing the understandings, dispositions, and intellectual skills necessary for mature participation in a participatory democracy later in life. In this developmental-democracy view of progress, school life would be democratic, and democratic life (both inside and outside the school) would be educational.

The *social-efficiency* view of progress focused on achieving an orderly society in which political and economic institutions represented the interests of the governed through the application of the best principles of scientific knowledge and expertise. Social-efficiency progressives did not think of themselves as opposed to democracy. On the contrary, they believed that under modern urban conditions, schools could best prepare students for participation in a democratic society by identifying the "evident or probable destinies"[56] of different groups of students and educating them for these respective destinies. It would be just as inefficient, in this progressive view, to provide a college-preparatory curriculum to a child destined for factory work as it would be to provide a vocational shop curriculum to a college-bound student.

Several primary ideas in progressive education were subject to these competing interpretations. For the purposes of this chapter, five of these ideas may be identified as most important and most illustrative of how developmental-democracy progressives differed from social-efficiency progressives in their views of progress. Each of these assumptions is stated sufficiently loosely to allow for the competing interpretations of the era, but each is stated substantively enough to distinguish it from the traditional, classical-curriculum approach that had been assumed in the 19th century.

Progressive education assumes that

1. The traditional classical curriculum should be replaced by a varied curriculum based on the interests and needs of students.

2. Learning should be based on activities rather than on rote.

3. School aims, content, and processes should reflect social conditions.

4. A primary aim of schooling is to help solve social problems.

How each of these ideas was interpreted differently in the two contrasting strands of progressivism is the subject of the remainder of this chapter.

Deweyan Developmental Democracy

Perhaps not very meaningful, but interesting nonetheless, is that John Dewey was born in 1859, a year which also marks Horace Mann's death and the publication of Darwin's *On the Origin of Species*. Certainly, something of the old order was passing and the new was beginning. Dewey would become one of the two or three most influential American philosophers of the 20th century, writing not just about education but about traditional philosophical questions such as the nature of reality, knowledge, and moral life. Although it is not known whether the Vermont town-meeting tradition of Dewey's childhood influenced his adult philosophy, Dewey would eventually articulate a democratic theory that would address the conditions of modern, urban, industrial life. As a professor at the University of Michigan, University of Vermont, University of Chicago, and later Teachers College, Columbia University, Dewey developed an educational philosophy he believed to be consistent with his democratic theory. There are others who held Dewey's democratic approach to education during the progressive period, but Dewey is featured here because of his recognized importance to this major stream of progressive thought.

Following 18th-century philosopher Jean-Jacques Rousseau and 19th-century philosopher John Stuart Mill, Dewey believed that democracy was important not only because it stood for freedom and equality but because of its educational consequences. To begin with, he recognized Jefferson's view that for a democracy to be successful, the people must be educated enough to recognize and express their own interests. But more important, Dewey believed, was the converse: *for education to be most successful, it is necessary that people participate in democratic forms of life.* That is, Dewey believed in a developmental argument for democracy which held that participation in democratic life is more educational for the population than is participation in any other form of political life. He stated it best in *Reconstruction in Philosophy,* in which he argued that the democratic "test of all the institutions of adult life is their effect in furthering continued education. . . . Democracy has many meanings, but if it has moral meaning, it is found in resolving that the supreme test of all political institutions and industrial arrangements shall be the contribution they make to the all-around growth of every member of society."[57]

John Dewey, the most famous advocate of "progressive education," believed that children are by nature curious and active. Given meaningful tasks that reflect their own purposes, they become active problem solvers.

Dewey believed that the school could be a "laboratory for democracy" in which children developed the understandings, skills, and dispositions required for democratic life not only by reading about them in books but by interacting democratically in their learning activities. His view of the child's nature was that while most children do not have a "distinctively intellectual interest" in learning out of books for the sake of learning itself, all children have a great capacity for intellectual development.[58] The schools as traditionally conducted, he believed, had failed to stimulate the intellectual capacities of most children because they had not taken the nature of the child into account.

The Nature of the Child

Dewey believed that first, children are by nature actively social creatures; second, they are by nature constructive—they like making things; third, they are creatively expressive; and fourth, they are by nature curious and inquiring. Dewey argued that the traditional school not only failed to encourage but actively *penalized* children for behaving in accord with these facets of their nature. The school required children not to interact with one another, to be passive receivers rather than actively and creatively constructive, to accept a fixed curriculum rather than exercise their curiosity by following up on things of interest to them. In *Democracy and Education*

Dewey remarked that children are prepared as if they were going to lead a life of slavery rather than a life as free individuals. Dewey stated in that volume and others that Plato's definition of a slave was one who accepts as a guide to his own activities the purposes of another, while for Dewey *a free person was one who could frame and execute purposes of his or her own.*[59]

Dewey argued that the classroom could be an environment where children, working together in social activity, could frame and execute their own purposes. He urged that these activities should be selected by the students and teacher together on the basis of the students' interests, for when students are interested, he believed, they will pursue an activity for its own sake and learn more readily. In the course of such student-chosen activities or projects, Dewey argued, the students would inevitably encounter obstacles and problems in reaching their goals, and such problems should be solved by children working together under the teachers' guidance. Such cooperative problem solving would exercise the students' abilities to think critically about the causes and consequences of things they were interested in, and thus they would grow intellectually just by participating in their chosen projects. This growth would lead to new interests, new choices of activities, new problems to overcome, and new growth in a cycle of learning driven by the ever-developing interests of the students. In this manner, Dewey believed, schools would respond to social problems by equipping students to become adults who could solve social problems for themselves.

For Dewey, the primary social problem of the time was not worker resistance to scientific management, poverty, or ethnic conflict. His primary concern was that problems brought about by urbanization, immigration, and industrialization were being solved non-democratically, by authoritarian methods that put some members of society in control of others. Dewey believed that the schools could be a part of, but not the whole, solution to this pervasive political, economic, and ideological problem.[60]

In the preceding brief sketch we can see how Dewey embodied three of the four main assumptions of progressive education: (1) replacement of the traditional curriculum with a varied, child-centered curriculum, (2) learning through activity, and (3) schooling as a response to social problems. The fourth dimension, that schools should reflect social realities, Dewey believed would be a function of the students' interests and the projects they would seek to pursue. Of Dewey's many books, the one most widely read during his lifetime, *The School and Society* (1899), argued that classrooms at the elementary level in particular should allow students to engage in activities based on occupations with which they were familiar. Such occupations would provide thematic unity to the students' constructive activities, reading, writing, and so on. The occupations would also provide connections to the world outside the classroom so that classroom experiences would inform and enrich student experiences outside school and nonschool experiences could motivate, inform, and enrich classroom experiences.

Dewey cautioned, however, against using these activities to prepare students for specific occupations or vocations in the workplace. He insisted that such occupation-based projects "should never educate *for* vocations, but should always educate *through* vocations." Dewey believed that progressive teachers could use such activities to develop experiences in discussing, reading, writing, arithmetic, problem solving, and other intellectual pursuits in ways that would stimulate students' interests in these areas much better than did the traditional methods. And part of the basis of this interest would be that the classroom would visibly reflect the social environment rather than be isolated from it.[61]

A Unique Meaning for Progressive Education

The meaning of "progressive" education, for Dewey, thus differed from the meaning as it was generally understood then—and as it is generally applied now. For most educators and observers during the progressive era, education was progressive because it was new and different from "traditional" education and because it was thought to result from and contribute to social progress in general (see, for example, the opening paragraph of this chapter). For Dewey, however, the primary meaning of "progressive" education was that it marked an arrangement of student activities that grew progressively out of the student's interests and past experiences, leading to new experiences and new interests in a continuous and progressive cycle. For Dewey, education that did not grow organically from the student in this way was not progressive at all.[62]

The key to understanding Dewey's theory of pedagogy, then, is the relationship between two key ideas: *experience* and *interest*. Students, even in early childhood, come to class not as blank slates, but already with a vast and varied set of *experiences* that make them *interested* in very different things. Their experiences may eventually

make many of them think they don't like "book learning" at all. Dewey argues that the task of the teacher is not to "sugarcoat" the curriculum to try to make it interesting to students, but to start with the *interests* of the students and help them shape new learning *experiences* that are chosen and guided in accord with those interests. Well-chosen experiences, Dewey argues, will help the students shape new interests that will then lead to new educational experiences. The teacher, who has mature ends in view, is a good judge and guide for which experiences will lead down a blind alley, or to trouble, and which experiences might actually help students learn things worth knowing. Reading a textbook is an experience, but not a very interesting one for many children.

Readers might reflect on their own past school experiences to try to recall when teachers were following something of a Deweyan path. The drama teacher who allows the students to choose the play they will produce and allows them to take roles in that production on the basis of their own interests—from lighting to writing to acting to stage-managing—believes that the children will learn by doing in ways consistent with Deweyan thought. The social studies teacher who invites students to create a class cultural journal on the basis of their interviews with people from the community whom they find interesting—this, too, can be an example. In both cases, teachers believe that the kind of learning that our culture values will emerge from these experiences. Deweyan pedagogy may be increasingly difficult to achieve, however, in an era in which all children are held to the same learning standards each year, and teachers feel an obligation to make sure each child performs to a prescribed level on standardized tests, which in some ways are an inheritance from the social efficiency strand of progressive education.

Charles W. Eliot and Social Efficiency

Dewey's interpretation of society's needs, and of how education should meet them, was not the dominant or the most influential view among progressive educators, if we are to judge by the claims of the social-efficiency progressives and by the actual school programs that took root during the progressive period. One of the most prominent educators of the time, Harvard president Charles W. Eliot, provides a good example of the social-efficiency stream of progressive thought, and through him the most important innovations of progressive education prior to 1920 can be examined. Although he was at one time an advocate of liberal education

Historical Context

The Progressive Era

Setting the Stage for the Progressive Period

1859	John Brown attempts to start slave insurrection at Harper's Ferry, West Virginia
1859	Darwin publishes *On the Origin of Species*
1859	Death of Horace Mann, birth of John Dewey
1867	U.S. Office of Education established
1869	Susan B. Anthony and Elizabeth Cady Stanton organize the National Woman Suffrage Association
1875	Alexander Graham Bell patents telephone
1879	Edison invents first practical electric lamp
1873	Influenced by German pedagogical theory, St. Louis schools establish the first public kindergartens

1880s

1881	New York Trade Schools are privately organized to provide vocational training
1885	Beginning of the "new immigration"
1886	Statue of Liberty is dedicated in New York Harbor
1886	American Federation of Labor is organized
1886	Bomb explodes in Haymarket Square, Chicago, killing and wounding over 80 police and workers
1888	Edward Bellamy publishes *Looking Backward, 2000–1887*
1889	*The Wall Street Journal* is established

1890s

1890	Sherman Anti-Trust Act is passed
1893	The National Educational Association's Committee of Ten, chaired by Charles Eliot, stresses mental discipline as the primary objective of secondary schooling
1894	Pullman Palace Car Company strike in Chicago, with sympathetic railroad strike in 27 states and territories
1896	John Dewey opens his laboratory school at the University of Chicago
1896	New York City abolishes the ward system of school administration; St. Louis does so in the following year
1896	*Plessy* v. *Ferguson,* Supreme Court decision supports separate-but-equal laws for Blacks and Whites.
1898	Jane Addams opens Hull House as immigrant settlement House in Chicago

1900s

1901	J. P. Morgan organizes U.S. Steel Corporation, the first billion-dollar corporation
1902	Chinese Exclusion Act is extended to prohibit Chinese immigrants from the Philippines
1903	Wright brothers achieve first airplane flight
1905	Albert Einstein proposes special theory of relativity and the equation $E = mc^2$
1907	All but nine states, all of which are in the South, now have compulsory attendance laws
1908	Henry Ford introduces Model T

1910s

1910	Ella Flagg Young becomes the first woman president of NEA
1910	National Association for the Advancement of Colored People (NAACP) is formed
1912	Maria Montessori publishes *The Montessori Method for Early Childhood Education*
1917	Congress passes law requiring literacy test for all immigrants
1917	Smith-Hughes Act provides federal money for vocational education
1918	NEA's *Cardinal Principles of Secondary Education* stresses social efficiency and development of personality as the primary objectives of secondary schooling
1919	Progressive Education Association is established

1920s

1920	League of Woman Voters formed in Chicago to educate women in the use of the vote and improve the economic, political, and social conditions of the country
1920	Nineteenth Amendment is passed giving women in the United States the right to vote

Thinking Analytically about the Timeline

What evidence do you see in this timeline that various groups in the United States were or were not increasing their influence in political–economic affairs (including immigrants, African Americans, women, corporate America, workers, and the federal government)?

for all secondary school youth, Eliot became an articulate spokesperson for the replacement of traditional educational goals by four new educational objectives for the schools: social stability, employable skills, equal educational opportunity, and meritocracy.

Although Eliot had favored universal, liberal education at the secondary level through most of his career at Harvard, he recognized that his position applied to fewer than 10 percent of secondary school children because of high dropout rates. As the sheer numbers and ethnic diversity of high school students increased, Eliot became an advocate of vocational education. Eliot had distinct prejudices against students not from "pure American stock," as he put it, and was especially prejudiced against African Americans and Native Americans. As Steve Preskill writes, "Frankly referring to blacks as savages, Eliot preached that they must learn the lessons of the six-day workweek and vigilant frugality before they could be accorded political and economic parity with whites." Eliot often lauded Booker T. Washington for his vocational approach to the education of African Americans, and he was a member of the national General Education Board, which just before the 1920s successfully instituted vocational education in schools for African Americans throughout the South.[63]

Eliot's prejudices extended also to southern and eastern European immigrants, and he declared that new immigrants in New England presented "the same race problem to that part of the country that Negroes do to the South."[64] Reflecting the influence of Darwin on many intellectuals of his day, Eliot also endorsed a plan to discourage unmarried southern and eastern Europeans from immigrating to the United States, reasoning that married immigrants would present a lesser threat to the gene pool of the "pure American stock" of the nation.[65]

Apart from discouraging immigration from "objectionable" countries, national leaders such as Eliot increasingly turned toward education as a means of responding to the immigrants already here. To Eliot and other new liberals, the new immigrants were identified with a set of social problems which they believed schools might help solve. For example, the immigrants were a large part of the factory labor force that had been resisting scientific management of the workplace, and the resulting strife was a part of the larger disorder of the overcrowded cities. Further, the increasingly stratified industrial order demanded very different skills among workers, managers, and professionals. Two social and educational goals that became newly emphasized in

Charles Eliot was president of Harvard from 1869 to 1909, during which time his social and educational views influenced the course of progressive education.

progressive schools, then, were social stability and employable skills. It was believed that the differentiated curriculum, offering both academic and vocational courses of study, could achieve both goals. Further, it was believed that such a differentiated curriculum could contribute to democratic schooling and democratic institutions by achieving two additional aims: providing equal educational opportunity to all students and basing the democratic leadership of society on merit in school performance.

While none of these goals for schooling—social stability, employable skills, equal educational opportunity, and meritocracy—was entirely new to American society, they took on an unprecedented emphasis and distinctive character in the progressive period. Like most educational leaders of his time, Eliot endorsed all of them. Although he differed from Dewey in his progressive vision, the differentiated curriculum, with its emphasis on vocational education, represented for Eliot an interpretation of progressivism that, like Dewey's, (1) abandoned the classical curriculum; (2) based learning on activities rather than on rote; (3) reflected social conditions in school aims, content, and processes; and (4) sought to help solve social problems. Yet these progressive characteristics, when put to the service of the four new aims of social stability, employable skills, equal educational opportunity, and meritocracy, helped shape progressive schooling in ways that were very different from Dewey's developmental-democracy approach.

Social Stability   Born to one of Boston's wealthier families in 1834 (only eight years after Jefferson's death and two years before Horace Mann assumed leadership of the Massachusetts Board of Education), Charles W. Eliot was tutored in the classics as a child and attended the Boston Latin School. After graduating from Harvard with a degree in chemistry at age 19 and later teaching there, Eliot studied in Europe before accepting the presidency of Harvard at age 35. It was at Harvard that his vision of the good society and the good school system took shape. Born before the common-school era, Eliot would preside over Harvard well into the age of automobiles and air travel. His impact on ushering in the modern educational era was enormous.

Given Eliot's unusually privileged background and Harvard's increasingly close ties with the business community of the nation, it is not surprising that Eliot was more supportive of business than of labor in the strife between the two. Although he expressed considerable sympathy for the plight of workers and argued against excessive skill dilution and division of labor, Eliot attacked labor unions as a threat to individual freedom. In contrast, he identified the corporations as "really great reinforcements of public liberty" and believed that one function of the schools should be to teach prospective workers a more accommodating and cooperative attitude toward management. Vocational education, thought Eliot, offered a particularly good way to address problems of labor unrest by adjusting students to the realities of the managed workplaces of business and industry.[66] Further, he believed that "governmental affairs must be conducted on the same principles on which successful private and corporate business is conducted" and that students should be taught to "respect and confide in the expert in every field of human activity."[67]

Other educators, too, emphasized the service schools could provide to social stability. A 1914 bulletin of the U.S. Bureau of Education declared, "The State maintains schools to render its citizenship homogeneous in spirit and purpose. The public schools exist primarily for the benefit of the State rather than for the benefit of the individual."[68] Stanford University's prominent progressive educator Ellwood P. Cubberley applauded this notion in 1919, claiming that not only vocational education but such progressive innovations as night school, adult education, supervised playgrounds, and vocational guidance programs would serve the interests of the state by helping achieve a more stable society.[69]

Cubberley was correct in noticing the wide range of activities emerging as a part of the new progressive school. The one-room schoolhouse that taught the academic basics to those who voluntarily attended was rapidly being replaced by a more total institution that represented, as Cubberley said, the "extension of education." Schooling was being extended from a voluntary to a compulsory institution, and therefore it was being extended from the privileged few to the mandatory many. The extended school was one which provided auditoriums for school assemblies, shops and kitchens for vocational education, and before- and after-school supervision of clubs and other extracurricular activities. Such activities were planned with the intention of preparing students to take their places in an urbanized, industrial order. In its extension from voluntary to compulsory, from the few to the many, from a unified to a differentiated curriculum, from traditional academic to new vocational subjects, and from classroom curriculum emphasizing intellectual learning to extracurricular activities emphasizing social learning, the progressive school reflected a consistent concern for social stability as a primary educational objective. But there were other objectives of equal importance.

Employable Skills   One of those objectives was that schools should prepare students with specific skills and attitudes for the workplace. Again, vocational education would play a major part in efforts to achieve this aim. Eliot, once a proponent of liberal education for all youth, was arguing by 1908 that modern American society was divided into four largely unchanging classes: (1) the small managing or leading class, (2) the commercial class devoted to buying and selling, (3) skilled artisans, and (4) "the rough workers." Failure to recognize these classes, argued Eliot, resulted in a system in which the "immense majority of our children do not receive from our school system an education which trains them for the vocation to which they are clearly destined."[70] He further argued before the National Education Association (NEA) in 1910 that "serious modifications of the programs" in schools required teachers and administrators to accept their new "functions of guiding children into appropriate life work."[71]

By the time Eliot addressed the NEA, the nation's largest organization of educators, a sharp distinction had come to separate established hands-on learning activities from the new vocationalism. "Manual training" had begun growing in popularity in the 1880s,

Exhibit 4.7   Enrollment of Public High School Students in Specified Subjects*

	School Year Ending				
	1900	1910	1922	1934	1949
Total Enrollment (000s)					
	519	739	2,155	4,497	5,399
Percentage Enrollment by Subject					
General science	—	—	18.3%	17.8%	20.8%
Biology	—	1.1	8.8	14.6	18.4
Chemistry	7.7%	6.9	7.4	7.6	7.6
Physics	19.0	14.6	8.9	6.3	5.4
Physiology	27.4	9.5	5.1	1.8	1.0
Earth science	29.8	21.0	4.5	1.7	0.4
Algebra	56.3	56.9	40.2	30.4	26.8
General mathematics	—	—	12.4	7.4	13.1
Geometry	17.4	30.9	22.7	17.1	12.8
Trigonometry	1.9	1.9	1.5	1.3	2.0
Spanish	—	0.7	11.3	6.2	8.2
French	7.8	9.9	15.5	10.9	4.7
German	14.3	23.7	0.6	2.4	0.8
English	38.5	57.1	76.7	90.5	92.9
Latin	50.6	49.0	17.5	16.0	7.8
U.S. and English history	38.2†	55.0†	18.2	17.8	22.8
Civil and community government	21.7	15.6	19.3	16.4	8.0‡
Industrial subjects	—	—	13.7	21.0	26.6
Bookkeeping	—	—	12.6	9.9	8.7
Typewriting	—	—	13.1	16.7	22.5
Shorthand	—	—	8.9	9.0	7.8
Home economics	—	3.8	14.3	16.7	24.2
Agriculture	—	4.7	5.1	3.6	6.7
Physical education	—	—	5.7	50.7	69.4
Music	—	—	25.3	25.5	30.1
Art	—	—	14.7	8.7	9.0

*Covers enrollment in last four years of school.

†Includes ancient history and medieval and modern history.

‡Civil government only.

Source: Adapted by Stuart McAninch from *Historical Statistics of the U.S., Colonial Times to 1970, Bicentennial Edition* (Washington DC: U.S. Department of Commerce, Bureau of Census, 1975), p. 377.

and it embraced hand-oriented learning as a way to enhance academic education for all students. The new "industrial education," however, focused on the development of workplace skills and attitudes considered appropriate for that majority of students who would one day be the industrial working class.

Eliot represents the predominant thinking of progressive educators who shifted their vision from a liberal education to a "workforce" model in which, as Ellwood Cubberley said, "Our schools are, in a sense, factories in which the raw materials are to be shaped and fashioned into products to meet the various demands of life. The specifications for manufacturing come from the demands of the 20th century civilization, and it is the business of the school to build its pupils to the specifications laid down."[72] Exhibit 4.7 illustrates the change in course offerings intended to teach employable skills in this workforce model.

In 1900, about half a million students were enrolled in secondary schools, and their courses were overwhelmingly traditional "academic" subjects: Latin, English, algebra, geometry, physiology, earth science, physics, and history. Negligible percentages of students were enrolled in vocational subjects. By 1922, however, secondary school enrollment had quadrupled, while the percentage of students in most traditional academic subjects had declined markedly. Conversely, hundreds of thousands of students were now enrolled in the new vocational courses: industrial subjects, bookkeeping, typewriting, home economics, and agriculture, for example. Other subjects, such as music, art, and physical education, illustrate extension of the curriculum into areas that were neither clearly vocational nor academic but were seen to have social value.

Before leaving Exhibit 4.7, note the predominance of new vocational subjects intended for female office workers: bookkeeping, typewriting, shorthand, and home economics were from their inception heavily gender-typed. Likewise, vocational courses in industrial arts almost exclusively enrolled boys. Similar differences, though less pronounced, persisted in such academic subjects as advanced math and science. These differences led some psychologists and educators to challenge the value of coeducation, arguing that schools should provide separate curricula to "make boys more manly and girls more womanly."[73] As office work became increasingly a female occupation in the progressive era, business-occupations courses increased also. The published curriculum of the Beaumont, Texas, public schools illustrates the sentiment that home economics courses should be offered for women for different reasons.

> However inviting civic honors may appear to the suffragette, or vocational life may be to the bread winning or to ambitious women, homemaking is the normal life activity of most womanly women. Our schools should accentuate this normal life for women by providing a course in Domestic Science. Thus our girls would have equal advantages with our boys in life training, as our boys for several years have had the advantage of a well-equipped and well-conducted manual training department.[74]

While such sentiment for keeping women in the home appeared to have greater support in southern schools than in the industrial North, both regions used the employment market to help justify the vocational curriculum. The San Antonio Board of Education in 1915 commissioned a survey which noted that "only nine of the boys leaving school each year, out of the thousand from all grades, will become lawyers. Only seven will become physicians. Only four will become teachers; an equal number clergymen. . . . The figures show clearly that the vocations for which training is needed by the large numbers are not professional. Into the professions only about five percent of the men go."[75] The president of the school board of Muncie, Indiana, put the matter more succinctly: "For a long time all boys were trained to be President. Then for a while we trained them all to be professional men. Now we are training boys to get jobs."[76]

While some vocational courses, particularly those in business classes for girls, provided training that would translate into immediately employable job-specific skills, the schools could not hope to provide adequate job-specific training in the many skills required by the workplace. Perhaps more important than specific skills, the schools sought to provide in their vocational courses proper *attitudes* for the workplace; as the Lewistown, Idaho, board of education stated it, "The senior high school is charged with developing a *spirit* of enthusiasm that will make every boy and girl who is prepared for the work eager to enter."[77]

One way in which this could be accomplished, it was believed, was by converting traditional academic subject matter into vocational "courses of study" or "tracks" that would not be limited to shop work and manual activities but would also include "vocational English," "vocational math," and so on. So presented, it was believed that students would see the relevance of their academic work to their vocational courses of study and would thus be more interested in them. The Deerfield, Illinois, public schools, for example, advertised their manual training course of study with the recognition that "the school does not teach an individual trade," but vocational students would achieve "a like-mindedness and a sympathy that cannot but help toward the preservation of American institutions."[78] By 1920, Eliot's call for "serious modifications of the programs" of American secondary schools was well under way, justified by the new progressive objective of schooling for employable skills.

Equal Educational Opportunity   Since Jefferson's time, the view that education could be a source of social mobility for the lower economic classes was a part of the liberal faith of American society. Horace Mann had proclaimed that schools would be "the great equalizer" of social conditions, providing opportunity for all citizens to achieve their economic goals. And John Dewey in 1916 stated, "Only through education can equality of opportunity be anything more than a phrase."[79] It was not until the progressive era, in fact, that the term "equal educational opportunity" entered educational discourse. It became a newly explicit aim for progressives, in part because the differentiated curriculum had to be defended against charges that it was undemocratic, that it provided children from different backgrounds different and unequal educations. What progressive reformers meant by "equal educational opportunity" was not that students should receive the same educational experiences, as Aristotle had claimed would be appropriate for a democratic society and as Mann had envisioned for the common schools. In fact, they meant just the opposite, as is illustrated in this 1908 explanation by the Boston superintendent of schools:

> Until very recently [the schools] have offered equal opportunity for all to receive *one kind* of education, but what will make them democratic is to provide opportunity for all to receive such education as will fit them *equally well* for their particular life work.[80]

That is, equal opportunity meant to this Boston educator that students would receive different kinds of education, but all students would have "equal opportunity" to receive the education appropriate to them.

This view of equal educational opportunity prevailed among the most influential progressive educators in part because it appeared to justify separating students into different curricula and preparing them for different occupational outcomes, both of which, while "socially efficient," seemed undemocratic. The progressive interpretation of equal educational opportunity seemed to answer such charges and make the differentiated curriculum appear democratic. Furthermore, differentiation among students didn't need to wait until secondary school. "The teachers of the elementary schools ought to sort the pupils and sort them by their evident or probable destinies," said Charles Eliot in 1908. "We have learned that the best way in education is to find out what the line is in which the child can do best, and then to give him the happiness of achievement in that line. Here we come back to the best definition of democracy."[81] The "best definition of democracy," for Eliot, might more fairly be called "meritocracy."

Meritocracy Eliot argued that the schools could contribute to a more democratic society if, first, they taught students to "respect and confide in the expert in every field of human activity," and second, they helped locate and educate the most talented members of society for democratic leadership. "[An] important function of the public school in a democracy," he wrote, "is the discovery and development of the gift or capacity of each individual child. This discovery should be made

at the earliest practicable age, and, once made, should always influence, and sometimes determine, the education of the individual. It is for the interest of society to make the most of every useful gift or faculty which any member may fortunately possess."[82] This, to Eliot, was democratic in that it provided equal opportunity for each student to be educated for his or her particular place in society. Since, as Eliot said, "there is no such thing as equality of gifts, or powers, or faculties, among either children or adults," such schooling would educate leaders and followers.

Thinking Critically about the Issues   #3

Critically analyze the differences between John Dewey's idea of education *through* the vocations and Charles W. Eliot's idea of education *for* the vocations.

By 1919 Ellwood Cubberley would write that "a thoroughly democratic ladder has everywhere been provided" in the nation's schools. This ladder, according to the view of many progressives, was there for everyone, but only the most talented could be expected to climb it. Thus, the truly meritorious would rise to the top as a result of equal opportunity, completing the democratic argument. The result, wrote Cubberley, would clearly differentiate the leaders from the followers on the basis of merit:

> In our high schools and colleges the more promising of our youth must be trained for leadership and service to the State . . . along the lines of the highest and best of our national traditions in statesmanship, business, science, and government. In our common schools and in special schools those who labor must be trained for vocational efficiency, and given a sense of their responsibility for promoting the national welfare.[83]

The use of mass IQ testing beginning in the second decade of the century gave progressive educators a more "exact" and "scientific" way to assess the "evident and probable destinies," as Eliot had said, of children in schools. The differentiated curriculum and placement in vocational tracks could now be based on scientific measurement of student abilities. The developer of the Stanford-Binet test, Louis Terman, wrote in 1923:

> Preliminary investigations indicate that an IQ below 70 rarely permits anything better than unskilled labor; that the range from 70 to 80 is preeminently that of semi-skilled labor, from 80 to 100 that of the skilled or ordinary clerical

labor, from 100 to 110 or 115 that of the semi-professional pursuits; and that above all these are the grades of intelligence which permit one to enter the professions or the larger fields of business. . . . This information will be of great value in planning the education of a particular child and also in planning the differentiated curriculum here recommended.[84]

For Terman, E. L. Thorndike, and other advocates of the social-efficiency brand of progressive education, intelligence testing was a way to make the meritocratic aims of schooling more democratic. Students in the vocational programs were placed there not only for the social good, it was believed, but for their own good, because their talents best suited them to nonprofessional occupations.

BUILDING A PHILOSOPHY OF EDUCATION

Educational reform movements today, as always, respond to particular social conditions and are shaped by particular ideological commitments. Chapter 4 has profiled the special social and ideological conditions of the era in which the progressive education reform movement took place in the United States. In very general terms, the political–economic conditions included urbanization, immigration, industrialization, labor unrest, and the increasing centralization of decision making in business and government. Ideologically, the beginning of the 20th century was marked by a shift from the laissez-faire, limited-government commitments of classical liberalism toward a new liberalism marked by ever-greater reliance on government and scientific expertise to solve persistent social and economic problems. Older scientific conceptions of a fixed, mechanistic universe were replaced by a new conception of an evolving, organic universe in which truth itself could and would change. In the area of human learning, faculty psychology was rapidly replaced by new psychologies of the human mind and learning. It was in response to such new conditions and perceptions that the progressive education movement took place.

Who were these progressive reformers? What were their aims? And what were the consequences of their efforts? Although these questions are addressed at length throughout Chapter 4, Exhibit 4.8 on page 117 might help organize some of the relevant information. Anyone who understands progressive education well will be able to explain the relationships among the items in the three columns.

It might seem odd, however, to place John Dewey and Charles Eliot in the same place in Exhibit 4.8, when the two of them differed so sharply in their educational visions. If they were so different, how could they both have contributed to the same general aims and outcomes of the progressive education era?

Although Dewey differed from Eliot and others on the aims and methods of progressive education, he gave great legitimacy to the central ideas that helped fuel the progressive movement: ideas such as the abandonment of the classical curriculum, the use of occupations in the classroom, notions of learning by doing, making schools relevant to changing social conditions and solving social problems, and tailoring learning to the needs of the child. While these ideas meant one thing to Dewey and quite another thing to Eliot, all the ideas were new and different from the traditional "book learning" that had dominated public schooling since Jefferson's time. Although Dewey helped the educational community accept these new ideas, it was the social-efficiency variety of progressive education rather than Dewey's developmental-democracy variety that took root. The political–economic and ideological conditions of the turn of the century provided a more fertile seedbed for the social-efficiency approach to progressive education. In short, Dewey's arguments for a new education helped nourish a form of schooling—complete with ability-grouping of students, vocational education, and top-down decision making by administrative "experts"—that he would later criticize.

Teachers today often find themselves caught within the tension we have inherited from the split between the social-efficiency and the developmental-democracy progressives. On the one hand, most teachers today are well aware of the Deweyan reminders that students learn best when they are genuinely interested in what they are learning, and not all children are interested in the

Exhibit 4.8 Progressive Educational Reform (1890s–1920s)

Reformers	New Objectives	Extension of Schooling
Business community	Employable skills	From the few to the many
Journalists	Social stability	From voluntary to compulsory
Social reformers	Equal educational opportunity	From unified curriculum to differentiated curriculum
New psychologists	Meritocracy	From academic curriculum only to extracurricular activities
Educators (e.g., Dewey, Eliot, Cubberley)		From local control to central administrative control

same things. On the other hand, nearly all teachers today are feeling the pressure of state learning standards that hold all children, and increasingly all school districts, to teaching what all children "should know and be able to do," as it is often phrased, by grade 3 or grade 8 or grade 11. Teachers ask, "How can I be expected to appeal to children's authentic and unique interests if they are all going to be tested on the same material a month from now?"

There may be at least some good news in this dilemma. One thing that seems genuinely different from the progressive era in this current standards movement is the expectation that students from all income levels and all ethnic backgrounds will be held to the same academic standards. Certainly that was not true of the progressive differentiated curricula that placed very different learning expectations on children on the basis of their "evident and probable destinies," as Eliot said, consigning many students to vocational education as early as

possible. But the challenge to teachers today is a significant one: how to take children from very different economic and cultural backgrounds, very different academic skill levels, and engage them all successfully in learning challenging academic material.

Perhaps the most important part of that challenge is for teachers to believe, genuinely and thoroughly, that all kids are capable of learning the tough material; and another part is for teachers to develop the skills to find links between what Dewey called the "ends in view" (the important learning outcomes) and the interests of each child. Outstanding teachers do find ways to make their classes interesting to all students; do find ways to enlist students' active motivation and engagement in their academic work; and do find ways to educate all children to high standards. Your philosophy of education can address all of those issues as you express your goals, your methods for achieving your goals, and why you think those goals and methods are justified.

Primary Source Reading

Both the social-efficiency progressives and the developmental-democracy progressives believed that schools could play a role in social change. These two kinds of progressives had different visions of what society should look like, but both believed that schools could help society get there. Similarly, each group had its own ideas about how schools could respond to the social

Source: From *The Social Frontier* 3 (May 1937), pp. 235–37.

changes already disrupting U.S. society—social changes including immigration, industrialization, corporate capitalism, and centralization of power in local and national government.

Today, as in the progressive era, many educators have high hopes for how education can respond to rapid social changes and how schools can help make a better society. In the following selection, John Dewey, at the age of 78, writes a reflective essay on how much we can expect from schools in the way of social change. Can schools lead social change, or are they better suited to support

...social changes are happen-
... people and some not, how
...social changes that educators
...ble? Dewey addresses these
...n important journal that existed
... first called *The Social Frontier*,
and la... ...ucation. It was a journal in which
reform-minded edu... ...s, including teachers and principals, debated such issues as the relationship between
schools and social change.

Education and Social Change

John Dewey

Upon certain aspects of my theme there is nothing new
to be said. Attention has been continually called of late
to the fact that society is in process of change, and that
the schools tend to lag behind. We are all familiar with
the pleas that are urged to bring education in the schools
into closer relation with the forces that are producing
social change and with the needs that arise from these
changes. Probably no question has received so much
attention in educational discussion during the last few
years as the problem of integration of the schools with
social life. Upon these general matters, I could hardly do
more than reiterate what has often been said.

Nevertheless, there is as yet little consensus of opinion
as to what the schools can do in relation to the forces of
social change and how they should do it. There are those
who assert in effect that the schools must simply reflect
social changes that have already occurred, as best they
may. Some would go so far as to make the work of schools
virtually parasitic. Others hold that the schools should
take an active part in *directing* social change, and share
in the construction of a new social order. Even among
the latter there is, however, marked difference of attitude.
Some think the schools should assume this directive role
by means of indoctrination; others oppose this method.
Even if there were more unity of thought than exists,
there would still be the practical problem of overcoming
institutional inertia so as to realize in fact an agreed-upon
program.

There is, accordingly, no need to justify further discussion of the problem of the relation of education to
social change. I shall do what I can, then, to indicate
the factors that seem to me to enter into the problem,
together with some of the reasons that prove that the
schools do have a role—and an important one—in
production of social change.

Schools Reflect the Social Order

One factor inherent in the situation is that schools *do*
follow and reflect the social "order" that exists. I do not
make this statement as a grudging admission, nor yet in
order to argue that they should *not* do so. I make it rather as a statement of a *conditioning* factor which supports
the conclusion that the schools thereby do take part in
the determination of a future social order; and that, accordingly, the problem is not whether the schools *should*
participate in the production of a future society (since
they do so anyway) but whether they should do it blindly and irresponsibly or with the maximum possible of
courageous intelligence and responsibility.

The grounds that lead me to make this statement
are as follows: The existing state of society, which the
schools reflect, is not something fixed and uniform.
The idea that such is the case is a self-imposed hallu-
cination. Social conditions are not only in process of
change, but the changes going on are in different directions, so different as to produce social confusion and
conflict. There is no single and clear-cut pattern that
pervades and holds together in a unified way the social conditions and forces that operate. It would be easy
to cite highly respectable authorities who have stated,
as matter of historic fact and not on account of some
doctrinal conclusion to be drawn, that social conditions
in all that affects the relations of human beings to one
another have changed more in the last one hundred and
fifty years than in all previous time, and that the process
of change is still going on. It requires a good deal of
either ignorance or intellectual naiveté to suppose that
these changes have all been tending to one coherent social outcome. The plaint of the conservative about the
imperiling of old and time-tried values and truths, and
the efforts of reactionaries to stem the tide of changes
that occur, are sufficient evidence, if evidence be needed
to the contrary.

Of course the schools have mirrored the social
changes that take place. The efforts of Horace Mann
and others a century ago to establish a public, free,
common school system were a reflection primarily of
the social conditions that followed the war by the colonies for political independence and the establishment
of republican institutions. The evidential force of this

outstanding instance would be confirmed in detail if we went through the list of changes that have taken place in (1) the kind of schools that have been established, (2) the new courses that have been introduced, (3) the shifts in subject-matter that have occurred, and (4) the changes in methods of instruction and discipline that have occurred in intervening years. The notion that the educational system has been static is too absurd for notice; it has been and still is in a state of flux.

The fact that it is possible to argue about the desirability of many of the changes that have occurred, and to give valid reasons for deploring aspects of the flux, is not relevant to the main point. For the stronger the arguments brought forth on these points, and the greater the amount of evidence produced to show that the educational system is in a state of disorder and confusion, the greater is the proof that the schools have responded to, and have reflected, social conditions which are themselves in a state of confusion and conflict.

Inconsistent Conservatism

Do those who hold the idea that the schools should not attempt to give direction to social change accept complacently the confusion that exists, because the schools *have* followed in the track of one social change after another? They certainly do not, although the logic of their position demands it. For the most part they are severe critics of the existing state of education. They are as a rule opposed to the studies called modern and the methods called progressive. They tend to favor return to older types of studies and to strenuous "disciplinary" methods. What does this attitude mean? Does it not show that its advocates in reality adopt the position that the schools can do something to affect positively and constructively social conditions? For they hold in effect that the school should discriminate with respect to the social forces that play upon it; that instead of accepting the latter *in toto,* education should select and organize in a given direction. The adherents of this view can hardly believe that the effect of selection and organization will stop at the doors of school rooms. They must expect some ordering and healing influence to be exerted sooner or later upon the structure and movement of life outside. What they are really doing when they deny directive social effect to education is to express their opposition to some of the directions social change is actually taking, and their choice of other social forces as those with which

education should throw in its lot so as to promote as far as may be their victory in the strife of forces. They are conservatives in education because they are socially conservative and vice-versa.

Alternative Courses

This is as it should be in the interest of clearness and consistency of thought and action. If these conservatives in education were more aware of what is involved in their position, and franker in stating its implications, they would help bring out the real issue. It is not whether the schools shall or shall not influence the course of future social life, but in what direction they shall do so and how. In some fashion or other, the schools will influence social life anyway. But they can exercise such influence in different ways and to different ends, and the important thing is to become conscious of these different ways and ends, so that an intelligent choice may be made, and so that if opposed choices are made, the further conflict may at least be carried on with understanding of what is at stake, and not in the dark.

There are three possible directions of choice. Educators may act so as to perpetuate the present confusion and possibly increase it. That will be the result of drift, and under present conditions to drift is in the end to make a choice. Or they may select the newer scientific, technological, and cultural forces that are producing change in the old order; may estimate the direction in which they are moving and their outcome if they are given freer play, and see what can be done to make the schools their ally. Or, educators may become intelligently conservative and strive to make the schools a force in maintaining the old order intact against the impact of new forces.

If the second course is chosen—as of course I believe it should be—the problem will be other than merely that of accelerating the rate of the change that is going on. The problem will be to develop the insight and understanding that will enable the youth who go forth from the schools to take part in the great work of construction and organization that will have to be done, and to equip them with the attitudes and habits of action that will make their understanding and insight practically effective.

Drift or Intelligent Choice?

There is much that can be said for an intelligent conservatism. I do not know anything that can be said for perpetuation of a wavering, uncertain, confused condition of social life and education. Nevertheless, the easiest thing is to refrain from fundamental thinking and let things go on drifting. Upon the basis of any other policy than drift—which after all is a policy, though a blind one—every special issue and problem, whether that of selection and organization of subject-matter of study, of methods of teaching, of school buildings and equipment, of school administration, is a special phase of the inclusive and fundamental problem: What movement of social forces, economic, political, religious, cultural, shall the school take to be controlling in its aims and methods, and with which forces shall the school align itself?

Failure to discuss educational problems from this point of view but intensifies the existing confusion. Apart from this background, and outside of this perspective, educational questions have to be settled *ad hoc* and are speedily unsettled. What is suggested does not mean that the schools shall throw themselves into the political and economic arena and take sides with some party there. I am not talking about parties; I am talking about social forces and their movement. In spite of absolute claims that are made for this party or that, it is altogether probable that existing parties and sects themselves suffer from existing confusions and conflicts, so that the understanding, the ideas, and attitudes that control their policies, need re-education and re-orientation. I know that there are some who think that the implications of what I have said point to abstinence and futility; that they negate the stand first taken. But I am surprised when educators adopt this position, for it shows a profound lack of faith in their own calling. It assumes that education as education has nothing or next to nothing to contribute; that formation of understanding and disposition counts for nothing; that only immediate overt action counts and that it can count equally whether or not it has been modified by education.

Neutrality Aids Reaction

Before leaving this aspect of the subject, I wish to recur to the utopian nature of the idea that the schools can be completely neutral. This idea sets up an end incapable of accomplishment. So far as it is acted upon, it has a definite social effect, but that effect is, as I have said, perpetuation of disorder and increase of blind because unintelligent conflict. Practically, moreover, the weight of such action falls upon the reactionary side. Perhaps the most effective way of re-inforcing reaction under the name of neutrality, consists in keeping the oncoming generation ignorant of the conditions in which they live and the issues they have to face. This effect is the more pronounced because it is subtle and indirect; because neither teachers nor those taught are aware of what they are doing and what is being done to them. Clarity can develop only in the extent to which there is frank acknowledgment of the basic issue: Where shall the social emphasis of school life and work fall, and what are the educational policies which correspond to this emphasis?

Revolutionary Radicals Believe Education Impotent

So far I have spoken of those who assert, in terms of the views of a conservative group, the doctrine of complete impotence of education. But it is an old story that politics makes strange bedfellows. There is another group which holds the schools are completely impotent; that they so necessarily reflect the dominant economic and political regime, that they are committed, root and branch, to its support. This conclusion is based upon the belief that the organization of a given society is fixed by the control exercised by a particular economic class, so that the school, like every other social institution, is of necessity the subservient tool of a dominant class. This viewpoint only takes literally the doctrine that the school can only reflect the existing social order. Hence the conclusion in effect that it is a waste of energy and time to bother with the schools. The only way, according to advocates of this theory, to change education in any important respect is first to overthrow the existing class-order of society and transfer power to another class. Then the needed change in education will follow automatically and will be genuine and thorough-going.

This point of view serves to call attention to another factor in the general issue being discussed. I shall not here take up in detail the basic premise of this school of social thought, namely the doctrine of domination of social organization by a single rather solidly-unified class; a domination so complete and pervasive that it can be thrown off only by the violent revolutionary action of another distinct unified class. It will be gathered, however, from what has been said that I believe the existing situation is so composite and so marked by conflicting criss-cross tendencies that this premise represents an exaggeration of actual conditions so extreme as to be a caricature. Yet I do recognize that so far as any general characterization of the situation can be made, it is on the basis of a conflict of older and newer forces—forces cultural, religious, scientific, philosophic, economic, and political.

But suppose it is admitted for the sake of argument that a social revolution is going on, and that it will culminate in a transfer of power effected by violent action. The notion that schools are completely impotent under existing conditions then has disastrous consequences. The schools, according to the theory, are engaged in shaping as far as in them lies a mentality, a type of belief, desire, and purpose that is consonant with the present class-capitalist system. It is evident that if such be the case, any revolution that is brought about is going to be badly compromised and even undermined. It will carry with it the seeds, the vital seeds, of counter-revolutions. There is no basis whatever, save doctrinaire absolutism, for the belief that a complete economic change will produce of itself the mental, moral, and cultural changes that are necessary for its enduring success. The fact is practically recognized by the school of thought under discussion in that part of their doctrine which asserts that no genuine revolution can occur until the old system has passed away in everything but external political power, while within its shell a new economic system has grown to maturity. What is ignored is that the new system cannot grow to maturity without an accompanying widespread change of habits of belief, desire, and purpose.

Is Indoctrination the Way Out?

It is unrealistic, in my opinion, to suppose that the schools can be a *main* agency in producing the intellectual and moral changes, the changes in attitudes and disposition of thought and purpose, which are necessary for the creation of a new social order. Any such view ignores the constant operation of powerful forces outside the school which shape mind and character. It ignores the fact that school education is but one educational agency out of many, and at the best is in some respects a minor educational force. Nevertheless, while the school is not a sufficient condition, it is a necessary condition of forming the understanding and the dispositions that are required to maintain a genuinely changed social order. No social change is more than external unless it is attended by and rooted in the attitudes of those who bring it about and of those who are affected by it. In a genuine sense, social change is accidental unless it has also a psychological and moral foundation. For it is then at the mercy of currents that veer and shift. The utmost

that can be meant by those who hold that schools are important is that education in the form of *systematic indoctrination* can only come about when some government is sufficiently established to make schools undertake the task of single-minded inculcation in a single direction.

The discussion has thus reached the point in which it is advisable to say a few words about indoctrination. The word is not free from ambiguity. One definition of the dictionary makes it a synonym for teaching. In order that there may be a definite point to consider, I shall take indoctrination to mean the systematic use of every possible means to impress upon the minds of pupils a particular set of political and economic views to the exclusion of every other. This meaning is suggested by the word "inculcation," whose original signification was "to stamp in with the heel." This signification is too physical to be carried over literally. But the idea of stamping in is involved, and upon occasion does include physical measures. I shall discuss this view only as far as to state, in the first place, that indoctrination so conceived is something very different from education, for the latter involves, as I understand it, the active participation of students in reaching conclusions and forming attributes. Even in the case of something as settled and agreed upon as the multiplication table, I should say if it is taught educatively, and not as a form of animal training, the active participation, the interest, reflection, and understanding of those taught are necessary.

The upholders of indoctrination rest their adherence to the theory in part upon the fact that there is a great deal of indoctrination now going on in the schools, especially with reference to narrow nationalism under the name of patriotism, and with reference to the dominant economic regime. These facts unfortunately *are* facts. But they do not prove that the right course is to seize upon the method of indoctrination and reverse its objective.

Democracy as a Frame of Reference

A much stronger argument is that unless education has some frame of reference it is bound to be aimless, lacking a unified objective. The necessity for a frame of reference must be admitted. There exists in this country such a unified frame. It is called democracy. I do not claim for a moment that the significance of democracy as a mode of life is so settled that there can be no disagreement as to its significance. The moment we leave glittering generalities and come to concrete details, there is great divergence.

I certainly do not mean either that our political institutions as they have come to be, our parties, legislatures, laws, and courts constitute a model upon which a clear idea of democracy can be based. But there is a tradition and an idea which we can put in opposition to the very much that is undemocratic in our institutions. The idea and ideal involve at least the necessity of personal and voluntary participation in reaching decisions and executing them—in so far it is the contrary of the idea of indoctrination. And I, for one, am profoundly sceptical of the notion that because we now have a rather poor embodiment of democracy we can ultimately produce a genuine democracy by sweeping away what we have left of one.

The positive point, however, is that the democratic ideal, in its human significance, provides us with a frame of reference. The frame is not filled in, either in society at large or in its significance for education. I am not implying that it is so clear and definite that we can look at it as a traveler can look at a map and tell where to go from hour to hour. Rather the point I would make is that the *problem* of education in its relation to direction of social change is all one with the *problem* of finding out what democracy means in its total range of concrete applications; economic, domestic, international, religious, cultural, economic, *and* political.

I cannot wish for anything better to happen for, and in, our schools than that this problem should become the chief theme for consideration until we have attained clarity concerning the concrete significance of democracy—which like everything concrete means its application in living action, individual and collective. The trouble, at least one great trouble, is that we have taken democracy for granted; we have thought and acted as if our forefathers had founded it once for all. We have forgotten that it has to be enacted anew in every generation, in every year and day, in the living relations of person to person in all social forms and institutions. Forgetting this, we have allowed our economic and hence our political institutions to drift away from democracy; we have been negligent even in creating a school that should be the constant nurse of democracy.

I conclude by saying that there is at least one thing in which the idea of democracy is not dim, however far short we have come from striving to make it reality. Our public school system was founded in the name of equality of opportunity for all, independent of birth, economic status, race, creed, or color. The school cannot by itself alone create or embody this idea. But the least it can do is to create individuals who understand the concrete meaning of the idea with their minds, who cherish it warmly in their hearts, and who are equipped to battle in its behalf in their actions.

Democracy also means voluntary choice, based on an intelligence that is the outcome of free association and communication with others. It means a way of living together in which mutual and free consultation rule instead of force, and in which cooperation instead of brutal competition is the law of life; a social order in which all the forces that make for friendship, beauty, and knowledge are cherished in order that each individual may become what he, and he alone, is capable of becoming. These things at least give a point of departure for the filling in of the democratic idea and aim as a frame of reference. If a sufficient number of educators devote themselves to striving courageously and with full sincerity to find the answers to the concrete questions which the idea and the aim put to us, I believe that the question of the relation of the schools to direction of social change will cease to be a question, and will become a moving answer in action.

Developing Your Professional Vocabulary

A good understanding of this chapter's content would include an understanding of why each of these terms is important to education.

Charles Eliot

developmental democracy

eugenics

John Dewey

monopoly capitalism

new immigration

new psychology

On the Origin of Species

populism

progressive educational reformers

skilled artisanship

social efficiency

Taylorization

vocational education

Questions for Discussion and Examination

1. Explain how and why reformers centralized power in both city and school government during the progressive era. What effect, in your view, did this have on American democracy?

2. Both the developmental-democracy and the social-efficiency approaches to progressive education abandoned the classical curriculum of the 19th century, in which all students studied the same academic subjects. What argument might be made in favor of keeping the traditional, classical curriculum, and how would you evaluate that argument? Take into account the major social changes occurring at the turn of the century.

3. This chapter appears to be heavily biased against vocational education in favor of a more "academic" education for all young people. What justification does the chapter provide for its criticism of vocational education, and do you think this justification is adequate, given the historical circumstances of the progressive era?

4. As a result of reading Dewey's article "Education and Social Change," what do you believe schools should accomplish in terms of achieving social change—and what do you believe it is possible for schools to accomplish? Explain how similar or dissimilar your point of view is to Dewey's.

5. This chapter marks a shift in psychological theories about the human learner, resulting in a 20th-century viewpoint that some kids are really smart, some are really slow, and most are in between. Is this a case of science supporting common sense, or is there something amiss with this point of view? Is it really true, as today's educators say, that "all children can learn" challenging academic material, or did the new liberal reformers have it right that we should have very different expectations for different groups of kids?

OLC Online Resources

Go to the Online Learning Center at **www.mhhe.com/ tozer7e** to take chapter quizzes, practice with key terms, access study resources, and link to related websites. Also available on the Online Learning Center are PowerWeb articles and news feeds.

Chapter 5

Diversity and Equity Schooling Girls and Women

Chapter Overview

Unlike the preceding chapters of Part 1, each of which emphasized one period in our national history, Chapter 5 examines school and society in several historical eras, from the colonial through the progressive periods. These periods have already been treated in Chapters 2 through 6, yet this chapter is not a review. It focuses on an issue that has appeared too briefly in the preceding chapters: the education of girls and women. Chapter 5 begins with a discussion of the ideological origins of the differential treatment of girls and women in society. Those ideological roots were in part religious. As the chapter notes, it should not be surprising that a nation founded by religious dissenters would show deep religious influences in its political thought and values. We begin with a brief discussion of how the early Christian tradition contributed to justifying differential expectations for men and women in society and schooling.

The chapter traces the development of schooling for girls and women from colonial times through the postrevolutionary period, the 19th century, and the major part of the progressive era. In each of those periods, prevailing forms (and absences) of schooling for girls and women are examined in the context of shifts in views about women's roles in society and the proper preparation for those roles. In the colonial period, the relative absence of girls from schools reflects the dominant view of women that discouraged intellectual development. In the post-revolutionary period, contrasts between boys' and girls' schooling show increasing schooling arrangements for girls, but within specific boundaries of preparation for "feminine" work. Emma Willard's Troy Female Seminary is shown to be an early-19th-century contribution to expanding educational and professional possibilities for women. By the middle of the 19th century, competing viewpoints on the role and education of girls and women had sharpened into identifiable ideological positions—conservative, liberal, and radical—each of which had antecedents in classical liberalism. This discussion of ideological hetero- geneity is illustrated by the two Primary Source Readings, one of which, the Seneca Falls Declaration of 1848, is briefly referenced in the chapter.

Nineteenth-century approaches to the higher education of women are discussed, including academies, normal schools, colleges, and high schools. As the 20th century approached, the vocational education movement discussed in Chapters 4 and 6 took on particular significance for the education of girls and women in secondary schools. Chapter 5 will show that a distinctly different position was articulated by the African American intellectual Anna Julia Cooper, an advocate for the *higher* education of African American women.

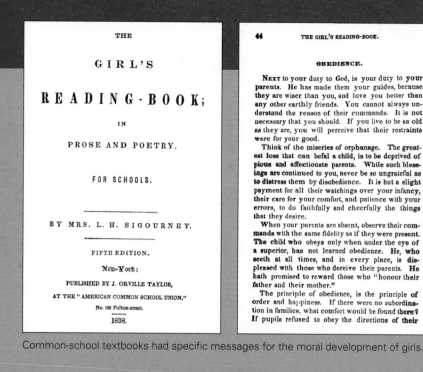

THE

GIRL'S

READING-BOOK;

IN

PROSE AND POETRY.

FOR SCHOOLS.

BY MRS. L. H. SIGOURNEY.

FIFTH EDITION.

New=York:

PUBLISHED BY J. ORVILLE TAYLOR,

AT THE "AMERICAN COMMON SCHOOL UNION,"

No. 129 Fulton-street.

1838.

---

44   THE GIRL'S READING-BOOK.

OBEDIENCE.

NEXT to your duty to God, is your duty to your parents. He has made them your guides, because they are wiser than you, and love you better than any other earthly friends. You cannot always understand the reason of their commands. It is not necessary that you should. If you live to be as old as they are, you will perceive that their restraints were for your good.

Think of the miseries of orphanage. The greatest loss that can befal a child, is to be deprived of pious and affectionate parents. While such blessings are continued to you, never be so ungrateful as to distress them by disobedience. It is but a slight payment for all their watchings over your infancy, their care for your comfort, and patience with your errors, to do faithfully and cheerfully the things that they desire.

When your parents are absent, observe their commands with the same fidelity as if they were present. The child who obeys only when under the eye of a superior, has not learned obedience. He, who seeth at all times, and in every place, is displeased with those who deceive their parents. He hath promised to reward those who "honour their father and their mother."

The principle of obedience, is the principle of order and happiness. If there were no subordination in families, what comfort would be found there? If pupils refused to obey the directions of their

Common-school textbooks had specific messages for the moral development of girls.

Chapter Objectives

Among the objectives that Chapter 5 seeks to achieve are these:

1. This chapter should help explain selected aspects of the history of the education of girls and women in the United States from colonial times through the early 20th century.

2. A second objective is to introduce the precolonial ideological origins of biases against women. Because of the religious origins of colonialism in the United States, particular attention is paid to the religious origins of views about women's essential nature.

3. Students should begin to assess the degree to which prevailing beliefs about women affected women's opportunities for education in the 18th, 19th, and early 20th centuries.

4. Students should also evaluate the degree to which educational arrangements for women served the ideals of women's equality that were expressed throughout this period.

5. This chapter offers an opportunity for students to evaluate whether conservative, radical, and liberal views on women's education were adequate to challenge the subordinate status of women.

6. The Primary Source Readings provide illustrations of how, despite prevailing social and educational practices, dissenting women have historically been able to formulate viewpoints that challenge those practices.

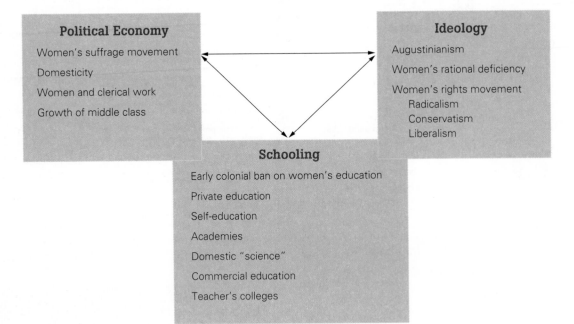

Analytic Framework
Girls and Women in the United States

Political Economy

Women's suffrage movement

Domesticity

Women and clerical work

Growth of middle class

Ideology

Augustinianism

Women's rational deficiency

Women's rights movement
     Radicalism
     Conservatism
     Liberalism

Schooling

Early colonial ban on women's education

Private education

Self-education

Academies

Domestic "science"

Commercial education

Teacher's colleges

Introduction: Why a Separate Chapter on Females?

Students may justifiably ask why it is necessary to devote a separate chapter to the education of women. Shouldn't the history of educational thought and the evolution of schooling be examined in a unified, gender-free treatment? Until recently this was the manner in which educational history was usually examined. Such examinations, however, ignore an important reality: the education of females in our culture, as in many cultures, has been importantly different, both in purpose and content, from the education of males. General statements about the history of education, then, may be misleading if they do not specifically attend to the experiences of girls as well as boys, women as well as men. While we have pointed out the significance of gender in specific instances in each chapter thus far, a more comprehensive treatment is needed to provide context for those instances. This chapter will provide an overview of the history of women's education to delineate the aspirations, limitations, and opportunities that American society held for half of its population through the first part of the 20th century. These gender themes will be revisited

repeatedly in Part 2 of the text, but this is the only chapter to attempt a comprehensive overview of the evolution of the education of girls and women in the United States.

Writing in the last decade of the 18th century, the Englishwoman Mary Wollstonecraft exposed her era's view of female education in observations such as the following:

> How grossly do they insult us who thus advise us to render ourselves gentile, domestic brutes! For instance, the winning softness so warmly, and frequently, recommended, that governs by obeying. . . . [A]ll writers who have written on the subject of female education and manners . . . have contributed to render women more artificial, weak characters, than they would otherwise have been, more useless members of society. . . . [M]y objection extends to the whole purport of those books, which tend, in my opinion, to degrade one half of the human species, and render women pleasing at the expense of every solid virtue.[1]

Unfortunately, Wollstonecraft's assessment remained true for over 100 years. During this period the primary goal of female education was to render women pleasing as wives and effective as mothers. The underlying assumptions behind this view were that women were fundamentally different from and inferior to men and consequently posed a danger to men. This assumption seems to have been tacitly accepted, apart from exceptions like Wollstonecraft, by both female and male proponents of women's education. This is not as surprising as one might think. Even today, evidence of belief in fundamental differences between the sexes and the idea of inherent inferiority of women can be found in many dimensions of our culture, as we shall see.

Ideological Origins in Early Christianity

In a country founded by religious dissenters, it is not surprising to find origins of basic ideological commitments in religious traditions. We have seen, for example, how such dimensions of classical liberalism as rationality and virtue were ascribed differently to men and women by liberals in Jefferson's era. This bias had roots in Christianity.

The point of this discussion is *not* that institutional Christianity has historically justified the subordination of women more than other religions have. Nor do we suggest that Christianity is the primary cause of social and political biases against women. Rather, we are noting that religious values contribute importantly to social ideology—and that the founding religious values and institutions of European America were Christian.

Early in the Christian era the tone for gender discussion was set by the apostle Paul in his instructions to Timothy regarding church organization. Paul said, "Let a woman learn in silence with all submission. For I do not allow a woman to teach, or go to exercise authority over men; but she is to keep quiet. For Adam was formed first, then Eve. And Adam was not deceived, but the woman was deceived and was in sin. Yet women will be saved by childbearing, if they continue in faith and love and holiness with modesty."[2] In this epistle Paul asserted the superiority of male over female because of Adam's earlier creation and Eve's submission to the temptations of the serpent. It would take another four centuries before the full implications of Paul's assertion would become central to Christian gender considerations.

One of the most significant developments in Western civilization's attitude toward gender occurred in the first part of the 5th century A.D. At that time, against the vigorous opposition of Pelagius and his followers, Augustine, Bishop of Hippo, successfully overturned previous Christian interpretations of Genesis 3.[3] Contrary to over

four centuries of Christian teaching, Augustine held that the story of the Fall meant that the sin of Adam was transmitted from the first parents through sexual reproduction to all future humans, and because of that "original sin," subsequent humanity was incapable of exercising free will. This interpretation placed a heavy burden on Eve in particular and women in general. She was, in this tradition, the first one to succumb to the temptations of the serpent. Being created out of Adam's body, Eve was purportedly more prone to bodily or sexual passion and thus easier to seduce. In Augustine's words, the serpent had deceitful conversation with the woman—no doubt starting with the inferior of the human pair so as to arrive at the whole by stages, supposing

The idea of women's rational inferiority to men and their consequent need for a less rigorous education was supported by the Christian belief that Eve, who was presumed to be more sensual and less rational than Adam, was chosen for seduction by the serpent.

that the man would not be as gullible.[4] Moreover, in this interpretation it was Eve who then persuaded Adam to join in her sin and thus condemned all future generations of humans. Historian Elaine Pagels succinctly summarizes the gender ramifications of Augustine's interpretation of Genesis 3:

> Although originally created equal to man in regard to her rational soul, woman's formation from Adam's rib established her as the "weaker part of the human couple." Being closely connected with bodily passion, woman, although created to be man's helper, became his temptress and led him into disaster. The Genesis account describes the result: God himself reinforced the husband's authority over his wife, placing divine sanction upon the social, legal, and economic machinery of male domination.[5]

Augustine's division of humankind into two inherently different kinds of beings contained all the necessary components for religiously justifying the subjugation of women and their inferior education for the next 15 centuries. Women were seen as complementary to, but different from, men. Properly fitted with men, women were the completing portion of humanity. They were seen as passionate and nurturing, while men were seen as rational and reserved. Women were prone to mercy, men to justice. Women were fitted for the domicile, men for work and public life. Men were to govern, women to obey. Because of their deficiency in rational capacity and unstable emotional nature, women were to be subject to the more rational nature of their fathers and later, their husbands.

Gender and Education in Colonial America

It was this Augustinian legacy that formed the consciousness and guided the gender behavior of most colonial and 19th-century Americans.[6] At their best, White Americans were concerned with educating their sons to become productive workers, effective political agents, and independent rational actors. However, when they thought of education for their daughters, the concern was to prepare them as wives and mothers, not as independent, rational beings. As long as the home remained the primary economic unit in society, most of a girl's education could be obtained there, emulating her mother and obeying her father.

As described in Chapter 2, Americans began to develop schools for their sons early in the colonial era.

Public elementary schools became common in New England, and a few colleges, such as Harvard, William and Mary, Yale, and Kings, were scattered among the colonies. Women were not admitted to the colleges and were only grudgingly admitted to the public elementary schools around the time of the Revolution. Most early school committees believed that the admission of girls to the common schools was "inconsistent with the design" of those schools.[7] Most girls who learned to read did so at home. Of course, such home schooling greatly disadvantaged girls whose parents were illiterate or unwilling to teach them to read and write.

Early colonial school records are scanty and obscure regarding the education of girls. Two historians, after searching the records of nearly 200 New England towns, could find only seven that had definitely voted to allow girls to attend common schools before the 1770s.[8] Among the earliest were Dorchester, Massachusetts (1639), Hampton, New Hampshire (1649), Ipswich, Massachusetts (1669), and Wallingford, Connecticut (1678). Only in the last two towns is there any evidence that girls actually attended those schools before the revolutionary era. Generally, when girls were given permission to attend a common school, they were only allowed to do so when boys were absent. For example, London, Connecticut, allowed girls to receive instruction from 5 to 7 A.M. during the summer of 1774.[9] Two years later Medford, Massachusetts, permitted girls to receive instruction from the schoolmaster two hours a day after the boys were dismissed. Later, in 1787, the Medford girls were admitted for instruction for one hour each morning and afternoon when the boys were not in attendance. Three years later the girls received instruction during the three summer months. Similar arrangements were common in other New England towns, such as Newburyport, Essex, and Salem, during the late colonial era. Not until 1834, two years before Horace Mann began his common-schooling campaign in Massachusetts, were Medford boys and girls allowed to attend the common school together during the entire school year.[10]

In 1900 George Martin succinctly summarized the history of girls' education in the American colonies and the new nation:

> First, during the first one hundred and fifty years of colonial history girls did not attend the public schools, except in some of the smaller towns, and there only for a short time; second, about the time of the Revolution, the subject of the education of girls was widely agitated; third, against much opposition the experiment of sending girls to the master's

During the colonial era, most girls received their education in their homes either from literate parents or from private tutors. Such home education was limited to families where the parents could either afford tutors or were literate enough to do the job themselves.

school for a few hours in a day during a part of the year, but never in the same rooms or at the same times with the boys; fourth, this provision extended only to the English schools, no instruction being provided in Latin or even in the higher English branches; fifth, it was not until the present century [i.e., the 19th] was far advanced that girls and boys shared alike the advantages of the higher public schools.[11]

Martin's dismal picture of early female education has not been much improved by subsequent historical investigations. With rare exceptions girls were barred from public schooling from the 1630s to the eve of the Revolution. The exceptions occurred in religious communities that were not dominated by the Augustinian tradition. For example, the Quakers and Moravians, principally in Pennsylvania and the Carolinas, did provide elementary education for girls.[12] This 150-year exclusion of girls from American public schools was not the result of neglect or oversight but rather the result of two factors. First, it was not considered necessary to

educate girls in an agrarian and frontier society when only few people required education. Just as important, however, was the common belief that females were basically unsuited for intellectual activities. On April 13, 1645, John Winthrop, the governor of Massachusetts Bay Colony, wrote the following entry in his journal:

Mr. Hopkins, the governor of Hartford upon Connecticut, came to Boston, and brought his wife with him (a godly young woman, and of special parts), who was fallen into a sad infirmity which had been growing upon her divers years, by occasion of her giving herself wholly to reading and writing, and had written many books. Her husband, being very loving and tender of her, was loath to grieve her; but he saw his error, when it was too late. For if she had attended her household affairs, and such things as belong to women, and not gone out of her way and calling to meddle in such things as are proper for men, whose minds are stronger, etc., she had kept her wits, and might have improved them usefully and honorably in the place God had set her.[13]

The historical record tells us that Governor Winthrop's view of women's appropriate place was clearly that of the majority. Nevertheless, in the face of considerable odds, some women were able to develop their intellectual interests during this 150-year era. The poetess Anne Bradstreet was taught by her father, Governor Dudley. Mercy Warren was tutored along with her brother by Rev. Jonathan Russell. Most remarkable, perhaps, was Phillis Wheatley, an African American slave girl in Boston, who during the 1760s taught herself to read English and Latin and write poetry. Other colonial women of extraordinary intellectual attainment included Anne Hutchinson, Elizabeth Ferguson, Debora Logan, Susanna Wright, Hanna Means, and Mrs. Stockton.[14] For most colonial women, however, there was no formal education, only the hope of rudimentary literacy acquired in the home from a literate and willing parent. Consequently, most colonial women remained illiterate.

Private Schools

Those colonial women who managed to acquire an education were overwhelmingly from affluent homes. Many of them were educated by tutors in the home. Others attended private female seminaries and academies. These private secondary institutions began to develop in the second quarter of the 18th century. Most were boarding schools. The Ursuline Convent for girls, established in New Orleans in 1727, was perhaps the earliest. Soon after, in 1742, the Bethlehem Female Seminary began educating girls in Pennsylvania.

During the first half of the 19th century a large number of these female seminaries came into existence; the most respected were in Philadelphia, Pennsylvania; Salem, Massachusetts; Troy, New York; and Endicott Mills, New York.[15] Unfortunately, many of these female institutions were more interested in fitting girls for marriage than in developing their minds. Much of the training focused on so-called polite accomplishments, such as dancing, music, drawing, and needlework.[16]

The social skills that dominated the formal education of colonial women flowed logically from contemporary opinion. Most colonial Americans believed that the only appropriate goal for a woman was matrimony. Typical of this attitude was the following poem, which appeared in 1805 in the *North Carolina Journal*:

> When first the nymph within her breast
> Perceives the subtle flame,
> She feels a something break her rest,

> Yet knows not whence it came,
> A husband 'tis she wants.[17]

Jane Austen's *Pride and Prejudice* provides a depressing account of the probable state of mind of many young women in this description of Charlotte Lucas just after she announced her engagement to Mr. Collins:

> The whole family . . . were properly overjoyed on the occasion. . . . [Her brothers] were relieved from their apprehension of Charlotte's dying an old maid. . . . Mr. Collins, to be sure, was neither amiable nor agreeable; his society was irksome and his attachment to her must be imaginary. But still he would be a husband. Without thinking highly of men or of matrimony, marriage had always been her object: it was the only honorable provision for well educated young women of small fortune, and, however uncertain of giving happiness, must be a pleasant preservation from want. This preservation she had now obtained; and at the age of twenty-seven, without ever having been handsome, she felt the good luck of it.[18]

If marriage was the approved goal for girls, it was understandable, perhaps, that a male-dominated society would try to fit women into the roles demanded by men. In early America, "a learned wife" was not sought after. A colonial poem often recommended to young women put this very clearly:

> One did commend to me a wife both fair and
>   young
> That had French, Spanish, and Italian tongue.
> I thanked him kindly and told him I loved
>   none such,
> For I thought one tongue for a wife too much,
> What! love ye not the learned?
> Yes, as my life,
> A learned scholar, but not a learned wife.[19]

An interesting feature of this poem is its evidence of the belief that women were capable of intellectual development but that it was not a feature men desired in them.

The Revolution and the Cult of Domesticity

Although the Revolution changed much in American society, it did not challenge most prevailing assumptions about the education of women. But independence brought considerable discussion about how a new nation could be forged, and that discussion would eventually bring about changes in the education of girls. As we

The "cult of domesticity" dominated female education from the time of the Revolution until well into the 20th century. It maintained that a woman's proper social role revolved around the home where she was to be (1) a proper wife, (2) a nurturing mother and teacher of the young, and (3) a moral exemplar to all.

saw in Chapter 2, the idea of using public schooling to build the nation was a major new concern.[20] Analysis of the requisite education for boys centered on (1) their future role as republican citizens, especially as informed voters, and (2) their role as economic agents, especially as producers. These considerations were not applied in the same way to girls, whose productive role would be limited to the family. It was their future role as wives and mothers that after the Revolution focused the discussion of appropriate female education. This nurturing role was to dominate thinking about girls' education until well into the 20th century.

By the 1820s many articles devoted to the "female role" appeared in educational journals such as the *Annals of Education,* the *Common School Journal,* and the *American Journal of Education.* Additionally, there appeared numerous books, such as Coxe's *Claims of the Country on American Females,* Butler's *The American Lady,* and Todd's *The Daughter at School.* These authors argued that women's first responsibility was to provide for the comfort and solace of husbands, who faced an increasingly competitive and inhospitable economic world. Beyond this, they should attempt to improve the

manners and morals of society by teaching and by example, and guide the development of the future generation during the early years of childhood.[21] Twentieth-century historians would name this shift in the understanding of the female role the "cult of domesticity."[22] It would provide a rationale for the formal education of increasing numbers of girls and young women in the new nation, rendering obsolete the colonial view that girls were simply not in need of schooling.

This cult of domesticity was first aimed at middle- and upper-class women, but in time its effects were felt in all but the lowest social classes. It was a double-edged sword. By considering homemaking and nurturing-teaching roles to be exclusively female, it encouraged the view that women should be educated. However, because of women's supposedly nurturing nature and the limits within which this nature was to be exercised, the education offered women was confined to the nurturing roles of wife, early educator, and moral exemplar.[23] It is fair to conclude that 19th-century Americans had not advanced much beyond Martin Luther's 16th-century admonition, "The world has need of educated men and women to the end that men may govern the country properly and women may bring up their children, care for their domestics, and direct the affairs of their households."[24]

Growing out of the combined cultural influences of sexist religious views, capitalism, and planning for nationhood, the cult of domesticity had a profound effect on female education. If women were to form morals and manners and provide initial education for children, they required some formal education. Consequently, most communities in the Northeast slowly began admitting girls to the common schools during the first quarter of the 19th century. The effect of this increased educational opportunity can be seen in the greatly increased rate of female literacy during this era.[25] As access to elementary schooling gradually was secured, proponents of female education turned to higher education.

During the 19th century higher education was less well defined than it is currently. Any schooling beyond the common school was considered higher. The "ladder" system, with secondary schools serving as a prerequisite for collegiate training, was not established until late in the century. Academies, seminaries, normal schools, the new public high schools, and colleges all offered what was considered higher education, and often they were seen as competing institutions. Women's access to these institutions and the curricula women were to be afforded constituted the major controversies concerning female education during the 19th century.

Competing Ideological Perspectives in the Nineteenth Century

Martha Maclear has shown that "three distinct currents of thought regarding the education of girls" emerged in the first half of the 19th century. The first current was that of the right wing, or conservatives, who wanted to maintain the status quo. The center, or liberals, while accepting the existing definitions of the appropriate female role, attempted to interpret those definitions in ways that would improve educational opportunities for women. Finally, radical, or left-wing, groups demanded both a new, expanded definition of female roles and the new education appropriate to the expanded opportunities they envisioned for women.[26] Both the conservative and liberal positions stood squarely within classical liberal ideology, with the liberals emphasizing progress

through change and the conservatives emphasizing traditional notions of female virtue. The radical position, however, challenged both streams of classical liberal thinking on the education of women and their role in society. Yet it, too, relied on such classical liberal constructs as natural law, rationality, and freedom in opposing the ideological mainstream.

The Conservative and Liberal Positions

The conservative position was typified by William Johnson, Esq., in an 1845 edition of the *Literary Emporium*. He offered the timeworn male-centric advice: "Women's chief ambition is gratified by a single conquest: the scope of her happiness and usefulness is circumscribed by the domestic and social circle. Beyond this, her influence is only felt by its moral reflection on the hearts and lives of mankind. Nor is this the result of any system of education—it is a distinguishing circumstance in her existence—one which God never intended to be otherwise."[27]

The liberals similarly held that women's destined role was exclusively as wife, mother, teacher of the young, and moral exemplar. Nevertheless, they differed from the conservatives by arguing that those roles required more and better education than was currently available for girls. No doubt America's growing trend toward a liberal Protestantism, exemplified by the transcendentalism of Emerson and the theology of Bushnell, made their arguments more palatable. This liberalizing trend deemphasized original sin and the evil side of human nature, lessening the special sin of Eve and its resulting stain on all women. Leaders of the liberal wing included Benjamin Rush, Emma Willard, Horace Mann, Catharine Beecher, and Mary Lyon.[28]

Benjamin Rush provided the prototype program for female education in his "Thoughts on Female Education" at the beginning of the 19th century. He contended that women should be the stewards of their husband's wealth, homemakers, and child caregivers. To fulfill those duties adequately, Rush proposed an education that included the English language, handwriting, arithmetic, bookkeeping, beginning astronomy, chemistry, natural philosophy, dancing, Christian religion, geography, and history. The last two subjects he recommended so "she might become an agreeable companion to a sensible man." Rush concluded his essay with the admonition to men that "a weak and ignorant woman will always be governed with the greatest difficulty."[29]

Horace Mann, who championed women's higher education in normal schools, announced the limitations that the liberals would project for women in an 1838 article in the *Common School Journal.* In advocating women's special role in the "peaceful ministry" of teachers of the young, he said:

> And why should women, lured by false ambition to shine in courts or to mingle in the clashing tumult of men, ever disdain this sacred and peaceful ministry?
>
> Why, renouncing this serene and blessed sphere of duty, should she ever lift up her voice in the thronged marketplace of society, haggling and huckstering to barter away that divine and acknowledged superiority *in sentiment* which belongs to her own sex, to exhort confessions from the other of a mere equality *in reason?* Why, in self-abasement, should she ever strive to put off the sublime affections and the ever-bearing beauty of a seraph, that she may clothe a coarser, though it should be a stronger spirit, in the stalwart limbs and highness of a giant? . . . If the intellect of women, like that of a man, has the sharpness and the penetration of steel or iron, it must also be as cold and hard. No! but to breathe pure and exalted sentiments into young and tender hearts . . . to take the censers which Heaven gives and kindle the incense which Heaven loves . . . this is her high and holy mission.[30]

It was not only men like Rush and Mann who promoted women's education in order to make women more effective in their "female" roles. Many liberal women shared the prevailing view of their social role and resulting education. During the 1830s the noted educator Mrs. Phillips similarly noted, "To females geology is chiefly important, by its effect in enlarging their sphere of thought, rendering them more interesting as companions to men of science, and better capable of instructing the young."[31] Moreover, the female leaders of the liberals accepted the traditional role for women. Emma Willard's memorandum to Governor Clinton of New York, requesting that the state provide normal schools for women, argued for women's nurturing role on the basis of natural law: "That nature designed our sex for the care of children, she has made manifest, by mental as well as physical indications." Moreover, Willard concluded, not only would women teach better than men, "they could afford to do it cheaper, and those men who would otherwise be engaged in this employment, might be at liberty to add to the wealth of the nation, by any of those thousand occupations, from which women are necessarily debarred."[32] Catharine Beecher, whose career as a proponent of women's education spanned most of the 19th century, said, "Heaven had appointed one sex superior and to the other the subordinate station."[33] And throughout her career she maintained that

Emma Hart Willard (1787–1870) wrote a classic appeal on women's education to the public and the New York State legislature in 1819, then opened the academically ambitious Troy Female Seminary in 1821.

Frederick Douglass (1817–1895), born a slave in Maryland, became an author, orator, U.S. Minister to Haiti, abolitionist, and defender of women's rights.

all education for women must center on some phase of domestic training or teaching.

It might be argued that the liberals developed a pragmatic program that was intended to achieve all that was possible within the constraints of popular prejudice. And they did achieve notable advances for women's education during the century. Nevertheless, their writings seem to indicate an acceptance of the common assumptions regarding the inherent and fundamental division of the sexes that ultimately restricts the life possibilities for women. The belief that national, ethnic, cultural, economic, racial, or gender groups possess some inherent social, emotional, moral, or intellectual characteristic(s) has been endemic in American history. It is based on unwarranted and malevolent assumptions. Almost universally this belief has been used to justify political, economic, or educational exclusion, which in turn fosters subordination and repression. Such assumptions continue to hamper women's full development as equals rather than as subordinates to men.

The Radical Position

The idea that a political or ideological position is "radical" stems from that word's meaning: "of or pertaining to the root." Radical thinking seeks to get to the root of a problem, and radical solutions thus require fundamental changes. While the liberals and the conservatives described by Maclear held similar views of women's role as wife, mother, teacher of the young, and moral exemplar, the radicals demanded a dramatically new vision of women's place in society: they demanded gender equality. The earliest expressions of these views were by such women as Frances Wright, Sarah M. Grimke, Margaret Fuller, and Ernestine Rose.[34] Grimke, writing in 1837, set the tone for the radical response to conservatives and liberals by constructing a different interpretation of the story of Adam and Eve:

> Adam's ready acquiescence with his wife's proposal, does not savor much of that superiority in *strength of mind* which is arrogated by man. . . . I ask no favors for my sex. I surrender not our claim to equality. All I ask of our brethren is, that they take their feet from off our necks and permit us to stand upright on that ground which God designed us to occupy. . . . All history attests that man has subjected woman to his will, used her as a means to promote his selfish gratification, to minister to his sensual pleasures, to be instrumental in promoting his comfort; but never has he desired to elevate her to that rank she was created to fill. He has done all he could to debase and enslave her mind; and now he looks triumphantly on the ruin he has wrought, and says, the being he has thus deeply injured is his inferior.[35]

The symbolic beginning of the radical women's movement can be located later, at the Seneca Falls Women's Rights Convention of 1848. As Gertrude

Martin has shown, this was more than simply a demand for the vote; it envisioned the opening of higher education on an equal basis to women and subsequent equality in all occupations.[36] The radicals were led by Susan B. Anthony, Elizabeth Cady Stanton, Elizabeth and Emily Blackwell, Sojourner Truth, Victoria Woodhull, Matthew Vassar, and Wendell Phillips. They formed a public resistance, which continues in various forms to the present, against male privilege and dominance in such institutions as the ballot box, the professions, and collegiate education. The convention's Declaration of Sentiments and Resolutions in the first Primary Source Reading at the end of this chapter illustrates the thinking of the leadership of the Seneca Falls convention, particularly its conscious appeal to the classical liberal ideals of rationality, natural law, and freedom.

Catharine Beecher: The Liberal Education of the Homemaker

These general ideological trends are easy to support as historical types, but when applied to the life of an extraordinary individual, the general is less illuminating than the particular. Catharine Beecher (1800–1878) was such an extraordinary individual. Her father Lyman was one of the nation's best-known preachers, her brother Henry Ward Beecher was more famous still, and her sister Harriet Beecher Stowe wrote *Uncle Tom's Cabin.* Catharine Beecher was an influential teacher and educational theorist whose work embraced commitments to liberal democracy, Christianity, and female domesticity and subordination. Her book, *A Treatise on Domestic Economy,* is on the one hand a discourse on the nature and duties of women in the home, as the title implies, and thus appears on its face to be conservative. But it goes well beyond that to emphasize the liberal education of women's God-given rational capacities. They were to exercise their developed reason and character in their domestic sphere, as she termed it, while males exercised their rational capacities in the public spheres of citizenship, politics, and work outside the home.

Like other liberal educational and social theorists of her time, Beecher did not challenge the second-class status of women in public life. She more than once defended that status for women, saying that "the highest degree of happiness" in the wife's relationship to the husband is one involving "the duties of subordination," at least in public and political affairs. She elaborates:

> In this country, it is established, both by opinion and by practice, that woman has an equal interest in all social and civil concerns; and that no domestic, civil, or political institution, is right, which sacrifices her interest to promote that of the other sex. But in order to secure her the more firmly in all these privileges, it is decided that, in the domestic relation, she take a subordinate state, and that, in civil and political concerns, her interest be intrusted [sic] to the other sex, without her taking any part in voting, or in making and administering laws.[37]

Nonetheless, Beecher embraced democratic ideals and believed women had a critical role to play in supporting them. Beecher believed that "the principals of democracy, then, are identical with the principals of Christianity." She arrived at this conviction partly because she believed that the moral core of the Golden Rule ("treat others as you would have them treat you") had the same moral core as the democratic principle that "all men are created equal." The role for women in democratic life becomes clear in this passage:

> The success of democratic institutions, as is conceded by all, depends upon the intellectual and moral character of the mass of the people. If they are intelligent and virtuous, democracy is a blessing; but if they are ignorant and wicked, it is only a curse, and as much more dreadful than any other form of civil government, as a thousand tyrants, are more to be dreaded than one. It is equally conceded that the formation of the moral and intellectual character of the young is committed mainly to the female hand. The mother forms the character of the future man . . . the wife sways the heart, whose energies may turn for good or for evil the destinies of a nation. Let the women of a country be made virtuous and intelligent, and the men will certainly be the same. The proper education of a man decides the welfare of an individual; but educate a woman, and the interests of a whole family are secured.

Beecher's educational and social vision may rightly be considered liberal because although it values a new education for women to develop their rational capacities, it does not challenge the established order, as the radical position would. It was a middle-class ideal, in that the household she envisions assumes that the well-educated woman supervises domestic servants. If there is a radical potential in her viewpoint, however, it lies in the education for women she proposes: an education not constrained by a narrow view of the role of women in the home, but by the belief that (1) the range of intellectual and moral qualities needed to be the ideal wife and mother and administrator of the household requires the broadest and deepest education possible, with depth specifically in knowledge of domestic sciences; and (2) that such an education will ensure the development of the critical, rational capacities that all humans are capable of, rather than a mere training for the domestic role, however demanding that role might be.

To accomplish such educational goals, Beecher recommended for girls after age 14 two hours a day of domestic chores and "a system of Calisthenic exercises." She had a faculty psychology (see Chapter 2) view of rigorous study in the disciplines, in which "the mere acquisition of facts . . . should be made of altogether secondary account." Instead, by studying "the same textbooks are used as are required at our best colleges," in mathematics, English grammar, history, philosophy, chemistry, astronomy, botany, geology, political economy, and Christianity, as well as other disciplines, higher-order thinking skills would be developed. As Beecher wrote:

> The formation of habits of investigation, of correct reasoning, of persevering attention, of regular system, of accurate analysis, and of vigorous mental action, is the primary object to be sought in preparing American women for their arduous duties.

In addition to a first-rate liberal education, Beecher believed young women should also pursue domestic science education and physical education. She placed a great emphasis on the physical health of girls and women, and advocated never more than an hour of classroom "confinement" without following that with "sports in the open air." And as for "domestic sciences," Beecher believed that proper homemaking and parenting was worthy of a professional level of study—that the knowledge base needed by the successful homemaker was equal to the knowledge base of the established professions.

> But are not the most responsible of all duties committed to the charge of woman? Is not her profession to take care of mind, body, and soul? And that, too, at the most critical of all periods of existence? And is it not as much a matter of public concern, that she should be properly qualified for her duties, as that ministers, lawyers, and physicians should be prepared for theirs? And is it not as important to endow institutions which shall make a superior education accessible to all classes—for females, as for the other sex?

Contemporary philosopher Jane Roland Martin observes that this idea, that an important body of knowledge should inform the nurturing functions expected by women, is a turning point in educational and social thought. She writes, "In introducing the concept of professionalism into women's education and women's work, Beecher is trying to transform both the traditional female role and the education intended for it."[38] That observation is an important one when we recognize that today there are those who question whether there really is a professional knowledge base in teaching, long considered "women's work" and long considered to be work that almost any educated person can do. These issues will be examined further in Chapter 10.

Ideology and Life: Emma Willard

Perhaps even more prominent an educator than Beecher was Emma Hart Willard. A brief examination of her life and work may help us better understand 19th-century conservative, liberal, and radical views regarding women. This biographical examination may also show that historical judgment is neither easy nor unambiguous. A cursory analysis of the ideological positions may suggest that the liberal position of Emma Willard was detrimental to women's education and their position in society. A closer examination, however, suggests that a more complex judgment is needed.

Emma Willard was born in 1787 in Berlin, Connecticut.[39] Her father, Samuel Hart, had been a captain in the revolutionary army. At the evening circle around the fireplace he shared with his family his great love for books, especially literature, history, political theory, and philosophy. As the 16th child, young Emma learned to participate in the evening discussions and acquired a lifelong love for learning. In many ways her early life was similar to that of her contemporary Horace Mann. Both were New Englanders born to farm life. She, like Horace, also attended the district elementary school. When Emma was 15, a new town academy opened at Worthington. She and her older sister Nancy entered it and studied for two years with Thomas Minter, a recent Yale graduate.[40]

Upon leaving the academy, Emma Hart began her teaching career. At age 17 she was employed to teach in Berlin's district summer school, and a year later in its winter session. This appointment to the winter session stands as strong testimony to the village's positive assessment of her teaching ability, for it was quite unusual for a woman to be allowed to teach during the winter session in district schools at that time. She soon had advanced from the village school to the Berlin Academy and from there to Westfield Academy and in 1807 to Middlebury. It was in Middlebury that she met Dr. John Willard, who had left medicine for politics. In 1809, although 28 years his junior, she married Dr. Willard and temporarily left teaching.

The next four years were important for Emma's intellectual development. She apparently spent considerable time studying her husband's medical books in an effort to become conversant with his interests. Lacking access to higher education institutions, 19th-century women intellectuals often educated themselves through the resources available to a father, brother, or husband. Emma Willard had the advantage of a supportive father and a supportive husband. Additionally, Dr. Willard's nephew, John Willard, lived with them while he attended Middlebury College. Emma and John spent considerable time discussing his college studies, and she eagerly read his course texts. Without doubt, this exchange illuminated for Emma the world of learning from which she and nearly all other young women were excluded. The birth of her son, John Hart Willard, in 1810 introduced her to the complexities of parenting. These activities would have lasting significance for her intellectual outlook.

A New Vision for Women's Education

By 1813 Dr. Willard's financial and political fortunes declined. In part to relieve her husband's financial woes, Emma returned to teaching, opening a boarding school for girls in their home. The following five years were instrumental in developing her educational ideas. Her school offered instruction more advanced than any then available in the United States for girls. In addition to the usual "refinements" of manners, she taught mathematics, geography, science, history, and languages. Because neighboring Middlebury College refused to allow her students to attend any of its courses, Emma was forced to teach all the courses in her school. This meant that she was not only required to train teachers but in some instances needed to learn new subjects herself. This self-education in new subjects at an ever-increasing level of complexity became a hallmark of her teaching career. It reinforced her earlier belief that women were capable of higher learning. Moreover, it led her to develop innovative teaching methods and materials. Soon her school had over 70 students, of whom 40 were boarders.

It was during this time that Willard systematically began to collect her ideas on female education. The result was a thesis she titled "A Plan for Improving Female Education," which she eventually sent to Governor DeWitt Clinton of New York in 1818. She published it under the title "An Address to the Public: Particularly to the Members of the Legislature of New York, Proposing a Plan for Improving Female Education." The Plan quickly attracted attention in the United States, although it stimulated little action. It even achieved international acclaim when the English educator, George Combe, published it in his *Phrenological Journal*.[41] Combe's phrenological theory would later be embraced by Horace Mann.

The primary purpose of the Plan was to convince the voters and legislators—males—to provide public funds for higher education for women. Toward this end Willard organized the Plan in four categories. The first deplored the existing state of female education. She pointed out that in most places opportunity for higher education did not exist for women. In the few places where it did, the schools were woefully inadequate. They were poorly funded and therefore temporary institutions with insufficient physical facilities. Moreover, these were "finishing" schools, which emphasized superficial social refinements and not intellectual attainments or sound moral qualities. Nowhere in the United States could young women receive an education even roughly equivalent to that offered in the abundant colleges for young men. Only when female schools received public funds could they be established on a permanent basis with resources to provide an adequate education.

The second aspect of Willard's Plan analyzed the principles that should regulate female education. Most important, she asserted: "Education should seek to bring its subjects to the perfection of their moral, intellectual and physical nature, that they may be of the greatest possible use to themselves and others."[42] A major error in existing female education, she argued, was that it sought to prepare females mainly to please men rather than to prepare them as humans. Willard quickly added, "I would not be understood to insinuate, that we are not, in particular situations, to yield to obedience to the other sex. Submission and obedience belong to every being in the universe, except the great Master of the whole. Nor is it a degrading peculiarity to our sex, to be under human authority. Whenever one class of human beings, derive from

another the benefits of support and protection, they must pay its equivalent, obedience. . . . Neither would I be understood to mean, that our sex should not seek to make themselves agreeable to the other. The error complained of, is that of the taste of men, whatever it might happen to be has been made a standard for the formation of female character."[43] She went on to note that the education advocated for females was to be likened to that for males in its permanency and uniformity of operation, yet "adapted to the difference in character and duties" of females. To emphasize the difference between male and female higher education she made the distinction between male "colleges" and "female seminaries."

Third, Willard outlined a "sketch of a female seminary." This seminary would be supported by public funds and include a building holding rooms for student lodging, recitations, scientific apparatus, and a domestic department. It would provide instruction in four areas: religion and morals, literary (this included the usual collegiate intellectual subjects), domestic (probably the first call for home economics instruction in the United States), and ornamental (drawing, painting, penmanship, music, and grace of motion). This proposed instructional program was far superior to any then in existence for females in the United States.

The last section of the Plan was titled "Benefits of Female Seminaries." Willard rightly claimed that the proposed seminaries "would constitute a grade of public instruction superior to any yet known in the history of our sex."[44] The main benefits of this instruction would be felt in two areas: the common schools and the nation at large. The graduates of these seminaries would become teachers in the common schools, where they would raise the level of instruction because of their specific training and Willard's belief "that nature designed for our sex the care of children." These seminary graduates "would be likely to teach children better than the other sex," and as we saw earlier, Willard had an economic argument. Not only could women teach at lower salaries than men, but men would increase productivity in male-dominated occupations because they would not be teaching.[45] Moreover, all seminary graduates would greatly lift the moral and cultural level of the nation and thus save it from the slide to barbarism and anarchy commonly predicted by its enemies. This national uplift would be accomplished, she believed, as these seminaries better suited their graduates to be mothers and wives of the nation's men. The female seminaries would regenerate the nation.

It is interesting how Emma Willard foreshadowed the arguments of Horace Mann for women teachers while representing views that 20th-century historians later called the cult of domesticity, discussed earlier in this chapter. Women had a special role because of their supposed "natural" differences from men, in this domestic perspective. Those differences included being more sensitive, empathetic, devoted to domestic duties and child rearing, and concerned with cultural affairs. These same qualities, which uniquely fitted women as teachers, wives, and mothers, according to her argument, "necessarily debarred" women from other occupations. While the exponents of the cult of domesticity mirrored many of Willard's ideas, they generally neglected to include her strong belief that women were equal to men in the ability to rationally understand academic subjects. This was a difference of considerable importance.

The Troy Female Seminary

After the positive reception of her Plan by Governor Clinton and the legislature, Willard was confident enough that the State of New York would fund her proposed seminary to move her school in 1819 from Middlebury, Vermont, to Waterford, New York. This confidence, however, was to prove misplaced. Repeatedly, the all-male legislature refused to appropriate funds for female seminaries. The Waterford school managed with precarious finances for two years. Then the city of Troy offered municipal backing for a female seminary. Willard accepted the offer and in 1821 relocated her school for the last time; it became the Troy Female Seminary.

For the next 17 years Willard continued to expand her experiment in female education in the relatively safe haven of the Troy Female Seminary.[46] The early years were greatly eased by the role of Dr. Willard, who acted as school doctor, financial director, and sympathetic supporter of his wife. His death in 1825 was not only a severe personal loss, it added a considerable workload to the already overextended headmistress as she assumed the financial management of the growing institution.

Willard made significant curricular contributions to 19th-century education. This was a time when most people considered females incapable of serious academic study. Fashionable opinion considered algebra or history beyond the capacity of the female mind, and physiology probably dangerous to it. Respectable authorities believed that if such study did not cripple the weaker female mind, certainly it would misshape it to an "unfeminine" mold. In the face of such attitudes, Willard broadened the curriculum at the Troy Female Seminary and was in the forefront of allowing "electives."

Troy Female Seminary became well known for teacher training.

Northwestern view of the Troy Female Seminary.

The required subjects included the Bible, composition, elocution, drawing, and physical education. Among the electives were modern foreign languages (including French, German, Italian, and Spanish), Latin, astronomy, algebra, geometry, trigonometry, geography, history, literature, logic, physiology, and other natural sciences. Not only did she pioneer in adding these subjects to female instruction, but because she was self-taught in most of them, she understood the difficulties of comprehending each subject. This understanding was partially responsible for her innovative instructional methods. Far in advance of most of her 19th-century colleagues, she developed teaching techniques and learning materials that facilitated student involvement and critical analysis rather than rote memorization. While at Troy Seminary, Willard wrote five major geography and history textbooks.[47] The geography texts became especially popular and earned considerable royalties.[48] They were widely used in female seminaries and in secondary schools for males as well.

The preparation of teachers at the Troy Seminary eventually became its most famous function. It occurred, however, almost accidentally. Early in the history of the Seminary, Willard received requests for admission from girls who could not afford the tuition or board. Her response was to provide for what she called "teacher scholars." These girls were provided tuition, board, and in some cases clothing. In return, they promised to repay the expense after they graduated and were employed as teachers. It was estimated that Willard loaned approximately $75,000 to students during her tenure at Troy.[49] Not all the teachers from Troy had been teacher scholars, but this device provided many young women an avenue to an education and a profession. Willard was particularly proud of her role in teacher training: "I continued to educate and send forth teachers, until two hundred had gone from the Troy Seminary before one was educated in any public normal school in the United States." She called her school the nation's "first normal school."[50] Troy Female Seminary became so well known for teacher training that Willard's signature on a letter of recommendation was often a guarantee of employment. It may have functioned as the first teacher certification in the country. Anne Firor Scott estimated that over 1,000 teachers may have been prepared at Troy Seminary by 1863.[51] Willard's normal school had preceded Horace Mann's by 16 years!

Willard's influence on these teachers did not cease once they left the Seminary. In 1837, the year Mann assumed leadership of the Massachusetts schools, she organized the Emma Willard Association for the Mutual Improvement of Female Teachers. Its purpose was to retain contact through letters and publications with former students in the teaching profession. The communications contained suggestions on a range of topics from pedagogy and textbooks to healthy exercise and sound psychological habits.[52] These suggestions seemed to reinforce the lessons Willard taught at the Seminary. In 1898 a group of Troy Seminary alumnae gathered testimony from former students. Over 3,500 of the 12,000 students who had spent time at the Seminary between its founding and 1871 responded. From these responses Professor Anne Firor Scott has constructed a convincing portrait of the influence of Willard on her students.[53] This portrait suggests that she provided them with a model of female independence fueled by intellectual competence and fiscal independence. Her students were expected to learn subjects previously thought to be "beyond" female comprehension. They were taught self-reliance, to prepare for self-support, and that the "women's sphere" included the professional work of teaching.

This brings us back to the question at the beginning of this section: how do we evaluate the effect of Emma Willard on the history of the United States? She seemed to champion the ideal of a "women's sphere," which was to be separate from the male sphere. Her belief in the "special" qualities of women led her to argue for women's place as mothers and teachers, but these qualities "necessarily debarred" women from other occupations and roles. The patriarchal family and women's domestic role seemed very dear to her. She admonished her students for even secretly debating the politics of the 1828 election and never fully embraced the idea of suffrage for women.[54] All this would seem to bode ill for improving women's position in society. Phillida Bunkle, without specific reference to Willard, has described this set of ideas as "a sexual ideology," which was an "antifeminist system of belief [that] dominated the perception of women in the nineteenth century."[55] And yet there is more to say about Willard's beliefs and achievements.

Her Troy Female Seminary educated over 12,000 women and inspired over 200 schools to follow its example. Willard provided a role model for her students and others, exemplifying a self-confident woman who was a successful administrator, author of respected texts, skilled teacher, and independent thinker. Moreover, she cultivated the same qualities in her students. Professor Scott pointedly noted that "nowhere else in the country in the 1820s were young women told that they could learn any academic subject, including those hitherto reserved to men, and that they should prepare themselves for self-support and not seek marriage as an end in itself."[56] With this observation Scott has uncovered the most significant contribution of Emma Willard to the education of American women. No doubt Willard did not inspire a "feminist" revolution, but her work provided an ideal of educated women and a critical mass of such women, who would eventually contribute to such a revolution.

Anna Julia Cooper

No discussion of the history of women's contributions to education in the United States would be complete without attention to Anna Julia Cooper. Born into slavery in North Carolina in about 1858, just after Booker T. Washington and just before W. E. B. Du Bois and John Dewey were born, Cooper lived over a hundred years, until 1964. A writer and intellectual, she was one of the first African Americans to receive a Ph.D. (in French, at the University of Paris in 1925). Cooper was also a multifaceted educator, serving as a school teacher and principal, and later as president of Frelinghuysen University, a school for working Black residents of Washington, DC.

Cooper was also a prominent activist for the rights of African American women. In 1892 she helped organize the Colored Woman's League of Washington, DC. The following year she and three others were the only Black women to address the Women's Congress, convened during the world Columbian Exposition in Chicago. In 1895 she took part in the first meeting of the National Conference of Colored Women, and throughout this period helped edit *The Southland* magazine, but her greatest publishing achievement had been her book, *A Voice from the South by a Black Woman of the South,* in 1892.

The article "Womanhood a Vital Element in the Regeneration and Progress of a Race" was published in *A Voice from the South,* but it was first a speech given before a convocation of African American clergy in Washington, DC, in 1886. It is not surprising, then, that she framed her remarks on an ideal for educated women within "that rich and bounteous fountain from which flow all our liberal and universal ideals—the Gospel of Jesus Christ."[57] For Cooper, as for other educators before her (such as Benjamin Rush or Catharine Beecher) Christian ideals and democratic ideals were a compatible foundation for educational theorizing. Unlike most who had gone

before her, however, Cooper argued for the higher education not only of African Americans, but particularly of African American women. She believed that the status of women in society was both a measure of the health of the society and of the capacity of a society to improve itself: "The position of woman in society determines the vital elements of its regeneration and progress. . . . And this is not because woman is better or stronger or wiser than man, but from the nature of the case, because it is she who must first form the man by directing the earliest impulses of his character." Her position on this was not too dissimilar from Catharine Beecher's, with the important exception that Cooper specifically was addressing African Americans as part of all womankind.

For Cooper, it was self-evident that women influenced social progress throughout "Christendom," and that it was important to recognize the special responsibility of women in an African American culture that had so recently been enslaved. She wrote: "Now the fundamental agency under God in the regeneration, the retraining of the race, as well as the ground work and the starting point of its progress upward, must be the *black woman.*"

Scholar Renea Henry remarks that Anna Julia Cooper was not alone among Black woman educators in her beliefs, though she may have been the most well known. Henry writes:

> Throughout the 19th and 20th centuries, African-American women intellectuals have grappled with the same issues dealt with by leading black male intellectuals. Their work has had added significance because they have almost always asserted the inextricable roles of gender and sexuality to the cultural conditions wrought by racial marginality and exclusion.[58]

Henry goes on to say that Cooper was a part of the Black intellectual community that nourished Du Bois's own thinking, and that it "seems clear" that Cooper influenced Du Bois, though there is no explicit acknowledgment in Du Bois's work that would allow identifying direct influence of her ideas. Henry notices that unlike Du Bois, Cooper focused on the education of African American *women* as means to political and social equality in a racist culture: "Every attempt to elevate the Negro, whether undertaken by himself or through the philanthropy of others, cannot but prove abortive unless so directed as to utilize the indispensable agency of an elevated and trained womanhood."[59]

For Cooper, well before Du Bois began fighting for the higher education of African Americans, the educational implication of her position for "the Colored Girls of the South" was that Black women should be educated as well as any members of society are educated—including becoming "lawyers, doctors, professors" and leaders of various kinds.

Higher Education for Women

Academies

The first inroads for female higher education were made in the academies. Although the first American academy was Franklin's Academy, established in 1751 in Philadelphia, the "age of the academy" was from 1820 to 1870. The academy was a curious institution. Sometimes it was a church foundation; at other times it was a private venture supported by public subscription or, in some instances, by public tax monies. Thus, it was usually a semipublic school. Its curriculum was so varied that it competed both with the Latin grammar schools and with the colleges. Moreover, it generally offered "practical" subjects such as surveying, pedagogy, and bookkeeping.[60] As a new institution, it was not bound to tradition like the colleges and Latin grammar schools. One prominent tradition that it increasingly violated in the 19th century was the exclusion of women. In fact, some academies were founded exclusively for women, including the Moravian's Friends Academy at Salem, North Carolina, in 1802 and the academies at Pittsfield, Massachusetts, in 1807; Derry, New Hampshire, in 1823; and Ipswich, Massachusetts, in 1828. Others were coeducational, such as Bradford Academy (1803) and Friends Academy (1812) at New Bedford, Massachusetts. The most famous, and probably the most rigorous, were Emma Willard's Troy Female Seminary and Mary Lyon's Mt. Holyoke Seminary.[61] At a time when women were barred from colleges and when public high schools were just beginning, the academies offered women the best opportunities for education beyond the elementary level.

The academy, however, had at least three fundamental problems with respect to women's education. First, attendance was restricted to those who could pay the tuition. Second, the academies reflected the early-19th-century bias against educating girls and boys together, and even many of the coeducational academies educated the girls in separate buildings or separate rooms. In 1852 the trustees of Rome Free Academy in New York were forced to resign due to the angry reaction against their proposal to admit girls to the same classes with boys. Eventually the new trustees enacted a program of "coordinate education" with a female department of the academy in a separate building.[62] Third, the girls' curriculum was usually

different from that of the boys, reflecting the reality that "separate" did not mean "equal" in educational resources or goals. In many academies the curriculum continued to focus on "ladylike" subjects.[63] Even the Mt. Holyoke curriculum emphasized teaching and domestic pursuits rather than the classical studies considered fundamental for the liberal education of young men.

Normal Schools

The opening of elementary school teaching to women and the subsequent development of normal schools to train those teachers demonstrate both strengths and weaknesses in the liberal position on female education. On the positive side, liberals such as Horace Mann, Henry Barnard, Dewitt Clinton, Emma Willard, Catharine Beecher, and Mary Lyon successfully opened higher education to women during the first half of the 19th century by establishing both private and state-supported normal schools. Samuel Hall's private normal school at Concord, New Hampshire (founded in 1823), was a pioneering example. Horace Mann's efforts to establish state normal schools in Massachusetts were decisive in the drive for trained elementary school teachers in America. A consummate rhetorician, he successfully employed an image of women as inherently nurturing and thus better common-school teachers than men. This public image substantially promoted female attendance at the normal schools, thus opening to tens of thousands of 19th-century American women education beyond the elementary level as well as respectable employment. The primary alternatives for young women at the time were factory work and domestic work in other people's homes.

While this public image of women as natural teachers due to their special nurturing qualities did open some doors to higher education and employment, it also helped keep other doors closed. Most professions, such as law, medicine, and commerce, together with virtually all branches of government, were thought to require such "manly" characteristics as logical reasoning abilities, stern discipline, and a sense of justice based on rationality rather than compassion and mercy. Therefore, while women were welcomed to teaching and to the normal schools, the rationale that justified their entrance into those arenas helped block their entrance into other areas of higher education and the professions. Outside the home and the elementary school, a "motherly" disposition was not a desired quality. Women's struggle for admission to secondary and collegiate education thus was won at a price.

High Schools

The English classical school, soon renamed the high school, began in the second decade of the 19th century as an "effort to create for youth a public institution which would do without cost what the academy had done for a fee."[64] In 1821 Boston opened its English classical school for boys. Five years later the Boston school committee opened a similar school for girls, directed by Ebenezer Bailey. The girls' school was so successful that it apparently could accommodate only about a quarter of those desiring admittance. However, the committee closed the school after three years, and Boston was without a public high school for girls until 1852, when the Girls' High School was opened as part of its Normal School.[65] Concurrently, George Emerson operated a private English classical school for girls in Boston whose long waiting list for admission was further evidence that Boston's females desired education beyond the common school.[66] The first public high school for girls opened in Worcester, Massachusetts, in 1824. It was followed by others in New York City in 1826; North Glastonbury, Connecticut, in 1828; East Hartford, Connecticut, in 1828; Buffalo, New York, in 1828; and Rochester, New York, in 1838. The first coeducational public high school opened in Lowell, Massachusetts, in 1841. This example was followed in the 1840s in New Hampshire, Connecticut, and Vermont.[67] These new high schools clearly extended the educational horizons for females. The Worcester school committee noted that it hoped to "provide an education for girls comparable to that provided for boys in the Latin Grammar School and the English School."[68]

Care should be exercised against an overly favorable evaluation of these developments. First, the justification for girls' high school education almost always followed traditional gender-biased lines. The Salem, Massachusetts, school committee discussed girls' education in the 1840s, saying:

> It is a matter of complaint in our city, and seemingly just, that girls have too much intellectual and too little home education. . . . Boys need, strictly speaking, a more intellectual education than girls, since the latter are destined for duties in the home, while the main province of the former, as men, is ever abroad, in the complications of business, requiring the rigid analysis and calculation happily spared to the wife and mother.[69]

The address by John T. Irving at the opening of New York's high school for females was typical. He noted that girls must be educated in order to ensure their "domestic happiness," to make them more "fit companions for their husbands," and for their role as mothers. He pointed out that "such a judicious selection has been made both of study and employment for the pupils as is suited to their sex, and will prepare them for presiding with skill and prudence in those domestic stations, for which Providence has designed them." Irving left no doubt regarding the nature of these "divinely" appointed female stations:

> It would be a great mistake if we were to consider female education as calculated merely to render ladies useful and agreeable companions in domestic life. That is undoubtedly one important object. But it has a higher and nobler purpose: the best and most durable lessons, and the most happy direction which the youthful mind receives, is from the mother. It is her task to inspire her sons with the earliest love of knowledge, to teach them the precepts of religion, the charities of life, the miseries of vice, and to lead them into the paths of a just and honourable ambition.[70]

In short, female education was still captive to the benefit it would bring to males—husbands and sons. Women were seen as destined exclusively for marriage and motherhood, with a few entering teaching before marriage. Like most visions that divide humanity into subordinate and dominating groups, this vision was rather myopic. By 1845 over 75,000 women were working in the textile industries in the United States. In 1837 women were engaged in over 100 different occupations. Women were listed as employers in many manufacturing and business concerns in the 1840s. By 1880 almost 15 percent of females age 10 or older were gainfully employed, while fewer than 60 percent of women were married.[71] Clearly the assumption that *all* women were "destined for duties of the home" while only men were to encounter the "complications of business" was less warranted by facts than by the wishful imagination of contemporary commentators.

A second cautionary note regards the limited impact of secondary education in the 19th century. By 1872 girls attending high school outnumbered boys by 43,794 to 37,978, but this figure represents less than 4 percent of the total number of girls age 15 to 18. By 1890 female graduates of public high schools outnumbered males by nearly three to two, but the figures represent less than 10 percent of the total high-school-age population in the United States at that time.[72] Finally, during the 19th

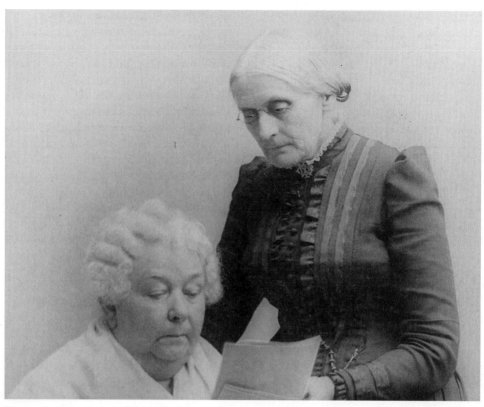

The symbolic beginning of the radical women's movement can be traced to the Seneca Falls Women's Rights Convention of 1848 where women like Susan B. Anthony (right) and Elizabeth Cady Stanton began to demand gender equality in such institutions as the ballot box, the professions, and higher education.

century high school attendance was generally limited to the most affluent.

Colleges

A fourth battlefield for female advancement in higher education was the American college. In 1836 six young women interviewed President Quincy in his office at Harvard. When one of them demanded to know whether there was any reason they could not be admitted with their brothers, Quincy's answer was simple, direct, and representative of the contemporary male opinion: "Oh yes, my dear, we never allow girls at Harvard. You know the place for girls is at home."[73] This answer was unacceptable to radical proponents of female education, who had already begun to work for female collegiate education. Their early struggle faced huge odds. For example, when the LeRoy Female Seminary in New York applied to the state legislature in 1851 for a charter as a

women's college, it was turned down simply because of precedent: there were no colleges for women.[74] During the 1860s the state's regents appointed a commission to study charters for female colleges. It did so not because the regents were favorably disposed to the idea but in order to respond to those "who would demolish all distinctions, political, educational and social between the sexes, ignoring alike the providence of God and the common sense of mankind."[75] The argument was grounded in classical liberal thought: the same Creator who endowed men with inalienable rights had ordained that men and women should occupy distinctly different spheres in society.

Nevertheless, substantial progress was already being made. The Georgia legislature chartered the Georgia Female College at Macon in 1836.[76] Antioch and Oberlin colleges in Ohio became coeducational during the 1840s, admitting women and men of color, as well. During the fourth and fifth decades of the century, four female colleges were opened in Ohio, three in Pennsylvania, one in Tennessee, and one in Illinois.[77] Before 1870, 11 colleges in New England and New York admitted women. In New York State the following colleges were chartered to admit females: Ingham University in 1842, Genesee College in 1851, Central College in 1851, Elmira College in 1855, St. Lawrence in 1856, Alfred University in 1858, Vassar in 1861, and Rutgers Female College in 1867. In Massachusetts several institutions were similarly chartered: Boston University in 1869, Wellesley in 1875, and Smith in 1875. With the exception of Vassar and Boston University, all the institutions that began admitting women before 1870 were plagued with similar problems: insufficient endowments, inability to overcome the weight of traditional opposition to female higher education, and lack of sufficient social and educational vision.[78]

A major breakthrough for female collegiate education was the establishment of Vassar College at Poughkeepsie, New York, in 1861. Founded by Matthew Vassar with an endowment of half a million dollars, Vassar began with a sound financial foundation. Moreover, its founder started from the premise that women were equal to men, and he demonstrated that liberal ideology could be used to justify equal rights for women: "It occurred to me that woman, having received from her Creator the same intellectual constitution as man, has the same right as man to intellectual culture and development."[79] Thus, from the outset, Vassar intended to provide women with collegiate educations equal to those provided in the best male colleges—and it had the financial resources to do so.

Thinking Critically about the Issues   #1
In your view, what were the strengths and weaknesses of the efforts made to provide education for women at the secondary and postsecondary levels in the 18th and 19th centuries?

Matthew Vassar understood that quality would be expensive and was willing to charge high tuition for superior education. He argued "to court public patronage by catering to cheap or low prices of instruction is to my mind ridiculous. . . . I go for the best means, cost what they may, and corresponding prices for tuition in return. . . . I am therefore giving the daughters of the public the very best means of education and make them pay for it."[80]

This attitude was reflected in Vassar's program. While other female colleges often taught "geography of

Heaven," for example, at Vassar Maria Mitchell used the second largest telescope in America to teach astronomy. Vassar's library had seven times the holdings of Elmira College and was nearly equal to the library at Columbia. Vassar's salary budget for instructors was one of the largest in the nation, and its male instructors' salaries compared favorably with those at Harvard and Yale. The entrance requirements and curriculum at Vassar were equal to those at the best male colleges.[81] The inevitable result was that Vassar provided an education for women that was at least equal to that of the best male institutions. Indeed, in 1870, after visiting Vassar's classes, Harvard's president Charles Eliot remarked, "the boys at Harvard did not recite so well in German, French or Latin or even in mathematics as did the girls at Vassar."[82] Perhaps most significant was that Vassar provided an obvious counterexample to the time-honored belief in female inferiority.

Women and Vocational Education

The Vassar example did not produce a revolution in American attitudes toward gender and education. As described in Chapter 4, the two decades surrounding the turn of the 20th century found Americans' attention focused on an array of other problems: major new immigration from southern and eastern Europe, urbanization, the demands of the new industrial enterprises, and the disquieting social and economic disturbances resulting from these phenomena. Not surprisingly, Americans turned to the schools to alleviate these difficulties. Educators and social commentators soon become enamored of the idea that vocational training would make schools more responsive to social and economic conditions. The demand for vocationalism became a roar that drowned out most other considerations in educational policy making. With respect to gender, most of the vocational training discussion assumed that girls should be trained for traditional women's activities while boys should be trained for men's occupations. Girls' vocational training was generally confined to domestic science and commercial education.

Domestic Science Training

Without exception, the literature on vocational training for girls emphasized the woman's natural role as wife and homemaker.[83] A leading educator, John D. Philbrick, while analyzing city school systems for the U.S. Commissioner of Education in 1885, set the tone for the era when he stated that "no girl can be considered properly educated who cannot sew."[84] The chairperson of the woman's branch of the Farmer's Institute of North Carolina, W. N. Hutt, put it more bluntly when she informed the 1910 National Education Association convention that regardless of what other vocation a woman might temporarily adopt, "She will, with it all, wake up some fine morning and find herself in some man's kitchen, and woe be unto her if she has not the knowledge with which to cook his breakfast."[85] A year earlier, in New York City, the city schools' director of cooking, Mary E. Williams, emphatically delineated women's "natural vocation." She argued that every girl should study domestic science because once a woman heard the "God-given call of her mate," she would desert all other vocations to assume the "position of the highest responsibility and the holiest duties of human life, those of homemaking and motherhood; upon which the progress of civilization and of human society depend."[86]

There was an ethnic and class bias in the campaign for domestic science. In the North these programs were specifically aimed at the daughters of immigrants and the working class, and in the South, at African Americans. Middle-class educators were convinced that these children came from homes that could offer no lessons on adequate diet, food preparation, home management, or family life. If they were properly trained in the school's domestic science classes, educators thought that girls would regenerate working-class homes and provide "stability" for industrial workers. New York City's superintendent of schools argued in 1910 that homemaking courses "have been a factor during the past years in helping to solve the economic questions of the nation."[87] Describing the impact of domestic science courses in Chicago's schools, the principal of Spry School said, "The evening meal of the factory hand may be made more tempting than the lunch counter, and the clothing of the family, as well as the arrangement and tidiness of the living room at home may be as attractive as the gilded home of vice. Domestic science may become the unsuspected, and yet not the least efficient, enemy of the saloon."[88]

Indeed, Chicago led the rush to implement domestic science training for girls in the middle grades. Almost three-fourths of Chicago's seventh- and eighth-grade girls were enrolled in household arts courses in 1900.[89] Ten years later, approximately half of New York City's girls in the seventh and eighth grades were in similar programs, and the superintendent announced that all high school girls would be required to receive domestic instruction.[90] By 1928, 30 percent of all female high school students in the United States were enrolled in domestic science courses.

The vocational education movement of the late 19th and early 20th centuries continued to pattern its female curriculum around the old domestic science pursuits such as sewing, cooking, hospitality, and keeping the family accounts.

Historical Context

Education of Girls and Women

1700s

1773	Phyllis Wheatley, first African American poet in America, bought from slave ship as a young child
1775	Thomas Paine proposes civil and political rights for women in *Pennsylvania Magazine*
1777	Abigail Adams, wife of President John Adams, writes that women "will not hold ourselves bound by any laws in which we have no voice"
1791	French feminist Olympe de Gouges issues *Declaration of the Rights of Women and of the Citizen*
1792	English feminist Mary Wollstonecraft writes *A Vindication of the Rights of Woman*
1793	Ex-slave Katy Ferguson establishes a school for poor children of all races in New York

1800–1850

1819	Emma Hart Willard (1787–1870) writes the classic appeal *An Address to the Public: Particularly to the Members of the Legislature of New York, Proposing a Plan for Improving Female Education;* though unsuccessful, it defines the issue of women's education
1820	Susan B. Anthony born
1824	Teacher Sophia B. Packard opens a college for African Americans in Georgia
1833	Oberlin is first U.S. coeducational college
1846	Catharine Beecher publishes *An Essay on Slavery and Abolitionism with Reference to the Duty of American Women to Their Country*
1848	Seneca Falls conference on women's rights is led by American feminists Lucretia Mott and Elizabeth Cady Stanton; not a single woman of color is present, though Frederick Douglass addresses conference
1850	Clara Barton founds one of New Jersey's first "free," or public, schools

1850–1900

1851	Sojourner Truth delivers an unplanned fiery address (now known as "Ain't I a Woman?") at the Women's Rights Conference in Akron, Ohio
1860	First English-language kindergarten established in United States
1869	National Woman Suffrage Association is founded by Cady Stanton and Susan B. Anthony
1869	Female lawyers are licensed in United States
1877	Helen Magill White (1853–1944) earns a Ph.D. in Greek from Boston University, the first woman to receive a Ph.D. from an American university
1878	U.S. constitutional amendment to grant full voting rights to women is introduced for the first time in Congress and every year thereafter until its passage in 1920

1900–1920

1903	American educator and children's rights advocate Julia Richman (1855–1912) opens many schools in New York City for troubled students and urges special classes for students with mental and physical disabilities
1904	Mary McLeod Bethune (1875–1955) founds a school for Black girls in Daytona Beach, Florida, which eventually becomes Bethune-Cookman College
1904	Susan B. Anthony cofounds the International Woman Suffrage Alliance and is made president of the International Leadership Conference in Berlin
1915	Jane Addams and Carrie Chapman Catt found Women's Peace Party
1916	Margaret Sanger forms New York Birth Control League
1920	Nineteenth Amendment is passed, giving women in the United States the right to vote

Thinking Analytically about the Timeline

What evidence in the timeline, if any, suggests women's struggle for education and equality intersected with issues of education and equality for African Americans?

Domestic science programs aimed at more than merely teaching girls to cook, sew, and order a household. They were sophisticated efforts at shaping reality for students. The method can be seen in the National Education Association's 1910 "Report of the Subcommittee on the Industrial and Technical Education in the Secondary Schools." In the section devoted to industrial training for girls, the report described programs at Boston's Girls' High School of Practical Arts and at Cleveland's Technical High School. The principal of the Boston school noted that a major aspect of the girls' mathematics course involved solutions to simple problems such as the maintenance of household accounts. He continued, "Our academic work, as well as the drawing, correlates with the shop. Descriptions of various processes, with materials in hand, are required as lessons in good English. The chemistry deals with questions of food, clothing, and shelter. The aim of these courses is to set before the girl the highest ideals of home life; to train her in all that pertains to practical housekeeping." The description of the industrial training department in Cleveland's Technical High School reveals a similar orientation. Domestic science topics were assigned in English classes, chemistry revolved around food preparation, and mathematics was devoted to adding household accounts and dividing cooking recipes. "In short, all technical subjects involving homemaking are taken as the basis of the course for girls, and the rest of the studies are grouped around these."[91]

In 1910 the National Education Association held that one important aim of girls' vocational education was to "train work in *distinctly feminine* occupations."[92] In 1906 the Massachusetts Commission on Industrial and Technical Training recommended that if a woman was obliged to work (outside the home), vocational education should "fit her so that she can and will enter those industries which are most closely allied to the home."[93] Secretarial practice, bookkeeping, and general office work were often seen as the office equivalent of the wife. Women in these positions were expected to do the routine and "housekeeping" chores of the office.

Commercial Education

As industry and business became increasingly bureaucratized and Taylorized at the turn of the century, the amount of paperwork greatly increased as instructions and reports were sent along the growing chain of managerial command. An efficient, technically trained, and cheap clerical workforce was required to process, send, store, and retrieve this mountain of paper. Women fitting this description were available in significant numbers, and so clerical work would quickly shift from a male occupation to be considered women's work. Public secondary schools quickly stepped forward to satisfy the desires of industry. As historian John Rury reports, "Commercial education was among the fastest growing areas of study in high schools across the country in this period. . . . Commercial education became an important aspect of female high school education in the opening decades of the twentieth century, and represents one of the earliest examples of the manner in which women's education responded to changes in the labor market."[94] The fact that clerical work was designed to mirror the supposed female qualities was reflected in business educators' assessment of the

appropriate kind of training needed by their students. Again Rury is instructive:

> [Business educators commented] repeatedly on the different career patterns men and women followed in business, and some argued that distinctive male and female curricula ought to be established to accommodate such differences. A survey of sixty-six high school principals in 1917 found that nearly two-thirds believed that businessmen wanted training for men and women to differ. Boys, it was felt, required preparation for careers in administration and management, while women needed training for relatively short-term employment as secretaries and typists. Consequently, men ought to be given a broader education commensurate with the responsibilities they were expected to assume, while the technical details of office procedure were considered sufficient for women, whose working careers were generally short. Surveys of the occupational status of men and women in business confirmed the accuracy of these expectations. One of the best known such surveys found in Cleveland that "regardless of the position in which boys and girls started in life, boys worked into administrative positions," while women remained secretaries or clerks until they left the office to get married.[95]

Rury points out that although few commercial education programs were actually sex-segregated, the commercial courses generally became women's education because "women were entering these courses more rapidly than their male counterparts." Commercial education was largely female because the labor market sought women for low-paying clerical positions.[96]

Most of the evidence suggests that like domestic science, commercial education was not only sex-segregated but class-biased. It was primarily a curriculum for women and especially for the daughters of less affluent families. Timothy Crimmins's study of Atlanta's Girls' High School is an excellent case in point. Girls' High School was opened in 1872. Its composition reflected both the caste system and the class system in contemporary Atlanta. African Americans were excluded; 29.9 percent of the students were from the upper class, and 61.3 percent were from middle-class families. None were from the lowest-class families.[97] Given this social class composition, what curriculum might we expect to find—classical or vocational? The curriculum included Latin, French, mathematics, physical science, composition, English literature, and philosophy.[98] By 1896 enrollment had doubled, the percentage from upper-class families had declined, and the percentage from the lower-middle and lower classes had increased substantially. The student body still had no girls from the lowest-class White families.[99] As the social composition of the school changed, however, so did its curriculum. In 1889 a commercial curriculum was added that allowed girls to "substitute typing, bookkeeping, and stenography for Latin, algebra, and philosophy." This curriculum "led directly to employment as secretaries, stenographers, and typists in the city's burgeoning bureaucracies."[100] The social class composition of the two curricula is enlightening: all the upper-class students and 224 of the 297 middle-class students were in the literary curriculum. All the girls in the commercial curriculum came from middle- and lower-class families.[101]

Thinking Critically about the Issues   #2

Evaluate whether the following is a valid reading of Chapter 5: The history of education for girls and women in this country was little more than an attempt to further subordinate women to men.

BUILDING A PHILOSOPHY OF EDUCATION

Chapter 5 illustrates how major social changes from Jefferson's time to the progressive era, accompanied by tensions in the dominant ideology from classical liberalism to modern liberalism, led to shifts in the nature and purposes of women's education, while the underlying assumptions about women's subordinate place in society were not radically altered. Some might argue that gaining the vote at the end of this period was indeed a radical improvement for the role of women in society, yet women remained second class in many other ways. The ideological tension portrayed in this chapter is that women were increasingly entitled to education, but they were still not to be regarded as equal to men. The resulting developments in schooling were on the one hand the increasing enrollment of girls in public schools and on the other hand the strengthening of the belief that women are naturally destined for domestic roles—and that schools should therefore prepare girls for those adult roles. Given the narrow range of employment options for women, the classical liberal era "cult of domesticity" would give way to the progressive period's "domestic sciences" curriculum, a new vocational solution to the problem of what schools should do for girls. During this period (as we saw in Chapter 3 as well), the teaching profession came to be seen as an extension of the domestic role and thus an appropriate occupation for women.

The Primary Source Readings for this chapter demonstrate that individuals don't need to allow the dominant ideology to completely define their own thinking, although one's thinking is inevitably influenced by one's cultural circumstances. The 1848 Seneca Falls Declaration of Sentiments and Resolutions clearly opposes the subordination of women in society, and over 60 years later Mary Leal Harkness opposed girls' vocational education in schools. Today, it might easily appear that the dominant ideology has finally accepted women as the legal, social, and political equals of men, in which case there would be no need for teachers to question that ideology. Yet, as we will see in Part 2 of this volume, social and economic inequalities based on gender still exist in American culture. Anyone who works with children and youth can see that the influences on young women—from advertising and the media more generally, for example—are very different than they are on young men. And, as we will see in Part 2, even the best-intentioned teachers may find themselves unwittingly reinforcing gender stereotypes in the classroom. It is still easy today for girls to lack confidence in the classroom in certain subjects if they believe that "boys are better" in that area, or if they are less assertive than boys by nature or by socialization or both.

Only recently have the laws been put in place to make the same curricular and extracurricular opportunities available for both boys and girls in schools, and they are still needing enforcement. Resentment can still persist in some schools and universities when a male athletic program, for example, is curtailed to make room for a girls' or women's program to balance athletic opportunities.

So the question arises: Does any of this have implications for how teachers think about their own practices with both boys and girls? Should anything in your philosophy of education make those implications explicit, or is this one of those things that "goes without saying"?

Primary Source Reading

Elizabeth Cady Stanton and Lucretia Mott, both of whom were deeply influenced by the antislavery movement, organized the Seneca Falls conference in July 1848 to bring men and women together to consider the subordinate role of women in the United States. The two organizers, together with others, drew up this declaration, using the Declaration of Independence as a model. At the conference, attended by some 300 persons and chaired by Lucretia Mott's husband, James, 11 resolutions were passed unanimously, and the 12th was narrowly passed after a stirring speech from the floor by Frederick Douglass. The language of Jeffersonian liberalism would come to be used by women and African Americans to extend the meaning of equality before the law for the next 150 years, right up to our own time.

The Declaration is presented here so students may see the political–economic conditions that were foremost in the minds of women's rights advocates in mid-19th century; consider the ideological tensions in classical liberalism, the ideology that justified the oppressions of women and yet provided the conceptual underpinning of this Declaration; and finally, examine the various educational issues implicit in these sentiments and resolutions.

Declaration of Sentiments and Resolutions

When, in the course of human events, it becomes necessary for one portion of the family of man to assume among the people of the earth a position different from that which they have hitherto occupied, but one to which the laws of nature and of nature's God entitle them, a decent respect to the opinion of mankind requires that they should declare the causes that impel them to such a course.

We hold these truths to be self-evident: that all men and women are created equal; that they are endowed by their Creator with certain inalienable rights; that among these are life, liberty, and the pursuit of happiness; that to secure these rights governments are instituted, deriving their just powers from the consent of the governed.

Source: Miriam Schneir, ed., *Feminism, the Essential Historical Writings* (New York: Vintage, 1972), pp. 76–82.

Whenever any form of government becomes destructive of these ends, it is the right of those who suffer from it to refuse allegiance to it, and to insist upon the institution of a new government, laying its foundation on such principles, and organizing its powers in such form, as to them shall seem most likely to effect their safety and happiness. Prudence, indeed, will dictate that governments long established should not be changed for light and transient causes; and accordingly all experience hath shown that mankind are more disposed to suffer, while evils are sufferable, than to right themselves by abolishing the forms to which they were accustomed. But when a long train of abuses and usurpations, pursuing invariably the same object evinces a design to reduce them under absolute despotism, it is their duty to throw off such government, and to provide new guards for their future security. Such has been the patient sufferance of the women under this government, and such is now the necessity which constrains them to demand the equal station to which they are entitled.

The history of mankind is a history of repeated injuries and usurpations on the part of man toward woman, having in direct object the establishment of an absolute tyranny over her. To prove this, let facts be submitted to a candid world.

He has never permitted her to exercise her inalienable right to the elective franchise.

He has compelled her to submit to laws, in the formation of which she had no voice.

He has withheld from her rights which are given to the most ignorant and degraded men—both natives and foreigners.

Having deprived her of this first right of a citizen, the elective franchise, thereby leaving her without representation in the halls of legislation, he has oppressed her on all sides.

He has made her, if married, in the eye of the law, civilly dead.

He has taken from her all right in property, even to the wages she earns.

He has made her, morally, an irresponsible being, as she can commit many crimes with impunity, provided they be done in the presence of her husband. In the covenant of marriage, she is compelled to promise obedience to her husband, he becoming, to all intents and purposes, her master—the law giving him power to deprive her of her liberty, and to administer chastisement.

He has so framed the laws of divorce, as to what shall be the proper causes, and in case of separation, to whom the guardianship of the children shall be given, as to be wholly regardless of the happiness of women—the law, in all cases, going upon a false supposition of the supremacy of man, and giving all power into his hands.

After depriving her of all rights as a married woman, if single, and the owner of property, he has taxed her to support a government which recognizes her only when her property can be made profitable to it.

He has monopolized nearly all the profitable employments, and from those she is permitted to follow, she receives but a scanty remuneration. He closes against her all the avenues to wealth and distinction which he considers most honorable to himself. As a teacher of theology, medicine, or law, she is not known.

He has denied her the facilities for obtaining a thorough education, all colleges being closed against her.

He allows her in Church, as well as State, but a subordinate position, claiming Apostolic authority for her exclusion from the ministry, and, with some exceptions, from any public participation in the affairs of the Church.

He has created a false public sentiment by giving to the world a different code of morals for men and women, by which moral delinquencies which exclude women from society, are not only tolerated, but deemed of little account in man.

He has usurped the prerogative of Jehovah himself, claiming it as his right to assign for her a sphere of action, when that belongs to her conscience and to her God.

He has endeavored, in every way that he could, to destroy her confidence in her own powers, to lessen her self-respect, and to make her willing to lead a dependent and abject life.

Now, in view of this entire disfranchisement of one-half the people of this country, their social and religious degradation—in view of the unjust laws above mentioned, and because women do feel themselves aggrieved, oppressed, and fraudulently deprived of their most sacred rights, we insist that they have immediate admission to all the rights and privileges which belong to them as citizens of the United States.

In entering upon the great work before us, we anticipate no small amount of misconception, misrepresentation, and ridicule; but we shall use every instrumentality within our power to effect our object. We shall employ agents, circulate tracts, petition the State and National legislatures, and endeavor to enlist the pulpit and the press in our behalf. We hope this Convention will be followed by a series of Conventions embracing every part of the country.

Resolutions

WHEREAS, The great perception of nature is conceded to be, that "man shall pursue his own true and substantial happiness." Blackstone in his Commentaries remarks, that this law of Nature being coeval with mankind, and dictated by God himself, is of course superior in obligation to any other. It is binding over all the globe, in all countries and at all times; no human laws are of any validity if contrary to this, and such of them as are valid, derive all their force, and all their validity, and all their authority, mediately and immediately, from this original; therefore,

Resolved, That such laws as conflict, in any way, with the true and substantial happiness of woman, are contrary to the great precept of nature and of no validity, for this is "superior in obligation to any other."

Resolved, That all laws which prevent woman from occupying such a station in society as her conscience shall dictate, or which place her in a position inferior to that of man, are contrary to the great precept of nature, and therefore of no force or authority.

Resolved, That woman is man's equal—was intended to be so by the Creator, and the highest good of the race demands that she should be recognized as such.

Resolved, That the women of this country ought to be enlightened in regard to the laws under which they live, that they may no longer publish their degradation by declaring themselves satisfied with their present position, nor their ignorance, by asserting that they have all the rights they want.

Resolved, That inasmuch as man, while claiming for himself intellectual superiority, does accord to woman moral superiority, it is preeminently his duty to encourage her to speak and teach, as she has an opportunity, in all religious assemblies.

Resolved, That the same amount of virtue, delicacy, and refinement of behavior that is required of woman in the social state, should also be required of man, and the same transgressions should be visited with equal severity on both man and woman.

Resolved, That the objection of indelicacy and impropriety, which is so often brought against woman when she addresses a public audience, comes with a very ill-grace from those who encourage, by their attendance, her appearance on the stage, in the concert, or in feats of the circus.

Resolved, That woman has too long rested satisfied in the circumscribed limits which corrupt customs and a perverted application of the Scriptures have marked out for her, and that it is time she should move in the enlarged sphere which her great Creator has assigned her.

Resolved, That it is the duty of the women of this country to secure to themselves their sacred right to the elective franchise.

Resolved, That the equality of human rights results necessarily from the fact of the identity of the race in capabilities and responsibilities.

Resolved, therefore, That, being invested by the Creator with the same capabilities, and the same consciousness of responsibility for their exercise, it is demonstrably the right and duty of woman, equally with man, to promote every righteous cause by every righteous means; and especially in regard to the great subjects of morals and religion, it is self-evidently her right to participate with her brother in teaching them, both in private and in public, by writing and by speaking, by any instrumentalities proper to be used, and in any assemblies proper to be held; and this being a self-evident truth growing out of the divinely implanted principles of human nature, any custom or authority adverse to it, whether modern or wearing the hoary sanction of antiquity, is to be regarded as a self-evident falsehood, and at war with mankind.

[At the last session Lucretia Mott offered and spoke to the following resolution:]

Resolved, That the speedy success of our cause depends upon the zealous and untiring efforts of both men and women, for the overthrow of the monopoly of the pulpit, and for the securing to woman an equal participation with men in the various trades, professions, and commerce.

Primary Source Reading

This article was written by journalist Mary Leal Harkness for a popular, well-educated audience in 1914. It illustrates a number of the issues raised in this chapter: a criticism of the prevailing view that a woman's place is in the home or in a limited number of "female" roles outside the home, the role of schooling in supporting these limited life options for women, the various ideological justifications for the subordinate place of women in society, and so on. Harkness's piece cannot be dismissed simply as just another tirade against the subordinate roles of

Source: Excerpted from Mary Leal Harkness, "The Education of the Girl," *Atlantic Monthly: A Magazine of Literature, Science, Art and Politics* 113 (1914), pp. 324–30. Dr. Karen Graves suggested this article.

women. She is thoughtful about the value of those creative dimensions of gendered domestic experience, such as cooking or sewing, that she finds rewarding. However, she strongly criticizes relegating any such experience to boys or girls alone. Moreover, she calls into question the entire progressive notion of using schools for vocational preparation, whether for girls or for boys, as a "wasting of children's time."

The Education of the Girl

Mary Leal Harkness

I do not know why an utterance on that subject in yesterday morning's paper stirred me up more than similar ones which I am constantly seeing in print. Perhaps it was because the utterer was advertised as an "authority" on "vocational education," for his words did not differ essentially from the current platitude. "The problem of girls education is simple," he said in effect, "since what you have to do is merely to train them to be home-keepers; to teach them the details of the management of the house and the care of children, and not to despise domestic duties."

. . . But why, I beg to ask, does everyone know that the vocation which is sure to delight every girl and in which she is sure to succeed (always provided, of course, that she is given the proper "practical" training in her school-days) is housekeeping and the rearing of children, when even the cocksure vocationalist has to admit that he cannot always foretell with absolute certainty whether a boy of fourteen was made to be a carpenter or an engineer, a farmer or a Methodist preacher? In our outward configuration of form and feature we women confessedly differ as greatly from one another as do men. Why this assumption that in the inward configuration of character, taste, and talent we are all made upon one pattern? I must say that the perpetual declaration on the "woman's page" of modern periodicals that "every woman should know how to cook a meal, and make her own clothes, and feed a baby" fills me with scorn unutterable. But then for that matter the mere fact of a "woman's page" fills me with scorn. Why not a "man's page," with a miscellany of twaddle, labeled as exclusively, adapted to the masculine intellect? The idea that literature is properly created male and female is no less absurd than the idea that there is one education of the man and another of the woman. And it is no more essential to the progress of the universe that every woman should be taught to cook than that every man should be taught to milk a cow.

I do not propose to enter into any discussion of the possible mental superiority of either sex over the other (although I cannot resist quoting in an "aside" the recent remark to me of a teacher of distinguished judgment and long experience: "the fact is, girls are much better students than boys"), but only to maintain this: that girls show as much diversity of taste in intellectual work as boys, that their aptitude for work purely intellectual is as great, and that, therefore, whatever variation is made in the present plan of their education, it should not be based upon the narrow foundation of preconceived ideas of differences inherent in sex. I do not believe that anything necessarily "becomes a woman" more than a man, except as our superstition has made it seem to do so.

Yet, as a matter of fact, superstition begins to hamper a girl's education almost at the very beginning, and one of the first forms which it takes is "consideration for her health." Consideration for the health of a child of either sex is more than laudable, if it be intelligently exercised; but I really cannot see why our daughters deserve more of such consideration than our sons. And the typical consideration for the health of the little girl and the young maiden is not infused with a striking degree of intelligence, as is evidenced by the very small amount of intelligence with which we invariably credit the girl herself. For absolutely the only kind of activity which we ever conceive to be injurious to her is mental activity.

One might perhaps agree to the reiterated parental excuse for half-educated daughters that "nothing can compensate a girl for the loss of her health," if parents would explain how they think that anything can compensate a boy for the loss of his. But they take that risk quite blithely, and send him to college. Personally I have never seen any evidence that the risk for either sex is more than a phantom, and I believe that it is yet to be proved that the study of books has ever in itself been responsible for the breaking down in health of any human being. Many foolish things done in connection with the study of books have contributed to the occasional failure in health of students, but there is, I firmly believe, no reason but prejudiced superstition for the unanimity with which the fond mamma and the family physician fix the cause of the break-down in the books, and never in the numerous and usually obvious other activities. And in the spasms of commiseration for the unfortunates whose "health has been ruined by hard study" nobody has taken the trouble to notice the by-no-means infrequent cases of young persons, and girls especially, of really delicate health, who have stuck to their studies, but with a reasonable determination not to try to stick to ten or a dozen other side issues at the same time, and have come out of college, not physical wrecks, but stronger than when they went in. And who shall say with what greater capacity for enjoying life than those who have devoted the principal energy of their adolescence to the conservation of their health—frequently with no marked success?

So far as the normal child is concerned, his—and her—brain is naturally as active as his body, and it is not "crowding," nor yet "overstimulation," to give that active and acquisitive brain material worth while to work with. Therefore, the pathetic picture which has been painted recently in certain periodicals of the lean and nervous little overworked school-girl may be classed, I think, among the works of creative art rather than among photographs taken from life. Such pictures, as Art, may rank very high, but do not deserve great commendation as a contribution to the science of education. I am not saying that there are not many abominations practiced in our schools, especially of primary and secondary grade; but they are not in the direction of overeducation.

The thing against which I pray to see a mighty popular protest is the wasting of children's time, and the dissipation of all their innate powers of concentration, through the great number of studies of minor (not to use a less complimentary adjective) educational value, which is now one of the serious evils in our schools. And I think that this evil is bearing rather more heavily upon the girls than upon the boys. . . .

But my objection to the whole movement to "redirect" the education of girls is not that many very good things are not put into the redirected curriculum, but that its whole direction is wrong. I cannot say that it is not a good thing for *some* women to know how to cook and sew *well,* for it is indeed both good and necessary to civilized life. I cannot say that some of the subjects introduced into a good domestic-science course are not educative and truly scientific, because I should be saying what is not true. But I do believe that the idea at the basis of it all is fundamentally false. For the idea is this: that one-half of the human race should be "educated" for one single occupation, while the multitudinous other occupations of civilized life should all be loaded upon the other half. The absurd inequality of the division should alone be enough to condemn it. The wonder is that the men do not complain of being overloaded with so disproportionate a share of the burden. I dare say it is their chivalry which makes them bear it so bravely.

This statement of the division is not inconsistent with my complaint that women try to do too many things. They do, but they are all things which are supposed to be included in some way or other within their "proper sphere," the maintenance of the home. Sometimes I grow so weary of The Home that if I did not love my own I could really wish that there were no such thing upon this terrestrial ball. I do love my own home, but I protest that the primary reason is not because my mother is a good cook, although she is, notably. Even as I write these words I thrill with the thought of my near return to her strawberry shortcakes. But I know other homes where there is also strawberry shortcake of a high order, in which I yet think that even filial devotion would have a hard task to make me feel much contentment. I might say the same of the various things that make my home attractive to look upon. Yet the course of study which would graduate "home-makers" is based upon the principle that "home" consists primarily of these things. I am aware that its makers would include certain studies supposed to contribute to "culture," but even where these are well taught, they are still, in my opinion, rendered largely ineffectual by the false motive for study inculcated from the beginning, which makes them all, for women, only side-issues.

I cannot see that girls were created essentially to be "home-keepers" any more than boys. Men and women, so far as they choose to marry, are to make a home together, and any system of education which so plans the division of labor between them that the woman shall "make" and stay in a place for which the man pays and to which he returns once in twenty-four hours, is wrong for at least two good reasons. It trains to two such different conceptions of responsibility that true companionship and community of interest is diminished, and often almost destroyed; and it so magnifies a specialized manual training for the woman that it places her at the end in the artisan class, and not in the educated. If a woman so trained knows how to care for the minds of her children as well as she knows how to feed and dress and physic and spank them, she owes it to the grace of Heaven and not to her "vocational" education "for motherhood." But I do not believe that girls should be "educated to be mothers" at all, in the absurdly narrow sense in which such education is now conceived.

Every form of special instruction as a preparation for parenthood that can be necessary for a girl is necessary for a boy also. For what does it profit a woman or her offspring to have kept herself strong and clean, to have learned the laws of sex-hygiene and reproduction, or of care of the child, if the father of the child has failed to do the same?

But I cannot see how the world can have gone so mad as it has over the idea that *the birth of the child,* and its few subsequent months of existence, constitute the epochal point, the climax, as it were, in the life of any married pair. Surely, it is a very narrow view of life which fails to see how much is to be done in the world besides rearing children. It is true that society does perhaps in a way recognize this, but it seems to wish all active doing relegated to the men, while the woman's contribution is confined to "influence" exerted while nursing a numerous progeny through the diseases of infancy in a happy and perfectly sanitary home.

It is time for a more general recognition that such "feminine influence," like honesty, *laudatur et alget.* The average woman only influences her husband or children to anything good through her brains and character, and the degree of power to express either brains or character depends mainly upon education. It sounds well to proclaim the mothering of the world as woman's greatest profession, her truest glory; but it would be well also to consider that such "mothering" as is mostly done—and will be, so long as women are taught to prepare only for its physical demands, its purely material services—is never going to be either great or glorious. An education which can give the greatest intellectual strength, the completest mental sanity, and so the broadest outlook upon life, is the need and the right of girls and boys alike.

But surely it cannot be said that their need is met alike unless the likeness in their education extends also to the ideal of the use that is to be made of it after school-days are past. If the colleges in which women are taught have failed at all in accomplishing their full possibility, it has been in the comparatively small degree to which they have succeeded in removing even from the minds of the young women themselves the hoary idea that, after all, the principal thing to be expected of the higher education of women is still the diffusion of an exceptionally exalted type of the aforementioned "influence." It does seem rather a small return for years of collegiate effort that the best that can be said of them is that a woman's mental attainments have proved a great assistance to her husband's career as a Cabinet officer. I cannot think that we shall have what wholly deserves to be called an educated womanhood until we have dissipated the idea, still so prevalent even among women themselves, that a woman needs to have a definite occupation only until she marries, or if she fails to marry.

That "a woman must choose between marriage and a career" is the most detestable of all the woman platitudes in the entire collection, because, while most of these platitudes are merely stupid, this one is wholly vicious. It has been so incessantly reiterated, to the accompaniment of much shallow sentimentalizing on the sacredness of home and mother, that the public has never been allowed a quiet moment to reflect on its injustice, and to realize how possible, and therefore imperative, is its removal along with other ancient injustices.

As I have urged in a previous article, the recently born and phenomenally growing department of education which styles itself variously Domestic Science, Household Economy, and I believe one or two other impressive things, might be the pioneer in this great work of justice, if it would. So far as that educational movement adds to woman's ability to become a good citizen by leading her to an intelligent interest in the civic problems of housing, feeding, teaching, and amusing not alone her immediate family group, but a whole community, it does more in the right direction. But the very women who are themselves making a successful profession of teaching this group of subjects (thanks mainly to their having received the sort of education they now deprecate for women in general) apparently claim for them no greater mission for the average young woman than ability to guard her husband from ptomaine poison in his ice-cream, or to make gowns and shirt-waists well enough so that she can earn a living, "if she ever has to work."

Shall we never cease to hear that contemptible reason for a girl's education? An age in which women have proved themselves possessors of intellects might naturally be expected to recognize as a province of their education the ability to discover some particular intellectual bent whose training and development for life-long use are not contingent upon matrimony and the financial condition of two men—their fathers and their husbands respectively. It is held rather reprehensible to say it, but I do not see why every girl has not as good a right as every boy to dream of fame, and to be put in the way of reaching fame. If ninety-nine percent of the girls fail of even the smallest title to fame, just as ninety-nine percent of the boys do, yet the level of their lives must inevitably be raised by the education and the educational ideals which we should provide for them all for the sake of the hundredth girl. The supreme ideal which I hope that our schools may some day inspire is that every girl should discover something, whether of fame-bringing probabilities or not, which will seem to be worthy of being a life-work.

In nearly every present plan for the education of girls there lurks the same fatal weakness; girls are not made to realize as boys are that they are being educated for a business which must last as long as life lasts; that they are to feel an interest in it and grow in it,—to develop it, if possible; they are not taught that a definite purposeful share in the outside world's work is a privilege not a misfortune. My own theory is that the only way in which such a state of feminine mind can be made general is by broadening woman's education on the purely intellectual side; but of course I am open to conviction that the result can be better attained by "scientific" bread-making,—even to the exclusion of Latin and Greek.

Developing Your Professional Vocabulary

A good understanding of this chapter's content would include an understanding of why each of these terms is important to education.

Catharine Beecher

college education of women

colonial education of women

cult of domesticity

Emma Hart Willard

Horace Mann's views on education of women

Mary Wollstonecraft

Sarah M. Grimke

Seneca Falls Convention of 1848

Troy Female Seminary

Questions for Discussion and Examination

1. Do you believe that any of Augustine's views on women and men influence the educational experiences of girls and women today? How, specifically? Explain your view.

2. If the Seneca Falls Declaration was purposely based on classical liberalism, which was the dominant ideology of that time, how could the document have been considered radical or extreme in its views? Explain.

3. Discuss the extent to which Emma Willard's views and accomplishments were evidence of the power of liberal change and the degree to which they reinforced the status quo for women in the 19th-century United States.

OLC   Online Resources

Go to the Online Learning Center at **www.mhhe.com/ tozer7e** to take chapter quizzes, practice with key terms, access study resources, and link to related websites. Also available on the Online Learning Center are PowerWeb articles and news feeds.

Diversity and Equity Schooling and African Americans

Chapter Overview

Chapter 6 examines the relationships among political economy, ideology, and schooling in the experience of African Americans after the Civil War. Political–economic developments of that period included the Thirteenth, Fourteenth, and Fifteenth Amendments to the Constitution, which granted civil and political rights to former slaves and other African Americans; the period of Reconstruction, in which African Americans achieved significant political power in the South and a number of higher education institutions were established for African Americans; and the subsequent period of "redemption," in which the oppression of African Americans by southern Whites through Jim Crow laws and revisions of state constitutions reached terrible proportions. Ideologically, racist European Americans believed that this oppression was justified on the basis of a "scientific" view that Whites were biologically more evolved than African Americans and that classical liberal commitments to freedom and equality did not therefore apply to "less evolved" human beings.

In terms of schooling, it is noteworthy that African Americans were successful during the Reconstruction period in establishing schools for Black children throughout the South. In general, southern Whites had less access to quality education than did southern Blacks. The redemption era, however, particularly the period marked by the ascendancy of Booker T. Washington to political and educational power, resulted in significantly reduced opportunities for the education of African American youth. While Washington often is regarded as a hero of African American advancement, this chapter shows that his commitment to vocational education and acceptance of disfranchisement and lack of civil rights for African Americans were opposed by some Black leaders, including W. E. B. Du Bois. The contrasts between the social, political, and educational analyses of Booker T. Washington and those of Du Bois are drawn in detail and underscored by the Primary Source Reading.

Vol. XVIII   OCTOBER, 1916   No. 2

MANUAL TRAINING MAGAZINE

DEVOTED TO THE
MANUAL ARTS IN
VOCATIONAL
AND GENERAL
EDUCATION

HEAVY FOUNDRY WORK AT WILLIAM L. DICKINSON HIGH SCHOOL, JERSEY CITY, N. J.

PUBLISHED BY
THE MANUAL ARTS PRESS
PEORIA, ILLINOIS

Education of African Americans has historically
emphasized manual skills and vocational training.

Chapter Objectives

Among the objectives that Chapter 6 seeks to
achieve are these:

1. This chapter should equip students to understand
   certain dimensions of African American history
   immediately after the Civil War. In particular,
   students should consider the nature of the racist
   oppression that was supported by legal measures
   in that period.

2. Students should begin to assess the degree
   to which political and economic power can be
   wielded purposefully to the advantage of some
   groups at the expense of others and understand
   that progress, contrary to classical liberal views,
   is not always inevitable.

3. This chapter should help students begin to
   assess the degree to which African Americans
   effectively took responsibility for their own
   education after the Civil War and the degree to
   which the efforts of Whites interfered with Black
   educational achievements.

4. Students should be equipped to evaluate the
   degree to which, in the context of racist political
   economy and ideology, Booker T. Washington's
   educational solutions served the interests of
   African Americans.

5. Students should assess the degree to which
   Washington's faith in social reform through
   educational means was adequate.

6. This chapter should equip students to
   evaluate the critique of Washington formulated
   by W. E. B. Du Bois and to discuss whether Du
   Bois's assessment of the problems of African
   Americans was more or less adequate than
   Washington's assessment.

Analytic Framework
The History of African Americans in U.S. Schools

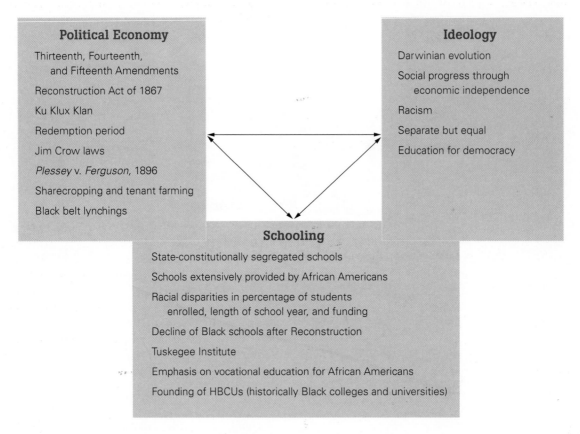

Political Economy

Thirteenth, Fourteenth,
    and Fifteenth Amendments

Reconstruction Act of 1867

Ku Klux Klan

Redemption period

Jim Crow laws

Plessey v. *Ferguson,* 1896

Sharecropping and tenant farming

Black belt lynchings

Ideology

Darwinian evolution

Social progress through
    economic independence

Racism

Separate but equal

Education for democracy

Schooling

State-constitutionally segregated schools

Schools extensively provided by African Americans

Racial disparities in percentage of students
    enrolled, length of school year, and funding

Decline of Black schools after Reconstruction

Tuskegee Institute

Emphasis on vocational education for African Americans

Founding of HBCUs (historically Black colleges and universities)

Introduction: Common Schools in the South

After the common-school movement began in the Northeast, it spread rapidly throughout the rest of the United States. State governments began to pass schooling legislation before the Civil War, and by the 1870s thousands of children were attending public schools in the North and the South. While state school legislation moved more rapidly in the North, one of the most significant developments of this postwar period was the increasing number of African American children attending school in the South. In fact, as early as the 1870s, in parts of the South, Black children attended school in proportionately higher numbers than did White children. However, the educational history of African Americans in the postwar South presented cause for concern as well as for celebration.

Political–Economic Dimensions of Reconstruction and Redemption[1]

On New Year's day in 1863, in the middle of the Civil War, President Abraham Lincoln issued the Emancipation Proclamation, announcing the end of slavery for all states in rebellion against the Union. It was not until several months after the war ended in the spring of 1865, however, that Congress passed the Thirteenth Amendment to the Constitution, which freed 4 million slaves, 3½ million of them in the South. By that time Congress had already created the Freedmen's Bureau as part of the effort to "reconstruct" the southern political economy. The South needed to be reconstructed not only because it had been ravaged by war but also because the new economic, political, and social order would not, for the first time in over 200 years, include slavery at its center.

The Reconstruction period was marked by radical changes and resulting tensions throughout the South. In 1866 the Fourteenth Amendment was passed by Congress, giving full citizenship to former slaves upon its ratification in 1868. Before that ratification, however, the Ku Klux Klan was founded by southern White people, in part to keep African Americans from voting. And just as quickly, southern state governments set up "Black Codes," which segregated African Americans from Whites and prohibited Black people from exercising their new freedoms. At the same time, many southern Whites resisted racial equality with violence. Riots in Memphis and New Orleans resulted in the murders of several Black people and brought increased national attention to Reconstruction conflicts.

In 1867 the North increased its influence in the South with the first Reconstruction Act, which gave Congress greater control over the southern political economy. Northern soldiers occupied the South in an effort to establish a new order, and southern resentment grew. By the end of 1870, all 10 former "rebel" states had been readmitted to the Union, and the Fifteenth Amendment established the right to vote for all African American males. The result: Black men constituted the majority of voters in five southern states and supported the majority party in the other five. Clearly, the South was being reconstructed with elements it had never known before.

One such mark of the new South was the construction of a number of institutions for the higher education of African Americans. Many of the colleges and universities that are known today as historically Black colleges were founded in the Reconstruction period, usually by missionary aid societies and other Protestant church groups. They include Howard University in Washington, DC; Fisk University in Nashville; Atlanta University; Hampton Institute in Virginia; and Talladega College in Alabama; among many others. That African Americans had a strong desire for education at all levels became clear immediately after the war, and their schooling efforts during Reconstruction were remarkably successful.

Reconstruction also meant dramatic change in the political life of Black southerners. Hundreds of African American politicians sought and won local, state, and U.S. congressional offices. During the first 15 years after the Civil War, two Black U.S. senators were elected from the South. This was double the number of Black senators elected over the next 100 years. That fact alone raises the question: why did the gains initiated in the Reconstruction period fail to develop as they should have? The answer lies in what happened after the withdrawal of federal troops from the South in 1877. That point marks the end of the Reconstruction era and the beginning of what White southerners referred to as the "period of redemption." At that point, White southerners were left to "redeem" the South by restoring almost total White domination over political and economic life.

Redemption

Throughout Reconstruction the Ku Klux Klan and southern "rifle clubs" had continued to fan the flames of White hostility toward Black people. Hundreds of African Americans were lynched by gangs of White racists during Reconstruction, and the northern military presence was often ineffectual. At the same time, the North became less and less committed to reconstructive efforts in the South as northern economic problems deepened. The major depression of 1873 focused the North on its own recovery, and the South became a less urgent concern for President Grant and northern lawmakers. Finally, in a political compromise in 1877, southern White support enabled Rutherford B. Hayes to assume the presidency in exchange for the removal of federal troops from the South, and the Reconstruction era effectively came to an end.

The South moved swiftly to "redeem" itself from northern influence. As C. Vann Woodward indicated in *Origins of the New South,* most powerful White southerners saw Reconstruction as an interruption in the working out of the place of free African Americans in the South.[2] As Woodward points out, despite the considerable educational and political gains Black people had made during Reconstruction, their economic gains were meager. In 1900, only 1 of every 100 African Americans in 33 predominantly Black Georgia counties owned land, only 1 Black in 100 in 17 Black Mississippi counties owned land, 1 of 20 in 12 other Black Mississippi counties owned land, and so on throughout the South. What this meant was that Black people, the overwhelming majority of whom were still engaged in agriculture, were working White people's land with White people's mules and plows and were required to give up a share of their crops as rent. By 1900, 75 percent of Black farmers in the South were sharecroppers or tenant farmers, working for subsistence only.[3]

During this time the southern redemption movement attacked the civil and political rights granted by the Fourteenth and Fifteenth Amendments and enforced during Reconstruction. After the end of Reconstruction in 1877 and into the 1890s, local White supremacy laws were passed to prohibit Black people from using public facilities, such as parks, buildings, cemeteries, railroad cars, and restrooms. "Pig laws" were passed, which imposed harsh, multiyear prison terms for minor crimes (such as stealing a pig) if they were committed by Black people. At the same time, "convict lease" programs were implemented so that White southern industrialists, lumber companies, and mine owners could lease chained convicts from the state and put them to work essentially for free. The death rate on these chain gangs was even higher than the death rate for slaves on the prewar plantations.

In 1890 Mississippi used a constitutional convention to establish literacy and poll-tax requirements that deprived most Black people of the vote, and 11 other states followed the "Mississippi Plan" in the next 20 years. In Louisiana, for example, the number of Black voters was cut from 130,000 to 1,300 in a six-year period. States were further encouraged to follow the Mississippi example when the U.S. Supreme Court upheld the Mississippi Plan as constitutional in 1898. Two years before, the Supreme Court had upheld the "separate but equal" laws that segregated Blacks from Whites in public places, even though it was clear that these "Jim Crow" laws were being used to create a caste system that institutionalized the inferior status of African Americans in southern social, political, and economic life.[4] The redemption period successfully destroyed most of the advances made by African Americans during Reconstruction.

Reconstruction, Redemption, and African American Schooling

This period of intense oppression of southern Black citizens included economic privation, violation of civil and political rights, and racially motivated lynchings that numbered in the thousands. In this atmosphere, an educator from Alabama's Tuskegee Institute became the most prominent African American leader of his time.

In part, Booker T. Washington achieved this leadership position by announcing, before a national audience at the Atlanta Exposition in 1895, that it was acceptable for Black people to remain separate from Whites in social and political matters but that Black people could help themselves economically by being more industrious and thrifty—and by obtaining the kind of education that would equip them for manual labor in the southern economy. Rather than calling for African Americans to directly confront their segregated and oppressed social and political status, Washington told his Black listeners, "Cast down your buckets where you are!" They would thus take their places as laborers and trade workers, earning the respect of Whites in the South. The "Atlanta compromise" speech was a message that southern White leaders and northern industrialists were delighted to hear.

Washington's accession to power and recognition was signaled in 1901 by dinner at the White House with President Theodore Roosevelt and his family. From his base at Tuskegee he gradually built what became known as the "Tuskegee machine," and from 1901 to 1915 he was in the heyday of his career. Yet "what was for Washington personally the best of times was for most Blacks the worst," writes Louis R. Harlan, "the most discouraging period since the freeing of the slaves."[5]

Indeed, as Washington's rise to power was crowned in 1901, White Alabama Democrats convened to crown their political supremacy over African Americans. The state's legislature authorized a constitutional convention for May 1901. The convention was so permeated with

At the very time when White America was hailing Booker T. Washington's efforts to improve the lot of African Americans through a combination of hard work and education, most Black southerners were losing the political and educational gains made during the Reconstruction era.

racially extremist convictions that former governor William C. Oates felt compelled to comment on the change in White politicians' opinions regarding the status of Black people. He was appalled by the increase in racial hatred since Reconstruction, when Black people were enfranchised and competing for political office. "Why, sir, the sentiment is altogether different now, when the Negro is doing no harm, why, people want to kill him and wipe him from the face of the earth." These were the times that historian Rayford Logan called the nadir of African American history.

The most virulent "anti-Negro" speakers at the 1901 Alabama constitutional convention were the Democrats from the Black belt or from counties bordering the Black belt.[6] The Black belt representatives successfully presented a resolution on education that brought the new state constitution into harmony with the 1890 House Bill 504, which allowed township trustees to fund White schools at a higher level than Black schools. The Black belt representatives substituted the phrase "just and equitable" for the corresponding phrase in the constitution of 1875, which required that all funds be appointed "for the equal benefit of all the children." During the convention the Black belt delegates indicated what they meant by justice and equity. One delegate said, "There is no necessity for paying a teacher for a colored school the same amount you pay to White school teachers, because you can get them at much less salary. Under the present laws of Alabama, if the law is carried out, the colored pupil gets the same amount of money per capita as the White pupil, and that is not justice."

In this atmosphere of racial animosity, the state's constitution was changed to permit local school officers to control apportionments and discriminate against Black schoolchildren. The concept of "just and equitable" expressed at this convention stood in marked contrast to the freed men and women's politics that had endorsed educational and political equality regardless of race. To the extent that Booker T. Washington aligned himself with the Black belt planters, he joined the most antidemocratic forces of his era.[7] But to assess Washington's approach to schooling for African Americans in the South, it is first necessary to examine those schools in the Reconstruction and redemption periods.

Schooling in the Black Belt

Few values and aspirations were more firmly rooted in the freedmen's culture than education. Their crusade for universal schooling was perhaps the most striking illustration of their postwar campaign for self-improvement. Their idea of universal public schooling, regardless of race or class, was a conception of education and democracy unprecedented in southern history. The prewar constitutions and laws of the Confederate states denied literacy and formal schooling to Black people and paid little attention to public education at all. South Carolina's constitution made no mention of education. Alabama, Arkansas, and Florida had brief general clauses about encouraging the means of education and using the proceeds of federal land grants to support schools. A clause in the Georgia constitution of 1777 about schools was omitted in later revisions, though provision was made in 1798 for promoting "seminaries of learning." Mississippi and North Carolina alluded to the value of learning in their constitutions but included no specifications about state schools. Virginia, which defeated Jefferson's proposals for public schools in the 18th and 19th centuries, later used a "capitation" (or per capita) tax for use of White primary schools. Louisiana and Texas went somewhat further than the others, providing for superintendents, a school fund, and state school systems but hedging the language regarding the implementation of public systems of education. For example, Louisiana's constitution of 1852 stated that the legislature might abolish the superintendent's office, while in Texas the legislature was to establish a school system "as early as practicable."[8]

These haphazard and halting constitutional provisions for education in the antebellum South were transformed into elaborate legal frameworks for universal public schooling in the Reconstruction era. The freed men and women helped set in motion customs, laws, and political movements that fundamentally altered the definition of public education. They formed the core of the political vanguard that inserted universal public education into the Reconstruction constitutions of the former Confederate states. The constitutional provisions for public schooling shifted from vague clauses to decisive "shall" declarations and highly specific requirements.[9]

Events in Alabama paralleled regional developments. In 1867, Alabama freedmen coalesced with other Republicans to enact constitutional laws that provided ample sources of public education revenue for the schools, discouraged private contributions to finance public education, promised equal opportunities regardless of race or class, and did not mandate racially separate schools, though the state constitution left the decision entirely to the discretion of the state board of education. Still, so far as the Black belt

Exhibit 6.1   Percentage of School-Age Population Enrolled in School by Race in Selected Alabama Counties: 1877, 1887, 1897, and 1915

County	1877		1887		1897		1915	
	Black	White	Black	White	Black	White	Black	White
Autauga	37.5%	25.4%	37.1%	48.9%	40.5%	69.4%	39.6%	70.3%
Barbour	35.3	53.9	54.5	54.0	51.4	60.0	35.3	71.6
Bullock	21.8	28.5	39.6	44.6	39.7	72.0	43.6	80.1
Butler	29.4	26.5	54.4	45.5	54.1	64.4	43.3	66.3
Chambers	25.8	25.0	67.0	60.8	78.5	70.8	31.8	80.2
Choctaw	35.2	27.7	59.0	55.2	70.9	86.1	55.3	84.4
Clarke	47.5	42.4	53.1	48.1	80.9	52.8	41.8	73.5
Dallas	28.7	26.3	37.2	44.4	40.3	26.8	37.4	72.2
Greene	27.8	32.0	45.6	41.6	47.5	48.1	51.8	93.1
Hale	24.6	25.4	42.5	50.5	40.1	68.5	51.9	69.2
Lee	45.6	38.5	57.0	40.3	47.4	53.4	42.5	71.8
Lowndes	30.5	36.4	36.8	41.0	24.7	68.1	38.2	72.2
Macon	41.0	36.4	58.4	37.4	49.5	59.6	61.4	69.4
Marengo	20.3	24.0	36.6	54.9	44.2	66.7	32.5	78.4
Monroe	71.3	64.1	97.3	63.4	52.3	65.4	47.4	80.6
Montgomery	14.5	19.3	34.2	26.6	44.0	73.5	36.6	68.9
Perry	32.3	29.9	32.5	39.6	26.1	59.6	43.1	68.5
Pickens	48.9	62.3	59.1	67.0	68.9	63.9	72.1	80.9
Russell	30.5	37.5	65.4	65.8	65.9	47.2	43.9	71.8
Sumter	32.5	32.3	55.9	52.0	46.6	69.9	29.7	73.0
Wilcox	27.7	32.2	50.1	55.5	37.3	71.4	19.6	78.9

Sources: Report of Superintendent of Education for the State of Alabama, 1878, with Tabular Statistics of 1876–7 (Montgomery: Barrett and Brown, 1879), pp. xlix–lvi; *Thirty-third Annual Report of the Superintendent of Education of Alabama, 1887* (Montgomery: W. D. Brown, 1888), pp. 99–116; *Report of Superintendent of Education of Alabama 1898* (Montgomery: Brown Printing Company, 1898), pp. 268–70, 327–28; *Annual Report of the Department of Education of the State of Alabama, 1915* (Montgomery: Brown Printing Company, 1915), pp. 110–16.

freedmen were concerned, the constitution of 1868 provided virtually every promise of equal opportunities. Further, their rights were ensured in part by the presence of Peyton Finley, an African American citizen from the Black belt, on the state board of education. He pressed constantly for an equal division of the public school fund among African Americans and Whites.[10]

Educational opportunities were not always equal, but Black people's political participation and the racial equality established in Alabama's Reconstruction constitution enabled them to make gains in public schooling between 1868 and the reestablishment of planter dominance in the late 1870s. For instance, in 1877, in 11 of the 21 Alabama Black belt counties, the percentage of Black children of school age enrolled in school exceeded the percentage of White children enrolled (see Exhibit 6.1). For the Black belt as a whole, the average length of public school terms for Black children was longer than that for White children, though the average length of

White school terms in 11 of the counties exceeded that for Black children (see Exhibit 6.2). The average monthly pay for Black teachers in 1877 exceeded that for White teachers in 18 of the 21 Black belt counties (see Exhibit 6.3). As long as the state funding of Alabama's Black belt remained nearly equal between the races, or even if the school fund was divided according to the poll tax and real estate taxes paid by the two races, Black communities, given their quest for education, could continue to foster the expansion and improvement of public schools. But this was all to change with the end of Reconstruction.

The seeds of the destruction of educational advancement in Black communities were planted in 1875, the year the redeemers—White Democrats—began to regain control of Alabama's Black belt. In Macon County, for example, in 1875 the county's two state representatives, both Black Republicans, were charged with and convicted of felonies—adultery and grand larceny—by the newly elected circuit judge, James Edward Cobb. They

Exhibit 6.2   Average Length of Public Schools in Days by Race in Selected Alabama Counties: 1877, 1887, 1897, and 1915

County	1877 Black	1877 White	1887 Black	1887 White	1897 Black	1897 White	1915 Black	1915 White
Autauga	86	60	89	61	63	63	93	140
Barbour	74	81	85	71	68	62	91	148
Bullock	71	69	106	70	63	64	86	163
Butler	105	67	82	65	72	60	84	122
Chambers	78	87	131	120	60	60	91	156
Choctaw	64	80	65	65	60	64	56	120
Clarke	74	72	82	72	65	80	72	110
Dallas	92	74	75	60	68	70	108	172
Greene	93	122	106	74	86	85	94	158
Hale	79	57	80	64	78	79	102	115
Lee	81	94	95	71	60	60	89	156
Lowndes	78	98	83	60	72	92	91	142
Macon	79	80	70	60	78	79	101	158
Marengo	71	63	95	70	78	71	93	126
Monroe	125	87	59	63	70	65	65	120
Montgomery	100	88	100	97	72	80	121	174
Perry	88	79	96	72	77	79	109	152
Pickens	68	84	60	60	60	75	80	108
Russell	76	81	83	71	62	64	80	152
Sumter	80	91	79	79	70	81	86	152
Wilcox	99	102	78	60	60	66	81	151
Total averages	84	82	86	71	69	71	89	143

Sources: Report of Superintendent of Education for the State of Alabama, 1878, with Tabular Statistics of 1876–7 (Montgomery: Barrett and Brown, 1879), pp. xlix–lvi; *Thirty-third Annual Report of the Superintendent of Education of Alabama, 1887* (Montgomery: W. D. Brown, 1888), pp. 99–116; *Report of Superintendent of Education of Alabama 1898* (Montgomery: Brown Printing Company, 1898), pp. 268–70, 327–28; *Annual Report of the Department of Education of the State of Alabama, 1915* (Montgomery: Brown Printing Company, 1915), pp. 110–16.

were sentenced by Cobb to chain gangs. Cobb, a Democrat and former Confederate colonel, had been captured at Gettysburg and had spent the remainder of the war in Union prisons. He charged the district's White Republican state senator with perjury, but the senator avoided prosecution by resigning from office. Throughout Alabama's Black belt in 1875 freedmen were driven from political office and either disfranchised or controlled firmly by White Democrats. Consequently, the state's constitution of 1875, reflecting the reestablishment of planter political supremacy, severely restricted the amount of money available for public schools.[11]

The constitution framed by the Black belt redeemers in 1875 legally required racial segregation in schools. It also altered the governance of public education in ways that placed it permanently in White hands. However, there was no wholesale demolition of the structures the former slaves and their Republican allies had created. Most important, the legal framework of school finance

in the 1875 constitution was strictly on a per capita child basis and for the equal benefit of each race, thus leaving no discretion to any official to discriminate for or against either racial group. Reconstruction had nearly ended in the Black belt in 1875, and the redeemers were committed to retrenchment in public education. But two key factors protected the continued development of education in the Black communities. First, Black people could still vote, and the redeemers knew that as long as they sought to win Black votes, it was politically dangerous to tamper excessively with Black public education. Second, Black public education was protected in part because of the legal safeguards for equal funding that the freedmen had inserted in the state constitution of 1868 and which remained a part of the 1875 constitution.[12]

Hence, even during a decade of redeemer government in Alabama's Black belt from 1877 to 1887, Black education continued to prosper. In 1887, as in 1877, the

Exhibit 6.3   Average Monthly Pay of Teachers by Race in Selected Alabama Counties: 1877, 1887, 1897, and 1915

County	1877		1887		1897		1915	
	Black	White	Black	White	Black	White	Black	White
Autauga	$34.36	$37.13	$22.08	$26.50	$19.51	$29.80	$24.78	$47.93
Barbour	23.50	13.50	29.30	23.33	18.99	24.93	27.54	55.72
Bullock	28.46	16.65	27.50	20.00	30.50	35.50	25.57	60.48
Butler	24.50	17.50	26.04	25.56	16.24	24.20	25.54	55.30
Chambers	18.00	18.75	31.57	38.00	27.30	27.30	30.87	49.76
Choctaw	26.70	23.00	25.93	22.95	18.60	20.00	22.12	52.58
Clarke	20.18	17.00	22.33	24.75	16.15	19.85	30.65	64.23
Dallas	17.80	12.50	34.33	17.00	28.00	27.00	22.93	71.73
Greene	32.77	13.50	29.22	19.30	18.16	17.65	24.29	55.89
Hale	31.00	16.00	36.86	19.53	21.33	30.65	25.68	63.55
Lee	19.41	14.57	20.75	18.00	18.52	26.45	32.93	62.28
Lowndes	29.00	22.00	29.47	26.44	25.00	50.00	27.84	74.58
Macon	15.00	18.00	20.00	20.00	15.06	20.20	28.87	56.65
Marengo	35.05	27.28	34.50	25.18	19.29	27.90	22.48	68.66
Monroe	25.00	22.58	19.93	21.77	10.01	15.50	30.52	49.27
Montgomery	27.60	18.06	22.00	30.00	21.11	30.05	31.52	78.96
Perry	27.96	17.35	32.39	20.57	11.70	15.79	26.08	53.65
Pickens	32.00	19.31	14.00	16.00	16.00	21.00	20.75	50.22
Russell	20.12	12.60	31.00	36.95	17.51	28.13	29.26	70.71
Sumter	30.07	21.80	27.75	27.07	19.25	34.93	26.46	66.68
Wilcox	22.44	13.76	25.60	16.30	14.30	31.98	19.88	62.63

Sources: Report of Superintendent of Education for the State of Alabama, 1878, with Tabular Statistics of 1876–7 (Montgomery: Barrett and Brown, 1879), pp. xlix–lvi; *Thirty-third Annual Report of the Superintendent of Education of Alabama, 1887* (Montgomery: W. D. Brown, 1888), pp. 99–116; *Report of Superintendent of Education of Alabama 1898* (Montgomery: Brown Printing Company, 1898), pp. 268–70, 327–28; *Annual Report of the Department of Education of the State of Alabama, 1915* (Montgomery: Brown Printing Company, 1915), pp. 110–16.

percentage of school-age Black children enrolled in school exceeded the percentage of White children enrolled in 11 of the 21 counties (see Exhibit 6.1). With respect to length of school terms, in 20 of 21 counties in 1887, the Black school terms were longer than or equal to the White school terms (see Exhibit 6.2).

Moreover, racial disparities in the average length of school terms had increased considerably in favor of Black children since 1877—from 84 to 86 days for Black pupils and from 82 to 71 days for White pupils. This represented significant improvement of educational conditions in Black communities between 1877 and 1887. Conditions for Whites declined as Black students took advantage of schooling opportunities that Whites did not have. These included schools supported by churches, the Freedmen's Bureau, and local Black citizens. Only in a few instances did Whites move toward parity. The average monthly pay of Black teachers in 1887 exceeded the average monthly pay of White teachers in 13 counties, but Blacks had earned more than

Whites in 18 counties in 1877 (see Exhibit 6.3). Hence, as we shall see, Booker T. Washington entered the Black belt in 1881 in the middle of an era of advancement in Black education dating back to the Reconstruction constitution of 1868.

Approximately 10 years after Washington's arrival, Black education fell on hard times. In 1890, State Superintendent of Education Solomon Palmer, in his annual report, introduced his discussion of major problems confronting public education by declaring that Alabama had to increase school revenues to keep pace with other states and meet the growing demand of its school population. He then proceeded to review the complaints against the way in which the school funds were apportioned and spent. The two principal complaints were that Blacks in the Black belt counties received nearly all the area's school funds while paying virtually no taxes and that Black pupils were not mentally advanced to the point where they needed as much education as White pupils, and therefore did not need as much money for their education. Palmer's response was to place public school funds in the hands of local White school authorities, to be spent at their discretion.

In 1890 Palmer's plan was introduced in the Alabama legislature as House Bill 504. It passed in the House and Senate in February 1891. The new law required the state superintendent to apportion the public school fund according to the school-age population but authorized township trustees to apportion funds as they deemed "just and equitable." This law effectively relieved the superintendent of education of the responsibility for apportioning the school fund between the races, and it was used to get around the state's constitutional provision requiring that the school fund be apportioned on a per capita basis and for the equal benefit of both races.[13]

No political faction in Alabama was more in favor of this new plan than the White Democrats of the Black belt counties. Representative Smith of Russell County thought it was the best bill ever introduced in the Alabama legislature and declared that the author of the bill "deserved a vote of thanks from the white people of the state." The superintendent of schools of Wilcox County, where in 1891 above 85 percent of the school-age population was Black, welcomed the new law by proclaiming that "Wilcox never had such a boom on schools. The new law has stimulated the Whites so that neighborhoods where no schools existed for years, are now building houses and organizing schools." It was clear both to Blacks and to Whites that this law assigned state funds to White county officials to allocate as they chose. The result in Black belt counties was to permit school officers to pour money into White schools and give tiny sums to the Black schools. Ironically, the Black belt Democrats favored a "color-blind" distribution of the school fund over creating a racially distinct tax base and apportionment because the former would permit them to take an even larger share of the tax base.[14]

The day after the passage of House Bill 504, a "colored convention" convened in Montgomery, the state's capital. The general purpose of the convention was to "discuss subjects which would benefit the Negro race in Alabama." A pressing concern was the newly passed school-fund apportionment law. In the evening session of the convention Booker T. Washington spoke against the law. His speech was described by a reporter for the Montgomery *Advertiser* as a "bitter" indictment of the Alabama legislature for authorizing school officers to bypass the 1875 constitutional provision for equal apportionment of the already meager school funds. Ironically, only three years earlier, Washington

had said, "The rate at which prejudice is dying out is so rapid as to justify the conclusion that the Negro will in a quarter of a century enjoy in Alabama every right that he now enjoys in Pennsylvania." He had spoken too soon. Black Alabamians were about to enter the era from 1890 to 1910, referred to by Benjamin Brawley as the "vale of tears." With the new school-funding statute in place, the campaign to shortchange Black education had an open field.[15]

After 1890 the Democrats in Black belt counties seized the school funds of the disfranchised Black citizens. Consequently, the general enrollment and school terms of Black children and the average pay of Black teachers came to a standstill and in many cases actually decreased, while educational conditions among Whites began to improve sharply (see Exhibits 6.1, 6.2, and 6.3). In vital respects, Black education in the Black belt counties, which had advanced steadily from 1867 to 1887, declined significantly from 1887 to 1897. In 10 counties, the percentage of school-age Black children enrolled in school was lower than in 1887. In 17 counties, the Black school terms were shorter than they had been in 1887, and the average monthly pay of Black teachers decreased in 19 of the 21 counties between 1887 and 1897. Hence, two years after Washington's "Atlanta Compromise" address, the speech that catapulted him into national prominence as educational statesman of Black America, the postwar struggle for education in Alabama's Black communities had reached its nadir.

This period of retrogression must have been difficult and peculiar for Washington. In general, as Louis Harlan has written, "Washington allied himself with the southern planters and businessmen against the poorer class of whites." The legal, political, and extralegal movements to crush the development of Black education were led by some of the same allies, the White planter Democratic coalition from the Black belt counties.[16]

As Louis R. Harlan has documented in his classic study *Separate and Unequal,* the campaign by local and state governments to improve public schools in the South from 1901 to 1915 was aimed at White people and sharply increased the disparities between the schools the two races attended. In short, law and government had been used successfully to re-create inequality.

White public education steadily gained ground on Black public education. In 1915, in every Black belt county the percentage of school-age White children enrolled in school exceeded that of Black schoolchildren (see Exhibit 6.1). This had not been the case in

African American commitment to education was so strong that 10 years after the end of Reconstruction, attendance at Black schools was still higher than at most White schools.

1877, 1887, or 1897. Moreover, in 14 counties in 1915, the percentage of school-age Black children enrolled in school had fallen below the 1897 rates (see Exhibit 6.1). Thus, relative to White enrollments and relative to their position in 1897, Black school enrollments declined significantly during the apex of Washington's career. Similarly, in 1915, the length of White school terms and the average monthly pay of White teachers exceeded those for Blacks, usually by significant margins, in every Black belt county. In all but four counties in 1915, the average monthly pay of White teachers doubled that of Black teachers (see Exhibit 6.3). This was a drastic turnaround from 1877, when the average monthly pay of Black teachers exceeded that of White teachers in 19 of the 21 Black belt counties. Finally, the percentage of Black teachers decreased, generally sharply, in 19 of the 21 Black belt counties (Exhibit 6.4). After 1890 and until Washington's death in 1915, African Americans' conception of community advancement turned inward. Assuming a defensive posture, they concentrated on

strengthening their institutions and surviving in the face of an undemocratic and unjust social order, since they no longer had political clout. Their educational advancement during the Washington era depended heavily on private sacrifice. In 1915, approximately 60 percent of the schoolhouses for Black children in Alabama's Black belt were privately owned (Exhibit 6.5). A large amount of money was contributed by Blacks to public education over and above that paid as taxes. It was through such traditions and customs of self-sacrifice that Black communities kept afloat a fragmented and feeble school system during the "vale of tears."[17]

Thinking Critically about the Issues   #1

Exhibits 6.1 through 6.5 provide a large amount of data, but data always must be interpreted. What is your interpretation of the story that is told in these five tables?

Exhibit 6.4 Black Percentage of School-Age Population, Schools, and Teachers in Selected Alabama Counties: 1877, 1887, 1897, and 1915

County	1877			1887			1897			1915		
	Percentage of School-Age Population	Percentage of Schools	Percentage of Teachers	Percentage of School-Age Population	Percentage of Schools	Percentage of Teachers	Percentage of School-Age Population	Percentage of Schools	Percentage of Teachers	Percentage of School-Age Population	Percentage of Schools	Percentage of Teachers
Autauga	44.8%	40.3%	40.4%	63.6%	53.3%	57.7%	65.2%	49.2%	49.2%	61.2%	43.7%	35.1%
Barbour	53.4	37.0	37.0	60.1	48.1	48.0	63.6	41.9	43.4	65.4	39.6	34.0
Bullock	69.8	50.0	49.0	74.7	54.9	52.2	80.5	54.7	54.7	87.8	60.2	47.8
Butler	41.7	18.7	18.5	45.4	37.5	35.0	48.1	38.8	43.5	58.2	39.0	33.8
Chambers	43.1	25.6	25.6	45.4	33.6	33.6	52.7	42.1	42.1	56.5	38.0	27.0
Choctaw	50.1	45.8	45.8	53.8	47.2	38.8	51.4	42.7	43.3	63.4	37.1	33.0
Clarke	53.4	38.4	38.5	56.9	52.3	60.0	53.1	41.5	41.5	59.5	38.7	34.8
Dallas	84.1	63.8	63.8	88.0	76.4	74.7	90.3	74.1	74.1	85.2	68.8	55.4
Greene	80.8	64.7	64.7	86.1	72.0	70.3	86.4	60.2	60.2	88.1	63.4	63.4
Hale	77.5	69.4	69.4	83.4	65.9	63.0	85.8	63.6	63.1	81.5	57.6	53.2
Lee	48.4	46.3	46.3	49.3	46.3	46.3	63.5	52.6	51.6	65.1	42.1	35.8
Lowndes	80.0	68.5	68.5	86.5	75.5	75.5	90.9	63.5	63.5	90.9	62.4	58.5
Macon	57.7	53.9	53.9	65.3	57.1	57.1	74.1	62.8	61.4	85.9	37.2	61.3
Marengo	73.9	48.4	48.4	76.0	58.4	58.0	76.9	50.0	50.0	74.4	39.5	33.5
Monroe	47.4	29.7	29.7	54.1	57.9	43.0	55.7	40.4	40.4	58.2	38.7	33.0
Montgomery	72.9	57.4	57.4	73.0	69.6	69.6	85.3	64.5	63.6	75.8	60.6	45.4
Perry	73.5	47.3	47.3	76.0	58.3	58.8	79.5	51.0	50.5	83.1	55.0	32.3
Pickens	49.1	32.9	32.9	55.3	47.0	41.8	55.1	44.0	37.9	53.5	40.3	36.9
Russell	66.5	61.9	61.9	71.5	54.7	54.7	73.0	64.6	64.6	83.9	61.1	50.0
Sumter	70.9	60.6	60.6	75.9	68.3	62.1	80.9	64.2	60.2	84.6	53.6	40.2
Wilcox	75.6	61.7	61.7	77.3	57.9	57.9	79.3	50.0	50.0	83.8	33.3	40.0

Sources: Report of Superintendent of Education for the State of Alabama, 1878, with Tabular Statistics of 1876–7 (Montgomery: Barrett and Brown, 1879), pp. xlix–lvi; Thirty-third Annual Report of the Superintendent of Education of Alabama, 1887 (Montgomery: W. D. Brown, 1888), pp. 99–116; Report of Superintendent of Education of Alabama 1898 (Montgomery: Brown Printing Company, 1898), pp. 268–70, 327–28; Annual Report of the Department of Education of the State of Alabama, 1915 (Montgomery: Brown Printing Company, 1915), pp. 110–16.

Exhibit 6.5   Number and Percentage of Schoolhouses by Race and Ownership in Selected Alabama Counties

County	Schoolhouses for Black Children				Schoolhouses for White Children			
	Public	Private	% Public	% Private	Public	Private	% Public	% Private
Autauga	4	26	13.4%	86.6%	30	10	75.0%	25.0%
Barbour	19	23	45.2	54.8	55	10	84.6	15.4
Bullock	17	30	36.2	63.8	24	9	72.7	27.3
Butler	30	17	63.8	36.2	63	8	87.5	12.5
Chambers	31	4	88.6	11.4	56	1	98.2	1.8
Choctaw	36	0	100.0	0	53	8	86.9	13.1
Clarke	31	21	59.6	40.4	74	9	89.2	10.8
Dallas	9	90	9.1	90.9	26	19	57.7	42.3
Greene	33	26	66.0	44.0	27	2	93.1	6.9
Hale	5	51	9.0	91.0	25	17	59.5	40.5
Lee	30	9	77.0	23.0	42	3	93.3	6.7
Lowndes	18	40	30.0	70.0	20	15	57.1	42.9
Macon	45	6	88.2	11.8	24	8	75.0	25.0
Marengo	8	37	17.8	82.2	49	20	71.0	29.0
Monroe	26	20	56.5	43.5	53	20	72.6	27.4
Montgomery	18	77	18.9	81.1	44	18	71.0	29.0
Perry	5	46	9.8	90.2	33	12	73.3	26.7
Pickens	31	19	62.0	38.0	65	9	87.8	12.2
Russell	14	30	31.8	68.2	27	2	93.1	6.9
Sumter	3	34	8.1	91.9	22	10	68.8	31.2
Wilcox	13	14	48.1	51.9	32	22	59.3	40.7
Totals	426	630	40.3%	59.7%	844	232	78.4%	21.6%

Source: Annual Report of the Department of Education of the State of Alabama for the Scholastic Year Ending September 30, 1915 (Montgomery: Brown Printing Company, 1915), pp. 110–16.

Booker T. Washington's Career

While appraising Booker T. Washington's influence on public education for Blacks in Alabama, African American reformer and historian Horace Mann Bond wrote that "the historian of educational events may find in the life of the builder of Tuskegee Institute perhaps the most illuminating point of departure from which to evaluate the times and the social and economic forces in which he was involved." Bond cautioned us not to make two grave errors. First, we should not attribute momentous social and economic changes to Washington's heroic leadership. Second, we should not judge his greatness by immediate quantitative and institutional results. After all, said Bond, Booker T. Washington had become a legend, and "who shall deny the importance of legends, as social forces, in affecting the course of human history?" The continuing interest in

Washington and his era gives at least some credence to Bond's observations.[18]

There is also much validity to Bond's suggestion that Washington's life is an "illuminating point of departure" from which to examine a critical historical moment in the development of African American education, the period from Reconstruction to the great migration of southern African Americans to the urban North from 1914 to 1930. Born a slave in 1856, he was already of school age when the former slaves mobilized to create in the South a system of universal public education. Washington, a part of this movement himself, described vividly their struggle for education: "Few people who were not right in the midst of the scenes can form any exact idea of the intense desire which the people of my race showed for education. It was a whole race trying to go to school. Few were too young, and none too old, to make the attempt to learn." As a schoolboy, he worked at a salt furnace from 4 to 9 A.M. before attending day school, and later, he worked in the morning and attended school for a few hours every afternoon. In 1872, at age 16 and crudely educated, he went off to the Hampton Normal and Agricultural Institute in Hampton, Virginia. He was one of hundreds of young African Americans who flocked to the normal schools and colleges in search of an education that would enable them to lead their people effectively.[19]

Washington started working as a teacher in 1875 and in 1879 became a teacher and assistant at Hampton Institute. In 1881, he went to Tuskegee and began his life's work. By that time Reconstruction had collapsed, and his career as an educational statesman was launched in a fundamentally different political context from the one in which he attended elementary and normal school. The South became a one-party region under the control of a reactionary ruling elite that sought to contain the freedmen's progressive campaign for democracy and universal schooling. In this context, Washington rose to great heights as an educational and political statesman for African Americans everywhere. Again we are reminded, as historian Louis R. Harlan has written, "Washington's rise coincided with a setback of his race."[20]

With Bond's cautions in mind, great social and political changes will not be attributed to Washington's influence here, nor will his contribution be evaluated in terms of institutional results. Nonetheless, it should be borne in mind that one of Washington's important claims and a central part of his legacy was the belief that despite political compromises, he had a favorable impact on the advancement of public education in Black communities. In *Up from Slavery* Washington wrote about teachers in Alabama's Black belt, where schools were in session only three to five months out of the year, and how he and his graduates worked to improve those conditions. He spoke frequently of Tuskegee graduates who were "showing the people how to extend the school term to 4, 5, and even 7 months." In 1911 he claimed that as a result of the Tuskegee program there existed in Macon County "a model public school system, supported in part by the county board of education, and in part by the contributions of the people themselves."[21]

Undoubtedly, Washington was a ceaseless advocate for education. On speaking platforms, through periodicals, and in the White and Black press, he lost no opportunity to plead for the advancement of public education. Indeed, the chief benefit that Washington intended Black people to receive from the "Atlanta Compromise" speech was the chance to attain an education that would fit them for useful employment. The central concern of this chapter is with what actually happened to Black public education during Washington's career, particularly in Alabama's Black belt, where he became the chief spokesperson for that struggle.

Washington and Schooling in the Black Belt

In the summer of 1881 Washington went to Macon County, Alabama, to become principal of the newly created Black state normal school in the town of Tuskegee. This was a place in the deep South—the Black belt—where he had never been before but where his people had struggled for generations to forge and nurture a culture that placed a high premium on literacy and formal schooling.

The "Tuskegee story" of Washington's era runs counter to the parallel development of Black education. The story is symbolized by a statue on Tuskegee's campus portraying Washington as "lifting the veil of ignorance from the Negro race." This particular legacy holds that there is plenty of room for debate over Washington's methods, but none over his results. He demonstrated that against overwhelming odds he could turn a dilapidated shanty and a run-down church in rural Alabama into the most famous Black institution of learning of its time. Over the years schools and colleges (normal schools) founded and taught by Tuskegee alumni sprang up throughout the rural South, helping downtrodden African Americans improve and expand their local school systems by finding a common ground of understanding with powerful White politicians. This pragmatic philosophy, which propelled Washington into national fame and power, is believed to have worked at the local level to systematically improve public educational opportunities in Black communities. Thus, despite the setbacks in politics, civil rights, and human rights that occurred during the age of Washington, his disciples were credited with steadily building an infrastructure of practical education that protected Black students from the worst tendencies of southern racism. Some even suggest that Washington's pragmatic approach, his emphasis on the work ethic, traditional morality, and industrial education, "may well have saved Negro education from total destruction." It is maintained that Washington's promises to keep Blacks in their "place" and educate them to be more efficient laborers "reconciled many whites to the idea of Negro education."[22]

Whatever grain of truth may be contained in this version of the Tuskegee story, it is largely mythology. The age of Booker T. Washington was characterized by

African Americans attended schools and newly founded colleges in great numbers as soon as the law allowed them a formal education. This photo is of a Tuskegee Institute history class, 1902.

the worst treatment of Black public education by state and local school officers since the end of slavery. Indeed, Washington's generation was sandwiched between two important progressive eras in southern Black public education: (1) the two decades (1877–1897) after Reconstruction and (2) the two decades (1915–1935) after Washington's death. Both progressive eras were sustained by grassroots movements in Black communities designed to challenge rather than cooperate with southern White authorities.

It is revealing that the post-Washington school campaigns were precipitated mainly by ordinary Black men and women who defied one of his sacred principles: "Cast down your bucket where you are." Washington urged African Americans to remain in the South and

find common ground with White planters and businesspeople. But many African Americans were willing to tolerate only one generation of state-enforced illiteracy. Hence, in 1915 Black southerners en masse picked up their "buckets" and headed north in search of better economic and educational opportunities. Just as the freedmen had used political power to foster universal schooling during the Reconstruction era, Black workers during the post-Washington era used the withdrawal of their labor power as a powerful form of protest against intolerable economic and social conditions. Many Black families remained in the South, however.

What they did in the two decades after his death was monumental. Their defiance of southern White authority, coupled with a grassroots campaign for universal schooling, radically altered educational opportunities for Black schoolchildren. The proportion of southern Black children ages 5 to 14 enrolled in school increased from 36 percent in 1900 to 78 percent by 1935, and the corresponding rate for Whites went from 55 percent in 1900 to 79 percent in 1935. Younger Black children, whose rates of enrollment were significantly lower than those of younger Whites in 1900, had reached parity by 1935. Black high school enrollment increased from 3 percent of the high-school-age Black population in 1910 to 18 percent in 1935, and White high school enrollment increased from 10 to 54 percent. There was far from parity at the secondary level, but the overall improvements in Black elementary and secondary schooling represented significant improvement since the age of Washington. Undoubtedly, Booker T. Washington would have been proud of the educational achievements of his successors, particularly of rural Black people. It was an educational awakening of the same kind as the freedmen's school campaigns he recalled with such pride. It was also a kind that he never witnessed during his career as educational statesman of Black America.[23]

Washington had tried in his own passive style to halt the Democrats' dismantling of the Black public school system. He urged White school reformers, especially northern White philanthropists who worked in the South, to take a strong stand on behalf of state support for Black rural schools. He arranged in 1909 for the publication and dissemination of a pamphlet by Charles Coon, a White county school superintendent in North Carolina, showing that more tax money was paid by Black North Carolinians than was allocated to their schools. Washington was propagandizing against the southern White claim that White taxpayers were paying for Black public schools, especially in Black belt counties. He hoped that such efforts would generate a greater spirit of fairness toward Black public schools.

In several ways Washington sought to expose the gross racial inequality in southern public education. For example, in 1909 he sent the members of the Southern Education Board evidence that in Lowndes County, Alabama, $20 per capita went to White schoolchildren and $0.67 per capita to Black schoolchildren. Lowndes was in Alabama's Black belt, just two counties west of Macon. However, there was virtually nothing that Washington could do through letters and propaganda to slow the decline of Black public education. In earlier times, particularly from 1868 to 1890, Black communities were able to check assaults on their public school

systems through political clout and legal safeguards. Ironically, it was Washington who made the observation in 1902 that "not one of his students had ever broke into jail or Congress." Now, to protect the reform movement he cherished the most—the advancement of education in Black communities—he found himself needing the very political involvement he had once discouraged. Without political clout, Washington could only stand by and observe quietly, as he did in 1909, that the advancement of White education "is being made at the expense of Negro education, that is, the money is actually being taken from the colored people and given to white schools."[24]

Historians have tended to see Washington's accommodationist style of leadership as appropriate to the context of its time, that is, as a pragmatic response to the racial injustices of the late 19th and early 20th centuries. They maintain that given the basic inhumanity of the era, it is hard to see how Washington could have preached a radically different philosophy in his time and place. However, other leaders in the same era did articulate a radically different philosophy, including W. E. B. Du Bois, William Monroe Taylor, Ida B. Wells-Barnett, and John Hope, to name only a few.

What is perplexing and interesting about Washington's era is the manner in which African American leaders of similar social experiences developed such divergent understandings of and solutions to the problem of racial oppression. This had much to do with their different perceptions of social reality and the political meanings they derived from their perceptions. One of the essential qualities of an effective leader is the ability to raise the consciousness of his or her people from the personal to the social. Common men and women experience an oppressive social system in a thousand personal and seemingly disconnected ways. It is a leader's challenge to help the masses see their oppression as flowing from a common social source and help them identify their oppressors. The quality of leadership is determined in large part by the ideological cohesion that leaders provide for their followers, which in turn stems directly from the leaders' perceptions of their social environment. Put another way, Washington, Du Bois, and other leaders held different perceptions of the causes of racial oppression, and those different perceptions led them to put forward different proposals for liberation. The remainder of this chapter will first examine Washington's perceptions of the so-called race problem during his time and then contrast his views with those of W. E. B. Du Bois.

An Ideology of African American Inferiority

Early in his career Washington was forced to examine his perceptions of racial conflict and formulate a coherent explanation of racial inequality in America. As he put it, "One of the first questions that I had to answer for myself after beginning my work at Tuskegee was how I was to deal with public opinion on the race question." For an answer to this question he resorted not to the social perceptions—folklore and slave-community perceptions of race and slavery—implicit in African American traditions or to his day-to-day experiences in an oppressive system of racial subordination but to the precepts and lessons he had learned at Hampton Institute under the tutelage of Samuel Chapman Armstrong, a White Union officer in the Civil War who worked for the Freedmen's Bureau in the South. The hallmarks of Washington's leadership, his conservative social philosophy, his accommodation with White supremacy and racial segregation, and his belief in industrial education and skilled labor as a means to overcome racial and class discrimination were well developed in the 1870s and early 1880s. What Washington learned as a student at Hampton Institute from 1872 to 1875 and as a postgraduate from 1879 to 1881 were perceptions of race development, politics, economics, and education that tended to rationalize historical and contemporary oppression while offering hope in the distant future.[25]

According to historian Louis R. Harlan, Washington found in Armstrong "the great White father for whom he had long been searching." Since Washington knew that his own father was White but was never certain of that man's identity, it is plausible that he longed for this father figure. What is more certain, however, is that Washington was overwhelmed by Armstrong and began to model his conduct and thought on Armstrong's. In his autobiography, *Up from Slavery,* Washington said of Armstrong, "I shall always remember that the first time I went into his presence he made the impression upon me of being a perfect man; I was made to feel that there was something about him that was superhuman." He described Armstrong as "the most perfect specimen of man, physically, mentally and spiritually" that he had ever seen, and he considered the best part of his education to have been the privilege of being permitted to look upon General Armstrong each day. Washington had the opportunity of observing Armstrong closely, for throughout his three years at Hampton he was a janitor in the academic building, close to the general and the other White teachers.[26]

A Liberal Justification for Racial Oppression: Darwinian Evolution

One of the first and more enduring lessons Washington learned from Armstrong was the meaning of race, its significance throughout human history, and its bearing on relationships between European Americans and African Americans. Armstrong sincerely believed that race was the key to understanding morality, industry, thrift, responsibility, ambition, and the overall social worth of human beings. He believed that the human race was appropriately divided into the White and the darker races. The White races were civilized, superior because they had centuries of Christian moral development, hard work, self-government, and material prosperity. The darker races, including Indians, Polynesians (Armstrong was a child of missionaries in Hawaii), and Africans, were weak in Christian morality, lacked industrious habits, and were incapable of self-government and political leadership. As Armstrong put it, "The [American] white race has had three centuries of experience in organizing the forces about him, political, social, and physical. The Negro has had three centuries of experience in general demoralization and behind that, paganism."[27]

Darwin published *On the Origin of Species* in 1859, on the eve of the Civil War, the year of John Dewey's birth and Horace Mann's death. A new era was dawning ideologically and educationally.

This theory of racial evolution was grounded in metaphors derived from Darwin's theory of biological evolution, which swept the European American intellectual world and fed the roots of new liberal ideology. The main purpose of race-evolution theory was to provide a rational explanation of the unequal distribution of wealth and political power among racial groups. The Hampton faculty taught Black students that the subordinate position of their race in the South, even in places where they were the overwhelming majority, was not the result of oppression but of the natural process of moral and cultural evolution. In other words, Black people had only evolved to a cultural stage that was 2,000 years behind that of White people, and their inferior position in society therefore represented the natural order of social evolution. The darker races were likened to children who must crawl before they can walk, must be trained before they can be educated. For it was only after the backward races put away childish things, stilled their dark laughter, and subordinated their emotional nature to rational self-discipline that they would be ready to vote, hold political office, and enjoy the rights and privileges of first-class citizenship.

Thinking Critically about the Issues   #2

Would Charles Darwin the scientist have condoned the philosophy of social Darwinism, which was used to justify social oppression through a theory of racial evolution? How would you research the answer?

Washington learned this lesson well while attending Hampton and internalized it as a lens through which he perceived and interpreted questions of race development, political inequality, and civil rights. As he said in 1900 before the General Conference of the African Methodist Episcopal Church, "My friends, the white man is three thousand years ahead of us, and this fact we might as well face now as well as later, and at one stage of his development, either in Europe or America, he has gone through every stage of development that I now advocate for our race." Instead of regarding the difficulties of his race as the result of arbitrary and unjust oppression, Washington interpreted them as the natural difficulties that almost every race had been compelled to overcome in its upward climb from uncivilized life. He cautioned White people not to overlook the fact "that geographically and physically the semi-barbarous Negro race has been thrown right down in the center of

the highest civilization that the world knows anything about." The Black race lagged behind the White race not because of slavery and racism but because a semibarbarous race naturally could not keep pace with a highly civilized race.

While Washington did not condone the enslavement of African people, he maintained constantly that during slavery African Americans' exposure to a highly civilized race gave them advantages over other uncivilized races. As he put it,

> The Indian refused to submit to bondage and to learn the white man's ways. The result is that the greater portion of the American Indians have disappeared, the greater portion of those who remain are not civilized. The Negro, wiser and more enduring than the Indian, patiently endured slavery; and contact with the white man has given him a civilization vastly superior to that of the Indian.[28]

Although this viewpoint did not condone slavery, it portrayed it as a school where the allegedly uncivilized Africans received a jump start on the road to civilized life by imitating the best they found in White culture. "The Indian and the Negro met on the American continent for the first time at Jamestown, in 1619," said Washington. "Both were in the darkest barbarism." Two hundred fifty years later the "Negro race" had learned "to wear clothes, to live in a home, to work with a high degree of regularity and system, and a few had learned to work with a high degree of skill." Not only this, the African race had learned a fair knowledge of American culture "and changed from a pagan into a Christian race." Thus, in Washington's mind slavery was a blessing in disguise since it gave "pagan" Africans the opportunity to have contact with highly civilized Europeans. This conception of history and progress as racial evolution led Washington to conclude that racial inequality was merely the natural order of evolutionary laws, which in turn would lead to equality as the darker, semibarbarous races became more civilized.[29]

Avoiding the Issue of Political Power

Directly and closely related to this perception of racial evolution was the question of whether the freedmen should vote and pursue political office, since such rights and privileges were reserved for the fully civilized. In Armstrong's view, the "colored people" should "let politics severely alone." African American voters, he maintained, were "dangerous to the country in proportion to their numbers." His desire to disfranchise the freedmen followed logically from his premise that the freedmen and women were not civilized and therefore incapable of self-government. Washington also internalized this view of Black participation in the body politic. Although he was opposed to depriving Black men of the legal right of franchise, like Armstrong he advised that it was a mistake for them to enter actively into politics. Washington went beyond urging Black people not to vote or run for political office; he also counseled them not to speak out against racial injustice. Race prejudice, he believed, was something to be lived through, not talked down.

In 1888, one of Tuskegee's employees, George M. Lovejoy, wrote a letter to a Mississippi Black newspaper protesting the effort of a White mob in Tuskegee to take a Black man from the county jail. The local White newspaper, the Tuskegee *News,* asked if it was the purpose of Tuskegee Institute to breed hatred of the White race and warned Lovejoy to leave town. Washington sent a card to the Tuskegee *News* bearing this message: "It has always been and is now the policy of the Normal School to remain free from politics and the discussion of race questions that tend to stir up strife between the races, and whenever this policy is violated it is done without the approbation of those in charge of the school." Thus, Washington publicly advised the general Black population to abstain from voting, running for political office, or speaking out against racial injustice.

This directive, however, was not a blanket condemnation of political activity by all African Americans. The White registrars in his Alabama county gave him a special invitation to come in and awarded him a lifetime voting certificate, which he framed and hung in his home. Washington voted and urged a few selected African Americans to vote, but both publicly and privately he favored restrictions that would prevent the propertyless and illiterate of both races from voting.[30]

During Washington's career as head of Tuskegee Institute, Macon County's Black population increased from 74 percent of the county's population in 1880 to 85 percent in 1910. The position he took encouraged the disfranchisement of the masses of Black voters. Meanwhile, the state constitution protected the White vote with various loopholes. The result was that the small White minority maintained exclusive control of the county's political system during Washington's era, a control that continued until after the passage of the Voting Rights Act of 1965. Washington's major complaint was that the Whites in power did not apply the voting restrictions equally to both races. Nevertheless, as state after state placed property and educational restrictions

on voting, he refused to take a public stand against ratification of the undemocratic constitutions. He sincerely believed in the disfranchisement of the propertyless, the illiterate, and "backward" races and therefore found it difficult to fight publicly against restrictions on popular voting even when such restrictions were more racially qualified than he preferred. Indeed, to Washington, the worsening position of African Americans since emancipation seemed to result from the reaction of White voters against Black participation in the body politic. He did not object to educational or property tests because he believed that citizenship rights were to be secured by education, property, and character, not by constitutional guarantees. Black people, he insisted, needed moral training, education, and property before they would be ready to vote and hold political office.[31]

A Liberal Faith: Social Progress through the Marketplace

The most critical dimension of Washington's perceptions of his social environment was his belief that hard labor and the accumulation of property were the keys to resolving all social problems. Although this component of his social perceptions diverged from reality to a breathtaking degree, in order to understand it, it is necessary to see how Washington viewed his world and posed solutions based on those perceptions. The gospel of thrift, industry, and property ownership had been instilled in Washington during his student years at Hampton Institute. Armstrong taught that southern White opposition to Black participation in politics did not exist in the arenas of education and economics. He insisted that "there was no power and little disposition on the part of leading white conservatives to prevent the colored people from acquiring wealth and education." He argued further that "competition in the North" held back skilled African American workers "more than prejudice at the South." Southern Black mechanics, according to Armstrong, had "a fair field." He was very careful to point out that it was only in the South that Black people had practically a fair field in the commercial world and the world of skilled labor.[32]

Washington, like Armstrong, made sharp distinctions between what did and could happen in the economic world and what did and could happen in the social and political worlds. "Man may discriminate," said Washington, "but the economic laws of trade and commerce cannot discriminate." He thought that economic life and all individuals's economic actions were controlled by natural laws, which individuals defied at their peril. These perfect laws disallowed anything so irrational as race prejudice. "When an individual produces what the world wants," Washington believed, "the world does not stop long to inquire what is the color of the skin of the producer." This perception distorted the fact that in reality the South was very conscious of skin color, especially in the realm of economics. The region had just emerged from two and a half centuries of slavery, a system of economic exploitation based exclusively on race. Washington saw slavery differently and interpreted it in a manner consistent with his perception of the natural laws of economics. In his view,

> Under God, as bad as slavery was, it prepared the way for the solving of this [race] problem by this [business] method. The two hundred and fifty years of slavery taught the Southern white man to do business with the Negro. If a Southern white man wanted a house built he consulted a Negro mechanic about the building of that house; if he wanted a suit of clothes made, he consulted a Negro tailor. And, thus, in a limited sense, every large plantation in the South during slavery was, in measure, an industrial school.[33]

Since emancipation, Washington perceived, "The Negro in the South has not only found a practically free field in the commercial world, but in the world of skilled labor." He often told Black southerners that "when one comes to business pure and simple, stripped of all ideas of sentiment, the Negro is given almost as good an opportunity to rise as is given to the white man." To Washington it followed that the South was a place where African Americans had equal opportunity to succeed in the labor market and the commercial world. "Whenever the Negro has lost ground industrially in the South," said Washington in 1898, "it is not because there is prejudice against him as a skilled laborer on the part of the Native Southern white man, for the Southern white man generally prefers to do business with the Negro as a mechanic rather than with a white one."[34]

What was peculiar about this article of faith was Washington's belief that racially neutral laws of labor and commerce existed in the South, the land of slavery and peasantry, but not in the North, the land of capitalism and free labor. In almost every speech or essay in which he extolled equal economic opportunity for Black southerners, he was quick to point out that racial prejudice was a key barrier to Black economic progress in the North. The following story, which he told to a

Booker T. Washington believed in the racial neutrality of the marketplace and felt that if African Americans achieved economic success, political and social gains would automatically follow.

Brooklyn, New York, audience in 1896, is typical of Washington's perception of economic opportunities for Black people in the North:

> Not long ago a mother, a black mother, who lived in one of your Northern states, had heard it whispered around in her community for years that the Negro was lazy, shiftless, and would not work. So when her boy grew to sufficient size, at considerable expense and great self-sacrifice, she had her boy thoroughly taught the machinist's trade. A job was secured in a neighboring shop. . . . What happened? . . . Every one of the twenty white men threw down his tools and deliberately walked out, swearing that he would not give a black man an opportunity to earn an honest living. Another shop was tried, with the same results, and still another and the same.[35]

In such instances Washington did not ignore the fact that racism was present in the labor markets and contradicted his notion that the natural laws of labor and commerce precluded race prejudice. "Hundreds of Negroes in the North become criminals who would become strong and useful men if they were not discriminated against as bread winners," Washington observed in 1900. But this was the North; he saw the South as the exact opposite. Throughout his career he held to the belief that race prejudice and discrimination did not influence occupational and commercial opportunities in the South.[36]

Although this perception of economic reality had virtually no basis in fact, Washington held to it unswervingly, in part because it was critical to his proposals for solving the problem of racial oppression. "There is almost no prejudice against the Negro in the South in matters of business, so far as the native whites are concerned, and here is the entering wedge for the solution of the race problem," said Washington in 1898. Economic development and its foundation, industrial education, were viewed by Washington as the entering wedge for solving the race problem because he believed strongly that material prosperity was the real basis of civil and political equality. "In proportion as the ignorant secure education, property and character," he said in 1898, "they will be given the right of citizenship." This social perception and its inherent resolution shifted the question of citizenship from rights guaranteed by federal and state constitutional law to a reward granted for material success.

Washington argued that when Black southerners demonstrated the virtues of good businesspeople by getting property, good jobs, nice houses, and bank accounts, White southerners would give Black people the ballot and other perquisites of full citizenship without a qualm. Consequently, he did not believe in political means toward liberation and equality, thinking that political action was at best a waste of time and at worst the cause of White backlash. "We have spent time and money in political conventions, making idle political speeches, that could have been better spent in becoming leading real estate dealers and leading carpenters and truck gardeners, and thus have laid an imperial foundation on which we could have stood and demanded our rights," he proclaimed in 1898. He said that it was right that all the privileges guaranteed to Blacks by the U.S. Constitution be sacredly guarded. But the "mere fiat of law," he cautioned, "could not make a dependent man an independent man" or "make one race respect another." "One race respects another in proportion as it contributes to the markets of the world," he contended. Washington alleged that "almost without exception, whether in the North or in the South, wherever I have seen a Negro who was succeeding in business, who was a taxpayer, a man who possessed intelligence and high moral character, that man was treated with respect by the people of both races." Hence, respect and first-class

citizenship would come to Blacks in proportion to their accumulation of property, education, and good jobs. In reality, from Reconstruction to 1915, Black people were acquiring significantly more property and education as they were being stripped of basic civil and political rights. As Washington perceived his social world, he stood reality on its head, believing that the accumulation of property and education would lead to respect and first-class citizenship precisely at the moment when the opposite was unfolding.[37]

The Washington Solution

Perhaps because he accommodated so easily to the southern system of racial inequality, Washington romanticized the region's economic life as providing a firm foundation for emancipation from racial oppression. Acquiescence in racial segregation was one of the prices he believed he had to pay for peace with White southerners. He also counseled Black people to stay away from politics and not to agitate for civil rights. Another concession was a rather sweeping abandonment of the First Amendment guarantee of free speech. It was his policy to refrain from discussions of controversial race-relations questions, and he forbade his faculty and students from speaking out against racial injustice. In his imagined world of southern economics no law could push individuals forward if they were worthless and no law could hold them back if they were worthy. Thus his solutions for solving the race problem—industrial education and economic development—flowed logically from his perception of the natural laws of southern economic life.[38]

In theory, Washington's proposal for Black progress worked like this: industrial education would provide the skills for business and occupational success, and this success would earn civil and political rights. This approach to solving the "race problem" called for the education of the masses in skilled occupations and business leadership. But Washington's theory about the natural laws of commerce and trade and equal opportunities for Black people to succeed therein was not borne out by day-to-day practices. Indeed, he often received information that described a real world of economic racism, the exact opposite of the racially neutral world of trade and commerce he imagined. In 1904, for example, Black businesspeople who exemplified Washington's ideal of success were molested in West Point, Mississippi. Isaiah T. Montgomery, entrepreneur and founder of the town of Mound Bayou, Mississippi, wrote him:

Historical Context

Schooling and African Americans

1800–1840

1806   New York City provides schools for Black children for the first time

1807   Bell School, the first school for Black children in Washington, DC, is established by freedmen George Bell, Nicholas Franklin, and Moses Liverpool

1818   Philadelphia free Blacks establish Pennsylvania Augustine Society "for the education of people of colour"; schools for Blacks receive public aid in Philadelphia

1823   Mississippi enacts laws that prohibit teaching reading and writing to Blacks and meetings of more than five slaves or free Blacks

1824   American teacher and church worker Sophia B. Packard (1824–1891) establishes a Negro college in Georgia

1827   About 140 antislavery groups exist in United States

1831   Slave Nat Turner leads rebellion against slavery

1832   Free Blacks petition the Pennsylvania state legislature to admit their children to public school; the petition is unsuccessful

1833   American educator Prudence Crandell defies White townspeople in Connecticut by accepting a Black girl into her school

1833   Oberlin College (Ohio), the first coeducational college, is integrated from the outset and serves as a leader in the abolitionist cause

1834   First Black-funded school for Blacks in Cincinnati, Ohio, opens

1837   Angelina and Sarah Grimke found the National Female Anti-Slavery Society, one of the few such societies to include women of color from the start

1837   Institute for Colored Youth, the first Black coeducational classical high school, opens in Philadelphia

1838   Ohio law prohibits the education of Black children at the expense of the state

1839   Benjamin Roberts, a Black printer, sues the Boston School Committee to gain admission to a common school for his daughter

1840–1880

1852   Antislavery novel *Uncle Tom's Cabin* is written by Harriet Beecher Stowe

1857   In Dred Scott case, U.S. Supreme Court rules slavery is legal in U.S. territories

1859   Harper's Ferry raid led by abolitionist John Brown in West Virginia is unsuccessful in attempt to start a slave uprising

1861   Civil War begins

1863   American abolitionist and "conductor" on the Underground Railroad Harriet Tubman leads a raid that frees 750 slaves

1863   Lincoln issues Emancipation Proclamation

1864   Lincoln signs a bill mandating the creation of public schools for Blacks in Washington, DC

1865   Thirteenth Amendment to U.S. Constitution abolishes slavery

1865–1867   Institutions of higher learning for African Americans are established (now known as historically Black colleges and universities, like Howard and Fisk)

1867   Peabody Fund is established to provide endowments, scholarships, and teacher and industrial education for newly freed slaves across the nation

1868   Congress passes Fourteenth Amendment, which grants Blacks full citizenship and equal civil rights; it is later ratified

1868   Hampton Institute is opened by ex-Union officer Samuel Chapman Armstrong in Hampton, Virginia

1877   End of Reconstruction and restoration of conservative state governments in the South hinder public education of African Americans

1880–1920

1881   Tuskegee Institute is founded by Booker T. Washington

1895   W. E. B. Du Bois receives the first doctoral degree awarded to a Black from Harvard University

1896   *Plessy* v. *Ferguson,* Supreme Court decision used to support constitutionality of separate schools for Whites and Blacks

1902   John D. Rockefeller establishes General Education Board, a powerful philanthropic foundation

1903   Du Bois's *The Souls of Black Folk,* a collection of essays, is published

1909   Du Bois and others, including Whites, meet and advocate a civil rights organization to combat growing violence against Black Americans; later the National Association for the Advancement of Colored People (1910)

1915   Carter G. Woodson founds the Association for the Study of Negro Life and History; much of its early support comes from women

Thinking Analytically about the Timeline

What evidence can you identify to support or refute the following interpretation of the timeline? The 19th- and early-20th-century history of African American schooling is not a story of steady progress, but one of partial progress punctuated by significant legal and educational setbacks of enduring influence.

Thomas Harvey runs a neat little Grocery, he kept a Buggy and frequently rode to his place of business, he was warned to sell his buggy and walk. Mr. Chandler keeps a Grocery, he was ordered to leave, but was finally allowed to remain on good behavior. Mr. Meacham ran a business and had a Pool Table in connection therewith, he was ordered to close up and don overalls for manual labor. Mr. Cook conducted a hack business between the Depots and about town, using two vehicles, he was notified that he would be allowed to run only one and was ordered to sell the other.

Another West Point businessman, a Black printer named Buchanan, had a piano in his home and allowed his daughter, who was his cashier and bookkeeper, to ride the family buggy to and from work until "a mass meeting of whites decided that the mode of living practiced by the Buchanan family had a bad effect on the cooks and washer women, who aspired to do likewise, and became less disposed to work for the whites." A White mob forced the family to flee without allowing them even to pack. So much for the economic panacea for solving the race problem. Economic reality was a far cry from the gospel of thrift, industry, and wealth preached in Washington's speeches and essays. The racist barriers against Black success in business stood tall and firm, and in the world of work the White South relegated the vast majority of Black people to the most disagreeable and poorest paid occupations.[39]

Underneath it all Washington, though preaching a gospel of material prosperity, seemed to accommodate to economic repression as he did to political and civil repression. Specifically, Tuskegee Institute did not attempt to supply the South with graduates trained in skilled trades or business leadership and therefore offered no direct competition to White dominance in those areas. Stories about Tuskegee were so filled with rhetoric about industrial education that both contemporary observers and later historians mistakenly assumed that trade, technical, and commercial training formed the essence of the institute's curriculum. In fact, Tuskegee placed little emphasis on trade and commercial training. In 1903 Daniel C. Smith, Tuskegee's auditor, made a study of the school's industrial training program. According to Smith, of 1,550 students, "there were only a dozen students in the school capable of doing a fair job as joiners. There were only fifteen boys who could lay brick." "Meanwhile," Smith continued, "the number of students who are doing unskilled drudgery work is increasing, and the number who receive no training through the use of tools is getting to be very large." The few students who did learn skilled trades seemed to learn them on the job.

There were insufficient classroom and shop facilities to teach skilled trades.

The situation was similar with respect to the teaching of commercial or business subjects. In 1906, while assessing Tuskegee's offerings in the teaching of business and commercial subjects, Robert E. Park discovered that "there is a large amount of business conducted by the school, but there is no school of business here." There were "a large number of stenographers employed on the ground but stenography and typewriting are not taught here." Three papers and a number of pamphlets were published at Tuskegee, but printing was not taught there. There was not even a formal course in bookkeeping.

In reality, Tuskegee was neither a trade school nor a business school. It was a normal school, and its chief aim was to train teachers. Its philosophical commitment to industrial education translated in practice into a routine of hard unskilled and semiskilled labor that was designed to teach prospective teachers the social–psychological value of hard work. The teachers in turn were expected to translate the Tuskegee work ethic to the millions of African American schoolchildren in the South. In a word, Tuskegee's industrial education was the teaching of the work ethic, not the teaching of trade and business skills. This constituted an accommodation to the South's economic system based on racial inequality, not a foundation from which to achieve economic independence and civil rights.[40]

Thinking Critically about the Issues   #3
The authors claim, "In reality, Tuskegee . . . was a normal school," lies at the heart of the authors' critique of Washington. But what's so bad about Tuskegee being a normal school?

Before leaving this critical interpretation of Booker T. Washington, it is important to recognize that W. E. B. Du Bois, one of Washington's strongest critics, wrote, "By 1905 . . . I had much admiration for Mr. Washington and Tuskegee," and, on another occasion, "One hesitates, therefore, to criticize a life which, beginning with so little has done so much" (see the Primary Source Reading). Like Du Bois, we can examine Washington's shortcomings while giving credit where it is due. Precious few citizens in the history of the United States have founded universities of the stature of Tuskegee, an institution that would later become a true university and educate generations of leaders in all walks of our national life. Such an accomplishment cannot be ignored. However, Du Bois and other Black leaders felt compelled to challenge Washington's social, political, and educational perspectives—and to challenge the way in which he went about building and protecting Tuskegee. Developing an appreciation of Washington's accomplishments while recognizing the source of Du Bois's criticisms is a challenge to anyone who wishes to understand the history of education in the United States.

William Edward Burghardt Du Bois

Although Booker T. Washington was clearly the most prominent Black leader in the United States from 1895 until his death in 1915, his vocational-education approach to the social and economic problems of Black people did not appeal to all African Americans. By 1903, he was being criticized publicly by William E. B. Du Bois, an influential leader in his own right.

"Among Negro Americans," writes historian John Hope Franklin, "there could hardly be a greater contrast than the careers of Booker T. Washington and W. E. B. Du Bois" (pronounced by Du Bois himself to rhyme with "toys").[41] Unlike Washington, who had been born into Virginia slavery, Du Bois was born in 1868 in Great Barrington, Massachusetts, where he recalled more ethnic discrimination against the Irish than against the 25 to 50 Black inhabitants among the population of some 5,000 people.[42] After excelling in school, Du Bois traveled south to attend Fisk University in Nashville, one of the historically Black institutions founded during Reconstruction. At Fisk, Du Bois studied a traditional liberal arts curriculum that emphasized the classics. He read Homer, Livy, and Sophocles but also studied the sciences, German, and philosophy. After graduating with a B.A., Du Bois entered Harvard University, but because he had graduated from a Black institution, he had to enroll as a junior. Majoring in philosophy, Du Bois graduated cum laude and then traveled to Berlin, where he pursued graduate study for two years. After returning to the United States, Du Bois received a Ph.D. degree at Harvard, and his dissertation on the African slave trade was later published as the first volume of the Harvard Historical Series.

In 1897 Du Bois accepted a faculty position at Atlanta University, where he and his graduate students began authoring what would become a series of 18 volumes

Unlike Booker T. Washington, who believed social and political success would follow naturally from economic success, W. E. B. Du Bois believed that economic and social gains would occur only as a result of political gains.

on African American life. He was at this time primarily a scholar and had little interest in political activism. "By 1905," he wrote, "I was still a teacher at Atlanta University and was in my imagination a scientist, and neither a leader nor an agitator; I had much admiration for Mr. Washington and Tuskegee."[43] Despite that admiration, Du Bois was also critical of Washington. In his early Atlanta years Du Bois came to see that when he did disagree with the Black leader's beliefs, such disagreements were considered to be an attack on Washington and were interpreted by Washington's followers as hostile to Black people in general. This stifling of criticism, perhaps more than any other fact of Washington's organization, aroused Du Bois's ire. As Du Bois records in his *Autobiography,* the "Tuskegee machine" was able to use White financial backing to buy up Black-owned newspapers that criticized Washington's leadership. In 1903, in *The Souls of Black Folk,* Du Bois took Washington to task for stifling the "earnest criticism" that Du Bois believed was the "soul of democracy."[44]

Thinking Critically about the Issues   #4

Imagine that you are a student about to graduate from Tuskegee Institute in 1900. Would you urge a friend to go to Tuskegee or to the liberal arts–oriented Fisk University? Why? What reasons would you give?

A second major problem for Du Bois was the unabated oppression of Black southerners. From his college days at Fisk until 1900, over 2,000 African Americans had been lynched. Black citizens were taken out of their homes by White gangs and executed in front of their families. Others were taken out of jails and hanged without trial. Washington preferred not to talk about such racist violence and in fact avoided discussing discrimination and prejudice in public whenever possible. Du Bois, however, like a number of other Black leaders in the South, soon came to believe that racist Whites were only too happy to see the energies of the only powerful Black leader in the nation directed toward vocational education.

As a direct result of a 1908 racially motivated street riot in Springfield, Illinois, which involved the lynching of two Black men, the National Negro Committee was formed in New York. Du Bois was one of the featured speakers at the inaugural meeting, and he chaired the committee that nominated its first governing body. Two years later, the committee became the National Association for the Advancement of Colored People (NAACP), and Du Bois was invited to be its director of publications and research. At the NAACP he founded and edited *The Crisis,* a magazine to educate Black and White people alike to the realities of racism. The magazine, which published such information as running totals of racist lynchings, reached a remarkable circulation of 100,000 by 1918. Not surprisingly, the Tuskegee machine opposed the formation of the NAACP. Also not surprisingly, Du Bois used the pages of *The Crisis* to criticize Washington. "To discuss the Negro question in 1910 was to discuss Booker T. Washington," Du Bois later wrote in his autobiography.[45] For example, after Washington had presented a series of speeches in England "along his usual conciliatory lines," Du Bois wrote the following to a British and European audience:

> Mr. Washington . . . is a distinguished American and has a perfect right to his opinions. But we are compelled to point out that Mr. Washington's large financial responsibilities have made him dependent on the rich charitable public and that, for this reason, he has for years been compelled to tell, not the whole truth, but that part of it which certain powerful interests in America wish to appear as the whole truth.

The "whole truth," for Du Bois, included attention to the institutionalization of racism and racist oppression in the United States: not just in the South but in the North as well. Du Bois believed that Washington's failure to confront and emphasize that racism—institutionalized

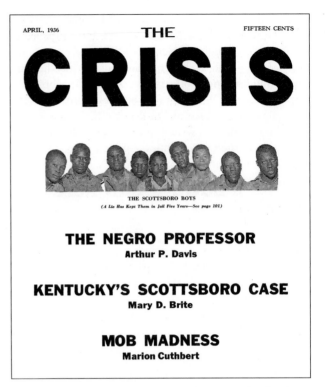

Du Bois edited *The Crisis* for the National Association for the Advancement of Colored People, in which he addressed issues of race and racism for a wide audience.

in the nation's laws, its educational system, political life, and economic practices—was tacit acceptance of the oppression of African Americans. Washington's route to assimilation of African Americans into mainstream American life was through acquiescence, charged Du Bois, who argued that assimilation should be obtained through self-assertion instead. Where Washington advocated that Black people should make the best of a bad situation by acquiring a vocational education and earning a living, Du Bois called for organized public protest, legal action against racist institutions, and higher education for Blacks. It was a source of great pain to Du Bois that Washington's approach to assimilation was as influential as it was, while his own emphasis on civil rights, political rights, and higher education was not implemented until the civil rights movement of the 1950s and 1960s. Du Bois lived until 1963, long enough to see some of his ideas influence civil rights legislation and higher education for African Americans. In fact, when news of Du Bois's death reached the leadership of a massive civil rights march on Washington, DC, on August 28, 1963, NAACP executive secretary Roy Wilkins told the assembled throng, "It is incontrovertible that at the dawn of the twentieth century, his was the voice calling you to gather here today in this cause."[46] It is that voice that we let speak for itself in the chapter-end Primary Source Reading from *Souls of Black Folk,* 1903.

Perhaps the most interesting summary of the basic differences between Booker T. Washington and W. E. B. Du Bois is contained in the following poem by Dudley Randall. The student who can readily provide an interpretation of each of its stanzas is likely to have a good grasp of several major issues in this chapter.

Booker T. and W. E. B.

by Dudley Randall[47]

"It seems to me," said Booker T.,
"It shows a mighty lot of cheek
To study chemistry and Greek
When Mister Charlie needs a hand
To hoe the cotton on his land,
And when Miss Ann looks for a cook,
Why stick your nose inside a book?"

"I don't agree," said W. E. B.
"If I should have the drive to seek
Knowledge of chemistry or Greek,
I'll do it. Charles and Miss can look
Another place for hand or cook.
Some men rejoice in skill of hand,
And some in cultivating land,
But there are others who maintain
The right to cultivate the brain."

"It seems to me," said Booker T.,
"That all you folks have missed the boat
Who shout about the right to vote,
And spend vain days and sleepless nights
In uproar over civil rights.
Just keep your mouths shut, do not grouse,
But work, and save, and buy a house."

"I don't agree," said W. E. B.,
"For what can property avail
If dignity and justice fail?
Unless you help to make the laws,
They'll steal your house with trumped-up clause.
A rope's as tight, a fire as hot,
No matter how much cash you've got.
Speak soft, and try your little plan,
But as for me, I'll be a man."

"It seems to me," said Booker T.—
"I don't agree,"
said W. E. B.

BUILDING A PHILOSOPHY OF EDUCATION

Entering the 20th century, not only the South but the entire United States was undergoing basic changes in its political economy and dominant ideology. Not surprisingly, the conflict of educational ideas between Booker T. Washington and W. E. B. Du Bois reflected similar conflicts among educational thinkers throughout the country. Nationally prominent St. Louis educator William Torrey Harris spoke for many other White educators when he observed that Washington's vocational approach to the education of Black people was of "so universal a character that it applies to the downtrodden of all races, without reference to color."

As Chapter 4 will also illustrate, educating "the downtrodden" became a primary concern for educators almost exactly a hundred years ago. If Booker T. Washington's approach was controversial for African Americans in the South, it was to become just as controversial for the education of poor and immigrant children throughout the nation. The differences between Washington and Du Bois can be viewed in terms of several basic controversies regarding the education of American youth in general—Black or brown or White, Italian or Swede, male or female, rich or poor. Five of these issues that would remain important throughout the revolution in American schooling in the early 20th century, remain important today.

1. *Education for social stability:* If schools take as one of their primary missions the education of children for a stable society, what becomes of developing in children the intellectual and critical capacities necessary for a free society? In general, do education for social stability and education for freedom mean the same thing?

2. *Education for employable skills:* If schooling is intended primarily to develop employable skills among students, might this not result in most students being educated at a level well below their highest intellectual capacities, which include the ability to think analytically and critically in the various disciplines of the humanities, social sciences, mathematics, and sciences? Are there times when education for employable skills tends to conflict with education for intellectual development?

3. *Schooling for social reform:* If schools are assigned the task of responding to deep social problems such as racial discrimination, civil rights inequities, and conflicts between labor and management, might this not result in failure to address these and other social problems in more direct and more effective ways—such as legislation for basic changes in civil rights or in the workplace? In general, does schooling for social reform take attention away from the more fundamental and achievable educational goal of education for individual human development?

4. *Education for group differences:* If differences among people (like skin color, gender, or class) are considered so important that different kinds of education should be provided for children from these different groups, might this not result in the most value—and valued—kinds of education being reserved largely for those who are already most privileged? In general, which is better—education for group differences or education for what people have in common?

5. *Education for whose interests?* If people in positions of economic power decide that schools should serve the interests of industry and the economic order, might this not fail to serve the interests of "those most nearly touched" by schooling—the students themselves? In general, are there dangers in a system in which the economically and politically powerful determine what education will best serve the interests of the majority of young people?

While each of these issues represents an area of disagreement between B. T. Washington and W. E. B. Du Bois, each also represents a problem for educational leaders and classroom teachers today. In the end, as we saw in John Dewey's article "Education and Social Change," schools serve certain roles for society, and that's why people pay taxes to support them (see the Primary Source Reading in Chapter 4). Citizens believe there are social goals being served, and these goals are often debated: employable skills or a liberal education for every child and youth? Should schools seek to enhance industrial competition with other nations or should they focus on each child as an end in himself or herself? Dewey also pointed out that when schools serve the interests of some parts of society, they may necessarily fail to serve others. Thus it might be said that teachers may have to decide whose interests they will serve first, and they may have to be able to articulate and defend those choices. Does your own philosophy of education make clear whose interests you intend your teaching to serve? How might that be communicated most clearly?

Thinking Critically about the Issues   #6

Some students familiar with Du Bois's criticism of Washington have defended Washington's approach as a "practical" solution that sought to accomplish what could be done for Black people under the conditions of that particular place and time. Yet Du Bois believed that Washington fundamentally misinterpreted those conditions and that given the political–economic and ideological realities of the period, Washington's solution was truly impractical as a route to Black advancement. Which leader had the stronger position, in your view, and why?

An African American Teacher's Reflection on Chapter 6

Chapter 6 on African American education in the United States causes me to reflect on how my students value education—and why. Teaching in a challenging school on the west side of Chicago, I constantly fought "learned helplessness." My students seemed to be placing themselves in a lose–lose situation by not doing their work and not even trying. As a teacher working with students whom some might call lazy and unmotivated, I began to see how important it is to develop a keen sense of discernment, to resist falling for the stereotypical view that blames these kids for their own failure.

As educators, we must take into account the history of the educational experience of African American people. Teachers must be more than just familiar with the historic background; they must understand the history of the triadic relationship of political economy, ideology, and schooling from both the White and Black perspectives. These understandings link directly to the subtle discernment needed in the classroom.

White teachers and Black teachers alike often arrive at a school like mine with the "baggage" of low expectations of their students. If they come with high expectations, they often quickly lower them to what they say is a "realistic" level. To change perspectives and deepen knowledge to improve instruction, teachers must have an unusually strong understanding of what's going on with the students.

For example, young Mr. B is a handsome, witty African American sophomore in my math class who does not take homework seriously, rarely studies, and is often talkative. Yet, he is a well-mannered and likable young man. The key factor that Mr. B never seemed to learn through my course was valuing learning and something we typically call a "work ethic." I have no doubt he could have worked consistently at an A level. Yet, devaluing the educative process resulted in consistent grades of C.

Here is precisely where understanding the historical background can affect instructing and learning. I could have easily labeled Mr. B as lazy and unconcerned with schooling. Actually, that is part of his personal challenge and he will have to learn to take responsibility for his behavior or suffer the consequences. The question for me as his teacher is, "What do I have to do to help him learn what he needs to learn if he is to succeed amidst the realities of a society with few options for uneducated people in general and uneducated Black people in particular?" To this end, the historical educational experiences of African Americans through slavery, reconstruction, Jim Crow, desegregation during the sixties, and present-day desegregation and choice schools offer a perspective worth considering.

These periods have all included challenges for African Americans where oppressive forces were predominant over the reforms and "equitable" policies being made for all children. Schooling has not had the same history as a route to success in the Black community, particularly for low-income Blacks, as it has in other communities; it has not been established as a trustworthy route to a better life. In the Black community, it is well known that you can "try hard" and still not get ahead. Why try hard, under those conditions?

This interpretation may be debatable, but it helps me see Mr. B as something other—something more—than lazy or unmotivated. The bottom line is we must be mindful of the way we make sense of our students, because we will teach them that way. I'm not sure that schools have changed very much since that time, although the world around us has changed dramatically. While our process of schooling would look familiar to time-travelers from the progressive era, our postindustrial, digital society would not.

—Clay Braggs, high school mathematics teacher

Primary Source Reading

Following is the full text of W. E. B. Du Bois's essay "Of Mr. Booker T. Washington and Others." In his essay, Du Bois criticizes Booker T. Washington's failure to challenge the racist ideology and social structure that were responsible for the oppression of Blacks in the United States. Students should read the selection carefully and critically, keeping in mind the historical context of the essay.

Primary Source Reading

Of Mr. Booker T. Washington and Others

W. E. B. Du Bois

> From birth till death enslaved; in word, in deed, unmanned!
>
> . . .
>
> Hereditary bondsmen! Know ye not
> Who would be free themselves must strike the blow?
>
> *Byron*

Easily the most striking thing in the history of the American Negro since 1876 is the ascendancy of Booker T. Washington. It began at the time when war memories and ideals were rapidly passing; a day of astonishing commercial development was dawning; a sense of doubt and hesitation overtook the freedmen's sons,—then it was that his leading began. Mr. Washington came, with a single definite programme, at the psychological moment when the nation was a little ashamed of having bestowed so much sentiment on Negroes, and was concentrating its energies on Dollars. His programme of industrial education, conciliation of the South, and submission and silence as to civil and political rights, was not wholly original; the Free Negroes from 1830 up to war-time had striven to build industrial schools, and the American Missionary Association had from the first taught various trades; and Price and others had sought a way of honorable alliance with the best of the Southerners. But Mr. Washington first indissolubly linked

Source: From *The Souls of Black Folk,* reprinted in John Hope Franklin, ed., *Three Negro Classics* (New York: Avon Books, 1965), 242–52.

these things; he put enthusiasm, unlimited energy, and perfect faith into this programme, and changed it from a by-path into a veritable Way of Life. And the tale of the methods by which he did this is a fascinating study of human life.

It startled the nation to hear a Negro advocating such a programme after many decades of bitter complaint; it startled and won the applause of the South, it interested and won the admiration of the North; and after a confused murmur of protest, it silenced if it did not convert the Negroes themselves.

To gain the sympathy and cooperation of the various elements comprising the white South was Mr. Washington's first task; and this, at the time Tuskegee was founded, seemed, for a black man, well-nigh impossible. And yet ten years later it was done in the word[s] spoken at Atlanta. "In all things purely social we can be as separate as the five fingers, and yet one as the hand in all things essential to mutual progress." This "Atlanta Compromise" is by all odds the most notable thing in Mr. Washington's career. The South interpreted it in different ways: the radicals received it as a complete surrender of the demand for civil and political equality; the conservatives, as a generously conceived working basis for mutual understanding. So both approved it, and today its author is certainly the most distinguished Southerner since Jefferson Davis, and the one with the largest personal following.

Next to the achievement comes Mr. Washington's work in gaining place and consideration in the North. Others less shrewd and tactful had formerly essayed to sit on these two stools and had fallen between them; but as Mr. Washington knew the heart of the South from birth and training, so by singular insight he intuitively grasped the spirit of the age which was dominating the North. And so thoroughly did he learn the speech and thought of triumphant commercialism, and the ideals of material prosperity, that the picture of a lone black boy poring over a French grammar amid the weeds and dirt of a neglected home soon seemed to him the acme of absurdities. One wonders what Socrates and St. Francis of Assisi would say to this.

And yet this very singleness of vision and thorough oneness with his age is a mark of the successful man. It is as though Nature must needs make men narrow in order to give them force. So Mr. Washington's cult has gained unquestioning followers, his work has wonderfully prospered, his friends are legion, and his enemies are confounded. Today he stands as the one recognized spokesman of his ten million fellows, and one of the most notable figures in a nation of seventy millions. One hesitates, therefore, to criticize a life which, beginning with so little has done so much. And yet the time is come when one may speak in all sincerity and utter courtesy of the mistakes and shortcomings of Mr. Washington's career, as well as of his triumphs, without being thought captious or envious, and without forgetting that it is easier to do ill than well in the world.

The criticism that has hitherto met Mr. Washington has not always been of this broad character. In the South especially has he had to walk warily to avoid the harshest judgements,—and naturally so, for he is dealing with the one subject of deepest sensitiveness to that section. Twice—once when at the Chicago celebration of the Spanish-American war, he alluded to the color-prejudice that is "eating away the vitals of the South," and once when he dined with President Roosevelt—has the resulting southern criticism been violent enough to threaten his popularity. In the North the feeling has several times forced itself into words, that Mr. Washington's counsels of submission overlooked certain elements of true manhood, and that his education program was unnecessarily narrow. Usually, however, such criticism has not found open expression, although, too, the spiritual sons of the Abolitionists have not been prepared to acknowledge that the schools founded before Tuskegee, by men of broad ideals and self-sacrificing spirit, were wholly failures or worthy of ridicule. While, then, criticism has not failed to follow Mr. Washington, yet the prevailing public opinion of the land has been but too willing to deliver the solution of a wearisome problem into his hands, and say, "If that is all you and your race ask, take it."

Among his own people, however, Mr. Washington has encountered the strongest and most lasting opposition, amounting at times to bitterness, and even today continuing strong and insistent even though largely silenced in outward expression by the public opinion of the nation. Some of this opposition is, of course, mere envy; the disappointment of displaced demagogues and the spite of narrow minds. But aside from this, there is among educated and thoughtful colored men in all parts of the land a feeling of deep regret, sorrow, and apprehension at the wide currency and ascendancy which some of Mr. Washington's theories have gained. These same men admire his sincerity of purpose, and are willing to forgive much to honest endeavor which is doing something worth the doing. They cooperate with Mr. Washington as far as they conscientiously can; and, indeed, it is no ordinary tribute to this man's tact

and power that, steering as he must between so many diverse interests and opinions, he so largely retains the respect of all.

But the hushing of the criticism of honest opponents is a dangerous thing. It leads some of the best of the critics to unfortunate silence and paralysis of effort, and others to burst into speech so passionately and intemperately as to lose listeners. Honest and earnest criticism from those whose interests are most nearly touched,—criticism of writers by readers, of government by those governed, of leaders by those led,—this is the soul of democracy and the safeguard of modern society. If the best of the American Negroes receive by outer pressure a leader whom they had not recognized before, manifestly there is here a certain palpable gain. Yet there is also irreparable loss,—a loss of that peculiarly valuable education which a group receives when by search and criticism it finds and commissions its own leaders. The way in which this is done is at once the most elementary and the nicest problem of social growth. History is but the record of such group leadership; and yet how infinitely changeful is its type and character. And of all types and kinds; what can be more instructive than the leadership of a group within a group—that curious double movement where real progress may be negative and actual advance be relative retrogression. All this is the social student's inspiration and despair.

Now in the past the American Negro has had instructive experience in the choosing of group leaders, founding thus a peculiar dynasty which in the light of present conditions is worth while studying. When sticks and stones and beasts form the sole environment of a people, their attitude is largely one of determined opposition to and conquest of natural forces. But when to earth and brute is added an environment of men and ideas, then the attitude of the imprisoned group may take three main forms,—a feeling of revolt and revenge; an attempt to adjust all thought and action to the will of the greater group; or, finally, a determined effort at self-realization and self-development despite environing opinion. The influence of all of these attitudes at various times can be traced in the history of the American Negro, and in the evolution of his successive leaders.

Before 1750, while the fire of African freedom still burned in the veins of the slaves, there was in all leadership or attempted leadership but the one motive of revolt and revenge,—typified in the terrible Maroons, the Danish blacks, and Cato of Stono, and veiling all the Americans in fear of insurrection. The liberalizing tendencies of the latter half of the eighteenth century brought, along with kindlier relations between black and white, thoughts of ultimate adjustment and assimilation. Such aspiration was especially voiced in the earnest songs of Phyllis, in the martyrdom of Attucks, the fighting Salem and Poor, the intellectual accomplishments of Banneker and Derham, and the political demands of the Cuffes.

Stern financial and social stress after the war cooled much of the previous humanitarian ardor. The disappointment and impatience of the Negroes at the persistence of slavery and serfdom voiced itself in two movements. The slaves in the South, aroused undoubtedly by vague rumors of the Haitian revolt, made three fierce attempts at insurrection,—in 1800 under Gabriel in Virginia, in 1822 under Vesey in Carolina, and in 1831 again in Virginia under the terrible Nat Turner. In the Free States, on the other hand, a new and curious attempt at self-development was made. In Philadelphia and New York color prescription led to a withdrawal of Negro communicants from white churches and formation of a peculiar socioreligious institution among the Negroes known as the African Church,—an organization still living and controlling in its various branches over a million of men.

Walker's wild appeal against the trend of the times showed how the world was changing after the coming of the cotton-gin. By 1830 slavery seemed hopelessly fastened on the South, and the slaves thoroughly cowed into submission. The free Negroes of the North, inspired by the mulatto immigrants from the West Indies, began to change the basis of their demands; they recognized the slavery of slaves, but insisted that they themselves were freemen, and sought assimilation and amalgamation with the nation on the same terms with other men. Thus Forten and Purvis of Philadelphia, Shad of Wilmington, DuBois of New Haven, Barbadoes of Boston, and others, strove singly and together as men, they said, not as slaves; as "people of color," not as "Negroes." The trend of the times, however, refused them recognition save in individual and exceptional cases, considered them as one with all the despised blacks, and they soon found themselves striving to keep even the rights they formerly had of voting and working and moving as freemen. Schemers of migration and colonization arose among them; but these they refused to entertain, and they eventually turned to the Abolition movement as a final refuge.

Here, led by Remond, Nell, Wells-Brown, and Douglass, a new period of self-assertion and self-development dawned. To be sure, ultimate freedom and

assimilation was the ideal before the leaders, but the assertion of the manhood rights of the Negro by himself was the main reliance, and John Brown's raid was the extreme of its logic. After the war and emancipation, the great form of Frederick Douglass, the greatest of American Negro leaders, still led the host. Self-Assertion, especially in political lines, was the main programme, and behind Douglass came Elliot, Bruce, and Langston, and the Reconstruction politicians, and, less conspicuous but of greater social significance Alexander Crummell and Bishop Daniel Payne.

Then came the Revolution of 1876, the suppression of the Negro votes, the changing and shifting of ideals, and the seeking of new lights in the great night. Douglass, in his old age, still bravely stood for the ideals of his early manhood,—ultimate assimilation through self-assertion and on no other terms. For a time Price arose as a new leader, destined, it seemed, not to give up, but to re-state the old ideals in a form less repugnant to the white South. But he passed away in his prime. Then came the new leader. Nearly all the former ones had become leaders by the silent suffrage of their fellows, had sought to lead their own people alone, and were usually, save Douglass, little known outside their race. But Booker T. Washington arose as essentially the leader not of one race but of two,—a compromiser between the South, the North, and the Negro. Naturally the Negroes resented, at first bitterly, signs of compromise which surrendered their civil and political rights, even though this was to be exchanged for larger chances of economic development. The rich and dominating North, however, was not only weary of the race problem, but was investing largely in Southern enterprises, and welcomed any method of peaceful cooperation. Thus, by national opinion, the Negroes began to recognize Mr. Washington's leadership; and the voice of criticism was hushed.

Mr. Washington represents in Negro thought the old attitude of adjustment and submission—but adjustment at such a peculiar time as to make his programme unique. This is an age of unusual economic development, and Mr. Washington's programme naturally takes an economic cast, becoming a gospel of Work and Money to such an extent as apparently almost completely to overshadow the higher aims of life. Moreover, this is an age when the more advanced races are coming in closer contact with the less developed races, and the race-feeling is therefore intensified; and Mr. Washington's programme practically accepts the alleged inferiority of the Negro races. Again, in our own land, the reaction from the sentiment of war time has given impetus to race-prejudice against Negroes, and Mr. Washington withdraws many of the high demands of Negroes as men and American citizens. In other periods of intensified prejudice all the Negro's tendency to self-assertion has been called forth; at this period a policy of submission is advocated. In the history of nearly all other races and peoples the doctrine preached at such crises has been that manly self-respect is worth more than lands and houses, and that a people who voluntarily surrender such respect, or cease striving for it, are not worth civilizing. In answer to this, it has been claimed that the Negro can survive only through submission. Mr. Washington distinctly asks that black people give up, at least for the present, three things,—

First, political power,

Second, insistence on civil rights,

Third, higher education of Negro youth,—

and concentrate all their energies on industrial education, the accumulation of wealth, and the conciliation of the South. This policy has been courageously and insistently advocated for over fifteen years, and has been triumphant for perhaps ten years. As a result of this tender of the palm-branch, what has been the return? In these years there have occurred:

1. The disfranchisement of the Negro.

2. The legal creation of a distinct status of civil inferiority for the Negro.

3. The steady withdrawal of aid from institutions for the higher training of the Negro.

These movements are not, to be sure, direct results of Mr. Washington's teachings; but his propaganda has, without a shadow of doubt, helped their speedier accomplishment. The question then comes: Is it possible, and probable, that nine millions of men can make effective progress in economic lines if they are deprived of political rights, made a servile caste, and allowed only the most meagre chance for developing their exceptional men? If history and reason give any distinct answer to these questions, it is an emphatic *No.* And Mr. Washington thus faces the triple paradox of his career:

1. He is striving nobly to make Negro artisans businessmen and property-owners; but it is utterly impossible, under modern competitive methods, for workingmen and property-owners to defend their rights and exist without the right of suffrage.

2. He insists on thrift and self-respect, but at the same time counsels a silent submission to civic inferiority such as is bound to sap the manhood of any race in the long run.

3. He advocates common-school and industrial training, and depreciates institutions of higher learning; but neither the Negro common-schools, nor Tuskegee itself, could remain open a day were it not for teachers trained in Negro colleges, or trained by their graduates.

This triple paradox in Mr. Washington's position is the object of criticism by two classes of colored Americans. One class is spiritually descended from Toussaint the Savior, through Gabriel, Vesey, and Turner, and they represent the attitude of revolt and revenge; they hate the white South blindly and distrust the white race generally, and so far as they agree on definite action, think that the Negro's only hope lies in emigration beyond the borders of the United States. And yet, by the irony of fate, nothing has more effectually made this programme seem hopeless than the recent course of the United States toward weaker and darker peoples in the West Indies, Hawaii, and the Philippines—for where in the world may we go and be safe from lying and brute force?

The other class of Negroes who cannot agree with Mr. Washington has hitherto said little aloud. They deprecate the sight of scattered counsels, of internal disagreement; and especially they dislike making their just criticism of a useful and earnest man an excuse for a general discharge of venom from small-minded opponents. Nevertheless, the questions involved are so fundamental and serious that it is difficult to see how men like the Grimkes, Kelly Miller, J.W.E. Bowen, and other representatives of this group, can much longer be silent. Such men feel in conscience bound to ask of this nation three things:

1. The right to vote.

2. Civil equality.

3. The education of youth according to ability.

They acknowledge Mr. Washington's invaluable service in counselling patience and courtesy in such demands; they do not ask that ignorant black men vote when ignorant whites are debarred, or that any reasonable restrictions in the suffrage should not be applied; they know that the low social level of the mass of the race is responsible for much discrimination against it, but they also know, and the nation knows, that relentless color-prejudice is more often a cause than a result of the Negro's degradation; they seek the abatement of this relic of barbarism, and not its systematic encouragement and pampering by all agencies of social power from the Associated Press to the Church of Christ. They advocate, with Mr. Washington, a broad system of Negro common schools supplemented by thorough industrial training; but they are surprised that a man of Mr. Washington's insight cannot see that no such educational system ever has rested or can rest on any other basis than that of the well-equipped college and university, and they insist that there is a demand for a few such institutions throughout the South to train the best of the Negro youth as teachers, professional men, and leaders.

This group of men honor Mr. Washington for his attitude of conciliation toward the white South; they accept the "Atlanta Compromise" in its broadest interpretation; they recognize, with him, many signs of promise, many men of high purpose and fair judgment, in this section; they know that no easy task has been laid upon a region already tottering under heavy burdens. But, nevertheless, they insist that the way to truth and right lies in straightforward honesty, not in indiscriminate flattery; in praising those of the South who do well and criticizing uncompromisingly those who do ill; in taking advantage of the opportunities at hand and urging their fellows to do the same, but at the same time in remembering that only a first adherence to their higher ideals and aspirations will ever keep those ideals within the realm of possibility. They do not expect that the free right to vote, to enjoy civic rights, and to be educated, will come in a moment; they do not expect to see the bias and prejudices of years disappear at the blast of a trumpet; but they are absolutely certain that the way for a people to gain their reasonable rights is not by voluntarily throwing them away and insisting that they do not want them; that the way for a people to gain respect is not by continually belittling and ridiculing themselves; that, on the contrary, Negroes must insist continually, in season and out of season, that voting is necessary to modern manhood, that color discrimination is barbarism, and that black boys need education as well as white boys.

In failing thus to state plainly and unequivocally the legitimate demands of their people, even at the cost of opposing an honored leader, the thinking classes of American Negroes would shirk a heavy responsibility—a responsibility to themselves, a responsibility to the struggling masses, a responsibility to the darker races of men whose future depends so largely on this American experiment, but especially a responsibility to this nation—this common Fatherland. It is wrong to encourage a man or a people in evil-doing; it is wrong to aid and abet a national crime simply because it is unpopular not to do so. The growing spirit of kindliness and reconciliation between the North and South after the frightful difference of a generation ago ought to be a source of deep congratulation to all, and especially to those whose mistreatment caused the war; but if that reconciliation is to be marked by the industrial slavery and civic death of those same black men, with permanent legislation into a position of inferiority, then those black men, if they are really men, are called upon by every consideration of patriotism and loyalty to oppose such a course by all civilized methods, even though such opposition involves disagreement with Mr. Booker T. Washington. We have no right to sit silently by while the inevitable seeds are grown for a harvest of disaster to our children, black and white.

First, it is the duty of black men to judge the South discriminatingly. The present generation of Southerners are not responsible for the past, and they should not be blindly hated or blamed for it. Furthermore, to no class is the indiscriminate endorsement of the recent course of the South toward Negroes more nauseating than to the best thought of the South. The South is not "solid"; it is a land in the ferment of social change, wherein forces of all kinds are fighting for supremacy; and to praise the ill the South is to-day perpetrating is just as wrong as to condemn the good. Discriminating and broad-minded criticism is what the South needs,—needs it for the sake of her own white sons and daughters, and for the insurance of robust, healthy mental and moral development.

To-day even the attitude of the Southern whites towards the blacks is not, as so many assume, in all cases the same; the ignorant Southerner hates the Negro, the workingmen fear his competition, the moneymakers wish to use him as a laborer, some of the educated see a menace in his upward development, while others—usually the sons of the masters—wish to help him to rise. National opinion has enabled this last class to maintain the Negro common schools, and to protect the Negro partially in property, life, and limb. Through the pressure of the moneymakers, the Negro is in danger of being reduced to semi-slavery, especially in the country districts; the workingmen and those of the educated who fear the Negro, have united to disfranchise him, and some have urged his deportation; while the passions of the ignorant are easily aroused to lynch and abuse any black man. To praise this intricate whirl of thought and prejudice is nonsense; to inveigh indiscriminately against "the South" is unjust; but to use the same breath in praising Governor Aycock, exposing Senator Morgan, arguing with Mr. Thomas Nelson Page, and denouncing Senator Ben Tillman, is not only sane, but the imperative duty of thinking black men.

It would be unjust to Mr. Washington not to acknowledge that in several instances he has opposed movements in the South which were unjust to the Negro; he sent memorials to the Louisiana and Alabama constitutional conventions, he has spoken against lynching, and in other ways has openly or silently set his influence against sinister schemes and unfortunate happenings. Notwithstanding this, it is equally true to assert that on the whole the distinct impression left by Mr. Washington's propaganda is, first, that the South is justified in its present attitude toward the Negro because of the Negro's degradation; secondly, that the prime cause of the Negro's failure to rise more quickly is his wrong education in the past; and, thirdly, that his future rise depends primarily on his own efforts. Each of these propositions is a dangerous half-truth. The supplementary truths must never be lost sight of: first, slavery and race-prejudice are potent if not sufficient causes of the Negro's position; second, industrial and common-school training were necessarily slow in planting because they had to await the black teachers trained by higher institutions,—it being extremely doubtful if any essentially different development was possible, and certainly a Tuskegee was unthinkable before 1880; and, third, while it is a great truth to say that the Negro must strive and strive mightily to help himself, it is equally true that unless his striving be not simply seconded, but rather aroused and encouraged, by the initiative of the richer and wiser environing group, he cannot hope for great success.

In his failure to realize and impress this last point, Mr. Washington is especially to be criticised. His doctrine has tended to make the whites, North and South, shift the burden of the Negro problem to the Negro's shoulders and stand aside as critical and rather pessimistic spectators; when in fact the burden belongs to the nation, and the hands of none of us are clean if we bend not our energies to righting these great wrongs.

The South ought to be led, by candid and honest criticism, to assert her better self and do her full duty to the race she has cruelly wronged and is still wronging. The North—her co-partner in guilt—cannot salve her conscience by plastering it with gold. We cannot settle this problem by diplomacy and suaveness, by "policy" alone. If worse comes to worst, can the moral fibre of the country survive the slow throttling and murder of nine millions of men?

The black men of America have a duty to perform, a duty stern and delicate,—a forward movement to oppose a part of the work of their greatest leader. So far as Mr. Washington preaches Thrift, Patience, and Industrial Training for the masses, we must hold up his hands and strive with him, rejoicing in his honors and glorying in the strength of this Joshua called of God and of man to lead the headless host. But so far as Mr. Washington apologizes for injustice, North or South, does not rightly value the privilege and duty of voting, belittles the emasculating efforts of caste distinctions, and opposes the higher training and ambition of our brighter minds,—so far as he, the South, or the Nation, does this,—we must unceasingly and firmly oppose them. By every civilized and peaceful method we must strive for the rights which the world accords to men, clinging unwaveringly to those great words which the sons of the Fathers would fain forget: "We hold these truths to be self-evident: That all men are created equal; that they are endowed by their Creator with certain unalienable rights; that among these are life, liberty, and the pursuit of happiness."

Developing Your Professional Vocabulary

A good understanding of this chapter's content would include an understanding of why each of these terms is important to education.

Black Codes

Booker T. Washington

The Crisis

Freedmen's Bureau

historically Black colleges

Mississippi Plan

NAACP

Reconstruction

redemption

Thirteenth, Fourteenth, and Fifteenth Amendments

Tuskegee Institute

W. E. B. Du Bois

Questions for Discussion and Examination

1. Critically analyze Dudley Randall's poem "Booker T. and W. E. B." at the end of the chapter.

2. Some students have defended Washington against Du Bois's criticism by saying that Washington had a "practical" solution that sought to accomplish for Black people the most that could be done under the circumstances of that time and place. Yet Du Bois believed that Washington fundamentally misinterpreted those conditions and that given the political–economic and ideological realities of the period, Washington's solution was impractical as a route to African American advancement. Which leader had the stronger position in your view, and why?

3. In the Primary Source Reading Du Bois wrote, "Honest and earnest criticism from those whose interests are most nearly touched— . . . this is the soul of democracy and the safeguard of modern society." Read that statement in context and explain the degree to which you find it consistent or inconsistent with Jefferson's views on intellectual freedom and the developmental value of democracy. Support your position.

4. Du Bois relied on Washington's autobiography in writing that "the picture of a lone black boy poring over a French grammar amid the weeds and dirt of a neglected home soon seemed to him the acme of absurdities" (see the Primary Source Reading). Why, in your view, did Washington see this image as so absurd, and why did Du Bois see Washington's view as being so wrong in this instance? Which position do you believe is stronger, and why?

5. As you look around you today in your community or communities that you know, do you see evidence of different educational expectations for African Americans and other school populations? Explain your position, and explain why the conditions you observe are what they are.

Online Resources

Go to the Online Learning Center at **www.mhhe.com/ tozer7e** to take chapter quizzes, practice with key terms, access study resources, and link to related websites. Also available on the Online Learning Center are PowerWeb articles and news feeds.

Diversity and Equity   **Schooling and American Indians**

Chapter Overview

Chapter 7 examines the ways in which progressive liberal ideology helped shape educational policy for Native Americans from the 1920s through the 1940s. This brief history raises questions about modern liberal commitments to cultural pluralism, in which cultural and linguistic differences in a society are valued and maintained, in contrast to a commitment to assimilation, in which the customs, habits, and languages of subcultures are absorbed into a dominant culture. It appears that the history of American Indian education since the late 19th century has reflected a commitment to scientific management of Indian acculturation and assimilation by European American administrators. This has resulted in part from a fundamental clash between an impulse toward "manifest destiny" tempered by corporate liberal democratic ideology and Native American approaches to life that did not emphasize liberal concepts of property, progress, scientific rationality, and nationalism. In its effort to assimilate Native Americans into the dominant ideology and economic life of 20th-century European America, the federal government turned to formal schooling as its primary agency of reform.

To illustrate how well-intentioned liberals sought to acculturate American Indians through scientific management, this chapter reviews the career of John Collier, who was commissioner of Indian affairs from 1933 to 1945. While Collier was a progressive advocate of Indian cultural values, he did not support a genuine cultural pluralism in which Native Americans could exercise self-determination regarding their cultural and educational futures. Instead, he tried to use modern psychology and administrative techniques to bring Indians to value modified forms of assimilation. Collier believed that principles of progressive education could be employed to make Native American children's attitudes more positive toward the dominant culture. Progressive educator Willard Walcott Beatty extended Collier's commitment to assimilation through progressive education for Native American children. The Primary Source Readings at the end of the chapter contrast an administrative-progressive view of Native American social policy with Native Americans' views about their desire for self-determination and education for cultural pluralism.

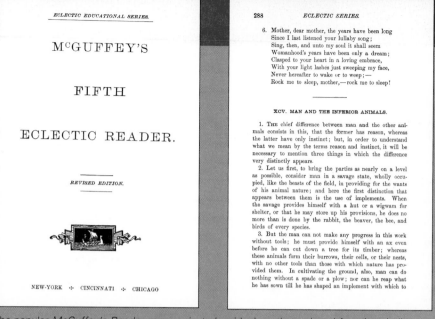

The popular *McGuffey's Reader* communicated an ideology that reduced American Indians to "savages."

Chapter Objectives

Among the objectives that Chapter 7 seeks to achieve are these:

1. This chapter seeks to exercise students' thinking about how modern liberalism operates in the context of a specific historical problem: the coexistence of European Americans and indigenous Americans in the 20th century.

2. Students may evaluate the degree to which modern liberal ideology has affected American Indians' efforts to determine their own lives and futures.

3. In particular, instructors should highlight the conflicts between modern liberal views of progress and Native American commitments to cultural traditions. Students may discuss the issue of school control and rights to curriculum.

4. This chapter should help students evaluate progressive education as conceived by American government officials, and whether it was an appropriate response to Native American educational needs.

5. Students should be able to discuss the careers and thinking of John Collier and Willard Beatty and how they apply liberal educational commitments to Native American culture.

6. A final objective is to engage students in discussing whether cultural pluralism was a more democratic educational and cultural aim than cultural assimilation for American Indians in the first half of the 20th century.

Analytic Framework
The History of European American Policies for Educating Native Americans

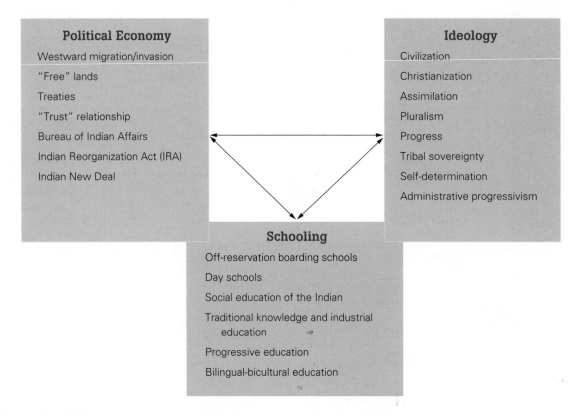

Political Economy
Westward migration/invasion
"Free" lands
Treaties
"Trust" relationship
Bureau of Indian Affairs
Indian Reorganization Act (IRA)
Indian New Deal

Ideology
Civilization
Christianization
Assimilation
Pluralism
Progress
Tribal sovereignty
Self-determination
Administrative progressivism

Schooling
Off-reservation boarding schools
Day schools
Social education of the Indian
Traditional knowledge and industrial education
Progressive education
Bilingual-bicultural education

Introduction: Assimilation through Scientific Management

Native American education is a unique set of stories that connect tribal history with the political–economic movement of European American hegemony. This chapter is an attempt to present an outline of the most important ways in which one of those stories illuminates the problem and promise of pluralist democracy in the United States.

Returning to the classical liberal ideal, we see how tribal peoples are denied membership in the polis of citizenship and democratic promise. In the classical ideal we saw how property ownership, tenure on the land, and long-standing occupancy were key elements of citizenship. Strangers, metics, immigrants, and others were not eligible for citizenship. The irony for Native Americans is that their citizenship was denied by those who came as strangers to their land. This denial came through rationalizations that denied Native people the freedom to determine how they would live. Colonizers could not very well justify taking lands from

fully rational human beings. Therefore Native Americans, much like Africans and Asians affected by the colonial project, were assigned subhumanity as a pretext for European rights to invasion and occupation.

Native American historian Jack Forbes has described how the ideological shift away from Native American human rights was accomplished in part by "Indianization." While the ideological use of Americanism has come to symbolize democracy and freedom, the invention of the term "America" and its use is freighted with colonial power and exclusion of its original people. This chapter section in part will be an exercise in reversing that habit, and when not quoting, will call "Indians" Americans, and European colonists, European colonials.

Forbes describes how the curriculum in European colonial schools today is devoid of accurate and comprehensive knowledge regarding the diversity and antiquity of American accomplishments in science, mathematics, religion, food development, oral literature, and medicine. School leaders eliminated the great and complex cultures of the thousands of American groups in a long hegemonic process of colonization. This process has proceeded to affect American children, who only find their cultures trivialized in school curricula and used as material for stereotypical mascots.[1]

This chapter will discuss reasons why the "reform" of education for Americans has been an exercise in progressivism. The two versions of progressive education described in Chapter 4 are here again, with a great emphasis on schooling for "evident and probable destinies."

There are 562 Native American tribal groupings recognized by the federal government. The U.S. population of indigenous American is just under one percent overall. There is an indigenous presence in every US metropolitan area, and significantly strong presence on tribal lands in nearly every state. The importance of indigenous peoples' contribution to the sweep history, and current life of the United States cannot be overestimated. Students from non-indigenous backgrounds might question why this study includes a chapter devoted to a significant Native American education story. For this there are several explanations. First, academic and honesty demands that important stories, previously neglected require re-examination. Native Americans have experienced significant neglect regarding their historic and ongoing presence in this country. Second, for all immigrant American experience, the heirs of that experience have homelands to which they may point, and gain understanding and strength in their search for meaning. When native people here lose their memory and identity, they risk losing their existence, for this land is the home they point toward. Third, many students from all backgrounds are completely unaware of the unique federal/ tribal government relationship that makes Native America, semi- independent as political entities. This degree of sovereign independence is demonstrated. The US constitution makes NO provision for the education of anyone, except for Native Americans. However, The school dropout rates and the achievement gap for Native American youth are greater than for any other American minority group.

During the progressive reforms described here, beginning at the end of the 19th century and through the end of World War II, several changes would be put in place that would benefit Americans. Chief among these were the end of land allotments that had helped move 100 million acres from American to Euro-American hands. In schooling the most corrosive and inhumane conditions of the Indian Boarding School were altered somewhat and public and community schools began to be established. We look at the career of John Collier, who as commissioner of Indian affairs, was instrumental in this change during the 1930s. The Collier legacy is torn by the effort, stimulated during his administration by such tribal scholars as D'Arcy McNickle to re-

establish a place for democratic pluralism in American schools. This effort at Deweyan "developmental democracy" was however, strongly influenced by the new liberal managerial impulse, which applied principles of "scientific social management" for the creation of "social stability" where Americans were concerned. This social stability effort included a democratic republicanism of tribal governments established through the Indian Reorganization Act (IRA). This form of government tended to disorganize the millennia of community consensus government that existed before European colonial arrival. Grassroots and traditional governance became overshadowed by tribal councils.

Currently the issues in American schools are numerous. The provisions of the No Child Left Behind legislation are working to undermine what little American community control of curriculum exists. American children, particularly in poor rural and urban communities, do perform poorly as compared to their Euro-American counterparts. However, starting a reform of American education with a regime of public humiliation through test score publication is a troubling step. Standardized testing mandates have vitiated efforts of teachers of American children to incorporate American languages, cultural practices, and intellectual traditions. This threatens to further alienate American students who are truants and dropouts at a much higher rate than other groups.

The two issues that are most important here are tribal sovereignty and the relationship of democratic education to curricular freedom. Both of these have been submerged beneath a schooling of ideology that has sought American student cultural obliteration, and has been blind to the treaty and Supreme Court history that reserves to Americans the right to control their education and social and religious life in ways unique to tribal members.

Pluralism versus Assimilationism

[Note: Following the example set by Native American writers, this chapter henceforth uses the terms *Native American, American Indian,* and *Indian* interchangeably. The Primary Source Readings by American Indians at the end of the chapter illustrate the use of all three terms.]

Any consideration of European American efforts to educate American Indians must take into account pluralist versus assimilationist visions of Native American life in the United States. In general, a regard for pluralism represents a recognition that the strength of a society depends in part on the extent to which cultural differences are honored for their contribution to healthy diversity. *Pluralism* thus conceived means valuing and maintaining cultural and linguistic differences within a society. It is also a yardstick of tolerance, a virtue inherent in the democratic belief that diversity of belief and outlook ultimately contribute to, rather than detract from, social and political life.

The concept of *assimilation* has come to mean the process by which diverse cultures—immigrant, racial, ethnic, and linguistic minorities—alter their customs, habits, and languages to allow absorption into a *dominant culture*. It can also be argued that assimilation produces a variety of effects on the dominant culture, both positive and negative. Assimilation into the dominant European American culture has meant radical change for most minority groups. When W. E. B. Du Bois called for assimilation for African Americans through "self-assertion" and not "acquiescence," he was favoring a form of cultural pluralism. For Native Americans in particular, as anthropologist Alexander Lesser has said, assimilation has a "crucial finality," since they have no other homeland to look to for cultural identification and regeneration.

Native American cultures were forged in a land that has been transformed from its original state. Yet despite great changes in the larger society, Native Americans have not forfeited their right to pursue a tribal life and culture distinct from the dominant American culture. The explicit Native American right to a distinct culture, protected by treaties, a special governmental relationship, and the maintenance of tribal homelands, has ensured that assimilation can never have the same meaning for Indian people that it has for other minority groups.

In this chapter we will be dealing with the impact of the new liberal ideology (described at length in Chapter 4) on the development of a unique pluralist vision for Native Americans in the United States. We will explore the impact of this developing ideology by examining the work of several crucial figures who shaped Indian education reform in the 20th century, particularly W. Carson Ryan, John Collier, and Willard W. Beatty. These individuals, more than any others, believed that the techniques of social-scientific rationality could be used to solve the problems of Indian America. For them, relations between Indians and Whites could be organized according to sophisticated social-science knowledge. Theirs was a vision of assimilation with elements of democratic participation, but it was to be carefully controlled participation, coordinated with "scientific" administration of Indian affairs. Although these men wished to alleviate the marginal living conditions of the Indian populace, the programs and policies they developed offered Indian citizens only limited involvement in the shaping of their social institutions.

In this clash between Native American and European American value systems in the first half of the 20th century education was seen as an important tool for achieving the distinctive kind of assimilation planned for Indians by new liberal reformers.

The American Indian relationship to formal schooling is a complex one that cannot be generalized. The expansion of efforts to bring formal schooling to Native Americans coincides with general expansion of schooling in the early 20th century. Thus, the emerging and changing nature of progressivism greatly affected Native Americans. Although many Indians during the progressive era lived in rural areas, the character of schooling was influenced greatly by the industrial education movement. Likewise, the Americanization efforts directed toward immigrants in the growing urban environment took an ironic twist in schooling for Native Americans. Curricular standardization, character education, and Protestant humanism affected Indian boarding and mission school efforts, as did the increasing effort to make compulsory public school a reality. The nearly successful genocide of the "Indian Wars" made way for more sophisticated efforts at "cultural adjustment."

Beginning with the early 20th century, administrative progressivism and managerial control were exemplified by the growth and influence of the Bureau of Indian Affairs and the institutionalization of tribal governments under the Indian Reorganization Act. Cultural and political research under the auspices of the Bureau of Ethnology illustrate the belief of that time that scientific experts could rationalize tribal culture and adjustment.

Part of the complexity of Indian education is due to the ambiguous and paradoxical nature of Native Americans' citizenship, sovereignty, and resistance to assimilation. Native Americans, like African Americans, have always been aware of the benefits of education. They seem often to have resisted schooling, however, as an institution that could damage the traditional spiritual and historic knowledge without which tribal survival was at risk or even meaningless. Like African Americans, Indian leaders often used whatever educational means they could: self-education, the military, boarding school, the home. All could be used to better their communities and wage legal and political battles. Understanding the complex relationships between American Indians and European American schooling requires historical perspective and a recognition that for most of their thousands of years of civilization, Indians have lived independently of White efforts to educate them.

The second quotation, dated 1886, reflects a usual view as to the types of emotion evoked in Indians by their own societies.

"To assist in the great work of redeeming these benighted children of nature from the darkness of their superstition and ignorance . . ."

"When they (Indian young people) return to their homes at night, and on Saturdays and Sundays, and are among their old surroundings, they relapse more or less into their former moral and mental stupor."

The presumption was one of administrative omnipotence. What was willed by authority, and put into action by authority—that was the thing which would be. The obscure complexes of personality and of group influence and ancient, present physical environment were ignored; good intention was deemed to be enough, without the need to measure results; and the law of the multiplication of effects was taken into account not at all. It followed, that not even the sense of reality of the Indian Service men and women out on the ground among the Indians was used in the making of headquarters policy. But I move into the immediate past, and the present.

. . . Change, at varying speeds, inhabits all of Indian life; change, at varying speeds, inhabits each group, each personality of the Indians. Is there any way to understand more surely, to predict more reliably, to act with knowledge more precise, so that we can know, genuinely, what worth our Indian effort has and how it may be made significantly more realistic, and so that our good (which we presume) may not become the enemy of a better?

The answer, if indeed there were one, must rest, it seemed to us, in the use of not one but many techniques of observation and measurement *integratively.* Our hypothesis—a truism, which yet leads to discovery when deeply meditated—was that the web of life and the world-field operate beneath as well as above the conscious threshold. And that the group and the individual are dynamically inseparable. And that the past, in the web of life and in the unconsciousness, is far more potent than can easily be known. And that trends of action and tensions of the body-soul are stubborn and imperious in men, though men may not know this fact at the conscious level.

From this hypothesis, there followed the method which we sought to have applied. Social history and the social present must be studied in relation to each other. The group structure, the group imperatives must be known, and the individual must be known as that personality-formation where the group forces clash and build (but not the group forces alone). Mind and performance in the individual must be measured, and through depth-psychology techniques, the types and trends of the individual unconsciousness must be explored. Bodily health must be examined. The physical environment, past as well as present, must be brought clearly, concretely into the picture. And finally, administration, in its subdivisions and as a whole, must be viewed afresh in the light of all of this data—data previously interrelated, so far as possible, within itself.

Into contact with the specialists—anthropologists, psychologists, physicians, and students of administration—the workers of Indian Service and, ideally, the Indians themselves, should be brought; and in the event, it has proved that important parts of the project have been done by the lay members (White and Indian) of Indian Service.

With this object in view—the scientific evaluation of Indian Service, and scientific planning—and under the sway of the hypothesis stated, and by the correlative or integrative use of the methods implied, the several monographs of this series have been produced. Supplements dealing with administrative application will be presented at dates soon after the publication of each of the volumes, and it is hoped that there will be a final volume devoted to principles of Indian administration treated as a special case of universal democratic administration, and another devoted to the utilization of the whole body of the material for its light upon the science of society.

I have stated a view of life (and in so far, the view is merely my own), and an intended goal of investigation, and intended use of methods. None is likely to realize as acutely as those who have given themselves to the present enterprise, how incomplete is the accomplishment. If it should prove to have carried forward by one critical fraction of a degree (in the vast arc which will be explored through centuries) the integrative use of the special sciences in the knowing of man and the helpful control of his destiny, this result will have been enough. Certainly into our problem of Indian Service the enterprise has cast many beams of light that reach far. Areas immanently important, never clearly brought into the light before, are now in a clear and growing light. Will we administrators, who include all the field forces of Indian Service, use the light?

In a recent issue of INDIANS AT WORK, I wrote, and my thought took form from a reading of some of the materials of the present and the forthcoming monographs:

"Does one seek to influence an individual or a group? Let him discover what is central to the being of that individual or group. Let his effort at influence be near to, and not deviate sharply from, the line of force of that which is central to the being of the individual or group. Thus, he may influence profoundly and helpfully. Remember that deep and central preoccupations, devotions and views of life can be helped to apply themselves to new practical ends. Here is the secret of efficient and democratic administration. Indian policies in the last ten or twelve years have come much nearer to the things central in the Indian's being than they came in previous decades. Hence the marked increase in the social energy of Indians, and their great and persevering response to the various practical programs. But we need to keep on trying, with greater, not with diminishing, energy, and we need to press ever inward toward discovery of those attitudes, hopes, fears, and patterns of functioning, and trends of the inner drive, which are central to the Indians. There is hardly any limit to the energy, the good-will, and the happiness which will meet us from within the Indian—if only we work with him at his own centers."

Primary Source Reading

Indians have seldom been asked what they want, nor have programs allegedly designed for their benefit often been developed with their participation. Indian initiative was so long repressed that it is only recently that Indians have rediscovered their own voice. The first effective national organization of Indians was the National Congress of American Indians, organized in 1944. Many large tribes, however, such as the Navajo, do not participate in it. The Indian cause has also been supported by White-initiated organizations, such as the Indian Rights Association (organized by Quakers in 1882) and the Association on American Indian Affairs (since 1923).

The following are excerpts first from Dillon Platero and second from Ethelou Yazzie, Navajo educators who were the second and third directors of the demonstration schools at Rough Rock. Platero's statement was drawn from a paper he prepared in 1973 entitled "Community Control-Historical Perspectives and Current Efforts, Both Public and Private." Yazzie's comments were drawn from

Source: Both selections from Robert A. Roessel, Jr., *Navaho Education and Action* (Rough Rock, AZ: Rough Rock Curriculum Center, 1977), pp. 138–40.

testimony she gave at Yellowknife, Northwest Territories, Canada, in 1976. These are followed by a discussion of a stipulated Native American curriculum and governance plan outlined by Patricia Locke, past president of the National Indian Education Association, who is affiliated with the White Earth Chippewa (Mississippi Band) and the Standing Rock Sioux-Hunkpapa Tribe.

These three statements, by different American Indian educational leaders, represent a view that differs significantly from the view represented in the John Collier piece—and Collier was one of the more enlightened liberal educators of his era. The Collier piece was written in the 1940s, and each of the selections below was written in the 1970s, but the differences are greater than the passage of three decades; they are differences in worldview.

Statements by Three American Indian Educators

I. Dillon Platero, *Second Director, Rough Rock Demonstration School*

Today a major and fundamental shift in Indian education is taking place. This new direction and emphasis has been selected and directed by the Indian People themselves: it is Indian control over Indian education. . . .

This principle of local control is characteristic of a democracy which is predicated upon reflecting the value and dignity of each individual and places on local communities major responsibilities for developing and molding an educational system uniquely tailored to the peculiar needs of each community.

It needs to be noted that this local responsibility and local control over education does not mean complete local financing of that education. While the principle of community control is recognized, it has rarely or never meant that community resources are the only, or even the major, source of education funds. . . .

It is necessary to distinguish between involvement and control. It is equally important to understand that control often comes in parts, or pieces. Involvement was a treasured objective in Indian education during the 1930s. During that period of time many 'community schools' were created and many provided for participation and involvement in the operation of schools on the part of parents and community residents. Parents were encouraged to visit schools, special adult programs were developed and community improvement activities centered around the school . . .

This was, and is, good. The parents felt the school filled an important need in the life of the community which exceeded merely the education of children.

Yet this was not control! Control ultimately and finally consists of hiring, firing, setting priorities, allocating funds and approving the curriculum. Forty years ago we had participation and involvement without control: today we are obtaining control and must consciously work toward community participation. . . .

While elsewhere in this great nation the principle of local control over education is accepted, it has been the exception rather than the rule in Indian education . . .

. . . The only viable option is that of community (Indian) control over Indian education. The obstacles which exist in realizing this objective can and will be overcome. There is no other acceptable alternative. Indian and non-Indian people must unite so that community (Indian) control over Indian education is a reality rather than a dream and so that Indian people enjoy the right to be wrong: the right to be right.

II. Ethelou Yazzie, *Third Director, Rough Rock Demonstration School*

One of society's purposes in requiring the formal education of its children is to use its power and its ability to transmit, preserve, and examine a society's history, language, religion and philosophy. This power was totally reversed in the education provided for the Navajo and other Native Americans. The purpose of that system was to *erase* Navajo history, language, religion and philosophy, and to replace it with the dominant culture of the Western European by means of an extensive and intensive resocialization process.

Through education, the dominant establishment tried to exert full control over the Navajo young. Navajo children were forcibly taken from their parents and families as early as seven years of age, and kept at distant boarding schools for ten months out of twelve. This severing of the young from their Indian backgrounds was supposed to make resocialization and cultural domination easier—and it was done through a show of power.

Cultural shock was inevitable. Disorientation and frustration occurred. To many children and parents the conflicting values were simply not acceptable. Other students, not knowing who to believe, resisted both sets of values. These students were then in a "no man's land" with little self-esteem, identity, or values to guide them. Even Indian teachers had difficulty teaching these students . . .

Failure to introduce varying languages and cultures in a positive light discourages the growing child's receptivity and his willingness not to pre-judge others and their cultures. Cultural domination has no place in education.

A Bicultural system respects both cultures and works with *all* segments of the community to the support of each. The family and the educational system need to work together as one with *all* parents knowing and caring about what goes on in the classroom. Neither group should be allowed to undermine the other, but must work together consciously to complement each other throughout the educational process . . .

Community members, if they are willing to assume the effort that it takes, can control their own schools, as does Rough Rock, right now. And in doing so, they transform more than an educational program. The involvement of the community in the school has ramifications far beyond the educational realm.

III. Patricia Locke, *Former President, National Indian Education Association*

An Ideal School System for American Indians: A Theoretical Construct

We are forced to adapt to the educational systems of the immigrant culture only because they are so numerous, insistent and all-pervasive. It would be ideal if Indian people could live, learn and die in the contexts of our cultures as they would have evolved, but we cannot. We have been forced to compromise educationally, to seem to adapt to some of the dominant society's mores in our educational patterns, because the prevailing educational hierarchy is so sure of its infallibility. And they impose laws and customs to make us conform.

We suffer in the name of education from their nursery schools, Head Start programs, secular and religious boarding schools, public day schools with formal hours and foreign curricula, non-Indian foster parent programs, vocational schools and other foreign post-secondary systems. Finally, there is the absurdity of "Golden Years" programs where our elders learn to plan for their retirement and funerals.

Source: From Thomas Thompson, ed., *The Schooling of Native America* (Washington, DC: American Association of Colleges for Teacher Education, 1978), pp. 120–31.

A listing of simple causes and effects of this educational system would illustrate the damage being done to tribal people:

Nursery schools include deprivation of family nurturing and interruption of the organic learning process. Head Start programs increase deprivation of the extended family influence, freeing the mother to enter the work force and causing marital disfunction. Secular boarding schools cause total deprivation of the family nurturing process; alienation from tribal language and culture occur. The same is true of religious boarding schools with the addition that the child is indoctrinated with alien myths and legends and becomes increasingly mutant as concepts of sin, hell and paganism are reinforced.

Non-Indian foster parents' boarding programs means the child loses his family and tribal contacts. Parents are bereaved as the child assumes a non-Indian identity and is lost as a contributing tribal member. At vocational schools the student accepts the Christian work ethic: he learns individualism, mercantilism, and acquisitiveness. Post-secondary school systems create continued alienation from the tribal environment. They impose useless curricula that impede the students' contribution to tribal support systems. Probable assimilation into the dominant society occurs if the student survives foreign counseling services. Finally gradual assumption of alien rhetoric and life styles takes place. "Golden Years" Programs involve the acceptance of the concept of "the generation gap." Elders are lost as teachers; apathy, senility, and death occur in isolation.

Education for American Indian tribal people must be related to the tribes' cosmologies, and integrated into the past and future of the particular tribe. A traditional Indian does not think of a career for self-fulfillment. He thinks of personal attainment only to serve tribal goals. Career satisfaction is often only a by-product of the degree of effectiveness reached in serving short and long range tribal goals.

The child normally begins learning at birth in an organic way. It is important to emphasize this intrinsic and non-formal learning procedure because it is a life-long process. The individual's uncles, aunts, grandparents and the respected elders of the tribe are the nurturers and teachers along with the parents. The function of tribal members as teachers, administrators, counselors, policy-makers and curriculum developers of the young Indian should be an integral part of the entire process of education.

Thinking Critically about the Issues   #5

The point of view informing this chapter suggests a strong connection between U.S. reform of American Indian education and the elimination of native culture and values. If Indian people could have controlled their own educational destinies, how might they have pursued an educational policy different from that imposed by the United States? In developing your response, consider differences in ideology between the dominant European American culture and the various Indian cultures.

A Conception of the Ideal Administration and Teaching Faculty

School administrators, supportive staff, teachers and teacher's aides will be tribal members. When this is not possible, personnel may be recruited from other tribes. Non-Indian persons will sometimes be recruited, especially from the Asian community where religion and life-styles are closer to American Indian Mores. For instance, it would be preferable to have English taught by an Asian teacher, since semantic understandings and interpretations would not be so diametrically opposed to Indian cosmologies.

Dillon Platero, head of the Navajo's Rough Rock Demonstration School at Chinle, Arizona, emphasized the disparity between Indian and non-Indian educational systems. He speculated that of both Indian and non-Indian graduates of this country's Schools of Education who become involved in Rough Rock's teacher training program, only thirty percent are retrainable. He further stated that a minimum of two and one-half years is required in the retraining and learning process.

Another controversial statement made at a national Indian education meeting was the effect that *no* college and university graduates should be allowed to teach Indian children. They should be used as consultants only. The obvious alternative would be to establish Indian Education Programs for Indian Teachers of Indian Children. This idea will be discussed later under the model for post-secondary education.

A vital and necessary part of the faculty would be respected persons of the tribe. They would receive remuneration commensurate with other teachers. The status of these older persons has traditionally been eminent. They are the repositories of oral literature and knowledge. They would serve a double function as guidance counselors, and would provide natural motivation by transmitting essential human knowledge for the continuance of tribal support systems.

The school board may wish to hire non-Indian custodians and janitors.

It is important that the child learns dual cultures and multi-cultures from the fourth grade onward. He must learn well the behavior of people from other cultures if he is to help his people survive. He will learn the values and behavior expectations of other cultures *as skills, not as values.* He may be chosen early by his tribe to pursue a non-Indian college education or a technological education in order to help the tribe survive. If he is to become an attorney or a physician, he will have to learn the necessary academic skills. But great care should be taken so that the student does not walk a path that will cause him to fall over the brink into complete acculturation and assimilation.

High schools will be located on the reservations. Policy will be mandated by the tribe's Education Committee, by elected representatives from the reservation districts or chapters, or by the tribe's Department of Education. All school personnel should be Indian except for individuals who teach foreign languages and white studies.

It is important that decisions be made about the individual students' direction of study for ensuing years. The Tribal Council will have determined short and long range goals—with help from consultants of the American Indian Tribes Research Institute (see below)—and will have made a human resource inventory. The tribe will know which areas of skill it is deficient in, and can pinpoint these needs to the secondary student so that he may prepare himself in these directions in keeping with specific tribal customs and ceremonies. Non-Indian holidays will not be observed. Classes will be open and students will not be grouped by age levels, but by aptitude and interest. Teacher discussions with parents and the student will take the place of a formal grading system. School attendance will not be mandatory. Beginning at eleven or twelve years, the student will participate in the tribe's "school on wheels." Groups of ten to twelve students will travel to nearby and selected distant reservations and off-reservation Indian communities, for "field work" in learning about other tribal people, and for the purpose of exchanging cultural programs with their peers. College students, who are members of the tribes to be visited, will "conduct" these traveling classes. Not only will the student learn about and come to appreciate the richness and diversity of the tribes,

but this understanding will help him to overcome latent tribal antagonisms that still persist. The groundwork will have been laid for improved *transtribal* communications and unity. Arrangements will be made so that the college student receives a stipend and course credit for the teaching experience.

The "traveling school" mechanism will also be integral to the secondary school system. Secondary school age youth will not be required to attend all White Studies courses unless it has been mutually determined that the individual will relate to external governments in later life for the benefit of the tribe.

Dual record systems will have to be maintained at the Tribal Council's Computer Center or one of the Regional Computer Centers so that the Indian student will not be *penalized* if he must leave the reservation and transfer to a non-Indian school. A report card with grades in such acceptable courses as American history, English, geography, spelling, social studies, home economics, reading and arithmetic will be maintained and made available for the transferring student.

Sample secondary curricula in Indian Studies and White Studies might be:

Indian Studies

Tribal Government Systems

Indian Reorganization Act Tribes

Terminated Tribes

Non-Federally Recognized Tribes

Tribes of Mexico

Tribes of Central America

Tribes of South America

Tribes of Canada

Modern Indian Religions

Ancient Indian Religions

American Indian History

American Indian Pre-Law

American Indian Medicine

Minority and Ethnic-Minority Relations

Land Reform

Comparative Minority Rhetoric

Introduction to American Indian Business Administration

American Indian Arts

American Indian Law and Order

Ecology

American Indian Literature and Poetry

Indian Communications Systems

Grantsmanship

Regional Languages and Dialects

White Studies

State Governments

The U.S. Constitution

The Congress

Federal Agencies, Bureaus, and Departments, i.e.:
    Department of the Interior
    (Bureau of Land Management,
    Bureau of Indian Affairs)
    Department of Labor
    Army Corps of Engineers
    Department of Commerce
    Department of Health, Education and Welfare

Comparative Religions

Christianity, Buddhism

Taoism, Hinduism

English Literature

Spanish Conversation

Caucasian Sociology

Black Sociology

Caucasian Law and Order Systems

European History

History of the Mexican Conquest

History of the U.S. Conquest

History of the Canadian Conquest

Caucasian Psychology

Caucasian Concepts of Real Estate

European Philosophy

Caucasian Art History

Caucasian Diseases

Caucasian Communications Systems

Computer Science

Mathematics

Economics

Caucasian Nutrition

Developing Your Professional Vocabulary

A good understanding of this chapter's content would include an understanding of why each of these terms is important to education.

assimilation

boarding school

Bureau of Ethnology

Bureau of Indian Affairs

Cherokee Nation v. *Georgia*

community control

cultural pluralism

Dawes Allotment Act

dominant culture

John Collier

Merriam Report

scientific administration

tribal self-determination

Willard Walcott Beatty

Worcester v. *Georgia*

Questions for Discussion and Examination

1. Most of the 3 million teachers currently teaching in the United States, and most of the over 300,000 currently in teacher education programs, will never have an American Indian student in their classrooms. How could a chapter like this be at all relevant to their teaching philosophy or teaching practice?

2. This chapter is framed in large part as a story of how progressive education ideals and practices were used to provide a Eurocentric version of education to American Indians. How does the lens of progressivism in society and education (a lens developed in Chapter 4 but revisited here) help us understand that story?

3. The history of the American "melting pot" idea suggests that all minority cultures share basically the same problem: how to fit into the larger dominant culture of the United States. Yet each minority group is different, with a different history and different needs. What particular issues associated with the development of a system of public education for Native Americans are different from those that apply to other American minorities? In developing your response, rely on your own experience as well as the material from this chapter.

4. Explain how U.S. policy toward Native American education may be seen as part of a larger cultural, social, and economic conflict between Native Americans and the dominant White culture.

 Online Resources

Go to the Online Learning Center at **www.mhhe.com/ tozer7e** to take chapter quizzes, practice with key terms, access study resources, and link to related websites. Also available on the Online Learning Center are PowerWeb articles and news feeds.

National School Reform The Early Cold War Era

By Stephen Preskill

Chapter Overview

Chapter 8 documents the emergence of the modern American secondary school—the comprehensive high school—in the post–World War II period. The analysis is grounded in the political–economic and ideological context of the cold war, but the components of modern liberalism remain explicit. Thus, the fundamental objectives of school reform that emerged in the progressive era—employable skills, social stability, meritocracy, and equal educational opportunity—remained central to the thinking of cold war era reformers. Chief among these was Professor James B. Conant, president of Harvard University and later U.S. high commissioner to Germany. Conant provides a lens through which the nationalism of the social and educational thinking of his day is examined. In contrast to Conant, the chapter presents a Primary Source Reading by Mark Van Doren, who provides students with a different way to think about the central role of education in a modern democratic society. This contrast suggests parallels with similar contrasts articulated elsewhere in the book: Dewey versus Eliot, Washington versus Du Bois, and Mann versus Brownson, among others.

GOOD-BY, LITTLE SOLDIER

Sometimes you want something
the minute you see it, and you
just can't stop thinking about it.

That's how it was with Tim
when Jack came over to Tim's house
with his new toy soldiers.

The minute Jack opened the box,
Tim thought, "Oh, I wish they were mine!"
And all the time that he and Jack
were playing, Tim was thinking,
"I wish they were mine!
I wish they were mine!"

32

But Tim really had no idea of trying
to keep any soldiers. It just happened.

When it was time for Jack to go home,
they put all the soldiers back in the box.
And then, without anyone knowing how,
the box fell over, and all the soldiers
fell out.

But even then, Tim did not take any.
He just did not say anything
about the soldier that Jack did not see.

"He has so many!" thought Tim,
after they put away the other soldiers
again, and Jack went home.
"He will not even see that one is lost."

33

Mid-20th-century-school texts continued the practice of teaching social values along with reading skills.

Chapter Objectives

Among the objectives that Chapter 8 seeks to achieve are these:

1. This chapter should deepen and extend students' ability to think critically about the presuppositions underlying the structure and content of modern schooling, particularly at the secondary level.

2. Another objective is to critically examine how modern liberal commitments to such values as expert knowledge, meritocracy, and nationalism influenced schooling in the latter half of the 20th century.

3. Students should also think critically about the school as an instrument of national political policy in the political–economic context of the United States after World War II.

4. This chapter asks students to question the notion of a nationalist agenda for schooling within the context of democratic ideals so that the idea of "national interest" itself becomes problematic.

5. Students should consider a relatively recent historical instance of how an expressed commitment to democracy and equality can, in modern liberal schooling policy, serve students inequitably.

6. Students should also consider Van Doren's alternative approach to democratic education in contemporary society, one that is committed not to social or political outcomes but to an ideal of human development applicable to all students.

7. This chapter can help examine our tendency to believe that the dominant way of thinking about school and society in a particular era was the only "sensible" approach or that it was a necessary "product of the times" and therefore a consensus view.

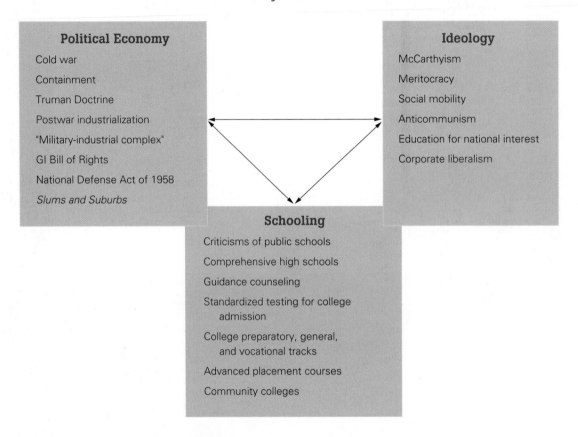

Analytic Framework
The Early Cold War Era

Political Economy

Cold war

Containment

Truman Doctrine

Postwar industrialization

"Military-industrial complex"

GI Bill of Rights

National Defense Act of 1958

Slums and Suburbs

Ideology

McCarthyism

Meritocracy

Social mobility

Anticommunism

Education for national interest

Corporate liberalism

Schooling

Criticisms of public schools

Comprehensive high schools

Guidance counseling

Standardized testing for college admission

College preparatory, general, and vocational tracks

Advanced placement courses

Community colleges

Introduction: The Best and Brightest . . .

By the turn of the 20th century most American children attended school, public or private. But only a minority proceeded beyond the eighth grade. Very few young people went on to high school, and even fewer graduated. The public high school did not become a mass institution until the 1930s. Even after World War II, educators continued to tinker with the high school's structure and curriculum as new populations of students sought to enter its doors and as policymakers increasingly looked to the high school for answers to society's problems. This period of American educational history, extending from the 1930s to the 1960s, not only witnessed the institutionalization of the public high school but led policymakers to link educational quality to national security. Fervently committed to

the notion that the schools could be used effectively to fight the cold war, James B. Conant became one of the chief architects of the public high school during this era. As educational philosopher James E. McClellan wrote in 1968, "If a foreign visitor to these benighted shores were required to take his views about the policies governing American education from one, and only one man . . . there could be only one sensible choice. . . . If any man spoke for and to American educational policy (granted that in a most important sense no man does or can)—that man would be James Bryant Conant."[1]

As the president of Harvard University from 1933 to 1953 and later as a public school investigator and reformer, Conant took advantage of an unprecedented opportunity to influence educational policy. For over 30 years Conant promoted his meritocratic vision, stressing the selective function of schooling and the advancement of the talented youngster. Through Conant's judicious use

consciousness. His affiliations with large corporations such as DuPont indicated to *The Nation* that Conant might be "of that category of technicians for whom the captains of industry loom as great men, wisely entrusted with the destinies of our social order."[15]

The early years of Conant's presidency were marked by his decision to upgrade the faculty and bring a broader range of students to Harvard. He sought first to clear the faculty ranks of what he regarded as dead weight, while hiring and promoting professors who had made important scholarly contributions to their fields. Some praised this new "up or out" policy, as it came to be called, but others attacked it as unfairly subordinating good teaching to the promotion of research. Conant maintained that the university gave equal consideration to both teaching and research in making faculty promotions and that up or out was a painful but effective way to enhance faculty quality.

Standardized Testing and Student Selection

Seeking to tear down some of the geographic and financial barriers that had traditionally limited Harvard's enrollment to students from the elite public and private schools of the Northeast, Conant proposed a National Scholarship Program. This program would identify able young scholars and make it feasible for them to attend Harvard. But Conant believed the program was doomed to fail unless a reliable and valid measure of academic aptitude could be found to ensure objectivity in determining scholarship eligibility. After much deliberation and consultation with his assistant deans, Henry Chauncey and Wilbur Bender, Conant settled on the Scholastic Aptitude Test (SAT). Assistant deans Bender and Chauncey favored the SAT for the efficiency with which the multiple-choice test could be administered and evaluated. Perhaps they were also impressed with the test developer's description of the exam as a series of progressively more difficult questions, each with its own unambiguous solution and increasingly tempting "traps."

By the mid-1930s Harvard had adopted the SAT, finding it a very satisfactory device for selecting promising scholars. Owing to this success, Harvard eventually employed the SAT as a standard by which all undergraduate applicants would be measured. As Conant said: "The record seems to show that Harvard's interest in the use of objective tests for selecting national scholars was an important factor in promoting the use of the tests for general admission purposes. My own interest in the new type of examinations certainly was aroused by the report of Bender and Chauncey and its outcome. Eventually it would lead to my playing a part in the establishment of the Educational Testing Service."[16]

Indeed, as Conant recalled it, his enthusiasm for the SAT represented an "almost naive faith" in standardized tests. He came to believe that exams such as the SAT offered a nearly foolproof method for ascertaining academic promise. He also thought that the testing movement provided a solution to some of the problems of public school instruction. With the help of testing, he maintained, a child's inherent abilities could be determined as early as age 12, and appropriate instruction then could be prescribed. Despite minor shifts in his point of view, for three decades Conant remained one of the most vigorous supporters of testing, vocational guidance, and the selective function of schooling.

Throughout the 1930s Conant traveled extensively to convince Harvard alumni and the general public of the need for national scholarships and standardized testing. Frequently, he referred to himself as an "educational Calvinist." By this Conant meant that most students were "predestined" to exhibit certain set capacities early in their school careers which were "highly resistant to change by external agencies." Moreover, as Conant saw it, a "strict educational Calvinist" was primarily concerned with sorting and classifying students according to their aptitude as measured by tests.[17]

Conant did not worry that standardized tests might penalize late bloomers, because he doubted that even education could help a previously undetected talent to emerge. He observed, "The percentage of those who have a delayed intellectual awakening was . . . too small to bother with." Conant's son, Theodore, later noted regarding his father's convictions: "He basically felt you were pretty well formed by heredity more than environment and you were going to pretty well act out in sort of a Greek tragedy."[18]

Conant's view of human nature and the education process suited him well for his leading role in the creation of the Educational Testing Service. In the 1930s the College Entrance Examination Board, the American Council on Education, and the Carnegie Corporation all provided colleges and universities with a variety of standardized tests for making admissions decisions. Advocates of testing, such as Conant and Henry Chauncey, thought that consolidating the testing divisions of these three agencies would strengthen the testing movement and give new impetus to the SAT as a leading admissions criterion. After many years of debate, the three divisions merged in 1947 to form the Educational Testing Service (ETS). As a member of its first board of trustees, Conant played a crucial role in the formation of ETS, stating in his memoirs, "The establishment of ETS was part of an educational revolution in which I am proud to have played a part." With the appointment of Henry Chauncey, Conant's former assistant dean, to the presidency of ETS, Conant boasted that he set Chauncey up in business. He also could have boasted that with the establishment of the ETS, America had moved one step closer to Conant's vision of the meritocratic society.[19]

> **Thinking Critically about the Issues   #2**
>
> To what degree did standardized testing affect your education or your life plans?

Who Merits a College Education?

Like many other Americans, Conant feared the long-term consequences of the great depression. The hard times dampened the traditional optimism of Americans, engendering skepticism about the value of free enterprise and democracy. Some found fascism and communism appealing, while others wanted to expand significantly the role of government in economic planning. Many Americans looked to Germany, Italy, and Japan for alternative roads back to prosperity. Developments abroad intensified Conant's sensitivity to the fragility of democracy and led to a redoubling of his commitment to capitalism and free enterprise. He concluded that the depression and totalitarianism jeopardized what he regarded as the very backbone of democracy—social mobility.

Redistributing wealth or achieving equality of condition would not resolve this crisis. But school reform could help forestall permanent class stratification. Scholarships and accelerated classes would encourage the intellectually gifted, while vocational education would meet the needs of the less academically able. Conant counted on Harvard and other elite institutions to awaken rank-and-file teachers to the new demands of modern society and to work with him to foster a new sense of community in the schools. Separate schools for the gifted and dull, although advantageous in some ways, would in the long run only contribute to further divisiveness and a continued

retreat from Conant's ideal of social mobility. Echoing Charles Eliot's fears and hopes, Conant wrote in 1940, "In short, a horde of heterogeneous students has descended on our secondary schools, and on our ability to handle all types intelligently depends in large measure the future of this country."[20]

> **Thinking Critically about the Issues   #3**
>
> Are excellence and equality compatible ideals? Explain.

In the dark days before World War II, Conant advanced the view that by giving recognition to the best students and helping the rest of the students find their educational niche, the schools would be promoting social stability and thus greatly enhancing national security. He feared, however, that in practice schools were not doing enough to discourage "marginal" high school students from pursuing a college education. In 1940, with 11 percent of high school students going on to college, Conant called them the wrong 11 percent and far more than American colleges could effectively teach without lowering standards. In addition to the problem of standards, Conant was concerned that an excessively large population of college students might cause disruptions in the social order. With social stability, not the intellectual fulfillment of each student, as his first priority, Conant warned: "I doubt if society can make a graver mistake than to provide advanced higher education of a specialized nature for men and women who are unable subsequently to use this training. Quite apart from economic considerations the existence of any large number of highly educated individuals whose ambitions have been frustrated is unhealthy for any nation."[21]

Near the end of World War II, the GI Bill of Rights provided full college scholarships to all veterans regardless of their academic "aptitudes." As a group, veterans had worse academic records and lower SAT scores than the average college student. Before the passage of this bill, Conant had lobbied vigorously for granting college subsidies only to a select group of veterans who had demonstrated high intellectual capacity. Given Conant's view that college should maintain a high level of selectivity, failure to win support for his version of the bill must have been a bitter defeat. Like his presidential counterpart at the University of Chicago, Robert Hutchins, Conant feared that an influx of nontraditional students

The college success of World War II veterans, many of whom had poor educational backgrounds, helped discredit the notion of Conant and others that the bill's nonselective nature would lead to massive academic failures.

would lead to a lowering of academic standards. Years later he complained that the passage of the GI Bill of Rights indicated America's unwillingness to accept the selective principle of education, which he regarded as essential in a free and fluid society.

Conant did not address the fact that his and Hutchins's fears of lowered standards had proved unwarranted. The GI Bill became one of the greatest academic successes in American history. Over two million veterans took advantage of the opportunity to attend college during the seven years the program was offered, and almost one-fourth of them probably would have never attended college without the bill's subsidies. Most impressive of all, more veterans than nonveterans distinguished themselves in academically rigorous courses. Veterans earned better grades than nonveterans, and contrary to Hutchins's predictions, they enrolled in liberal arts courses in far greater numbers than nonveterans. Although Congress passed the GI Bill partly to forestall massive postwar unemployment, the results of the bill showed that mature students, even from nonacademic backgrounds, could flourish in an academic atmosphere.[22]

What may have eluded Conant, or at least what he chose never to comment on, was the striking fact that the GI Bill provided millions of "academically promising" students the opportunity to prove themselves as "late bloomers." Undeterred, Conant never wavered from his belief that the "late bloomer" was a myth perpetuated by an American public unwilling to accept fully what he regarded as one of education's chief functions—to sort and to classify students by their cognitive ability.[23]

School Reform Reports and Social Stratification

In 1945, with World War II coming to a close and concerns about the postwar era becoming increasingly acute, a spate of reports appeared on the future needs of American education. Three of the most widely read and discussed of these documents were Harvard University's *General Education in a Free Society,* the Educational Policy Commission's *Education for All American Youth,* and a sociological study, *Who Shall Be Educated?* The Harvard report set forth lucidly and eloquently the theory and philosophy of general education. In searching for an overall logic or unity to secondary school instruction, the authors emphasized the goals of effective thinking and clear communication of thought. Moreover, the authors of this report affirmed that the great majority of high school students would benefit from a challenging course of study largely derived from the liberal arts.

The goals of the Harvard report stood in stark contrast to the objectives of the Educational Policy Commission's (EPC) *Education for All American Youth* and Lloyd Warner, Robert Havighurst, and Martin Loeb's *Who Shall Be Educated?* The EPC, with its life-adjustment orientation, asserted that only the 15 or 20 percent of students going on to college should be encouraged to take a full complement of academic subjects. Less able students, the EPC explained, would focus on three practical goals during their four years of high school: vocational efficiency, civic competence, and personal development. Largely agreeing with the EPC, Warner, Havighurst, and Loeb argued that schools should be used to increase the degree of social mobility only moderately. To try to do more than this, the authors maintained, would be to encourage more students to rise to the top of the social pyramid than could be accommodated by the status system. The authors thus called for a secondary school that would differentiate students according to measured ability and use an experienced staff of guidance counselors to carry out a sorting function closely corresponding to society's vocational needs.

As the initiator of the Harvard report, a member of the commission that had produced *All American Youth,* and an admirer of *Who Shall Be Educated?* Conant sought to offer a picture of American education that would draw liberally on all three documents. He got his chance when Columbia University invited him to deliver the prestigious Julius and Rose Sachs Lectures in November 1945. In the three lectures, which he collectively titled *Public Education and the Structure of American Society,* Conant focused on what he regarded as the necessary relation between education and equality of opportunity. Although education had the potential to foster a high degree of social fluidity and reduce the emphasis on class distinctions and hereditary privilege, he lamented that in the first decades of the 20th century education had tended to increase stratification in the United States. Without progress toward greater social mobility, Conant feared that more discontented Americans would endeavor to foment social change through violent action. He thus concluded that "the chances of a nonrevolutionary development of our nation in the next fifty years seem to me to be determined largely by our educational system."

As Conant saw it, if Americans would accept his vision of the ideal democracy, the potential violence and disruption of the postwar years could be averted. In his history of the Scholastic Aptitude Test, Nicholas Lemann has said that the big question for Conant was this: "How can you build a classless society through the mechanism of relentlessly classifying the entire population?"[24] First, Conant answered, Americans must acknowledge the important place of the well-trained, meritorious expert in every important field. Second, they must reject advancement through hereditary privilege and embrace a fluid social structure that would allow talented people from any social class to rise to positions of importance and responsibility. Third, all types of labor must be regarded as equal, with no position being accorded more social status than any other. Once these values were accepted, Conant observed, students would no longer feel compelled to attend college to reap the rewards of high status. Higher education, then, would be attractive only to those who genuinely merited it and required it in their eventual occupations. Public schools would play a crucial role in this process by sorting students according to their ability, and guidance counselors would assume the important job of selecting students for college preparatory courses. In response to those who feared that guidance counselors

might use their positions of authority to coerce students, Conant stated that school personnel could be counted on to employ "the democratic method of enlightenment and persuasion."[25]

To make all of this work, Conant asserted, "there should be no hierarchy of educational discipline, no one channel should have a social standing above the other." But as an exasperated Nicholas Lemann has exclaimed: "Was this touchingly naïve, or willfully naïve, or just unpardonably naïve?"[26] What hope was there really of creating such an academic culture, Lemann wondered, or was Conant merely attempting to mollify those who stood to benefit the least from his meritocratic vision?

Thinking Critically about the Issues   #4

Critically analyze the degree to which Conant's educational recommendations might be characterized as elitist in nature.

Education in a Divided World

Three years later, with tensions between the United States and the Soviet Union steadily increasing, Conant expanded the Sachs Lectures into a book titled *Education in a Divided World.* In this book, Conant argued that by promoting greater cultural and social unity, the American public schools could serve as the first bulwark of defense against the Soviets. As Conant saw it, the United States would prevail in the protracted struggle between the two superpowers if American students learned to recognize and condemn the defects of the Soviet system while absorbing "the historic goals of our unique society."

In one section of *Education in a Divided World* Conant attempted to demonstrate the superiority of American ideology by contrasting Soviet and American attitudes toward the individual in society. Whereas the United States regards the individual as sacrosanct, Conant offered, the Soviets subordinate the individual's welfare to the demands of the state. Yet as we have seen, Conant had consistently treated the individual as a means to the end of greater cultural, social, and political unity. Ironically, Conant employed quotations from Arthur Koestler's novel *Darkness at Noon* to heighten this contrast. Yet as educational philosopher James McClellan had pointed out, Conant did not fully explore the implications of Koestler's work. A major theme in *Darkness at Noon* is that even more important than making a choice of values or demonstrating the superiority of one ideology over another is the necessity of keeping responsible discourse and inquiry going. Conant, however, appeared willing to sacrifice the pursuit of knowledge and mutual understanding to the pursuit of American dominance.[27]

Conant's contribution to a 1951 pamphlet called *Education and National Security* extended the theme of how educators could help the United States compete more effectively with the Soviet Union. While the school must impart certain moral and spiritual values, its overriding purposes involved supplying the armed forces with adequate personnel and training people to meet the nation's critical needs. Whereas they condoned the study of history and critical thought, the authors also praised instructors for teaching their charges to accept and support American foreign-policy engagements such as the "police action" that then raged in Korea. The authors also wrote approvingly that teachers determine "how readily the young recruit adapts himself to military life, how the industrial employee learns his assigned operation, and with what speed and accuracy the new stenographer transcribes her notes."[28]

In his last year before leaving Harvard in 1953 to become the U.S. high commissioner to Germany, Conant published *Education and Liberty*. Based on a series of lectures delivered at the University of Virginia, this book again affirmed Conant's faith in American public schools. It also showed his growing mastery of the complexities of educational systems in Australia, New Zealand, Scotland, and England. Conant's recent investigations of Australian and New Zealand schools (made possible by a grant from the Carnegie Corporation) and increasingly broad knowledge of British educational history considerably sharpened his ability to draw parallels between those school systems and public education in the United States. Although he noted the effectiveness of those nations in educating talented youngsters, Conant's comparative study amounted to a celebration of both the diversity and the democratic unity of American public education.

For the first time in his major writings, Conant stressed the unique function of the American comprehensive high school. By mixing students of vastly different backgrounds and abilities in the same school, he observed, the comprehensive high school minimized class distinctions and avoided many of the social cleavages that characterized the other societies he had investigated. Whereas

schools in most other countries were highly centralized and run by the state, local communities administered American schools, greatly increasing educational diversity and the opportunity for experimentation. Conant conceded that inferior schools tended to emerge under America's decentralized system and that some of those schools were poorly equipped to prepare the academically talented for college. In general, however, he acclaimed the American comprehensive high school for its role in nourishing democratic unity.

Thinking Critically about the Issues   #5

Did the comprehensive high school form a part of your school experience? If so, how did it affect the education of your fellow students?

Although Soviet communism largely remained a tacit backdrop to *Education and Liberty,* at one point Conant articulated the chief assumption of his educational proposals. "If the field of Waterloo was won on the playing fields of Eton, it may well be that the ideological struggle with Communism in the next fifty years will be won on playing fields of the public high schools of the United States. That this may be so is the fervent hope of all of us who are working to support and improve these characteristic American institutions."[29]

As Conant left Harvard, he continued to reflect on the role of the American comprehensive high school. In *Education and Liberty* he had accumulated and presented more firsthand knowledge of Australian and New Zealand schools than he had of American schools. By closely studying test results and directly observing selected American high schools, Conant hoped to demonstrate that comprehensive secondary schools educated the academically talented as thoroughly as did European-style homogeneous secondary schools. This objective would serve as the initial basis for Conant's investigation of the American high school, a task he would undertake after serving his country for four years in Germany.

School Reform in the Postwar Era

In the postwar years educational debate in the United States centered on the value of schooling for "life adjustment." In 1945 Charles Prosser, one of the early boosters of vocational education, declared that schools had failed to educate the majority of high school youth for

One of Conant's major victories was helping establish the Educational Testing Service, which was responsible for developing the Scholastic Aptitude Test (SAT).

the demands of modern life. Claiming that most students had spurned the traditional academic curriculum or had rejected vocational education, Prosser argued that those students needed instruction in the practical arts of home and family life and civic competence. Although the life-adjustment curriculum would not omit science, math, and the humanities, those courses would stress hands-on experience and focus on contemporary problems. As one life-adjustment document put it, "citizenship training must concentrate on understanding the present, not studying the past."[30]

Although life-adjustment educators intended to make schooling more relevant and "functional," many of the courses that appeared in school districts around the country in the half decade after the war appeared to reflect a powerful anti-intellectual bias. In some school districts, entire instructional units were devoted to the etiquette of dating, including discussion of such questions as "Do girls want to 'pet'?" and "Should you go in with a girl after a date (to raid the ice box)?" As educational historian Diane Ravitch has pointed out, time and again one could find evidence of school instruction during this period which taught "children what kind of behavior was socially acceptable and how to adjust to group expectations."[31]

Beginning in 1949 and continuing for about a decade, a torrent of articles and books appeared that censured the public schools for lowering standards and in general miseducating American youth. Almost all these observers of the educational scene agreed that progressive reforms and especially life adjustment had sadly diminished the importance of academic achievement. By stressing personality development and meeting each student's individual needs, the critics argued, the schools were neglecting the traditional intellectual subjects and were thus failing to impart mental and moral discipline.

Of all the critics, perhaps the most interesting and perceptive were former urban school board member Mortimer Smith and noted professional historian Arthur Bestor. Both adamantly maintained that the primary purpose of schooling should be intellectual training, and both tenaciously clung to the belief that even the most ordinary student could profit from a rigorously intellectual course of study. While conceding the importance of serving a student's needs, interests, and abilities, Smith insisted that to develop well-roundedness, all students should be required to work at things for which they might not have talent. Bestor affirmed the importance of giving all students a solid liberal arts education regardless of how deficient their family or cultural background might appear. As Bestor saw it, the school could have no more important function than to overcome educational handicaps, thereby achieving its true democratic mission of meeting the fundamental need of all people for intellectual enrichment.

In 1956, Smith, Bestor, and colleagues of theirs formed the Council for Basic Education (CBE). The CBE's commitment to making intellectual training the highest priority of the public schools was as strong as its opposition to the differentiation of students by ability. The CBE's original statement of purpose declared "that only by the maintenance of high academic standards can the ideal of democratic education be realized—the ideal of offering to all the children of all the people of the United States not merely an opportunity to attend school, but the privilege of receiving there the soundest education that is offered any place in the world."[32]

Another critic of life-adjustment education, Admiral Hyman Rickover, took a different view. For Rickover, a naval engineer and nuclear submarine designer, technical and scientific education for a small, talented elite took precedence over all other kinds of schooling. As a naval admiral and stalwart cold warrior, Rickover asserted that "education is America's first line of defense" in competing with the Soviet Union. Although Rickover spoke of educating all children well, he focused attention on the 15 or 20 percent he regarded as academically talented. The future mathematicians, physicists, and linguists, he believed, must be trained in homogeneous, European-style secondary schools where academic standards would be maintained and sentimental attachments to the slow child would not impede the main task at hand. Rickover not only rejected mixed-ability classes but also regarded the comprehensive high school as an unfortunate vestige of a less complicated era. Rickover envisioned a school system that would identify talented students at an early age and enroll them in accelerated educational programs. In the long run, he argued, this highly selective process would enhance American freedom by helping the United States keep pace with the Soviets. Rickover's envisioned school system might slight the majority of students, but as Rickover reminded his readers, "The future belongs to the best educated nation. Let it be ours."[33]

After the Soviets launched *Sputnik* in 1957, alarming the American public and making them think that their schools had failed to teach science and math to an entire generation of students, Rickover's elitist perspective sparked new interest. In response to spreading fears that the United States was losing the cold war because of its intellectually feeble school system, Congress passed the National Defense Education Act of 1958. With strong endorsement from President Eisenhower, this legislation allocated millions of dollars for upgrading the teaching of science and math and improving procedures for identifying and educating gifted students. The hearings that led up to this legislation and the general concern regarding Russian technological superiority launched a new round of attacks against the public schools.

In the middle of this continuing debate, in the late winter of 1959, James B. Conant released his first study of secondary schools, *The American High School Today*. Conant asserted that the comprehensive high school, by educating academic and vocational students under the same roof, contributed to democratic unity while also doing an adequate job of preparing both populations for their respective post–high school destinations. Most important to school people, who had grown tired of defending themselves against an unremitting barrage of educational criticism, Conant appeared to accept the educational status quo with only minor modifications. Indeed, Conant's skillful manipulation of public opinion ensured *The American High School Today* wide and favorable exposure, which tended to defuse subsequent educational criticism. How Conant accomplished this feat requires us to examine closely some of the events that led up to the publication of *The American High School Today*.

The Great Talent Hunt

Between 1953 and 1957, while Conant served as high commissioner to Germany, John Gardner, the president of the Carnegie Corporation, and Henry Chauncey, the head of the ETS since 1947, indicated in their annual reports that their thinking about the education of the academically talented closely paralleled Conant's. At ETS, which had quickly become the most powerful institution for sorting young people in American society, Chauncey referred year after year to the role standardized tests were increasingly playing in identifying scientific and technical talent. He feared Soviet technological superiority but suggested that testing and guidance could become America's "secret weapon" by making "our education system fit the needs of youth better than the Russian system meets the needs of Russian youth."[34]

Although less concerned with the Soviets, John Gardner also emphasized the importance of educating talented youth. In his first annual report for the Carnegie Corporation, Gardner showed that he put great faith in IQ tests. He stated that a student with an IQ score between 108 and 115 would barely qualify for admission to a four-year college and that an IQ below 108 just about eliminated a student's chance to compete effectively in college. Increasingly, Conant frequently referred to an IQ of 115 as an appropriate cutoff for identifying the academically talented.

Thinking Critically about the Issues   #6

Explain the role that concern about national security played in at least five of James B. Conant's educational proposals.

In 1956 Gardner titled his second annual report "The Great Talent Hunt." He described at length the important new role that the gifted must play in American society and the special obligation of educators to challenge those students and develop their talents. In subsequent reports Gardner continued to stress the education of the talented but also tried to make a case for counseling students away from college who he believed were not suited for it. In his book *Excellence,* which appeared shortly after the first Conant report, Gardner wrote that the educational system must work effectively as a "sorting-out process." As Gardner put it, "The Schools are the golden avenue of opportunity for able youngsters; but by the same token they are the arena in which less able youngsters discover their limitations." Thus, in the late 1950s Gardner was advancing the same themes that Conant had been voicing since the late 1930s: identifying and promoting the talented while discouraging the rest of the students from enrolling in college preparatory programs.[35]

In December of 1956 Conant proposed to Gardner that the Carnegie Corporation finance his investigation of the education of talented youth in comprehensive high schools. Although he sought to ascertain whether a school containing college-bound and non-college-bound students could educate both populations effectively, he was chiefly interested in the academically talented. Could the comprehensive high school identify and develop students with IQs of 115 or better and provide them with solid instruction in a foreign language, mathematics through calculus, physics and chemistry, English

literature and language, and several years of history? If this important task could be accomplished in a school also attended by less able students, the comprehensive high school would be realizing its crucial mission: the identification and development of the most academically talented and the social integration of both college-bound and non-college-bound students.

On May 16, 1957, the board of trustees of the Carnegie Corporation announced that it was approving the appropriation of $350,000 to the ETS for the administration of the study of the American high school by James B. Conant. By that time the objectives of the study had been clarified, the staff had been hired, the schools to be studied had been identified and contacted, and a tentative schedule of school visits had been worked out.

Between September 1957 and July 1958 Conant conducted the first phase of his study. During that period Conant and an associate visited over 50 comprehensive high schools in 18 states, filing a detailed report after each visit. According to Conant, those schools all had a "high degree of comprehensiveness"—that is, with more than half the students enrolled in vocational programs and with a significant minority taking college preparatory classes. Conant and his staff deemed a comprehensive high school satisfactory if it gave "a good general education for *all* the pupils as future citizens of a democracy, provide[d] elective programs for the majority to develop useful skills, and educate[d] adequately those with a talent for handling advanced academic subjects—particularly foreign languages and advanced mathematics."[36]

At the conclusion of his investigations Conant reported that eight schools were successfully fulfilling his objectives for the comprehensive high school. Although reluctant to make sweeping generalizations about the condition of public secondary education in the United States, Conant admitted that "no radical alteration in the basic pattern of American education is necessary in order to improve public high schools." By so uncritically accepting the educational status quo, Conant ensured a favorable reception for his report. While Conant did offer 21 recommendations for improving public high schools, as historian Raymond Callahan has said, "Any superintendent who could say he was adopting Conant's recommendations, or better yet, that his school system had already been following them for years, was almost impregnable." Consequently, shortly after the publication of *The American High School Today,* Conant achieved wide renown as America's premier educational statesman. To express its gratitude formally, the American Association of School Administrators presented Conant with a specially inscribed award:

> Thomas Jefferson, more than any other man, convinced the new nation that education is essential to a free people. Horace Mann, more than any other man, convinced the expanding nation that public schools supported by all and open to all must be established if the nation was to achieve its destiny. A century later, with the people frightened, the nation threatened, free institutions held in doubt, and the public schools under severe criticism, James Bryant Conant, more than any other man, by his logic, keen analysis, patriotic sacrifice, and courageous vision rekindled the nation's flame of faith in free men's basic human values and rebuilt confidence in the public schools of America.[37]

Although the upbeat message Conant communicated to public educators partly explained the favorable reception his first report received, a skillfully engineered media blitz also greatly increased its chances for success. Both Conant and the Carnegie Corporation/ETS conglomerate maintained important ties to leading book publishers, newspapers, and magazines that helped keep Conant's name constantly in the public eye. Furthermore, the publicity campaign for *The American High School Today* was planned meticulously. The campaign organizers designated themselves the "joint chiefs"; they called the Carnegie Corporation offices the "control center" and often wrote of the best way to deploy their forces. To sustain media coverage over a period of months, the "joint chiefs" built a news release structure that ensured the appearance of a continuing stream of newspaper and magazine articles about Conant and his study. As the joint chiefs put it, they wanted to treat the publication of *The American High School Today* as a news story, not a literary event that might put them at the mercy of unfriendly book reviewers. With McGraw-Hill lined up to publish the Conant reports, a key pillar of the envisioned release structure was intact. One of McGraw-Hill's initial advertisements indicated the firm's willingness to promote Conant's study forcefully. In boldface letters, it read

THE CONANT REPORT—A BOOK THAT WILL AROUSE NATIONAL ATTENTION AND MAKE EDUCATIONAL HISTORY.[38]

Careful timing also helped *The American High School Today* attract attention. After spending his first year personally investigating secondary schools, Conant had planned to spend another full year talking to school boards and getting their reactions to his findings and tentative recommendations. Conant curtailed these visits in order to hurry the report's release. As Conant and his advisers knew, by January 1959 the public was ready for an affirmative and constructive study on public education. Conant consciously wrote the report to give the public exactly what it wanted.

Conant praised the comprehensive high school and condemned radical solutions, but two major concerns tempered his upbeat message. First, the small high school (with a graduating class of fewer than 100 students) would have to be eliminated. According to Conant, it was expensive and inefficient to maintain good academic and vocational programs for so few students. Since the small schools rarely bore the necessary costs willingly, inferior education was the usual result. Second, Conant believed that too many schools, both large and small, were not sufficiently challenging the academically talented. Especially troublesome were the number of boys neglecting courses in science and mathematics. Conant also lamented the dearth of four-year foreign language programs in the high schools he visited. In addition to believing that foreign language study exposes the future scientist or engineer to another culture, Conant stressed that "our grim competition with the Soviet Union in the newly developing countries calls for people who can pick up a language quickly and match their Russian counterparts who realize the importance of linguistic competence."[39]

Even before *The American High School Today* had become a best-seller, positioning him as the nation's number-one educational expert, Conant wrote a confidential memo to his staff that took the public schools to task for failing to challenge the academically talented. In the memo he admitted that he presented his findings more positively than he would have if he had not been writing in reaction to a negative and tense atmosphere of debate. Still, he confided that the vast majority of the schools he visited were badly neglecting the education of the most gifted students. Conant particularly blamed the educational establishment in state universities for graduating so many teachers who tended to give the same amount of attention to all their students regardless of academic aptitude.[40]

In *The American High School Today*, Conant did not reveal his underlying reasons for vigorously promoting the training of the best students. Although his earlier writings showed that concerns about the Soviet threat had spurred his school reform efforts, school people unfamiliar with these ideas had to consult a lesser-known companion volume to understand the full thrust of Conant's educational message. Titled *The Child, the Parent, and the State,* this book represented in a sense the social and philosophical underpinnings of *The American High School Today.* Throughout this work, Conant maintained that the divided world he had described 10 years earlier still prevailed and that the schools had the same responsibility to take up the challenge of halting the spread of Soviet communism. Conant believed Americans had adjusted too easily to living in a "divided world" and had failed to take seriously the role of the schools in effectively competing with the Soviets. If Americans conceded the gravity of the rivalry between the United States and the Soviet Union, Conant argued, they would actively work to eliminate the small inefficient high school, increase foreign language study, and in general see to it that talented youth developed their abilities as fully as possible. After all, Conant warned, these future scientists, engineers, and professionals would prove to be invaluable weapons in the technological race with the Soviets.

Conant rejected Admiral Rickover's proposal that Americans support separate schools for the academically talented. He believed that the public high school should enroll students preparing for vocations along with those preparing for college, but his rationale was largely social, not educational. First and foremost, this arrangement would foster greater democratic feeling. It would forge closer relationships among future professional people, craftspersons, engineers, and labor leaders and help promote "not only equality of opportunity but equality of esteem in all forms of labor." Conant wavered on the direct benefits of vocational education, however. At times he thought it could effectively prepare students for particular vocations. At one point he compared vocational education to the advanced placement program, because, like the gifted college preparatory student, the able vocational student should be in a position to assume the responsibilities of a second-year apprentice in many skilled trades. But more often and more realistically, Conant referred to vocational education as a "motivating force" that would keep the potential dropout in school, where he would learn the vocational habits and citizenship responsibilities demanded by modern American society.[41]

One of Conant's blind spots, even within this narrow vision of educational opportunity, was the education of females. As he proceeded with his investigations of American high schools, he came to realize that many of the academically talented students who were not being challenged and encouraged to go on to college were girls. He was not troubled by this, because he particularly wanted to recruit males for strategically important careers and, at the same time, sought to reduce college enrollments. As Conant put it, "a good deal of the talk about the bright people who don't go to college just may be a question of the girls."[42] In response to a letter from the president of Bennington College, inquiring why Conant put so much emphasis on hard, male-oriented subjects like science, math, and engineering, Conant explained matter-of-factly: "If we were not living in such a grim world, I doubt that I should advocate the high school program I recommend in my report. From the academically talented will come the future doctors, lawyers, engineers, scientists and scholars, as well as . . . business executives. These professional people will be 97 percent men."[43] Ever eager to avoid controversy, Conant confined his thoughts on these matters to private correspondence. But these sentiments remained still another sign of Conant's willingness, indeed, his intent, to restrict the education of the majority to further the education of that small, predominantly male elite whom he believed would uphold the national interest.

Slums and Subversives

Conant's continuing interest in the comprehensive high school as a source of social cohesion led him eventually to investigate the segregated urban and elite suburban high schools of the Northeast and Midwest. The schools Conant visited, which formed the basis for his next book, *Slums and Suburbs,* were the very antithesis of the comprehensive high school. At one extreme, the urban schools in low-income and poverty neighborhoods stressed vocational education and direct preparation of students for the workplace. At the other extreme, the wealthy suburban schools educated almost all their students for college. Conant particularly regretted the tendency of suburban parents to push their children into college preparatory courses regardless of their academic ability. Wider use of guidance services and standardized test scores would encourage more students to enter vocational programs, Conant thought, and increase the comprehensiveness of these elite schools. When it came to the impoverished urban schools, however, as historian Clarence Karier has said, Conant's "sense of ideal community gave way to what he judged was practically possible."

Historical Context

The Early Cold War Era

The following events should help you situate the educational developments in this chapter in a broader historical context. These events are illustrative; you might have chosen different ones if you were constructing such a timeline. For any item, you should be able to consider, What is its educational significance? Some of these events are not mentioned in the chapter and might lead you to further inquiry.

1940s

1940	U.S. Department of Labor reports that less than 17 percent of all married women in the United States are employed outside the home
1941–1945	United States enters World War II after the bombing of Pearl Harbor; women enter the workforce while men are at war; African Americans pressure Roosevelt to establish Fair Employment Practices Committee
1944	GI Bill of Rights is passed, paving the way for masses of World War II veterans to attain a college education at government expense
1945	Thousands of White students walk out of classes to protest integration in Gary, Indiana; this walkout becomes a precedent for future resistance to integration
1945	United States destroys Hiroshima and Nagasaki with first use of atomic bomb, bringing an end to World War II in the Pacific
1948	Truman orders end to segregation in armed forces
1949	Nuclear arms race between the United States and the Soviet Union begins when Soviets test atomic bomb

1950s

1950	Senator Joseph McCarthy whips up national fears of communists in media, entertainment, government, and public life
1953	Julius and Ethel Rosenberg executed for atomic secrets spying
1954	Supreme Court rules in *Brown* v. *Board of Education of Topeka* that segregated schools are "inherently unequal" and thus unconstitutional, reversing *Plessy* v. *Ferguson; Brown* also establishes that other public facilities separated on basis of race are inherently unequal
1955	Supreme Court orders that the integration of schools proceed "with all deliberate speed"
1955	Montgomery bus boycott begins as result of Rosa Parks's refusal to sit in the back of the bus
1957	Launching of *Sputnik I* by the USSR leads Americans to believe that the Soviets are ahead in missile technology; schools blamed for "technology gap"
1957	Southern Christian Leadership Conference forms; led by Martin Luther King, Jr., it is dedicated to nonviolent protest of racial discrimination
1958	U.S. National Defense Education Act promotes teaching of sciences, foreign languages, and mathematics
1959	Fidel Castro takes power in Cuba, forming first communist government in Latin America
1959	James B. Conant publishes *The American High School Today*

1960s

1961	Michael Harrington publishes *The Other America,* revealing that millions of Americans live below poverty level
1962	Students for a Democratic Society leads student protests against Vietnam throughout the nation
1962	Supreme Court orders University of Mississippi to admit student James H. Meredith; Ross Barnett, governor of Mississippi, tries unsuccessfully to block Meredith's admission
1963	Publication of *The Feminine Mystique* by Betty Friedan revitalizes feminist movement
1963	More than 200,000 marchers from all over the country stage the largest protest demonstration in the history of Washington, DC; Rev. Dr. Martin Luther King, Jr., delivers "I Have a Dream" speech
1963	Medgar Evers, field secretary for NAACP, is assassinated outside his home in Jackson, Mississippi
1963	Assassination of John F. Kennedy in Dallas
1964	Civil Rights Act of 1964 is passed, granting equal voting rights to African Americans
1964	Martin Luther King, Jr., awarded Nobel Peace Prize
1964	Escalation of U.S. presence in Vietnam following alleged Gulf of Tonkin incident
1965	Medicare Act, Housing Act, Elementary and Secondary Education Act, a new immigration act, and voting-rights legislation are enacted
1966	National Organization for Women is formed

Thinking Analytically about the Timeline

Besides "cold war fever," how do you interpret what is going on in the United States during the cold war that will change the nation markedly?

Thus, in considering ways to improve urban schools, Conant rejected both racial integration and expansion of academic offerings as impracticable and unnecessary.[44]

Few readers of *Slums and Suburbs* were aware that the threat of Soviet communism again played a key role in arousing Conant's sympathy for the plight of urban schoolchildren. Although he mentioned this threat in only one paragraph of the book, Conant had not lost his talent for dramatically drawing parallels between America's social problems and the waging of the cold war. He wrote: "I do not have to remind the reader that the fate of freedom in the world hangs very much in the balance. . . . Communism feeds upon discontented, frustrated, unemployed people. . . . These young people are my chief concern, especially when they are pocketed together in large numbers within the confines of the big city slums. What can words like 'freedom,' 'liberty,' and 'equality of opportunity' mean to these young people? With what kind of zeal and dedication can we expect them to withstand the relentless pressures of communism? How well prepared are they to face the struggle that shows no sign of abating?"[45]

Conant believed that the struggle to win the hearts and minds of urban youth depended on the effectiveness of vocational education programs. He cited a number of examples of how vocational education in predominantly Black high schools had fostered stability and other desirable social behaviors. Dunbar Vocational High School in Chicago provided a paradigm. While the school tailored its curriculum to meet the students' vocational needs, the academic program also had successfully prepared a handful of students for college, though this was clearly not the school's primary purpose. In fact, students at Dunbar could not remain in the academic program without successfully completing all shop classes. One cannot help wonder how many more students would have gone on to college from Dunbar, or simply enjoyed new intellectual challenges, if academic courses had been stressed as much as vocational ones. Conant approved of some academic courses for minority students and claimed they should constitute at least half of the curriculum. But the entire tone of the "Slums" section of *Slums and Suburbs*—with hardly a reference to the education of the academically talented—had a decided bias toward vocational education.

Conant's advocacy of a system of vocational education for slum schools followed logically from the rest of his educational philosophy. If most Black students scored poorly on IQ and SAT tests and other accepted measures of academic aptitude, and if students performing below the expected levels of excellence (IQ below 115) were to be counseled away from academic courses, then guidance counselors almost by default would be steering most African American students toward vocational studies. Somehow, the thought that these schools, with their vocational emphasis, might be contributing to the "social dynamite" in the cities never occurred to Conant; he just studied the data and offered his recommendations accordingly. He did not seem to understand, as historian Henry Perkinson has pointed out, that "instead of enhancing and fulfilling his expectations of determining his own destiny, this educational 'equality of opportunity' simply corroborated the black child's feelings of powerlessness." By condoning vocationally oriented education for most urban Black youth, Conant was harking back to the theory of "Negro education" promulgated by Booker T. Washington, which relegated Black youth to the least challenging forms of education to prepare them for the most menial jobs.[46]

A bitter irony resides in Conant's vocationalist thinking for students who didn't meet his definition of "academically talented," a definition that excluded all but a few urban African American students. The irony is that in 1954 the U.S. Supreme Court had just ruled that segregation of the races in public schooling is unconstitutional. This ruling, *Brown* v. *The Board of Education,* overturned the Supreme Court ruling of 1896, *Plessy* v. *Ferguson,* which had made "separate but equal" the law of the land shortly after Booker T. Washington had delivered his Atlanta "Cast down your buckets" address. While the *Brown* decision made school segregation illegal, Conant's policies had the consequence of segregating Black students from White students in the college preparatory and advanced placement classes Conant so vigorously endorsed. While separate vocational schools for African Americans would no longer be legal after 1954, a more insidious kind of segregation, which Conant did nothing to curtail, would come to be seen as normal in comprehensive high schools throughout the latter half of the 20th century.

As the 1960s wore on, Conant's fears of the communist bogey gave way to new fears of social unrest. The "social dynamite" he had observed in America's cities began exploding in the middle 1960s. Conflagrations in almost every major city alerted the nation that urban Blacks were fed up with second-class treatment. On college campuses students staged numerous protests against the Vietnam War and authoritarian educational practices. Conant especially feared these developments. He thought that the emergence of the new left posed the latest threat to a stable American democracy. He also became increasingly convinced that the colleges' willingness to accommodate larger and more diverse populations of students had strengthened the position of radical elements on campus. In response to these campus disruptions, Conant actively promoted the junior college movement. Not only would the junior colleges absorb some of those students whom Conant believed had fueled the fires of the protest movement, these colleges would also satisfy the educational ambitions of the most "marginal" students. Moreover, the junior colleges would meet technical training needs rarely addressed in high school and would appear to enhance equal opportunity without sacrificing meritocratic principles and the high standards of the four-year college.[47]

Whatever success the junior colleges might have had in "cooling out" the discontented and defusing the explosive atmosphere on some college campuses, Conant was dismayed that his school reforms had not opened the door to a better world. He applauded the new attention that teachers were giving the academically talented as a result of his efforts, but he regretted the new round of attacks the schools were forced to endure. This time the attacks came from the left, with most critics inveighing against the rigid structure and "mindlessness" that characterized public schools. Nevertheless, Conant adamantly maintained that a properly conceived educational system could help bring about his version of the ideal society. Yet it remained a very unimaginative vision, with an education system designed to help most people seek satisfaction in mind-numbing employment or the periodic opportunity to choose between two nearly identical political candidates. Despite his constant references to democracy, Conant sought a government run by experts with only limited participation by the masses. The education system he had worked for throughout his career would make an important contribution to shaping what the nation's citizens would come to take for granted about how high schools should serve the social order.

Thinking Critically about the Issues   #7

Who determines the "national interest"? How do education and schooling influence the national interest? How are they influenced by the national interest?

Thinking Critically about the Issues   #8

What political outcomes were most important for Conant? Were they compatible with democratic ideology? Explain.

BUILDING A PHILOSOPHY OF EDUCATION

A number of issues in this chapter have great significance for how teachers and other educators see their work today: (1) Is the concept of "meritocracy" a useful one to explain why some students succeed academically and others do not, or is meritocracy more myth than reality? (2) If not everyone is going to attend college, what should high school do for students who, by their own choice or by circumstances they can't control, are not "college bound"? and (3) Whose interests should guide the education of our nation's youth, and who gets to decide that question? A coherent philosophy of education can guide any educator in thinking more clearly about each of these issues.

James B. Conant initially used his Harvard power base to promote what he saw as a more meritocratic society, striving to make the university and the public school adhere to the principles of selectivity and excellence as he understood them. Conant repeatedly warned that the school must first prepare talented youth for strategically necessary scientific, professional, and technological occupations. Only secondarily, he believed, should the school train the rest of the students for occupational roles that played less significant supporting roles in advancing the national interest. Conant's views demonstrate the importance of all three questions above. Is it really a meritocracy, for example, when children from some neighborhoods consistently and predictably do better than children from other neighborhoods? Are we really selecting the most talented, or are we just using schools to select those who started school as the most advantaged? Furthermore, what do we mean by "talent" and how does that affect how we teach and evaluate students from different backgrounds? A teacher's answer to that is likely to influence how he or she teaches and evaluates students. If we assume all kids start at the same place in the competition for school success, then it makes sense to treat them all the same and see who "wins." But if we assume they start at very different places, depending on cultural and economic background, then different strategies are necessary to support the success of different students. In such an environment, the idea of a competitive "meritocracy" makes little sense.

Despite his enduring interest in public education, Conant's first allegiance was to college and university training, which he believed should be reserved strictly for the most meritorious. Only at the college level did the immense investments in the education of young people begin to pay dividends in the production of urgently needed engineers and scientists. It followed that if the lower schools were to serve the more essential colleges, university leaders had to exert considerable influence on the public secondary schools. Believing that the strength of higher education depended on the sorting efficiency of the elementary and secondary schools, Conant and his universities pioneered the SAT, advanced placement, and the academic inventory (a survey of advanced courses available to "talented students in each school") to differentiate more sharply the bright from the dull and the gifted from the average. Accordingly, these reforms increased the schools' abilities to funnel qualified students into colleges to meet more directly the technological and strategic needs of the nation. Not surprisingly, Conant and his other university counterparts gave only the most superficial consideration to the education of non-college-bound students.

When Conant did attend to the problem of educating students he regarded as less able, his solution was vocational education. Instead of seeking to produce self-education and self-cultivating men and women, he favored an education that would psychologically prepare students for a future occupation, thus ensuring a smooth transition from school to work. He opposed giving all students a liberal education, because even if they could profit from such an education, he reasoned, they could

not possibly find jobs commensurate with their educational experience. Knowing the unchallenging nature of most modern work, Conant feared that the resulting frustration would disrupt the social order. Of course, vocational education carried the additional virtue of keeping potential troublemakers in school. At least they would be off the street, perhaps picking up some useful skill while absorbing the responsibilities of citizenship in a pluralistic society. In general, Conant's fears of instability and his belief that most people were incapable of deriving benefit from rigorous teaching and learning impelled him to renounce liberal education for all but a small minority.

But the teacher who wishes to serve democratic ideals may well pause to consider whether the schools should be in the business of predicting and shaping the vocational futures of students. Surely, for the foreseeable future, there is little reason to expect that every single high school student will go on to achieve a baccalaureate degree. But for many teachers, the point of a public education through high school is simply this: to equip each young person with the knowledge and skills to choose the best postsecondary step for himself or herself, and to have the preparation necessary to succeed at that choice. Young people with a strong college-preparatory high school diploma can choose college, the military, technical training, or a job, for example; whereas vocationally trained youth may not be in the position to choose college education or to succeed if they do choose it. Yet, it may be argued, all young people in a democratic culture should be equipped to make that choice for themselves.

The progressive education goals examined in Chapter 4, including social stability, employable skills, meritocracy, and equal educational opportunity, continued to shape school reform in the post–World War II era. The Conant era reforms did not establish new directions for schooling but consolidated old gains from the social efficiency approach. Two dimensions of that approach were embraced by most American educators and the public at large during the Conant era. First, it became a largely unquestioned assumption that the first priority of schooling was promoting "the national interest" as defined by designated leaders. Second, it followed that schools could protect national interests in a cold war by selecting and preparing students for their vocational futures in an expert-led society. As a result of Conant's years of efforts, the role and functions of the American comprehensive high school became increasingly defined by those assumptions.

But in a democratic society, school teachers and administrators need to be wary of having the interests of their students defined as the national interests. Who gets to decide what the national interest is? The party in power at the time? The rich, who dominate the U.S. Senate decade after decade? Big businesses and financial interests, who dominate U.S. economic policy and influence military policy? Is it in the national interest for parents to have a voice in what is in their children's interests? Should teachers, who are the professionals who teach the children and youth? When it comes to how each child is educated, what *is* in the national interests, and who gets to decide? In a democratic culture, how are differences among these different groups' perspectives resolved? Notice that in the Primary Source Reading for this chapter, poet Mark Van Doren expressly addresses the question of educational goals and national interests, and his ideas may have an impact on your own educational philosophy.

The long lament about the ineffectiveness of public schools continues. While a variety of educational officials scramble to assign blame and provide explanations, few of them have assessed the situation historically. Yet the historical record shows clearly that reformers such as Conant used enormous power to consolidate the current structure of American public education. The result of this structure, with standardized testing, tracking, and the differentiated curriculum as its base, has been that the vast majority of students avoid the most academically challenging subjects in favor of courses deemed more appropriate to their skill levels and presumed vocational futures. Although Conant and other reformers claimed to weigh the best interests of all students, in effect they shifted the focus of educational concern from educating each schoolchild

to promoting political, economic, and social stability. Consequently, only a small group of ostensibly "talented" students have been provided with the sort of intellectual challenge that might otherwise be the birthright of every American youth.

In *The Big Test,* Nicholas Lemann concludes his provocative history of the SAT by condemning the assumption of Conant and his accomplices like Henry Chauncey and John Gardner that education at its best is a rigorous sorting-out process. He warns that this is, in fact, the worst possible model for education in a democratic society. He writes: "The chief aim of school should be not to sort out but to teach as many people as possible as well as possible, equipping them not for work but for citizenship. The purpose of schools should be to expand opportunity, not to determine results."[48] This is a sharp and accurate critique, because Conant consistently treated the school as an identifier of talent, not as an institution designed to enlarge and develop ability. Conant always worked from a scarcity model. Talent is both fixed and rare, he insisted. It must be found, not so much to make a good society as to sustain a society capable of holding its own against external or internal threats. Lemann contends that "the best and most distinctive tradition in American education is the tradition of pushing to educate more people."[49] He notes as well that this tradition is not necessarily what traditional leaders have supported, but has been carried forward by everyday leaders in neighborhoods, communities, and schools who have always believed "ordinary people are capable of more," much more than government officials or policymakers or college presidents have ever thought possible.

The lesson for all of us who care about education and making it better is simple. The problems of education should be addressed directly and most powerfully by those closest to children—teachers, parents, community members, and the children themselves. Only they have the knowledge and the commitment to help individual schools reach their full potential. Surely this is one of the major lessons of David Tyack's and Larry Cuban's important history of public school reform—*Tinkering toward*

Utopia. Government must increase its support for education, policymakers can assist, courts often can set new initiatives in motion, and colleges and universities should provide expertise and needed resources. Yet, "unless practitioners are also enlisted in defining problems and devising solutions adapted to their own varied circumstances and local knowledge, lasting improvements will probably not occur in classrooms."[50] In other words, when it comes to educational change and renewal, the best and wisest reformers reside in our local schools and our local communities. With adequate resources, societal backing, and the liberty to make constructive and appropriate changes tailored to the needs of these communities, there is no telling how far American education might go in finally living out John Dewey's democratic ideal of ensuring "the all-around growth of every member of society."[51]

Primary Source Reading

The following selection presents a view of the aims of education in contrast to James B. Conant's position that the conditions of the cold war world should influence how different people should be educated and to what purposes. Columbia University English professor and poet Mark Van Doren argued instead that education should not prepare people for any particular kind of society or political system but should treat people "as ends in themselves." In Van Doren's view, the only proper aim of education was to develop the intellectual and personal capacities of each person to the greatest degree possible, after which society would be well taken care of by such well-educated people. If this selection seems particularly difficult to read, the student might consider whether it is Van Doren's prose or the relative unfamiliarity of his ideas that causes one to stop frequently to review the course of the argument.

Van Doren's essay was first published in 1943, during World War II, and then republished in his book *Liberal Education* in 1959—the same year that Conant published *The American High School Today*. Van Doren's use of masculine pronouns was typical of the time.

Excerpts from "Education for All"

Mark Van Doren

Education is for all, and there can be no compromise with the proposition. "Just as in his mother's womb each man receives his full complement of limbs—hands, feet, tongue, etc.—although all men are not to be artificers, runners, scribes, or orators; so at school all men should be taught whatever concerns man, though in after life some things will be of more use to one man, others to another." Thus Comenius, the title page of whose *Great Didactic* promised that it would set forth "The whole art of teaching all things to all men"—to "the entire youth of both sexes, none excepted."[1] It was a noble vision, and it has never been realized. We teach our entire youth, but we do not teach them enough.

What was once for a few must now be for the many. There is no escape from this—least of all through the sacrifices of quality to quantity. The necessity is not to produce a handful of masters; it is to produce as many masters as possible, even though this be millions. An ancient sentence about liberal education says it is the education worthy of a free man, and the converse is equally ancient; the free man is one who is worthy of a liberal education. Both sentences remain true, the only difficulty being to know how many men are capable of freedom. The capacity was once a favor bestowed by fortune; the gentleman was a rare fellow whose father was rich or famous. It is also, however, a capacity which nature bestows, and nature is prodigal. Liberal education in the modern world must aim at the generosity of nature, must work to make the aristocrat, the man of grace, the person, as numerous as fate allows. No society can succeed henceforth unless its last citizen is as free to become a prince and a philosopher as his powers permit. The greatest number of these is none too many for democracy nor is the expense of producing them exorbitant. "A new degree of intellectual power," said Emerson, "is cheap at any price," and this

Source: Excerpt from Mark Van Doren, *Liberal Education* (New York: Beacon Press, 1959), pp. 28–42. First published in 1943 by Henry Holt and Company. © 1943 by Mark Van Doren.

[1]John Amos Comenius was a Czech educational reformer born in Moravia. He lived from 1592 to 1670.

is true no less for a country than for one of its citizens. In proportion as the theory is clear it will not confound itself with notions that the education of men, as distinguished from the training of animals, is something for a class—say a leisure class. The only slaves in our society ought to be its machines. There is a myth that machines have minds and so are educable, but no man will admit this. "We Americans," says Alexander Meiklejohn, "are determined that there shall not be in our society two kinds of people. We will not have two kinds of schools—one for gentlemen and ladies, the other for workers and servants. We believe that every man and woman should be governed. All the members of our society must have both liberal and vocational education. There shall be one set, and only one set, of schools for all people. The first postulate of a democracy is equality of education. The gospel of Comenius is still true." In proportion as our theory is clear it will agree with the foregoing.

What, then, of the fact that education when liberal, when occupied with human discipline, is arduous beyond all other known pursuits? Sufficient wisdom sometimes seems almost esoteric, an accomplishment of genius which the mass is bound to find unintelligible, no surface difference appearing between the subtlety of the philosopher and the caprice of the tyrant. Socrates supposed that philosophers would be useless only in a democracy, where he assumed they would not be heard. It is a question once more of the few and the many. And the answer is never that all men will be the best men. The sensible desire is simply that all men should be as good as possible. The higher the average the safer the state. But the pyramid will have symmetry only if the same attempt is made with every person: to produce in him the utmost of his humanity, on the assumption that this is what he possesses in common with every other person.

A democracy that is interested in its future will give each of its members as much liberal education as he can take, nor will it let him elect to miss that much because he is in a hurry to become something less than a man. It is obvious that all must not be less than they are; and a democracy must be prepared to give the entire quantity of itself that can be taken.

"A state which dwarfs its men in order that they may be more docile instruments in its hands even for beneficial purposes will find that with small men no great thing can really be accomplished." The warning of John Stuart Mill has lost no force. The good state wants great democrats; and gets them by teaching the love of truth; and teaches that by teaching the importance of thinking well. It does not achieve its end by pretense or coercion, or by a conspiracy to confuse the attempt with the deed. "There is no such thing," says Albert Jay Nock, "as democratic manners; manners are either bad or good."[2] So with anything else that is human. There is no such thing as democratic morals and ideas. Morals are either bad or good; ideas are either shallow or profound. Democracy's business is with morals as such, and with the deepest ideas available to its citizens.

Democracy cannot survive a loss of faith that the best man will make the best citizen. It certainly cannot afford to educate men for citizenship, for efficiency, or for use. Its only authority is reason, just as its only strength is criticism. It will not distinguish between its own good and the happiness of its members. It will study how to distribute well the things that are good for men, but it will study with equal care the goods of men, which incidentally make more sense in the singular: the good of man. The citizen will never forgive a society, democratic or otherwise, which taught him to do what time has shown to be wrong or silly. He can never blame a society which encouraged him to be all that he could be. If the teaching was good, he has no one else to blame. Democracy does not provide alibis.

The circle of the relation between the state and the individual, a circle which is drawn when we say that each depends upon the other for its good, can be broken only if we distinguish between the individual and the person. The individual has no relation to anything except the state or society of which he is a member, and to which he is a relative. But the person is not a member. He is the body of himself, and such is always to be understood as an end, not a means. As a ruler, he has first ordered his own soul. As the ruled, he likewise orders his soul. And this is something which he is unique among creatures in knowing how to do, even though he many never do it perfectly. The good state—democracy—will let him try, on the theory that good citizenship will follow naturally from even moderate success; though it will let him try anyway. For without autonomy he cannot find the center in himself from which in fact emanate the very generosity and lawfulness, the respect for others that is a form of respect for himself, necessary to the operation of society at all. Society may command fear and obedience; it cannot force love or friendship, which are

---

[2]Professor Albert Jay Nock was a humanist professor at Columbia University early in the 20th century.

irreducibly personal, and developed in places to which politics as most conceive it has no access. Yet they are the foundation of good politics, which in this sense must be personal to succeed greatly. Democracy wants millions of one-man revolutions, if only because the result might be a nation of persons worth organizing. Norman Foerster has suggested that "the individual, while learning to live wisely, becomes progressively more fit to be lived with."[3] He supports the remarks with a line from Aeschylus: "The wise have much in common with one another." The only common good is that which is common to good men.

The powers of the person are what education wishes to perfect. To aim at anything less is to belittle men; to fasten somewhere on their exterior a crank which accident or tyrants can twist to set machinery going. The person is not machinery which others can run. His mind has its own laws, which are the laws of thought itself. A congressman recently recommended that American youth be "taught how to think internationally." It would be still better to teach them how to think. Democracy depends for its life upon the chance that every man will take all the judgments he can. When he falls short of that he gives the government another name. He is no longer at home in the republic of the mind, where, since thought is free and only merit makes one eminent, he is less than a slave.

The state is doubtless superior to the individual on many counts. But when the question is one of good or bad, right or wrong, true or false, democracy must appeal to insight, imagination, and judgment; and these are personal things—things, that is, of man rather than society. By personal, it should be clear, the eccentric is not signified. Insight into what? Imagination about what? Judgment concerning what? Not, surely, the accidents of individual belief, but the essentials of the human situation. The individual, thinking about these, becomes personal in the grand dimension. The trivial dimension is something with which we happen to be more familiar, but this should not discourage us from using the word, which has a long and important history. To be personal in the trivial dimension means that in politics we cultivate little areas of freedom where we can live in isolation from the wilderness of compulsion. We have secrets; we lead the buried life. The large area of human freedom is a better place to breathe in. It is a general area, and in it

some of our license is lost. But it is the only region where personality is finally possible. For the paradox once more emerges: an individual, thinking the best thoughts of which he is capable, and mastering the human discipline without jealousy for his own rule, becomes more of himself than he was before. "Certain men," wrote Plato in one of his letters, "ought to surpass other men more than the other men surpass children." If that is a definition of aristocracy, the definition of democracy would be a condition in which all men surpass themselves, putting behind them childish things.

Democracy when it is secure will not deny its inferiority to persons. The superiority of its persons is its only strength. To say as much is to say that democracy lives dangerously. For humanity is dangerous, and is not to be controlled by committees of men. But the danger from its freedom—from a program which asks it what it can be rather than tells it what to do—is less than the blind risk that is run when the program is to mislead and miseducate it; or, what amounts to the same thing, to educate it partially. No risk is as real as that. There is danger anyway, as all teachers of pupils and parents of children know. Good teachers, parents, and states, however, will prefer the high danger to the low.

"The question, 'What is a good education?'" says Mortimer Adler, "can be answered in two ways: either in terms of what is good for men at any time and place because they are men, or in terms of what is good for men considered only as members of a particular social or political order. The best society is the one in which the two answers are the same."[4] That best society, doubtless, is still to exist on earth. But when it completely exists, perhaps at the end of history, its name will be democracy. And all of its citizens will be educated persons.

Thinking Critically about the Issues   #9

Compare the major educational recommendations of James B. Conant with those advocated by Mark Van Doren in "Education for All," assessing their relative significance for democratic life.

---

[3]Professor Norman Foerster was a humanist professor at the University of Iowa early in the 20th century.

[4]Mortimer Adler is a University of Chicago philosopher, educator, and, most recently, author of *The Paideia Proposal*, a humanist educational approach for school-age pupils.

Developing Your Professional Vocabulary

A good understanding of this chapter's content would include an understanding of why each of these terms is important to education.

The American High School Today	life-adjustment education
community college	provisional freedom
containment	Scholastic Aptitude Test
Educational Testing Service	Senator Joseph McCarthy
GI Bill of Rights	*Slums and Suburbs*
John Birch Society	*Sputnik*

Questions for Discussion and Examination

1. This chapter suggests a significant connection between standardized testing in schools and what might be called cold war ideology. What connection is being suggested, and do you believe this is a valid association to make? Explain.

2. Children who attended schools in the 1950s and 1960s were acutely aware of the threat of the cold war and news-media warnings of possible Soviet aggression. How does this compare with what students experienced after the terrorist attacks in the United States in September 2001? Has the threat of terrorism affected the consciousness of American schoolchildren or American educational policy? Explain your view.

3. Van Doren argues that "Democracy . . . cannot afford to educate men for citizenship, for efficiency, or for use." Throughout this Primary Source Reading, he makes clear that the aims of education cannot be based on the economic or political needs of any particular society, even a democracy, but on the needs and capacities of individuals as human beings. Can a school system actually operate on such premises? Explain.

4. Show the degree to which modern liberal ideology and modern psychology were important for Conant's educational reforms.

5. In your view, which educational thinker—Conant or Van Doren—offers an educational vision that is more likely to serve the needs of all the members of a diverse society such as ours: male and female, rich and poor, and of African, Asian, European, and Latino descent, among others?

 **Online Resources**

Go to the Online Learning Center at **www.mhhe.com/ tozer7e** to take chapter quizzes, practice with key terms, access study resources, and link to related websites. Also available on the Online Learning Center are PowerWeb articles and news feeds.

Part Two

Educational Aims
in Contemporary Society

Liberty and Literacy Today Contemporary Perspectives

With Arlette I. Willis, contributing coauthor

Chapter Overview

Chapter 9 is the first chapter in Part 2 and is thus the first chapter to develop Part 1 themes in a contemporary context. This chapter revisits the themes of liberty and literacy presented in Chapter 2. The contemporary perspective of Chapter 9 shows that the term "literacy" identifies more than one concept; that is, the meaning of literacy changes with historical setting and ideological orientation.

This chapter presents ideological hegemony theory as an explanation for the general absence of critical literacy that would allow most Americans to develop an alternative to the corporate liberal perspective. The Primary Source Reading at the end of the chapter raises questions about literacy, the Internet revolution and the degree to which this has changed students' chances for a literacy that will allow them to critically question standing social arrangements.

Year after year they bump-bumped along in their rusty old car. "Mamá," whispered Tomás, "if I had a glass of cold water, I would drink it in large gulps. I would suck the ice. I would pour the last drops of water on my face."

Tomás was glad when the car finally stopped. He helped his grandfather, Papá Grande, climb down. Tomás said, *"Buenas noches"*—"Good night"—to Papá, Mamá, Papá Grande, and to his little brother, Enrique. He curled up on the cot in the small house that his family shared with the other workers.

Early the next morning Mamá and Papá went out to pick corn in the green fields. All day they worked in the hot sun. Tomás and Enrique carried water to them. Then the boys played with a ball Mamá had sewn from an old teddy bear.

288

Contemporary textbooks are increasingly inclusive of multiple cultural practices.

Chapter Objectives

Among the objectives that Chapter 9 seeks to achieve are these:

1. Students should be able to discuss Jefferson's conception of the connection between literacy and democracy, and to compare it with the critical literacy perspective. To what degree are the methods of critical pedagogy necessary to achieve critical literacy?

2. Students should be able to discuss the basic tenets of cultural and ideological hegemony theory, and the extent to which that theory is supported by data in this chapter and in their experiences.

3. Students should be able to discuss whether contemporary society is marked more by hegemonic than by participatory democratic processes, and to what extent schools serve one or the other of those ideals.

4. This chapter should enable students to describe and explain how the different perspectives on literacy—conventional, functional, cultural, and critical—potentially serve different social groups and different ideological orientations in contrasting ways.

5. Students should be able to explain how the three different literacy perspectives serve different educational goals.

6. Students should be able to explain the importance of media access and consolidation of media as it relates to current trends in information technology.

7. Students should be able to explain the arguments for and the critiques of the unique yet related construct of cultural literacy.

Analytic Framework
Liberty and Literacy in the United States

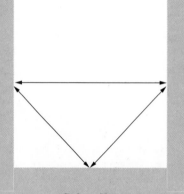

Political Economy

"Military-industrial complex"

War in Iraq and Afghanistan

Governmental and economic "elites"

Two-party system of government

Corporate control of mass media

Worst economic recession since Great Depression

Increasing gap between rich and poor

Rapid growth of digital technology

Ideology

Emergence of neoliberalism

Social consensus versus ideological hegemony

Free marketplace of ideas versus "information marketplace"

Democracy and critical literacy

Schooling

Corporate control of textbooks

Hidden curriculum of schools

Inculcation of social values

Selective omission in the curriculum

Political socialization for passivity

No Child Left Behind

"Market competition" in new schools and pathways to teaching.

Introduction: Revisiting Literacy

Chapters 1 through 3 in this text form a particularly useful foundation for our examination of literacy. Chapter 1 begins our reflection on the relationship between education and the development of human reason. We consider the legacy of ethnic, racial, and gender exclusion from that *liberal* or "freeing" education that, as Aristotle characterized it, is "worthy of a free man." We also begin our examination of property relations, which worked to limit access to this education, and the intertwined gender, race, and colonial relations, which served to justify an education for what Rousseau would call "role-playing" rather than free choices in acquiring the freedoms that Jefferson would intone as central to "the pursuit of happiness." Chapter 2 described Thomas Jefferson's faith in the ability of an educated populace to safeguard its liberties. In particular, Jefferson believed that the skills of reading and writing would equip people to stay informed about

social, economic, and political events and thus help them recognize and protect their interests. Popular literacy was for Jefferson and other classical liberals one of the cornerstones of a free society. Our current condition has left educators to ponder the relationship between a local emphasis on access to fair education and education policy forged by national imperatives. For example, the overarching federal No Child Left Behind (NCLB) policies have left us with challenging questions regarding rhetorical and real goals of education. Students and teachers are facing new strictures regarding the relationship between classroom time spent in search of equal educational goals or spent in search of the pedagogical recipe that will result in more correct answers on standardized tests. Critics such as the *National Center for Fair & Open Testing* have questioned whether this emphasis, which is purported to benchmark success, holding schools accountable for those traditionally underachieving, has paradoxically deprived those children. They argue that these students are less likely to learn higher levels of critical and creative thinking, which are essential for fair access to higher education.

One ideal of literacy is that students learn to negotiate multiple texts and prepare for democracy and its communication challenges. Under NCLB and the larger reform agenda, students most at risk for missing access to high literacy are subjected to reading programs scripted to be read by teachers. Schools and districts that adopt these reading programs are required to sign assurances that scripts will be followed to the letter. Education critic Jonathan Kozol describes a school where one of these programs, Success For All, is implemented. Consistent with scripted teaching, educational behaviors are strictly monitored. He writes: "There was, it seemed, a formal name for every cognitive event within this school: 'Authentic Writing,' 'Active Listening,' 'Accountable Talk.' The naming systems are allied to a re-Taylorization of curriculum. Like that earlier effort, these regimes have 'a way of ordering cognition . . . [that] disproportionately affects low SES and minority schools.'"[1]

Thus, while scripted reading and regimes of order and discipline are prescribed to address the "achievement gap" between minority and middle-class students, research results show few positive effects on achievement. These techniques are more likely to be approaches in which students are only asked to respond mechanically, not creatively, nor to bring in their personal backgrounds and knowledge. Only correct recall of factual information and accuracy are emphasized. In middle-class schools where children come to school with requisite social capital to meet benchmarks, there is still in-district competition for scores, but fewer interruptions in teacher autonomy on curriculum.

Meanwhile the USA Patriot Act works to increase surveillance on information outlets and library borrowing for the stated purpose of tracking terrorism. Education in the "national interest" may compete with the freedom to teach for developing a democratic appraisal of current conditions. At stake is the ideal of an education that, again as Jefferson cited, enables one to identify and affect conditions that either "secure or endanger" one's freedom.

At the same time, Jefferson's view of literacy reveals serious limitations in his social and political thought. Like his contemporaries, for example, he limited non-Whites' access to literacy. His Bill for the More General Diffusion of Knowledge provided for literacy for White children but not for children of African American or Native American descent. Jefferson's classical liberal assumptions about the inherent superiority of Whites undergirded his views about literacy and political participation.

Chapter 3 sends us in search of the foundations of freedom *and* exclusion, which continue to trouble the "public" education Mann inspired. Our public schools tantalize us with the promise of a free, fair, and humanizing universal education, while they also taunt us with the vestiges of exclusion, education for "evident and probable destinies," blind patriotism, and inadequate fair access to the goods of an increasingly crucial credential market, upon which individual economic opportunity and security are based.

Chapter 4 serves as a springboard for the world of public education where the promise of literacy for all is placed before us in the comprehensive education system with which we live. We are required to observe competing definitions of the educated person, where the gravity of differentiated wage labor and monopoly capitalism bends the light of reason, altering our perception of fairness in the distribution of educational goods.

In this chapter we will explore the social construct of literacy. We will discuss several ways in which this term has been used in educational policy discussions, and focus on its connection to the basic themes of educational promise and real school practice.

For example, during the previous national push for "excellence" in education, starting with the Nation at Risk movement in the Reagan administration, great emphasis was placed on international comparisons of learning and literacy. Currently, when compared to international standards of literacy as defined by the U.S. Department of Education, it is children in high poverty U.S. schools who are left behind. Fourth-graders in U.S. public elementary schools with the highest poverty levels "score lower on the combined reading literacy scale compared to their counterparts in schools with lower poverty levels," levels being defined by free and reduced school lunch access.[2] Under the No Child Left Behind policy, supporters, which included conservative Republican President Bush and liberal Democrat Edward Kennedy, argue that rigorous statewide assessments will be the impetus for change that will work to level the crisis in literacy and education. This movement has continued and even accelerated under President Obama and his "Race to the Top" theme in national policy. However, critics have charged that it is just those children traditionally left furthest behind that will fare worst in the current effort to benchmark success with a standardized test.

The issue of literacy, when reflectively considered, tells us a great deal about school and society in the United States today. This chapter focuses on literacy as a way to illuminate the relationships between schooling, political economy, and ideology in contemporary culture. First, as a fundamental objective of education, the study of literacy helps us understand particular features of schooling, for example, how schools serve some groups in society more successfully than others. Second, because literacy is affected not only by schools, but also by social processes and institutions outside the schools, the study of literacy illuminates important details of the political economy of today's society. Social context must always be examined in judging the successes and failures of schools. Finally, the study of literacy helps us recognize the competing ideologies within our society. Different opinions prevail regarding why literacy is important, and these different views often are grounded in differing ideological perspectives. For example, recent growth of neoliberal ideology has been a challenge to the idea of free public education. It has been successful partly because it has reconstituted the notion of positive freedom by reinvigorating the classical liberal ideology of laissez-faire, negative freedom (freedom from government interference), and privileged property rights as against rights to public goods, like public education. Yet neoliberalism is a redefinition of rights. For example, the "privatization" of schooling refers not to a return of private fee schooling to replace public school. Rather it argues that private groups should have access to public funds and licensure to run public schools. These arrangements also privilege parents with the "social capital"—educational background, discretionary time, transportation options, and so on. For the neoconservatives this is a recaptured "freedom" to choose. For the critic of these changes it further restricts access to educational capital by those whose needs are the greatest.

A Brief Historical Perspective

Literacy often refers to general reading and writing skills. One way the concept of literacy is used, then, is to describe rates of reading and writing ability. This is difficult to quantify and may lead to differing conclusions. It is difficult to compare literacy rates in contemporary society with literacy rates in earlier times. First of all, there is lack of agreement about how to define literacy. Second, in the 18th and 19th centuries there were no widespread, systematic studies of literacy such as exist today. Available studies of early American literacy are generally based on the ability of individuals to sign their names on legal documents such as wills. By that standard, illiteracy was near zero for males in some New England communities by 1800, and it is near zero throughout the country today. The ability to produce a signature, however, leaves

unanswered fundamental questions about someone's ability to read and write. It really isn't clear how much literacy existed in the Jeffersonian and common-school eras discussed in Part 1. Further, these studies of crude literacy, known as signature literacy, have led some researchers to conclude that the literacy rate of White males exceeded that of White females and was nearly universal in New England and the Middle Atlantic and southern regions in the 1800s. The self-reports of adults to the U.S. Census Bureau in 1850, however, indicate that White male and female signature rates were nearly equal.[3]

Still, some things do seem clear about literacy in the last two centuries, and they are instructive. It appears certain, for example, that people from upper social classes were more literate than those from lower social classes. Wealthier people had access to more forms of education—including schools, tutoring, and parental instruction—than did poorer people. Gender, too, was an obstacle to literacy. Because formal schooling and participation in public and commercial life were considered important primarily for men, women of the last two centuries had lower literacy rates than men.[4] Ironically, however, mothers and women in "dame schools" provided the earliest literacy instruction that most children received.

Racism also affected the chances of acquiring literacy. Before the Civil War, in most southern states it was illegal for a slave to learn to read and write, because it was widely believed that a literate slave would not be an obedient slave. Despite such laws, many African Americans learned by individual or group efforts to acquire literacy, including secret lessons held in privately funded schools housed in churches. In addition, schools were established for African Americans as early as 1770 in Philadelphia, 1787 in New York, and 1792 in Baltimore. Nonetheless, it is estimated that in 1865, 90 percent of African Americans, slave or free, were illiterate.[5] After emancipation, political and economic discrimination together with educational segregation created new obstacles to literacy among the Black population.

We saw how two prominent Black leaders, Booker T. Washington and W. E. B. Du Bois, differed regarding the purposes of literacy. For Du Bois, liberal education and preparation for higher education were desirable goals for students, some of whom (his talented tenth) would move into leadership roles. Washington, rather, saw African Americans best prepared with vocational studies, on a long developmental road to eventual leadership and power.

Native Americans offer a special case worthy of mention. Many Native American nations resisted White values, customs, and ways. However, members of the Cherokee nation sought to emulate Whites by adapting themselves to White ways. They formed a governing body, schools, and a newspaper and owned African slaves. Chief Sequoya developed a syllabary for the Cherokee language. Many people were taught to read, and children attended schools where they learned to read and write Cherokee. On February 21, 1828, their first newspaper, *The Cherokee Phoenix,* written in Cherokee and English, was published. Like Whites, the Cherokee viewed their newspaper as a source of information about events important to them.[6]

Literacy rates also varied by region in 18th- and 19th-century America. New England, with its more urban demography and commercial base, tended to emphasize schooling and literacy more than did the South, which was more rural and almost feudal in its social order. With fewer schools, inhabitants of the western frontier were also less literate in general than people of the Northeast. It should be remembered, however, that many pre-20th-century Americans learned to read and write outside of schools, especially at home.

Local community ordinances, however, could make schooling a public, not simply a personal, issue. The Massachusetts Education Act of 1789 allowed for the equal education of males and females. In addition, the law did not prevent the use of public funds to educate African Americans. Historian Stanley Schultz reports that in Boston at the beginning of the 19th century, few African American children attended school. Schultz attributed the low attendance patterns to poor economic conditions and overt acts of prejudice experienced by African American children in schools. In 1798, African American parents petitioned the school board for separate schools for their children. The request was initially rejected and later accepted by the school board. By the 1820s, however, African American parents, frustrated by the poor quality of teaching in the segregated schools, began to request that schools be reintegrated. In 1855, the governor of Massachusetts signed into law an act preventing communities from denying access to school on the basis of race or religious belief.[7]

Literacy and Power: Literacy as a Social Construction

Literacy can be discussed as a general condition of access and ability to gain information that can be useful for the pursuit of general freedom and happiness.

It can be redefined in context and evaluated according to criteria that reflect access to freedom. Simply, if as a society we value choices, do we equally value fair access to the information-gathering skills and information sources that makes choice meaningful? Past and present literacy rates are not only affected by differences in social class, race, gender, and region; they are also closely tied to social need. To be illiterate in today's culture is to be significantly handicapped in the conduct of everyday affairs, to be so regarded and to be relegated to the "margins" of mainstream life. This was not as true in earlier centuries, when the everyday requirements for literacy were less demanding. In that predominantly agrarian society, literacy was not so essential to employment and the conduct of daily affairs. In fact, an illiterate person could be a respected and productive member of the rural community.[8] Most people could not vote anyway, for example, and thus were not in that way disadvantaged by illiteracy. Although Jefferson and others considered literacy necessary to the conduct of republican government, it is important to note that in 1800 women, people of African descent, and Native Americans had no voice in government, and only a small minority consisting of White, male property owners was eligible to vote. Nor did religious life depend absolutely on literacy. Bible reading was considered essential in Protestant culture and was therefore an inducement to literacy, but people could participate in religious life without reading. Thus being illiterate in the 18th century and throughout much of the 19th did not necessarily mean being handicapped in the pursuit of well-being and full participation in society. The socioeconomic marginality of the illiterate is largely a 20th-century phenomenon, though the valuing of literacy is deeply rooted in Western culture. Nevertheless, all powerless groups in U.S. history, African, Asian, Native, and Mexican and their descendants, have desired access to literacy. They have valued literacy and education. The history of each group in the United States reveals that they desired to educate themselves, often in the hope of economic and social advancement. Parents did not want to see their children experience the servitude they had endured. Employers, landowners, and overseers, however, had limited interest in educating the children of workers. They wanted to maintain a cheap source of labor and often feared an educated workforce. Unlike slaveholders who denied African slaves any access to literacy, however, most employers have historically encouraged literacy. Early in the 20th century this meant allowing children to be educated up to the sixth or eighth grade. The emphasis in schooling was often on the development of a "good" worker and on vocational training, as Chapter 4 described.

Ideological Hegemony Theory: Democracy and the Consolidation of Economic Power[9]

Jefferson believed that popular literacy could ensure the democratic distribution of power; however, the 20th century witnessed power flowing into business and government in ways he could not have foreseen. Especially since World War II, the complex relationship between corporate power and the mass media requires a reexamination of the relations between liberty and literacy in the United States today. Here we examine the sources of information against which individuals may test their powers of judgment regarding political and social arrangements. We also examine a powerful theory of political and social stability that challenges our notions of freedom and a "free" marketplace of ideas. The public debate that followed the Iraq war placed a focus on the availability of accurate information and the role of corporate media companies as stewards of fair, balanced information gathering and public dissemination.

In 1961, two events revealed contrasting assessments of power in the United States: the publication of Robert Dahl's *Who Governs?* and President Dwight Eisenhower's farewell address to the nation.[10] Dahl's book was a major

contribution to the pluralist school that dominated political science in this country during the 1950s. Pluralists argued that despite being governed by a very small group of decision makers, modern societies are consistent with democratic ideals so long as the governing groups represent competing political interests and are accountable by election to the general population. That this normative account of democracy described political conditions in the United States was virtually an article of faith in the pluralist camp, and *Who Governs?* was intended to provide empirical data to bolster that faith.

It came as some surprise, then, that President Eisenhower would warn the nation in 1961 of "the potential for the disastrous rise of misplaced power" of a "military-industrial complex" under which "public policy itself could become the captive of a scientific technological elite."[11] Whereas Dahl's work strengthened our traditional view of political power, Eisenhower's speech echoed the leftist critique of power C. Wright Mills had advanced five years earlier in *The Power Elite*.[12] In Mills's analysis, which the pluralists took pains to reject, the important power in the United States was concentrated in the hands of an elitist group made up of those in leadership positions in government, the military, and the corporate establishment. For Mills, this elite was neither open to competition from other interests nor significantly accountable to the citizenry. Eisenhower was warning the nation, in effect, that Mills was closer to the truth than the pluralists cared to admit.

Some forms of literacy, such as the ability to create and interpret youth graffiti, are not highly valued by the dominant culture.

To what degree is the exercise of power in contemporary society "open"? In *Who's Running America?* first published in 1976 and then revised during each subsequent presidential administration through George W. Bush, Thomas Dye agreed with Mills that power resides not primarily in individuals but in institutions.[13] Dye's approach provided a concrete look at the most powerful positions in three major sectors of American society: corporate, public interest, and government. By identifying the most powerful positions in each of the top 100 industrial corporations; the top 50 utilities, communications, and transportation companies; the top 50 banks; the top 50 insurance companies; and the top 15 investment firms, Dye found that 4,325 positions carry extraordinary influence in the corporate sector. In the public interest sector, he identified 2,705 positions in the mass media, in education, in philanthropic foundations, in the most prestigious law firms, and in civic and cultural organizations. In the government sector, Dye identified the most influential committee positions in Congress, the most powerful positions in the legislative and executive branches, and the key positions in the military for a total of 284 government positions. The total from these three sectors is 7,314 positions that, according to Dye, wield the major decision-making power in the most influential institutions in political and economic life.

The influence of these institutions and of those who run them is remarkable. In Dye's account, 100 corporations account for roughly 60 percent of all corporate revenues and all corporate assets. The latest available Census data show that there were 6 million firms with employees in 2007. For example, in 1996 over 75 percent of the nation's industrial assets were concentrated in 100 corporations. In 1950 that percentage was 39.8. The positions in Dye's list control over half the nation's industrial assets; over half the utilities, banking, and transportation assets; over two-thirds of the nation's insurance assets; over half the endowed assets in the nation's private colleges and universities; one-third of the nation's daily newspaper circulation; and over nine-tenths of broadcast news. In addition, these positions dominate the legal field and investments and securities, all the major standing committees in the House and Senate, the Supreme Court, and the four branches of the military. These are the positions occupied by those whom Mills called "the power elite" and whom Prewitt and Stone have more recently called "the ruling elite."

In *Power and Powerlessness,* John Gaventa found that his efforts to study the power relations in an Appalachian community required asking "not why rebellion occurs in a 'democracy' but why, in the face of massive inequalities, it does not."[14] It is tempting to ask similarly of U.S. society in general: If power relations are as undemocratic as elite theorists describe, why do citizens not only accept it, but also continue to think of the social order as

Social analysts have warned of an undemocratic power elite that controls major institutions in this country.

democratic? Answering this question raises issues that are fundamentally educational in character.

If the concentration of power has been accurately portrayed by elite theorists, what are the educational consequences? First, it is necessary to miseducate a population in important ways for people to perceive a nondemocratic society as democratic, thereby sustaining unequal power relations. Second, the processes of participating in such a society are not as educational as Jefferson, Dewey, and others would have us believe. Each of these points will be treated in turn.

The theory that best contributes to our understanding of how society miseducates in order to sustain nondemocratic power relations is that of ideological hegemony. The term "hegemony" refers to unequal power relationships between two or more cultures, ideologies, socioeconomic groups, and so on. Since there is no single, definitive account of ideological hegemony theory, it is regarded as one of the most suspect collections of concepts in the social sciences. Some formulations are better than others, however, and the intent of this section is to provide a coherent account of the available literature. T. Jackson Lears's essay on cultural hegemony is an exemplary discussion, and parts of our account rely on his treatment.[15]

The first thing to note about hegemony theory is that, like all theories, it is an effort to explain selected facts. These general facts appear to be most relevant in contemporary society: The United States is made up of many individuals and groups with different and often conflicting interests; the social order benefits some groups far more than others in terms of health, wealth, access to positions of power, and freedom to pursue personal interests. Despite conflicting interests and differing benefits, U.S. society is a very orderly one, with stable economic, government, and social institutions and a class structure that did not change appreciably throughout the 20th century. This stable social order is maintained not at gunpoint or through threat of force but through the cooperation of its citizenry. Hegemony theorists seek to explain the basis of this cooperation as the foundation of the social world itself.

A first attempt to explain hegemonic social order might be expressed this way: A small minority of U.S. citizens control the political and economic institutions that shape the civic beliefs, values, and behavior of most of the population. In contrast to traditional democratic theory, which holds that the social order is based on public consensus, ideological hegemony theory argues that the social, political, and economic institutions of this society serve a relatively small group at the expense of the majority of citizens. Hegemony theory can be summarized in four general propositions, each of which requires further development:

1. Institutional elites who share common economic and political interests control the dominant political and economic institutions of the United States.

2. Though they may disagree on particular policies or strategies, these institutional elites share a common worldview, or ideology, which reflects and justifies the organization of dominant institutions.

3. Through such institutions as the government, the workplace, the school, and the mass media, the general populace is socialized into accepting these ruling ideas.

4. Although ruling ideas do not reflect the experience of all social classes, they serve to limit discussion and debate, prevent the formation of alternative social explanations, and promote a general acceptance of the status quo.

It is not possible to document all the ways in which various social institutions structure experience to legitimize the dominant ideology, but we can examine two institutions that have particularly concerned hegemony theorists: the popular media and the schools. These two institutions are particularly important to hegemony theorists because they explicitly communicate ideological perspectives to the general population. It is valuable in this regard to recall Jefferson's high regard for both newspapers and schools as pillars of a democratic society. Jefferson's faith in a free marketplace of ideas led him to claim that newspapers were even more important to democracy than government was. Cultural hegemony theorists argue that we now have reason to doubt the effectiveness of both the news media and the schools in preserving democratic understandings and lifestyles.

Mass Media and Ideological Hegemony

Jefferson's concepts of the free marketplace of ideas and the power of human reason both depend on adequate access to ideas and information. The steady consolidation of media sources is a challenge to this notion. The Internet offers an important but complex counterweight to this. For example, now the best, most current information on media consolidation was in book form. At the time of this writing, the most current and widest and deepest source is the website by Anup Shah (www.globalissues.org/humanrights/media/corporations/owners.asp).[16]

There are currently six media companies that control the large majority of information consumables. AOL/Time Warner is the largest, having completed the largest media merger in history. On January 10, 2000, America Online and Time Warner announced a merger in a stock swap valued at $350 billion. The Federal Trade Commission supported this merger, and saw no conflict of national interest or antitrust issues. Supporters saw nothing negative. Gerald Levin, chief executive of AOL/Time Warner predicted global media would become the dominant industry of the 21st century—so powerful that they might in fact become more powerful than governments. "So what's going to be necessary is that we're going to need to have corporations redefined as instruments of public service," he said, adding, "It's going to be forced anyhow because when you have a system that is constantly available everywhere in the world immediately, then the old-fashioned regulatory system has to give way." Robert McChesney notes the "massive paradox" that with the explosion of information and technology, "sitting atop this golden web are a handful of media firms—exceeding by a factor of 10 the size of the largest media firms of just 15 years earlier."[17] Detractors say that media conglomerates must be most carefully regulated to ensure competition, because they define, by their production of video, audio, publishing, news and entertainment, the free marketplace. Here the freedom to pursue property rights, in the form of media holdings, lays in stark contrast to the freedom of citizens to pursue the truth from a healthy variety of sources.[18] However, Robert Pitofsky, chair of the U.S. federal Trade Commission said, "Antitrust is more than economics. And I do believe that if you have issues in the newspaper business, in book publishing, news generally, entertainment, I think you want to be more careful and thorough in your investigation than if the very same problems arose in cosmetics, or lumber, or coal mining. . . . I mean, if someone monopolizes the cosmetics field, they're going to take money out of consumers' pockets, but the implications for democratic values are zero. On the other hand, if they monopolize books, you're talking about implications that go way beyond what the wholesale price of books may be."[19]

The Paradox of Media Property Rights and Public Information Rights: From NBC to GE to Comcast

Thus the tendency toward corporate consolidation pursued, with government regulatory support, as a liberal property right, works to conflict with the citizen's right to a free market of ideas. Thus the very economic freedom of the market moves in ways to limit freedom in the political social marketplace. As another case in point, while NBC, the National Broadcasting Company, was, until recently, an unconsolidated singular media entertainment and news company, it was owned by industrial giant General Electric. The ninth-largest corporation in the world, GE revenues are equivalent to the Gross National Product of Norway. If it were a national economy it would be larger than 130 countries.[20] For example, GE benefits from its defense contracts for profit, how might this have affected balanced news coverage of military conflict? A GE website, *GE in the News,* reported, just prior to the outbreak of war in Iraq, "a war in Iraq could clip air traffic, which in turn would hurt the sale of spare parts by GE's aircraft-engines unit. Still, the company currently expects aerospace operating profits to jump by 5% to 10% this year, as GE benefits from cost reductions, a growing services segment and military sales."[21]

GE purchased the largest Spanish-language television network and The History Channel, a prime cable network source of political and historical interpretation. *Time* magazine, a center-conservative news magazine, is cited as the source of an article identifying GE as easily the most globally diversified company in the world, with increasing global market share, and the company most aggressive in increasing profits through "corporate welfare" to enable job cuts in the United States. It was an enthusiastic proponent of NAFTA, the North American Free Trade Agreement, and, according to its workers' news outlet, has aggressively fought labor gains by internationalizing production.[22]

The classical liberal faith in the power of the market cuts two ways in the GE case. Adam Smith would not flinch when noting the tendency of GE to seek profit at the expense of its labor force. It would also tend, by the same principle, to seek advantage by encouraging information dissemination consistent with its military, global, and international interests. At the beginning of 2007, eight media companies dominated the U.S. news business: Disney, Time Warner/AOL, Viacom, GE (NBC), News Corporation, Yahoo!, Microsoft, and Google. Here the classical liberal notion of free markets, which assumes, also, new markets, meets modern liberalism's and modern capitalism's radical reduction of markets, strangling the diversity of opinion and ideas that are required for any political economic arrangement to serve the ideal of democracy. We use the GE example to indicate how the interests of ownership can taint the process of delivering news.[23] In 2010 General Electric completed its sale of NBC Universal, which includes all its media outlets, to media giant Comcast. This creates a media behemoth. Comcast is also the nation's largest provider of broadband cable and Internet, controlling media across distribution platforms.[24]

Thinking Critically about the Issues   #1

What are the possible educational responses to the paradox of freedom in *information markets?*

Beyond NBC we must examine the information-shaping power of the corporate consolidated media. The news media outlets of these corporations report a great many negatives about American society, but these criticisms nearly always stay within clearly acceptable bounds. For example, even though criticisms often address problems faced by American institutions, they do not address problems in how those institutions are structured. The media may criticize how the game is being played, but it never questions the rules of the game itself. A few detailed examples can illustrate this point.

Reports on the domestic economy of the United States often point out unemployment, job layoffs, welfare cuts, and the flight of corporations to third-world nations. This is presented as bad news, but the American public is given no way of understanding how such bad news is an inevitable outcome of the structure of corporate capitalism itself. A structural critique would examine how unemployment is built into our capitalist system and how it benefits capitalists by keeping workers in competition with one another for scarce jobs. Such a critique could show how the interests of corporate owners make it rational for them to sometimes act against the interests of the workers, for example, by investing their profits in the less expensive workforces of foreign countries rather than in industries that would benefit workers in the United States.

Given our present economic structure, the interests of labor are dependent on the interests of capitalists, and the interests of capitalists are best met, as they themselves proclaim, by developing third-world labor markets. Thus, what is represented as our national interest is largely determined by the interests of corporate directors who readily abandon the American worker for cheap foreign labor and support a foreign policy that ultimately relies on the American worker to die in foreign battles to protect the interests of capitalists. The Great Recession has been in part due to consolidation in financial markets and banking, and the success of those industries to wield great influence on Congress to weaken regulations that required their activities to be transparent to the public. Critics also argued that the consolidation of news media and their alignment with corporate finance also resulted in less critical coverage of financial fraud during this period. This perspective, which has been developed by a number of scholars in the United States and abroad, is typically not made available to the American public through the news media.[25] News corporations in America are, after all, capitalist institutions; their interests would be threatened if they alienated advertisers who depend on current American foreign policy for their profits. Further, many representatives of U.S. multinational corporations serve as directors of major U.S. news corporations.

When Thomas Jefferson argued that daily newspapers were so essential to democratic life that he would rather see a society without government than a society without newspapers, he had no way of knowing that multinational corporations would one day control the public's exposure to the media, and that the independent newspaper would become a species close to extinction.

The most extensive treatment of this relatively recent development is *The Media Monopoly,* written by Ben H. Bagdikian, a Pulitzer Prize–winning journalist and professor of journalism at the University of California, Berkeley. Bagdikian writes:

> At the end of World War II . . . 80 percent of the daily newspapers in the United States were independently owned, but by 1989 the proportion was reversed, with 80 percent owned by corporate chains. In 1981 twenty corporations controlled most of the business of the country's 11,000 magazines, but only seven years later that number had shrunk to three corporations.[26]

Again, for Jefferson, the notion of a "free marketplace of ideas" was predicated on a diverse array of privately owned newspapers and pamphlets with competitive points of view. Each citizen would be free to accept or reject those publications on the basis of how well his or her own interests were reflected. In a controlled marketplace of ideas, however, such choice has largely evaporated. Bagdikian notes that "in order to have the power of rejection, the public needs real choices and choice is inoperative where there is monopoly, which is the case in 98 percent of the daily newspaper business, or market dominance of the few, which is the case with television and most other mass media."[27]

In 1930 there were 132 newspapers sold daily per 100 households in the United States. By 1965 the number was reduced to 111 papers per 100 households, and in 1986 the number had declined to 72.[28] Bagdikian reports that the 1982 edition of the *World Press Encyclopedia* ranked the United States 20th in papers sold per person, with only 272 daily papers sold per 1,000 population. This compares, for example, with 572 sold per 1,000 people in Sweden, 526 in Japan, 472 in East Germany, and 447 in Luxembourg, to cite the top four. UNESCO's 1990 *Statistical Yearbook* shows that by 1990 the United States had fallen still farther behind the leading nations.[29] By 2003, another 150 daily papers had disappeared from the scene in the United States. The percentage of Americans who read a daily paper declined from 62 percent in 1990 to 55 percent in 2002.

In 1983, the men and women who headed the 50 mass media corporations that dominated American audiences could have fit comfortably in a modest hotel ballroom. The people heading the 20 dominant newspaper chains probably would form one conversational cluster to complain about newsprint prices; 20 magazine moguls in a different circle denounce postal rates; the broadcast network people in another corner, not being in the newspaper or magazine business, exchange indignation about government radio and television regulations; the book people compete in outrage over greed of writers' agents; and movie people gossip about sexual achievements of their stars.

By 2003, five men controlled all these old media once run by the 50 corporations of 20 years earlier. These five, owners of additional digital corporations, could fit in a generous phone booth. Granted, it would be a tight fit and it would be filled with some tensions.[30]

Of course, the pervasiveness of television and the Internet has contributed to the decline of newspaper circulation in the United States, but this is not encouraging news. Ownership of television stations, even when cable TV is taken into account, is more concentrated than ownership of newspapers in part because there are so few TV stations in comparison to newspapers.[31] There is much more that could be written—and has been written—about the ways in which the communications media have institutionalized violations of a

free marketplace of ideas. And the news media perhaps make up a smaller part of that picture than do the entertainment media. Todd Gitlin is one of several writers who have described the ways in which television programming, apparently designed for entertainment, reinforces rather than questions the dominant ideology.[32]

Further, it can be argued that it is not just the messages on television that affect people's ability to think about their culture. The technology itself may have an impact on our ability to develop the literacy skills to read deeply and critically. A U.S. government study, for example, showed the following:

> Students who watched 3 or fewer hours of television a day showed higher levels of reading proficiency than those who watched 6 or more hours each day. In 1994, 57 percent of 4th-graders and 59 percent of 8th-graders watched 3 or fewer hours daily, while 75 percent of 12th-graders did so.[33]

Bagdikian's work in 1980 was groundbreaking and provides us with a benchmark for his later work.[34]

Communications Technologies: From Jefferson's "Free Marketplace of Ideas" to the "Information Marketplace"

Computer technology and the World Wide Web are providing a tantalizing if sometimes troubling platform to look at literacy in this century. On one hand, the alternative press and opinion developing in numerous websites and weblogs (blogs) is one of the main challenges to the consolidation of media information power. Indeed, Danny Scheckter, executive director of MediaChannel.org, points out the illusion of Internet diversity. The total number of companies that control 60 percent of all minutes spent online in the United States dwindled 87 percent, from 110 in March 1999 to 14 in March 2001. It is functioning strongly in the world of opinion and in political campaigning and fundraising. However, the access to this new form of "property" implies new issues regarding the information marketplace and the question of who owns the means of knowledge production and distribution. In *What Will Be: How the New World of Information Will Change Our Lives,* Michael Dertouzos writes about the future of technology and society in the United States and the world. In this volume Dertouzos, director of the MIT Lab for Computer Science, compares the current information technology revolution with the industrial revolution in England and the technology revolution of the early 20th century: "The Industrial Revolution began in England when the steam engine was invented in the middle of the eighteenth century. . . . Technical change had largely stopped by the end of the nineteenth century when a new wave of innovations appeared: the internal combustion engine, electricity, synthetic chemicals, the automobile. . . . Both revolutions had dark sides as well as bright." The author goes on to assert that the current "Information Revolution will trigger a similarly sweeping transformation," which he calls "the Information Marketplace." In 1980 he wrote this about the information marketplace:

> By Information Marketplace I mean the collection of people, computers, communications, software, and services that will be engaged in the intraorganizational and interpersonal information transactions of the future. These transactions will involve the processing and communication of information under the same economic motives that drive today's traditional marketplace for material goods and services. The Information Marketplace already exists in embryonic form. Expect it to grow at a rapid rate and to affect us as importantly as have the products and processes of the industrial revolution.[35]

In addition to the growth of the use of computers and the Internet in society in general, concerns about access and the "digital divide" continue. According to 2005 and 2010 reports from the National Center for Education Statistics (NCES):

- 81 (2005) and 92 percent (2010) percent of high school sophomores who were White non-Hispanic and 83 percent of Asian American sophomores used a personal computer at home at least once a week, but only 56 (2005) and 82% (2010) percent of African American and Hispanic sophomores did so.

- 53.7 percent of low-income high school sophomores reported using a computer at least once a week at home, while 88 percent of high-income sophomores did so.

- By 2003, 99 to 100 percent of schools in urban and rural environments alike were connected to the Internet, but student access to school computers varied with family income across all grade levels.[36]

Given this dramatic growth in the availability of computers and the Internet in schools and homes, we can expect to see many studies being conducted with titles similar to this one by Ronald D. Owston: "The World Wide Web: A Technology to Enhance Teaching and Learning?" Owston asks, Does the Web increase access to education? Does it promote improved learning? Does it contain the costs of education? He finds that "a promising case exists for the Web in all three areas. The case is rooted largely in how educators are actually using the Web today."[37] Owston's study illustrates the great potential of the Web but also shows that this potential is not always tapped.

The Rise of Social Media

Social media are a developing hybrid of technologies, including Internet forums, weblogs, social blogs, microblogging, wikis, podcasts, and instant text messaging. Social media are distinct from industrial or traditional media, such as newspapers, television, and film. They are relatively inexpensive and accessible to enable anyone to write, publish and access information. Our discussion of media consolidation has focused on corporate industrial media, which generally require significant resources to publish information. By contrast, these media are characterized by diffusion and personalized control of information, with links to the hyperexpanding world of the Internet. Beyond but including this social content media such as YouTube and Facebook have created alternative spaces for information sharing. The radical redistribution of information is still a question of platform consolidation, with increasing monopolization of the Internet search power. The promise of social media as a means toward an expanded and democratized marketplace of ideas is real. However, the following ongoing issues remain: information surveillance, private access to and secret use of public posts, governments employing censorship and surveillance.

Educators have begun to work with such media as a way of involving students more fully in the world of ideas, academic studies, and news. While great progress has been made, however, one issue has emerged that is central to the media explosion, monopolization of student attention, not with one idea or corporate media message, but with the media themselves. Social networking via Facebook is the main source of communication for college students. Social bullying and isolation have emerged as a problem. With social networking and

Internet-mediated knowledge production multiplying exponentially, some worry that the rise in immediacy will be paid for in a loss of social memory. Earlier media connections in a print world constituted a special kind of record that demanded attention and a logical focus from topic to topic and event to event. Hyperinformation has attracted the attention of critics who claim that social media in fact create an illusion of interpersonal connection, monopolizing time during which interpersonal relationships might otherwise develop. Some argue deterioration of language, writing and conversational skills. Still others talk about the addictions to social media that particularly affect the young during which the opportunity to develop socially and emotionally and intellectually is lost, perhaps permanently. Social media are a new challenge to our models of literacy and democracy. They have been a real presence in movements for change in the Arab world in the past several years, and in the mobilization of citizens, the power of monopoly finance in the Great Recession and foreclosure crises, and the "Occupy" movement. While you are reading this, some of your classmates are attending deeply to a world that is both intimate to their private world and connected to the most public of social spaces. Where this heads will be a part of your educational journey and legacy.

Recall Dertouzos's claim that each revolution in technology has a bright and a dark side and notice that in the data presented earlier, it is clear that some segments of society—those with greater economic resources—have greater access to new technologies in homes and schools. Dertouzos believes this is a matter of great concern, given the political economy of the United States and the influence of capitalism on the market economies of the world:

> With the productivity gains made possible by all the information and information tools at their disposal, the rich nations and rich people of the world will improve and expand their economic goods and services, thereby getting richer. As they get richer they will leverage the Information Marketplace even further, thereby experiencing exponentially escalating economic growth. The poor nations and poor people, by contrast, can't even get started. . . . The painful conclusion is that, *left to its own devices, the Information Marketplace will increase the gap between rich and poor countries and between rich and poor people.*[38]

Later, Dertouzos argues: "We must help ensure that with respect to this critical gap the Information Marketplace is not 'left to its own devices.'" This resolution, however, is far from easy to attain. If public or governmental intervention is being advocated, the specter of Orwell's Big Brother is immediately raised: Do we want a strong central government to control powerful information technologies? If the government does not play a role, however, is it not inevitable that the haves will move further ahead of the have-nots in information, power, and wealth?

Dertouzos recognizes that the political economy of capitalism will play a major role in the nature and distribution of technology resources. He writes that market forces will coerce national policies in some directions and not others:

> Already, the world is moving with giant strides in the quest for massive economic growth. The Information Marketplace is a central factor in this growth and can even be regarded as the largest potential market in the world. A nation that seeks economic growth in the global economy has no choice but to join in. Most of the control over the machinery of the Information Marketplace will be exerted by the industrially wealthy nations, which are democratic nations as well. . . . By its very definition, this control distributed in the hands of the bulk of the people who will use the Information Marketplace runs counter to centralized control by Big Brother. . . . [N]o self-respecting dictator would want it.[39]

George Orwell wrote in the dystopian novel *1984* of a world in which technology would be used to control citizens, not liberate them.

Thinking Critically about the Issues   #2

Examine textbooks used in your classes. Using library sources, find examples of inclusion or exclusion that bear out the ideological hegemony thesis.

At the same time that our system of capitalist democracy and its founders are praised, a number of important details of American social history are selectively omitted. One of these is the role of conflict in producing progressive social change. Jean Anyon's study of high school social studies texts reveals that positive social changes in civil rights, the resolution of the Vietnam War, labor unions, and the women's movement are presented as triumphs of the legal system and of processes of discussion and bargaining. The role of disruptive protests that often involved violent repression by the police and military is ignored. The message explicitly communicated in these texts is that consensus rather than power or conflict is what makes history and leads to progress. The effectiveness of protest and militant collective action is selectively omitted.

A related example is omission from history texts of the success of the Socialist party early in the 20th century. If portrayed at all, it is most often portrayed negatively, as an insignificant movement on the part of an irresponsible few.[40]

As Michael Apple points out, a fundamental linkage exists between the overt and implicit messages in school texts and the economics of textbook publishing itself. Some states regulate the political content of their texts, and publishers cannot afford to ignore those guidelines if they want to sell books.[41]

Just as schools strengthen the prevailing ideological hegemony through both their processes and their academic content, so society as a whole strengthens the prevailing ideological hegemony through the decision-making processes of most workplaces and through the ideology that underlies and controls the media. The decision-making processes of the great majority of workplaces, for example, are characterized by authoritarian, hierarchical structures in which workers do not participate in major decisions that affect their working lives. On the one hand, this hierarchy is legitimized by claims of talent and training on the part of superiors and by the need for efficiency in decision making. On the other hand, the resulting forms of work life are decidedly nondemocratic. This nonparticipatory experience in the workplace contrasts markedly with the prevailing political rhetoric that U.S. society is democratic. This conflict between the nondemocratic relations of daily experience and the culture's proclamations of democracy is rarely analyzed and evaluated in popular discourse. Instead, people live with the contradictions, generally not recognizing them as such.

Antonio Gramsci, an important ideological hegemony theorist, argued this position some 50 years ago, saying that the working person in a capitalist society tends to be paralyzed into passivity and inactivity by this basic contradiction between democratic political rhetoric and the daily experience of nondemocratic forms of life.[42] Gramsci's account perhaps goes a long way toward answering Gaventa's question cited earlier: "not why rebellion occurs in a 'democracy' but why, in the face of massive inequalities, it does not."

If correct, the hegemony theorists' analysis has many implications for education, two of which are fundamental. First, it appears that society is educating in deeply contradictory ways. On the one hand, citizens are taught in the schools and through the media that they live in a democratic society. On the other hand, they are taught through daily experience not to expect participation in fundamental decisions affecting their lives. Finally, they are not educated by either school or society to examine and question such contradictions between rhetoric and reality. Instead, citizens learn from an early age to tolerate the contradictions *if they see them at all*. It requires nothing less than indoctrination to convince people in a hegemonic, nondemocratic society that democracy is working well. If the hegemonic theorists are correct in arguing that American education contains a stiff dose of indoctrination, we should not be surprised that the most literate classes are the most convinced.[43]

Second, hegemony theory points out a more subtle form of popular miseducation, which Peter Bachrach contrasts to the "developmental" view of democracy.[44] This view holds that democratic forms of life place upon citizens demands that are themselves uniquely educative. As Jefferson believed in the 18th century and John Dewey in the 20th, there is no democratic justification for a ruling class that monopolizes decision making, no matter what its credentials and expertise. A democracy stripped of significant, systematic participation by people in the fundamental decisions affecting their lives is not a democracy at all, and it therefore fails to educate the populace through political participation. Democratic decision makers continue to learn about the world around them in order to make their decisions; they learn from the consequences of their decisions and go on. Those who do not participate in the decision-making process are not required to learn, and if hegemony theorists are correct, the already large educational gap between the powerful and the powerless grows greater.

Historical Context

Significant Events

In Part 2 of this text, significant events of the last 40 years of U.S. social and educational history, from the 1970s through 2008, are listed in each chapter. As in Part 1, these events are illustrative; you might have chosen different ones if you were constructing such a timeline.

1960s

1960	Six years after the 1954 *Brown* v. *Board of Education* decision against school segregation, the modern "sit-in" movement begins when four Black students from North Carolina A&T College sit at a "Whites-only" Woolworth's lunch counter and refuse to leave when denied service
1962	Students for a Democratic Society formed at Port Huron, Michigan
1962	The Supreme Court orders the University of Mississippi to admit James H. Meredith; Ross Barnett, governor of Mississippi, tries unsuccessfully to block Meredith's admission
1962	Supreme Court upholds ban on public school prayer
1963	More than 200,000 marchers from all over the United States stage the largest protest demonstration in the history of Washington, DC; the "March on Washington" procession moves from the Washington Monument to the Lincoln Memorial; Reverend Dr. Martin Luther King delivers "I Have a Dream" speech
1964	Student Mario Savio leads Free Speech Movement at University of California at Berkeley
1964	Civil Rights Act of 1964 is passed
1966	Former teacher Margaret C. McNamara founds Reading is FUNdamental (RIF)
1968	Bilingual Education Act passed
1969	Theodore Roszak publishes *The Making of a Counter Culture*
1969	250,000 antiwar protesters (the largest antiwar demonstration ever) march on Washington, DC, calling for the United States to leave Vietnam
1969	The Stonewall rebellion in New York City marks the beginning of the gay rights movement

1970s

1970	A subcommittee of the U.S. House of Representatives holds hearings on sex discrimination in education, the first in U.S. history
1972	Title IX Educational Amendment passed, outlawing sex discrimination in educational institutions receiving federal financial assistance
1973	Native Americans defy federal authority at Wounded Knee, South Dakota
1975	Congress passes Education for All Handicapped Children Act (Public Law 94-142)
1979	Moral Majority is founded, forming a new coalition of conservative and Christian fundamentalist voters in resistance to "liberal excesses" of 1960s and early 1970s

1980s

1980	Ronald Reagan is elected president, promising to reverse the "liberal trends in government"
1980	Microcomputers begin to appear in U.S. classrooms
1983	*A Nation at Risk,* a report by the Presidential Commission on Excellence in Education, advocates a "back to basics" education; becomes the first major document in the current reform movement
1984	Carl D. Perkins Vocational Education Act continues federal aid for vocational education until 1989

1990s

1992	Americans with Disabilities Act, the most sweeping antidiscrimination legislation since the Civil Rights Act of 1964, guarantees equal access for people with disabilities
1994	Number of prisoners in state and federal U.S. prisons top 1 million, giving United States the highest incarceration rate in the world
1996	Clinton signs the Defense of Marriage Act, denying federal recognition to same-sex marriages
1999	Kansas Board of Education votes against testing any Kansas students on science curriculum related to theory and science of evolution (but it would be restored in 2001 by new school board)
1999	Federal Communications Commission loosens restrictions on any one company controlling too much of the cable industry, allowing AT&T to win more than a third of the nation's TV, phone, and high-speed Internet franchises

(continued)

Historical Context *(concluded)*

2000s

2000	Campaigning on a platform emphasizing ethical character, George W. Bush loses popular vote to Vice President Al Gore but wins the presidency by a 5–4 Supreme Court ruling ending the recount of disputed votes in Florida
2001	Media giants AOL and Time Warner merge, increasing concentration of media ownership
2001	September 11, 2001: Two hijacked commercial airliners destroy the twin towers of the World Trade Center in New York City, marking the worst-ever terrorist attack on American soil; a third hijacked airliner crashes into the Pentagon in Washington, DC, while a fourth crashes into rural Pennsylvania; about 3,000 people are killed
2001	The United States launches a retaliatory attack in Afghanistan against terrorist organization al-Qaeda, and the Office of Homeland Security is created; cabinet-level Department of Homeland Security is created in November of the following year
2001	Congress passes bipartisan USA Patriot Act, intended to assist the war on terrorism by providing new powers to law enforcement agencies; American Civil Liberties Union and other critics claim the act removes or weakens essential checks against government invasion of privacy
2002	The US. House (voting 296–133) and the U.S. Senate (77–23) give President Bush support to use military force against Iraq, which the White House had mistakenly claimed was developing a program of using weapons of mass destruction; by July 2003, the White House acknowledges inaccuracy of intelligence information
2002	Republicans emerge from midterm elections with a new majority in the U.S. Senate and an increased majority in the House of Representatives
2003	U.S. and allies launch war against Iraqi regime and declare victory on May 1; resistance continues, however, and far more U.S. casualties are sustained after May 1 than before; deposed Iraqi leader Saddam Hussein is captured December 13
2004	President Bush reelected over Senator John Kerry of Massachusetts; victory attributed to Bush campaign's success in increasing participation among conservative voters impressed with Bush's strong stand on terrorism and Iraqi war
2005	Press coverage lags as Hurricane Katrina devastates New Orleans, LA; delayed federal response raises questions about uneven national commitments to public welfare and race equity
2006	The Chinese government censors activist websites with the tacit approval of Google, the U.S.-based and world's largest search engine
2007	Subprime mortgage lending triggers extensive mortgage crises and foreclosures in the U.S. housing market
2008	In Iraqi war, U.S. military death toll surpasses 4,000 and Iraqi death toll surpasses 1 million
2009	The U.S. Labor Department reports that January 2009 saw 598,000 jobs lost, the highest number since December 1974 General Motors files for bankruptcy and announces it will close 14 plants in the United States
2010	Sept. 16: The percentages of American living below the poverty line ($10,830 for an individual and $22,050 for a family of four) reached a 15-year high, according to the U.S. Census Bureau. Over 44 million people, or 14.3 percent of Americans, are considered living in poverty. The United States is experiencing its worst economic period since the Great Depression
2011	The Arab Spring movement begins in Tunisia when demonstrators take to the streets to protest chronic unemployment and police brutality. Occupy Wall Street, an organized protest in New York's financial district, expands to other cities across the United States, including Boston, Chicago, Los Angeles, and San Francisco. Occupy Wall Street defines itself as a group of activists who stand against corporate greed, social inequality, and the disproportion between the rich and poor

Thinking Analytically about the Timeline

For the purposes of studying Chapter 9 you might ask of each decade: Which five events from this decade (1970s, 1980s, and so on) have the most *direct significance* for the issues discussed in this chapter?

Contemporary Perspective on Literacy: Conventional Literacy

Probably the simplest definition of "conventional" literacy is that which appears in most dictionaries: "the ability to read and write." It is this simple form of literacy that most citizens of the United States have in mind when we think about ourselves as a highly literate nation. After all, virtually the entire population of this country has attended school, where reading and writing are taught in the earliest grades.

This is exactly the reasoning employed by the U.S. Bureau of the Census, which found in the 1980 census, for example, that 99.5 percent of U.S. adults are literate.[45] The Census Bureau defined literacy as "the ability to read and write a simple message in any language." The literacy rate was determined by asking people what grade level they had completed in school and, for those who completed fewer than five grades, whether they could read. Nearly all the respondents claimed either to have finished the fifth grade or to be able to read anyway. Thus the Census Bureau concluded that only 0.5 percent of the nation's adults are illiterate.

As linguist Shirley Brice Heath notes, many scholars and policymakers have challenged the Census Bureau's findings and its simple definition of literacy.[46] First, its findings are highly suspect because they rely heavily on written questionnaires and telephone interviews. The former method is very ineffective for reaching the illiterate, and the latter method ineffective for reaching the poor, among whom illiteracy is most common.

More damaging to the Census Bureau's findings, however, is its definition of literacy. In the view of Heath and other critics of the conventional literacy perspective, even if people respond that they are able to read and write—the conventional notion of literacy—the most important questions remain unanswered. One unanswered question is what the 99.5 percent of U.S. adults are able to read and write. If, for example, they can read and write their own names, they can legitimately answer the Census Bureau in the affirmative. This standard, after all, was used to judge the literacy rates of Americans in the 18th and 19th centuries. But we do not know what level of literacy is reflected in the Census Bureau's data.

The conventional literacy perspective does not focus on the vast differences in literacy that prevail among different population groups in the United States. African Americans, Latinos, Asian Americans, Native Americans, recent immigrants from Europe and elsewhere, and poor people of all ethnic backgrounds call attention to the fact that some population groups in our society are much more literate than others and that these differences greatly influence their lives. By claiming that virtually everyone in society is literate, we obscure important questions about levels of literacy among the various groups in our society and what this means in terms of social benefits and costs. In sum, the conventional literacy perspective appears to emphasize social and educational progress and obscure the social and educational inequalities that other conceptions of literacy might reveal.

Functional Literacy

Shifting definitions of literacy have helped obscure accurate literacy rates. In the social construction of literacy debate the term "functional literacy" has had perhaps the most discussion. In 1993 the National Center for Education Statistics redefined literacy beyond reading and writing, asked participants to complete tasks, defined an adult as someone 16 years of age or older, and scored responses in a range of literacy achievement. The definition of literacy used in the survey is illustrative of the shifting concerns about literacy. In the report, literacy was defined as "using printed and written information to function in society, to achieve one's goals, and to develop one's knowledge and potential."[47] This report, the National Adult Literacy Survey (NALS), provides useful data on 26,000 adults and will be referred to at several points in this chapter.

The origin of the term "functional literacy" says something important about its nature. The term was first used by the U.S. Army during World War II to mean "the capability to understand written instructions necessary for conducting basic military functions and tasks . . . a fifth-grade reading level." Rather than using a fixed definition of literacy such as the ability to read and write, the Army recognized that literacy needed a definition that was adjustable to particular contexts. If a recruit could read and write, but not well enough to function in the context of the written materials provided by the Army, that recruit was judged functionally illiterate.[48]

Because functional literacy is conceived with respect to particular social contexts, being functionally literate may differ greatly in different societies. This makes functional literacy difficult to define with precision. The United Nations suggested the following definition in 1971: "A person is literate when he has acquired the essential knowledge and skills which enable him to engage in all those activities in which literacy is required for effective functioning in his group or community."[49] The Literacy Volunteers of America, Inc., also invokes the notion of "effective functioning" in its definition of functional literacy:

> Functional literacy relates to the ability of an individual to use reading, writing, and computational skills in everyday life situations. For example, a functionally illiterate adult is unable to fill out an application, read a medicine bottle [or] newspaper, locate a telephone number in a directory, use a bus schedule or do quality comparison shopping. In short, when confronted with printed materials, such people cannot function effectively.[50]

One well-known early effort to investigate functional literacy was conducted in the mid-1970s at the University of Texas, using an index called the adult performance level (APL).[51] The APL project tested how well adults could function in 65 tasks requiring literacy skills in everyday life. From 20 to 60 percent of those tested failed to perform successfully at tasks such as writing a check that a bank would process, addressing an envelope adequately, figuring the difference in price between a new and a used appliance, making change for a purchase, matching personal qualifications to a written job application, and determining whether a paycheck was correct. The APL researchers concluded that 30 million people are "functionally incompetent" and that another 54 million "just get by." Author Jonathan Kozol, in his acclaimed book *Illiterate America,* argues that approximately 60 million people cannot read well enough to understand the antidote instructions on a bottle of kitchen lye, the instructions on a federal income tax return, or the questions on a life insurance form. He writes that these 60 million people are "illiterate in terms of U.S. print media at the present time." In other words, one-third of the adult population was functionally illiterate. The more recent NALS findings suggest that Kozol's figures may somewhat overstate functional illiteracy in the nation today but that 40 to 44 million adults function at the lowest of the five levels of literacy identified.[52]

Such definitions, although leaving open what it means to "function effectively," help raise important questions about society and education. For example, the functional literacy perspective shows how social groups differ in literacy rates, something the conventional literacy perspective obscures. The APL study, for example, suggested that now, just as in Jefferson's time, gender affects the chances of being literate: About 23 percent of women over age 18 were identified as functionally illiterate, compared with 17 percent of men. The more recent NALS data, however, did not confirm these gender differences, except in quantitative literacy activities.[53]

Perhaps more disturbing were the differences in literacy among different ethnic groups. The APL study indicated that 16 percent of White people, 44 percent of Black people, and 56 percent of Latinos over age 18 were functionally illiterate at that time. Although the illiteracy rate among minority youth is lower than that among adults, it is still scandalous.

Limitations of the Functional Literacy Perspective

The value of the functional literacy perspective is that it shows how our society educates (in terms of literacy, at least) different social groups to different degrees. There are, however, limits to this approach. As we have seen earlier, despite his own use of the functional perspective to illustrate the severe problem of illiteracy in the United States, Jonathan Kozol argues against the term "functional." He writes, "If there is a single word we would do well to wipe away from the vocabulary of a literate society, it is the invidious modifier 'functional.' It is a bad word, chosen by technicians but unfortunately accepted without protest by the humanistic scholar and the pedagogic world alike."[54] Kozol's basic objection to the functional literacy perspective is that it denotes as a goal "the competence to function at the lowest levels of mechanical performance" instead of indicating a more ambitious conception of literacy. Certainly Jefferson did not have only minimum competence in mind when he described the connections between literacy and a free society.

Educator Colin Lankshear and others have added to Kozol's criticism of the functional literacy perspective. A second limitation on this perspective, according to Lankshear, is its tendency to blame the victims of social inequality for illiteracy. The emphasis tends to fall on the personal deficiency of the illiterate person. Consequently, the concept of functional illiteracy, in practice, tends to initiate illiterate people into a powerful series of assumptions.

> (i) The problem is within me. If I cannot get a job, or the job I want, it's because of something about me rather than something about the world (such as a shrinking or shifting labor market, or an economic crisis);
>
> (ii) If others do better than I do, that is because they are better than I am. If I want to do as well, then I have to improve. The "game" or "race" itself is proper, legitimate, beyond question. I'm just not a sufficiently skilled or competitive "player";
>
> (iii) To get better I will have to have my faults diagnosed and be taught how to improve. Others have this knowledge. It is not for me to determine the problem or the cure.[55]

In sum, says Lankshear, the functional literacy perspective leads people to see the illiterate person as someone who must be improved by others. This view, Lankshear argues, is "an initiation into passivity." It also implies that the illiterate person need only be trained to the minimum work levels that industry needs. Who does this benefit most, the learner or industry? Lankshear asks.

Under NCLB, educators have witnessed a renewal of curricular "Taylorization." Mechanical, scripted reading programs such as Success For All (SFA) and Reading First (RF) have increasingly deskilled the teaching of reading. Like the methods of Frederick Taylor, as we have seen, these programs disproportionately affect students and teachers in low-SES and minority schools.[56]

With Reading First we see an intriguing intersection between literacy, corporate influence peddling, and consolidation. In a recent case, these two giants of the reading industry, RF and SFA, battled over the curricular moral high ground. In 2007 a federal inspection of RF found evidence that program directors steered the grant-application process for the $1 billion annual initiative to ensure that particular reading programs and instructional approaches were widely used and that others were essentially left out.[57] Indeed, recent studies have shown that while RF increased some functional/basic reading skills, comprehension, the building block of advanced literacy, in fact declined.

This limitation of the functional perspective becomes apparent in popular news articles on illiteracy as a threat to institutions—"The Scourge of Adult Illiteracy," as the *New York Times* put it.[58]

Popular news stories warn that illiteracy is so high that soon "there won't be enough people equipped to handle complex new technology" and that "these functional illiterates exact a high national price" in terms of the costs of welfare and unemployment compensation. Or, as literacy advocate Barbara Bush, mother of President George W. Bush, argued, "Most people don't know we spend 6.6 billion dollars a year to keep 750,000 illiterates in jail. I'm trying to remind people that there's a direct correlation between crime and illiteracy, between illiteracy and unemployment."[59] These comments emphasize that functional illiteracy is dysfunctional for society. It is a "social disease that affects us all," proclaims an advertisement by Gulf & Western Corporation. To help people become functionally literate, from this perspective, is to indicate how they can help institutions function better. Educator Neil Postman notes in this connection that "some minimal reading skill is necessary if you are to be a 'good citizen,' but 'good citizen' here means one who can follow the instruction of those who govern him."[60]

Two other perspectives on literacy have been developed in an effort to overcome the limitations of the functional perspective. The more conservative of the two has become known as cultural literacy, while the more radical may be regarded as critical or emancipatory literacy.

> ### Thinking Critically about the Issues   #3
>
> What, in your view, does the functional literacy perspective contribute to our understanding of the political economy of literacy in the United States? If these are valuable contributions, is the functional approach an adequate view of literacy on which to base educational policy? Explain.

> ### Thinking Critically about the Issues   #4
>
> E. D. Hirsch argues that his conception of cultural literacy preserves the connection between literacy and liberty found in the views of Thomas Jefferson and Martin Luther King, Jr. Do you agree? Explain.

Critical Literacy

Critical literacy is a multidisciplinary perspective that refocuses us on the issue of knowledge and the distribution of power in educational communities working to maintain and improve their democratic institutions and hopes. This is a refocusing on education as nurturing the ability to see what will "secure or endanger" freedom. Those who embrace the critical literacy perspective most frequently pay respect to the work of Brazilian educator Paulo Freire, whose 1973 book *Pedagogy of the Oppressed* remains the most creative and influential work in critical literacy. Freire explicitly avoids making recommendations for literacy education in the United States but approves of the efforts of U.S. educators to do so. In particular, Freire cites the work of Henry Giroux, a professor of curriculum theory who has done a great deal to define the significance of Freire's work for schooling in the United States. Giroux is so committed to the theoretical importance of Freire's approach to critical literacy that he writes, "The principles underlying Freire's pedagogy are essential to any radical theory of literacy." Indeed, other major contributors to radical or critical theories of literacy—among them Stanley Aronowitz, Jonathan Kozol, and Ira Shor—all cite Freire extensively in their work. Freire continued to develop his thinking until his death in 1997.[61]

In *Theory and Resistance in Education,* Henry Giroux points out that Freire's work long ago showed how literacy has the potential not only to liberate people but to make oppressed people believe that the dominant culture is correct in portraying them as "inferior and responsible for their location in the class structure." Giroux continues: "In this case—largely as a result of what it does not say—literacy produces powerlessness, making people voiceless and denying them the tools they need to think and act reflectively."[62] These comments illustrate several important features of the critical literacy perspective. First, critical literacy draws attention to power relations in society by focusing on oppression. Usually this oppression is defined in terms of economic and political discrimination on the basis of race, ethnicity, gender, or (perhaps most pervasively) social class.

Second, the critical literacy perspective, unlike the other literacy perspectives examined in this chapter, particularly attends to how knowledge and power are interrelated. In modern capitalist society, as in other societies, what knowledge is of most worth is determined by those who dominate the culture's institutions. The dominant ideology is dominant because its proponents are those people who control the social institutions. People without such class-defined knowledge, usually the poor and otherwise oppressed, are considered inferior to those in the dominant educated class.

Third, for critical literacy theorists, the basis of literacy is the capacity to think and act reflectively, not the ability to read lines on a page. That is, the connection between literacy and liberty is taken so seriously in this perspective that the skill of reading words is considered less significant than the skill of "reading the world," as Freire says. The point of critical literacy is not reading words but understanding the world—and acting to change the social relations of oppression to relations of liberation. Giroux writes:

> Literacy, for Freire, is a quality of human consciousness as well as the mastery of certain skills. The uniqueness of this approach is that it is situated in a critical perspective that stresses the transformation of relations between the dominated and the dominant within the boundaries of specific historical contexts and concrete cultural settings.[63]

Simply put, the critical literacy perspective redefines literacy as the ability to understand and act against the social relations of oppression. Because they lack an account of this combined ability to understand and to act, argue critical literacy theorists, the other forms of literacy—conventional literacy, functional literacy, and cultural literacy—miss the essential value of literacy, which is its potential for human liberation. This is why critical literacy is sometimes referred to as emancipatory literacy. Freire and Macedo write:

> In our analysis, literacy becomes a meaningful construct to the degree that it is viewed as a set of practices that functions to either empower or disempower people. In the larger sense, literacy is analyzed according to whether it serves as a set of cultural practices that promotes democratic and emancipatory change.[64]

For critical theorists, the other three forms of literacy examined in this chapter serve primarily to support established relations of oppression and thus disempower people rather than empower them.

Critical Literacy Method

The first three literacy perspectives are all compatible with the teaching methods most commonly used in U.S. schools—methods that emphasize learning the skills of reading and writing and learning information about U.S. and world culture. The methods for teaching from a critical literacy perspective, however, are not so familiar. In *Education under Siege,* Aronowitz and Giroux provide some beginning principles on which a critical literacy pedagogy could be based:

> In the first instance, critical literacy would make clear the connection between knowledge and power. It would present knowledge as a social construction linked to norms and values, and it would demonstrate modes of critique that illuminate how, in some cases, knowledge serves very specific economic, political, and social interests. . . . Thus, critical literacy is linked to notions of self- and social empowerment as well as to the process of democratization. In the most general sense, critical literacy means helping students, teachers, and others learn how to read the world and their lives critically and relatedly; it means developing a deeper understanding of how knowledge gets produced, sustained, and legitimated; and most importantly, it points to forms of social action and collective struggle.[65]

Exactly what this might mean in terms of specific classroom practice is a matter that remains to be worked out by both theorists and teachers. Helping "students, teachers, and others learn how to read the world critically" is not something that theorists claim to know exactly how to do in the context of the United States, so they look to the achievements of Paulo Freire in Brazil and elsewhere. Instead of teaching Brazilian peasants the language and cultural information of the educated

Critical literacy equips people to form independent judgments about relations of power and domination.

classes, Freire took as his starting point the experiences, understandings, and language of the peasants themselves. He based his pedagogy on the importance of "dialogue," in which teacher and students educated one another with respect to their understandings of the world. The knowledge of the peasants was not regarded as inferior or inadequate but as legitimate learning that could be critically examined for its strengths and weaknesses. In particular, the dialogue took seriously the peasants' discontent with their conditions at the bottom of the socioeconomic order and sought to develop an understanding of why those conditions prevailed. In constructing such an understanding, both teacher and students developed a greater awareness of the ways in which inequality and oppression were built into the social and economic order of Brazilian society—and they began to develop ways to change that order.

In relying on Freire's theories and practices in Brazil, Henry Giroux offers the following as an initial step toward a corresponding pedagogy in U.S. schools:

> The type of critical pedagogy being proposed here is fundamentally concerned with student experience; it takes the problems and needs of the students themselves as its starting point. This suggests both confirming and legitimating the knowledge and experience through which students give meaning to their lives. Most obviously, this means replacing the authoritative discourse of imposition and recitation with a voice capable of listening, retelling, and challenging the very grounds of knowledge and power. . . .

> It is important to stress that a critical pedagogy of literacy and voice must be attentive to the contradictory nature of student experience and voice and therefore establish the grounds whereby such experience can be interrogated and analyzed with respect to both strengths and weaknesses.[66]

One might legitimately ask of such an approach, "But what about reading and writing? Doesn't critical literacy include reading and writing?" E. D. Hirsch wrote an article citing the high written and "cultural" literacy requirements in the pedagogy of hegemony theorist and critical theory avatar Antonio Gramsci.[67] Indeed, Gramsci argued for a traditional curriculum and against what might have been termed a "life adjustment" curriculum, as a guard against an intellectually and politically crippled society.

The most direct answer to this question is yes. The critical literacy perspective does include reading and writing, but it defines them in important new ways. Reading and writing are not perceived as a set of skills for merely functioning in existing society or as a way to become "culturally literate" but rather as a means to understand, express, and change the social relations that favor some people at the expense of others. Giroux, Kozol, Shor, and others recognize that those who are unable to read and write are easily victimized by a society that values reading and writing so highly. But mere functional literacy drill endangers the stimulation of interest and meaning, which may make schooling for marginalized children more meaningfully a promise for fair chances to advance their education, and will not in itself prevent such victimization. For critical literacy to exist, there must be a combination of critical understandings and actions together with the ability to use the language tools of the dominant culture.

Cultural Literacy: Arguments for High-Status Curriculum

Recognizing the limitations of the functional literacy perspective, scholars such as de Castell, Luke, and MacLennan have called for a conception of literacy that takes into account particular cultural contexts and "the broader literacy needs for social and political practice, as determined by the needs of any truly participatory democracy."[68] This is an expansion of the meaning of literacy cited in national reports, and includes the importance of knowledge underlying the decoding process used in message decoding and interpretation. Perhaps the most prominent and influential effort to describe a conception of literacy consistent with the cultural context and democratic ideals of U.S. schools is E. D. Hirsch, Jr.'s, best-selling 1987 book *Cultural Literacy*. Hirsch deplores any conception of literacy that reflects only a technical "skills orientation" to reading. In a related article written for educators, Hirsch argues that language cannot be disentangled from the cultural knowledge and understandings that give language meaning. Thus, "if one believes in literacy, one must also believe in *cultural* literacy."[69] Hirsch claims that his conception of cultural literacy goes beyond the technical reading of functional literacy to embrace the democratic ideals of Thomas Jefferson and Martin Luther King, Jr. His critics, of course, disagree.[70]

Hirsch's approach could also be described as cultural "fluency" with a focus on "acquaintanceship" with a multiplicity of persons, terms, and concepts, which Hirsch argues are indispensable to the furnishing of a cultivated or cultured mind. Critics would argue that disembodied term collections lead away from the stimulation of interest and meaning-making that is essential to the development of critical literacy.

Hirsch and two colleagues—a historian and a natural scientist—compiled a 63-page categorized list of names, places, events, titles, and other items to illustrate the kinds of things with which culturally literate people should be familiar (see Exhibit 9.1). The list is an effort to reflect unexplained information that writers typically mention

in everyday publications, information that "truly literate" people must bring to the act of reading. In part, this list is intended to serve as an educational checklist: Are we teaching these items in school? If not, says Hirsch, we are teaching only the mechanics of reading and writing, something far short of true literacy in his view.

Cultural Literacy: Whose Interests Are Served?

The cultural literacy perspective seems well suited to the educational aims of those who would return to a "knowledge-based" curriculum that emphasizes familiarity with the traditional elements of the nation's dominant cultural perspectives. These perspectives are largely grounded in the achievements of White, male, middle-class culture, as a look at Hirsch's list in Exhibit 9.1 reveals—and as he himself readily admits. Hirsch's argument for the need to employ language and cultural knowledge and understandings in reading and writing suggests that there is one culture, one language, and one set of knowledge and understanding needed for a person to become culturally literate.

Hirsch is by now familiar with the concern of his critics: that his list is culturally exclusive and privileges Euro-American language and perspective. His book with Joseph F. Kett and James Trefil has a response curriculum for nationalism:

> We know from the history of Europe that national schools can achieve high literacy ". . . for everyone in a multicultural population. France did so with a population that, up to the eighteenth century, spoke at least four different languages. . . . Viewed in a long historical perspective, it has been the school, not the home, that has been the decisive factor in achieving mass literacy. . . . When the schools of a nation fail adequately to transmit the literate national language and culture the unity and effectiveness of the nation will necessarily decline."[71]

This idea of transmission of the national language and culture is a conservative approach to education, but Hirsch et al. argue that literacy is by its very nature conservative, because in any culture's literacy, "Some of its elements do not change at all."

Kwame Anthony Appiah and Henry Louis Gates, Jr., might be two of the "elitists" Hirsch has in mind, because they would like the conception of cultural literacy to be more transformative than conservative. Their 1997 book *The Dictionary of Global Culture* attempts to embrace a view different from Hirsch's. They are trying to show that contemporary culture in the United States

Exhibit 9.1 Excerpt from 1066 through AIDS

E. D. Hirsch's Introduction to "What Literate Americans Know"

E. D. Hirsch, Jr., is William R. Kenan Professor of English, Joseph Kett is chair of the Department of History, and James Trefil is professor of physics, all at the University of Virginia, Charlottesville. This list is provisional; it is intended to illustrate the character and range of the knowledge literate Americans tend to share. More than 100 consultants reported agreement on over 90 percent of the items listed. But no such compilation can be definitive. Some proposed items were omitted because they seemed to us known by both literate and illiterate persons, too rare, or too transitory. Moreover, different literate Americans have slightly different conceptions of our shared knowledge. We see the list as a changing entity, partly because inappropriate omissions and inclusions are bound to occur in a first attempt. Comments and suggestions are welcome and should be sent to Dr. Hirsch at the Department of English, University of Virginia, Charlottesville, VA 22903. Correspondents should bear in mind that we do not seek to create a complete catalog of American knowledge but to establish guideposts that can be of practical use to teachers, students, and all others who need to know our literate culture.

The List*

1066	academic freedom	Adam and Eve	Aeneas
1492	a capella	Adams, John	Aeneid, The (title)
1776	accelerator, particle	Adams, John Quincy	aerobic
1861–1865	accounting	Adaptation	Aeschylus
1914–1918	acculturation	Addams, Jane	Aesop's fables
1939–1945	AC/DC	Addis Ababa	aesthetics
1984 (title)	Achilles	Adeste Fideles (song)	affirmative action
Aaron, Hank	Achilles' heel	ad hoc	affluent society
Abandon hope, all ye who enter here.	acid	ad hominem	Afghanistan
abbreviation	acid rain	adieu	aficionado
Aberdeen	acquittal	ad infinitum	AFL-CIO
abolitionism	acronym	adiós	Africa
abominable snowman	acrophobia	Adirondack Mountains	Agamemnon
abortion	Acropolis	adjective	Age cannot wither her, nor custom stale/Her infinite variety.
Absence makes the heart grow fonder.	Actions speak louder than words.	Adonis	
absenteeism	act of God	adrenal gland	aggression
absolute monarchy	actuary	adrenaline (fight or flight)	agnosticism
absolute zero	acupuncture	adultery	agreement
abstract art	A.D.	adverb	agribusiness
abstract expressionism	ad absurdum	AEC (Atomic Energy Commission)	Ahab, Captain
	adagio	Aegean, the	AIDS

*The portion reprinted here represents about one-sixtieth of the total list.

Source: E. D. Hirsch, Jr., *Cultural Literacy: What Every American Needs to Know* (New York: Vintage Books, 1988), pp. 146, 152–55.

---

has multicultural roots and that to know our culture deeply, we should know those diverse origins:

> [L]argely because of Europe's involvement in half a millennium of trade and of empire, her economy, technology, religion, and culture are not the products only of "white" people, of Europeans and their descendants outside Europe. Take two entirely different, but representative examples: that the rebirth of European philosophy in the European Renaissance owed a great deal to the Arab scholars who had kept alive Greek classical learning during the European Dark Ages; and the idea of democracy in the United States was refashioned in part out of the contributions of African-Americans whose understanding of freedom was deepened by their understanding of the Old Testament and by their experience of racial slavery.
>
> What we are suggesting, in effect, is that we all participate, albeit from different cultural positions, in a global system of culture. That culture is increasingly less dominated by the West, less Eurocentric, if you like. And so there must be more and more people in the West, like ourselves, who are both aware of their ignorance of many of the "other" traditions and want to know more. . . . [W]e have placed some of the achievements of Western culture alongside those of many other cultures and traditions. We have done this in part because those juxtapositions enrich our understanding and appreciation of the achievements of "our" culture;

in part because we think that in preparing the new generations for culture that is more global, it is essential for them to learn about William Shakespeare as they learn about Wole Soyinka from Nigeria, Murasaki Shikibu from Japan, Rabindranath Tagore from India.[72]

Appiah and Gates chose an interesting method. They contacted scholars from cultures around the world, asking them for their views of the most important components of their respective cultures—components so significant that all well-educated people in a global society should know something about them. The first 10 entries reveal something about what this method yielded. The definitions of these terms range from half a column to two columns in length, but the abbreviated phrases below will give you some idea of the breadth of the entries.

Abakwa, Sociedad—a secret society of African extraction based in Cuba.

abangan—an Indonesian term referring to a large Javanese peasant community there.

'Abbasid—the second major dynasty of Islamic rulers, or caliphs.

'Abd al-Nasir, Gamal (Nasser, 1918–1970)—Egyptian political leader, one of the Arab world's greatest 20th-century leaders.

Achebe, Chinua (1930–   )—Nigerian essayist and novelist, author of *Things Fall Apart.*

adab—Arabic term meaning "manners" and "literature."

adat—Arabic term for a particular system of customs and legal arrangements.

Ade, King Sunny (1946–   )—Nigerian musician internationally known for his dance-pop Yoruba juju music.

adobe—building material made of heavy clay soil, sun-dried into bricks.

Aeschylus (525–456 B.C.E.)—Greek playwright, author of oldest extant body of Greek drama, including *Seven Against Thebes* and *Agamemnon.*[73]

In one sense, both dictionaries of cultural literacy share in common the commitment to a notion of literacy that goes beyond the technical skill of decoding symbols into words. Each seeks a deeper understanding of ourselves and our culture's ideals and processes. And each approach reflects an understanding that cultural literacy—in the sense of knowing a little bit about a lot of cultural concepts—is not the same as an ideal of a well-educated person. As Hirsch et al. say:

> We also hope and expect that no one will be willing to stop with cultural literacy as a final educational aim. Cultural literacy is a necessary but not sufficient attainment of an educated person. Cultural literacy is shallow; true education is deep. But our analysis of reading and learning suggests the paradox that broad shallow knowledge is the best route to deep knowledge.[74]

Some educators believe that one route to deeper knowledge is implied in the concept of critical literacy, to which we now turn.

Surely the cultural literacy perspective is correct in seeking to go beyond the mechanics of reading and writing to a deeper understanding of ourselves and our society's ideals and processes. However, the question remains: Does cultural literacy, as Hirsch advocates it, really embody the best aims of literacy? Advocates of critical literacy answer with an emphatic no.

Schooling and Ideological Hegemony

A number of researchers have investigated ways in which schooling socializes students into an authoritarian and unequal social order that claims allegiance to freedom and equality. So examined, the school can be seen as a status quo institution that reinforces dominant values and ideologies and teaches uncritical acceptance of the existing social order. Ideological hegemony theory suggests that it is not consent but compliance that is fostered in the schools and that both the organization and the curriculum of schools are responsible for this compliance.

Hegemony theory focuses importantly on the content of school curriculum material. Students are socialized into the existing political–economic system not just by practicing it in schools but by having it portrayed in their texts as desirable and legitimate. Texts routinely praise our economic and political system and routinely criticize other systems. Likewise, texts rarely criticize our system. The first kind of political socialization is sometimes referred to by hegemony theorists as positive inculcation; the second is referred to as selective omission. These can be illustrated by statements from social studies textbooks.

An example of positive inculcation is the praise of the free market system that routinely appears in social studies textbooks, the corresponding claim that the U.S. free market economy is democratic, and the delegitimation of alternative political–economic systems. Such claims are in some measure misleading: There is no completely free market economy in the United States, and if there were, it would not necessarily be democratic. Slavery and some of the most antidemocratic abuses of immigrants, women, and children occurred in a historical period when our economy was much less regulated by government than it now is. Similarly, trumpeting the U.S. political–economic system over the systems of other nations obscures important truths. As Derek Bok has shown, citizens of the United States lag behind the citizens of most other industrialized nations in the majority of measures of quality of life.[75]

A critical consciousness, while of primary importance, is not enough; it must be accompanied by reading and writing skills, which have the potential to enhance personal and social liberation. Donaldo Macedo writes that the radical educator "will enable students to become literate in their culture as well as in the codes of the dominant classes." Freire elaborates on this point by using the illustration of Black students in U.S. schools:

> The successful usage of the students' cultural universe requires respect and legitimation of students' discourse, that is, their own linguistic codes, which are different but never inferior. . . . In the case of black Americans, for example, educators must respect black English. . . . The legitimation of black English as an educational tool does not, however, preclude the need to acquire proficiency in the linguistic code of the dominant group.[76]

A tension clearly exists here. What balance should the critical perspective seek between criticism of the dominant culture on the one hand and learning its "linguistic code" on the other? Such tension is inherent, from the critical literacy perspective, in learning both to "read the world" critically and to "read the word," which may be uncritical and biased. Without the critical reading of the unequal power relations that structure society, however, literacy does not realize its essential value of liberating the literate—at least in the critical literacy perspective. Contemporary curriculum theorist Cameron McCarthy is among those who argue that teachers can effectively engage students in examining how knowledge is produced and sustained in U.S. schools and the wider cultures and that such an investigation will necessarily have to consider relations of power in the wider culture.[77]

Teachers can think critically about curriculum and textbook use and seek participation in the widening of source material selection. They can also intervene prudently yet effectively by encouraging democratic processes in school space use and in student learning activities.

In the educational reform movement of the 1980s a great many different "literacies" were advocated: functional literacy, computer literacy, civic literacy, aesthetic literacy, and so on. Each use of the term *literacy* focuses on a different realm of learning that its advocates wish to designate as fundamental to education as the three Rs. Using the word *literacy* seems to accomplish this. As a result, the term is often used to mean that which the one using it believes should be learned. Thus, the meaning of the term becomes altered in ways that serve different social and educational aims.

From this perspective, one can see what kind of education is being promoted by the advocates of each kind of literacy treated in this chapter. Those who advocate functional literacy want people to function in society's existing social and economic roles; those who promote cultural literacy want a greater understanding of the established culture; those who advocate critical literacy focus on empowering people to criticize and change political and economic oppression. There are no advocates of conventional literacy as an educational goal because it is so minimal. Are all these perspectives on literacy equally good and valuable? Now that we have examined how they fit into different educational orientations, how can we use them?

The usefulness of the various perspectives on literacy depends on the goal we have in mind. For example, if we want to provide evidence of the successes of the U.S. social and educational systems, the conventional literacy perspective is the most useful and valuable, because it indicates that illiteracy has been virtually eliminated in the United States. Yet we have seen that this perspective obscures the way illiteracy and power are distributed among the various social groups in this country.

If our goal is to measure people's ability to function at a minimum level within existing social and economic institutions, the functional literacy perspective will seem most valuable. However, we have seen that this perspective tends to settle for a minimum-skill view of literacy that does not attend to higher-order thinking and that may promote passivity in the learner. Further, there is reason to question this view because it seems to locate the source of illiteracy primarily in individuals themselves rather than in the larger social order—a social order that seems systematically to allocate illiteracy to some socioeconomic groups but not to others.

Finally, if the goal is to emphasize the relationship between literacy and empowerment, the critical literacy perspective seems most valuable. It begins with the notion that power is unequally and undemocratically distributed in contemporary society; it emphasizes that those in power define *their* knowledge as the most worthwhile; it recognizes that traditional definitions of literacy serve the interests of those who have the greatest wealth and power, not those who have the least; and it asserts that literacy should help those with the least power understand these relationships and act to change them. Paulo Freire has long practiced such an approach to literacy in Brazil and elsewhere, but the practice of critical literacy in the United States lags behind the theory.

We can evaluate the different literacy perspectives, then, by reference to various goals. It is therefore important to choose perspectives carefully. Which one, for example, is best suited to the interests of inner-city schoolchildren? An inner-city teacher or school that embraces a functional literacy perspective may be largely satisfied if all students can read at the sixth-grade level when they graduate from high school, because such students will be able to function in society. But a teacher who embraces cultural literacy might ask, "What understandings do such students have of Western civilization, of U.S. economic, social, and political institutions? Enough to participate as citizens and voters or only enough to choose the best buy at the supermarket?" And a teacher of critical literacy could ask, "And what if students *did* have such knowledge of historical and contemporary institutions? Whose interests would such knowledge serve: their own interests in becoming equal participants in political life or the interest of those who benefit from leaving political power and participation unequal?" Different perspectives on literacy reflect different educational aims.

Teachers seeking to engage their students in a curriculum that empowers students in democracy and a pedagogy of human rights are frustrated by the recent growth of deskilling and what theorist Michael Apple has termed the conservative "restoration" of property privileges in education.[78] Freire wrote an elegant book that is a signpost toward inclusive democratic literacy. Titled *Teachers as Cultural Workers: Letters to Those Who Dare Teach,* Freire urges students to identify with their

students' struggles and nurture their voices and writing toward developing a critical literacy.

The journal *Rethinking Schools* is an invaluable source for teachers looking for models of critical pedagogy. In just one issue Hawaiian educator Wayne Au emphasizes how critical teacher practice is possible and desirable. There the curriculum emphasizes student voices blending with the stories in curriculum. There the diversity of functional and cultural literacy are incomplete without this blend of democratic practice. He also emphasizes that critical literacy practice is a team sport. Nurturing local regional and national networks is a key element in teacher professional life.[79]

It is instructive at this point to reflect upon Thomas Jefferson's view of the importance of literacy in the United States (see Chapter 2). Clearly Jefferson thought literacy was important for the everyday reading and writing, buying and selling functions that people had to do at that time. He also valued literacy for the cultural understanding it made possible; he advocated the teaching of history, for example, in the elementary grades. And Jefferson was clearly fond of the cultural achievements of civilized humanity; he valued reading the works considered classics for the pleasure of learning and enjoyment of literature.

But Jefferson was not satisfied with a literacy that was restricted to everyday functioning and cultural appreciation, though he valued those things. He argued that literacy was necessary for political power and freedom and particularly necessary for guarding against undemocratic abuses of power. In proclaiming that "knowledge is power," Jefferson was recognizing a relationship between knowledge and power that the critical literacy theorists of today have elaborated on and extended. Unlike the critical theorists, however, Jefferson was content to allow members of the nonmajority culture to be excluded from the benefits of literacy and the benefits of power. Nor was he sensitive to the potential of a genuine cultural pluralism that honored the cultures of people of color. According to historian Ronald Takaki, "Jefferson had envisioned . . . a nation of racially homogeneous people covering the entire continent."[80]

Jefferson recognized that literacy is in part minimum reading, writing, and computational skills, and he thought that these skills could be taught to most students in three years of elementary instruction. He did not think, however, that it was enough to employ such skills mechanically; he did not settle for a conception of learning that overlooked the relationship between literacy and liberty. Similarly, both the cultural literacy perspective and the critical literacy perspective claim to preserve an indispensable relationship between liberty and literacy, yet they do so in different ways. The cultural literacy perspective emphasizes traditions of representative government and participation in established institutions. The critical literacy perspective asserts that when these institutions are themselves constituted undemocratically, only by developing a critical perspective on power and knowledge can literacy serve the goal of rejuvenating political and economic liberty for all citizens, not just the privileged classes.

Jefferson believed he had articulated a conception of literacy that, for his own time, was consistent with democratic ideals. There is one question we may ask of each perspective on literacy examined in this chapter. To what degree is it consistent with democratic ideals in our own time and place? It is a question we may rightfully ask of any educational approach in our society and one that recurs in various forms throughout the remainder of this text.

Thinking Critically about the Issues   #5

What elements in the school community or the wider community might object to teaching for critical literacy in public schools? Why?

Thinking Critically about the Issues   #6

To what degree do you find the critical literacy perspective consistent with John Dewey's democratic ideal, expressed in Chapter 4, of "the all-around growth of every member of society"? Explain how critical literacy theory does or does not serve this ideal.

 BUILDING A PHILOSOPHY OF EDUCATION

Early in U.S. history, the primary purpose of schools seems to have been to teach children to read, write, and "know their numbers." But from the very beginning, schools have also sought to shape the beliefs and values of the young, who were expected to absorb religious or moral or political "truths" as they learned the skills of literacy. Teachers today need to recognize that their teaching is not just about reading, writing, 'rithmetic, or calculus, or foreign language. It is also about imparting social and political values, whether teachers mean to do this or not. Schools don't just teach lessons about literacy; they teach lessons about how society works, who succeeds and who does not, and why. And to an important degree, teachers can influence what kinds of social and political messages get delivered in their classrooms.

As this chapter illustrates, the literal and political significance of "literacy" has changed as society has changed. Although one who could read and write a bit was considered literate in Jefferson's era, such rudimentary literacy skills do not necessarily qualify one as literate in our time. To some extent, the definition of literacy has changed with society. The various dimensions of literacy in contemporary life are coined in such terms as *functional literacy, cultural literacy,* and *critical literacy,* all of which differ from the conventional notion of literacy as the simple ability to read and write. While there is no universal agreement on the meanings of those coined terms, each points to a different way in which literacy is embedded in social contexts. Each reminds us that different teachers can settle for, or aspire to, different levels of literacy for their students—and that teachers can communicate different expectations of literacy to different students, whether they intend to or not.

The concept of *functional literacy,* for example, is grounded in a view of the degree of literacy that people need to function well or independently in a world pervaded by the written word. In this respect, functional literacy in one time and place may differ from functional literacy in another. A question arises regarding what it is to function well or independently. Are the skills of reading and writing, however fluently, enough to interpret written text well? Or are some kinds of background knowledge also important in the uses of functional literacy?

Such a question lies at the foundation of the notion of *cultural literacy,* which proposes that fluent reading and writing skills alone are not adequate for interpreting written text. Embedded in all such text are cultural meanings, and the reader's understanding

Access to computer literacy may well serve to exacerbate the differences between social classes if a "technology gap" persists in schools.

of those meanings will influence the interpretation of the text. One task of educators, in this view, is not just to teach functional literacy skills but to teach the background knowledge necessary to interpret written text in its cultural context. Thus, knowledge of history, literature, politics, science, and other dimensions of human experience is necessary to make sense of written text. As the background knowledge differs so will the reader's interpretation of the text differ. As a teacher in any subject, knowing that students bring different backgrounds to class, should you help the students connect new learning with the necessary background knowledge? Do some students need more help with this than others? Does your philosophy guide you to give different kinds of help to different students?

Advocates of *critical literacy* argue that any adequate conception of literacy should include a conceptual connection to human liberty. They assert that it is important for citizens to develop the knowledge, skills, and dispositions to reflect critically on their experiences and the power relations within their daily lives. They further argue that

functional or even cultural literacy is a tool that can be used to liberate or to dominate; if literacy is to be liberating, people need to be educated to think carefully about power.

The power of functional and cultural literacy to assist in dominating a population's ways of understanding the world is illustrated by the concept of *ideological hegemony,* sometimes referred to as *cultural hegemony.* Consideration of the decision-making processes of modern capitalist culture suggests that while Jefferson may have been correct that a society cannot be ignorant and free, neither is education a guarantee of freedom. The popular press and other news and entertainment media, together with the schools, can inculcate ways of thinking and valuing in a population that leave gross concentrations of economic and political power in the hands of a very small minority while a society proudly proclaims itself as democratic. Nor is there strong reason to believe at this time that new communications technologies will seriously challenge the concentration of wealth and power in the hands of a few.

We are left to wonder what Jefferson would think of the role today's schools play in the process of developing self-governing citizens. It would appear that our schools—and the kind of literacy they develop—play at least some role in helping students accept that participatory self-government is no longer a realistic goal in modern society. Moreover, as Dewey pointed out, schools are only one agency of socialization, and there are many others in society. Some, like family, peer groups, and the media, may be more powerful than schools at instilling values that you as a teacher might find objectionable: among these could be sexism, consumerism, glorification of violence, desire to win or succeed even if cheating is necessary, and so on. Good teachers know what social values they stand for, and which they stand against. How can you justify to others the fostering of values that may seek to resist certain social norms? In the public schools, a religious position is not an appropriate justification for a teacher's choice of values. How might democratic values constitute a basis for your choices of what values to embrace, and which to reject, in your classroom? Your philosophy of education should be able to make that clear.

Primary Source Reading

"Is Google Making Us Stupid?" That's the question that writer Nicholas Carr posed in a 2008 article in *The Atlantic*. That same year, the *New York Times* published a page one article by Mokoto Rich on the Internet's effects on literacy. We have reproduced that piece for you here, not because it's a good example of critical literacy, but because it addresses *some* of the issues raised in this chapter—and because it challenges the reader to raise issues that this article omits.

The Mokoto Rich article is a good example of mainstream journalism: interesting, informative, and focused on an important issue that confronts all of us: the impact of the Internet on literacy in young people. But does it go far enough? In reading this piece, ask yourself what concept of literacy lies at the foundation of the article: functional literacy, cultural literacy, critical literacy, or something else altogether? In your opinion, does this article address the literacy issues that you as an educator are most concerned about in a democratic society? Put differently: The article is interesting and informative, but is it sufficiently critical? How could this article have been more critical, in your view?

A version of this article appeared in print on July 27, 2008, on page A1 of the New York edition.

The Future of Reading

Literacy Debate: Online, R U Really Reading?

MOTOKO RICH

BEREA, Ohio—Books are not Nadia Konyk's thing. Her mother, hoping to entice her, brings them home from the library, but Nadia rarely shows an interest. Instead, like so many other teenagers, Nadia, 15, is addicted to the Internet. She regularly spends at least six hours a day in front of the computer here in this suburb southwest of Cleveland.

A slender, chatty blonde who wears black-framed plastic glasses, Nadia checks her e-mail and peruses myyearbook.com, a social networking site, reading messages or posting updates on her mood. She searches for music videos on YouTube and logs onto Gaia Online, a role-playing site where members fashion alternate identities as cutesy cartoon characters. But she spends most of her time on quizilla.com or fanfiction. net, reading and commenting on stories written by other users and based on books, television shows or movies.

Her mother, Deborah Konyk, would prefer that Nadia, who gets A's and B's at school, read books for a change. But at this point, Ms. Konyk said, "I'm just pleased that she reads something anymore."

Children like Nadia lie at the heart of a passionate debate about just what it means to read in the digital age. The discussion is playing out among educational policy makers and reading experts around the world, and within groups like the National Council of Teachers of English and the International Reading Association.

As teenagers' scores on standardized reading tests have declined or stagnated, some argue that the hours spent prowling the Internet are the enemy of reading—diminishing literacy, wrecking attention spans and destroying a precious common culture that exists only through the reading of books.

But others say the Internet has created a new kind of reading, one that schools and society should not discount. The Web inspires a teenager like Nadia, who might otherwise spend most of her leisure time watching television, to read and write.

Even accomplished book readers like Zachary Sims, 18, of Old Greenwich, Conn., crave the ability to quickly find different points of view on a subject and converse with others online. Some children with dyslexia or other learning difficulties, like Hunter Gaudet, 16, of Somers, Conn., have found it far more comfortable to search and read online.

At least since the invention of television, critics have warned that electronic media would destroy reading. What is different now, some literacy experts say, is that spending time on the Web, whether it is looking up something on Google or even britneyspears.org, entails some engagement with text.

Setting Expectations

Few who believe in the potential of the Web deny the value of books. But they argue that it is unrealistic to expect all children to read *To Kill a Mockingbird* or *Pride and Prejudice* for fun. And those who prefer staring at a television or mashing buttons on a game console, they say, can still benefit from reading on the Internet. In fact, some literacy experts say that online reading skills will help children fare better when they begin looking for digital-age jobs.

Some Web evangelists say children should be evaluated for their proficiency on the Internet just as they are tested on their print reading comprehension. Starting next year, some countries will participate in new international assessments of digital literacy, but the United States, for now, will not.

Clearly, reading in print and on the Internet are different. On paper, text has a predetermined beginning, middle and end, where readers focus for a sustained period on one author's vision. On the Internet, readers skate through cyberspace at will and, in effect, compose their own beginnings, middles and ends.

Young people "aren't as troubled as some of us older folks are by reading that doesn't go in a line," said Rand J. Spiro, a professor of educational psychology at Michigan State University who is studying reading practices on the Internet. "That's a good thing because the world doesn't go in a line, and the world isn't organized into separate compartments or chapters."

Some traditionalists warn that digital reading is the intellectual equivalent of empty calories. Often, they argue, writers on the Internet employ a cryptic argot that vexes teachers and parents. Zigzagging through a cornucopia of words, pictures, video and sounds, they say, distracts more than strengthens readers. And many youths spend most of their time on the Internet playing games or sending instant messages, activities that involve minimal reading at best.

Last fall the National Endowment for the Arts issued a sobering report linking flat or declining national reading test scores among teenagers with the slump in the proportion of adolescents who said they read for fun.

According to Department of Education data cited in the report, just over a fifth of 17-year-olds said they read almost every day for fun in 2004, down from nearly a third in 1984. Nineteen percent of 17-year-olds said they never or hardly ever read for fun in 2004, up from 9 percent in 1984. (It was unclear whether they thought of what they did on the Internet as "reading.")

"Whatever the benefits of newer electronic media," Dana Gioia, the chairman of the N.E.A., wrote in the report's introduction, "they provide no measurable substitute for the intellectual and personal development initiated and sustained by frequent reading."

Children are clearly spending more time on the Internet. In a study of 2,032 representative 8- to 18-year-olds, the Kaiser Family Foundation found that nearly half used the Internet on a typical day in 2004, up from just under a quarter in 1999. The average time these children spent online on a typical day rose to one hour and 41 minutes in 2004, from 46 minutes in 1999.

The question of how to value different kinds of reading is complicated because people read for many reasons. There is the level required of daily life—to follow the instructions in a manual or to analyze a mortgage contract. Then there is a more sophisticated level that opens the doors to elite education and professions. And, of course, people read for entertainment, as well as for intellectual or emotional rewards.

It is perhaps that final purpose that book champions emphasize the most. "Learning is not to be found on a printout," David McCullough, the Pulitzer Prize–winning biographer, said in a commencement address at Boston College in May. "It's not on call at the touch of the finger. Learning is acquired mainly from books, and most readily from great books."

What's Best for Nadia?

Deborah Konyk always believed it was essential for Nadia and her 8-year-old sister, Yashca, to read books. She regularly read aloud to the girls and took them to library story hours.

"Reading opens up doors to places that you probably will never get to visit in your lifetime, to cultures, to worlds, to people," Ms. Konyk said.

Ms. Konyk, who took a part-time job at a dollar store chain a year and a half ago, said she did not have much time to read books herself. There are few books in the house. But after Yashca was born, Ms. Konyk spent the baby's nap time reading the Harry Potter novels to Nadia, and she regularly brought home new titles from the library.

Despite these efforts, Nadia never became a big reader. Instead, she became obsessed with Japanese anime cartoons on television and comics like "Sailor Moon." Then, when she was in the sixth grade, the family bought its first computer. When a friend introduced Nadia to fanfiction.net, she turned off the television and started reading online.

Now she regularly reads stories that run as long as 45 Web pages. Many of them have elliptical plots and are sprinkled with spelling and grammatical errors. One of her recent favorites was "My absolutely, perfect normal life . . . ARE YOU CRAZY? NOT!," a story based on the anime series "Beyblade."

In one scene the narrator, Aries, hitches a ride with some masked men and one of them pulls a knife on her. "Just then I notice (Like finally) something sharp right in front of me," Aries writes. "I gladly took it just like that until something terrible happen . . . ."

Nadia said she preferred reading stories online because "you could add your own character and twist it the way you want it to be."

"So like in the book somebody could die," she continued, "but you could make it so that person doesn't die or make it so like somebody else dies who you don't like."

Nadia also writes her own stories. She posted "Die-ing Isn't Always Bad," about a girl who comes back to life as half cat, half human, on both fanfiction.net and quizilla.com.

Nadia said she wanted to major in English at college and someday hopes to be published. She does not see a problem with reading few books. "No one's ever said you should read more books to get into college," she said.

The simplest argument for why children should read in their leisure time is that it makes them better readers. According to federal statistics, students who say they read for fun once a day score significantly higher on reading tests than those who say they never do.

Reading skills are also valued by employers. A 2006 survey by the Conference Board, which conducts research for business leaders, found that nearly 90 percent of employers rated "reading comprehension" as "very important" for workers with bachelor's degrees. Department of Education statistics also show that those who score higher on reading tests tend to earn higher incomes.

Critics of reading on the Internet say they see no evidence that increased Web activity improves reading achievement. "What we are losing in this country and presumably around the world is the sustained, focused, linear attention developed by reading," said Mr. Gioia of the N.E.A. "I would believe people who tell me that the Internet develops reading if I did not see such a universal decline in reading ability and reading comprehension on virtually all tests."

Nicholas Carr sounded a similar note in "Is Google Making Us Stupid?" in the current issue of the *Atlantic* magazine. Warning that the Web was changing the way he—and others—think, he suggested that the effects of Internet reading extended beyond the falling test scores of adolescence. "What the Net seems to be doing is chipping away my capacity for concentration and contemplation," he wrote, confessing that he now found it difficult to read long books.

Literacy specialists are just beginning to investigate how reading on the Internet affects reading skills. A recent study of more than 700 low-income, mostly Hispanic and black sixth through 10th graders in Detroit found that those students read more on the Web than in any other medium, though they also read books. The only kind of reading that related to higher academic performance was frequent novel reading, which predicted better grades in English class and higher overall grade point averages.

Elizabeth Birr Moje, a professor at the University of Michigan who led the study, said novel reading was similar to what schools demand already. But on the Internet, she said, students are developing new reading skills that are neither taught nor evaluated in school.

One early study showed that giving home Internet access to low-income students appeared to improve standardized reading test scores and school grades. "These were kids who would typically not be reading in their free time," said Linda A. Jackson, a psychology professor at Michigan State who led the research. "Once they're on the Internet, they're reading."

Neurological studies show that learning to read changes the brain's circuitry. Scientists speculate that reading on the Internet may also affect the brain's hard wiring in a way that is different from book reading.

"The question is, does it change your brain in some beneficial way?" said Guinevere F. Eden, director of the Center for the Study of Learning at Georgetown University. "The brain is malleable and adapts to its environment. Whatever the pressures are on us to succeed, our brain will try and deal with it."

Some scientists worry that the fractured experience typical of the Internet could rob developing readers of crucial skills. "Reading a book, and taking the time to ruminate and make inferences and engage the imaginational processing, is more cognitively enriching, without doubt, than the short little bits that you might get if you're into the 30-second digital mode," said Ken Pugh, a cognitive neuroscientist at Yale who has studied brain scans of children reading.

But This Is Reading Too

Web proponents believe that strong readers on the Web may eventually surpass those who rely on books. Reading five Web sites, an op-ed article and a blog post or two, experts say, can be more enriching than reading one book.

"It takes a long time to read a 400-page book," said Mr. Spiro of Michigan State. "In a tenth of the time," he said, the Internet allows a reader to "cover a lot more of the topic from different points of view."

Zachary Sims, the Old Greenwich, Conn., teenager, often stays awake until 2 or 3 in the morning reading articles about technology or politics—his current passions—on up to 100 Web sites.

"On the Internet, you can hear from a bunch of people," said Zachary, who will attend Columbia University this fall. "They may not be pedigreed academics. They may be someone in their shed with a conspiracy theory. But you would weigh that."

Though he also likes to read books (earlier this year he finished, and loved, "The Fountainhead" by Ayn Rand), Zachary craves interaction with fellow readers on the Internet. "The Web is more about a conversation," he said. "Books are more one-way."

The kinds of skills Zachary has developed—locating information quickly and accurately, corroborating findings on multiple sites—may seem obvious to heavy Web users. But the skills can be cognitively demanding.

Web readers are persistently weak at judging whether information is trustworthy. In one study, Donald J. Leu, who researches literacy and technology at the University of Connecticut, asked 48 students to look at a spoof Web site (http://zapatopi.net/treeoctopus/) about a mythical species known as the "Pacific Northwest tree octopus." Nearly 90 percent of them missed the joke and deemed the site a reliable source.

Some literacy experts say that reading itself should be redefined. Interpreting videos or pictures, they say, may be as important a skill as analyzing a novel or a poem.

"Kids are using sound and images so they have a world of ideas to put together that aren't necessarily language oriented," said Donna E. Alvermann, a professor of language and literacy education at the University of Georgia. "Books aren't out of the picture, but they're only one way of experiencing information in the world today."

A Lifelong Struggle

In the case of Hunter Gaudet, the Internet has helped him feel more comfortable with a new kind of reading. A varsity lacrosse player in Somers, Conn., Hunter has struggled most of his life to read. After learning he was dyslexic in the second grade, he was placed in special education classes and a tutor came to his home three hours a week. When he entered high school, he dropped the special education classes, but he still reads books only when forced, he said.

In a book, "they go through a lot of details that aren't really needed," Hunter said. "Online just gives you what you need, nothing more or less."

When researching the 19th-century Chief Justice Roger B. Taney for one class, he typed Taney's name into Google and scanned the Wikipedia entry and other biographical sites. Instead of reading an entire page, he would type in a search word like "college" to find Taney's alma mater, assembling his information nugget by nugget.

Experts on reading difficulties suggest that for struggling readers, the Web may be a better way to glean information. "When you read online there are always graphics," said Sally Shaywitz, the author of *Overcoming Dyslexia* and a Yale professor. "I think it's just more comfortable and—I hate to say easier—but it more meets the needs of somebody who might not be a fluent reader."

Karen Gaudet, Hunter's mother, a regional manager for a retail chain who said she read two or three business books a week, hopes Hunter will eventually discover a love for books. But she is confident that he has the reading skills he needs to succeed.

"Based on where technology is going and the world is going," she said, "he's going to be able to leverage it."

When he was in seventh grade, Hunter was one of 89 students who participated in a study comparing performance on traditional state reading tests with a specially designed Internet reading test. Hunter, who scored in the lowest 10 percent on the traditional test, spent 12 weeks learning how to use the Web for a science class before taking the Internet test. It was composed of three sets of directions asking the students to search for information online, determine which sites were reliable and explain their reasoning.

Hunter scored in the top quartile. In fact, about a third of the students in the study, led by Professor Leu, scored below average on traditional reading tests but did well on the Internet assessment.

The Testing Debate

To date, there have been few large-scale appraisals of Web skills. The Educational Testing Service, which administers the SAT, has developed a digital literacy test known as iSkills that requires students to solve informational problems by searching for answers on the Web. About 80 colleges and a handful of high schools have administered the test so far.

But according to Stephen Denis, product manager at ETS, of the more than 20,000 students who have taken the iSkills test since 2006, only 39 percent of four-year college freshmen achieved a score that represented "core functional levels" in Internet literacy.

Now some literacy experts want the federal tests known as the nation's report card to include a digital reading component. So far, the traditionalists have held sway: The next round, to be administered to fourth and eighth graders in 2009, will test only print reading comprehension.

Mary Crovo of the National Assessment Governing Board, which creates policies for the national tests,

said several members of a committee that sets guidelines for the reading tests believed large numbers of low-income and rural students might not have regular Internet access, rendering measurements of their online skills unfair. Some simply argue that reading on the Internet is not something that needs to be tested—or taught.

"Nobody has taught a single kid to text message," said Carol Jago of the National Council of Teachers of English and a member of the testing guidelines committee. "Kids are smart. When they want to do something, schools don't have to get involved."

Michael L. Kamil, a professor of education at Stanford who lobbied for an Internet component as chairman of the reading test guidelines committee, disagreed. Students "are going to grow up having to be highly competent on the Internet," he said. "There's no reason to make them discover how to be highly competent if we can teach them."

The United States is diverging from the policies of some other countries. Next year, for the first time, the Organization for Economic Cooperation and Development, which administers reading, math and science tests to a sample of 15-year-old students in more than 50 countries, will add an electronic reading component. The United States, among other countries, will not participate. A spokeswoman for the Institute of Education Sciences, the research arm of the Department of Education, said an additional test would overburden schools.

Even those who are most concerned about the preservation of books acknowledge that children need a range of reading experiences. "Some of it is the informal reading they get in e-mails or on Web sites," said Gay Ivey, a professor at James Madison University who focuses on adolescent literacy. "I think they need it all."

Web junkies can occasionally be swept up in a book. After Nadia read Elie Wiesel's Holocaust memoir *Night* in her freshman English class, Ms. Konyk brought home another Holocaust memoir, *I Have Lived a Thousand Years*, by Livia Bitton-Jackson. Nadia was riveted by heartbreaking details of life in the concentration camps. "I was trying to imagine this and I was like, I can't do this," she said. "It was just so—wow."

Hoping to keep up the momentum, Ms. Konyk brought home another book, *Silverboy*, a fantasy novel. Nadia made it through one chapter before she got engrossed in the Internet fan fiction again.

Developing Your Professional Vocabulary

A good understanding of this chapter's content would include an understanding of why each of these terms is important to education.

conventional literacy

critical literacy

cultural literacy

functional literacy

hidden curriculum

ideological hegemony

the "information marketplace" versus a "marketplace of ideas"

literacy as a social construction

mass media

NAEP (National Assessment of Educational Progress)

Paulo Freire

Questions for Discussion and Examination

1. What features of contemporary U.S. ideology and political economy come to light in the critical literacy perspective that do not emerge in the other literacy perspectives? In your view, should teachers try to take these features into account in their approaches to teaching? Explain.

2. From the point of view of the primary source reading, discuss, using examples, ways that digital communication may impact attention, access to accurate information, and development of critical literacy.

3. Which of the perspectives on literacy presented in this chapter do you think is the most important for individual teachers and for schools in general to embrace in the United States today? Defend your view, taking into account relevant dimensions of political economy and ideology as you understand them.

4. In what ways do social media both contribute to and create issues for general student literacy, for critical literacy, and for the quality of communication in school and out?

 Online Resources

Go to the Online Learning Center at **www.mhhe.com/ tozer7e** to take chapter quizzes, practice with key terms, access study resources, and link to related websites. Also available on the Online Learning Center are PowerWeb articles and news feeds.

Teaching in a Public Institution **The Professionalization Movement**

Chapter Overview

Chapter 10 brings a contemporary perspective to the issues raised in Chapter 3 on schooling as a public institution. Chapter 10 explores the meaning of the "professionalization" movement to improve schools by improving teachers and teacher preparation. A key consideration in this discussion is whether teaching is a profession. This chapter points out that unlike other occupations called professions, teaching serves the entire childhood and youth population and is both publicly funded and publicly controlled. In addition, most of its practitioners are women, who have historically earned less and have had less professional autonomy than men. Despite teaching's comparatively lower status among professions, this chapter maintains that teaching is clearly a profession nonetheless, with its own characteristics and ethical mission. Moreover, despite social forces that might work in favor of the success of some students and against the success of others, teachers are challenged to identify the sources of authority from which they can operate effectively in their own classrooms. The education of teachers, at the university level, and during a career, can work toward Building an intellectual and practical foundation for the exercise of meaningful authority. This process is addressed in the primary source reading.

Chapter Seven

Making the Most of Classroom Time

On the first day of school, the academic year seems to stretch out endlessly. If you're a beginning teacher, you may wonder how you'll ever fill all the hours of school that lie ahead (especially if you're not even certain what you're going to do *tomorrow*). And yet, as the days go by, you may begin to feel that there's never enough time to accomplish everything you need to do. With assemblies, fire drills, announcements over the intercom, recess, clerical tasks, and holidays, the hours available for instruction seem far fewer than they did at first. Indeed, by the end of the year, you may view time as a "precious resource" (Goodlad, 1984)—not something that has to be filled (or killed), but something that must be conserved and used wisely. (Of course, your students may not share this view, as Figure 7-1 illustrates!)

This chapter focuses on the issues of time and time management. First, we look at the amount of school time that is actually available for teaching and learning. Much of our discussion draws on the Beginning Teacher Evaluation Study (BTES: Fisher, Filby, Marliave, Cahen, Dishaw, Moore, and Berliner, 1978), an influential project that examined how time is used in elementary schools and the relationship between time and achievement. Our purpose here is to provide you with a set of concepts that you can use to think about the way time is used in your school and classroom.

The second part of the chapter considers strategies for using classroom time efficiently. We discuss four complementary approaches—maintaining activity flow, minimizing transition time, holding students accountable, and limiting the disruption caused by students leaving the room for special instruction ("pull-outs.") As Linda Shalaway (1989) has commented, "Students only have so much time to learn in your classroom and you only have so much time to teach them" (p. 51). The wise use of time will maximize opportunities for learning and minimize opportunities for disruption.

138

Textbooks for teachers attempt to communicate knowledge of the profession.

Chapter Objectives

Among the objectives that Chapter 10 seeks to achieve are these:

1. Students should consider whether teachers can uncritically accept district goals and practices for their classrooms, if the school system's goals and practices systematically produce unequal outcomes in different ethnic and economic classes of K–12 students. Prospective teachers are helped to explore their sources of professional authority for holding their classrooms to a higher standard than the district might support.

2. This chapter seeks to discuss the origins of teaching as an occupation, and the extent to which that occupation has become a profession.

3. Students should consider whether there is a definition of a profession to which teaching or any other profession must adhere.

4. Students should be able to discuss whether and how teaching is unique compared with other occupations that are called professions.

5. Students should be able to discuss how the profession of teaching has evolved with different historical eras, and that in the 21st century, a new view of school organization—and therefore a new view of teaching—is rapidly developing.

6. Finally, teachers as well as school leaders are seeing that for the diverse learning needs of children to be met, schools need to be places where teacher learning is highly valued—and that schools can be organized for such teacher learning.

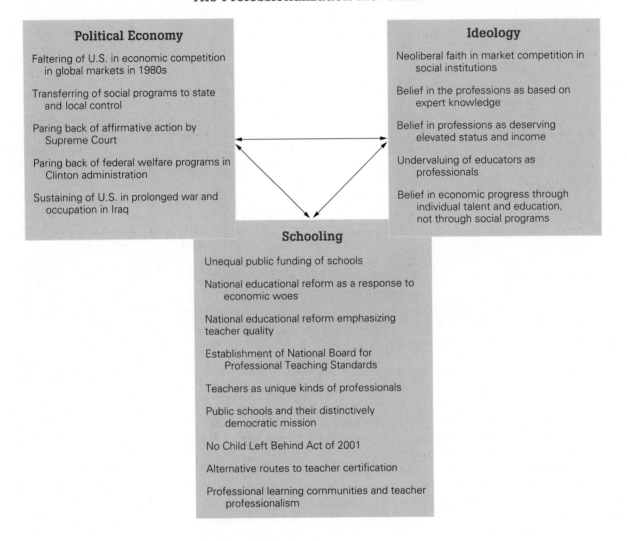

Analytic Framework
The Professionalization Movement

Political Economy

Faltering of U.S. in economic competition in global markets in 1980s

Transferring of social programs to state and local control

Paring back of affirmative action by Supreme Court

Paring back of federal welfare programs in Clinton administration

Sustaining of U.S. in prolonged war and occupation in Iraq

Ideology

Neoliberal faith in market competition in social institutions

Belief in the professions as based on expert knowledge

Belief in professions as deserving elevated status and income

Undervaluing of educators as professionals

Belief in economic progress through individual talent and education, not through social programs

Schooling

Unequal public funding of schools

National educational reform as a response to economic woes

National educational reform emphasizing teacher quality

Establishment of National Board for Professional Teaching Standards

Teachers as unique kinds of professionals

Public schools and their distinctively democratic mission

No Child Left Behind Act of 2001

Alternative routes to teacher certification

Professional learning communities and teacher professionalism

Dominant Ideology and the Teacher's Professional Authority

As Chapter 9 suggests, the past 30 years of educational research have marked a growing interest in the role of ideology in schooling.[1] By developing the notion of "dominant ideology," scholars have given a new direction to the old observation that schools transmit culture.

This new direction emphasizes that it is not just culture in general that schools help sustain, but it is a particular ideological view of one's culture that is put forward in schools: an ideological view that supports the institutional and economic dominance of a society's ruling class. This dominant-class ideology is put forward not only by schools but by other information-producing institutions such as news media, government, and economic agencies as well. It is understood as the "dominant ideology" because (1) it is this ideological perspective, and no other, that is

relationships are, and what people need in order to participate in them; about what a good society is, and what kind of people it takes to have one.

If such an educational point of view is developed, teachers can employ all their bases of authority—the authority of rules, of expertise, and of the community, real and ideal—to teach students what they will need to know in order to take their places in a more adequate community than the one they presently know. This is not to say that teachers should prepare students for some nonexistent utopia. Rather, teachers must develop an understanding of the community as it exists *and* an understanding of what kind of people will be required to make it better. They can try to develop for themselves an ideal of the community their students should strive for, and they should help their students with the knowledge, the values, and the skills they will need if they are to be resiliant enough to maintain high standards of belief and conduct in an imperfect society.

To do all of this, teachers must learn to develop for themselves an educational philosophy that will guide them in locating the community they wish to serve. Such a community is not found on a roadmap; it is a community that may exist only as a set of ideals and principles that history and careful reflection provide us. But the authority of those ideals may be for teachers the strongest authority of all.

The Professional Teacher: Remembering Horace Mann

In Chapter 3 we examined the early history of the common-school movement, which sought to reform schooling to meet what influential leaders saw as the needs of Massachusetts in the 1830s. Part of this reform movement included Horace Mann's efforts to improve the quality and quantity of teachers available to the new common schools. It led also to Mann's successful effort to centralize state control of schooling. We thus saw how an early instance of school reform produced changes in how teachers were prepared and how schools were governed.

Of particular interest was the development of *normal schools,* which were devoted to what Mann saw as teachers' educational needs. The curriculum in these schools included pedagogy, some psychology of learning, and the subject matter that teachers were expected to teach.

By establishing for the first time a specialized body of knowledge that all teachers were expected to master and using that knowledge as the basis for establishing

state-controlled certification standards, Mann pushed teaching in the direction of becoming a *profession.* Previously it had been a loosely organized occupation that was open to anyone regardless of training and certification. We also saw in Chapter 3 how Mann actively sought to recruit women into the normal schools for this newly professionalizing occupation, a development that would seem to be good for women and good for teaching. It would appear to open professional opportunities for women and provide a core of better-prepared practitioners for an emerging profession. Yet today, prominent school reformers are still trying to "professionalize" an occupation that, unlike other, more established professions, is predominantly female. Their efforts may have to take into account the subordination of women in American culture. If the feminization of teaching has contributed to its comparatively low status among the professions, it may also be true that teaching has not been the route to professional autonomy for women that other professions have been (though for fewer women).

Can an occupation with over 3 million practitioners, most of whom are women, be expected to achieve professional status similar to that of such professions as medicine, law, and architecture? Or is teaching so conditioned by its history as a gendered, publicly funded occupation that it is unsuited to certain kinds of professionalization? If so, efforts to improve education by professionalizing teaching may be misplaced.

Efforts to professionalize teaching are currently centered, as they were in Mann's time, on the intention to improve schooling. Just as in the 1830s and 1840s, the current professionalization movement raises questions about the funding and control of the profession of teaching as well as questions about who should become teachers and how they should be prepared. Four of the most important issues to consider in the contemporary debate on professionalism are these:

- Preparation and licensure of practitioners for a mass profession that must serve the entire population, not just private clients who seek services.

- The consequences of public funding of the profession compared with private funding.

- The role and status of women in the profession.

- The tension between public and professional control over teaching practice and what will be accepted as the specialized knowledge base of the profession.

Each of these issues has an impact on the status and rewards of the profession. Taken together, they define teaching as unique among the professions. They also help us understand whether the movement to professionalize teaching is likely to have an impact on the quality of schooling in the 21st century.

Professionalization of Teaching: Historical Perspective

Common-School Reform

Each of the main periods of school reform we have examined, from the common-school reforms through the Conant era, included as part of its reform agenda the effort to improve teaching and teachers. Horace Mann, for example, sought to make teaching more effective and respectable by treating pedagogy as a field worthy of study for all teachers. His primary purpose was not to give teaching the status of a profession but to provide sufficient numbers of practitioners with the

skills necessary to provide high-quality education to the common-school children of Massachusetts. To establish these skills, he believed, specific programs of education and training were necessary, and the normal school was born. In the normal schools we see the beginning of one of the most critical features of any profession: the pulling together of a specialized body of knowledge that all practitioners are expected to master through extended study. Government licensure or certification is used to ensure mastery of the professional knowledge base. In fact, these two features—an identifiable body of specialized knowledge and government licensure—are identified by educational historian Joel Spring as the most important defining elements of a profession.[2]

There were other ways in which Mann began to confer professional status on an occupation whose practitioners varied greatly in the quality of their preparation and methods. For example, his effort to establish and enforce a moral code of behavior through both the state and local school councils can be viewed as a way to achieve something like a professional code of ethics to which practitioners could be expected to adhere. And by standardizing both the content and the conduct of schooling through the state board of

The basic configuration of the typical classroom, with student desks facing the teacher's desk, has remained largely intact since the 18th century.

education, Mann was seeking to standardize the quality of professional practice. As states gained the power to influence and even control the school day and the school curriculum, however, the decision-making autonomy of teachers was severely constrained. This tension between state control and teacher autonomy, both of which are components of professionalism, would prove to have very different consequences for teaching than for private-practice professions such as medicine and law. In those fields, professional licensure did not so severely limit the control of the field by the professionals themselves.

Yet it would seem on the face of it that what resulted from Mann's ambitious reforms in Massachusetts was a solid foundation for the establishment of a true profession. But as John Goodlad pointed out, the 20th century dawned with teaching still far short of professional status. Goodlad notes, for example, that the typical two-year normal-school curriculum provided poor professional preparation. The body of professional knowledge it presented was ill defined, its students often did not plan to go into teaching, and its atmosphere was both unscholarly and submissive. Such characteristics do not fit well with the preparation of a professional capable of autonomous practice based on specialized expertise.[3]

Progressive Era Reform

These, in fact, were some of the concerns that led progressive educational reformers in the late 19th and early 20th centuries to reexamine the nature of teaching and teacher preparation. A development that came about at that time was the attachment of teacher preparation programs to four-year baccalaureate degrees, such as law and medicine had come to require. These new four-year programs sought to provide a greater theoretical base in the psychology of learning and the history and philosophy of education. William R. Johnson's research suggests that normal schools had already begun extending to four years of study by the end of the 19th century and were increasingly emphasizing academic subject matter over pedagogy.[4] With the location of teacher education programs in four-year state colleges and universities, the age of the two-year normal school ended relatively early in the 20th century.

The impulse for such improvement through more rigorous academic preparation came from the larger school reform movements of the progressive era. That era introduced the notion of the scientific management of schooling, and both the efficiency progressives and the democratic-development progressives wanted teachers to have a better understanding of the newly emerging research on the psychology of learning and the principles of group management. In addition, teacher educators with a social-reconstructionist orientation at Columbia Teachers College in the 1930s argued that teachers should have distinctive preparation in the history, sociology, and philosophy of education. They could then become "educational statesmen," capable of leading the schools and their students to the forefront of democratic changes in America.[5]

An interesting tension developed here as teachers colleges and other four-year institutions began paying increasing attention to the preparation of educational administrators. On the one hand, *professional administrators* were being educated to play a greater role in school management and decision making; on the other hand, teachers were also being given more extensive education so that they could, presumably, exercise greater autonomy in their work. By the beginning of World War II, the normal-school era had ended and teacher education was primarily a four-year state university enterprise. The fact that teachers were increasingly required to have a baccalaureate degree and that teaching and teacher education had come under the governance of state regulations gave the appearance of moving teaching closer to being a profession. In truth, however, increased control of schools and school districts by administrative experts, as described in Chapter 4, meant that teachers' autonomy was increasingly threatened. "Administrative progressivism" becomes a legacy that is not easily sidestepped in the current move to reform teaching.

Conant Era Reform

Within a few years after the end of World War II, both teaching as an occupation and the education of teachers came under increasingly hostile criticism from those who considered schooling in the United States to have gone academically "soft" (see Chapter 8). In the early 1950s, books such as Arthur Bestor's *Educational Wastelands* attacked schools' curricula. In the late 1950s, after the launching of the Soviet *Sputnik,* the Conant reforms called for greater academic rigor, "ability grouping," and increased emphasis on math, science, and vocational training. Then, in 1963, two books were published attacking teacher education: James D. Koerner's *The Miseducation of American Teachers* and James B. Conant's *The Education of American Teachers.* Consistent with the reform movement's increased emphasis on academic rigor for the presumably academically talented, both men disparaged teacher education courses, which they believed to be intellectually unchallenging and professionally useless, and emphasized preparation in academic content areas.[6] In addition, Conant emphasized the importance of an intensive period of practice teaching, which was seen to be more consistent with the clinical or internship training of such professions as medicine and law. In the end, however, Conant, Koerner, and others did little during this reform period to professionalize teaching. Johnson writes:

> Teachers came to be seen as less central to the improvement of the schools during the early 1960s because, beyond a consensus among lay critics that more intensive academic training was needed, there was no agreement on how to train teachers. This was not a matter of disagreement over which models of professional training ought to be supported. There were no models. Not even imperfect ones which might, through renovation and reform, hold promise for the future.[7]

Johnson goes on to suggest that given this skepticism concerning the preparation of teachers, the accountability movement of the 1970s and thereafter, which linked teacher evaluation to student test scores, can be understood as an effort by legislators and policymakers to control the quality of teaching from the top down. Insofar as the accountability movement emphasizes the management of teachers rather than their professional autonomy, it appears to step away from professionalism in teaching rather than toward it. But as Jurgen Herbst argued, professionalization in teaching has historically taken on the trappings and bureaucratic control of *managed occupation.* This, of course, is opposed to professionalism, which emphasizes "the recognition and practice of a teacher's right and obligation to determine his or her own professional tasks in the classroom."[8] It would appear that the period following the Conant reforms produced movement away from professionalism in teaching despite Conant's recommendations for how to achieve better schooling through reformed teacher education. And if the school reform movement of the 1980s and 1990s is any indication, educational policymakers are still not satisfied with the achievements of schools or the preparation of teachers.

Professionalism and Contemporary School Reform

The "excellence" reform movement of the 1980s continued into the 1990s, and school performance has remained a topic in the forefront of news coverage and political campaigns.

For example, days after taking office, President Bush announced his intent to pass the No Child Left Behind law. Enacted in January 2002, the bipartisan law reauthorized the Elementary and Secondary Education Act of 1965. It seeks to raise accountability of local school systems for educating all students. Its primary provisions include the following:

- **increased accountability** for states, school districts, and schools

- **greater choice** for parents and students, particularly those attending low-performing schools

- **more flexibility** for states and local educational agencies (LEAs) in the use of federal education dollars

- **a stronger emphasis on reading,** especially for our youngest children

All of these have implications for the quality of teachers who are expected to "leave no child behind" (see the Primary Source Reading).

A key dimension of this reform movement has been renewed attention to the education of teachers, with strong arguments made again for the professionalization of the teaching occupation. The present reform movement has emphasized, perhaps above all else, improving the measured academic achievement of students in our schools. From the early reports in 1983, such as *A Nation at Risk,* to the Clinton administration's Goals 2000: Educate America Act, to Bush's No Child Left Behind Act improved achievement in so-called basic academic areas has been touted as necessary for the United States to compete economically in the world marketplace. NCLB requires that teachers test students in reading and math every year in grades 3 through 8. Schools with low test scores face numerous sanctions. While few students are taking the option, one NCLB proviso allows children in low-performing schools to transfer. Some schools will be publicized as "underperforming" and will be required to respond successfully or face governance changes. Many educators have criticized the early results of NCLB. They

As the progressive era ideology of expert top-down management began to pervade schools, colleges of education began preparing professional administrators to run schools using principles of scientific management taken from business.

cite the punitive nature of the Act, forcing schools to abandon critical thinking or enrichment in favor of rote learning. Students in high-poverty schools face exposure to learning goals that emphasize "training" rather than the liberal education preparation most valued in higher education.

In the recent spate of educational reform reports, discussion of the professionalization of teaching always begins with concern for the quality of schooling in the United States. Once it is established that education in schools is deficient, it is a logical step to hold the teachers responsible for it. If there are problems in schooling, it is asserted, they are due in part to inadequacies among the teachers. But what is inadequate about teachers? In attempting to answer this question, scholars and critics turn to professionals in other fields, such as medicine and law, for comparison. This appears at first to be appropriate, since we are accustomed to thinking of teaching as a profession that requires a college degree, claims a body of specialized knowledge, and requires a license to practice.

Comparing Teaching to Other Professions

When we look to other professions for standards of comparison, it is said, teaching as a profession fails to measure up in several ways. To use a crude production model, we might say that the quality of the raw materials (teacher education candidates), the quality of the processing (teacher education), and the quality of the final product (teachers and the organization of the profession) are all lacking—or so goes the rhetoric. In terms of the quality of the input, it is asserted that the talent or background of the candidates entering teacher training is inferior to those entering other professions. In terms of the processing, it is asserted that teacher education programs are not as rigorous as the programs in medicine, law, architecture, and other professions. And in terms of the output, it is asserted that teachers, with their inferior academic talents and inadequate preparation, are often not competent to perform the complex tasks expected of them; further, they populate a profession that is structured with less autonomy, lower status, and fewer material rewards than other professions.

This three-part comparison of teachers to other professions is explicit in *Tomorrow's Teachers,* the first of three manifestos of the Holmes Group, a consortium of deans from the colleges of education of major research universities in the United States. In the middle of the school reform movement of the 1980s, the Holmes Group began its "Agenda for Improving a Profession" with the following comparison between teaching and other professions. In this comparison, the candidates, the preparation, and the structure of the profession fare poorly:

> Professional education prepares people for practical assignments: to teach, to heal, to design buildings or to manage organizations. . . . Unhappily, teaching and teacher education have a long history of mutual impairment. Teacher education long has been intellectually weak; this further eroded the prestige of an already poorly esteemed profession, and it encouraged many inadequately prepared people to enter teaching. But teaching long has been an underpaid and overworked occupation, making it difficult for universities to recruit good students to teacher education or to take it as seriously as they have taken education for more prestigious professions. Teaching, after all, comes with large responsibilities but modest material rewards. Good teachers must be knowledgeable, but they have few opportunities to use that knowledge to improve their profession, or to help their colleagues improve. And, despite their considerable skill and knowledge, good teachers have few opportunities to advance within their profession.
>
> As we try to improve teaching and teacher education, then, we cannot avoid trying to improve the profession in which teachers will practice.[9]

The Holmes Report argued that teaching compares unfavorably to other professions, and it offers recommendations for how to make teaching more closely resemble those professions. Yet if teaching is so distinctive an enterprise that it is difficult to compare with other professions, professionalizing teaching may be the wrong way to improve schooling. To examine whether making teaching "more professional" is best for schools, it becomes appropriate to ask, Should teaching be viewed as a profession like others, or is it so different that the differences make comparisons misleading?

After discussion of such questions, members of the Holmes Group chose to pursue the "professionalization" model for teaching, as did the Carnegie Forum's Task Force on Teaching as a Profession. These groups will be discussed in the following text because both made highly publicized recommendations for standardizing the teaching profession for greater professionalization and improved schooling. Their approach to standardization, as we will see, is in some ways reminiscent of Horace Mann's, but with new ideological justification and in a different historical context.

Professionalism versus Neoliberal Market Competition

All the attempts to define professionalism presented in this chapter are grounded in modern liberalism, particularly its commitment to specialized expertise and scientific rationality. The proponents of professionalizing teaching use as their criteria for a profession such characteristics as the existence of a scientific knowledge base that practitioners can master through prolonged study, state licensure based on demonstrated mastery of that knowledge base, and decision-making autonomy for practitioners who demonstrate such mastery. This approach also confers elevated social status and material rewards on those who have been licensed as having acquired this specialized expertise.

As we saw in Chapter 3, these professionalization measures all got their start in the common-school era, when we saw a turning point in the teaching profession in the United States. By creating the first state normal school, Horace Mann tried to prepare teachers who would help the schools achieve their fundamental tasks of 3 Rs and political and moral socialization. Since morality was so closely tied to religion, it meant religious teaching in schools alongside 3 Rs and Republican forms of government. Mann thought that the challenge to teaching was too great to be left to chance, so there had to be places where teachers learned subject matter content as well as how to teach.

Mann's teacher preparation movement resulted in the beginnings of a profession of teaching. Though some may question whether teaching is a profession or a quasi-profession, there is probably little to be gained by such a discussion. Teaching, like other professions, has characteristics unique to it—there is no single model to which all professions conform. Mann's efforts also resulted in the shifting of teaching from a male to a female occupation, which preserved and even exacerbated teaching as a low-status, low-pay occupation. Further, Mann's effort to "standardize" the profession—by establishing consensus about what good professional practices were—represents an effort that continues today in the work of the National Board for Professional Teaching Standards. Finally, it could be said that in the era of one-room schoolhouses, school masters and mistresses, and the early normal schools, a particular view of teaching as an isolated profession was established. This stands in contrast to a view of the teacher as a member of an organized body of professionals who through teaming and collaboration can accomplish things that individuals cannot.

Since the 19th century, other developments took place that further affected the profession of teaching:

- Schools changed from one-room schoolhouses to factory-style buildings that required new methods of organization if they were to serve equal education for all kids, but the model of the teacher as isolated practitioner prevailed.

- With urbanization, industrialization, and immigration at the dawn of the 20th century, school systems began differentiating their curricula—tracking working-class kids into factory futures and middle-class kids into management and professional futures. The truly rich didn't need public schools, and more and more private schools opened themselves to a select few middle-class kids with the "talent" to attend private prep schools.

- In the post–World War II era, high schools further institutionalized tracking with advanced placement (AP) and vocational education tracks, so teachers saw themselves preparing kids for the workplace, or some degree of postsecondary education (community colleges or maybe the state school); or for competitive colleges and universities where AP tracks could lead. During this period the Jim Crow era was ended by law, resulting in the integration of thousands of formerly segregated schools and the eventual "achievement gap" that showed differences in learning outcomes for different ethnic groups. At the same time, as national priorities seemed increasingly to drive school policy, teachers began turning to their unions—American Federation of Teachers (AFT) and International Education Association (IEA)—to gain some voice and pay. They were looked on by many as blue-collar union people rather than as members of a profession.

- In the 1980s, the contemporary school reform movement began, and one of its most significant initiatives has been the development of professional standards for teachers at the state and national levels. These standards have attempted to codify in writing what good teaching is, and the National Board for Professional Teaching Standards was formed partly to demonstrate that good teaching can reliably be assessed.

- If the primary purpose of schools in Mann's time was a common education for all in literacy, political principles, and moral training, it changed in the progressive era to preparation for employable skills and for social stability; changed again in post–World War II to competition in a cold war world; then changed again in the 1980s to economic competition in world capitalism in a rapidly

developing post–cold war world. In all of these phases, teaching remained largely a female, low-status, low-pay (in comparison to other professions), mass public occupation in which practitioners worked in isolation from one another.

A neoliberal response to the problems of the profession   If the professionalization movement can be described as a modern liberal response to the needs of schools through expert training of a professional class of teachers, it is clear that a neoliberal response has developed over the past 20 years: Alternative Routes to Teacher Certification (ARTC). These alternative routes range from Teacher for America to Troops to Teachers to a new national exam that college graduates can take to become teachers without having to go through any teacher preparation program at all. These alternative routes are defended by neoliberal advocates in part because they break the "monopoly" of schools and colleges of education and thus will improve the profession through greater competition (deregulation) among routes to the teaching profession.

In general, ARTC programs do not look like traditional undergraduate or even graduate teacher preparation programs that require completion of a degree and/or certification before full-time teaching can begin. Martin Haberman's idealized summary of a "pure" ARTC is intended to reveal the "deregulator" rationale behind each program component:

> The essential knowledge base for alternative certification programs is the competence of candidates in the cognate disciplines (#1). This base can be readily assessed by written tests of subject matter (#2). All professional studies are merely skills and information that can be readily learned on the job, through common sense, practice, having a colleague in the school (#4) and an occasional meeting (#5). The basic assumption is that candidates learn to teach by teaching (#3) and can do so in the most difficult school situations (#6) if they know their subjects. Finally the determination of who should be licensed is based on performance, including student achievement (#7), and that those most capable of making these decisions are the candidates' employers (#9 and #10).[10]

The years 2001, 1996, and 1986 provide benchmarks for thinking about significant events in this history. Earlier still, the year 1983 deserves special mention for the Reagan White House publication of *A Nation at Risk,* the launching point for the late-20th-century school reform movement. The *A Nation at Risk* demand for improved student learning and improved teacher quality helped fuel the alternative certification movement. Also in 1983, New Jersey governor Tom Keane convened a task force, headed by the late Ernest Boyer, to create an alternative to teacher certification that would attract liberal arts graduates to the teaching profession. C. Emily Feistritzer, a participant, has called the task force "officially the beginning of the alternative certification movement."[11] The National Center for Educational Information was founded at that time to begin tracking developments in alternative certification, and it remains today one of the best sources of information in that area.

By 1986, when the Holmes Group and the Carnegie Commission published manifestos on the future of the teaching profession, New Jersey had created a national stir with its Provisional Teaching Certificate, and other states soon followed. Holmes and Carnegie called for teacher preparation to be more rigorous and more grounded in professional research, even calling for extended programs of teacher preparation. Meanwhile, the nascent alternative certification movement was putting teachers into classrooms with only a summer of preparation. By the end of 1985, six states had produced nearly 300 ARTC teachers. By 1996, this number had grown to some 7,000 ARTC graduates in 16 states. Even the American Association of Colleges for Teacher Education (AACTE), widely regarded as a main pillar in the teacher education establishment, was in the ARTC business, publishing a volume titled *Alternative Paths to Teaching: A Directory of Postbaccalaureate Programs* (1996).

In 1986, ARTC programs were still in their infancy. Despite considerable growth, by 1996 the movement was still far from what it has become today. In 1996, alternative certification was still not fully on the radar screen in most educational discourse. It was not, for example, on the agenda of the national governors conference on education that year which called for an annual accounting of education progress. *Education Week* began writing its *Quality Counts* series in response to the governors' conference, but did not include ARTC as one of the many indicators of progress in its first Teaching Quality report—nor for several years thereafter. By January 2006, *Quality Counts* included ARTC programs as a mainstream indicator of "Efforts to Improve Teacher Quality."[12] Today, the National Center for Educational Information reports that 47 states have produced over 200,000 ARTC teachers. In Texas, for example, the majority of new teachers are now trained in alternative certification programs, compared with none in 1986.

In 2001, two more events, this time on the federal level—passage of No Child Left Behind (NCLB) and funding for the American Board for Certification of Teacher Excellence—promised to have significant impact on the ARTC movement. Among the many far-reaching provisions of NCLB was the stipulation that by the end of the current school year (2005–2006) all teachers must be fully qualified. While it is largely the responsibility of each state to determine the precise meaning of fully qualified, the Act in effect holds ARTC programs to the same standards to which all teacher education programs are held. The chief difference between the two is that ARTC candidates are allowed to work full-time as teachers while earning their teaching certificates. Moreover, the second major event of 2001—the American Board for Certification of Teacher Excellence (ABCTE)—demonstrates that the NCLB "highly qualified teacher" standard for alternative routes to certification may be more accommodating than many anticipated.

The ABCTE is potentially more significant to the teaching profession than NCLB because it reduces teacher certification requirements. A project of what Haberman calls the "deregulators" and the U.S. Office of Education, ABCTE has developed a "Passport to Teaching," described on the ABCTE website as the "premier national teacher certification program . . . ideal for knowledgeable and motivated professionals who want to change careers and pursue their dreams of becoming teachers, and for current teachers who need to earn their certification" (www.abcte.org/passport).

The ABCTE website presents a five-step individualized program of study intended to prepare postbachelor candidates to "demonstrate mastery on rigorous examinations of subject area and professional teaching knowledge." All of this can be done without the assistance of a college of education or any teacher preparation program other than the individualized study plan. Currently, this method can lead to certification in five states—Florida, Idaho, New Hampshire, Pennsylvania, and Utah—but efforts are in place to extend the initiative to all other states as well. The website ensures that "All teachers certified through Passport to Teaching are considered highly qualified according to the No Child Left Behind Act of 2001."

Political–Ideological Perspective   Certainly, the advent of ABCTE has changed the future field of play in alternative certification. While schools and colleges of education can embrace the opportunity to provide their own ARTC programs, ABCTE allows prospective teachers with undergraduate degrees to forgo higher education programs altogether. ABCTE and the Passport to Teaching are as staunchly opposed by those whom Haberman terms the "professionalists," as they are energetically supported by those he terms the "deregulators." In a 2006 Web article on alternative routes, Haberman offers a concise and colorful account of the ideological tensions dividing the two camps— both of whom profess to improve student learning by improving the quality of classroom instruction. First, he describes the professionalists, sometimes referred to as the "educational establishment," as including:

> faculty and administrators in education departments and colleges, the administrators and staffs of the 50 state education departments, the NEA and the AFT, the National Council for the Accreditation of Teacher Education (NCATE), and until the year 2000, the United States Department of Education. . . . Professionalists firmly believe that colleges and universities are capable of preparing teachers and indeed are the only organizations capable of doing so. Essentially, the professionalist position is based on the existence of their knowledge base, which they equate with the knowledge bases used to prepare other professionals, e.g., physicians, nurses, lawyers, engineers. . . . The stated goal of the professionalists is to limit the power to certify teachers to schools and departments of education in colleges and universities. They are dedicated to the proposition that no one should enter a classroom as a licensed teacher who has not completed a state approved program of professional studies offered by an accredited school of education.[13]

Opposing the professionalists, says Haberman, are the deregulators, who are viewed by the "educational establishment" as driven by a conservative, market-based ideology:

> The constituencies comprising the deregulators group hold a range of opposing views. . . . They believe that what teachers know is not a "professional knowledge base" known only to teachers but common sense known to anyone who is a college graduate, a parent, or anyone in the general public who is willing to think about their own school experiences. The deregulators believe that in place of education courses people learn to teach by actually teaching. . . . The essence of the deregulators' argument is that what is wrong with schooling in America is that the teachers don't know enough of the subjects they teach, and that the whole structure of licensing teachers is a protectionist plot to keep people who possess the requisite knowledge in the cognate fields from teaching children. Some of the constituencies comprising the deregulators group include

those who support private, parochial, charter, voucher and home schools; the United States Department of Education since 2000; several prominent foundations; many academics in the liberal arts and in fields outside of education; large numbers of the general public and many elected officials. The stated goal of the deregulators is to do away with current state systems of teacher licensing and allow schools to hire knowledgeable teachers in a free market system.[14]

There can be no doubt that a rift like Haberman describes is both real and persistent. The evidence goes back to educators' vigorous resistance to New Jersey's provisional certification in 1985; it continues in the current conflict between supporters and critics of ABCTE over whether any national test by itself can provide adequate evidence of an individual's preparedness to be a teacher.[15] It is well documented in the extensive references in journal articles such as "Does Teacher Certification Matter? Evaluating the Evidence."[16] At the same time, as the title of that article suggests, it is fair to question whether the rift is based on political–ideological differences or simply on an empirical question: Do teachers really need extensive preparation in professional education courses to learn how to teach well? Would the consequences of ABCTE for the teaching profession be positive, negative, or negligible?

Traditional Criteria for the Professions

Those who, like the Holmes and Carnegie commissions, look to the traditional professions as models for the occupation of teaching take what might be called a traditional sociological perspective. They identify several traits that characterize a profession's place in the larger society—such as autonomy grounded in certifiably expert knowledge or social status and rewards— and argue that if teaching adequately exhibited those traits, it would clearly be a profession and that public schooling would be improved.

There is, however, no full agreement on what constitutes a profession. The National Labor Relations Act attempted in 1948 to define a professional as one who is

> engaged in work predominantly intellectual . . . involving the consistent exercise of discretion and judgment . . . of such character that the output produced cannot be standardized . . . requiring knowledge of an advanced type in a field of science or learning customarily acquired by a prolonged course of specialized intellectual instruction and study.[17]

By this definition, is a teacher a professional? Certainly the work is more "intellectual . . . involving the consistent exercise of discretion and judgment" than simply physical and routine. At least among teachers we consider to be good at their craft this is true. What about the other criteria expressed earlier? How do teachers measure up in terms of acquiring a specialized body of knowledge through prolonged study?

While an argument could be made that teachers are professionals by the previous definition, one of the most recent and comprehensive studies of professional preparation for teaching argues emphatically that teaching is "not quite" a profession. In the 1990 volume *Teachers for Our Nation's Schools,* John Goodlad writes, "The conditions necessary to a profession simply have not been a part of either teacher education or the teaching enterprise." Goodlad identifies the following as the necessary conditions for professional status:

- A reasonably coherent body of necessary knowledge and skills.

- A degree of homogeneity in groups of program candidates with respect to expectations and curricula.

- Rather clear borders demarcating qualified candidates from the unqualified, legitimate programs of preparation from the shoddy and entrepreneurial, and fads from innovation in theory and research.[18]

While Goodlad asserts that these conditions are "largely lacking," he goes on to say that teaching may be considered a profession, but a "weak" one, "not quite" the profession that others are:

> Our studies have led us to several conclusions (and related hypotheses) supporting the proposition that teaching is a weak profession. . . . First . . . there is not a knowledge base sufficient to justify the claim that teaching warrants classification as a profession. . . . Our second conclusion, related to the first, is that the knowledge underlying and relevant to teaching has been little codified. The process is just beginning. . . . Our third conclusion is that curriculum development in teacher education is largely absent, inadequate, primitive, or all of these.[19]

Goodlad is reflecting the view, found in the Holmes and Carnegie reports, that teaching is not a profession in the sense that the major professions are but that it could become such a profession if certain reforms in teacher education were enacted. Unlike the Holmes and Carnegie reports, he focuses only on professional *preparation* and does not go on to talk about the conditions of work (autonomy, rewards, and so on) in the occupation. As indicated earlier, the Holmes and Carnegie reports do make recommendations for restructuring the profession of teaching as well as preparation for it.

Thinking Critically about the Issues   #1

Some readers of this book will be teachers who are going through alternative routes to teacher certification, while others will be graduates of "traditional" routes. Are ARTCs good for the profession and good for Pre-K–12 students in schools, or not? What's your argument, and what's your evidence?

Teaching as a Public Profession

Earlier we considered briefly the issue of the relatively low status of teaching among the occupations. In considering school teaching as at best "a quasi-profession," educator Dee Ann Spencer presents a brief summary that identifies three factors that must be considered in assessing the prospects for the improvement of teaching. Spencer writes:

> In summary, teaching is considered a quasi-profession because of low pay and teachers' lack of control over their work place. The conditions under which teachers work are more similar to those of blue-collar workers than to those of other professionals. The way in which the organizational structure of schools has developed over time and the predominance of women in teaching have created and perpetuated these conditions.[20]

Each of these issues—low pay, lack of control over workplace decisions, and the predominance of women—interacts with the others in shaping the nature and status of teaching as a quasi-profession, and each will be examined briefly here.

In doing so, however, we will examine an alternative hypothesis: teaching is a "partial" or "quasi" profession only if the concept of "profession" is narrowly defined. If we accept the notion that there are different kinds of professions, teaching can be understood as a distinctive type of profession with distinctive features of its own. How one defines professions is to some degree an ideological choice. For example, to define professions by the characteristics of medicine and law, which contract private clients on a competitive basis, are male-dominated, and resist public, democratic control in favor of control by privileged expertise, is to ensure that publicly funded and controlled, female-dominated, and noncompetitive professions appear deficient. Given these defining criteria, rectifying that "deficiency" seems like a sensible

Teaching is sometimes called an "isolated" profession because teachers spend most of their work day apart from the company of other adults.

thing to do. If, however, one starts from the point of view that the modern liberal emphasis on expert control of decision making might not be appropriate to all professions, different reasoning is possible.

Teaching "Job" versus Teaching Profession: The Issue of Professional Control

Like the term "progressive," the term "professional" is fraught with equivocated historical uses. In an interesting way these two terms overlap to create some contemporary teaching control paradoxes. In Chapter 4 we saw how the term "progressive" takes on two different meanings. In the case of Deweyan progressivism, educators were urged to expand their locus of authority, to celebrate the democratic life by increasing possibilities for control by teachers and by students. On the other hand, Eliot's progressivism is focused, not on democratic workplaces, but on the differentiation of labor and the role of administrative "experts" in the design and planning of work, in this case teacher work. This legacy remains with us. We have two definitions of profession. The first we will call academic professionalism, following the work of Jurgen Herbst. In this definition we describe the teacher as a member of a public profession that works to elevate the quality of teaching and teacher's lives from within the "guild" of teachers and scholars. This approach centers on a definition of teacher excellence that is both responsive to the public, the school boards, parents, and state and national authority, and maintains the power to define quality of education from within the sources of authority that constitute the life of the scholar, the world of scholarship in the arts and sciences, social and behavioral sciences, and all the disciplines that impact the minds of citizens. "Administrative professionalization," on the other hand, is the term we use to describe efforts to improve teaching from outside or on the tangent of the academy. This is bureaucratic profession building that treats teachers as employees more than as "academic" colleagues, whose performance is judged by "expert" administrators, and "management professionals."

Herbst contrasts *professionalization* (credentialing, career ladders, increasing specialization, more administration) with *professionalism,* which emphasizes "the recognition and practice of a teacher's right and obligation to determine his or her own professional tasks in the classroom."[21] He, like other theorists critical of the administrative professionalization model, does not assume that teaching needs to be like other professions. He seeks instead the conditions under which teachers could determine for themselves what they want their profession to be. For the nation as a whole to move in that direction would require an ideological shift away from faith in experts as decision makers and toward a commitment to democratically shared decision making among teachers in schools.

One difficulty with that vision, however, and a potentially severe one, is that there are many stakeholders in the schools: teachers, parents, students, the business community, legislators, and others. If democratic decision-making processes require dialogue among all stakeholders, teachers become one voice among many—and an often devalued, female voice at that. Given a commitment to democratically shared decision making, the movement toward professionalism, based on a liberal view of progress through expert autonomy, becomes suspect. A tension develops between administrative professionalization and the special role of the teacher who seeks to serve the democratic ideals of the community.

The dominant modern liberal ideology of top-down decision making and administrative professionalization operates to rule some issues out of the public debate. The fact that the ongoing school reform movement has focused less on these underlying social issues than on academic professionalism is evidence of how powerful is the legacy of administrative progressivism. Currently, the national political agenda has increased greatly the leverage on efforts to set criteria for good teaching as good standardized test scores. No Child Left Behind legislation has turbocharged the move away from teacher-made assessment and local academic standard setting, toward standardized, one-size-fits-all, indicators of quality. These indicators are increasingly threatening to create a class of pariah schools, and teachers, ignoring the effects of socioeconomic disparity on school achievement. On the other hand, the legislation offers encouragement that districts place "highly qualified" teachers and aides in every classroom.

Political–Economic Dimensions of Teaching as a Public Profession

Teaching as a Mass Public Profession   The often-cited problems of low status and low rewards for teaching are not sufficient evidence that teaching is a weak or quasi-profession. Although teacher pay is inevitably related to teacher status in a materialistic society, it is also related to many other factors. Among them is the need to use public funds to support 2.5 million public school teachers. This dependence on public funding (along with other factors that follow) has contributed to low pay for teachers relative to other professions. Teachers cannot ordinarily "hang out a shingle" as members of other professions can, that is, go into private practice,

because the institutions in which they conduct their practice are primarily public institutions supported by public taxes. In private schools (where about 12 percent of teachers work), teachers are supported by tuition that often provides them with less income than the public schools provide. For the most part, teachers are considered public servants, who, like police and firefighters, must depend on the public for their support. In addition, teachers greatly outnumber such public servants as police and firefighters. Consequently, their salaries are often lower than those in other public-servant positions that do not require a college degree. There are currently over 3.5 million teachers in public and private elementary, middle, and secondary schools, and projections suggest there may be over 4.2 million by 2016 (see Exhibit 10.1.)[22] Furthermore, their services are selectively, not universally, available, most often on a private contractual basis as the need arises. Imagine what would happen to physicians' salaries if their numbers were quintupled and they were paid with tax dollars. Would we say that physicians were no longer professionals?

Public versus Private Funding   Using 3.0 million as a conservative estimate of public school teachers, one can quickly see the enormous increase in public expenditures that would be necessary if salaries were raised even $10,000 across the occupation. An additional expenditure of $30 billion annually, or even half that amount, is not one that state governments or the public is likely to support (see Exhibit 10.2. Partly as a consequence of such large numbers of teachers, a rough leveling effect has operated historically to keep teachers at about the median point of all full-time occupations. In the period 1929–1930, teachers earned 2 percent more than the average for full-time employees working for wages or salary in all industries *if supervisors and principals are included in these figures.* During World War II the average for teachers dropped to 15 percent less than other workers, but by 1972 it had risen to 24 percent more. Since then, the average has fluctuated between 11 and 22 percent more than the pay for other workers.[23] Although this shows some improvement, it may well be a function of the increased numbers of higher-paid school administrators since World War II.

The fact that teacher salaries are state and locally funded is part of the nation's historical commitment to state-level control of education, and the fact that there is no national policy on teacher salaries accounts for the wide discrepancies even in the same region. But discrepancies among average teacher salaries within a state are typically greater than those between states or

Exhibit 10.1   Actual and Middle Alternative Projected Numbers for Elementary and Secondary Teachers, by Control of School: Fall 1991 through Fall 2016

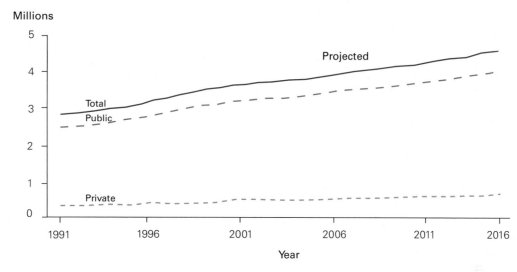

Source: U.S Department of Education, National Center for Education Statistics Common Core of Data (CCD), "State Nonfiscal Survey of Public Elementary/Secondary Education," 1990–1991 through 2003–2004; Private School Universe Survey (PSS), selected years, 1991–1992 through 2003–2004; and Elementary and Secondary Teacher Model, 1973–2003. Retrieved April 22, 2008, from http://nces.ed.gov/programs/projections/projections2016/figures/figure_29.asp?referrer=list.

regions, because in a given community, local resources can play the decisive role in funding local schools. Some towns and cities are simply much wealthier than others. Exhibit 10.2 indicates the extent to which state and local revenues have contributed most of the funding for schooling in the United States.

Whether teaching is a weak profession, not quite a profession, or a profession unique among the professions, it is clear that it is not materially rewarded as much as other professions tend to be. In 1992, when the average pay for public elementary and secondary school teachers had risen to $34,434, this represented more than a doubling of the average salary earned in 1980 and a tripling of the average salary earned in 1972. Yet after adjustment for inflation, *the salaries had increased only $92 per year since 1972.*[24] In 2008, public school teachers earned an average of about $50,000, which represents an increase since 1990 of just over $1,000 if held constant for inflation (see Exhibit 10.5).

These differences in salary may or may not account for the fact that teaching seems to draw fewer academically skilled students than other professions do. The National Center for Education Statistics reports that in 2002, SAT verbal scores of college-bound high school seniors intending to major in education lagged behind the scores of students intending to major in social

science/history, engineering, and physical sciences by 49, 43, 63, and 81 points, respectively.[25]

Educational researcher Geraldine Clifford writes that teaching has been underpaid throughout history regardless of the gender of the majority and the method of paying for teaching.[26] She asserts that this is due in part to the low social status of its clients, who are children. While the client status of children may be a factor, it seems clear that the preponderance of women in the field of teaching has also kept salaries depressed. Typically, occupations dominated by women provide earnings that are much lower than those in male-dominated occupations requiring similar skill levels. In 2002, women earned just 75 percent of men working in the same occupation. Even in female-dominated occupations, women on average earn significantly less than do men working in the same occupations.[27]

Thinking Critically about the Issues   #2

In *When Best Doesn't Equal Good* (New York: Teachers College Press, 1994) Sears, Marshall, and Otis-Wilborn conclude that the "best and the brightest" are not the best teacher candidates because they leave the field. In that case, is it necessary to recruit middling people but train them well?

Exhibit 10.2

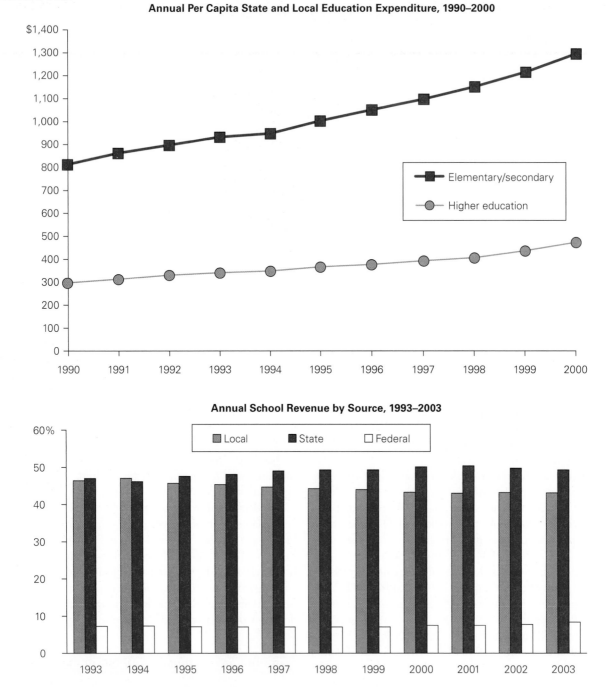

Annual Per Capita State and Local Education Expenditure, 1990–2000

Annual School Revenue by Source, 1993–2003

Teaching as a Predominantly Female Profession
The question that arises, of course, is whether the movement toward professionalization of teaching will be likely to change significantly the status, rewards, and lack of control over their occupations that teachers experience. If Spencer is correct that the predominance of women in the field is a major obstacle to teachers' obtaining professional status comparable to that of other professions, there is cause to be skeptical of the professionalization approach because teaching

Exhibit 10.3   Percentage Distribution of Revenues of Public Elementary and Secondary Education in the United States, by Source: Fiscal Year 2006

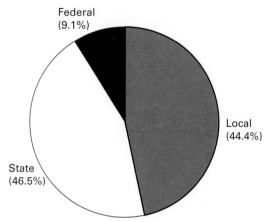

Federal
(9.1%)

Local
(44.4%)

State
(46.5%)

Note: Detail may not sum to totals because of rounding.

Source: U.S. Department of Education, National Center for Education Statistics, Common Core of Data (CCD), "National Public Education Financial Survey (NPEFS)," 'fiscal year 2006, Version 1a. Retrieved April 22, 2008, from http://nces.ed.gov/pubs2008/expenditures/figures/figure_01.asp.

promises to remain predominantly female for some time to come. Further examination reveals additional relationships between gender and teaching.

As the Holmes Group notes, occupations that are female-dominated tend to earn lower income and enjoy lower status than male occupations that require comparable skills and training. And as Spencer notes, increasing the proportion of women in a field has historically tended to expand the number of male administrative professionals who control that field.[28] Since the 1860s women have been the majority of teachers, and this condition is not likely to change. In 1999–2000 women made up the majority of the U.S. teacher workforce: A total of 2,590,000 teachers were female while 860,000 teachers were male (75 vs. 25 percent). The percentages of female and male teachers were similar in both public and private schools: Female teachers made up 75 percent of public school teachers and 76 percent of private school teachers. However, the distribution of teachers by sex differed widely by grade level. Among those teaching in the elementary grades, 1,340,000 teachers were female, while 140,000 teachers were male (91 vs. 9 percent). In contrast, at the high school level, 570,000 teachers were female, while 470,000 teachers were male (55 vs. 45 percent) In the middle grades, there were 660,000 female and 250,000 male teachers (73 vs. 27 percent).[29]

Historical Perspective   Historically women have been thought by some to be ideally suited to the occupation of

teaching. From the standpoint of town councils and local school boards, female teachers in Horace Mann's time were considered to be more malleable than men for the various demands and limitations of the job. Further, as schooling spread throughout the populace, the notion grew that teachers should be a bridge between the personal, nurturing environment of the home and the more impersonal, group-oriented environment of the school and outside world. By virtue of their experience as homemakers, as well as their nurturing instincts, women were considered ideally suited to help children cross this bridge.[30]

As the low status and salaries of 19th-century schoolmasters made the job increasingly unappealing to its traditional male candidates, there arose a simultaneous need for more teachers to staff the growing number of schools. As these new teaching positions were increasingly filled by women, any potential demands for perquisites were stifled by the fact that the only alternative occupations available, factory and domestic labor, were unappealing to many women. At the same time, as John Rury has pointed out, more rewarding management and commercial opportunities were drawing men out of teaching.[31]

One reason that other occupations have historically drawn men away from teaching is the fact that teaching is a "flat" occupation. That is, good job performance does not naturally lead to a higher-paying managerial or ownership position. Except when given additional administrative chores, such as curriculum specialist or department chair, teachers at the beginnings and ends of their careers have

Exhibit 10.4   Inflation–Adjusted Current Expenditures per Pupil for Public Elementary and Secondary Education in the United States: Fiscal Years 1985–2006

Inflation-adjusted
current expenditures
per pupil (in 2006 dollars)

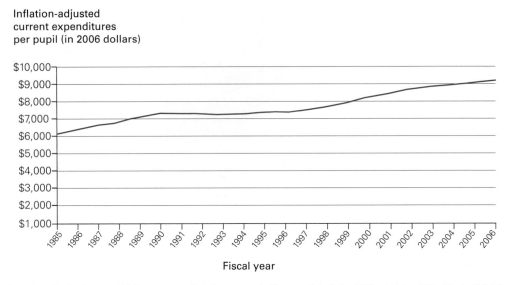

Fiscal year

Note: Data have been adjusted to fiscal year 2006 dollars to account for inflation using the Consumer Price Index (CPI), which is published by the U.S. Labor Department, Bureau of Labor Statistics. This price index measures the average change in inflation of a fixed market basket of goods and services purchased by consumers.

Source: U.S. Department of Education, National Center for Education Statistics, Common Core of Data (CCD), "National Public Education Financial Survey (NPEFS)," fiscal year 1985, Version 1a; fiscal year 1986, Version 1a; fiscal years 1987–2001, Version 1b; fiscal year 2002, Version 1c; fiscal years 2003–2005, Version 1b; fiscal year 2006, Version 1a. Retrieved April 22, 2008, from http://nces.ed.gov/pubs2008/expenditures/figures/figure_02.asp.

similar responsibilities. In contrast, educational administration has a hierarchical structure that progresses from school to district to state levels. As opposed to teaching, which is female dominated, administrative jobs, which are higher paying and more prestigious, have historically been dominated by men.

Current Reform Activity   In the liberal women's movement of the 1970s, one goal was to redress the balance of female policymakers in schools and school districts. That effort continues, although part of the focus has shifted to addressing the empowerment of teachers who choose not to leave the classroom for administrative posts. The choice is often made not because teachers do not value administrative tasks or desire more responsibility for policymaking and implementation but because they do not want to leave teaching—and the choice is often either/or. Teaching remains a valued set of activities for them, and classroom life is not traded for central administration offices.

An important national report to emerge from the professionalization movement expressly seeks to support and reward the professionalism of teachers who remain in the classroom. This report, *What Matters Most: Teaching*

for America's Future, was released in late 1996 by the National Commission for Teaching and America's Future (NCTAF), funded by the Rockefeller and Carnegie Foundations (see the Primary Source Reading at the end of this chapter). *What Matters Most* adds substantially to the work of the earlier Carnegie Commission and Holmes Group reports. The National Commission began with three fundamental premises:

1. What teachers know and can do is the most important influence on what students learn.

2. Recruiting, preparing, and retaining good teachers is the central strategy for improving our schools.

3. School reform cannot succeed unless it focuses on creating the conditions in which teachers can teach, and teach well.

When one focuses on the teaching conditions necessary for optimal student learning, the issue of professionalism is framed not by seeking to make teaching look like other professions. Instead, the issue of professionalism in *What Matters Most* is grounded in how *the distinct knowledge and skills of the teaching profession* can be incorporated into the governance of teacher licensing and the nature of teacher

Exhibit 10.5   Estimated and Alternative Projected Numbers for Average Annual Salaries of Classroom Teachers in Public Elementary and Secondary Schools: 1990–1991 through 2015–2016

School Year	Constant 2003–04 Dollars[1]	Current Dollars
Estimated		
1990–91	$45,979	$33,084
1991–92	45,875	34,063
1992–93	45,747	35,029
1993–94	45,477	35,737
1994–95	45,378	36,675
1995–96	45,339	37,642
1996–97	45,024	38,443
1997–98	45,274	39,350
1998–99	45,854	40,544
1999–2000	45,960	41,807
2000–01	46,128	43,395
2001–02	46,651	44,660
2002–03	46,777	45,776
2003–04	46,752	46,752
2004–05	46,476	47,750
Middle alternative projections		
2005–06	46,561	48,533
2006–07	47,017	49,907
2007–08	47,185	51,124
2008–09	47,373	52,446
2009–10	47,768	—
2010–11	47,989	—
2011–12	48,231	—
2012–13	48,405	—
2013–14	48,489	—
2014–15	48,553	—
2015–16	48,580	—

—Not available.

[1]Based on the Consumer Price Index for all urban consumers, Bureau of Labor Statistics, U.S. Department of Labor.

Note: Calculations were made using unrounded numbers. Some data have been revised from previously published figures.

Source: U.S. Department of Education, National Center for Education Statistics, Elementary and Secondary Teacher Salary Model, 1970–1971 through 2002–2003; and National Education Association, *Estimates of School Statistics*. (Latest edition 2005. Copyright 2005 by the National Education Association. All rights reserved.) (This table was prepared November 2005.) Retrieved April 22, 2008, from http://nces.ed.gov/programs/projections/projections2015/tables/table_36.asp.

preparation and professional development. In addition, the report recommends the recognition and reward of teachers who have demonstrated advanced professional achievement, using rigorous standards and teacher assessments developed by the National Board for Professional Teaching Standards, which the Carnegie Commission had recommended early in the 1980s, earlier in the contemporary school reform movement.

Thinking Critically about the Issues   #3

Doesn't the public have a legitimate interest in the quality of teachers and schooling? Criticism of schooling has prompted the current reform movement. Is this criticism warranted?

Public Control versus Professional Autonomy

Who Controls the Schools? Who Should?

It is not easy to determine "who controls the schools," to borrow the title of a well-known book on the subject. It is instructive to note the various agencies and constituencies that seem to be legitimate stakeholders in determining what counts as important knowledge and values in the schools and how they should be taught. In a 1991 U.S. Department of Education survey, for example, two-thirds of public school teachers reported that they did not have complete control over decisions concerning classroom

The nurturing side of teaching has been used to classify it as a "helping" profession that is more suitable to women than men. Is there any reason that a helping profession should have less status than a more impersonal one?

discipline. But, it might be argued, this is as it should be. Do we want each teacher to decide, on the basis of his or her best professional judgment, how to discipline each child regardless of what state or local school board policy or the federal courts have ruled? It would appear that all these constituencies have a legitimate role to play in the teacher's decision making, and the teacher's professional duty is to be influenced by these agents. Under NCLB, teachers are subjected to a new fixation on "state content standards" and test results, altering the notion of teacher judgment and authority considerably.

Similarly, it is difficult to hold teachers accountable to a codified body of knowledge that is influenced by so many groups. The Educational Testing Service reports that 41 states test students to demonstrate accountability to the taxpayers. Teachers are ill advised to ignore the content of those tests when they are teaching. On the other hand, a 1992 article in the journal *School Administrator* was titled "School Reform by University Mandate" to indicate the influence that university entrance requirements have over school curricula.[32] Meanwhile, schools and colleges of education have the responsibility of preparing new teachers, but state mandates are designed to influence what schools of education can and should do in such preparation. State legislatures are in turn subject to a variety of political and economic forces exerted by various pressure groups. Among these, for example, is Citizens for Excellence in Education, based in Costa Mesa,

California, a conservative Christian group that claims 120,000 members in 868 chapters in all 50 states. This group was one of several that in 1993 fought to use the courts to ban certain public school textbooks because of their "secular humanist" content.

Influence of yet a different kind comes from major foundations with the resources to sponsor research studies and policy documents. The Rockefeller Brothers Fund, for example, has weighed in on the professionalism debate with a booklet called *A Shared Vision: Policy Recommendations for Linking Teacher Education to School Reform.* Teachers are also influenced by such professional organizations as the National Council of Teachers of Mathematics and the National Council of Teachers of English, organizations that attempt to set the curriculum and teaching standards for their respective fields. And finally, those who are calling for more systematic licensure in the teaching profession seek to influence what teachers will learn by holding teacher education programs and teachers accountable to specific expectations regarding what teachers should know and be able to do. The major national teachers' unions, the American Federation of Teachers and the National Education Association, have supported such recommendations.

All these organizations represent various elements of the public that the public schools are expected to serve. Who should determine the public interest if not the people themselves, through governmental bodies and special interest groups? The authority for what should be taught in schools must ultimately lie with the public as well as with professional teachers and administrators. Consequently, teachers must ultimately learn how to balance a great number of competing perspectives while focusing on the best interests of each child in every classroom. The task is truly challenging even to the wisest and most experienced teachers.

To appreciate the relationship of public control and professional autonomy in American education, it is necessary to understand the role of the governmental structure that undergirds public education and the various legal and extralegal considerations that affect students, teachers, parents, and others with involvement and interest in public schools.

Statutory Control Structure

An understanding of U.S. educational governance begins with the Tenth Amendment to the United States Constitution, which states: "The powers not delegated to the United States by the Constitution, nor prohibited by it to the States, are reserved to the States respectively, or to the people." Because education is not mentioned anywhere in the Constitution, the individual states have plenary power over public education. However, given the early American tradition of placing government control as close to the people as possible, a form of educational government developed in which a significant portion of state control of public education was delegated to local school districts created by the state. Because government education policy is under the control of each state, there is no uniform pattern to school districts. They vary in size, number, and even in regard to whether they exist at all. For example, Illinois has about 2,000 local school districts and Hawaii has not created any.

State Government and Local Control   It is important to understand that while most states have delegated authority for daily operations to local districts, school districts remain creatures of the state. The state legislature may create new ones or dissolve existing ones. A Michigan court decision provides a good description of this relationship: "The legislature has entire control over the schools of the state. . . . The division . . . into districts, the conduct of the school, the qualifications of teachers, the subjects to be taught therein, are all within its control."[33]

State education policy is administered through boards of education and state departments of education. State boards exercise general control over state educational policy and recommend legislation to the state legislature. State departments advise their boards on policy and legislation and execute policy set by state boards. State departments also promulgate rules and regulations for the conduct of public education. As a general rule, states exercise authority for establishing minimum standards, which individual school districts must meet and may exceed if they wish. These minimum standards include teacher certification requirements, the minimum number of days public schools must be in session, compulsory student attendance rules, required subjects to be taught, graduation requirements, school health and safety standards, school finance policy, responsibilities of local boards of education, and more. Some states, for example, California and Texas, require state approval of any textbooks used in local schools. It is important to understand that once the state has delegated specific authority to local districts, that authority cannot be arbitrarily superseded.

Local school board members, whether elected by citizens living in the school district or appointed by the local government in which the school district is set, are representatives of state government in their communities and generally serve without pay. School boards are empowered to set school district policy within the broad framework established by state law. Among the most important powers exercised by a local school board are appointing the school superintendent, approving the school district budget, negotiating collective bargaining agreements with teachers' unions, and acting on all district employee hiring and dismissal decisions. The role of the school superintendent has two basic components. The superintendent of schools serves as the leader of the educational staff, responsible for providing direction and supervision for all aspects of school district activity. The superintendent's other, equally important role is to advise the school board on all matters before it, recommend policy to it, and implement the policy decisions of the school board.

Three of the most important national acts that have exerted enormous influence over the direction and conduct of education deserve mention. The National Defense Education Act of 1958 funded program improvements and student study grants in science, mathematics, foreign languages, and guidance because Congress deemed educational improvements in these areas necessary for national defense during the cold war. The Elementary and Secondary Education Act of 1965 (currently reauthorized as No Child Left Behind) provides large amounts of funding to schools directed at improving the education of

A sizeable portion of the teaching force still teaches in rural environments.

students whose education is limited by poverty. Finally, the Education for All Handicapped Children Act of 1975 (currently reauthorized as the Individuals with Disabilities Education Act) requires school districts to serve the needs of disabled students according to rules and regulations established by the U.S. Department of Education. Even though federal funding is authorized to enable school districts to meet federal guidelines for serving handicapped students, the amount of funds provided has proved inadequate, requiring schools to divert large proportions of their budgets to this purpose.[34] This last act illustrates that federal support for new mandates can be a mixed blessing for school districts.

Federal control over education extends far beyond the requirements of these and related acts. This is so because many of these acts provide that if school districts refuse to implement them or improperly implement them, all of their federal funds may be at risk. This is a serious concern for all public school districts, since an average of about 8 percent of their budgets comes from federal funds, which most districts can ill afford to lose.

The second source of federal influence over education comes from civil rights amendments to the Constitution, primarily the First Amendment (protection of religious freedom and freedom of expression), the Fourth Amendment (privacy protection), and the Fourteenth Amendment (rights of due process and equal protection of law). It is important to understand that public school districts are agents of state government and therefore subject to

constitutional safeguards against government abuse of the rights of the people as set forth in civil rights amendments and statutes. Even though the language of the First and Fourth Amendments prevents only the national government from abusing civil rights, the U.S. Supreme Court has decided that state government (including public schools) is similarly forbidden from violating these fundamental rights. State and federal courts have the role of hearing complaints from students, educators, and other citizens regarding charges of civil rights abuses by public schools. Since the mid-20th century, there has been a large increase in educational litigation that affects all those involved in schooling. The extent of school-related court suits has been great enough for many to call the justices of the U.S. Supreme Court "the black-robed school board." Prospective teachers should be familiar with the major court decisions that influence school policy.

While many federal education cases focus on constitutional civil rights amendments, others are litigated on the basis of various federal civil rights acts affecting education. Chief among these is the Civil Rights Act of 1964, which forbids discrimination because of race, color, religion, sex, or national origin by any agency receiving federal funds. Other congressional civil rights statutes that have been the source of educational litigation include Title IX of the Education Amendments of 1972, which forbids schools to discriminate in their programs on the basis of gender; the Rehabilitation Act of 1973, which forbids discrimination based on a disability by any agency receiving federal funds; the Family Educational Rights and Privacy Act of 1974, which requires schools to allow teachers to inspect their personnel files and challenge material in them as well as make all student records available for inspection by parents or by students aged 18 or above and to challenge material in those records; and the Equal Access Act of 1984, which forbids schools allowing various groups to meet in the school to deny access to groups on the basis of religious, political, or philosophical views. Teachers receive specific protections against hostile actions by school boards because of pregnancy (Pregnancy Discrimination Act of 1978) or age (Age Discrimination in Employment Act of 1967).

Thinking Critically about the Issues   #4

Increasingly, children and youth are attending schools with pagers and cell phones on their persons, sometimes for bad reasons (drug dealing) and sometimes for good reasons (maintaining contact with home after school). If schools try to restrict the use of such communications devices, what issues of due process and privacy need to be considered? Explain.

Who Controls the Schools? Extralegal Influences

Government legal structure, laws, and court decisions are not the only influences on school control. Government personalities, particularly the personal influence of the president, serve as a powerful extralegal influence on education policy. A prominent example of this is the influence exerted by President Reagan during the 1980s. The issuance by his administration of the *Nation at Risk* report, which criticized poor school performance as an internal threat to national security that was more serious than the external threat of Soviet communism, is a prime example. The result of Reagan's use of the "bully pulpit" was a wave of school reform in which almost every state participated. This has resulted in efforts to make both teachers and students more accountable for school performance.

A variety of nongovernmental forces exert influence equal to that exerted by government. For example, private foundations such as Carnegie, Ford, Lilly, Kellogg, and MacArthur dispense millions of dollars to support higher education research directed at improving school practices and support of school programs for improving teacher ability and student programs. Foundation funds are directed to applicants whose proposals address the issues deemed appropriate by the funders. As a result, the boards of these private organizations exert influence over the direction of American education equal to that of the research and development funding provided by national and state governments.

Textbook publishers also exert a powerful influence on school policy (see Chapter 9). It is estimated that 75 percent of classroom time and 90 percent of homework time are spent with text materials.[35] The major textbook-publishing firms exercise care in seeing to it that textbooks designed for broad national sales avoid offending large buyers. Thus, when states with statewide adoption policies or very large districts are seen to be offended by the treatment of a particular topic, publishers may try to chart a course that produces maximum sales. The result may be harm to the intellectual integrity of their products, reducing them to a lowest common denominator of treatment designed to avoid offending any potential buyers. For example, some districts dominated by Christian fundamentalist groups complain that social studies texts fail to provide appropriate space to the contributions of Christianity to Western civilization, while districts influenced by minority groups voice the same complaint regarding treatment of the contributions to civilization of their race or ethnicity.[36] Textbook publishers' attempts to please everyone are often the result of the profit motive rather than a concern for scholarly rigor and pedagogical effectiveness.

A more recent pressure on the nature of textbooks has developed from the aforementioned national reform effort emphasizing school accountability. Many states now require standardized testing of students on both national and state-prepared tests. This has caused school districts to demand textbooks and related materials that emphasize the particular types of learning demanded by the state and national tests. Again, national textbook publishers attempt to respond to their largest buyers, creating problems for schools without sufficient buying power to influence textbook development.

This influence exerted by national tests in the current reform movement is only the most recent extralegal influence of tests on school policy. For many years schools have used nationally standardized tests to track students into various ability levels, including assignment of students into various special education categories. Those dissatisfied with the predominance of testing as a student sorting mechanism call attention to the fallibility of tests for this purpose, particularly when they serve as the only, or even primary, determinant of student classification. In California, the Association of Black Psychologists sued the California State Department of Education on the basis of its claim that the major standardized intelligence tests, which were used to classify children as "mentally retarded," were culturally biased against Black children. The resultant appellate court decision (*Larry P.* v. *Riles,* 1984) found that the tests did contain enough bias against Black students to find a violation of the equal protection rights of minority students. An opposite conclusion was reached on the same issue in the Illinois federal court (*PASE* v. *Hannon,* 1980). Since the U.S. Supreme Court has never ruled on the issue, it remains a matter of controversy. The proper resolution of the problem advocated by most educators is to consider a number of sources of evidence in making decisions about the appropriate placement of students in school programs. Test results should be used, but in conjunction with evidence of school grades, teacher judgments, and other relevant information that sheds light on the educational potential of the student.

A final extralegal influence deserving attention is that of the two nationwide teacher organizations, the American Federation of Teachers (AFT) and the National Education Association (NEA). Both focus on influencing teacher welfare and educational improvement by lobbying for legislation at the national level and at the state level through state affiliates and representing teachers in local district collective bargaining agreements. There was a time when the NEA preferred professional sanctions to teacher strikes as a way to influence school district and state education policy and concerned itself mainly with general improvement of education rather than concentrating on teacher welfare issues such as salary and fringe benefits. In contrast, the AFT operated more in the mold of a traditional labor union, using labor strikes as its most powerful weapon. Because of the success of the AFT at winning teacher salary increases and related teacher welfare concessions in large urban districts, thereby winning teachers from the NEA to its side, the NEA has developed a stance more consistent with labor movement tradition, including strikes, that rivals that of the AFT. Although the NEA is far larger than the AFT, both are very active in supporting candidates for political office who favor their positions and opposing those with contrary platforms, both publish professional journals, and both support a variety of teacher development programs for members.

As time has passed, the traditional NEA–AFT rivalry has been replaced by increasing cooperation in recognition of the important political influence that can be exerted by combining forces. This has resulted in the merging of some local NEA and AFT affiliates in California and elsewhere. However, enough differences remain between the two national agencies to make a merger unlikely. Even while divided, the two organizations converge on a number of national issues, making their influence a powerful force on the direction of national education policy.

Professional Satisfaction and Professional Ethics

Researchers increasingly are turning to teachers to find out what is right, wrong, and possible in the teaching occupation. NEA research revealed in 2002 that 88 percent of teachers wish for more influence over curriculum and instruction decisions in their schools.[37]

Studies of what teachers find most and least satisfying about their work reveal factors similar to those that operate in most occupations. Researcher Karen Seashore Louis, in studying the general literature on quality of work life, found several conditions that teachers, like other workers in various occupations, find important.[38] These conditions include

1. Respect and status in the larger community.

2. Participation in decision making that influences control over their work setting.

3. Frequent and stimulating professional interaction among peers within the school.

4. Opportunity to make full use of existing skills and knowledge and to acquire new ones (self-development) and the opportunity to experiment.

5. Procedures that permit teachers to obtain frequent and accurate feedback about the specific effects of their performance on student learning.

6. A pleasant physical working environment and adequate resources for carrying out the job.

7. A sense of congruence between personal goals and the school's goals, or a low degree of alienation.[39]

Since the student Free Speech Movement began on the University of California–Berkeley campus in 1964, students have tested the limits of court rulings on freedom of speech in educational settings.

Louis writes that her interviews with teachers reveal that the first of these may well be the most critical factor, followed by the second, third, and fifth.

The U.S. Office of Education confirms Louis's study with regard to teachers' felt need for greater respect for their profession. While most teachers (53 percent) in a 1986 study indicated that greater respect for their profession would exert a major impact on keeping them in teaching, more involvement in decision making also was a high priority. But if asked to rank factors, a plurality (26 percent) chose better pay (with more room for future increases) as the one factor that would have the greatest impact on their decision to continue or leave teaching.[40]

One clear effect of the school reform movement of the 1980s was the effort to increase teachers' salaries. As illustrated earlier in Exhibit 10.5, however, the average teacher salary has barely kept up with inflation over the past 25 years. And teachers still work long hours. The average elementary school teacher, according to recent survey data, spends 47 hours per week on school duties, while the average secondary school teacher spends an average of 51. The difference may well be due to the fact that on average, elementary school teachers have about 25 students in class, while secondary education teachers have an average of 23 students in each of five classes.[41]

Despite the importance of salary to teachers who said better pay would affect their decision to continue or leave teaching, recent studies remind us that other conditions are important to job satisfaction and that job satisfaction in teaching leaves something to be desired. Yet 50 percent of private school teachers said they certainly would become teachers again, whereas only 40 percent of public school teachers said that. Why would this be? The same study indicates that overall, only 11 percent of public school teachers were highly satisfied with their working conditions, compared with 36 percent of private school teachers.[42] These conditions include those that Louis identified above. Some of these, such as

Historical Context

Teaching as a Public Profession

This timeline is different from the one in Chapter 9, though they both cover the last 40 years or so. For the purposes of studying Chapter 10, you might again ask of each decade: Which events from this decade (1970s, 1980s, and so on), have the most *direct significance* for the issues of teaching as a public profession discussed in this chapter?

1960s

1960   Six years after the 1954 *Brown* v. *Board of Education* decision against school segregation, the modern "sit-in" movement begins when four Black students from North Carolina A&T College sit at a "Whites-only" Woolworth's lunch counter and refuse to leave when denied service

1960   President Dwight Eisenhower signs the Civil Rights Act of 1960, which acknowledges the federal government's responsibility in matters involving civil rights

1963   Publication of *The Feminine Mystique* by Betty Friedan revitalizes the feminist movement

1964   Head Start, U.S. educational program for low-income preschool children, is established

1964   Student Mario Savio leads Free Speech Movement at University of California at Berkeley

1966   Former teacher Margaret C. McNamara founds Readings Is Fundamental (RIF)

1968   Bilingual Education Act passed

1969   250,000 antiwar protesters (the largest antiwar demonstration ever) march on Washington, DC

1969   The Stonewall rebellion in New York City marks the beginning of the gay rights movement

1970s

1970   A subcommittee of the U.S. House of Representatives holds hearings on sex discrimination in education, the first in U.S. history

1970   Supreme Court upholds new 18-year-old voting age

1972   Title IX Educational Amendment passed, outlawing sex discrimination in educational institutions receiving federal financial assistance

1975   Congress passes Education for All Handicapped Children Act (Public Law 94-142)

1975   Congress votes to admit women to Army, Navy, and Air Force academies

1978   Proposition 13 in California begins U.S. "taxpayer revolt" against government spending

1980s

1982   Equal Rights Amendment fails to win state ratification

1982   Reagan establishes "new federalism," transferring social programs to local and state control

1983   *A Nation at Risk,* a report by the Presidential Commission on Excellence in Education, advocates a "back to basics" education; becomes the first major document in the current reform movement

1984   Education for Economic Security Act (Public Law 98-377) passed, adding new science and math programs at all levels of schooling

1984   Carl D. Perkins Vocational Education Act continues federal aid for vocational education until 1989

1990s

1991   Unemployment rate rises to highest level in a decade

1992   Americans with Disabilities Act, the most sweeping antidiscrimination legislation since the Civil Rights Act of 1964, guarantees equal access for people with disabilities

1993   United States follows other industrialized nations with Family Leave Act that guarantees workers up to 12 weeks of unpaid leave for medical emergencies

1995   Supreme Court rules against any affirmative action program that is not "narrowly tailored" to accomplish a "compelling government interest"

1996   Clinton signs welfare reform legislation, ending more than 60 years of federal cash assistance to the poor and replacing it with block grants to states to administer

1996   Clinton signs the Defense of Marriage Act, denying federal recognition to same-sex marriages

1997   Supreme Court rules 5–4 that public school teachers can work in parochial schools that need remedial or supplemental classes

1998   Students at schools in Jonesboro, Arkansas, and Springfield, Oregon, open fire on students and teachers, killing seven and injuring many others

1999   Kansas Board of Education votes against testing any Kansas students on science curriculum related to theory and science of evolution (but it would be restored in 2001 by new school board)

2000s

2001   The No Child Left Behind Act expands the federal government's role in elementary and secondary education

2003   Millions of demonstrators around the world take to the streets to protest the planned U.S. invasion of Iraq

2003   President Bush orders the invasion of Iraq

2003   The Pentagon says major combat operations are ended in Iraq after the takeover in April of the last Iraqi stronghold

2003   U.S. Supreme Court votes 6–3 to strike down Texas sodomy law banning sexual conduct between gay people

2003   Massachusetts Supreme Judicial Court holds a 4–3 decision that gay couples in Massachusetts have the right to marry

2004   President Bush declares his support for an amendment to the Constitution that would ban gay marriage

Thinking Analytically about the Timeline

How does the recent history of the gay and lesbian rights movement have potential impact, if any, on teaching as a profession?

opportunity for frequent peer interaction and participation in decision making, are clearly conditions that school systems can address.

Teaching and Teacher Learning as Collaborative Activities

In the 21st century, a new view of school organization—and therefore a new view of teaching—is rapidly developing. To meet the learning needs of children, schools need to be places where teacher learning is highly valued. This is because:

- What teachers can learn in a brief teacher education program is limited. Imagine learning to play a musical instrument at the professional level by reading about that instrument for three years in college, observing it being played for a semester, then playing it yourself for a semester before taking your place on the concert stage. Virtually no one could do it, and no one is expected to. Yet we expect teachers to perform at a high professional level by preparing them in just that manner. And it could be argued that meeting the varied learning needs of an entire classroom of children or youth is a far more complex and demanding task than playing in a concert orchestra.

- Moreover, what teachers can learn in a teacher ed program is necessarily general so it can apply to many kinds of school settings, while teachers need to learn a lot about the particulars of one school setting when they begin teaching there. This includes the culture and practices of the school as well as the culture and practices of the community of the school.[43]

- The level of teaching expertise required to meet the needs of children who are not learning well is huge, and good teachers take years to learn their craft.

To meet the learning needs of children schoolwide, teachers need to learn how to work together, and this can best be learned by doing it with the particular teachers in that school. If student learning is valued, then teacher learning must be highly valued, and therefore teacher collaboration must be valued. The theory and practice of professional learning communities has developed dramatically in the past decade. We have learned that teachers who are supported in their efforts to work together to solve problems in the school can have a significant impact on student learning.[44]

Therefore, schools must be organized to eliminate, as much as possible, the isolated, privatized practice of teaching that was characteristic of the one-room schoolhouse. When schools began looking like factories, they did not reorganize the work of teaching into collaborative teams solving problems together. Union organization did not create such teaming, either, around the learning needs of students. But in this new view of teaching as a collaborative professional activity, a clear consensus is emerging from administration and unions alike that teachers need to work together to create the spaces for teachers to collaborate in professional learning communities that focus on the learning needs of students.

Even within that collaborative mode, the teacher must be concerned about newly developed professional norms and standards, as well as laws, that affect each teacher as an individual. Teachers ignore the laws and the relevant professional standards at their peril. Ultimately, the teacher is not a Lone Ranger in the classroom, but a representative of several wider communities:

- The community of subject matter specialists that determines what is true, not true, or debatable in each subject, whether it's history or mathematics or literature, and so on.

- The community of teaching researchers and practitioners who have established a knowledge base about what is effective and ethical in the classroom.

- The local community in which the school resides, because that community has cultural and linguistic norms, practices, and expectations of teachers to which teachers must be sensitive.

- The community of the particular school that determines what the norms and expectations are for teachers in the school, whether they pertain to personal appearance or professional conduct in the hallways or peer relationships.

These are some of the communities of values and practices that give teachers the authority to act in some ways and not others. Teachers who represent these communities well are usually on safe professional and ethical ground. However, sometimes those communities may have expectations that do not fit the teacher's own philosophy. One or another of these communities may endorse physical punishment or belittling of children as good methods of classroom management, for example. Or the history text may be clearly mistaken about something the teacher knows well r true. When there is conflict between a teacher's valu the values of the communities he or she represents in the classroom, it is important to be thoughtful and strategic about how that conflict is addressed. The way in which it is done will be, for better or worse, a learning occasion for the teacher, the students, and the environing communities. If the occasion is well planned by the teacher for optimal adult learning as well as student learning, good outcomes can result. Poorly addressed, these conflicts can become damaging for all concerned.

Democratic Ethics and the Profession of Teaching

That teaching is situated amid the competing values and demands of the public provides another component of its uniqueness as a profession: the professional ethics of teaching. Each profession has its own ethical codes, and teaching is no exception. The ethical codes of each profession are shaped by the activities and responsibilities unique to that profession, and since each profession has different responsibilities, the ethical codes vary accordingly. According to philosopher Michael Scriven, examples of the professional ethical responsibilities of teaching include

> respecting confidentiality of student and personnel records; avoiding favoritism or harassment (sexual or otherwise) of particular students—as well as avoiding the appearance of favoritism or harassment; not presenting oneself as representing the school's viewpoint unless specifically empowered to do so; ensuring that cheating does not occur and is punished and reported when it does; avoiding all versions of "teaching to the test" and other test invalidation such as requesting that less able students stay home on test day . . . ; assisting with activities such as the development and enforcement of professional ethical standards.[45]

In this list of examples, Scriven focuses on the ethical responsibilities that derive from day-to-day activities of teaching, just as ethical codes are derived from the activities of other professions. A distinctive dimension of the ethical conduct of teaching, however, goes beyond these day-to-day activities to the underlying mission of the public school. This underlying mission is grounded in the special relationship between education and democracy: Each is needed for the other to reach its full potential. No other profession takes as its fundamental goal the nurture of the knowledge, skills, and dispositions necessary for young people to take independent places in democratic life. The teacher therefore finds that professional ethics are determined not just by the activities of the profession, not just by the need to balance

fairly competing values of the various constituencies to be served by the schools, but also by each teacher's understanding and ethical commitment to serving democratic ideals. But where does one go for guidance concerning what is meant by "democratic ideals"? For example, John Dewey's belief that the moral meaning of democracy is its commitment to "the all-around growth of every member of society."[46] Among all our social institutions, only the schools have accepted such a broad mandate. Translating this ideal into classroom practice, for the "all-around growth of every member" of the class, is part of the ethical challenge that teachers may elect to meet. This challenge is thus one of the defining features of the profession of teaching.

 BUILDING A PHILOSOPHY OF EDUCATION

For the school reform movement to focus on the quality of teaching is a signal to teachers, school administrators, and the public that the connections between good schooling and good teaching are strong. Efforts to improve schooling necessarily take teachers, their preparation, and their practice into account, and the professionalization effort also seeks to do this. The push for professionalization could result in increased status and benefits for teachers, yet the acknowledgment and protection of teacher interests require a close examination of the ways in which professionalization could both serve and undermine them.

Teachers are a vital but not solitary component in the massive American educational system. Although more power and autonomy could change the nature of teaching practice, teachers cannot be held accountable for systematic failures in the wider society that adversely affect their work. Good teaching can open new life possibilities for young people in even the harshest living conditions, but good teaching is not likely to solve problems of drugs, violence, poverty, economic recession and resulting unemployment, or other societal conditions that require direct solutions of their own. Yet because the ultimate authority for what is to be taught in schools lies in the knowledge and values of the wider society, teachers tend to be held accountable by a great many different segments of the public—parents, local governments, state governments, the business community, representatives of minority groups the schools have not served well, and others. How to remain responsive to these various groups that have a legitimate stake in schooling, and yet remain autonomous professionals whose educational judgments are trusted, remains a problem for the professional educator.

As the possibilities of improving the status of teaching are considered and implemented, the various constituencies that have influence over schools need to take the history and particularities of teaching into account. It is possible that such study would reveal the strengths of an occupation that carries historically feminized values such as nurturing, support, and attention to personal relationships. Those values could then be integrated into the strategies that evolve for the improvement of the conditions under which teachers are educated and become responsible for the education outcomes and futures of subsequent generations. We can question whether a historically feminized occupation with 3 million practitioners can ever be expected to achieve the material rewards and status enjoyed by male-dominated professions with a fraction as many practitioners. If this likelihood is remote, one can further ask which dimensions of professionalization would be of benefit to teachers and their students and how. If teaching is to have higher professional status than it now has, it will be likely nevertheless to occupy a distinct niche among the professions. One mark of the success of the professionalization of teaching will be the degree to which teachers achieve significant influence in making the fundamental decisions that affect their working lives while successfully engaging representatives of the many educational constituencies in dialogue over what should be taught, to whom, and how.

Making teachers look more like other professionals, however, may be a mistaken approach to the original question that gave rise to the professionalization discussion: How can schooling be improved? Professionalization proves to be a misleading line of thought if it leads to a protracted discussion of whether teaching is really a profession or leads to

reforms that make teaching more like other professions but leave the quality of schooling little improved. If the problem to be addressed is the quality of schooling, a better question would be, What do teachers need to *be* to accomplish their educational tasks best? The questions that follow from that would include:

- What kinds of people make the best teachers?
- How can we select and prepare them?
- How should schools be structured for the education of the students?

Perhaps Holmes and Carnegie are correct and the answers to those questions lead to the conclusion that teaching should be more like the other professions. But that claim needs to be persuasively argued, not just asserted through comparisons with established professions. What matters in the end is not the designation of "professional" but that teachers have a range of knowledge, skills, and dispositions to respond to distinctively educational problems effectively. Such knowledge, skills, and dispositions are not likely to be simply lay knowledge or common sense. This specialized knowledge, however, doesn't itself define a profession, for there is specialized knowledge in many crafts and occupations. But the debate whether teaching is really a profession becomes a red herring brought about by calls to professionalize teaching. The problem at hand is to determine what teachers need to accomplish their educational tasks. One issue you may wish to address in your philosophy of education is the kind of working climate you wish to be a part of and to contribute to, and how you would or should respond to the new regimes of accountability mandated under NCLB. Should it be one in which it's every person for himself or herself, or one in which colleagues work together for common school goals? One in which you have no voice in school decision making, or one in which your ideas are sought out by school leaders? While you might not find the ideal working environment, are you prepared to work collaboratively to achieve it? If so, how? If not, why not?

Primary Source Reading

This chapter has criticized the teacher professionalization movement as a way to reform schooling in the United States. Yet, the chapter endorses a view of professionalism in teaching that embraces strong professional preparation, professional commitment, and professional standards of ethics and performance. Clearly, this chapter finds encouragement in the 1996 report on teaching and learning in the United States, *What Matters Most: Teaching for America's Future.* Students are encouraged to consult the website of the National Commission on Teaching and America's Future to learn more about the commission's high expectations for teachers.

Professional teacher preparation, especially the connection between teacher practice and higher education, is crucial to meaningful school improvement. This article, by Jennifer Epstein, demonstrates the level of concern regarding the fit between the university, the teaching profession and the American school.

Making Teaching a Profession

Jennifer Epstein

WASHINGTON—After spending much of the fall calling for major reforms to the nation's teacher preparation programs, Secretary of Education Arne Duncan's pleas appear to have begun to encourage action, as a major accreditor begins an effort this week aimed at bringing major changes to colleges of education and school districts alike.

More than two dozen teacher educators and education policy leaders will converge here Wednesday and Thursday for the first meeting of the National Council for Accreditation of Teacher Education's (NCATE) Panel on Clinical Preparation, Partnerships and Improved Student Learning, charged with recommending scalable ways to improve in-the-classroom training and strengthen relationships between school districts and the colleges and universities that prepare their teachers. The recommendations, in turn, would probably form the basis for revisions to the council's accreditation standards.

Source: http://www.insidehighered.com/news/2010/01/05/teachers.

NCATE—which accredits more than 600 colleges and programs nationally that graduate two-thirds of new teachers—has initiated what James Cibulka, its president, called a "redesign and transformation" aimed at making teaching a more respected profession with heightened preparation standards throughout.

The panel, he said, will "identify what the best practices are in strong clinical preparation and in preparing teachers to more effectively teach diverse learners." Efforts will focus on building partnerships between universities and making sure ideas are "relevant to policies at the national, state and local level." After this week's sessions, the panel will meet again in April before issuing a final report in May, a timeline he said is accelerated because the change is badly needed and the national environment is ripe for change.

In an October speech at Columbia University's Teachers College, Duncan said "America's university-based teacher preparation programs need revolutionary change—not evolutionary tinkering." In another speech that month, at the University of Virginia, he suggested that "teaching should be one of our most revered professions, and teacher preparation programs should be among a university's most important responsibilities," an opinion he voiced again in a column published in the magazines of the National Education Association and American Federation of Teachers.

Among the ideas to be seriously considered by the panel: the restructuring and rebranding of teaching as a practice-based profession like medicine or nursing, with a more closely monitored induction period—akin to a doctor's residency—and career-long professional development.

Tom Carroll, a member of the panel and president of the National Commission on Teaching and America's Future, said he wants the group "to respond with a very proactive, forward-looking vision of what we need to do to reinvent teacher preparation."

Panelist Arthur Levine, president of the Woodrow Wilson National Fellowship Foundation and former dean of Teachers College, said he hopes to see the group take steps to bridge "the yawning chasm of practice and theory between the universities and the schools." Schools, he said, should "become teaching hospitals," environments where undergraduate and graduate students preparing to become teachers can learn as they contribute to the instruction of primary and secondary students. Levine published a series of highly critical (and controversial) reports about the problems in teacher education several years ago.

Most teacher preparation programs already include some element of clinical practice, or student teaching, but Levine said the problem he has seen at dozens of programs was that there was "no connection between the clinical experience and what went on in the university." Ideally, he said, students "would teach in the morning, spend the afternoon learning theory connected to what went on that morning, and then preparing for the next day."

To Catherine Emihovich, a panelist who is dean of the University of Florida's College of Education, "the time has come" for major changes to teacher preparation. "Secretary Duncan has been pushing for change and the true understanding of teaching as a profession, and we are too," she said. "We must treat teaching as a recognized profession that occurs in stages rather than to see it in the old model where students study it in college, graduate in four years . . . and then are working in the field and done with their education."

Sona K. Andrews, provost of Boise State University, said her institution's college of education is "actually one of the few that puts students in the classroom throughout the entire tenure that the student is here." The university has strong relationships with local school districts to ensure that the two entities are serving one another's needs.

The ivory tower and the little red schoolhouse must learn how to work together, Cibulka said. Student teachers must be placed with master teachers rather than "the teachers that say they need a student teacher." They need "strong relationships with supervising teachers and with other teachers in the school and other students learning in the preparation program."

That's possible, he said, only if the two kinds of institutions work together. "To be successful it is going to have to be done in partnership. Working together, I think we're going to begin to actually change the profession."

Developing Your Professional Vocabulary

A good understanding of this chapter's content would include an understanding of why each of these terms is important to education.

Brown v. *Board of Education*

democratic ethics

due process protection in schools

expert management

Holmes Report

Lau v. *Nichols*

National Board for Professional Teaching Standards

profession

professional autonomy

professional ethics

professionalization versus professionalism

Title IX

Questions for Discussion and Examination

1. This chapter lists several reasons, from the economic to the ideological to the demographic, for the relatively low professional status of teaching. In your view, are there other reasons that should be included, or do the reasons presented have adequate explanatory value? Explain.

2. Given that professional status, autonomy, and the material reward structure in teaching compare poorly to those of other professions, what do you expect to derive from teaching in terms of personal rewards? What evidence do you find in this chapter that your expectations are likely or not likely to be met? How adequate is that evidence, in your view? Explain your position.

3. What issues of teacher professionalism are raised by the Primary Source Reading? Are these issues relevant to your own administrative aspirations as a teacher? Explain.

 Online Resources

Go to the Online Learning Center at **www.mhhe.com/ tozer7e** to take chapter quizzes, practice with key terms, access study resources, and link to related websites. Also available on the Online Learning Center are PowerWeb articles and news feeds.

Differentiated Schooling, Labor Market Preparation, and Contemporary School Reform: The Post–Cold War Era

Chapter Overview

Chapters 11 through 13 correspond to Chapters 4 and 7 in their emphasis on race, ethnicity, economic class, and gender as elements of social and economic inequity. Chapter 11 corresponds to Chapter 4 in its attention to the contrast between vocational education and the liberal ideal in education. Some readers view this chapter as the most important one in the volume. It makes explicit a theme that has pervaded the text up to this point: While the historical ideals of liberal education have come from cultures that were structured in racist, sexist, and class-based ways, key dimensions of liberal education ideals are worth preserving. These ideals emphasize both the full development of the intellectual and emotional capacities of each person and the idea that as human beings we have more in common than in contrast with one another; accordingly, these ideals are worthy of shaping our educational aims for all students.

This chapter argues that the democratic ideal of "the all-around growth of every member of society" that Dewey advocated and that remains compelling today has not been well served in the historical development of "labor force" education goals, programs, and results. The chapter then examines a different approach to work preparation education that uses vocational methods to achieve traditional liberal education ideals and leaves open a wider opportunity for students to make a variety of postsecondary choices, regardless of their primary and secondary schooling. Examples of current practice illustrate the Deweyan approach to education *through* vocations instead of *for* vocations.

PART

I

THE TRIUMPH OF
MODERNISM

Since the birth of civilization, no age has broken with tradition more radically or more self-consciously than the twentieth century. In part, this break represents the willful rejection of former values. The modernist break with the past also registers the revolutionary effects of science and technology on all aspects of life. Electronic technology has transformed the planet earth into what Canadian sociologist Marshall McLuhan has called a "global village." In the global village of the twentieth century, communication between geographically remote parts of the world is almost instantaneous, and every new development—technological, ecological, political, and intellectual—potentially affects every villager. Social and geographic mobility, receptivity to change, and a self-conscious quest for the new, the different, and even the outrageous are the hallmarks of this largely secular and materialistic world community.

The metaphoric "shrinking" of the planet actually began at the end of the nineteenth century, with the invention of the telephone (1876), wireless telegraphy (1891), and the internal combustion engine (1897), which made possible the first automobiles. By 1903, the airplane joined the string of enterprises that ushered in an era of rapid travel and communication. Such technology was as revolutionary for the twentieth century as metallurgy was for the fourth millennium B.C.E.

(opposite) Pablo Picasso, detail of *Guernica*, 1937. Oil on canvas, whole painting 11 ft. 5½ in. × 25 ft. 5¾ in. Prado, Madrid. Museo Nacional Centro de Arte Reina Sofía, Madrid. Photo: Oronoz, Madrid. © Succession Picasso/DACS 1997.

However, while metallurgy ushered in the birth of civilization, modern technology (machine guns, poison gas, and nuclear power) gave civilization the tools for self-destruction.

The end of the nineteenth century was a time of relative peace and optimistic faith in technological progress and human productivity. Throughout the world, however, sharp contrasts existed between rich and poor, between democratic and totalitarian ideologies, and between technologically backward and technologically advanced nations. As the powerful nations jockeyed for political and economic primacy, and as Europe and the United States continued to build their industrial and military might, few anticipated the possibility of armed conflict. In 1914, that possibility became a reality in the outbreak of the first of two world wars. The "Great War," the first total war in European history, ended forever the so-called age of innocence. And by the end of World War II, in 1945, nothing would ever seem certain again.

The modern era—roughly the first half of the twentieth century—has yielded a rich diversity of ideas and art styles. These are addressed thematically: Chapter 32, "The Modernist Assault," surveys the arts of the first decades of the twentieth century, especially as they reflect revolutionary changes in technology and new perceptions of time, space, and motion introduced by the science of atomic physics. Imagist poetry, abstract and nonrepresentational art, international-style architecture, and atonal music all demonstrate the modernist's quest to "make it new." Chapter 33, "The Freudian Revolution," takes as its subject the nature

Public education can introduce all students to the life of the mind as well as to employable skills.

Chapter Objectives

Among the objectives that Chapter 11 seeks to achieve are these:

1. This chapter should demonstrate the supporting arguments for labor market education in public schools and analyze how well this education has served the population it has been intended to serve.

2. Students should be able to discuss how the rhetoric of advocates of differentiated education contrasts with the available data on the nature of the American workplace in the foreseeable future.

3. Another objective is to discuss whether a revised view of workplace education that focuses on traditional liberal educational goals instead of preparation for the workplace is more supportable for educational and economic reasons.

4. Students should be able to consider the historical ideal of liberal education and how that ideal can be used to serve the interests of all students. Further, they should consider the potential of liberal education for embodying democratic ideals more thoroughly than a vocationalist or differentiated-curriculum approach does.

5. This chapter should explain how the four major themes of the contemporary reform movement have influenced the conduct of schooling in the United States.

6. Students should be able to identify who decides on and who benefits from the recommendations and policies of the contemporary reform movement.

7. Students should be able to evaluate the political–economic analysis presented in this chapter and discuss whether it captures the meaning of the contemporary reform movement.

8. Finally, this chaper should equip students to analyze the extent to which the contemporary reform movement can improve educational outcomes.

Analytic Framework

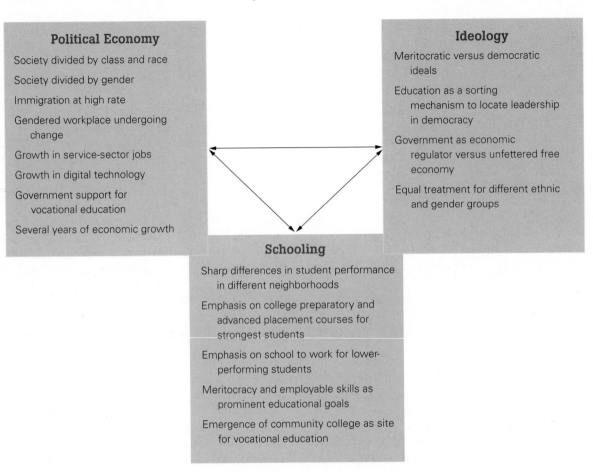

Political Economy

Society divided by class and race

Society divided by gender

Immigration at high rate

Gendered workplace undergoing change

Growth in service-sector jobs

Growth in digital technology

Government support for vocational education

Several years of economic growth

Ideology

Meritocratic versus democratic ideals

Education as a sorting mechanism to locate leadership in democracy

Government as economic regulator versus unfettered free economy

Equal treatment for different ethnic and gender groups

Schooling

Sharp differences in student performance in different neighborhoods

Emphasis on college preparatory and advanced placement courses for strongest students

Emphasis on school to work for lower-performing students

Meritocracy and employable skills as prominent educational goals

Emergence of community college as site for vocational education

Introduction: The Purposes of Schooling

In the 18th and 19th centuries the primary purpose of schooling was to teach young people academic skills. Young men and women developed workplace skills not in schools but in apprenticeships and other on-the-job training, whether for skilled crafts or for the newly developing factories. The beginning of the 20th century, however, brought with it the effort to mix job preparation with academic schooling, a mix that remained controversial throughout the century. Just as some Black educators questioned Booker T. Washington's emphasis on vocational education for African American youth, educators from John Dewey to Mark Van Doren to contemporary curriculum theorists have criticized the class, gender, and race biases of vocational education in public schools.

Historian Edward Krug, in his classic work *The Shaping of the American High School 1920–1941,* identifies one source of ideological and political–economic contest and change in education. He called it the "cult of business" This was an extension of the social stability proponents—schoolmasters who sought in the 1920s to respond to those arguing that the academic life of learning and inquiry was hostile to the orderly development of American life and unsuited to the majority of students. Along with this cult of business came an ideology of anti-intellectualism, social and political conformity, and the ritual of high school culture. This relationship between commerece, industry, and education was not new at this time and not uniform.

For example, while business elite were influencing the differentiation of education for industrial efficiency, organized labor fought back largely rejecting the deformation of teachers' work. For example, in 1923 the New York Federation of Labor called for class size and teacher load reductions, provisions for teacher tenure, and elimination of supervisory ratings, and significantly limited vocational training to students over 16. Also, in 1923 the American Federation of Labor's committee on education rejected censorship and business interference with teachers' academic authority. This movement also saw labor reject the junior high school, which was developed during this period as a mechanism for early vocational tracking toward economic efficiency.[1]

John Dewey had called these business values a part of the "religion of prosperity" and was concerned that such prosperity would not be fairly distributed. He also noted that it would foster a knee-jerk patriotism, "industrial fodder" equivalent to the "efficient cannon fodder" turned out by other nations. This comes on the heels of the Great War and the role of imperialist militarized Germany, whose own waves of 19th-century public education reform spawned both the 20th-century research-model university and the most comprehensive system of public education and template for anti-intellectual working-class education.

The culture of business influence in education reform is firmly established in the 20th century during times of wealth creation, as in the 1920s' insecurity and in the 1930s. These movements are characterized by vocational and custodial goals. Ironically, business elites in the 1980s would retool this language in a new narrative of testing and standards.

As we saw earlier in Booker T. Washington's arguments, the arguments of social-efficiency educators of the progressive era, James B. Conant's arguments in the early cold war era, and similar arguments presented early in the 21st century, the primary purpose of schooling is often defined in terms of the economic conditions and needs of the larger society rather than in terms of what each individual needs to be a well-educated person.[2] Many teachers have not had the opportunity to think carefully about the difference between the ideals of liberal education and those of vocational education, as Mark Van Doren did in Conant's time, for example. This chapter affords an opportunity to think about those purposes of education in today's world.

We have seen how labor force preparation and responses to workplace changes are a leading political–economic discourse at least since the early 19th century. Liberal education and high school as postsecondary school preparation dominate the discussion in the early 20th century. College prep and trades/vocational schooling characterize early-century efforts to academically track students. However, there are political and economic forces that drive schooling. David Angus and Jeffrey Mirel argue that the most significant 20th-century development is the so-called general track. It points to another interesting development in school and labor preparation. Market conditions such as the surplus population of unemployed youth led this trend.[3] Angus and Mirel write, "In the 1910s and 1920s the primary mission of high schools was the preparation of young people for adult roles and responsibilities in the economy either through academic or vocational education. While that mission did not disappear during the 1930s and the 1940s, it was rapidly relegated to a secondary position as the need to keep young people out of the labor market became a crucial social and economic necessity."[4] As the president of the American Youth Commission (AYC) Howard Bell put it, "If they [high school–age youth] get jobs, they displace adults and thus aggravate the national problem of unemployment."[5]

This "custodial" mission of the American school must be kept in mind whenever we observe reform breaking out in the United States, and, indeed now, in the global marketplace.[6] Ginsburg's volume is a compilation of papers each pointing to international, noneducational schooling functions: labor pool adjustment, political stability, certainly vocational and academic tracking. The reforms discussed in this text are mainly idiosyncratic to the United States, but labor markets and state-sponsored education dovetail wherever wage-labor and managerial differentiations exist in mature or emerging economies.

The general track courses later metamorphosed into a curriculum of "life adjustment" and were heavy on leisure studies, lighter noncollege preparatory "adapted" versions of general science, some social studies, language "arts," "work experiences," practical math, "modern problems," hygiene, and other commercially focused versions of academic subjects.[7]

The 1960s witnessed a revival of vocational education. As we saw in Part 1, James B. Conant emphasized vocational education in his much-discussed 1959 book *The American High School Today*. Conant argued, for example, that a comprehensive high school could be regarded as successful if one of the three major things it accomplished was to offer an extensive elective program that prepared the majority of students for the workplace immediately after high school. The other two items that he identified as marking a successful comprehensive high school were the provision of a good education for all students as future citizens and an advanced curriculum aimed at the most "talented" students.[8]

Three of Conant's 21 recommendations attempted to systematize the vocational education direction established in the progressive era. Conant argued in recommendation 1, for example, that "a meaningful sequence for a majority of the students would be a series of courses leading to the development of marketable skills."[9] In recommendation 2 Conant advised that each student should choose either an academic or a vocational or commercial sequence of courses, though he cautioned that any student at any time should be able to switch from one of these sequences to another. In recommendation 7 Conant focused on diversified vocational education programs, which he believed ought to be provided in any good comprehensive high school. He meant secretarial and home economics courses for girls and trade and industrial courses for boys. He argued that these programs should be geared to employment opportunities in the local community.[10]

Conant's widely publicized recommendations signaled renewed emphasis on vocational education in the late 1950s and early 1960s. One of his most significant contributions was to provide an emphatic answer to a debate that had endured since the inception of vocational education at the turn of the century. This dispute concerned whether there ought to be separate high schools for students in vocational and academic programs. Conant clearly argued that such a separation was inadvisable and that a comprehensive high school should offer different kinds of curricula under the same roof.

The Future of the Workplace

Thus the stage was set early in the 20th century for the kinds of labor force training and custodial "holding" of the needs of markets in labor. This section examines the kinds of information that might be shared with students to help them more fully understand the realities of work in the 21st century.

Future Jobs

Wirth writes about the ongoing shift in the American workplace from manufacturing to service industries:

> In the steady trend toward a computer-driven society, there continues to be a strong shift from manufacturing to

high-tech and service industries. The skills of highly paid factory workers continue to become obsolete. By the year 2000, some 75 percent of [manufacturing] employees will need to be retrained in new jobs or taught fresh skills for their old ones. On the average, workers now change jobs from four to six times in their work lives. There is a striking trend toward a requirement of more education for the fastest-growing kinds of jobs, those in technical, managerial, and professional areas. A projection of new jobs to be created between 1984 and 2000 shows that more than half will require education beyond high school, with about a third to be filled by college graduates. The median years of education required for new jobs for 2000 will be 13.5 compared with 12.8 for 1984. In absolute numbers, most new jobs will be in service occupations such as administrative support, marketing, and sales. By the year 2000, some 88 percent of the work force will hold jobs in the service sector. While the rate of growth will be greatest in higher-skill areas, the largest *number* of jobs will be for cooks, nursing aides, waiters, and janitors; for cashiers in marketing and sales; and for secretaries, clerks, and computer operators in administrative support. Other than the computer operators, most of these categories require only modest skills. But even here there will be increased expectations that these workers can read and understand directions, do arithmetic, and be able to speak and think clearly. The unskilled clearly will be the most vulnerable.[11]

Wirth points out that the model of the American workplace on which vocational education programs of the progressive period were based no longer accurately represents the American economy (see Exhibits 11.1 and 11.2). The American workplace has shifted significantly from heavy manufacturing industries to services-producing businesses, in particular small firms that require people with flexible, multiple skills.

For example, the U.S. government reports that from 1990 to 1992 nearly a million jobs among operators, fabricators, and laborers were eliminated while significant increases were recorded among jobs designated as managerial, professional, technical, sales, and service.[12]

Many of the fastest-growing occupations are in fact related to high technology, as indicated in Exhibit 11.2. For example, the fastest-growing jobs (in terms of *percentage* growth) were computer service technicians, computer systems analysts, computer engineers, and so on. On the other hand, it is important to note that these high-tech positions actually constitute a very small percentage of the total job growth. That is, although such jobs are growing rapidly, relatively few of them are available. The fastest-growing job

Exhibit 11.1   Employment in the 10 Occupations with Largest Projected Job Growth, 1996 and Projected 2006

Occupations	Employment		Change		Quartile Rank by 1996 Median Weekly Earnings of Full-Time Workers	Education and Training Category
	1996 (in thousands of jobs)	2006 (in thousands of jobs)	Number (in thousands of jobs)	Percentage		
All occupations	132,353	150,927	18,574	14%	—	—
Ten Occupations with Largest Job Growth: 1996–2006						
1. Cashiers	3,146	3,677	530	17%	4	Short-term on-the-job training
2. Systems analysts	506	1,025	520	103	1	Bachelor's degree
3. General managers and top executives	3,210	3,677	467	15	1	Work experience plus bachelor's or higher degree
4. Registered nurses	1,971	2,382	411	21	1	Associate degree
5. Salespersons, retail	4,072	4,481	408	10	3	Short-term on-the-job training
6. Truck drivers, light and heavy	2,719	3,123	404	15	2	Short-term on-the-job training
7. Home health aides	495	873	378	76	4	Short-term on-the-job training
8. Teacher aides and educational assistants	981	1,352	370	38	4	Short-term on-the-job training
9. Nursing aides, orderlies, and attendants	1,312	1,645	333	25	4	Short-term on-the-job training
10. Receptionists and information clerks	1,074	1,392	318	30	4	Short-term on-the-job training
Total	19,486	23,627	4,139	21	—	
Share of all jobs (percentage)	14.7%	15.7%	22.3%	—	—	

—Means not applicable.

Source: G. Silvestri, "Occupational Employment Projections to 2006," *Monthly Labor Review,* Bureau of Labor Statistics, Office of Employment Projections, November 1997.

category, database administration, for example, represented a small percentage of the job growth in American society and even a smaller percentage of total jobs. The same can be said for the other high-tech jobs in Exhibit 11.2.

For a truer picture of job growth in American society we need to look at the growth in *numbers* of jobs in the job market. For example, although the category of computer engineers is one of the fastest-growing job categories in terms of percentage growth, it accounts for only 235,000 new jobs. On the other hand, as Exhibit 11.1 shows, the fastest-growing job category in terms of total *number* of jobs available is cashiers, with 530,000 new jobs. In fact, by far the greatest numbers of new jobs available are service jobs or professional jobs that require the kinds of skills that most secondary

vocational education programs are not well suited to provide. Examples include cashiers, salesclerks, general office clerks, registered nurses, food servers, teachers, and truck drivers. Only a few of these jobs—such as secretaries, nursing aides, and orderlies—are positions for which high school curricula are preparing students. The question arising from such data is, is an entire vocational education curriculum needed to prepare someone to be a secretary or a nursing aide or an orderly? Notice the kind of training and education each job in Exhibit 11.1 requires.

Educating for the Workplace

This question of what kind of high school education is most productive for non-college-bound workers must

Exhibit 11.4   Fastest-Growing Occupations, 2002–2012 (Numbers in thousands of jobs)

2000 Standard Occupation Classification Title	Employment		Change		Quartile Rank by 2002 Median Annual Earnings*	Most Significant Source of Postsecondary Education or Training†
	2002	2012	Number	Percentage		
Medical assistants	365	579	215	59%	3	Moderate-term on-the-job training
Network systems and data communications analysis	186	292	106	57	1	Bachelor's degree
Physician assistants	63	94	31	49	1	Bachelor's degree
Social and human service assistants	305	454	149	49	3	Moderate-term on-the-job training
Home health aides	580	859	279	48	4	Short-term on-the-job training
Medical records and health information technicians	147	216	69	47	3	Associate degree
Physical therapist aides	37	54	17	46	3	Short-term on-the-job training
Computer software engineers, applications	394	573	179	46	1	Bachelor's degree
Computer software engineers, systems software	281	409	128	45	1	Bachelor's degree
Physical therapist assistants	50	73	22	45	2	Associate degree
Fitness trainers and aerobics instructors	183	264	81	44	3	Postsecondary vocational award
Database administrators	110	159	49	44	1	Bachelor's degree
Veterinary technologists and technicians	53	76	23	44	3	Associate degree
Hazardous materials removal workers	38	54	16	43	2	Moderate-term on-the-job training
Dental hygienists	148	212	64	43	1	Associate degree
Occupational therapist aides	8	12	4	43	3	Short-term on-the-job training
Dental assistants	286	379	113	42	3	Moderate-term on-the-job training
Personal and home care aides	608	854	246	40	4	Short-term on-the-job training
Self-enrichment education teachers	200	280	80	40	2	Work experience in a related occupation
Computer systems analysts	468	653	184	39	1	Bachelor's degree
Occupational therapist assistants	18	28	7	39	2	Associate degree
Environmental engineers	47	65	18	38	1	Bachelor's degree
Postsecondary teachers	1,581	2,184	603	38	1	Doctoral degree
Network and computer systems administrators	251	345	94	37	1	Bachelor's degree
Environmental science and protection technicians, including health	28	38	10	37	2	Associate degree
Preschool teachers, except special education	424	577	153	36	4	Postsecondary vocational award
Computer and information systems managers	284	387	103	36	1	Bachelor's or higher degree, plus work experience
Physical therapists	137	185	48	35	1	Master's degree
Occupational therapists	82	110	29	35	1	Bachelor's degree
Respiratory therapists	86	116	30	35	2	Associate degree

*The quartile rankings of Occupational Employment Statistics annual earnings data are presented in the following categories: 1 = very high ($41,820 and over), 2 = high ($27,500 to $41,780), 3 = low ($19,710 to $27,380), and 4 = very low (up to $19,600). The rankings were based on quartiles using one-fourth of total employment to define each quartile. Earnings are for wage and salary workers.

†An occupation is placed into one of 11 categories that best describes the education or training needed by most workers to become fully qualified. For more information about the categories, see *Occupational Projections and Training Data,* Bulletin 2572 (Bureau of Labor Statistics, 2004).

were lower in each category. In short, as the number of manufacturing jobs declines, the jobs that are replacing them tend to pay much lower wages.[16]

Another related point is that "both employed and unemployed people are experiencing a substantial erosion of benefits." Serrin argued that the number of Americans with no health insurance is growing by a million a year, and fewer than half of U.S. workers are now covered by pension plans—a significant decline from the 1970s. It is also important to note that in the new labor market only 60 percent of U.S. workers are employed full-time, year-round. Those preparing to enter the workforce need to know which jobs are full-time jobs with full benefits and which are seasonal or tend toward part-time rather than full-time employment.[17]

In examining income and benefits, students in vocational programs could also study employment and income differentials among different population groups. To examine why full-time working women only earn 72 percent of the income of men, for example, would raise opportunity for understanding gender discrimination in the workplace.[18] Similarly, study of the employment patterns of different population groups would show that African Americans are unemployed over the decades at a rate consistently double that of the White population despite having closed the education gaps dramatically. Thus, the effects of race on employment could be examined. Such inequities will be further addressed in Chapter 12.

Vocational Education as a Teaching Method[19]

When Dewey wrote in 1916 that "the only training *for* occupations is training *through* occupations," he was advocating an educational approach that has never been well understood.[20] Like many vocational training programs today, the vocational education Dewey advocated was activity-oriented and project-centered rather than "book-centered." Although his approach was based on activities and projects related to actual occupations, its primary objective was not preparation for a particular occupation or even a specific range of occupations but rather "intellectual and moral growth."[21] Dewey argued that vocational education programs were not primarily aimed at such growth and that students were instead being prepared for specific occupational futures that closed off other alternatives. As Dewey put it:

To predetermine some future occupation for which education is to be a strict preparation is to injure the possibilities of present development and thereby to reduce the adequacy of preparation for a future right employment.

When educators conceive vocational guidance as something which leads up to a definitive, irretrievable, and complete choice, both education and the chosen vocation are likely to be rigid, hampering further growth. . . . If even adults have to be on the look-out to see that their calling does not shut down on them and fossilize them, educators must certainly be careful that the vocational preparation of youth is such as to engage them in a continuous reorganization of aims and methods.[22]

It appears clear that the changing nature of the workplace in the 1990s and beyond makes it very risky to train students for specific jobs. Most vocational educators recognize this fact. More difficult to articulate is an education that uses vocational activities as a means to educate students in the kind of intellectual skills and capacities that will give them maximum flexibility. If students are educated through vocations rather than for them, they may choose to attend either two-year or four-year colleges, enter the military, pursue job-specific training, or enter the working world. Allen Weisberg's words are worth recalling: "We know that general literacy skills are more likely than any other factor to yield success in the labor market."[23]

The value of using vocations as a means to teach general literacy skills lies primarily in the motivational value of vocational activities and projects. Hands-on problem solving can be a powerful motivator to students alienated from conventional academic teaching methods. This is partly why in *Democracy and Education* Dewey saw such pedagogical potential in school shops and laboratories.[24] Many teachers in "academic" classrooms have much to learn about motivating students through activity-centered teaching, an area where vocational educators have the opportunity to provide genuine leadership. Further, vocational educators who find ways to make intellectual development come alive through concrete projects and activities may well attract a broader student clientele than they currently attract. So conceived, vocational education courses would be dramatically different from those now seen in comprehensive high schools. Their aims would not be, as they now are, very different from the aims of the academic courses. Consequently, groups of students would not be tracked into separate vocational futures, yet different teaching approaches would all seek the same academic ends.

The authors of this volume first emphasized Dewey's notion of "education *through* vocations" in 1988 and then again in 1993, when the first edition of this textbook was published. It was therefore with considerable interest that we noted the publication in 1995 of W. Norton Grubb's two-volume edited collection of essays, *Education through Occupations in American High Schools.* Grubb, a longtime respected critic of traditional approaches to vocational education, relies heavily on Dewey's theoretical perspective as the foundation for the two volumes. The books were written in an effort to explore the theoretical and practical potential of the notion of curriculum integration as it is described in only general terms in the Perkins Amendments of 1990.

In the concluding essay of the two volumes, "Achieving the Promise of Curriculum Integration," Grubb writes, "Integrating academic and vocational education is a reform rich with possibilities precisely because there are so many purposes it can serve." These purposes include the following innovations:

1. Programs of greater intellectual sophistication for students who for various reasons have been labeled academically incompetent and presumed "manually minded" and then segregated from the high-status academic programs.

2. A new conception of vocational education that prepares students for employment after high school, postsecondary education, or the combination of postsecondary education and employment that has become increasingly common.

3. Getting students to think about their occupational futures, the curricular choices they make in high school, and the relationship between school-based learning and future work life.

4. The "greatest ambition": to reshape the entire high school, for all students and all teachers . . . by replacing the aimless choice of electives with a more coherent set of academic and elective courses unified by a broadly defined occupation, an industry, or some other intrinsically important theme.

5. A way to reduce the tracking and segregation that permeates the high school by giving students genuine choice among coherent programs of study that respond to their interests.

6. Better motivation of students by engaging them in constructing their own learning and making clear how such learning is related to their own purposes.

7. A way for high schools to establish connections to institutions outside their walls, including postsecondary institutions (community colleges, four-year colleges, technical training programs) and employers.[25]

4-H projects often provide excellent examples of learning *through* vocations, not necessarily *for* vocations.

The Meaning of a Liberal Education[26]

Historical Perspectives

The Deweyan notion of educating through vocations, rather than for them, abandons the fundamental rationale for vocational education as Conant and others developed it: preparation of non-college-bound students for specific occupations. If that rationale is to be abandoned, there is no longer any reason to advocate vocational education in public schools at all. Under Dewey's approach, what is now termed "vocational education" would simply become an alternative approach to educating students for academic, intellectual, and personal growth. In other words, the traditional aims of a *liberal education* would be embraced for all students throughout their public school years, and "vocational education" would be reserved for postsecondary instruction. In fact, our nation is currently witnessing just such a shift of vocational programs from secondary schools to community colleges.

Students rarely have the opportunity to consider what the term *liberal education* means or why anyone would advocate such an education. Most efforts to understand the term focus attention on the educational ideals of classical Athens and on ideals that informed Jefferson's thinking as described in Chapter 2. In *The Politics,* which Jefferson read, Aristotle argues that in the best kind of education, "it is the whole of excellence which ought to be cultivated, and cultivated for its own sake."[27] For Aristotle, such an education equips citizens for "a life of action and war" and other such "necessary or useful acts." Even more important is the development of the qualities that equip citizens "to lead a life of leisure and peace" and "to do good acts." How to accomplish this? For Aristotle, "The exercise of rational principle and thought is the ultimate end of man's nature," and education should be planned "with a view to the exercise of these facilities."[28] Aristotle recognizes that young people will not always choose the studies that most exercise their rational faculties, for their appetites may lead them elsewhere, "but the regulation of their appetites should be intended for the benefit of their minds."[29] For Aristotle, one of the roles of the teacher, and of good government, is to see that the appetites of the young are cultivated toward wisdom and virtue.

John Dewey recommended the use of vocationally oriented activities as a method of teaching traditional academic subject matter. The activity pictured here could be used to teach science and problem-solving skills as well as how to work together.

Aristotle's remarks might seem like a cloud of idealistic words at first, but three features of his educational thought are relevant here:

1. Educating for the "whole of human excellence" means educating for both vocational ends and other ends that are useful "for their own sake" in the development of the good person. This is the primary reason for Aristotle's emphasis on philosophy and music and, more broadly conceived, literature and the arts.

2. Each person's education should emphasize not just "useful" and "good" acts but the qualities of mind and character needed to perform both kinds of acts. Here Aristotle argues for the development of the rational capacities, for in his view, goodness and wisdom are both grounded in reason.

3. If left to their own devices, young people may not choose their studies wisely, and so they need to be guided in the cultivation of their appetites so their highest human capacities will be served.

It is worth noting that Aristotle accused the Greek states, as well as individuals, of choosing unwise forms of education: "The Greek states of our day which are counted as having the best constitutions . . . have fallen

Historical Context

Social Diversity, Differentiated Schooling, and Contemporary School Reform

For the purposes of studying Chapter 11, you might ask of each decade: Which events have the most *direct significance* for the issues of liberal education and vocational education discussed in this chapter?

1960s

1960	Six years after the 1954 *Brown* v. *Board of Education* decision against school segregation, the modern "sit-in" movement begins when four Black students from North Carolina A&T College sit at a "Whites-only" Woolworth's lunch counter and refuse to leave when denied service
1960	President Dwight D. Eisenhower signs the Civil Rights Act of 1960, which acknowledges the federal government's responsibility in matters involving civil rights
1963	More than 200,000 marchers from all over the United States stage the largest protest demonstration in the history of Washington, DC; the "March on Washington" procession moves from the Washington Monument to the Lincoln Memorial; Reverend Dr. Martin Luther King, Jr., delivers his "I Have a Dream" speech
1964	Economic Opportunity Act funds Job Corps and Head Start programs
1964	Civil Rights Act passes Congress, guaranteeing equal voting rights to African Americans
1964	President Johnson elected; calls for "Great Society" programs as part of his "war on poverty"
1966	The Medicare Act, Housing Act, the first Elementary and Secondary Education Act, a new immigration act, and voting-rights legislation are enacted
1968	Large-scale antiwar demonstrations (Columbia and other universities and Democratic Convention)
1968	Rioting in poor urban neighborhoods
1968	American Indian Movement (AIM) launched
1968	Alicia Escalante forms East Los Angeles Welfare Rights Organization, the first Chicano welfare rights group
1968	Bilingual Education Act passed
1968	Richard Nixon is elected president and begins emphasizing his platform of law and order and government responsiveness to the silent majority, dismantling many of the Great Society programs of Kennedy–Johnson era
1969	The Stonewall rebellion in New York City marks the beginning of the gay rights movement

1970s

1972	Title IX Educational Amendment passed outlawing sex discrimination in educational institutions receiving federal financial assistance
1975	Congress passes Education for All Handicapped Children Act (Public Law 94-142)
1979	Moral Majority is founded, forming a new coalition of conservative and Christian fundamentalist voters in resistance to "liberal excesses" of 1960s and early 1970s

1980s

1980	Ronald Reagan is elected president, promising to reverse the "liberal trends in government"
1982	Unemployment exceeds 10 percent for first time since Great Depression of 1930s; federal budget deficit exceeds $100 billion for first time ever

(continued)

Historical Context *(concluded)*

1983	*A Nation at Risk,* a report by the Presidental Commission on Excellence in Education, adovcates "back to basics" education; becomes the first major document in the current reform movement
1984	Education for Economic Security Act (Public Law 98-377) passed, adding new science and math programs at all levels of schooling
1984	Carl D. Perkins Vocational Education Act continues federal aid for vocational education until 1989

1990s

1990	Congress passes $1.3 billion amendments to Carl D. Perkins Vocational and Applied Technology Act
1991	Unemployment rate rises to highest level in a decade
1992	Americans with Disabilities Act, the most sweeping antidiscrimination legislation since the Civil Rights Act of 1964, guarantees equal access for people with disabilities
1992	With unemployment at 7.8 percent, Bill Clinton defeats George Bush and Ross Perot for presidency
1993	United States follows other industrialized nations with Family Leave Act that guarantees workers up to 12 weeks of unpaid leave for medical emergencies
1993	Supreme Court rules unanimously that public schools must permit religious groups to use their buildings after hours if they allow community groups to do so
1995	Economy signals strong recovery, with Dow Jones index topping 4,000 for the first time ever
1996	Census Bureau reports that the gap between the richest 20 percent of Americans and everyone else has reached postwar high
1997	U.S. economy continues to grow, driving unemployment below 5 percent for first time in 24 years; Dow Jones industrial average tops 7,000 in February and 8,000 in July; mergers and acquisitions of major corporations reach all-time high
1997	Supreme Court rules 5–4 that public school teachers can work in parochial schools that need remedial or supplemental classes
1998	President Clinton announces budget surplus of over $70 billion, the first since 1969 and largest ever
1999	Kansas Board of Education votes against testing any Kansas students on science curriculum related to theory and science of evolution (but it would be restored in 2001 by new school board)
1999	Federal Communications Commission loosens restrictions on any one company controlling too much of the cable industry, allowing AT&T to win more than a third of the nation's TV, phone, and high-speed Internet franchises

2000s

2000	Campaigning on a platform emphasizing ethical character, George W. Bush loses popular vote to Vice President Al Gore but wins the presidency by a 5–4 Supreme Court ruling ending the recount of disputed votes in Florida
2001	Energy-trading company Enron becomes the largest firm ever to file for bankruptcy, leading to far-reaching financial and political scandal
2001	Days after taking office, President Bush announces the intent to pass the No Child Left Behind law; enacted in January 2002, the bipartisan law reauthorizes the Elementary and Secondary Education Act of 1965 and seeks to raise account-ability of local school systems for educating all students
2001	The No Child Left Behind Act expands the federal government's role in elementary and secondary education
2001	On September 11, two hijacked planes strike and destroy the World Trade Center, while a third plane destroys a portion of the Pentagon, and a fourth crashes in Pennsylvania; some 3,000 people die in the worst terrorist attack on American soil
2003	U.S. unemployment rises to highest level in 9 years, 6.4 percent; White House projects $450 billion budget deficit for 2003, the largest in U.S. history
2003	Millions of demonstrators around the world take to the streets to protest the planned U.S. invasion of Iraq
2003	President Bush orders the invasion of Iraq
2003	The Pentagon says major combat operations are ended in Iraq after the takeover in April of the last Iraqi stronghold
2004	J. P. Morgan Chase acquires Bank One for $58B and stock, further concentrating wealth
2004	At State of the Union address, President Bush announces a record-strong economy
2005	Skyrocketing oil prices and unresolved issue of privatizing Social Security lead the economic news
2006	Consensus builds toward alarm over impacts of global climate change
2007	Housing market free fall caused by fraudulent subprime lending schemes and rampant indebtedness

Thinking Analytically about the Timeline

Quite a few of these items concern either (1) economic indicators in the United States, or (2) the politics of race, class, and gender. What do each have to do with public schools? In your view, which wave of school reform from the 1980s and 1990s, the first or the second wave, seems to be most evident in the George W. Bush era of No Child Left Behind? Explain.

short of this ideal. . . . There has been a vulgar decline into the cultivation of qualities supposed to be useful and of a more profitable character."[30] Aristotle's complaint is echoed today by critics who hold that the vocational curriculum (or in higher education, professional studies) is given too much attention at the expense of liberal studies.

If Aristotle's ideal is admirable in its concern for the whole of human excellence, it is worth remembering that he did not intend his ideal for the whole of Athenian society. Only Athenian citizens were to be liberally educated, and citizens constituted a minority of that society. Women and the non-Athenian workforce known as metics were excluded from citizenship. What is more, the citizen's opportunity for leisure and the cultivation of artistic sensibilities was made possible by the institution of slavery. Aristotle reflected classical Athenian society in promoting education for all its *citizens,* rich and poor, but classical Athens excluded the majority of its inhabitants from citizenship and failed to provide a liberal education for them. Neither women nor non-Athenians—the latter considered to be of inferior racial stock—were believed to have the rational capacities necessary for citizenship or wisdom.

This historical tendency to reserve liberal education for the social elite was also echoed by the noted Renaissance educator Vergerius:

> We call those studies liberal which are worthy of a free man; those studies by which we attain and practice virtue and wisdom; that education which calls forth, trains, and develops those highest gifts of body and of mind which ennoble men, and which are rightly judged to rank next in dignity to virtue only.[31]

Examined in its Renaissance context, the ideal of liberal education expressed here is again reserved for the few—in this case, males of courtly society. There is some temptation today to reject the vision of liberal education offered by Aristotle and Vergerius as a thoroughly elitist, sexist, and racist ideal. However, some educators read into these classic statements the possibility that *all* people might be educated in the qualities of mind and character that are most appropriate to freedom and virtue. The difficulty is to develop an educational ideal that can be embraced by all races and both genders that is conducive to the development of all of us.

Reconstructing a Liberal Education Ideal   Although it is important to begin any consideration of liberal education with a careful examination of its historical tradition, anyone seeking to carry that tradition forward must inevitably leave parts of the past behind. In "The Study of the Past—Its Uses and Its Dangers," Alfred North Whitehead wrote:

> For each succeeding generation, the problem of Education is new. What at the beginning was enterprise, after the lapse of five and twenty years has become repetition. All the proportions belonging to a complex scheme of influences upon our students have shifted in their effectiveness. In the lecture halls of a university, as indeed in every sphere of life, the best homage which we can pay to our predecessors to whom we owe the greatness of our inheritance is to emulate their courage.[32]

Despite the stubborn resistance to ideological change that is characteristic of modern, liberal, capitalist society, our nation's history is in part a story of the reconstruction of liberal ideals. When Jefferson wrote about equality and inalienable rights, he had no intention of applying these ideals to women, for example, or to African Americans and Native Americans. Yet since Jefferson's time American activists have reconstructed those ideals and used them as leverage to gain civil and political rights for women and people of color.

Likewise, if the ideals of liberal education are worth salvaging, it takes a certain amount of courage to articulate and fight for their value in an educational environment as devoted to vocationalism as ours is today. For non-college-bound students in the secondary schools, "getting a good job" is presented as the primary rationale for staying in school, and for those who plan to go on to college, "getting a good job" is too often the fundamental rationale for a college degree. College faculty groups, educational researchers, and educational foundations are once again busy with the task of reconstructing the liberal education ideal, illustrating again Whitehead's words: "For each succeeding generation, the problem of Education is new."

These contemporary efforts have in common, first, a commitment to recognizing a distinction between learning that is an instrument in an occupation and learning that is intrinsically valuable for the way it shapes a person's understandings, character, and experience. Second, these various efforts recognize the value of both breadth of study (across areas of knowledge) and depth of study (within at least one specialized area). Finally, contemporary educators attend not only to the disciplinary content (usually expressed as required subjects or courses) of liberal education but also to the qualities of mind that are historically associated with the educated person. But what it is to be an educated person remains a disputed and problematic concept.

Analytic Framework

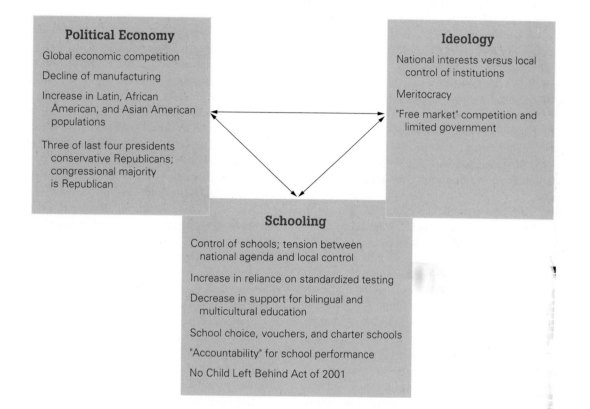

Political Economy

Global economic competition

Decline of manufacturing

Increase in Latin, African American, and Asian American populations

Three of last four presidents conservative Republicans; congressional majority is Republican

Ideology

National interests versus local control of institutions

Meritocracy

"Free market" competition and limited government

Schooling

Control of schools; tension between national agenda and local control

Increase in reliance on standardized testing

Decrease in support for bilingual and multicultural education

School choice, vouchers, and charter schools

"Accountability" for school performance

No Child Left Behind Act of 2001

The business interests and values that we identify with 20th-century schooling have not disappeared. These interests are not mutually exclusive of liberal education, but we have seen the developing tension between these values and the instrumental, commercial values of current arrangements in American capitalism. Central to this has been the mobilization of schooling in its service. This produces a tension between the needs of business for an "efficient" workforce with appropriate investment in particular skills and attitudes consistent with corporate competition. Yet these same skills may not serve well with what Dewey called the "overall growth and development" or the "flourishing" of the student.

Contemporary School Reform

One route to understanding American educational history concerning labor market preparation is to examine the various reform movements that have shaped American schooling. With the publication of *A Nation at Risk* in 1983, policymakers and social critics predicted that the weakness of American education would usher in an era of economic decline. Although unprecedented prosperity by the end of the 1990s dispelled those warnings, the reform movement, fueled by critical teacher shortages and the need for educational responses to changing demographics, presses forward. Four themes characterize the current reform movement: standardized assessment as indicative of educational excellence; tension between concern for excellence and concern for diversity and equity; student and parent choice in schooling; and restructuring in school governance, school processes, and the teaching profession. A critical analysis shows that the earlier economic problems resided in economic and political policies, not in school policies.

Social Changes and School Reform

It is possible to view the evolution of American society through periodic efforts to reform the educational system.

Large-scale social changes inevitably produce corresponding changes in schools. For example, we saw in Chapter 2 how Jefferson and the other colonial leaders committed themselves to the notion of a statewide community school network through which all potential voters could acquire the knowledge and literacy skills needed to function effectively in a democratic society. The ideals of literacy and political freedom were inextricably intertwined in the minds of those colonial leaders. Thus, America's great experiment in political democracy brought an equally radical experiment in mass education. As the right to vote gradually spread throughout the population, so too did access to some form of community- or state-sponsored education.

Vocationalism and custodial schooling are not to be separated from goals set by reformers for the preparation of immigrants and migrants in the burgeoning industrial centers. In Chapters 3 through 4 we saw how wave after wave of late-19th-century immigration and migration not only radically increased America's overall population but radically changed its racial and ethnic composition. Northern cities were increasingly populated with ethnically diverse people looking for work, and the newly emerging factory system had much work to offer. It is no accident that common school improvement, which sought to socialize these diverse masses to American values and language and to a factory-oriented work ethic, arose during this period. The schools were seen as a panacea for handling the massive urbanization and industrial problems of the 19th century.

Just before this period of industrialization came the emancipation of 4 million Black Americans after the Civil War. Once again the schools were expected to solve the attendant problems of social, political, and economic integration into mainstream American life. During this period an educational revolution took place in the South as African Americans swarmed to various kinds of schools in an attempt to achieve the education that was rightfully theirs under a system that was supposed to guarantee political and economic equality.

School reform took another major turn in the first half of the 20th century with the emergence of progressive education. Driven by the belief in progress through scientific management, leaders in American government, industry, and education began supporting larger, more centrally controlled institutions directed by scientifically trained experts. Schools broadened their curricula to include extensive vocational educational programs and infused into their academic programs the practice of classroom democracy and student-centered learning. School reform was driven by the idea that classrooms should reflect the reformers' view of the "real world" of work and citizenship. Once again, schools were seen as primary for socializing a diverse population into a culturally homogeneous one with appropriate vocational and political skills and attitudes.

Whereas citizenship goals dominated the discourse of colonial school reform, socialization and economic goals dominated school reform agendas during the late 19th and early 20th centuries. Then, after World War II, America experienced yet another wave of school reform. This time, however, it was motivated largely by fear of an external military and political threat. The Soviet Union had successfully launched *Sputnik,* the world's first artificial satellite. This scientific achievement, coupled with the Soviets' aggressive program of political expansion, caused American leaders to launch a massive investment in defense-oriented school reform. As we saw in Chapter 8, defense-related subjects such as math, science, and foreign languages became the focus of the new "core" curricula that sprang up around the country. Simultaneously, comprehensive high schools sponsoring new, advanced curricula for students scoring high on standardized achievement tests began appearing. Reform leaders were concerned with the development of elite students capable of shoring up the national defense.

This brief historical account of past school reform efforts is offered as a prelude to the following discussion of the present school reform movement. We will begin with a general examination of reform activity during the past decade and then look at the three stages that have characterized this and other reform movements. We will then conclude, as we began, by looking briefly at the political– economic and ideological context of the current reform effort. Gene Glass notes how the term "reform" has mutated away from its lexical definition "to remake or reshape." Citing Ansary's work, Glass notes the shift in meaning: to call yourself a reformer now is to say you are concerned, well-meaning, insightful, and that your prescription entails *solutions* to a problem you have named.[33]

Schooling as a Response to New Social and Economic Conditions

During the progressive era, urbanization, new immigration, and the emerging corporate-capital industrial system convinced a coalition of business, political, and professional leaders that the classical approach to schooling was inadequate. Partly as a result, progressive reformers introduced compulsory public schooling to instill necessary skills and industrial values in all citizens, a differentiated curriculum for students with different skill levels, vocational education to prepare students for the world of work, and extracurricular activities to further socialize students with values appropriate to the new industrial order.

In strikingly similar fashion, in the 1980s political and business leaders began pointing to changing social and economic conditions that they felt necessitated school reform. The three new economic and social realities most frequently cited were (1) the decline of manufacturing as the economic base of the United States and the concurrent rise of information processing, service industries, and high technology; (2) our declining ability to compete in world markets, with the result that the United States has gone from being a major lending nation to perhaps the world's leading debtor nation; and (3) the apparent decline in the academic skills of American students, whether measured against past American performance or against that of students from other industrialized nations. An often cited demographic factor in this declining academic picture is the rising proportion of Latino and African American students in the nation's schools, with attendant problems of poverty and cultural and language difficulties. Not since the new immigration of the progressive era has cultural pluralism been such a central concern of our nation's schools.

These economic and demographic changes led business and government leaders to the view that our schools should respond to an economy "at risk" by elevating the academic performances of all students at all levels of achievement. These better-educated students would then be able to perform well in an information-processing economy and help the United States become more competitive in the world marketplace. The argument of the policymakers was helped considerably by data showing what appeared to be genuinely dismal academic performance by U.S. students. SAT and ACT scores had been declining steadily since the early 1960s; approximately 700,000 students were dropping out of school each year, and of those who remained in school, fewer than 40 percent of 17-year-olds could analyze moderately complicated reading passages about topics studied in high school; finally, our 13-year-olds ranked behind such nations as Korea, Spain, and Ireland, and several Canadian provinces in mathematics performance[34] (see Exhibits 11.5 and 11.6).

The data for African American and Latino students were even more discouraging, with dropout rates in some Chicago and New York schools ranging from 63 to 68 percent. Further, "disadvantaged urban 17-year-olds" lagged 22 points behind the national average in a 1984 national reading assessment[35] (see Exhibit 11.7). Members of the business community were quick to translate such educational problems

Exhibit 11.5   Trends in SAT College Entrance Examination Scores That Led to Current Reform Movement

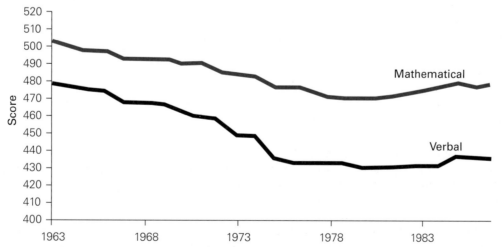

Source: National Center for Education Statistics, U.S. Department of Education, *The Condition of Education—Volume 1* (Washington, DC: U.S. Government Printing Office, 1988).

Exhibit 11.6   Trends in ACT Composite Entrance Examination Records That Led to *A Nation at Risk* Reform Movement

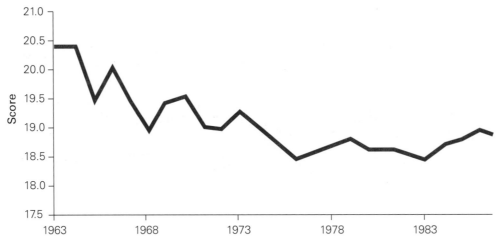

Source: National Center for Education Statistics, U.S. Department of Education, *The Condition of Education—Volume 1* (Washington, DC: U.S. Government Printing Office, 1988).

Exhibit 11.7   Percentage of In-School 17-Year-Olds at or above Various Reading Levels in the Mid-1980s

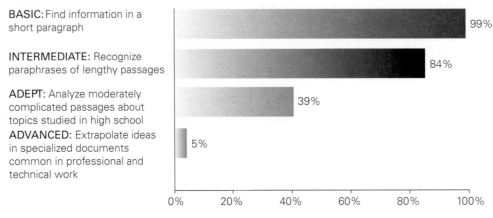

Source: National Assessment of Education progress, *The Reading Report Card* (Princeton, NJ: Educational Testing Service,1986.

into financial costs to the nation. The dropout rate, for example, was estimated to cost the nation some $240 billion annually[36] (see Exhibits 11.8 and 11.9).

On January 8, 2002, President George W. Bush signed into law the No Child Left Behind Act (NCLB) of 2001, which was part of a legislative package that included the reauthorization of the Elementary and Secondary Education Act (ESEA). It represents the most sweeping change of ESEA since its passage in 1965. In the following ways,

NCLB ratchets up the call for higher standards and test-based accountability:

- Improved teacher training and test-based licensure

- Annual tests in elementary reading and mathematics

- The chance for children in failing schools to transfer out

These are among the central features that link NCLB to the reforms of the 1980s and 1990s.

Exhibit 11.8 **Mid-1980s High School Completion Rates among 18- and 19-Year-Olds by Race and Hispanic Origin**

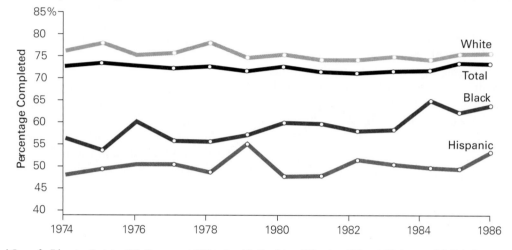

Source: National Center for Education Statistics, U.S. Department of Education, *The Condition of Education—Volume 1* (Washington, DC: U.S. Government Printing Office, 1988).

Exhibit 11.9 **Dropout Rates among Youth Ages 16 to 24 by Race and Hispanic Origin, October 1972–2005**

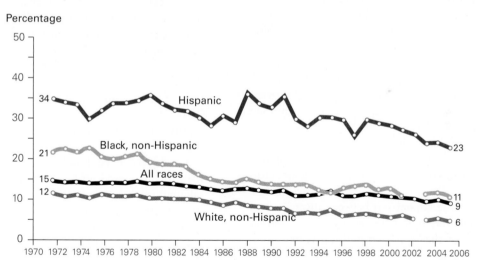

Note: This indicator uses the status dropout rate which measures the percentage of young adults aged 16 to 24 who were not enrolled in a high school program and had not received a high school diploma or obtained an equivalency certificate. Due to changes in the race categories, estimates from 2003 are not strictly comparable to estimates from 2002 and before. Prior to 2001, the black race catergory included Hispanics.

Source: Reproduced from: Sources: Data for 1972–2001: U.S. Department of Education, National Center for Education Statistics, The Condition of Education 2003. NCES 2003-067. Washington, DC: 2003. Figure on p.42. Data for 2002: Child Trends' calculations of U.S. Census Burreau, *School Enrollment–Social and Economic Characteristics.of Students: October 2002:* Detailed Tables: Table 1. Data for 2003: Child Trends' calculations of U.S. Census Bureau, *School Enrollment–Social and Economic Characteristics of Students: October 2003: Detailed Tables:* Table1. http://www.census.gov/population/www/socdemo/school/cps2003.html. Data for 2004: Child Trends' calculations of U.S. Census Bureau, *School Enrollment–Social and Economic Characteristics of Students: October 2004: Detailed Tables:* Table 1. http://www.census.gov/population/www/socdemo/school/cps2004.html. Data for 2005: Child Trends' calculations of U.S. Census Bureau, *School Enrollment–Social and Econnomic Characteristics.of Students: October 2005: Detailed Tables:* Table 1. http://www.census.gov/population/www/socdemo/school/cps2005.html.

The New Consensus on Excellence in Education

In order for there to be widespread agreement that these were indeed the economic and social conditions to which schools should respond and agreement on *how* the schools should respond, consensus had to be consciously built among government, business, and educational leaders at the state and national levels. Mark G. Yudof wrote early in the reform movement:

> Perhaps the most noteworthy aspect of the new era in educational policy, the one that partially explains the popular appeal of the many recent reports on the status of education, is the attempt to generate, locate and reinforce a consensus on U.S. public schooling. *A Nation at Risk* helped to serve that consensus-building role, proclaiming that "the Federal Government has *the primary responsibility* to identify the national interest in education."[37]

The specific issue of national interest will be discussed later in the chapter. What is notable here is the early 1980s perception among policymakers that one of the ills affecting American education was precisely the *lack* of consensus about what schools should achieve and why. In 1986, Secretary of Education William J. Bennett urged just such a consensus when he argued for the "three Cs: character, content and choice." In calling for schools to teach a common culture of "common values, common knowledge, and a common language," Bennett recalled Horace Mann's efforts to build universal values and a uniform curriculum into the common-school movement in Massachusetts.[38]

This effort to establish common cultural values, knowledge, and language has met with great resistance from those who hold what they regard as democratic commitments to diversity of values, knowledge, and language. This close connection between diversity and democracy, however, is not viewed by the consensus builders as part of the "common political vision" they feel to be the national interest.[39] In their consensus-building campaign, several major themes have emerged, and all of these themes, with some shifts in emphasis, have been sustained within the second wave of reform efforts. The four major themes running through nearly two decades of school reform (as well as from early reports) may be identified as follows:

1. **An academic-achievement definition of "educational excellence."** *A Nation at Risk* sought to define excellence primarily in terms of measurable results in standardized achievement tests targeted at traditional academic curricula. Bennett's concern for a common content is reflected in the Reagan and Bush administration reports, each of which argues for a common core of five academic subjects similar to Horace Mann's "five Rs." The "five new basics" for secondary school graduation articulated in *A Nation at Risk* are English, mathematics, science, social studies, and computer science. The Clinton administration's *America 2000* replaced these five with a slightly different list: English, mathematics, science, history, and geography. Both reports called for greater rigor in academic standards, assignments, homework, and time on task for all students, not just those considered college bound. NCLB would enjoin a school's failure in reading and math test results by listing that school as failing to make "adequate yearly progress." This can be used then as a basis for students to transfer and for the school to be denied funding if school improvement plans (SIP) don't produce results.

   The call for higher standards was accompanied by a call for greater "accountability." School report cards, state report cards, and national achievement testing, for example, are all ideas that have been proposed or implemented since *A Nation at Risk*. They are seen as measurable ways to hold schools and districts accountable for their "products," the students. In addition, the early reports called for lengthening the school day and the school year as a means to achieve the new vision of excellence. Finally, a number of reports identified the need for better trained and more talented teachers as a necessary component of this new excellence. The increased use of standardized tests is one of the clearest characteristics separating recent reform from those reformers earlier in the 20th century who focused on curriculum, pedagogy, and course taking. Assessment replaces curriculum as the standard of judgment.

2. **A tension between concerns for "excellence" and concerns for diversity and equity.** Distinctly at odds with some aspects of the purported new consensus is the view that democratic schooling will suffer if the various forms of diversity—racial, ethnic, gender, and disabling conditions—are not adequately understood and respected in the

teaching–learning processes of schools. To focus on a narrow core of common values and content stemming almost entirely from a male-dominated European tradition may well exclude or disadvantage children with backgrounds that are not White, male, and middle-class; on the whole, the schools did not serve those children well in the 20th century. Further, it is argued, the standardized tests, which have historically been used as accountability measures, will further disadvantage students from cultures that are unaccustomed to the language and codes of such tests.

3. **Choice in schooling.** Bennett's reference to "school choice" reflects a theme that has run steadily through the school reform movement since the beginning—weakly at first but strongly and explicitly advocated in *America 2000*. According to this concept, parents and students should be allowed to select any school of their choice, whether or not it is in their neighborhood, on the basis of its perceived quality and its compatibility with their personal educational goals. Some schools might be very traditional, and others very innovative, but parents and students should be able to "vote with their feet," in this view. The schools would be supported by a "voucher" system in which each family would receive a voucher for the tuition of each child and the school that the child attended would be paid by the state on the basis of the number of vouchers it received. The system would thus be designed so that the better schools would flourish because of high state revenues derived from high attendance, and poor schools would have to improve or perish. The philosophy here is grounded in the notion of a laissez-faire, free market economy. More will be said on this as we examine the ideology of reform. School choice is also a centerpiece of NCLB.

4. **Restructuring school governance, school processes, and the teaching profession.** *A Nation at Risk* and other reports recommended an increased role for citizens, especially for the business community, in school governance and leadership. Despite the tension between greater teacher autonomy and greater community and business input into school decision making, the thrust toward restructuring the teaching profession and school governance grew in importance throughout the 1980s and became for some analysts synonymous with the second wave of school reform.[40] For some, the restructuring movement meant primarily the movement to decentralize school governance, while for others, as we shall see, restructuring referred to new approaches to school curriculum. Although restructuring in one form or another has been central to every major school reform movement in U.S. history, the particular character of the current restructuring movement merits its own discussion.[41]

Restructuring

Historian David Tyack observes that the concept of restructuring "has become a magic incantation" that "is now gaining the popularity of *excellence* in the early 1980s or *equality* in the 1960s."[42] Tyack notes, however, that school "restructuring" has come to mean very different things to different people. In general he agrees with Passow, Kirst, and others that restructuring is partly a response to the failures of the early "excellence" movement of the 1980s to produce the reforms envisioned in *A Nation at Risk*. In reading Tyack's characterization of what restructuring has come to mean in the second wave of reform, we can see distinct elements of the first wave still contained within it:

> People regard restructuring as a synonym for the market mechanism of choice, or teacher professionalization and empowerment, or decentralization and school site management or involving parents more in their children's education, or national standards in curriculum with tests to match, or deregulation, or new forms of accountability, or basic changes in curriculum and instruction, or some or all of these in combination. Slogans suitable for bumper stickers proclaim the new dogmas: Choice is the answer; small is beautiful; blame the bureaucrats.[43]

Certainly one major stream of the restructuring effort has to do with the processes of decision making in schools and school districts. Perhaps the most ambitious example of this kind of restructuring is found in Chicago, which in 1989 elected 542 local school councils, or local boards of education, one at each of Chicago's public schools. Each council consists of six parents, two teachers, two community representatives, and the principal. Thus, nearly 6,000 citizens now exercise genuine authority in Chicago schools, including the power to hire principals, draft local school improvement plans, and control the school budget to accomplish their aims.[44]

Contemporary School Reform: A Critical View

At this point it is useful to return to our analytical framework and use the notions of political economy and ideology to think critically about the contemporary school reform movement.

The Political–Economic Origins of the Contemporary School Reform Movement

Basing his analysis on work by economists critical of the policies of corporate capitalism and an education reform report, *Action for Excellence,* that was published within two months of *A Nation at Risk,* educator Frank Margonis offers an alternative perspective on the political economy of school reform.[45] *Action for Excellence* was published in 1983 by the Education Commission of the States Task Force on Education for Economic Growth. It was supported by liberal as well as conservative governors and other leaders at the state level because it suggested a national economic and educational strategy for helping the economies of the states, which were enduring the worst recession since the Depression of the 1930s. Rather than accepting the standard argument that American industry was failing in world markets because American schools were doing their jobs poorly, Margonis argues that the poor performance of the American economy was due to economic factors apart from the schools. The growing inability of the United States to dominate world markets through military might since the Vietnam War, the rise of union participation at home, and federal regulation of corporate activity had led many businesses to reinvest in nonunion states and in foreign countries. Margonis cites one study estimating that 38 million jobs were lost to these processes in the 1970s, losses that severely damaged the economies of many states. Holding these events responsible for the economic plight of the United States is very different from holding schools responsible, and so Margonis's analysis is important to consider.

One notable exception to the states that were suffering economically in the early 1980s was Massachusetts, which had been very successful in attracting high-technology firms into and around the highly educated Boston area. This highly publicized feat eventually provided much of the political leverage for catapulting Governor Michael Dukakis into the Democratic party's presidential nomination for the 1998 election, but before that it had sent a message to other states about what was needed for economic recovery: high-tech industry, which requires a strong educational environment.

Deteriorating economic conditions in the United States in the 1980s combined with an increasingly global economy that requires a competitive labor force were behind the current reform movement in education.

Other states naturally sought to duplicate Massachusetts's success in attracting high-tech firms. However, lacking equivalent educational resources, they turned to the federal government for support in upgrading their educational facilities. The resulting coalition between corporate America, the states, and the federal government produced what has come to be known as the "excellence" movement in education. As was previously noted, the goal was to upgrade the academic skills of all students, both those who were gifted and those who were "at risk," for the workplace of the future.

This brief scenario explains how in the early 1980s deteriorating economic conditions together with an increasingly international economy led to a new era of educational reform. The movement was economically motivated. The cause of our economic problem was seen largely as a failure of our educational system to provide an internationally competitive labor force, and the way to correct this failure was to form a new educational coalition between state and federal governments and corporate America. At this point it is worth taking a look at each of these underlying assumptions.

The first assumption, that the motivating force behind the current reform movement lay in a deteriorating economy, is proclaimed in the language of the early reform documents. It is also evident in the organizations that sponsored these educational reform documents: the Business Higher Education Forum, the Economic Commission of the States, the Carnegie Forum on Education and the Economy, and so on.

The second proposition, that the failure of the educational system is the principal cause of the depressed economy, deserves the sort of detailed analysis that Margonis, among others, has offered. Rather than accepting the standard argument that American schools were doing their jobs poorly, Margonis argues that this poor performance of the American economy was due to economic factors apart from the schools, as noted above. Citing economists Carnoy, Shearer, and Rumberger, Margonis sums up his analysis in the following paragraph:

> By systematically directing investment away from factories located in the U.S. major corporations struck back at labor and citizen groups which had infringed upon business control of production [through minimum wage laws, fair labor standards, occupational health and safety provisions, equal employment opportunity, extended unemployment benefits, and improvements in worker compensation]. The devastation of regional economies resulting from such disinvestment set the conditions for many businesses to gain greater public subsidization for corporate research,

favorable tax laws, a weakening of anti-trust legislation and environmental regulation, and a new educational policy. More than anything else, the educational reforms of 1983 testify to the indirect power capital can exercise over political processes by constantly shopping for desirable plant locations.[46]

This loyalty to the free market rather than to the public good, argues Margonis, should warn us of the dangers of the states' strategy of trying to attract business through educational upgrades:

> While high-technology industries are likely to locate research facilities near educational centers, nationalistic rhetoric should not lead us to expect loyalty from them. Such firms, because of their high labor intensity, are particularly mobile and have played states off against one another, abandoned plants, and located much of their production in low-cost labor markets. An educational program designed to serve these industries does not amount to a unified national mobilization; rather, it is a part of a corporatist movement in which greater public resources are expected, in [Senator Paul] Tsongas's words, to "reflect the priorities of the private sector."[47]

If Margonis is right that corporate policy rather than educational failure is the principal cause of our economic woes, what can be said regarding the third proposition underlying current reform efforts? That proposition, you might recall, maintained that a new educational coalition between state and local governments and corporate America was the way to upgrade the nation's educational system and thereby upgrade its labor force. According to Margonis, such a coalition is suspect, since the analysis of the origin of the nation's economic problems is mistaken: It is not education that lies at the heart of the problem but economic policy itself, and economic policy is not being addressed in the school reform movement.

This view is echoed by educational historian Christine Shea, who agrees with Margonis that the educational strategy of the reform movement was designed to benefit business first and the citizenry second. She argues that a basic claim of the reform consensus builders—that a new education for all students is needed for the labor demands of high technology—simply misrepresents the reality of the high-technology industry. Shea, like Margonis, cites *Action for Excellence,* noting that the education most emphasized in this document is the development of "learning to learn" skills for the new technological labor market. "Most factory and service industry jobs in America today," says the report, "fall into this category." *Action for Excellence* then goes on to describe the minimal communication and computation skills it designates as "learning to learn" skills. This leads Shea to conclude that the liberal reform agenda

> has been designed for an increasingly small sector of American youth. For the vast majority of noncollege-bound/minimal-competency students, the end of formal schooling is expected to occur as soon as they demonstrate acquisition of "learning to learn" minimal-competency skills. As such, the school reform proposals are intended to do little more than to prepare minority children for a series of dead-end, low-paying jobs in the secondary labor market. . . . [*Action for Excellence*] admits that highly skilled labor will not likely be in great demand in America's high tech future, but it "sugar coats" this bitter reality in the soothing rhetoric of "advancing technology, upward mobility, and increasing opportunity."[48]

Shea goes on to cite data similar to those presented earlier showing that most of the jobs in the new service economy are not going to require high-technology knowledge. Yet this reality is obscured by the corporate liberal ideology behind the reform proposals.

Understanding the political economy of the origins of the contemporary school reform movement thus requires recognition of several factors. First, the sources of the nation's economic problems resided primarily in economic and political policies, not in schooling policies. Even though the educational achievement of the nation's youth in the early 1980s was deficient and the economy was in serious trouble, the former did not cause the latter; therefore, improving educational achievement is not likely to cure the nation's economic woes. In fact, the nation's economy improved tremendously after the 1980s, leading to President Clinton's reelection, *without* a corresponding improvement in student learning. Correspondingly, despite the establishment of new standards of course taking in the 1980s with the *Nation at Risk,* the minority achievement gap, dropout rates, and college attainment of the student cohort first were affected by these changes have not changed and in some cases are worse.

Second, it appears clear that the emerging technological and service workplace does not require a great many highly educated people, because *most* new jobs do not require advanced understanding of math, science, and technology. Insofar as the state governments are increasing requirements in those areas, and insofar as business is intervening to help fund advanced learning, it appears that the "high-tech" rationale for school improvement

can justify concentration of resources only in a relatively small minority of skilled students. It would take a rationale different from the economic argument—for example, a rationale emphasizing the right of each citizen in a democratic society to be educated to participate fully in the political processes of that society—to justify school reform that would benefit all citizens regardless of skill level, social class background, or ethnicity. Third, if the contemporary school reform movement reflects "the priorities of the private sector," it can be expected to remain limited in its impact on the educational lives of most students in most schools. In a later section, we will examine that thought more thoroughly.

Thinking Critically about the Issues   #3

Do you believe the school reformers of the 1980s and 1990s adequately understood the basic social and economic problems that undergird problems in student learning? Explain.

School Reform Today: New and Continuing Initiatives

We have seen how different themes were emphasized at different points in the course of the last 25 years of school reform and that these different points of emphasis—first on centralizing standard setting, then on "restructuring" and having site-based decision making, for example—led to different efforts at change. Some areas of emphasis in the late 1990s were not emphasized at all in the early 1980s (computer technology, for example), and others can be traced right back to the beginning—not just the beginning of this reform era but the beginning of common schools. Teacher professionalization would be a prime example. These are two of five areas of prominent school reform activity as we move further into the 21st century. The others are school choice, parent involvement in schools, and school-to-work reforms.

Computer Technology   Desktop computers did not become widely available until the late 1980s, and now, two decades later, schools are rarely without them. Computers are part of a wider information revolution in society rather than simply a component of school reform. We have already noted, in Chapter 9, the rapid growth of the World Wide Web in educational settings and homes and recent research suggesting that the Web can, if used appropriately, enhance teaching and learning. We have also raised cautions about whether the Web might, as educational innovations and reforms often do, serve economically privileged youth and children better than lower-income youth who have less access to the equipment and to well-prepared teachers.

The president of the United States proclaimed in his 1996 State of the Union Address that "every classroom in America must be connected to the information highway." This is an enormously expensive goal that must necessarily compete with other approaches to improving student learning. Larry Cuban argues that the "techno-reformers" are part of a significant problem in introducing computer technology to schools in that the techno-reformers do not understand the social organization of classrooms and schools, tend to make inflated claims for what computers can accomplish, help cause administrators to invest massive sums in a technology that is not being used productively, and end up blaming the teachers for the waste.[49]

Given the pace of technological change, it is very difficult to predict the eventual impact of the Web on schools and school reform. It might serve to bring teachers and administrators into more immediate contact, for example, with "best practices" and successful reforms in schools and districts. The federally funded North Central Regional Educational Laboratory in Oak Brook, Illinois, for example, has an Internet server, Pathways to School Improvement, that any teacher in the nation can use to investigate a wide range of innovations in areas such as curriculum, school organization, and student assessment. The address is www.ncrel.org/sdrs/. Communication of the best ideas in schooling is more readily available than ever before, though the distance from an idea to its successful implementation still requires complex professional and personal qualities from those who would want to accomplish change.

School Choice, Vouchers, and Charters

The "choice movement" in public schooling has its roots in the alternative school or "free school" movement of the 1970s. Early in the 1980s, school reformers such as Hofstra University's Mary Anne Raywid saw that some parents wished to send their children to nearby public schools rather than the ones to which their children were assigned by the district. Research found that parents and children who were able to choose which public school to attend tended to have greater investment in the school and had higher morale as a result. As Berliner and Biddle write:

Thus, if larger school districts really want to promote higher morale and greater involvement among parents, one simple thing they might consider is to allow parents to choose among schools in the district. Some urban districts fear that this would cause chaos, unwanted competition among local schools, and increased ethnic or racial segregation, but the evidence so far available does not support such fears.[50]

So far, so good. But soon the call for "public schools of choice" underwent what seemed to be a logical transformation: a movement to provide every school-age child or youth with a tax voucher—a kind of coupon in the amount the district would ordinarily spend on that child's education—to be "spent" at whatever school the family wanted, public or private. The argument was (and is) that in a free market system, private schools should have as much right as public schools to be supported by the government, and the best schools would attract the most students, thereby thriving and multiplying, while inadequate schools would simply die or have to improve due to lack of "customers." School-choice advocate Raywid objected strongly:

> In the cities, vouchers would quickly solidify a two-tiered educational system consisting of nonpublic schools and pauper schools. That development would impoverish us all, because it would represent an abandonment of efforts to improve education for disadvantaged youngsters, who are already a majority in most U.S. cities.[51]

By examining the inequitable and inefficient voucher system currently used in Australia and then comparing it with the much more successful and equitable public school system in France, Berliner and Biddle concur that Raywid's concerns are well founded.[52]

Not only would vouchers for private schools be likely to serve those with money at the expense of the poor, another problem quickly becomes evident: Using tax money to fund religious education or religious schools violates the First Amendment separation of church and state. But some school reformers are happy to use the choice movement to move to a voucher movement, with something called "charter schools" as a transition between the two. National Education Association president Bob Chase quotes one such school reformer:

> "What is called for is an incremental strategy that helps acclimatize the public to school choice, readying them for phase two, vouchers," said voucher activist Roxane Premont, in a speech at the Christian Coalition's annual conference in September [1996]. "Christians can enjoy the control they exercise in charter schools even as they push for vouchers."[53]

The future looks mixed for such a strategy. In 1997 a court decision declared the Cleveland, Ohio, voucher system unconstitutional after nearly a year of operation. The issue was church–state separation, because most of the 1,900 students using the voucher plan were doing so for religious institutions. The state had been providing for low-income students to attend religious schools at state expense.[54]

But what is this "charter school" to which Premont refers? A charter school is one for which the school district grants a group of people, which could include parents, community members, and teachers, a charter, or authorization, to open a school that reflects their shared educational philosophy. The district then funds that school like any public school. NEA president Chase concedes that charter schools have become laboratories for innovation, helping strengthen public schools, but he is concerned that they have also attracted privatization abuses. "In states such as Massachusetts, Michigan, and Arizona, these groups have succeeded in passing laws that grant charter status not just to legitimate public schools, but also existing private schools, to home-schoolers, and even to individuals and for-profit companies with no track record in education."[55] Chase is seeking to protect what he perceives as the public, democratic mission of the tax-supported school system, which he believes is threatened when tax dollars are used to support private beliefs, interests, and even profits.

Despite such objections, new plans for "privatizing" schooling continue to be developed and acted on. One of the most recent is the idea of "contract schools," which would extend the charter school approach to all public schools by having each one set up a contract with the local school board for its funding, its mission, and its accountability. The board would then have the right to terminate weak schools and fund promising ones— much like the practice of firing employees who don't perform well and giving raises to those who do.[56] But should this principle be applied to schooling in a democratic society? The state of Florida believes the answer is yes, and it recently legalized school vouchers statewide. Similarly, President George W. Bush has expressed strong support for school vouchers.

Critics of vouchers and their variants say that they are incapable of having any major reform impact on the massive public school system and that at best they will amount to "tinkering on the fringe of reform," as Gerald Tirozzi says.[57] He argues that with 46 million public school students, the private school capacity of 6 million students will never expand sufficiently to address the needs of the great majority. Political scientist John Witte agrees. He has written that the choice movement is like a pack of terriers nipping at the heels of the public school system. The terriers will not go away, but they won't have the power to change the system in fundamental ways.[58]

Despite a generation of school reform since *A Nation at Risk,* the promise of the fair distribution of life and work opprtunities and the chance for a postsecondary education seems elusive. One example is illustrative and exemplary. Melissa Roderick of the University of Chicago has found that the college attendance and retention rates among graduates of Chicago public schools (CPS) is still seriously lacking. She finds that test scores and advisement are key obstacles. CPS is a predominantly Black and Hispanic school landscape, reflecting the White middle-class exodus to suburbia. In 2005 72 percent of 12th graders stated they hoped to complete a bachelor's degree or higher. Forty-one percent actually enrolled, and among Black males, just 10 percent actually graduated.[59]

Far greater rates of college attendance would be an expectation, a greater equity among SES, ethnic, and racial groups. This will require deeper commitments to teacher academic preparation, fair distribution of all the conditions required for postsecondary success beyond hollow standards, teacher proof scripts, and the politicized rhetoric of schooling as merely a function of a socialized response to politicized economic "crises."

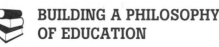

BUILDING A PHILOSOPHY OF EDUCATION

This chapter has examined the contemporary legacy of two conflicting educational traditions: (1) vocational or "general" education, with its roots in the era of progressive education, and (2) liberal education, with its roots in classical Athens.

Such a discussion raises questions about the fundamental aims of education for all citizens of a democratic society. As you articulate and justify your educational goals and methods, the following questions become important: Can a democracy afford to socialize major parts of its population to accept less education and intellectual development than the society is capable of offering? Or should Dewey's "all around growth for every member of society" (see Chapter 4) be the fundamental aim for all citizens? Can the limited intellectual demands of low-skill occupations define our educational aims for the millions of people who will one day fill those occupations? Or should they be educated to the limits of their capacity, partly because each parent should (and usually does) want the greatest possible intellectual, emotional, and moral development of his or her children? And if human development for its own sake is our educational ideal, what kind of school experiences will help bring about such development?

It should be instructive that the children of the upper and upper-middle classes are not typically counseled into vocational education curricula, for such curricula are not considered by members of those classes to be adequate for their children, even if their children are not particularly strong academically. If this is so, the belief that vocational education as it now exists is adequate for the children of the poor and working classes should be questioned and resisted. If, on the other hand, we find that schools are largely unsuccessful in teaching such students using approaches found to be successful for upper- and middle-class children, it may well be that our approaches to teaching should be expanded to fit the learning styles and dispositions of all students. In your philosophy of education statement, do you see greater evidence that your position is guided more by a liberal educational ideal, or by a vocational ideal?

Citizens of the United States, perhaps more than any other people, seem to have a deep-seated, even exaggerated faith in the ability of their schools to solve major social problems. Certainly this is true of those businesspeople, professionals, and other reform leaders who have expressed *this* faith throughout the nation's history. Yet the particular nature of school reform in any historical period varies with the perceptions of the problems to be solved, at least among those people who have the power to implement reform. Regardless of what their own philosophies of education might be, teachers typically work in a system not of their making, implementing educational reforms they rarely have a hand in shaping. Society's priorities

for schooling change as social conditions change. A teacher's head can be turned this way and that in an effort to keep up with new demands and new expectations. Successful teachers have their own philosophical compasses to keep their heads on straight.

We have seen, for example, how early American political leaders were primarily concerned with freedom from despotic, centralized political control and how this perception framed their vision of schools dedicated to democratic values and central literacy. Then, during the late 19th century, school reform was driven by the realization of the socialization problems that accompanied the massive immigration of ethnically diverse Europeans and the emancipation of 4 million African Americans. Again, during the cold war era, perceptions of an external military threat from communist Russia sparked school reforms intended to strengthen the national defense by identifying America's most academically able students and developing their intellectual abilities. Finally, the current reform movement, although multidimensional, received its start in the 1980s amidst a growing sense of insecurity in the face of international economic competition. It has transformed into something else in the 21st century, however: an effort to transform the role of government to import the logic of the "competitive marketplace" from business into education, in the hope that a deregulated competition among education providers, private and public, will stimulate innovation and excellence that a "government monopoly on education" presumably stifles.

The above sketch of major school reform movements deals only with what classical liberal and then modern liberal reformers (including those who are popularly called conservatives because of their commitment to principles of corporate liberalism) perceived to be the dominant problem of each historical period. Also, embedded in most reform movements are perceptions of other, lesser problems. For example, the current reform movement, although primarily focused on economic rehabilitation, also contains a host of issues related to the education of an increasingly multicultural population and the empowerment of teachers and parents. Likewise, such national problems as sexually transmitted diseases, drug abuse, childhood obesity, character education, and coping with terrorism seem to find their way into the reform agenda.

The discussion of the relationship between perceived social problems and school reform leads us back to such perennial education questions as these:

- Have we perceived our social problem(s) correctly?

- *Who* should have a voice in deciding what the problems are and how schools should go about solving them?

- Does our school reform agenda address too many social problems and too few distinctly educational problems?

- How amenable are these social problems to an educational solution?

- And finally, in the face of one reform movement after another, what is a teacher to do? Again, it seems important to learn from the most successful teachers, whose philosophies of education enable them to find in each reform era something they can learn that will help their students learn.

Primary Source Reading

Pathways to Prosperity: Meeting the Challenge of Preparing Young Americans for the 21st Century

Pathways to Prosperity Project, Harvard Graduate School of Education

February 2011

THE CHALLENGE

The Persistence of "The Forgotten Half"

One of the most fundamental obligations of any society is to prepare its adolescents and young adults to lead productive and prosperous lives as adults. This means preparing all young people with a solid enough foundation of literacy, numeracy, and thinking skills for responsible citizenship, career development, and lifelong learning. For over a century, the United States led the world in equipping its young people with the education they would need to succeed. By the middle of the 19th century, as Claudia Goldin and Lawrence Katz write in their book, *The Race between Education and Technology*, "the U.S. already had the most educated youth in the world." At the turn of the 20th century, just as Europe was catching up, the rapid spread of the "high school movement" helped the U.S. vault ahead again.

By 1940, the typical 18-year-old had a high school diploma, up from just 9 percent who had achieved this milestone in 1910. After World War II, the GI Bill helped usher in a huge expansion in higher education. As a result, members of the U.S. Baby Boom generation far surpassed their counterparts in other countries in educational attainment.

This surge in educational attainment laid the foundation for the staggering increase in American wealth and power that came to be known as the American Century. By 2000, per capita income, adjusted for inflation, was five to six times as large as it had been in 1900.

Yet as we end the first decade of the 21st century, there are profoundly troubling signs that the U.S. is now failing to meet its obligation to prepare millions of young adults. In an era in which education has never been more important to economic success, the U.S. has fallen behind many other nations in educational attainment and achievement. Within the U.S. economy, there is also growing evidence of a "skills gap" in which many young adults lack the skills and work ethic needed for many jobs that pay a middle-class wage. Simultaneously, there has been a dramatic decline in the ability of adolescents and young adults to find work. Indeed, the percentage of teens and young adults who have jobs is now at the lowest level since World War II.

These problems have been building for years. In 1988, the William T. Grant Foundation published a report that called the then 20 million non-college-bound youth "the forgotten half," and warned: "they are in danger of being caught in a massive bind that can deny them full participation in our society." A decade later, the American Youth Policy Forum issued *The Forgotten Half*

Revisited, and concluded that these ill-equipped young adults "have lost considerable ground versus their counterparts only a decade earlier." Since then, there have been many other reports—such as the National Academies' study, *Rising above the Gathering Storm*—that have sounded similar alarms. Yet for all the attention, we have failed to take effective action. Meanwhile, the challenge has become increasingly urgent.

A More Demanding Labor Market

The "forgotten half" challenge has deepened with the growing importance of postsecondary education to success in the labor market. In 1973, nearly a third of the nation's 91 million workers were high school dropouts, while another 40 percent had not progressed beyond a high school degree. Thus, people with a high school education or less made up 72 percent of the nation's workforce. In an economy in which manufacturing was still dominant, it was possible for those with less education but a strong work ethic to earn a middle-class wage, as 60 percent of high school graduates did. In effect, a high school diploma was a passport to the American Dream for millions of Americans.

By 2007, this picture had changed beyond recognition. While the workforce had exploded nearly 70 percent to 154 million workers, those with a high school education or less had shrunk to just 41 percent of the workforce. Put another way, while the total number of jobs in America had grown by 63 million, the number of jobs held by people with no postsecondary education had actually fallen by some 2 million jobs. Thus, over the past third of a century, all of the net job growth in America has been generated by positions that require at least some postsecondary education.

Workers with at least some college have ballooned to 59 percent of the workforce, from just 28 percent in 1973. Over the same period, many high school dropouts and those with no more than a high school degree have fallen out of the middle class, even as those who have been to college, and especially those with bachelor's and advanced degrees, have moved up. The lifetime earnings gap between those with a high school education and those with a college degree is now estimated to be nearly $1 million. And the differential has been widening. In 2008, median earnings of workers with bachelor's degrees were 65 percent higher than those of high school graduates ($55,700 vs. $33,800). Similarly, workers with associate's degrees earned 73 percent more than those who had not completed high school ($42,000 vs. $24,300).

Going forward, these trends will only intensify. Although labor market projections, like all economic forecasts, are inherently uncertain, we are struck by the work of the Center on Education and the Workforce at Georgetown University. The Center projects that the U.S. economy will create some 47 million job openings over the 10-year period ending in 2018. Nearly two-thirds of these jobs, in the Center's estimation, will require that workers have at least some postsecondary education. This means, of course, that even in the second decade of the 21st century, there will still be job openings for people with just a high school degree, and even for high school dropouts. But the Center projects that applicants with no more than a high school degree will fill just 36 percent of the job openings, or just half the percentage of jobs they held in the early 1970s. Even if the Center has overestimated demand for postsecondary credentials, the long-term trend is undeniable.

The message is clear: in 21st century America, education beyond high school is the passport to the American Dream. But how much and what kind of postsecondary is really needed to prosper in the new American economy?

The Georgetown Center projects that 14 million job openings—nearly half of those that will be filled by workers with postsecondary education—will go to people with an associate's degree or occupational certificate. Many of these will be in "middle-skill" occupations such as electrician, and construction manager, dental hygienist, paralegal and police officer. While these jobs may not be as prestigious as those filled by B.A. holders, they pay a significant premium over many jobs open to those with just a high school degree. More surprisingly, they pay more than many of the jobs held by those with a bachelor's degree. In fact, 27 percent of people with postsecondary licenses or certificates—credentials short of an associate's degree—earn more than the average bachelor's degree recipient.

Demand for middle-skilled professionals is exploding in the nation's hottest industry, healthcare, which has added over half a million jobs during the Great Recession. Openings for registered nurses and health technologists—positions that typically require an associate's degree—are expected to grow by more than 1 million by 2018. There will also be exceptionally rapid growth in such healthcare support jobs as nursing aide, home health aide, and attendant. Though such positions are still open to high school graduates, they are increasingly filled by people with some postsecondary education or a certificate. Similarly, over half of massage therapists and dental assistants now have a postsecondary certificate.

There will also be a huge number of job openings in so-called blue-collar fields like construction, manufacturing, and natural resources, though many will simply replace retiring baby boomers. These fields will provide nearly 8 million job openings, 2.7 million of which will require a postsecondary credential. In commercial construction, manufacturing, mining and installation, and repair, this kind of postsecondary education—as opposed to a B.A.—is often the ticket to a well-paying and rewarding career.

CONCLUSION

The American system for preparing young people to lead productive and prosperous lives as adults is clearly badly broken. Failure to aggressively overcome this challenge will surely erode the fabric of our society. The American Dream rests on the promise of economic opportunity, with a middle-class lifestyle for those willing to work for it. Yet for the millions of young Americans entering adulthood lacking access to marketable skills, the American Dream may be just an illusion, unlikely ever to come within their grasp. If we fail to better prepare current and future teens and young adults, their frustration over scarce and inferior opportunities is likely to grow, along with economic inequality. The quality of their lives will be lower, the costs that they impose on society will be higher, and many of their potential contributions to society will go unrealized. This is a troubling prospect for any society and almost certainly a recipe for national decline.

As President Obama has said, we now need every young American not only to complete high school, but to obtain a postsecondary credential or degree with currency in the labor market. Most Americans now seem to have gotten the message that a high school education is no longer sufficient to secure a path to the middle class. As we have noted, college enrollment has been steadily rising over the past decade. The problem is completion: nearly half of those who enroll leave without a degree. While the economic returns to "some college"—a category no other country uses in calculating higher education outcomes—are greater than those for young people with only a high school diploma, they vary widely depending on family background. Because of family connections and social networks, a middle-class student dropping out of a selective college is much more likely to find his way into a decent job than a working-class student dropping out of a less selective urban university. However, a young person of whatever background who leaves community college after completing a one-year occupational certificate program—also counted in our "some college" category—may earn more than many students who complete a four-year degree program. As the recent OECD reports suggest, other countries manage to equip a much larger fraction of their young people with occupationally relevant skills and credentials by their early twenties. Consequently, these young people experience a much smoother transition into adulthood, without the bumps and bruises so many of our young are now experiencing. The lessons from Europe strongly suggest that well-developed, high-quality vocational education programs provide excellent pathways for many young people to enter the adult workforce. But these programs also advance a broader pedagogical hypothesis: that from late adolescence onward, most young people learn best in structured programs that combine work and learning, and where learning is contextual and applied. Ironically, this pedagogical approach has been widely applied in the training of our highest status professionals in the U.S., where clinical practice (a form of apprenticeship) is an essential component in the preparation of doctors, architects, and (increasingly) teachers.

When it comes to teenagers, however, we Americans seem to think they will learn best by sitting all day in classrooms. If they have not mastered basic literacy and numeracy skills by the time they enter high school, the answer in many schools is to give them double blocks of English and math. Northern European educators, by contrast, believe that academic skills are best developed through embedding them in the presentation of complex workplace problems that students learn to solve in the course of their part-time schooling. These educators also focus on helping students understand underlying theory—not only how things work, but why.

This philosophy isn't simply about learning: it's also about how to enable young people to make a successful transition to working life. What is most striking about the best European vocational systems is the investment, social as well as financial, that society makes in supporting this transition. Employers and educators together see their role as not only developing the next generation of workers, but also as helping young people make the transition from adolescence to adulthood. If we could develop an American strategy to engage educators and employers in a more collaborative approach to the education and training of the next generation of workers, it would surely produce important social as well as economic returns on investment. Let us embark on this vital work.

Developing Your Professional Vocabulary

A good understanding of this chapter's content would include an understanding of why each of these terms is important to education.

charter schools

custodial education

educational excellence

general academic track

general education

Goals 2000: Educate America Act

heterogeneous grouping

homogeneous grouping

labor market

liberal education

A Nation at Risk

No Child Left Behind Act of 2001

school choice

school restructuring

service occupations

standardized achievement testing for accountability

tracking and detracking

voucher system for schools

Questions for Discussion and Examination

1. This chapter contrasts the aims of vocational or general track and liberal education. To what degree are these aims significantly different, and to what degree are they similar? Explain and defend your point of view.

2. This chapter appears to take the position that (1) all students are capable of benefiting from an academic as opposed to a vocational or general track education and (2) an academic curriculum is the most appropriate one for all students. To what degree does the chapter adequately support this position, and to what degree do you agree with it? Justify your position.

3. Discuss the potential of blogs to figure into the way education debates might unfold in the 21st century.

4. Discuss how NCLB is an extension and a revision of ideas from earlier reforms.

5. Most of today's college students attended school during the contemporary school reform movement. To what degree has your education been influenced by such school reform? Explain.

 Online Resources

Go the Online Learning Center at **www.mhhe.com/ tozer7e** to take chapter quizzes, practice with key terms, access study resources, and link to related websites. Also available on the Online Learning Center are PowerWeb articles and news feeds.

Diversity and Equity Today Defining the Challenge

Chapter Overview

Chapter 12 begins by defining the differences between two similar concepts: equity and equality. It then reviews the history of efforts to address educational equity since the 1954 Supreme Court decision *Brown* v. *Board of Education of Topeka, Kansas.* Current social inequalities are explained, including such political–economic dimensions as income, employment, housing, and political power differences among different ethnic and gender groups.

The chapter then turns from social inequalities to educational inequalities among various social groups. The social construction of different ethnic, gender, and economic groups' status in schools is considered. While particular attention is paid to African Americans and Latinos, Asian Americans and students with disabilities are also considered. The Primary Source reading points out specifics regarding socio-economic, ethnic and racial dimensions of the "achievement gap.

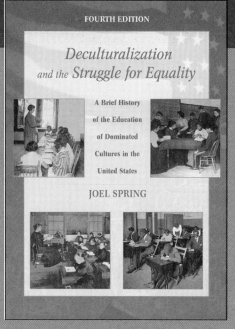

Authors increasingly investigate how education
serves different social groups differently.

Chapter Objectives

Among the objectives that Chapter 12 seeks to
achieve are these:

1. Students should be able to assess the validity
   of the assumption that differences in children's
   success in school are due largely to differences
   in children's native capacity for learning.

2. This chapter should help students examine
   variables that might affect student learning, and
   analyze how and to what degree race, ethnicity,
   social class, and gender play important roles.

3. Another aim is to evaluate the assertion that
   students should be "treated as individuals"
   without regard to gender or cultural background
   and discuss how important gender and cultural
   background are in shaping individual identity.

4. Students should be able to discuss how the
   political–economic context of schooling influences learning outcomes from one generation
   to the next.

5. Students should be able to discuss specific
   points of similarity and difference between
   today's struggles with cultural diversity and
   educational equity, and the struggles of the
   progressive era.

6. Finally, students should understand how the
   dimensions of social and economic inequality in
   this chapter are related to inequalities in
   schooling experiences and discuss whether
   cultural deficit theory adequately explains these
   differences.

Analytic Framework
Diversity and Equity Today

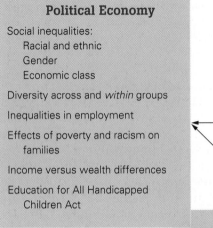

Political Economy

Social inequalities:
  Racial and ethnic
  Gender
  Economic class

Diversity across and *within* groups

Inequalities in employment

Effects of poverty and racism on
  families

Income versus wealth differences

Education for All Handicapped
  Children Act

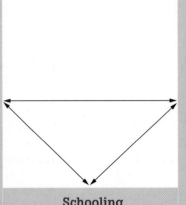

Ideology

Equal opportunity

Meritocracy

Genetic deficit theory

Cultural deficit theory

Racism

Sexism

Class bias

Disability bias

Social construction of which
  human differences matter

Schooling

Inequalities in educational resources

Inequalities in educational expectations

Standardized achievement test
  differences

Educational attainment differences

Language differences and school
  achievement

Inclusion of students with disabilities
  in "mainstream" classrooms

Gender and learning differences

No Child Left Behind

Introduction: Inequity and Inequality

From its very origins American society has struggled with questions of equity and equality. Although these terms derive from the same linguistic stem, they carry substantially different meanings. Equality denotes "equal"; equity, "fair." Even as an ideal, democracy does not call for an identical existence for each citizen or promise to equalize outcomes. In theory, democratic ideals of freedom marry well with ideals of economic freedom.

Robert N. Carson wrote the original draft of this chapter.

Those who have the most skill and talent, work hardest, and have the best luck are expected to prosper in a free market economy. The free market is supposed to structure a system of rewards that bring out the productive best in people. In practice, however, this theory is questionable. It assumes that the starting conditions for everyone allow for fair competition or, at the very least, that social institutions treat everyone fairly. British economic historian R. H. Tawney draws the distinction in this manner:

> [To] criticize inequality and to desire equality is not, as is sometimes suggested, to cherish the romantic illusion that men are equal in character and intelligence. It is to hold that, while their natural endowments differ profoundly, it is

the mark of a civilized society to aim at eliminating such inequalities as have their source, not in individual differences, but in its own organization, and that individual differences, which are the source of social energy, are more likely to ripen and find expression if social inequalities are, as far as practicable, diminished.

... it is by softening or obliterating, not individual differences, but class gradations, that the historical movements directed towards diminishing inequality have attempted to attain their objective.[1]

Liberal Ideology: Meritocracy Reexamined

Social theorists and educators have long been concerned with the origins of inequality. Does inequality stem from deficiencies within certain individuals or groups or from external social and economic conditions? It is important to remember that inequalities which have their source in social organization mean that some, the socially privileged, have advantages which are denied to others in the society. The privileged often find it comforting as well as expedient to interpret these socially derived inequalities as intrinsic personal qualities. Not only do they claim personal ownership of their advantages, they often charge the socially disadvantaged with personal ownership of their deficiencies, justifying the low socioeconomic benefits accruing to the disadvantaged.

In addition to frequent misuses of the terms *equity* and *equality,* much confusion has resulted from inadequately analyzing the implications of inequality. What sorts of educational and social policies are needed as a result of inequality, whatever its origin? Are some individuals so unequal that they cannot benefit from the kind of education others receive, and if so, should they be denied access to decision-making authority?

As we have seen, these equity and equality issues were settled during the first decades of the 20th century as psychologists such as E. L. Thorndike and Lewis Terman along with sociologists such as E. A. Ross and Charles H. Cooley convinced the American public that African Americans and the "new immigrants" were innately inferior to Anglo-Saxon Americans.[2] This conclusion led to the development of different and inferior educational programs for these groups. Thus, differentiated curricula soon became standard in American schools and were seen as a major component in the American system of meritocracy.[3]

The meritocracy issue reemerged during the 1960s, as we saw in the cold war era of Chapter 5, and remained at the center of educational discussions for the next 20 years. Fueling the new debate, as we shall see, was the *Brown* v. *Board of Education of Topeka, Kansas* decision and the ensuing Coleman study. These in turn led to several "cultural deprivation" studies, which will be analyzed briefly in the next section. The cumulative effect of these works was to reestablish the idea that some individuals and groups are inherently unequal. The source of inferiority was not considered to be social or economic conditions but flaws residing in some individuals and groups. Moreover, because their inherent deficiencies were considered to be of such magnitude, it was argued that they could not benefit from the kind of education their superiors received. Thus, the 1960s debate appeared to confirm the fairness of America's meritocratic economic structure. If some children succeeded in school while others failed, it was believed, the fairness of the system ensured that children succeeded due to their own individual merit.

Social Conditions behind the New Debate

It is instructive to examine the social conditions out of which this new meritocracy debate emerged. Perhaps the first major challenge to the meritocratic conclusions reached at the beginning of this century resulted from the "GI Bill," which appeared near the end of World War II as members of the Roosevelt administration began planning for the demobilization of the American armed forces. Their primary concern was to entice GIs to enter college rather than the labor market and thus help prevent massive unemployment. Many of these GIs came from poorly educated families that earlier had been judged inferior, and so they were not expected to succeed in college. In accordance with prevailing meritocratic ideas, many educators were horrified at the prospect of this horde of unprepared and ill-suited students leaving their lower-class backgrounds and crashing the citadels of learning. Educators forecast widespread failure for these new students. Much to their surprise, however, most of the GIs were very successful. As a group, they graduated at a higher rate than did the regular students and achieved higher grades en route to their diplomas. This success presented a new reality, a new set of social facts that most social analysts and educators chose to ignore.

Brown v. *Board of Education* in 1954 opened the way to scenes such as this, in which U.S. Marshals forceably protected the right of a young African American student to attend a previously all-White elementary school.

Nevertheless, it represented a potential chink in the armor of the meritocratic ideology.

In 1954, immediately after the positive experience of the GI Bill, came the Supreme Court's *Brown* v. *Board of Education* ruling, which stated, "It is doubted that any child may reasonably be expected to succeed in life if he is denied the opportunity of an education . . . [and such opportunity] must be made available to all on equal terms."[4] This reopened the debate about equity in American society. Michael Harrington's 1962 best-seller, *The Other America,*[5] added fuel to the debate as he reminded the middle class that one-third of Americans were still ill fed, ill housed, and ill clothed. Apparently, the umbrella of the "middle class" did not cover as much of the populace as conventional wisdom had assumed. This awareness of widespread inequality and inequity was heightened by the growing civil rights movement led by Dr. Martin Luther King, Jr., and the urban riots that followed his murder in 1968.

Meanwhile, the nation was becoming increasingly entangled in the Vietnam War and the social inequities that the war protest movement uncovered. And if the preceding events were not enough to unsettle the national psyche, President Lyndon Johnson, in an attempt to secure a political coalition of urban ethnics, African Americans, and liberal intellectuals, declared a war on poverty that found domestic foes almost as intractable as those in the rice paddies of southeast Asia. To round things out, events in the area of industrial labor relations were equally contentious, as seen in the conflict at General Motors' Vega plant, where workers demanded democratic control of the workplace.

It became clear to many that such events were causing a major reassessment of the modern liberal ideology undergirding meritocracy. Many critics questioned the "new liberal" faith in scientific expertise and scientific rationality as the best ways to organize the workplace and plan domestic and foreign policy. Expert and elite control of social institutions did not seem to be producing the progress that modern liberalism promised. Further, the uncritical nationalism that modern liberalism had fostered in so many Americans was being questioned. And the promise of freedom for all Americans seemed to be an illusion, given the pervasive conditions of poverty that seemed to constrain millions of Americans who simply didn't have an equal chance at the American dream of a self-sufficient life.

As if these concerns were not enough, there were simultaneous attacks on the schools that were preparing children for their future roles in the meritocracy. These attacks ranged from Admiral Hyman Rickover's demand for a technological elite to defend America from the onslaught of world communism,[6] to Arthur Bestor's charge that the schools were an intellectual "wasteland"[7] that threatened the very existence of American democracy, to Nat Hentoff's assertion that the inner-city schools were so underfunded that they could not educate.[8] Thus, education, the major institutional support for meritocracy, was also under severe assault.

Thinking Critically about the Issues   #1

A basic assumption in American schooling has been that students' success in school and in economic life is based on their learning abilities in an equitable educational system. How does this assumption relate to the idea of our society as a meritocracy?

The Coleman Report

To fulfill one of the provisions of the 1964 Civil Rights Act, the U.S. Office of Education commissioned James Coleman to conduct a survey "concerning the lack of availability of equal educational opportunity for individuals by reason of race, color, religion, or national origin." This study initiated the new debate on equity. Coleman's team of researchers gathered data on over 6,000,000 schoolchildren, 60,000 teachers, and 4,000 schools across the United States. His findings were startling. To summarize them briefly:

1. Most African American students and White students attended different schools.

2. According to "measurable" characteristics (e.g., physical facilities, curricula, material resources, and teachers), these schools were quite similar.

3. Measured student performance on standardized tests showed considerable differences, with White students well ahead of African American students in test results.

4. The measured differences in school resources seemed to have little or no effect on the differences in students' performance on standardized tests; that is, educational inputs (facilities, curricula, teachers) seemed to make no meaningful difference in outcomes (academic achievement).

5. The only variable that seemed to affect educational achievement ("outcomes") was "quality of peers."

6. Minority children, especially African Americans, Latinos, and Native Americans, entered school with lower achievement scores, and this gap increased throughout their stay in school.

Although it was profoundly influential in the national discussion about schools and inequality, the Coleman study was seriously flawed. According to Samuel Bowles and Henry Levin, for example, the statistical method used to analyze the data grossly underestimated the positive effects of schooling on student achievement.[9] In other words, if the study had been conducted differently, it would have shown that schools do matter a great deal—that different levels of school input produce very different outcomes in student learning. In addition to flaws in the statistical method used, the data collected by Coleman's team were in themselves misleading: Teacher quality, for example, was measured primarily by years of schooling and years of teaching experience.

Despite its flaws, the Coleman Report succeeded in focusing attention away from educational inputs (what schools bring to students) and toward what children bring to school. It seemed to invite the scientific investigation of unequal education achievement by looking for flaws in the children rather than in the schools or in society.

The Cultural Deprivation Studies

During the winter of 1966–1967, the Carnegie Foundation sponsored a seminar at Harvard University to examine the implications of the Coleman Report. Two books were conceived during the seminar: *On Equality of Educational Opportunity,* edited by Daniel P. Moynihan and Frederick Mosteller, and *Inequality,* by Christopher Jencks and his associates. Both books reanalyzed the Coleman database; that is, they used the data collected by the Coleman researchers rather than gathering new data. Thus both books suffered most of the same flaws as the original Coleman study.

The Moynihan–Mosteller work[10] concluded that since educational inputs are roughly the same for all children, America had achieved equal educational opportunity. The authors argued that educational expenditures were already high, and since further expenditures were not likely to raise educational achievement for minorities, such increases would be economically unwise. America, according to these writers, had already reached the point of diminishing returns regarding educational expenditures. In retrospect, it is interesting to note that the argument for a halt in rising educational expenditures did not originate with the conservative Nixon or Reagan administrations but with liberal Harvard social scientists who were supported by the Carnegie Foundation. This occurred because the Moynihan–Mosteller work reinforced the Coleman Report's suggestion that the achievement problems faced by minority students rested not with the schools but with the students and their cultural backgrounds. More money for the schools, in that interpretation, would provide little benefit. By implication, the book also bolstered the notion that poverty stems from personal problems within the poor rather than from problems within the social system.[11]

Christopher Jencks and colleagues' *Inequality*[12] was even more explicit, although perhaps unintentionally so, in its attempt to rescue the economic system from charges of inequity. The authors began by arguing that the Coleman data showed substantial equality of inputs in public schools. They also asserted that cognitive inequality was not affected by schooling but was largely dependent on the characteristics of the child upon entering school. Like Moynihan and Mosteller, they noted that unequal achievement was caused by deficiencies in the child, not in the school.

The conclusions of Jencks et al. regarding economic inequality were not as predictable as their assertions about educational inequality. They argued that nothing in the Coleman data could be shown to affect future economic success. According to Jencks et al., family background, schooling, IQ, and cognitive skills had little or no predictive value on future economic success. They did hazard a guess, which they acknowledged lacked data support, that economic success was probably related to "luck" and special competencies, such as the ability to hit a baseball. Nevertheless, they recommended that society spend more money on schooling—even though schools do not make any difference in a person's future—because most people spend 20 to 25 percent of their lives in school and thus schools should be "pleasant."[13] During the following decade many educators worried, talked, and planned about making schools more "pleasant" places. The real cost of this kind of activity was to deflect attention away from questions about how to make schools more effective learning centers for children.

Henry M. Levin's review[14] of Jencks and colleagues' work points out many of its major flaws. Levin notes that the authors' conclusion that family background has little effect on future income, especially for the rich and the poor, defies the results of many studies of intergenerational mobility which show that the effect of family is quite significant. Regarding their conclusion that schooling has only a small effect on income, Levin suggests that their interpretation of what constitutes "small" may be open to interpretation. The data showed that the difference in annual income between high school graduates and elementary school graduates who were otherwise identical was 16 percent in favor of the high school graduates; between college graduates and elementary school graduates, the difference was 48 percent in favor of the college graduates. Levin notes, "Jencks apparently believes that such differences are small, but two men separated by such income disparities might not agree."[15]

In light of the massive flaws in these studies and the fact that they nevertheless exerted, and continue to exert, considerable influence on educational and social policy, the question arises, How did this happen? The most reasonable explanation seems to be that these ideas were congenial to the powerful in our society because they served to justify and explain their own positions of privilege. In other words, these ideas were powerful because they accorded well with the dominant ideology: modern liberalism. They reinforced and appeared to justify a meritocratic arrangement of society and schooling. They deflected arguments that questioned the validity and fairness of such arrangements. Regardless of the reasons these studies became so influential, they continue to affect the way Americans think about equity and schools.

Let us now examine some of the data concerning income, race, social class, gender, and schooling. Subsequently, we shall examine theories that attempt to explain the relationships found in these data.

The Political–Economic Context

The Demographics of Modern American Society

The United States has been known from its beginning as a "land of opportunity," and today it ranks near the top of all industrialized nations in per capita purchasing power.[16] The United States is also one of the most schooled countries, in terms of years of schooling per capita. Per capita education spending in the United States compares well with other countries: Over 85 percent of U.S. students graduate from high schools, and U.S. college and university systems enroll nearly 20 million students, attracting applicants from all over the world.[17]

These statistics give an encouraging picture of American society. Unfortunately, this picture is misleading. For example, almost half of those who go on to college will drop out. And of those who drop out, a disproportionate number are from minority backgrounds. For example, six different states have school districts where the high school dropout rate is over 25 percent, and nationwide the dropout rate for African American and Hispanic students far exceeds the dropout rate for other populations. Although the nation is prosperous overall, income inequality is among the highest in the industrialized world. According to the U.S. Census Bureau, recent median income for White and Asian American families ranged from $55,000 to $60,000, while for Black and Hispanic families it ranged from $33,000 to $34,000.[18] These are huge differences not only in paying for college, but even for buying adequate clothing and housing a family in neighborhoods where good public schools prevail.

To gain a more detailed picture of how wealth and power are distributed in society, social scientists examine data on income, educational level, childhood mortality, teenage pregnancy, substance abuse, home ownership, capital stock, and other social indices. These variables are then matched against different demographic groups organized by age, race, ethnicity, social class, gender, and so forth. (See Exhibits 12.1 and 12.2 for years of school completed related to age, through 2000, with 2010 census verifying continuation of those trends.) The next few sections step back from this larger picture of general prosperity to examine outcomes for several different demographic groups. The intent is to reinforce with statistics what is already common knowledge: Social, economic, and political outcomes generally favor men over women, White people over people of color, and upper- and middle-class people over the urban poor and the working class.

Race, Ethnicity, and the Limits of Language

In this section we examine data for specific minority groups. Bear in mind that both *race* and *ethnicity* are socially constructed terms that are difficult to define. There

Exhibit 12.1   Years of School Completed by Persons 25 Years Old and Over, 1940–2000

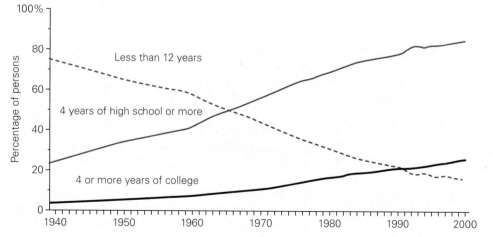

Sources: U.S. Department of Commerce, Bureau of the Census, *1960 Census of Population,* Volume 1, part 1; and *Current Population Reports,* Series P-20; and Current Population Survey, unpublished data.

Exhibit 12.2   Years of School Completed by Persons 25 to 29 Years of Age, 1940–2000

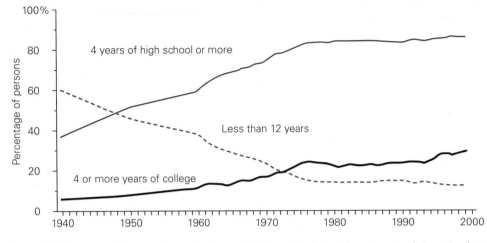

Sources: U.S. Department of Commerce, Bureau of the Census, *1960 Census of Population,* Volume 1, part 1; and *Current Population Reports,* Series P-20; and Current Population Survey, unpublished data.

is, for example, no definition of race that will stand up to scientific analysis, and so it must be understood that race is not a purely biological term. For example, the distinction between White and African American is largely determined by legal ruling, as is the case in Louisiana. There the courts have held that a person is African American if the equivalent of one great-great-great-great-grandparent was African American (i.e., if a person is one sixty-fourth African American). Hispanics are usually classified by virtue of a Spanish surname—clearly a cultural rather than a biological distinction. The important point is that these terms refer less to innate biological differences than to socially constructed differences in how people are perceived to be members of various groups (see the American Anthropological Association Statement on "Race" in Table 12.1).

There are several difficulties with trying to talk or write about issues of race and ethnicity. One, as the *Dictionary of Race and Ethnic Relations* points out, is that every time we use the word *race,* we appear to be perpetuating a concept that has no basis in science.[19] The Human Genome Diversity Project, for example, has demonstrated that the darkest-hued African and the lightest-skinned Scandinavian are 99.99 percent identical in their genetic composition.[20] Yet the concept of race has historically operated as if the differences among large groups of people (traditionally "Caucasoid, Mongoloid, and Negroid") are so significant as to identify us as subspecies of the larger human species, a division that has no scientific basis. To continue to use the term *race*

seems to perpetuate that mistaken notion. It might be better, it seems, to eliminate the term altogether from the way we refer to ourselves as humans—unless to affirm that we are all one race.

However, the term *race* has been historically used to differentiate us from one another, not to unite us. (For the African and the Scandinavian to say they are of the same race seems like nonsense to most people, as if the language were being used in a way it was not meant to be used.) Therefore, focusing on race draws our attention to the differences among us rather than to the similarities. The same might be said for *ethnicity,* a term which *does* have a strong basis in social science. Focus on this term, too, can make people uncomfortable, because in the middle of the effort to affirm what we have in common with one another—our essential humanness—social scientists and educators use a term that emphasizes our differences. This may be perceived as divisive. It separates us by different languages and different cultural histories. In short, focus on ethnicity, like focus on race, seems to divide us rather than unite us, but for different reasons.

There is still another difficulty with the language of race and ethnicity: Our terms of ethnic identification are disputed and often inaccurate. There is not full agreement among Native Americans (or American Indians, or Indians, or indigenous peoples) about which identifying term to use. Some of these terms (Indians, Americans) are the historical legacy of conquering Europeans, and most cultures resist having their names imposed by other cultures. One's identity is in part shaped by one's name, and we resist having our own names for ourselves replaced by someone else's names for ourselves. Similarly, most Asian Americans now resist being called "Orientals," and most African Americans resist being called "Negroes." While some African Americans and Hispanics and Asian Americans use the term *people of color* to refer to non-White, non-Hispanic people in the United States, this obscures the fact that some Hispanics in the United States identify strongly with their European origins, are in all outward respects "White," and do not want themselves described as "people of color." In their view, they are as "white" as any other U.S. language or ethnic group (Polish, German, Irish) of European descent. Alternatively, some Hispanics would choose to self-identify as Latino or Chicano (about which more later), terms that are chosen in part to make specific political statements about identity and

self-representation. The term *white* is itself a cultural construction with ideological baggage.

Even when we respect the names different peoples prefer for themselves, our efforts to talk about ethnicity are stymied by the fact that broadly inclusive terms are misleading. For example, to generalize about Hispanics or Asian Americans overlooks profound cultural differences, even historical hostilities, within each of those subgroups. While Japanese and Chinese and Cambodians are very different culturally and economically in the United States, the term *Asian American* seems to allow us to generalize about them as if they were basically similar. Similarly, Cubans, Puerto Ricans, and Mexicans have different histories and important differences in their status in the U.S. economic and educational system, but they are all Hispanics in our use of the language.

If our language is such a clumsy tool for talking about these matters, why talk about them? Why can't we all be

Table 12.1 AAA Statement on "Race"

The following statement was adopted by the AAA Executive Board, acting on a draft prepared by a committee of representative American anthropologists. It does not reflect a consensus of all members of the AAA, as individuals vary in their approaches to the study of "race." We believe that it represents generally the contemporary thinking and scholarly positions of a majority of anthropologists.

In the US both scholars and the general public have been conditioned to viewing human races as natural and separate divisions within the human species based on visible physical differences. With the vast expansion of scientific knowledge in this century, however, it has become clear that human populations are not unambiguous, clearly demarcated, biologically distinct groups. Evidence from the analysis of genetics (e.g., DNA) indicates that there is greater variation within racial groups than between them. This means that most physical variation, about 94%, lies *within* so-called racial groups. Conventional geographic "racial" groupings differ from one another only in about 6% of their genes. In neighboring populations there is much overlapping of genes and their phenotypic (physical) expressions. Throughout history whenever different groups have come into contact, they have interbred. The continued sharing of genetic materials has maintained all of humankind as a single species.

Physical variations in any given trait tend to occur gradually rather than abruptly over geographic areas. And because physical traits are inherited independently of one another, knowing the range of one trait does not predict the presence of others. For example, skin color varies largely from light in the temperate areas in the north to dark in the tropical areas in the south; its intensity is not related to nose shape or hair texture. Dark skin may be associated with frizzy or kinky hair or curly or wavy or straight hair, all

of which are found among different indigenous peoples in tropical regions. These facts render any attempt to establish lines of division among biological populations both arbitrary and subjective.

Historical research has shown that the idea of race has always carried more meanings than mere physical differences; indeed, physical variations in the human species have no meaning except the social ones that humans put on them. Today scholars in many fields argue that race as it is understood in the USA was a social mechanism invented during the 18th century to refer to those populations brought together in colonial America: the English and other European settlers, the conquered Indian peoples, and those peoples of Africa brought in to provide slave labor.

From its inception, this modern concept of race was modeled after an ancient theorem of the Great Chain of Being which posited natural categories on a hierarchy established by God or nature. Thus race was a mode of classification linked specifically to peoples in the colonial situation. It subsumed a growing ideology of inequality devised to rationalize European attitudes and treatment of the conquered and enslaved peoples. Proponents of slavery in particular during the 19th century used race to justify the retention of slavery. The ideology magnified the differences among Europeans, Africans and Indians, established a rigid hierarchy of socially exclusive categories, underscored and

(continued)

Table 12.1 *(concluded)*

bolstered unequal rank and status differences, and provided the rationalization that the inequality was natural or God-given. The different physical traits of African-Americans and Indians became markers or symbols of their status differences.

As they were constructing US society, leaders among European-Americans fabricated the cultural/behavioral characteristics associated with each race, linking superior traits with Europeans and negative and inferior ones to blacks and Indians. Numerous arbitrary and fictitious beliefs about the different peoples were institutionalized and deeply embedded in American thought.

Early in the 19th century the growing fields of science began to reflect the public consciousness about human differences. Differences among the racial categories were projected to their greatest extreme when the argument was posed that Africans, Indians and Europeans were separate species, with Africans the least human and closer taxonomically to apes.

Ultimately race as an ideology about human differences was subsequently spread to other areas of the world. It became a strategy for dividing, ranking and controlling colonized people used by colonial powers everywhere. But it was not limited to the colonial situation. In the latter part of the 19th century it was employed by Europeans to rank one another and to justify social, economic and political inequalities among their peoples. During World War II, the Nazis under Adolf Hitler enjoined the expanded ideology of race and racial differences and took them to a logical end: the extermination of 11 million people of "inferior races" (e.g., Jews, Gypsies, Africans, homosexuals and so forth) and other unspeakable brutalities of the Holocaust.

Race thus evolved as a world view, a body of prejudgments that distorts our ideas about human differences and group behavior. Racial beliefs constitute myths about the diversity in the human species and about the abilities and behavior of people homogenized into racial categories. The myths fused behavior and physical features together in the public mind, impeding our comprehension of both biological variations and cultural behavior, implying that both are genetically determined. Racial myths bear no relationship to the reality of human capabilities or behavior. Scientists today find that reliance on such folk beliefs about human differences in research has led to countless errors.

At the end of the 20th century, we now understand that human cultural behavior is learned, conditioned into infants beginning at birth, and always subject to modification. No human is born with a built-in culture or language. Our temperaments, dispositions and personalities, regardless of genetic propensities, are developed within sets of meanings and values that we call "culture." Studies of infant and early childhood learning and behavior attest to the reality of our cultures in forming who we are.

It is a basic tenet of anthropological knowledge that all normal human beings have the capacity to learn any cultural behavior. The American experience with immigrants from hundreds of different language and cultural backgrounds who have acquired some version of American culture traits and behavior is the clearest evidence of this fact. Moreover, people of all physical variations have learned different cultural behaviors and continue to do so as modern transportation moves millions of immigrants around the world. How people have been accepted and treated within the context of a given society or culture has a direct impact on how they perform in that society. The racial world view was invented to assign some groups to perpetual low status, while others were permitted access to privilege, power and wealth. The tragedy in the US has been that the policies and practices stemming from this world view succeeded all too well in constructing unequal populations among Europeans, Native Americans and peoples of African descent. Given what we know about the capacity of normal humans to achieve and function within any culture, we conclude that present-day inequalities between so-called racial groups are not consequences of their biological inheritance but products of historical and contemporary social, economic, educational and political circumstances.

Source: Reproduced by permission of the American Anthropological Association from *Anthropology News* 39, no. 6 (September 1998).

one and stop emphasizing differences among us? (In fact, some would prefer that U.S. Census Bureau and other official documents would stop requiring us to identify ourselves as African American, Asian and Pacific Islander, American Indian, and so on.) One very important reason, as indicated in Cornel West's *Race Matters*,[21] is that people in the United States are deeply affected—privileged, damaged, even killed—according to their *perceived* membership in one racial or ethnic group or another. To stop talking about race and ethnicity is to lose an important tool for understanding why some people are treated differently from others in our society. Without race and ethnicity as categories, we can't find answers to important questions about whether schools are serving all children equally well—or whether skin color or cultural background might be factors in why some children perform better than others. We would not be able to learn that Minnesota, a state with a highly regarded school system, ranks "dead last of all the states among African American fourth-graders," to cite a 1996 study of academic achievement. If we take away race and ethnicity as tools for analysis, we can't notice that

African American males are more likely to be killed or to go to prison in our society than they are to graduate from college. Without the tools for noticing that this is happening, we cannot begin to ask why. Without asking why, we cannot begin to do anything about it.[22]

On the one hand, our language about race and ethnicity is imprecise and often misleading. The very use of the term *race* seems to perpetuate a wrong-headed idea about human beings. Yet these seem to be the best tools we have for pointing out one huge category of problems that must be addressed if a school system seeks to serve democratic ideals. Those problems exist when children experience different educational outcomes not on the basis of their individual talents and interests but on the basis of their membership in a cultural group—whether that group is defined by race, ethnicity, family income, gender, or another characteristic. Even when the tools of language are clumsy, they are often sufficient to help us inquire into whether all children are receiving the education they deserve in a democratic society. Put differently, race may not be a coherent concept, but racism is a real phenomenon.

Ethnicity, Income, and Wealth   If race and ethnicity were of no consequence in American society, we would not expect great differences in income among different racial and ethnic groups. Where income varied among individuals, we would expect the differences to be due not to race and ethnicity but to such factors as education and individual talents or interests. Where income varied among families, we would consider such factors as the number of income earners in the household. In fact, as Sheldon Danziger points out, educational differences do not explain very much of the disparity between income earnings among non-Hispanic Whites, African Americans, and Hispanic individuals; correcting for educational differences does not eliminate most of the income differences.[23] Other differences, such as age, region, and racial bias in employment and promotion practices, are among those which must be examined. Similarly, Andrew Hacker has found that the difference between the number of two-income White households and two-income Black households does not explain the large gap in household income between those two groups, especially because a higher percentage of Black married women than White married women work outside the home.[24]

What is most salient for our purposes here is that the income differences are very real for different racial and ethnic groups, and these income differences lead to different life chances for children in different groups. Further, family income correlates highly with school achievement, which means that children from low socioeconomic status (SES) families will tend to perform less well in school than do high-SES children. Harold Hodgkinson pointed out more than 15 years ago, for example, that high-SES African American eighth-graders perform better in an advanced mathematics than do low-SES White or Asian American eighth-graders.[25]

Given that SES and race interact in complex ways, income disparities among different ethnic groups can have great consequences for children. And income disparities among different racial and ethnic groups are significant in the United States today. The U.S. Bureau of the Census reported, for example:

- While the income median of White families was well above the median household income of the United States overall ($57,073 in 2003 dollars), median earnings of African American and Hispanic families were much lower: respectively, $38,674 and $38,718.[26]

- Over 21 percent of White households earned over $100,000 in 2003, while 9 percent of African American households earned over $100,000 and 7 percent of Hispanic households of any race earn over $100,000.[27]

- At the opposite end of the income distribution, 12 percent of White households earn below $20,000, while 26 percent of African American households and 21 percent of Hispanics of any race earn below this figure. Only 15 percent of Asian/Pacific Islander households fall below this figure.[28]

- When family wealth is measured, which considers not just annual income but a family's full financial assets, such as real estate and stocks, the differences are much greater. In 2001, White families had a median net worth of $117,722. African American families had a median net worth of $18,510 and for Latino families it was $11,149.[29]

- The poverty level in 2000 was established at $17,650, well under half the median household income for the nation. Among Asian/Pacific Islander families, 12 percent fell below poverty level, compared to 10 percent of White families. In contrast, 22 percent of Hispanics and 24 percent of African Americans fell into this poverty category.[30]

In seeking explanations for such marked differences among different ethnic groups, we should avoid the simple suggestion that the higher levels of education attained by Whites and Asian Americans provide the answer. It is instructive, for example, that while the education gaps between Blacks and Whites have steadily narrowed since the late 1960s, the poverty levels for Whites have remained between 9 and 11.3 percent, while for Blacks they have remained much higher, between 21 and 30 percent.[31] Furthermore, Blacks and Hispanics with the same level of education as Whites, whether a high school diploma or a college or graduate degree, continue to earn less than their White counterparts.[32] The discouraging message here is that differences in employment and income are due to factors other than a person's education. While additional education can create opportunities for individuals in all ethnic groups, the historical record shows that it is not likely in itself to overcome differences among groups as long as various forms of ethnic discrimination exist.

Ethnicity and Employment   Hacker shows that for the last 30 years unemployment rates for African Americans have remained steadily at two to two and a half times the unemployment rates for Whites. Again, we are tempted to look for an explanation in educational differences. But as Hacker tells us, African Americans with college degrees have even worse unemployment, compared to college-educated Whites, than African Americans who have only a high school diploma as compared to their White counterparts. Perhaps even more discouraging to African Americans is the comparison of their recent unemployment rates with those 20 or 30 years ago. In the 1960s, Black unemployment went above 11 percent only in one year and stayed at or below 8 percent for the last half of the decade. In the 1980s and early 1990s, despite dramatic educational increases for African Americans, Black unemployment rates never went below 11 percent and for most years hovered in the range of 14 to 18 percent.[33] The message is that unemployment differentials, like income disparities, are dependent on socioeconomic conditions other than education. While additional education can create opportunities for individuals in all ethnic groups, it is not likely in itself to overcome differences among groups as long as various forms of discrimination based on ethnicity persist.

Discrimination interacts with cultural practices and traditions differently in different ethnic groups. In the section on social theory and education in the next chapter,

for example, we will see a theory suggesting a certain amount of resistance to school norms among children in some ethnic groups but not in others. A group's cultural practices, together with how groups are differently perceived by people who hire and fire in the workplace, have different consequences for different groups. The nation's unemployment rates for Whites and Asian/Pacific Islanders in 2004, for example, were 4.5 and 6.3 percent, respectively. Regarded as the "model minority" by employers as well as by some educators, Asian/Pacific Islanders do not encounter the sort of discrimination directed against African Americans or Hispanics, the unemployment rates for whom in 2004 were 10.7 and 7.0 percent, respectively.[34]

Such data tell us some important differences *among* groups but obscure important differences *within* groups. For example, the relatively high household income levels cited above for Asian/Pacific Islanders hide differences among different Asian groups. A 2006 study, for example, shows that median family income in the United States ranged from $70,849 for Japanese and $70,708 for Asian Indians to about half that for Cambodians and Hmong. Among "Hispanics," unemployment rates for Puerto Rican men tend to be double those for Cuban American men.[35] The general labels *Hispanic* and *Asian/Pacific Islander* can cause us to overlook important cultural and economic differences among the many different groups comprised by them. Similarly, discouraging data about Black poverty and unemployment can obscure the reality of the growing Black middle class, which has more in common with the White middle class than with the Black underclass in terms of economics, employment, and education.

Ethnicity and Family   We are learning from many quarters that changes in the American family affect all ethnic groups, but some more severely than others. The great majority of the 17.5 million children living in single-parent households, for example, are White non-Hispanic. It might seem, therefore, that information on the changing family structure in our society might better be discussed as a subtopic of economic class or gender rather than ethnicity. We mention family characteristics here largely because of the particular significance that single-parent families have for African American children. For 80 years, from 1880 to 1960, the proportion of Black children living with a single parent held steady around 30 percent, according to the new research by the University of Minnesota. During the same time, the proportion of White children living with only one parent stayed at about 10 percent. But in recent years, those figures have climbed—to 63 percent for Black children and 19 percent for White children. In data averaging from 2000 to 2002, 25 percent of White children were living in low-income or poverty-level families. This figure is 58 and 62 percent for African American and Latino families, respectively. The federal poverty level is $18,400 per family of four. Low income is below 200 percent of that level.[36] As Hodgkinson notes about correlations between poverty and single-parent families, "when both parents work, family income does not double; it *triples*."[37] Single-parent families are thus a significant reason that over 8.3 million White children, 4.6 million Black children, and nearly 3 million Hispanic children were listed as living in poverty in 1991 by the U.S. Bureau of the Census. Put in percentages, 16.1 percent of White non-Hispanic children, 45.6 percent of African American children, and 39.8 percent of Hispanic children lived in poverty in 1991. There is little doubt that these deep economic differences will contribute to different educational and life outcomes for these children.[38]

Some of these life opportunities are eliminated very early, even before birth. Hodgkinson reports that one-fourth of pregnant mothers receive no medical care during the crucial first trimester of pregnancy, when some 20 percent of disabilities might have been prevented by early prenatal care.[39] The United States has the highest infant mortality rate of any industrialized nation, due significantly to the effects of racism and poverty on African Americans. African American infants die at a rate twice that of White infants, and in some inner-city areas (such as Detroit, Chicago, and Philadelphia), infant mortality rates exceed those in Jamaica, Costa Rica, and Chile.[40]

Compared with White children, African American children are twice as likely to be born prematurely, suffer low birth weight, live in poor housing, have no parent employed, and see a parent die. Compared with White children, African American children are three times more likely to be poor, live in a female-headed family, be placed in an educable mentally handicapped (EMH) class in school, die of known child abuse, and have their mothers die in childbirth.[41]

Ethnicity and Housing Half the nation's African Americans are concentrated into just 25 major metropolitan areas. Two-thirds of all African American youth still attend segregated schools.[42] Patterns of segregation in housing nationwide have changed surprisingly little in the past 30 years despite the rise of a highly visible African American middle class and laws aimed at desegregating society.

The job market has changed, however, shrinking the middle class by eliminating manufacturing jobs and shifting many of the remaining jobs away from the central city to the suburbs or overseas to sources of cheap labor. Many African Americans in the inner city have been left behind without jobs and without opportunities for upward mobility. The breakdown of the family, the exit of African American professionals from the inner city, the erosion of the tax base, and the increase in drug use, violence, and crime have all served to leave the inner city a disastrous place to grow up. By the early 1990s housing and employment problems had actually worsened as the Bush administration tightened budgetary restraints on social spending.

For the purposes of illustrating socioeconomic inequalities, many of the examples presented here have contrasted African Americans with non-Hispanic Whites. This is partly because of the status of African Americans as the largest American ethnic minority group but also because discrimination against African Americans is uniquely grounded in a history of enslavement and subsequent related prejudice and oppression. As Marian Wright Edelman, founder of the Children's Defense Fund, wrote in an open letter to her own children:

> It is utterly exhausting being black in America— physically, mentally, and emotionally. While many minority groups and women feel similar stress, there is no respite or escape from your badge of color. . . . It can be exhausting to be a Black student on a "white" campus or a Black employee in a "white" institution where some assume you are not as smart as comparable whites. The constant burden to "prove" that you are as smart, as honest, as interesting, as wide-gauging and motivated as any other individual tires you out.[43]

While the African American experience in the United States has been distinctively oppressive, the fastest-growing minority groups in the nation are Asian Americans and Hispanic Americans, groups with great internal variation that are affected by different kinds of discrimination. More will be said about Asian Americans and Hispanics as we move later to the issues of education and ethnicity.

Gender

Originally, political representation in America excluded women. The family rather than the individual was assumed to be the political unit, and men represented the family unit. Remaining single for men and for women was discouraged by social censure and at times by political and economic means as well. As documented in Chapter 5, paternalistic social arrangements drawn from European society dated back through medieval times to the classical formulations of Greece and Rome. *Paternalism* refers to a male-dominated social arrangement embedded in traditional family, state, and church structures. When the purpose of education is seen as preparing individuals for places in society, there are clear implications for the education of females in a male-controlled society. Although the proportion of women completing high school and college and ascending to positions of responsibility, power, and wealth has increased dramatically since the days when women were legally subordinate to men, significant differences still exist between the conditions and experiences of modern men and women. A closer look at some of these differences will establish a foundation for later discussions of gender issues in American education.

Gender and Employment Most people, men and women, feel that an occupation is important to their well-being. In a survey conducted by the U.S. Department of Education 20 years ago, 84 percent of males and 77 percent of females indicated that being successful in work was far more meaningful to them than having a high income. Furthermore, most of those surveyed felt that a woman could successfully balance career aspirations and family obligations. And

an impressive 98 percent of the respondents felt that a woman should have exactly the same educational opportunities as a man.[44] Almost as many felt that women should have the same pay for equal work as well as the same opportunity for management and other positions of responsibility. In attitude at least, the public seems to have adjusted to the notion that women are entitled to equality in the workplace. Most women felt that the equal rights movement had made their lives better. One important trend is clear: Women of all races are closing the education gap with men, and in some cases outperforming men in completing college.[45] This is expected to have a significant effect on who gets hired for which jobs in the future, even if employment discrimination persists.

There seems to be a "glass ceiling" that prevents women from reaching the top positions in the economic world, although it does not prevent women from *seeing* the top echelon. Most commentators agree that this barrier has been constructed by the materials of gender discrimination rather than by any inherent deficiency in women. Nevertheless, some gains are clearly visible. Women have entered into the ranks of lawyers, doctors, and other professionals in numbers unparalleled in previous generations. Between 1972 and 1990, the proportion of lawyers who were women rose from 4 to 21 percent. In the same period, the proportion of women physicians nearly doubled, to 19 percent, according to the U.S. Department of Labor Bureau of Labor Statistics.

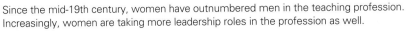

Since the mid-19th century, women have outnumbered men in the teaching profession. Increasingly, women are taking more leadership roles in the profession as well.

Despite these gains, many occupations remain predominantly female. Dental hygienists, preschool and elementary teachers, secretaries, receptionists, practical nurses, day care workers, domestic servants, typists, dressmakers, registered nurses, dietitians, speech therapists, teacher's aides, and bank tellers are still over 93 percent female, and some of these jobs are nearly 100 percent female. Some 59 percent of all female workers are employed in sales, clerical, and service work. Conversely, some jobs remain over 95 percent male: loggers, auto mechanics, tool-and-die makers, skilled building tradesmen, millwrights, engineers, mechanical engineers, aircraft mechanics, carpenters, civil engineers, industrial engineers, welders and cutters, machinists, and sheet metal workers. And of course, in the U.S. Congress, males constitute the overwhelming majority of the senators and representatives who make the laws of the land.

Gender and Income   Income differences between men and women have persisted since the beginning of the industrial era. That gap had been shrinking until recently. In 1980, for example, full-time year-round women workers earned 60 percent of what men earned, while in 1991 women earned 70 percent of men's salaries. But in 2006, full-time year-round working women earned 70.7 percent of men's salaries, which is essentially zero progress in 15 years. This rate of progress would not be encouraging to millions of women who are heads of their households.[46]

More recently, Census Bureau data give us more detailed ways to examine male–female income differences. For example, in 2006 the majority of full-time women workers earned less than $35,000 annually, while only 37 percent of men earned such a low salary. At the other end of the scale, more than 20 percent of men earned $75,000 or above, a figure surpassed by some experienced teachers in well-funded school districts. Nationwide, 6.3 percent of women make that amount or more. Perhaps more distressing is that women with a college degree make less than men who did not graduate from college, and women with a graduate degree make less than men who only graduated from college.[47]

Gender and Parenting   The 56.5 million working women in America represent 45 percent of the entire labor force over age 16, and over 10 million of these women are heads of households. Having children can be economically dangerous for working women, since the United States is the only Western democracy that fails to protect the careers of young working mothers. By the mid-1980s, for example:

- Swedish working women received a nine-month maternity leave at 90 percent of pay.

- Italian working women received a five-month maternity leave at 80 percent of pay.

- Hungarian working women received 20 weeks' leave at 100 percent of pay.

In 1992, Shapiro reported that the United States was the only industrialized nation without a mandated maternity leave policy; paid leave at 60 to 100 percent of salary is the norm in most of the other nations. In 1993, the United States passed the Family Medical Leave Act, which partly closed the gap with other nations by providing workers with up to 12 weeks of paid leave for specified family medical emergencies. U.S. employers continued to resist paying for advanced education and additional training for female employees on the grounds that they may subsequently have children and quit. This ignores the fact that male employees also quit: Men change jobs every seven years on average and are encouraged to do so to keep from stagnating.[48]

Since the 1990s, maternity leave has increased in other nations. *USA Today* recently reported that Canadian women can receive up to 14 months of family leave, with up to a year in Australia. *USA Today* reports: "Out of 168 nations in a Harvard University study last year, 163 had some form of paid maternity leave, leaving the United States in the company of Lesotho, Papua New Guinea and Swaziland."[49] By 2006, reports the Institute for Women's Policy Research, only 8 out of 100 companies offered the full 12 weeks encouraged by the 1993 law, while 14 out of 100 offered 2 weeks or less. Sixty-two percent of the 100 best companies for working mothers offered 6 weeks or less, half what the law encourages.[50] Why does the United States lag so far behind the rest of the industrialized world in supporting women's time off for infant care? Students are invited to reflect together on what dimensions of ideology and political economy in the United States best explain such differences.

Socioeconomic Class

Socioeconomic class is an arbitrary designation intended to group people whose social interests coincide by virtue of similar levels of wealth, income, power, occupational responsibility, social prestige, and cultural identity.

Although it is difficult to establish criteria separating one class from another, the notion of class is still useful for noting group differences. As we saw in Chapter 4, the dominant ideology of American society derives from an essentially middle-class, Enlightenment vision of progress which holds that rational people can control their own destiny and get what they deserve. Some social critics now charge that this vision is deeply flawed. The world is not as rational as was once believed, nor is human society so easily perfected. These critics also maintain that modern liberalism cannot protect the interests of certain groups in society. The values and worldview of one class do not necessarily apply to people situated elsewhere in the social structure.

The myth that virtually all Americans are middle class obscures what the numbers say. It neatly hides the fact that a small percentage at the top is fabulously wealthy and obscures the reasons why a disproportionate number of people at the bottom are truly distressed. Finally, our long-cherished faith in social mobility is not very well supported by the evidence. Class structure tends to be more rigid than most of us realize or care to admit. This rigidity has been maintained partly in the interest of social stability.[51]

The news media do depict a poverty class, but all too often as a problem of minority populations. Although African American poverty rates are three times White poverty rates, White non-Hispanics still account for 23.7 million of the more than 40 million people living in poverty in the United States. And though 32.7 percent of African Americans and 28.7 percent of Hispanics live in poverty, most members of both groups do not. Still, poverty is a problem that hits ethnic minorities and women, as well as the young, at disproportionate rates.[52]

These poverty rates are particularly disturbing on two counts: their stability over time and their resistance to the increasing educational attainment of all the groups involved. After 1969, for example, White poverty rates increased from 9.5 to 11.3 percent in 1991. During that period African American poverty rates remained essentially stable: In 1969 poverty among Blacks stood at 32.2 percent, and in 1991 it was 32.7 percent. Since 1975, when the government began keeping records on Hispanics, the Hispanic poverty rate remained relatively stable at about 27 to 29 percent, with some slightly better years in the late 1970s. It would appear that in economic periods, good and bad, poverty is a fact of life for large segments of American society, particularly minority populations. Yet for all three of these broad population groups, the educational levels have improved considerably since 1969–1970. White high school graduation rates since then have increased from 54 to 81 percent, while White poverty has increased. Black high school graduation rates have increased from 31 to over 67 percent, while poverty has not abated. And Hispanic graduation rates have increased from 37 to 52 percent, while poverty among Hispanics has slightly deepened.[53]

Class, Income, and Power   If the middle class is defined by income level, it is shrinking. However, if it is defined according to the percentage of white-collar jobs, it has grown overall, since many well-paid manufacturing jobs are being replaced with white-collar jobs at or near the minimum wage. Perhaps the simplest and most common way to designate class is by income bracket. Many economists define the middle class by income levels between $25,000 and $100,000, which includes about 60 percent of the American population, according to the nonpartisan, nonprofit Drum Major Institute for Public Policy.[54]

But there is something very limiting about the emphasis on income shared by liberal and conservative treatments of class differences today. Although the concept of different "classes" of society goes back hundreds of years, and Ben Franklin used the term freely in describing how little class difference existed in American colonial society, a new conception of class was introduced in 1848. In that year, Karl Marx and Friedrich Engels declared in the *Manifesto of the Communist Party,* "The history of all hitherto existing society is the history of class struggle," which may be the most famous single remark on class in the history of social science.[55]

Marx and Engels had a view of class that was very much about power and conflict. It was at once an economic concept, defining classes in terms of who did the wage labor to produce goods versus who owned the production facilities and profits—and a power concept that emphasized the power of one class over the other, and the resulting conflicts between them (see Chapter 4).

Within 100 years, Marx's notion of class as the power of one economic group over another was essentially replaced in American social science. One example of this is W. Lloyd Warner's 1949 book *Social Class in America,* subtitled *A Manual of Procedure for the Measurement of Social Status.* Warner replaced Marx's two opposing classes with multiple gradations of class that would become known as socioeconomic status (SES): upper class, upper-middle class, lower-middle class, upper-lower/ class, and lower-lower class. These gradations were based on family income, educational attainment, occupation, and type and location of dwelling.

The Marx–Engels notion of class was based on division of people into two classes according to their different places in the production of goods: either owning the means of production or working for those owners. The SES version is based more on the idea of people as consumers of goods, defined by their incomes, their purchases, and their ability to buy such social goods as education.

Education: Ethnicity, Gender, and Class

We now turn to the issue of social equity in schooling. Do schools promote the success of some members of society while hampering the success of others? Do schools uniformly serve the needs of all children, or do they contain mechanisms that subtly and systematically discriminate against some students? We do know, contrary to the conclusions of the Coleman Report, that schools in poor areas where academic achievement is low tend to be poorly staffed, overcrowded, underfunded, undersupplied, and wrought with physical and emotional dangers. These conditions represent one form of social inequity. Are there others, perhaps more subtle and even more effective in maintaining the status quo? Are there fundamental differences in the way African American, White, Indian, Latino, or Asian children experience the institution of schooling? Are there fundamental differences between the experiences of male and female, rich and poor? And do schools provide equitable treatment to students who are judged to have physical or psychological disabilities or handicapping conditions? Let us begin this portion of our inquiry by returning to the general demographic categories described earlier to examine the outcomes of schooling for children according to racial and ethnic characteristics, gender, and class differences.

Race, Ethnicity, and Education

In examining the data on schooling, bear in mind the distinction between equality of results and equity of social conditions. Inherited talents and dispositions may vary from student to student, and so different outcomes can be expected for different students. What intrigues and disturbs social scientists is the situation in which whole groups of people systematically perform below the levels of other groups. We must question the institutional arrangements that produce unequal results for certain groups.

We should also bear in mind that much progress has been made in spreading formal education to broader segments of society. This tells us that reform is not futile and that problems can be addressed. In 1900, for example, only about 10 percent of the population graduated from high school. In 1940, 24.5 percent graduated from high school and 4.6 percent completed college. In 1998, in one century's time, 78 percent of White students graduated from high school, while 56 percent of African American students and 54 percent of Latino students graduated from high school.[56] With each successive stage of formal schooling, the pool of minority students eligible for the next stage gets further reduced. About 38 percent of White students enter and 23 percent complete college; 29 percent of African American students enter and only 12 percent complete college. Notably, for African American students entering the nation's 100 highest-ranked institutions, the graduation rate is over 40 percent.[57] Chicanos, Puerto Ricans, and Native Americans complete college at the rate of roughly 9 percent of the population. Completion of graduate or professional school is 8 percent for White Americans, 4 percent for African Americans, and 2 percent each for Chicanos, Puerto Ricans, and Native Americans.[58]

Admission to higher education depends on standardized tests such as the SAT and the ACT.[59] These tests do not measure intelligence. They measure the acquisition of ideas, information, and patterns of thought that are representative of the dominant culture and, as such, are used as predictors of first-year success in college. What they correlate with most strongly is the economic background of the student, with some differences also attributable to gender and ethnicity.[60] This economic variable helps account for the fact that the average SAT score of African American students is 200 points lower than that of White and Asian students on a scale ranging from 400 to 1600. Desegregation has not succeeded in bringing minority students into sufficient contact with the White majority—that is, with the culture that the system rewards. Both neighborhood segregation and school segregation result in isolation from a cultural norm whose values and icons are often different, for example, from those of the African American culture. The following details are illustrative:

- Unbelievably, a recent Harvard study showed that racial segregation in America's schools has been growing, not shrinking, since the 1980s.[61]

In 1968, when the United States first began to survey racial and ethnic population of its public schools, 80 percent of students were white. Today, 44 percent of public school children are minorities. School desegregation reached its peak over 20 years ago. In 1988, one-third of black students attended schools that were at least 90 percent black. Today, partly due to more a more conservative judiciary, 40 percent of black students attend such a school. Black and Latino children are more segregated in 2009 than they were at the time of **Martin Luther King** Jr.'s death.

- Many desegregated schools display *de facto* in-school segregation. The upper-level courses enroll almost all White students, while the lower-level courses enroll mostly Latino and Black students.

- And finally, while the percentage of minority students grows in American schools, and while segregation increases, most teachers are White, whether experienced or new to the profession. Despite a great deal of talk about increasing the diversity of the teaching profession in the past 20 years, more than 85 percent of all pre-K–12 teachers are White—a figure that has changed little over time.[62]

Given the significance of cultural differences and economic deprivation for school performance, it is not surprising that so many African American children encounter difficulty in schools and on standardized tests.

But other ethnic groups also lag behind the performance of the non-Hispanic White majority in ways that must be attributed to socioeconomic factors rather than to native learning ability.

Since the *Brown* v. *Board of Education* decision in 1954, national concern about educational equity has focused largely on the education of African Americans, the second largest American minority group, behind Hispanics. In 2005, the nation's minority population totaled 98 million, or 33 percent of the country's total of 296.4 million.

- Hispanics continue to be the largest minority group at 42.7 million. With a 3.3 percent increase in population from July 1, 2004, to July 1, 2005, they are the fastest-growing group.

- The second largest minority group was Blacks (39.7 million), followed by:
    - Asians (14.4 million)
    - American Indians and Alaska natives (4.5 million)
    - Native Hawaiians and other Pacific Islanders (990,000)
    - The population of Non-Hispanic Whites who indicated no other race totaled 198.4 million in 2005.

Of the national population increase of 500,000 in 2005, about 300,000 was because of natural increase, with 200,000 attributed to immigration.[63] Because the track record of American schools in dealing with some minority groups has not been good, the challenge to educators in the next 10 years is considerable.

Scholastic Achievement Tests do not measure intelligence. They measure the acquisition of the ideas, information, and thought patterns of the dominant culture and, as such, are used as predictors of first-year college success.

Already, according to the U.S. Census Bureau, 2.9 million U.S. households, or 3.2 percent of the nation's total, are linguistically isolated, meaning that "no person above age 14 speaks English fluently." Of these households, 1.6 million speak Spanish and 0.5 million speak an Asian language. The greatest growth since 1980 has been in Asian languages, which are now 4 of the top 10 spoken. Chinese has doubled, and Korean and Vietnamese have more than doubled; with the addition of Tagalog (spoken in the Philippines), they represent over 3 million people. Nationwide, 13.8 percent of all residents speak a language other than English at home.[64]

The Model Minority Historian Ronald Takaki writes that "today, Asian Americans are celebrated as America's 'model minority.'" Takaki cites feature stories in *Fortune* and the *New Republic* applauding Asian Americans as "America's Super Minority" and "America's greatest success story." Takaki objects to this characterization as inaccurate, however. "In their celebration of this 'model minority,' the pundits and the politicians have exaggerated Asian American 'success' and have created a new myth. . . . Actually, in terms of personal incomes, Asian Americans have not reached equality." Income inequalities among Asian American men were evident in Takaki's data: Korean men earned only 82 percent of the income of White men, Chinese men 69 percent, and Filipino men 62 percent.[65] Takaki explains:

> The patterns of income inequality for Asian men reflect a structural problem: Asians tend to be located in the labor market's secondary sector, where wages are low and promotional prospects minimal. Asian men are clustered as janitors, machinists, postal clerks, technicians, waiters, cooks, gardeners, and computer programmers; they can also be found in the primary sector, but here they are found mostly in the lower-tier levels.[66]

Takaki notes that although they are highly educated, Asian Americans are generally not represented in positions of executive leadership and decision making. A comment that appeared in the *Wall Street Journal* is telling: "Many Asian Americans hoping to climb the corporate ladder face an arduous ascent. Ironically, the same companies that pursue them for technical jobs often shun them when filling managerial and executive positions."[67] We are reminded that Asians have a long history of discrimination in the United States, including the Chinese Exclusion Act of the 1880s and the imprisonment of Japanese American citizens during World War II.

Counter to the view that Asian Americans are uniformly successful in school, a Seattle study showed that one-fifth of the school population was Asian American and that as a whole over 39 percent of this group scored in the "at risk" category on the district's standardized reading test, about the same as the Hispanic students. Some Asian American subgroups, notably the Vietnamese, Samoan, and Southeast Asian students, did appreciably worse than the Hispanic students in reading and language skills together, while other groups, such as the Japanese and Chinese, did nearly as well as or better than the White American students.[68] The effects of economic, cultural, and linguistic differences are further revealed in the 1993 study, *Adult Literacy in America*. This massive inquiry shows White non-Hispanic adults to be significantly more proficient in all three literacy areas under investigation than all other population groups, including African Americans, Asian/Pacific Islanders, American Indians, and five different groupings of Hispanic origin.[69]

As we have seen, a term such as "Asian American" can usefully draw our attention to a general classification of people even if there are significant differences among cultural histories within that larger classification. Those cultural histories need further attention. Historian Sucheng Chan notes that almost a million people from China, Japan, Korea, the Philippines, and India came to the United States and Hawaii from the mid-1800s to the early 1900s (in contrast to 35 million European immigrants from 1850 to 1930). Of those Asian and Pacific immigrants, the Chinese (about 370,000) came first, pushed out by poverty and strife in China and attracted by California gold and jobs in Canada and the American West. Next, in the late 1800s and early 1900s, about 400,000 Japanese came, followed by 180,000 Filipinos and less than 10,000 Koreans. They were recruited by Hawaiian sugar plantation owners who needed thousands of workers, and these workers and their families often migrated east to the United States, which soon created an independent flow of immigration from the Asian and Pacific countries.[70] These immigrants, like immigrants from Europe, took jobs, started businesses, sent their children to school, and over time began to assimilate into the mainstream culture, language, and values while still retaining some cultural values and practices from their home countries.

After a sharp reduction in Chinese and Japanese immigration brought about by the world wars and the subsequent cold war, Europeans, Canadians, and Mexicans constituted the great majority of new immigrants to the

United States. Then a new source of Asian American immigration developed during and after the war in Vietnam. The 1965 Immigration Act and its amendments, the 1975 Indochina Migration and Refugee Assistance Act, the 1980 Refugee Act, and the 1987 Amerasian Homecoming Act have facilitated increased immigration from Southeast Asia. Since 1965, Asian/Pacific immigration has increased to the point where it now constitutes half of all immigration into the United States.[71]

Today, the fastest-growing minority group in the nation is Asian and Pacific Americans, more than doubling in size since 1980. It is projected to more than double again by 2020, resulting in an Asian/Pacific population of nearly 20 million in the United States (see Table 12.2). By the early 1990s there were nearly 2 million Asian American children and youth between the ages of 5 and 19 in school in the United States, with heavy concentrations of that population in major cities, where Asian languages are spoken in the home and the community. Interestingly, it was the 1970 class action suit brought by Kinney Lau and 11 other Chinese American students against Alan Nichols and the San Francisco Board of Education that led to the historic Supreme Court case *Lau* v. *Nichols*. The Court's ruling provided the basis for the nation's bilingual education mandates, which in turn have had a profound effect on the education of Hispanic Americans. The Court unanimously ruled that

> there is no equality of treatment merely by providing students with the same facilities, textbooks, teachers, and curriculum;

for students who do not understand English are effectively foreclosed from any meaningful education.[72]

The public at large, and perhaps some educators as well, perceive Asian Americans to be high achievers in school, students who don't need the support of the courts. We have seen, however, that different Asian American groups perform differently in school, and language can be an element of the problem for some students. It will be important for educators not to make assumptions about the growing number of Asian American students in their schools and classrooms other than that all children will need our best educational support. The Asian American experience has been a difficult one even when success is apparent for some families. As Chan writes:

> Thus the acculturation process experienced by Asians in America has run along two tracks: even as they acquired the values and behavior of Euro-Americans, they simultaneously had to learn to accept their standing as racial minorities—people who, because of their skin color and physiognomy, were not allowed to enjoy the rights and privileges given acculturated European immigrants and native-born Americans. In short, if they wished to remain and to survive in the United States, they had to learn how to "stay in their place" and to act with deference toward those of higher racial status. . . . Asian Americans, more so than black or Latino Americans, live in a state of ambivalence—lauded as a "successful" or "model minority" on the one hand, but subject to continuing unfair treatment, including occasional outbursts of racially motivated violence, on the other.[73]

Table 12.2   Asian/Pacific Americans: Population by Ethnicity: 1980 and 1990

	1980	1990	Percentage Growth
Total Asian/Pacific	3,726,440*	7,273,662	95%
Chinese	806,040	1,645,472	104
Filipino	774,652	1,406,770	82
Japanese	700,974	847,562	21
Asian Indian	361,531	815,447	125
Korean	354,593	798,849	125
Vietnamese	261,729	614,547	135
Hawaiian	166,814	211,014	26
Samoan	41,948	62,964	50
Guamanian	32,158	49,345	53
Other Asian/Pacific	226,001	821,692	264

*The 1980 number for Asian/Pacific Americans in this table is slightly higher than that used in other published reports because it includes the count for "other" Asian/Pacific American groups. Other published census reports include only nine specific Asian/Pacific American groups for the 1980 count. Therefore, our calculation of percentage growth is 95 percent, which is lower than the published 108 percent growth.

Source: The State of Asian Pacific America: Policy Issues of the Year 2020 (Los Angeles: LEAP Asian Pacific Public Policy Institute and the UCLA Asian American Studies Center, 1993), p. 12.

- The Asian population rose by 3 percent, or 421,000 people, between 2004 and 2005.

- Of the increase of 421,000 in the Asian population between 2004 and 2005, 182,000 was because of natural increase and 239,000 was attributed to immigration.

- The Asian population in 2005 was younger, with a median age of 33.2 years compared to the population as a whole at 36.2 years. About 26 percent of the Asian population was under 18, compared with 25 percent of the total population.[74]

Hispanic American Diversity   Just as it is an error to generalize about the experience of all 17 different Asian immigrant groups now part of the American culture, it is a mistake to think of "Hispanic" as describing a single people. As Holli and Jones write:

> Hispanic is an umbrella term encompassing Spanish-speaking people of different races and twenty separate nationalities. Hispanics come from as far as Uruguay, at the edge of South America, or as near as Texas, once a part of Mexico. Some have been here since the First World War, while others arrived only yesterday. They include high skilled professionals, political refugees trying to regain what they have lost, and peasants who never had much to lose. They share a language and a culture.[75]

These regional differences remind us of the very different cultural histories of different Hispanic groups. While Cubans began making their presence felt in the 20th century, for example, most heavily immigrating after the communist revolution in Cuba in 1959, Mexican Americans had a long history in the Southwest before it became the southwestern United States. Thousands from Texas to California did not immigrate to the United States at all but found themselves inside this nation's borders when their lands were conquered. It has sometimes been said of that historically Mexican population that they did not cross the border but the border crossed them. Yet people readily assume that most Mexican Americans and other Hispanics are immigrants, if not "illegal aliens." However, three-fourths of the Hispanic population in this country was born in the United States.[76]

Different Hispanic groups have very different migration histories. They have come from different parts of the hemisphere—North America (Mexico), Central America, the Carribean (Puerto Rico and Cuba), and South America—and they have tended to concentrate in different parts of the United States. Carrasquillo writes:

> In general, Mexicans settled in the southwest, the Puerto Ricans and Dominicans in the northeast, the Cubans

Bilingual education and ESL (English as a second language) are designed to enable limited English proficiency (LEP) students to learn better in all subject areas, not just language.

in the southeast and northeast, and South and Central Americans have spread out in the United States with large numbers found in the west and south (Nicaraguans) and in the northeast (Colombians, Peruvians and Ecuadorians) of the United States.[77]

Immigration and migration patterns have had a profound impact on the U.S. population. According to the U.S. Census Bureau, nearly one-fifth of Americans, or 47 million U.S. residents aged 5 and older, spoke a language other than English at home in 2000. That was an increase of 15 million people since 1990, and most of them were Spanish speakers. Spanish speakers increased from 17.3 million in 1990 to 28.1 million in 2000, a 62 percent rise.[78] And in 2008, the Official Census Bureau count is that the Hispanic population has reached 45 million in the U.S., 15 percent of the population.

Then in 2006, the Census Bureau released data on the most comprehensive survey of immigration in the United States ever performed. Immigrants living in U.S. households increased by 16 percent, to a current total of 35.7 million foreign-born residents in the country. The dramatic increase is from 2000 to 2005, with many newcomers moving to states that traditionally have not had many immigrants. The number of immigrants living in American households rose 16 percent, fueled largely by recent arrivals from Mexico, according to fresh data released by the Census Bureau.[79]

Despite their common language and some shared cultural practices and despite their grouping under the designation "Hispanic" for political purposes, differences among these cultures are significant. Referring to the Hispanic experience in Chicago, where half a million Hispanics reside, Holli and Jones write:

> As a result of migration history, each Hispanic group holds deeply felt concerns and attitudes not shared by others. For example, many Cubans share a strong anti-communist sentiment reflected in several organizations formed to oppose Cuban leader Fidel Castro. . . . Cubans, therefore, are suspicious of communist influences in the community-based development efforts that are prevalent in Mexican and Puerto Rican areas. . . . Immigrants from Cuba and South America, because many are affluent, are dismissed by some Mexicans and Puerto Ricans as not really Hispanic.[80]

Such social class differences can influence the experiences of Hispanic children in schools. Those from the lower economic rungs are all too often struggling academically even if they are born in this country.

As Laura E. Perez points out in quoting the National Council of La Raza,

> *Hispanic undereducation has reached crisis proportions.* By any standard, Hispanics are the least educated major population in the United States; Hispanic students are more likely to be enrolled below grade level, more likely to drop out, less likely to be enrolled in college, and less likely to receive a college degree than any other group.[81]

Yet Perez notes different experiences of different subgroups within the Hispanic population and notes that the largest group, Chicanas and Chicanos (Americans of Mexican descent) have the lowest educational attainment. Cubans, in contrast, have the highest, with Puerto Ricans falling closer to the Mexican Americans. The low educational attainment is paralleled by low socioeconomic measures for the Mexican American community. The per capita income cited by Perez for Mexican Americans is about 60 percent that of Whites, and about 38 percent of Mexican American children live in poverty. Perez cites research showing that "Chicanao primary and secondary students are in significant disproportion held back grades and tracked into programs for slow learners or the mentally retarded or 'special' inferior academic or vocational tracks."[82]

Not only economic class differences but language differences as well influence the school experiences of Hispanic young people. Limited English Proficiency (LEP) refers to a level of listening/speaking and/or reading/writing in English that is not at or near native-level proficiency, and by far the largest group of these in the United States is Spanish-speaking. Cisneros and Leone report that of the 2.2 million LEP students in U.S. schools, federal bilingual program funds are provided only for 251,000 of them, or about 11 percent. These authors believe that bilingual programs would assist LEP students' success in schools and that the problem of developing a sound bilingual educational policy will increase as numbers of LEP students rise in the coming years. If the data cited by Cisneros and Leone are reliable, as much as 20 percent of the population of the United States will be Hispanic by the year 2040, though it is not yet clear how many of these will be LEP. Table 12.3 indicates the 10 states with the highest LEP enrollments today. Chapter 13 will address the question of whether we are prepared to meet the challenge of educating these young people in our schools.

Table 12.3 States with Highest LEP Enrollments and Increases

State	1992	2003	Percentage growth
California	1,151,819	1,599,542	39%
Texas	344,915	630,148	83
New York	194,593	302,961	56
Florida	130,131	292,077	124
Illinois	94,471	164,414	70
Arizona	83,643	149,354	79

Source: OELA: Office for English Language Acquisition (formerly OBEMLA), State Resource Pages, 2004, www.ncela.gwu.edu.

Thinking Critically about the Issues   #2

What does the shift from the "Office of Bilingual Education" to "Office for English Language Acquisition" indicate about the policy and ideological drift from the Clinton to Bush administration? Discuss.

Socioeconomic Class and Education

Thomas Toch has observed that the links between family economic status and school labeling are significant:

By far, the nation's economically disadvantaged students pay the highest price for the pervasiveness of tracking in public education. . . . In other words, disadvantaged students [as measured by an index that includes parental income and education, parental occupation, and the presence of consumer goods in a household] are three times less likely to be in the academic track than affluent students are, but three times *more* likely than affluent students to be in the vocational track.[83]

Social class may prove to be a more effective determinant of future opportunities than either race or gender. With the breakdown of housing segregation, minority families that succeed financially can now move into the suburbs, where their children will experience life very much as the children of White middle-class families do. And girls born into middle- and upper-class families now tend to experience a climate more supportive of personal autonomy and professional aspirations than did their mothers and grandmothers. In the case of poor and working-class children, however, the evidence strongly indicates that neither the processes nor the outcomes of schooling are the same as they are for children of the upper classes. Social scientists are now exploring several evident patterns.

Children who are poor tend to go to schools with other children who are poor. Minority students attend school with other minority students of similar socioeconomic

Historical Context

Diversity and Equity Today—Defining the Challenge

For the purposes of studying Chapter 12, you might ask of each decade: Which events have the most *direct significance* for the issues of teaching different social groups of children for different educational outcomes discussed in this chapter?

1960s

1960	Six years after the 1954 *Brown* v. *Board of Education* decision against school segregation, the modern "sit-in" movement begins when four Black students from North Carolina A&T College sit at a "Whites-only" Woolworth's lunch counter and refuse to leave when denied service
1960	President Dwight D. Eisenhower signs the Civil Rights Act of 1960, which acknowledges the federal government's responsibility in matters involving civil rights
1961	Michael Harrington publishes *The Other America,* revealing widespread poverty in the United States
1962	The All-African Organization of Women is founded to discuss the right to vote, activity in local and national governments, women in education, and medical services for women
1962	The Supreme Court orders the University of Mississippi to admit student James H. Meredith; Ross Barnett, the governor of Mississippi, tries unsuccessfully to block Meredith's admission
1963	More than 200,000 marchers from all over the United States stage the largest protest demonstration in the history of Washington, DC; the "March on Washington" procession moves from the Washington Monument to the Lincoln Memorial; Reverend Dr. Martin Luther King, Jr., delivers his "I Have a Dream" speech
1963	Medgar Evers, field secretary for the NAACP, is killed outside his home in Jackson, Mississippi
1964	Civil Rights Act passes Congress, guaranteeing equal voting rights to African Americans
1964	Head Start, U.S. educational program for low-income preschool children, is established
1964	Civil Rights Act of 1964 is passed

1965   United Farm Workers strike
1966   The Medicare Act, Housing Act, Elementary and Secondary Education Act, a new immigration act, and voting-rights legislation are enacted
1966   Black Panther Party founded by Huey P. Newton and Bobby Seale
1968   Dr. Martin Luther King, Jr., and Robert Kennedy are assassinated
1968   Bilingual Education Act passed
1968   American Indian Movement (AIM) launched
1968   Alicia Escalante forms East Los Angeles Welfare Rights Organization, the first Chicano welfare rights group
1969   The Stonewall rebellion in New York City marks the beginning of the gay rights movement

1970s

1971   Busing to achieve racially balanced schools is upheld by the Supreme Court
1972   Title IX Educational Amendment passed, outlawing sex discrimination in educational institutions receiving federal financial assistance
1973   Native Americans defy federal authority at Wounded Knee, South Dakota
1975   Congress passes Education for All Handicapped Children Act (Public Law 94-142)
1978   In *University of California* v. *Bakke,* the Supreme Court disallows a quota system in university admissions but gives limited approval to affirmative action plans

1980s

1980   One million African American students enrolled in colleges and universities in the United States
1980   Ronald Reagan is elected president, promising to reverse the "liberal trends in government"
1982   Equal Rights Amendment fails to win state ratification
1984   Reverend Jesse Jackson becomes first African American to challenge for major party nomination for president
1986   New Hampshire teacher Christa McAuliffe killed along with six astronauts when space shuttle *Challenger* explodes on national TV

1990s

1991   Unemployment rate rises to highest level in a decade
1992   Americans with Disabilities Act, the most sweeping antidiscrimination legislation since the Civil Rights Act of 1964, guarantees equal access for people with disabilities
1993   Pentagon rules "don't ask, don't tell": gays and lesbians may serve in military but may not proclaim or openly practice their sexual orientation
1994   Number of prisoners in state and federal prisons tops 1 million, giving United States the highest incarceration rate in the world
1995   Supreme Court rules against any affirmative action program that is not "narrowly tailored" to accomplish a "compelling government interest"
1996   Census Bureau reports that the gap between the richest 20 percent of Americans and everyone else reached postwar high
1996   Clinton signs welfare reform legislation, ending more than 60 years of federal cash assistance to the poor and replacing it with block grants to states to administer
1996   Clinton signs the Defense of Marriage Act, denying federal recognition to same-sex marriages

2000s

2001   The No Child Left Behind Act expands the federal government's role in elementary and secondary education
2001   A Massachusetts company announces the first-ever clone of a human embryo
2002   Republican Trent Lott, recently chosen as Senate Majority Leader, left office because of remarks that appeared to many to be supportive of racial segregation
2003   Millions of demonstrators around the world take to the streets to protest the planned U.S. invasion of Iraq
2003   In an attempt to stem the widespread practice of Internet filesharing, the recording industry files 261 lawsuits against people of all ages
2003   By a vote of 5–4, the Supreme Court upheld an affirmative action program providing preference to minority candidates for admission to the University of Michigan law school; by a vote of 6–3, however, the Court rejected undergraduate admissions policies that favored ethnic minorities using a numerical formula
2006   The U.S. Census Bureau releases data on the most comprehensive survey of immigration in the United States ever performed; the number of immigrants living in American households rose 16 percent in five years, fueled largely by recent arrivals from Mexico, and dispersing to areas across the United States other than traditional centers of immigration

2008   In U.S. presidential primary elections, the last two candidates vying for the Democratic party nomination, for the first time in history, are an African American man (Barack Obama) and a woman (Hillary Clinton); another prominent Democratic contender was former governor Bill Richardson, a Latino; this is hailed as evidence of dramatic progress for women and for minority populations in the United States, but candidates and commentators observe that the campaign repeatedly surfaces issues of race and gender discrimination in the country

Thinking Analytically about the Timeline

Knowing what you do about economic, social, and educational inequality today, how successful was the activisim of the 1960s in the effort to achieve equality among different social groups?

background. The suburbs, where the wealth tends to be located, are not part of the general tax base that supports inner-city schools, and so there is little or no cross-fertilization of resources or equalization of conditions. The "better" schools get more qualified teachers and the best science labs, computer systems, reading materials, and other resources. Poor children are not expected to be as smart or to work as hard as middle- and upper-class children. They are not expected to know as much or learn as much. They are not expected to do as well in life.[84] These lower expectations lead to differential treatment by teachers.

Parents of upper- and middle-class standing are more likely to become involved in the process of their children's education. They tend to feel welcome in the school environment and to feel that they are equipped to make a contribution.[85] Conversely, the parents of lower-class children tend to feel alienated from their children's schools and education. The cultural patterns and icons of poor and working-class children are different from those of the dominant class, are not a part of the school's culture, are not rewarded, and are not generally understood by teachers whose background differs from that of the students. Disputes over bilingual education further illustrate the separation of culture between schools and their minority students.[86] Chapter 13 will revisit bilingual education as a response to the needs of LEP students.

Thinking Critically about the Issues   #3

Using evidence from this chapter, evaluate the validity of this statement: The demographic and educational data on Asian Americans suggest that educational and social equity efforts should be focused on other ethnic groups, such as African Americans and Hispanics.

Equity, Education, and Disabling Conditions

We have seen how membership in an ethnic or economic group can influence how individuals in that group perform and are evaluated and rewarded in schools and in the larger society. Questions of equity arise, as noted early in the chapter, when individuals' standing in school or society seems to be influenced by their group membership rather than by their individual merits. Such questions apply to children and adults with physically or psychologically disabling conditions. It is not always clear whether such individuals are allowed to succeed on the basis of their own merits, especially when they are labeled and treated as a group for whom expectations of success are lower than for others who have not been so labeled and grouped.

In 1975 Congress sought to address such equity questions with the Education for All Handicapped Children Act (EHA). As Judith Singer and John Butler write:

> Hailed as a "Bill of Rights" for children with handicaps, the law outlined a process whereby all children, regardless of the severity of their handicap, were assured the same educational rights and privileges accorded their non-handicapped peers: "a free appropriate public education." EHA was to transform special education practice across the nation by bringing all states up to the standard that some states, prompted by court action and advocacy by handicapped rights groups, already had adopted.[87]

One result of this act, for reasons soon to be mentioned, has been to increase the number of students designated by the schools as disabled. Currently, 4.3 million students out of a total K–12 public school population of over 47 million students have been designated as students with some sort of special needs. Between 1991 and 2002 there was a 35 percent increase in the number of children designated as "special needs," adjusted for general enrollment increase. The largest and fastest-growing of these categories throughout the 1980s was "learning disabled," which grew from 32 percent of the special education population in 1980 to 46 percent by 1991. In 1991 there were 2,129,000 of 4,710,000 and in 2003 there were 2,846,000 of 6,407,000. That figure has remained stable between 1991 and 2003. According to the *American Almanac*, "speech impaired" was the next largest group, with 22.8 percent of special needs students in 1991, followed by "mentally retarded" (12.4 percent), "emotionally disturbed" (9.0 percent), and then several categories each with no more than 2.2 percent of the population of students designated with disabilities: hard of hearing and deaf, orthopedically handicapped, other health impaired, visually handicapped, multihandicapped, and deaf-blind.[88]

Education analyst Thomas Toch explains part of the reason why learning disabled has become the largest of these categories. First, it "has proven particularly hard to define." Toch elaborates:

> The U.S. Department of Education's definition of the term, "a disorder in one or more basic psychological processes involved in understanding or in using language spoken or written . . . ," is broad. And it is only one of approximately fifty official but often vague and overlapping definitions of the term in use in public education today. As a result, in many school systems "learning disabled" has become a catchall category, and an increasing number of disadvantaged but otherwise "normal" students are being relegated to it, even though P.L. [Public Law] 94-142 prohibits inclusion in the category of students whose learning problems stem from "environmental, cultural or economic disadvantages."[89]

Even Madeleine C. Will, the U.S. Department of Education's official in charge of special education between 1983 and 1989, acknowledged that the "misclassification" of learning-disabled students has become a "great problem."[90] Toch also cites Alan Gartner, a former director of special education in the New York City school system, who wrote, "The students in such programs are not held to common standards of achievement or behavior." Toch elaborates, noting that "only rudimentary skills and topics are taught in classes for the learning disabled, homework is rarely if ever assigned, and the instructors for the learning disabled typically have little or no background in the academic subjects they teach."[91]

The issue of labeling is a critical one in the delivery of services to children with disabling conditions, real or perceived. Certainly some children have such obvious

physical challenges—sightlessness, cerebral palsy, or another multidisabling condition—but the growth of the learning-disabled category suggests that some students are being labeled as disabled who in another social environment might not be perceived as different from other children. Yet with extra funding tied to the identification of students as disabled, there is an incentive for well-meaning educators to label students in ways that might prove damaging. Toch addresses both the labeling and the incentive issues as follows:

> There is a powerful stigma attached to "special education" in the school culture; to be labeled a learning disabled student in a public school is to suffer the disparagement of peers and teachers alike. And rarely do students who have been labeled learning disabled return to the mainstream of school life. Indeed, since schools receive additional funding for learning-disabled students, . . . they have an incentive to continue classifying a student as "LD."[92]

Another incentive for schools to identify more students as learning disabled is that the performance scores of these students will then not be averaged into those of the school district when standards of accountability are implemented as part of the educational reform movement. Even the U.S. Education Department has issued a warning that raised standards may be "exaggerating the tendency to refer difficult children to special education."[93]

Gender and Education[94]

We have discussed how race, ethnicity, economic class, and disabling conditions may influence the experience of schooling of different groups of students. The largest of all "minority" groups (often a majority) is females. In studying the relationship between gender and education, we need to ask, (1) Are the processes of education different for girls than for boys? and (2) Are the outcomes of schooling different for women than for men? The answer appears to be yes on both counts.

During most of Western history, as we saw in Part 1, women were characterized differently from men and those characterizations were used to certify their inferior and subordinate status. Generally women were characterized as emotional, affectionate, empathetic, and more prone to sensual behavior. Men were characterized as rational, just, more directly in the "image of God," and susceptible to seduction by women's sensual intrigues. Thus, men were seen as naturally more fit for social and family leadership roles. Educational institutions and ideals usually reflected these male–female characterizations. Consequently, women were often relegated to education at the mother's side rather than in schools.

Thinking Critically about the Issues   #4

The Coleman Report was a major document in post–World War II American schooling debates. Critically analyze the role that this report—and the response to it by modern liberals (e.g., Daniel Patrick Moynihan and Christopher Jencks et al.)—plays in developing the arguments of this chapter.

Societal Definitions of Gender

Chapter 5 presented a historical account of exclusions and limitations on the education of girls and women in American schools and colleges. The central issue of female education in the last quarter of the 20th century was not *de jure* equal access to educational institutions and curricula. Girls and women are no longer denied equal access to education by law; indeed, since Congress enacted Title IX in 1972 and the subsequent Women's Educational Equity Act in 1974, sex bias in school access, services, and programs has been illegal. However, women are still in practice excluded from educational opportunities through processes more subtle and complex than those prior to Title IX. This *de facto* exclusion of some women from educational opportunities revolves around gender definitions. The central issue in female education today is therefore the problems related to gender and the way those problems affect women's self-concept and academic performance.

Sex refers to the biological characteristics of males and females; *gender* refers to societal expectations, roles, and limitations placed on a person because he or she is male or female. It is the *socially* sanctioned expectations and limitations, not the fact of biological sex differences, that cause the greatest difficulties for females in contemporary educational settings. Gender definitions compose a complex and sometimes subtle set of problems. The powerful impact of gender definitions may be more easily understood when one considers that gender definitions result in learned or socialized "roles."

Most of our social behavior stems from learned roles. There are roles associated with race, social class, occupations, and religion as well as gender. All humans begin to learn some of these roles almost at birth. Other roles are learned at other life stages. It is important to understand that individuals are not entirely passive recipients in this socialization process. Each brings somewhat different experiences to the process. Thus, different individuals will learn slightly or even vastly different roles when exposed to the same socializing conditions.

It is also vital to understand that the socialized roles and the resulting expectations become "reality" for individuals, groups, and society. For example, many 19th-century White southerners believed the role assignment to African American slaves that designated them as happy, passive, shiftless, lacking rationality, and needing direction. The fact that society or a group in society assigns a role to a particular group and believes the reality of that role does not make the role assignment natural, fair, or moral. Nevertheless, it does make it very difficult for anyone to renounce or reject it because one seems to be contradicting reality. The process of role socialization reflects what social theorists call "social construction of reality." One of the factors that contributes to the strength of this social construction of reality regarding roles is that the content of a role always serves a social function. The role content assigned to African American slaves provided the structure of justification for slavery and for the labor system of the antebellum South. The fact that the role assignment serves some social function should not lead one to assume that it is therefore desirable or fair. This assumption is made especially often in the case of gender roles.

Early in the 20th century George Herbert Mead and other social psychologists explained how an individual develops her or his sense of self primarily through interaction with groups. It is the way that others react to the individual which helps define that person's identity. On a simpler level, the nursery story "The Ugly Duckling" demonstrates the process. As long as the baby swan was in the company of ducks who responded to her as if she were ugly, she believed and acted as if she were ugly. Only when she grew into a swan and was confronted with other swans who reacted to her as if she were truly beautiful did she change her understanding of herself. Unfortunately, for most humans it is much more difficult to move from the society of ducks to that of swans.

Sex Roles in Infancy   It is instructive to examine the messages contemporary American society provides for girls at every stage of their maturation. Barbara Sinclair Deckard provides a revealing account of social interactions that confront girls and from which girls must construct their self-identification:

> Before a newborn baby leaves the delivery room, a bracelet with its family name is put around its wrist. If the baby is a girl, the bracelet is pink; if a boy, the bracelet is blue. These different colored bracelets indicate the importance our society places on sex differences, and this branding is the first act in a sex role socialization process that will result in adult men and women being almost as different as we think they "naturally" are. . . . Perhaps because sex is such an obvious differentiating characteristic, almost all societies have sex roles. Women are expected to think and behave differently. The societal expectation and belief that women and men are very different tends to become a *self-fulfilling prophecy.*[95]

These societal expectations strongly influence the way parents react to children. Deckard reports one study where parents described their girl babies as "significantly softer, finer featured, smaller, and less attentive than boy babies, even though there actually was no difference in the size or weight of the two sexes." Another clinical study of college students' descriptions of babies found that the students described a baby as "littler," "weaker," or "cuddlier" when informed that the baby was a girl.[96] Thus, even at birth our evaluations of a baby are directed by social expectations of gender.

Babies are brought home to a gender-directed color-coded world. It is not that blue is better than pink but that all girls are seen as different from boys. This difference continues, according to Deckard, into early infancy as the child begins play activities. Parents encourage boys to take chances and develop independence, while girls are protected and shepherded toward dependence. Boys are praised for aggressiveness, and girls for willingness to take direction. Boys are counseled to be like Dad; girls, like Mom. Parents buy dump trucks for their sons and Barbie dolls for their daughters.

Research indicates that these gender lessons are learned by children. At age 2 or 3 children use the terms *boy* and *girl* as "simple labels rather than the conceptual categories." A year or so later they begin to view the sexes as opposite and distinguish between girls' things and boys' things. And by age 6 both girls and boys begin to enforce sex roles. "Boys more consistently choose and prefer sex-typed toys and activities, and these preferences accelerate with age throughout early childhood."[97] This seems to be the natural outcome of the fact that society generally values male roles and denigrates female roles. Children learn these gender values early. Lawrence

Kohlberg found that among 5- and 6-year-old children, "Fathers are perceived as more powerful, punitive, aggressive, fearless, instrumentally competent and less nurturing than females. . . . Thus, power and prestige appear as one major attribute of children's sex-role stereotypes."[98] Observers should not be surprised that one of the most hurtful epithets to be hurled at a boy is to call him a girl. Gender lessons are among the earliest and most powerful lessons of infancy and early childhood.

Sex Roles in Early Education   Sex roles continue to play a significant role in early education. When children enter preschool, they are confronted with constant reminders of gender differences. Kirsten Amundsen's study found that teachers encouraged boys to be aggressive, assertive, and independent. Girls were discouraged when they exhibited daring or aggressiveness and were encouraged to be timid, cooperative, and quiet.[99] Preschool classroom research shows that girls receive less instructional time, less affection, and less teacher attention than boys.[100]

This pattern continues in primary school. Studies have found that primary school teachers talk more to boys. They talk to boys even when the boys are in remote classroom locations, but they talk to girls only when the girls are close to the teacher. Boys are asked higher-order questions more often than girls. Teachers tend to give boys instructions about projects, while they often show girls how to complete the work. Boys are praised more frequently for the intellectual quality of their work, while girls tend to be praised for neatness and following directions.[101] The lessons are clear: Boys are important and expected to be competent, and girls are unimportant and expected to need help. One study of elementary and middle school students showed that boys shouted answers eight times more often than girls. Moreover, when boys called out answers, teachers tended to listen, but when girls responded in a like manner, they were most often told to raise their hand if they wished to speak.[102] Moreover, teachers are more apt to ask questions of boys when they do not volunteer.[103] Such teacher behavior reinforces the subtle messages girls receive from home and society.

One study asked groups to evaluate a variety of items ranging from paintings to résumés. When the subjects were led to believe that the author of the item was male, they consistently valued it more highly. When a second group was asked to evaluate the same items with the supposed authors' sexes reversed, they consistently evaluated the item lower when they believed its author was a woman.[104] A similar study asked college students to evaluate scholarly articles. In this study both women and men rated the articles higher when they believed they were written by men.[105] Societal messages reinforce school gender lessons. Women are viewed as less capable, and their work is devalued. The result is to emphasize to girls that they are not expected to be independent, creative, intellectually competent, or aggressive. Surely these messages must contribute to the general lack of self-confidence that researchers find in girls at the secondary school level and beyond.[106]

Unfortunately, instructional materials communicate many of the same messages to students. During the last few decades several studies analyzing sex bias in instructional materials have been published.[107] The seminal work was *Dick and Jane as Victims: Sex Stereotyping in Children's Readers.* It analyzed almost 2,800 stories in 134 elementary school readers used in three New Jersey suburbs during the 1970s. Most of the stories were about males: there were two and one-half times as many stories about boys as there were about girls, three times as many stories about men as about women, six times as many male biographies as female biographies, and even twice as many male animal stories as female animal stories. In the stories boys and men were portrayed as brave, creative, smart, diligent, and independent. Girls were most often timid, passive, adventureless, and dependent on boys to help them. Men were shown in 147 different occupations; women were shown in 26, mostly traditional female occupations.[108]

Gender Bias in Secondary Schools   The problem persists in secondary school curriculum materials. A 1971 study of popular secondary U.S. history texts found that women were almost totally absent and that the little material devoted to women tended to be less than complimentary.[109] The 1992 study by the American Association of University of Women, *How Schools Shortchange Girls,* concluded:

> Studies from the late 1980s reveal that although sexism has decreased in some elementary school texts and basal readers, the problem persists, especially at the secondary school level, in terms of what is considered important enough to study.
>
> A 1989 study of book-length works taught in high school English courses reports that, in a national sample of public, independent, and Catholic schools, the ten books assigned most frequently included only one written by a woman and none by members of minority groups. This

research, which used studies from 1963 and 1907 as a base line, concludes that, "the lists of most frequently required books and authors are dominated by white males, with little change in overall balance from similar lists 25 or 80 years ago."[110]

The report noted that research during the 1980s and 1990s in other secondary school subject areas, such as social studies and foreign languages, showed similar developments. Research on social studies texts indicated that "while women were more often included, they are likely to be the usual 'famous women,' or women in protest movements. Rarely is there dual and balanced treatment of women and men, and seldom are women's perspectives and cultures presented on their own terms."[111] In instructional material for foreign languages the research commonly found "exclusion of girls, stereotyping of members of both sexes, subordination or degradation of girls, isolation of materials on women, superficiality of attention to contemporary issues or social problems, and cultural inaccuracy."[112]

Linda K. Christian-Smith's "Voices of Resistance: Young Women Readers of Romance Fiction" highlights an important curriculum issue with respect to young women with low reading ability in secondary schools.[113] Since the early 1980s teen romance novels have become the third most widely read young adult books. They are now a $500-million-a-year industry.[114] The teen romance novels are designed for "reluctant readers" and are sold through school book clubs to students. Often students are allowed to substitute these works for more traditional English readings that they see as too difficult or boring. The books are gender-differentiated, with mystery and adventure books for males and romance, dating, and problem-solving novels for females. Christian-Smith investigated the use of these romance novels in a midwestern city and intensively studied the reactions of about 30 young women to this literature. Not surprisingly, teachers were reluctant to allow their students to abandon traditional literature but quickly acquiesced to pressure from both the students and educational authorities who demanded improvement in reading scores. The young women reported that the romance novels offered "escape, a way to get away from problems at home and school," "better reading than dreary textbooks," "enjoyment and pleasure," and "a way to learn about romance and dating."[115] Christian-Smith found that the young women often developed their own interpretations for the social situations portrayed in the novels. However, because teachers did not require discussion of these readings, the young women seldom had any opportunity to understand the novels in a way that would help them "locate the contradictions between popular fiction's version of social relations and their own lives as well as help them to develop the critical tools necessary to make deconstructive readings that unearth political interests that shape the form as well as content of popular fiction."[116] Thus, "when young women read teen romance novels similar to Quin-Harkins's *California Girl,* they become parts of a fictional world where men give meaning and completeness to women's lives and women's destinies are to tend the heart and hearth."[117]

The teen romance novel issue points to two problems faced by teenage women in American schools. The first is the double burden of gender and class. Working-class and lower-class young women are faced with many curricular choices. Usually they are without guidance. Their families often do not have the experience, information, or knowledge necessary to provide useful guidance. The schools normally abrogate their responsibility to provide the essential guidance. Christian-Smith indicated that teachers did not long insist on providing reading guidance, and when students chose romance novels, teachers did not follow with discussions of the materials, which might have provided an educationally sound experience. Carl A. Grant and Christine E. Sleeter note that schools generally provide resources for students but tend to take a laissez-faire attitude toward students, especially working-class students.[118] These students often follow the "path of least resistance," taking the courses or completing the readings that are easiest or require the least amount of time and work. Often the students do not realize what is at stake when they make these decisions. Schools do not help make the issues clear.

The second problem highlighted by the teen romance novel issue is related to puberty, dating, and romance. As young women enter puberty, they are presented with gender roles by parents, television, movies, magazines, romance novels, and commercials. Most of these sources emphasize the importance of popularity. To be popular in contemporary American society, a young woman must cultivate the interest of young men. This requires both socially conditioned beauty and socially sanctioned demeanor. One of the young women in Christian-Smith's study put the issue succinctly: "The prettiest and most popular girls have their pick of the boys."[119] Girls are constantly bombarded by television and other mass media with models of beauty. Few indeed are the young women who can fit the conventional mold for beauty: slim, long slender legs, large—but not too large—breasts, blond, full-bodied hair, clear and fair complexion, between five feet two inches and five feet five inches tall, fashionable clothes, and the latest cosmetics. It is little wonder that most young women spend a large amount of money, time, and energy on their physical appearance. And the results do not lead to self-satisfaction. A 1990 national survey discovered that only 29 percent of high school girls were "happy the way I am."[120] One should not be surprised that many young women are often depressed or that eating disorders are a problem among teenage girls.

If appearance concerns are not sufficient to distract many young women from academic matters, the demands of demeanor certainly do not contribute to their academic success. By the time young women reach the teen years they have learned the appropriate demeanor for a "popular" girl. Deference to male pride is essential. Girls must never "show up" boys. It is an unusual young woman who does not know that she is not supposed to seem smarter than the boys if she is to be popular. Deckard states, "The really popular, successful high school girl is not a 'brain' or even an athlete; she is a cheerleader. She embodies the supportive and admiring role assigned to girls. She is defined in terms of her relationship to boys."[121] It is relatively certain that this aspect of gender roles does not contribute to the academic success of young women. How much it detracts is a complex and difficult question. Unfortunately, little research has been devoted to it.

Gender and Academic Achievement   There is an enormous amount of research data on academic achievement and participation. Much of it is discussed in the AAUW report. Summarizing some significant recent studies, the report states:

> Despite a narrowing of the "gender gaps" in verbal and mathematical performance, girls are not doing as well as boys in our nation's schools. The physical sciences is one critical area in which girls continue to trail behind. More discouraging still, even the girls who take the same mathematics and science courses as boys and perform equally well in tests are much less apt to pursue scientific or technical careers than their male classmates. This is a "gender gap" our nation can no longer afford to ignore.[122]

It is well documented that as young women advance in high school and college, they increasingly lower their estimation of their academic abilities and lower their goals.[123] Although the process leading to this condition is complex, it is difficult to ignore the central role of gender in the decline of self-confidence among young women. This decline results in many missed academic and career choices.

Thinking Critically about the Issues   #5

What role has gender played in the ways Americans have organized and conducted schooling in recent years? Does your own experience tend to confirm or challenge the portrayal of gendered education in this chapter? Explain how.

Evidence of Concern for Gender Equity It would be comforting to believe that since the passage in 1972 of Title IX, which mandates equal educational opportunity for girls and boys, there has been an increased awareness and marshaling of resources to eliminate gender inequality in American education. Indeed, there have been some encouraging signs. Female participation in high school athletics has increased from 4 to 26 percent, and the success of U.S. women in team sports beginning with the 1996 Olympics was directly attributed to the success of Title IX.[124] There has been a narrowing of the achievement gap between males and females as measured by standardized tests. In some areas curriculum materials are less gender-biased. Some important research on gender equity and education has been published. On the whole, however, it is fair to say that the effort has been poorly financed and its results have been less than sterling.

Between 1983, when the U.S. Department of Education issued its report *A Nation at Risk,* and the release of the AAUW report in 1992, there were at least 35 reports by major educational task forces. Only one addressed the question of gender equity.[125] At least part of the problem may be the fact that few women were members of the 35 groups issuing the reports. One group had no women. In only two did women constitute at least 50 percent of the membership. The 35 groups had a total of 834 male and only 171 female members.[126] Perhaps it should not be a surprise that there was very little mention and almost no discussion of gender issues as part of the problems facing American education.

Lack of adequate female representation in leadership positions is a continuing problem in American education. In 1991 only 9 of the 50 chief state school officers were women. Female representation on American local school boards increased from 10 percent in 1927 to only 33 percent in 1990. Also in 1990, 72 percent of all schoolteachers were women; however, 72 percent of school principals and 95 percent of superintendents were men.[127] According to research by Professor Linda Skrla of Texas A&M, 90 percent of district superintendents are male. Given that 75 percent of teachers are female, the odds that a woman will rise from teaching to the superintendency are 40 to 1.[128] These numbers represent only a slight improvement in the percentage of females in administrative posts in the past 20 years: In 1971, 99 percent of superintendents were men and 72 percent of principals were men.[129]

This disparity does not exist because there are many fewer qualified women available for administrative positions or because men are better educational administrators. One study in the mid-1970s showed that about the same number of male and female teachers had the necessary credentials, the major difference being that the median number of years of teaching experience before appointment to the principalship was only 5 for men while it was 15 for women.[130] There is no evidence to suggest that women are less effective than men as educational administrators. Indeed, a 1960s study by Neal Gross and Anne Trask showed that "professional performance of teachers and the amount of student learning were higher on the average in schools with women principals. Further, the morale of the staff did not depend on the gender of the principal."[131]

Remaining Barriers Many of the obstacles colonial American women faced have been removed. The *de jure* barriers that kept women from educational institutions and professions in the early eras have been dismantled. Women can now enter primary and secondary schools and institutions of higher education. It is illegal to bar a woman from any educational setting simply because she is a woman. Unfortunately, we have discovered that admission to a school does not necessarily mean equal access to an education. Most of the current barriers that deny women equal access to education involve societal definitions of gender and resulting social and educational practices.

Until American society begins to believe that all *persons* are equal and treats everyone as an individual rather than typing people according to group membership, we will continue to experience problems of equal educational opportunity. As long as we believe that women are different from men, with qualitatively different characteristics and abilities, we will continue to believe that certain occupations are for males and certain others are for females. The corresponding denigration of women's gender roles will continue to contribute to the vast inequality of income between women and men. The inevitable result is a lowering of self-esteem and a closure of opportunity for women.

The fact that societal attitudes and behaviors are central to the problem of equal educational opportunity for women is not an excuse for inaction on the part of schools or teachers. If we believe that every child has the right to the best education she or he can absorb, we must act to counter the damaging educational effects of gender bias. As teachers we have an obligation to understand the causes of any problem that inhibits the learning of any group of children. While this is much more easily said than done, schools in several communities throughout the country are showing us ways to teach all groups of children more successfully. We turn to this challenge in Chapter 13.

BUILDING A PHILOSOPHY OF EDUCATION

This chapter has challenged a basic assumption underlying 20th-century schooling in the United States. This chapter's challenge was grounded in a critical examination of social science theories that purport to explain why some racial, ethnic, and social class groups consistently perform more poorly than others in schools and in the economy. In addition, gender differences in school and society were examined briefly for their contribution to understanding inequality and inequity in schooling. The belief that in our educational system a person's success in school and in economic life is based only on his or her innate learning ability has been shown to be unfounded.

Yet liberal ideology locates the source of school success and failure in individuals, and some educators are fond of the maxim that treating all students as individuals will ensure equitable educational experiences. Research indicates, however, that the group differences (among ethnicities or social classes, for example) in school performance cannot be attributed simply to individual talent and motivation without taking into account the cultural contexts that shape individuals. If individuals are

importantly influenced by their cultures and if students in American schools come from identifiably different cultural backgrounds, treating all students as individuals requires attention to the cultural differences.

There is significant evidence that the content and processes of American schools have been relatively hospitable to the achievement of White middle-class students and especially to White middle-class male students. Certainly, females succeed in schools too, as do a great many children from African American, Hispanic, Native American, Asian, and other racial and ethnic backgrounds. But if members of any of those groups perform disproportionately poorly in schools, educators should become alerted to a possible mismatch between the school culture and the home culture of the student. All too often such an observation leads to two destructive misunderstandings. The first is that students from such mismatched cultural backgrounds are culturally (and, it is often thought, linguistically) deficient, and therefore the schools have to correct these deficiencies; the second is that any Native American, African American, or Hispanic child necessarily has cultural barriers to surmount in school.

The cultural deficiency misunderstanding is grounded in the failure to recognize that students from different racial and ethnic backgrounds are already living in full and rich cultures with customs, histories, and linguistic systems that don't need correcting. Educators have no reason to believe that such students are not capable of learning rigorous academic material; to the contrary, there are shining examples of how schools can respond to such students to support their academic success. What needs to be recognized is that the American school's content and processes reflect the values and practices of a dominant culture that devalues the language, values, and practices of many minority cultures. Moreover, such students are too easily judged deficient by inadequate standards that are class- or race-biased. It would be more educationally sound for educators to examine the interaction of the school and the child rather than just the performance of the child as measured by dominant standards. Some educators have developed an analysis of school experience which suggests that schools can indeed respond in ways that secure the success of students from subordinated cultures. Such responses demand a conception of cultural pluralism that respects diversity among peoples and among students' different ways of encountering the school culture. Such a conception may not come "naturally" to a profession that is largely White and socialized by the dominant culture's value and practices.

Gender theory suggests a way to avoid the second misunderstanding: that an individual possesses certain characteristics just by virtue of belonging to a racial, ethnic, or gender group. To make such an assumption conforms to the definition of bias, and this is something most educators wish to avoid. Yet to ignore ethnic or gender differences—to be "gender-neutral" or "race-neutral" in the treatment of students, for example—may overlook a variable that is crucial to understanding a student's experience of the world and of school. If students come to school with very different preparations for success in the distinctively White middle-class school culture, to ignore important differences in the effort to achieve "equal treatment" may lead to very inequitable results. It seems we are caught on the horns of a dilemma: To take account of students' group differences may be biased, but not to take account of them is to treat different learners as if they were the same, which will benefit some learners at the expense of others.

To treat students as individuals is, at its best, to try to take account of and respond to differences among students that have consequences for learning. If gender or cultural background is significant in making a student the individual learner he or she is, there are times when that factor needs to be taken into account. Yet to assume that an African American student should be treated differently simply because he is African American or that a girl needs special treatment because she is a girl is to risk racial or gender bias. Jane Roland Martin's contribution to the solution of this dilemma has been the notion of "gender sensitivity," in which the teacher seeks to recognize when gender is a significant variable in student learning and when

it is not. In addition, part of gender sensitivity is learning to celebrate and reward certain socialized feminine characteristics, such as caring, cooperation, and nurturance—which are often not well rewarded in society or in schooling—while at the same time helping female students develop the skills and self-confidence to succeed in traditionally male domains such as mathematics, science, and community leadership. Similarly, the contributions of all minority groups can be celebrated and affirmed while students from African American, Native American, Asian, and Hispanic cultures are helped to succeed in the linguistic and academic skills that the dominant culture rewards. Culture sensitivity, however, is not just recognizing African American History Month; it is learning to recognize when the subordinating forces of the dominant culture are interfering with a student's learning potential and then seeking to equip students to respond to those forces. Not all African American students, or all American students, experience such interference, and those who do may not experience it all the time. Being culturally sensitive and pluralistic requires one to learn to recognize when race or ethnicity, just like gender or social class, is a significant variable in a student's learning experience.

The consequences of all this for building a philosophy of education are several, but one of the most important is the teacher's commitment to what has by now become a modern cliché: All children can learn. Well, it might be said, of course they can, and some learn quickly and well, while others learn just a little. But some teachers and school leaders maintain the conviction that when every student isn't learning well, something is amiss and needs correction. They know that there are schools in which low-income children of majority and minority backgrounds succeed at very high academic levels, and that such schools serve as proof that all children really can learn well. The most successful teachers try to locate the sources of failure to learn not in the child, or in the child's home, but in the interactions between the child and home and school. With such a conviction, teachers know that the school (and the teacher) bears a major part of the responsibility for improving the learning outcomes.

If you were a parent of a low-income minority child, which kind of teacher would you want your child to have: one who was truly convinced of the ability of all children to learn challenging academic material, or one who was not? *For a teacher to have such a conviction means that he or she does not begin to doubt it when some students do poorly.* Rather, the teacher asks, what are the reasons why these children with so much ability are not learning, and how do we address those reasons? With such a teacher, the classroom becomes a learning environment in which all children really do learn. How the teacher's conviction translates into classroom and school practices to support student success is the focus of the next chapter.

Primary Source Reading

A Public Education Primer: Basic (and Sometimes Surprising) Facts about the U.S. Educational System

This report was written by Nancy Kober, a CEP consultant, and Alexandra Usher, CEP research assistant. Diane Stark Rentner, CEP's director of national programs, and Jack Jennings, CEP's president and CEO, provided advice and assistance. Based in Washington, D.C., and founded in January 1995 by Jack Jennings, the Center on Education Policy is a national independent advocate for public education and for more effective public schools. The Center works to help Americans better understand the role of public education in a democracy and the need to improve the academic quality of public schools. We do not represent any special interests. Instead, we help citizens make sense of the conflicting opinions and perceptions about public education and create the conditions that will lead to better public schools.

Introduction

Public education matters, whether you're a student, parent, teacher, administrator, employer, or taxpayer. Although you undoubtedly know something about public education, you may be unaware of important facts about the U.S. educational system or may be surprised to learn how things have changed in recent years. This edition of *A Public Education Primer* updates and expands on the version originally published by the Center on Education Policy in 2006. Like the first publication, this revised edition pulls together recent data about students, teachers, school districts, schools, and other aspects of elementary and secondary education in the U.S. Included are facts and figures on the distribution of students, student demographics, educational entities and their responsibilities, funding, student achievement, teachers, and other school services. As much as possible, the data compiled here come from the federal government—primarily the National Center for Education Statistics (NCES), the data-gathering arm of the U.S. Department of Education. Where NCES data are not available, we've carefully chosen data from other reliable sources. This primer is meant to give an overall snapshot of elementary and secondary education in the nation's public schools. In general, we've used data for the most recent year available. In many cases, these recent data are compared with data from ten years earlier or with future projections to show how things have changed or are expected to change. A few indicators, such as those relating to student achievement, show trends going back two or more decades to provide a historical perspective. The data in this report represent national averages. The experiences, trends, and issues in your local community may vary somewhat from the broad picture presented here. We hope this primer will provide you with sufficient background information about public education to encourage your interest in education issues and your involvement in your local schools.

Since the 1990s, most racial/ethnic groups have made gains on NAEP in reading and math at grades 4 and 8, but not in grade 12 reading. Moreover, progress in narrowing achievement gaps has been inconsistent. At grades 4 and 8, average scores on the main NAEP have gone up for African American, Latino, and white students since 1992 in reading and since 1990 in math.

Much of this improvement occurred before 2005. Asian American students have also made gains in both subjects since the 1990s, except in grade 8 reading. Native American students have not made significant progress in either subject compared with 1994.

In grade 12 reading, the average 2011 scores for all major racial/ethnic groups did not differ significantly from their 1992 scores. In grade 12 math, average scores for all groups increased from 2005 to 2009.

Reading: Trends by Racial/Ethnic Group in Average Scores on the Main NAEP

Grade and group	1992	1994	1998	2000	2002	2003	2005	2007	2009	2011
Grade 4 (scale of 0–500)										
White	224[†]	224[†]	226[†]/225	224	229	229	229	231[*]	230[*]	231
African American	192[†]	185[†]	193[†]/193	190	199	198	200	203	205[*]	205
Latino	197[†]	188[†]	195[†]/193	190	201	200	203	205[*]	205[*]	206
Asian American	216[†]	220[†]	221[†]/215	224	224	226	229	231[*]	230[*]	231
Native American		211[*]		214[*]	207[*]	202[*]	204[*]	203[*]	204[*]	202
Grade 8 (scale of 0–500)										
White	267[†]	267[†]	271[†]/270		272	272	271	272	273	274
African American	237[†]	236[†]	243[†]/244		245	244	243	245	246	249
Latino	241[†]	243[†]	245[†]/243		247	245	246	247	249	252
Asian American	268[*†]	265[†]	267[*†]/264[*]		267	270	271	271	273	274
Native American		248[*]			250[*]	246[*]	249[*]	247	251[*]	252
Grade 12 (scale of 0–500)										
White	297[†‡]	293[†]	297[†‡]/297[‡]		292		293		296	
African American	273[†‡]	265[†‡]	271[†‡]/269[‡]		267[‡]		267[‡]		269	
Latino	279[†‡]	270[†‡]	276[†‡]/275[‡]		273[‡]		272[‡]		274	
Asian American	290[†‡]	278[†]	288[†‡]/287		286		287		298	
Native American		274[†‡]					279[‡]		283	

[*]Not significantly different from 2011
[†]Accommodations not permitted
[‡]Not significantly different from 2009

Sources: NCES, *The Nation's Report Card: Reading 2011*, figures 4, 5, 6, 7, 20, 21, 22 and 23, http://nces.ed.gov/nationsreportcard/pdf/main2011/2012457.pdf; and *Grade 12 Reading and Mathematics 2009 National Pilot and State Results* (2011), figure 4, http://nces.ed.gov/nationsreportcard/pdf/main2009/2011455.pdf

Math: Trends by Racial/Ethnic Group in Average Scores on the Main NAEP

Grade and group	1990	1992	1996	2000	2003	2005	2007	2009	2011
Grade 4 (scale of 0–500)									
White	220[†]	227[†]	231[†]/232	234	243	246	248	248	249
African American	188[†]	193[†]	199[†]/198	203	216	220	222	222	224
Latino	200[†]	202[†]	205[†]/207	208	222	226	227	227	229
Asian American	225[†]	231[†]	226[†]/229		246	251	253[*]	255[*]	256
Native American			217[*]	208	223[*]	226[*]	228	225[*]	225
Grade 8 (scale of 0–500)									
White	270[†]	277[†]	281[†]/281	284	288	289	291	293[*]	293
African American	237[†]	237[†]	242[†]/240	244	252	255	260	261[*]	262
Latino	246[†]	249[†]	251[†]/251	253	259	262	265	266	270
Asian American	275[†]	290[†]		288	291	295	297	301[*]	303
Native American				259[*]	263[*]	264[*]	264[*]	266[*]	265
Grade 12 (scale of 0–300)									
White							157		131
African American							127		138
Latino							133		175
Asian American							163		161
Native American							134		144

[*]Not significantly different from 2011
[†] Accommodations not permitted

Sources: NCES, *The Nation's Report Card: Mathematics 2011*, figures 4, 5, 6, 7, 21, 22, 23 and 24, http://nces.ed.gov/nationsreportcard/pdf/main2011/2012458.pdf; and *Grade 12 Reading and Mathematics 2009 National Pilot and State Results* (2011), figure 14, http://nces.ed.gov/nationsreportcard/pdf/main2009/2011455.pdf

At grades 4 and 8, progress has been made in narrowing the achievement gap between African American and white students, except in grade 8 math. Latino–white gaps have not narrowed significantly, except in grade 8 reading. Native American–white gaps have not narrowed in either grade or subject. In grade 12 reading, achievement gaps have not narrowed significantly since the 1990s for any racial/ethnic group.

Students from low-income families have lower average test scores than students from higher-income families.

To compare achievement among different income groups, NAEP uses students' eligibility for free or reduced-price school lunches. Students are eligible for free lunch if their family income does not exceed 130% of the poverty level and for reduced-price lunch if their family income is above 130% but below 185% of the poverty level. Students with family incomes above 185% of the poverty level are not eligible for either free or reduced-price lunches. NAEP trends based on family income go back to 2003. On the main NAEP, higher-income students outperform lower-income students. At grades 4 and 8, both reading and math scores are highest for students not eligible for subsidized lunch and lowest for students in the free lunch group. Scores for students eligible for reduced-price lunch fall in between.

Reading: Trends by Income Group in Scores on the Main NAEP

Grade and group	2003	2005	2007	2009	2011
Grade 4 (scale of 0–500)					
Not eligible	229	230	232	232	235
Reduced-price lunch	211	212	215	216	218
Free lunch	199	201	203	204	206
Grade 8 (scale of 0–500)					
Not eligible	271	270	271	273	275
Reduced-price lunch	258	255	255	256	261
Free lunch	244	245	246	247	250

Source: NCES, *The Nation's Report Card: Reading 2011*, figures 11 and 27, http://nces.ed.gov/nationsreportcard/pdf/main2011/2012457.pdf

Math: Trends by Income Group in Scores on the Main NAEP

Grade and group	2003	2005	2007	2009	2011
Grade 4 (scale of 0–500)					
Not eligible	244	248	249	250	252
Reduced-price lunch	230	234	236	235	239
Free lunch	220	224	225	226	228
Grade 8 (scale of 0–500)					
Not eligible	287	288	291	294	296
Reduced-price lunch	271	270	274	276	279
Free lunch	256	260	263	265	268

Source: NCES, *The Nation's Report Card: Mathematics 2011*, figures 11 and 28, http://nces.ed.gov/nationsreportcard/pdf/main2011/2012458.pdf

Similar data by student income groups are not available at grade 12. But NAEP does compare the average grade 12 scores in high-poverty and low-poverty schools, based on the percentage of students in the school who are eligible for free or reduced-price lunch. Since 1998, low-poverty schools have done better on the grade 12 NAEP than high-poverty schools.

As all of these data indicate, large achievement gaps exist between higher-income and lower-income students.

Average Grade 12 Scores by School Poverty on the Main NAEP, 2009

School poverty (percentage of students In school eligible for free or reduced-price lunch)	Average grade 12 reading score (scale 0–500)	Average grade 12 math score (scale 0–300)
0–25% (low-poverty)	299	166
26–50%	286	150
51–75%	276	140
76–100% (high-poverty)	266	130

Source: NCES, *The Condition of Education 2011*, tables A-11-2 and A-12-2, http://nces.ed.gov/pubs2011/2011033.pdf

Developing Your Professional Vocabulary

A good understanding of this chapter's content would include an understanding of why each of these terms is important to education.

cultural deprivation
  studies

Education for All
  Handicapped Children
  Act

equality

equity

ethnicity

GI Bill of Rights

glass ceiling for women

Hispanic versus Latino

meritocracy

model minority

race

racism

sex-role socialization

sex versus gender

socioeconomic class

Questions for Discussion and Examination

1. Using your reading and any pertinent, reliable outside source, identify and discuss the educational and social consequences of the trend in school segregation.

2. We often think of "motivation" as a highly individualistic character trait. Individuals in any racial or ethnic group may be highly motivated to achieve or apparently lacking in motivation altogether. Yet some authors argue that ethnicity is important in shaping motivation to learn and other attitudes toward schooling. Evaluate this argument.

3. This chapter focuses on gender as well as on race, ethnicity, and social class in considering the issue of educational and social equity as it concerns different groups of students. To what degree do you find that considering all these different variables in one treatment obscures important differences among them, and to what degree does it illuminate similarities that are profitably considered together? Defend your view.

 Online Resources

Go to the Online Learning Center at **www.mhhe.com/tozer7e** to take chapter quizzes, practice with key terms, access study resources, and link to related websites. Also available on the Online Learning Center are PowerWeb articles and news feeds.

Diversity and Equity Today **Meeting the Challenge**

Chapter Overview

Chapter 13 extends the discussion of social and educational inequality in Chapter 12 to examine some of what we know about meeting the challenges of diversity and equity in today's schools. Whereas Chapter 12 might be described as a "language of critique" in its description of social and educational inequality, Chapter 13 presents a "language of possibility." It is possible to understand teaching and learning differently and to teach in ways that include more children in successful learning experiences.

How teachers understand the complex relationships between the school and the child plays a major role in how they respond to the learning needs of their students. This chapter explores several different theoretical approaches to understanding why different social groups perform differently in school. These approaches include genetic deficit theory, cultural deficit theory, and critical theory. The last theory incorporates cultural difference theory, cultural subordination theory, and resistance theory in trying to explain educational inequality in the United States.

Finally, the chapter turns to a variety of pedagogical (teaching) approaches to supporting success for all students. These approaches include multiculturalism, culturally responsive pedagogy, bilingual and ESL instruction, and gender-sensitive teaching, among others. The Primary Source reading highlights the importance of teaching which includes students' cultural references in all aspects of learning.

Bilingual and multicultural education remain controversial in the 21st century.

Chapter Objectives

Among the objectives that Chapter 13 seeks to achieve are these:

1. This chapter should help students examine the arguments regarding the power of social inequalities and inequities to influence unequal educational outcomes in schools today, and discuss to what degree they agree or disagree with the authors that teachers and schools can have a significant influence that resists the impact of social inequalities.

2. Students should consider Jane Elliott's famous classroom experiment, the Discrimination Day exercise, and discuss what sense can be made of it today.

3. Students should be able to assess and discuss which main theories of social and educational inequality seem best able to explain the data on social and educational differences described in Chapters 12 and 13.

4. Another aim is to consider the degree to which the gender-sensitivity concept applies to race sensitivity or ethnicity sensitivity in the effort to respond to the needs of different children. How similar are these ideas to culturally responsive pedagogy?

5. Students should be able to consider the examples of successful learning by low-income and minority students and discuss whether these examples are applicable to other teaching settings.

6. Students should be able to analyze different approaches to multicultural, culturally responsive, and inclusive pedagogy and discuss which seem most valuable for achieving the national teaching standards described in Chapter 10.

7. Finally, students should understand the importance of school organization to teacher success. If teachers want to have maximum impact on student learning, they must better understand how schools must be led and organized for that impact to be optimal.

Analytic Framework
Diversity and Equity Today: Meeting the Challenge

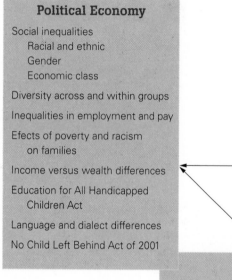

Political Economy

Social inequalities
   Racial and ethnic
   Gender
   Economic class

Diversity across and within groups

Inequalities in employment and pay

Efects of poverty and racism
   on families

Income versus wealth differences

Education for All Handicapped
   Children Act

Language and dialect differences

No Child Left Behind Act of 2001

Ideology

Equal opportunity for all

Meritocracy

Genetic deficit theory

Cultural deficit theory

Racism

Sexism

Disability bias

Social construction of which
   human differences matter

Neoliberal commitment to
   market competition

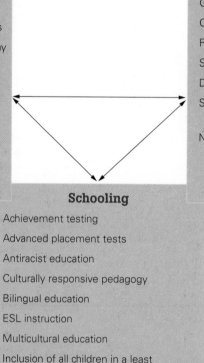

Schooling

Achievement testing

Advanced placement tests

Antiracist education

Culturally responsive pedagogy

Bilingual education

ESL instruction

Multicultural education

Inclusion of all children in a least
   restrictive environment

Organizing schools for student success

Rise of charter schools

Introduction: Does Social Inequality Necessarily Determine Educational Outcomes?

Chapter 12 explored how such variables as race, ethnicity, gender, and economic class can affect different groups' experiences in school and in the wider society. It seems clear that many people experience social institutions differently, often according to their group memberships. Further, these differences seem regularly to advantage those whose group membership is White, economically middle class or better, and male. This is not to claim that people of color, people from low-income backgrounds, and females never achieve as much as White middle-class males do in this country's educational and social institutions; virtually anyone reading this book knows of such successes. Rather, we tried to show that trends or patterns of inequality often influence an individual's life chances. Individuals succeed or fail not simply due to their native abilities and applied efforts but also on the basis of their membership in one or more ethnic, gender, or economic groups.

Institutional biases along lines of class, ethnicity, and gender are, as Chapter 12 demonstrated, alive and persistent in the 21st century. Simply watching the newspapers carefully can reveal dimensions of the challenge to educators, as research studies are often reported in the press. For three decades, for example, girls have scored substantially lower than boys on the SAT exam, thus receiving only 40 percent of the National Merit Scholarships despite outnumbering boys 56 to 44 percent in taking the PSAT, the first step in that scholarship competition.[1] Turning to the performance of Hispanic and African American students on standardized measures of academic proficiency, recent comparisons to White non-Hispanic students show that the gaps between minority and majority students are once again growing.[2] Meanwhile, despite a booming national economy, the poverty rates for African Americans and Hispanics are more than double, almost triple, the poverty rate of White non-Hispanics, which bodes ill for future educational attainment for large numbers of people from those ethnic groups.[3]

These inequalities take place in two (among many) problematic institutional contexts: The first is the wider U.S. society, in which countless acts of overt racism (including prosecutable hate crimes) are committed every day, while institutional racism is thoroughly embedded in the socioeconomic system.[4] The second context is school, in which taken-for-granted approaches to testing, grouping, and tracking students work against the success of low-income and minority students while appearing to many educators and the public to be consistent with good educational and democratic practice.[5]

It is important to engage in critical study of the nature and consequences of racism and sexism in this country's social institutions, especially in schools, which influence young people's perceptions of themselves and others in important ways. But critique is not enough; it is also important to examine ways in which schools and teachers can serve the interests of all children equally well rather than contributing to the position of advantaged groups. Although we can certainly locate the sources of school inequities outside the schools, in the larger socioeconomic system, this wider system does not necessarily *determine* what goes on in schools and classrooms. It would be more accurate to say that the wider society *influences* the classroom. Just as individuals from disadvantaged groups can succeed against the statistical odds, individual schools and classrooms can chart independent courses against prevailing patterns of inequality. But how? What do we know about schools and teachers that might help us see what must be done so that children from low-income groups, for example, will be allowed to succeed on the basis of their talents rather than on the basis of whether they were born into the "right" demographic category? The purpose of this chapter is to examine what we know about meeting the challenges of diversity and equity in contemporary schools.

Jane Elliott's Experiment

It is enlightening to reflect on the following experiment conducted by an elementary school teacher. She was initially motivated toward the experiment in April 1968 while watching the television coverage following the murder of Martin Luther King, Jr. The death of a national figure was sad enough, but Jane Elliott was stunned by the insensitivity of newscasters interviewing African American leaders: "Who is going to hold your people together now? What will they do? Who will control their anger?"[6]

Elliott was a third-grade teacher in Riceville, Iowa, an all-White, all-Christian farming community, population 898. When she arrived at class the next day, her children had already heard the news and Elliott had already made up her mind to teach them what prejudice and discrimination were really about. The experiment she conducted that day and repeated in subsequent years would eventually make national news. It would also project Elliott to national prominence following a documentary special by ABC News titled "The Eye of the Storm."[7]

Most of the children had had little contact with African American people. What they knew of African American people would have come from their parents and from television, and so Elliott started there. As the children described their impressions, a pattern began to emerge: African American people were poor; they did not manage as well as White people; they were not as smart, not as honest, not as civilized, not as moral; they fought a lot and were prone to riot; they smelled bad. The children were not being mean or vindictive. They were saying matter of factly what they had picked up here and there regarding the nature of African American people. Elliott pressed further. Are African

Strong teachers find ways to create connections with all their students.

Americans discriminated against? Yes. Do they deserve it? Well, maybe not. How would you feel if you were discriminated against? Not very good. These were all nice, appropriate responses. But Elliott knew from experience and observation that these are the common sentiments of a nation that is, by common consent, fundamentally racist.[8]

How would it feel to be an African American boy or girl? Would you like to find out what discrimination feels like? she asked. Her students said they would. The children were lumped into two status groups. The 17 children in her class who had blue eyes became one group. The other group, called the "brown eyes," consisted of the 11 children whose eyes actually were brown and the 3 children who had green eyes.

"Today, the blue-eyed people will be on the bottom and the brown-eyed people on the top," Elliott explained. To their questioning looks she added, "What I mean is that brown-eyed people are better than blue-eyed people. They are more civilized than blue-eyed people. And they are smarter than blue-eyed people."

Because of these traits, Elliott continued, different rules would have to apply, depending on whether a child had blue eyes or brown eyes. Brown-eyed children could use the drinking fountain, but blue-eyed children had to use a paper cup. Brown-eyed children would have five extra minutes of recess. But inferior, blue-eyed children were not allowed to play with them unless specifically invited to do so. Nor could blue-eyed children use the big playground equipment. Brown-eyed children got to go to lunch first, could go back for seconds, and could choose their lunch-line partners. None of the blue-eyed children were allowed those special privileges. When asked why these various rules should apply, the brown-eyed children eagerly supplied reasons. Jane Elliott nodded her approval.

The children caught on very quickly and assumed their various roles with chilling realism. Once the sense of it was clear, the roles became real and the children entered into the constructed reality. Elliott continued to play her role. Every time a blue-eyed child made a mistake, she identified it as evidence of inferiority. Every time a blue-eyed child had difficulty reading, she shook her head and asked a brown-eyed student to take over. She said later:

> By the lunch hour, there was no need to think before identifying a child as blue- or brown-eyed. I could tell simply by looking at him. The brown-eyed children were happy, alert, having the time of their lives. And they were doing far better work than they had ever done before. The blue-eyed children were miserable. Their posture, their expressions, their entire attitudes were those of defeat. Their

classroom work regressed sharply from that of the day before. Inside of an hour or so, they looked and acted as though they were, in fact, inferior. It was shocking.

The following Monday she reversed the scheme: "I lied to you on Friday. I told you brown-eyed people were better than blue-eyed people. That's not true. The truth is that blue-eyed people are better than brown-eyed people. They are smarter than brown-eyed people. They are more civilized. They are. . . ."

As easily as that she reversed the roles, and once again the children entered into their assigned identities. Those children who had been discriminated against on Friday were gleeful, and many of them were bent on revenge. Those brown-eyed children who had felt like "hot shots," who had felt "smarter, bigger, better, and stronger," quickly learned how demoralizing it is to be categorized and treated as inferior.

Later, Elliott would write:

All of the children enjoyed being considered superior. . . . But some of them took a savage delight in keeping the members of the "inferior" group in their place, in asserting their superiority in particularly nasty ways. . . . Nor had I realized until I saw it how destructive a feeling of inferiority really is, how it can literally change a personality, how it can drag down efficiency, destroy motivation.[9]

An Important Note of Caution

Jane Elliott's Discrimination Day exercises were repeated for many years, and at the request of business and government she has subjected adult audiences to the same experience, with strikingly similar results. With few exceptions, members of a group identified as superior tend to act and feel superior. Curiously, Elliott discovered that members of the "superior" group gained new confidence in their schoolwork, glimpsed new capabilities in themselves, and actually shot ahead academically. Those identified as inferior tended to accept the constraint, lost confidence in themselves, could not concentrate, and suffered a measurable decline in academic performance. When the experiments were over, Elliott conducted a skillful debriefing, restored shattered friendships and crushed egos, and helped her students draw from the experience the important lessons it contains. However, we urge you *not* to conduct this experiment in your own classrooms. The primary reason is that experiences of discrimination are so hurtful that they can be damaging. It is doubtful, for example, that

a university research ethics committee would approve Elliott's experiment today because of the very real potential for psychological harm. It is particularly sobering to consider that such harm can occur in a day or two of experiencing discrimination, while some people suffer discrimination all their lives.

Thinking Critically about the Issues   #1

What are the lessons teachers might learn from Jane Elliott's experiment? How would these lessons be important to a teacher's effectiveness, in your view? What dangers can you see in trying to implement such an experiment in today's classroom? Explain.

Theories of Social Inequality

Elliott's experiment can help us develop a theory, or at least hypotheses, about factors that lead to school success or failure. If we are to understand how to respond to social and educational inequalities, we need to understand them. In this section we will examine three different theoretical approaches to explaining inequality in society and school performance. These theories differ significantly in where they locate the source of inequality. A theory of genetic inferiority locates it in the individual; a theory of cultural deprivation, also recognizable as cultural or linguistic deficit theory, locates it in the individual's home culture; finally, a theory of cultural subordination locates it in the structural relationships of power differences between different social groups. These labels suggest which theory Elliott may have found most compatible with her own view. Can you identify it?

The first two theories, genetic inferiority and cultural deficit, are taken from liberal social and intellectual traditions which assume that individuals craft their own destinies. The theories often lead to the conclusion that society and the law should leave individuals alone to rise or sink according to their own merit. Most important, these theories tend to embrace a particular view of the world that we have previously identified as a middle-class, scientific worldview, a cultural orientation that Henry Giroux refers to as technocratic rationality.[10] As we shall see, theories of genetic or cultural inferiority stem from modern liberalism because they leave the existing social order essentially intact, vindicate the liberal resistance to a government role in individual (but not corporate) economic success and failure, and locate the source of social inequalities in the victims.

The third type of theory derives from that branch of thought called critical theory, which is characterized by a willingness to question the existing rules of society and locate the source of inequalities in social structural arrangements rather than in inherent characteristics of individuals or groups. Critical theorists see inequitable power relations in society as the fundamental source of social, economic, and educational inequality among social groups.

Genetic Inferiority Theory

Long ago, Plato wrote that one social group could subordinate another social group only if it were able to tell convincingly a certain "necessary lie." The full account is in the *Republic,* Book III (414A–415E). Here is the essential passage:

> "[You] are all brothers in the city," we shall tell them in our fable, "but while God molded you, he mingled gold in the generation of some, and those are the ones fit to rule, who are therefore the most precious; he mingled silver in the assistants; and iron and brass in farmers and the other craftsmen."

This necessary lie is known as the "myth of the metals." It is the classic statement of that imagined, God-given superiority that justifies social inequalities in the minds of those whose chances for success have been greatly enhanced by inclusion in the dominant social group. Later, during medieval times, the nobility was sanctioned by church authorities as having been ordained by God to rule over commoners. The myth of the metals persists to the present. Here, in a passage written in 1923 by educational psychologist Lewis Terman, is its modern equivalent dressed in scientific terminology:

> Preliminary investigations indicate that an I.Q. below 70 rarely permits anything better than unskilled labor; that the range from 70 to 80 is preeminently that of semi-skilled labor, from 80 to 100 that of the skilled or ordinary clerical labor, from 100 to 110 or 115 that of the semi-professional pursuits; and that above all these are the grades of intelligence which permit one to enter the professions or the larger fields of business.[11]

Terman played a leading role in applying the Stanford-Binet intelligence test to the mass testing of students in the United States. The myth of the metals has thus been transformed into the myth of the IQ score, whose scientific appearance makes it seem even more convincing and potent. Terman's passage offers an explanation of social classes in terms of genetic intelligence. The same criteria can easily be adapted to racial and ethnic inequalities. Here is a sample from a passage written during the early part of the last century by Henry Garret, in a pamphlet titled *Breeding Down:*

> You can no more mix the two races and maintain the standards of White civilization than you can add 80 (the average I.Q. of Negroes) and 100 (average I.Q. of Whites), divide by two and get 100. What you would get would be a race of 90s, and it is that 10 percent differential that spells the difference between a spire and a mud hut.[12]

Garret does not specify to which aspects of White civilization he is referring—certainly not the period of the Thirty Years' War in Europe, when ignorance, disease, poverty, filth, and sheer animal savagery prevailed. Nor does he specify which standards of African civilization he has in mind, though he probably does not mean the ancient dynasties of Egypt, which influenced the culture of all modern European civilizations.

The genetic, or biological, argument has been used repeatedly to rationalize the suppression of racial minorities, females, and people from lower socioeconomic classes. It has been particularly evident in White discrimination against African American people, in part because of its continuity with the racist beliefs that once sustained slavery. Terman, like many other leading educators of his time, actively supported the *eugenics* movement in the United States. Various eugenics societies sought to create policies that would control the gene pools of Americans by means of selective marriage, sterilization, and immigration restrictions. Genetic deficit theory has received its modern, pseudoscientific defense by Arthur Jensen, William Shockley, and Richard Herrnstein, each of whom has over the past 30 years used interpretations of IQ and standardized test scores as part of the effort to explain the "findings" of the Coleman, Moynihan–Mosteller, and Jencks et al. studies.[13]

The Jensen and Herrnstein studies, conducted in the late 1960s, were built on the following assumptions: (1) IQ tests are valid measures of intelligence, (2) intelligence is mainly inherited, (3) lower IQ test scores indicate that African Americans are less intelligent and therefore less educable than Whites, (4) occupational level and income are dependent on intelligence and resulting academic achievement, and (5) poverty therefore results from inherited deficiencies in the poor, not from unequal school and employment opportunities.

Critics of the Jensen–Herrnstein thesis quickly replied that IQ test scores measure the cultural knowledge of children from middle- and upper-class families, not intelligence. They also pointed out that Jensen and Herrnstein offered no evidence linking intelligence with heredity and that their database was a patchwork accumulation of old, flawed data that had been compiled over 60 years by various researchers under varying conditions and for various purposes. It is ironic that as a result of the Jensen–Herrnstein episode, IQ tests have lost much of their credibility, although they continue to reinforce racial stereotypes of "deficient" minority groups.

The breakdown of genetic inferiority theory began as a result of the Army Alpha test administered to 1,750,000 draftees during the 1917 call-up for World War I. The test purported to show the mental age of White recruits as several years higher than that of African Americans. In fact, 89 percent of the African American men tested were ranked as "morons," and thousands of men who had recently immigrated from Europe scored as "feeble-minded." In 1945 Harvard anthropologist Ashley Montague made a more detailed analysis of the data. He pointed out that the gap between White and African American test scores was greatest in the deep South and smallest in the North. Furthermore, African Americans in the northern states had scored better than Whites in the southern states. The claim that the test measured "intelligence" was finally called into question, as was the conclusion that African Americans were less intelligent than Whites. Since scores varied by location, it was clearly not the case that genetic endowment was being measured.

Theories of genetic inferiority break down anytime social and educational programs successfully close the gap between test scores for different groups—a phenomenon that is happening with increasing frequency as educational practice becomes better adapted to cultural differences. Finally, genetic theories of inequality have lost favor because they deal with only a small amount of evidence and because the conclusions drawn from them do not lead in a useful direction. They neither stimulate strong research nor contribute to the resolution of social and educational inequalities. Nonetheless, in 1994 Herrnstein drew national attention with publication of *The Bell Curve,* in which he and his coauthor,

C. Murray, again claimed to have found genetic origins of intelligence differences among different groups. Again their research was widely refuted.[14]

Cultural Deficit Theory

After modern theories of genetic inferiority lost favor in the early 1970s, liberal social scientists began searching for another model that would help organize the data and explain the persistence of low achievement rates in minority youth. They began to reason that these children were not biologically inferior but came from an inferior home environment. Poor and minority children did not have the same social, cultural, and intellectual opportunities as middle-class White children; they did not travel, visit libraries and art museums, go to zoos, or participate on a daily basis in sophisticated adult conversations. Their poorer, less-educated parents were unable to prepare them for school. So went the cultural deficit argument.

The language of the "ghetto" was brought into question and attacked as an inadequate linguistic vehicle. Poor children, especially poor African American children, did not grow up in circumstances that would teach them to think, reason, and speak in the manner generally approved by the dominant social order. Thus, it was reasoned, they were victims of linguistic or cultural deficiencies. When these children entered the formal stages of their public education, many of them could not compete with White children whose preschool experience had prepared them for the cultural environment and the social structure of the school.[15] This preparation gap served as the pretext for grouping poor and minority children into vocational and nonacademic curricula and placing them into educable mentally handicapped (EMH) classes at a rate three times that of their White peers. The penalty for not coming to school equipped with the approved social and cultural graces was relegation to an education devoid of challenging intellectual content. In short, poor and minority students were expected to fail and were put into programs that encouraged failure.

Since some children entering school could not read or count, did not know the letters of the alphabet, and could not name the colors, claims of cultural deficiency were not entirely groundless. Poverty does take its toll on children. Thus, there was enough evidence supporting the theory of cultural deficiency that it gained widespread acceptance.

Programs such as Project Head Start were designed to equip minority and poor children from "underprivileged backgrounds" with the same school-readiness abilities as their better-off peers from the mainstream culture.

Theories of cultural and linguistic deficiency guided the whole compensatory education movement during the 1960s and 1970s. These programs were attractive because they left existing social and cultural arrangements intact, located the problem of low achievement in the student's home culture, and seemed to point the way toward a solution. If children were growing up with an inadequate grounding in the basics, society merely needed to provide remedial education to older students and compensatory or preventive schooling for young children. Programs such as Project Head Start were designed to equip minority and poor children from low-income backgrounds with the same abilities and knowledge that their better-off peers had.

These programs did show results. Follow-up on Project Head Start and similar programs revealed positive effects for children on standardized tests, dropout rates, and so forth. But despite these encouraging results in the area of schooling, inequalities persist. One major problem is the fact that cultural deficit theory takes for granted the legitimacy of the dominant culture and does not call into question its privileged status as the cultural norm. Since children from minority cultures are tested and evaluated using the language and social knowledge of the dominant culture, they are operating at an obvious disadvantage. Standardized testing procedures do

not test for the competencies developed in other cultural and linguistic systems.

Critics argue that there is not a single American culture but numerous cultures competing, intermingling, and informing one another. And in each culture, or subculture, ways of behaving and relating to others, ways of knowing, ways of thinking, modes of expression, shades of meaning, icons and symbols, memories and history—the thousands upon thousands of subtle associations on which a cultural system is built—are different. What was needed, some scholars argued, was a theory to help investigate the relationships among these several cultures in order to understand social, economic, and political patterns of dominance and subordination.

Critical Theory

Liberal theories are characterized by the tendency to take for granted the existing social, economic, and political organization that has come down from classical and Enlightenment conceptions of humanity and society (see Chapter 2). In the two liberal social theories we have examined so far, middle-class, Anglo-American, Protestant culture serves as the conceptual frame of reference from which all other groups are considered. This cultural

Cultural deficit theorists view bilingual education as an attempt to overcome cultural "deficiencies," while cultural difference theorists view it as the school's attempt to help students from different but equal cultures adapt to the mainstream culture.

hegemony has been allowed to happen, critics charge, because the dominant social group has accumulated sufficient power to make its standards prevail.

Whereas liberal theories derive from the entrenched position of the dominant culture, critical theory is characterized by a willingness to call into question the whole social order and to place the concept of *power relations* at the center in discussing a problem. In the critical theories we are about to examine, the point of view of each party or group involved is legitimated and their relationships are considered. Critical theories rely on multiple frames of reference, as the following examples illustrate.

If a child from a minority family is having trouble in school, the quality of any assessment of the conflict depends greatly on what is taken for granted. School authorities may point to the child as the source of the problem. The child acts bored, seems uncommitted, uninterested; the child fantasizes, skips school, gets into fights. Since Anglo children do well at the same school, how can the problem lie with the school? School officials blame the child. Yet the parents know that the child does well at home, relates appropriately to family and peers, and is curious and generally cheerful. So how can the problem lie with the child? The parents suspect the school of discriminatory practices toward the child.

Although the authority of the school probably will prevail in a situation like this, there is clearly a problem here that cannot be resolved merely by recourse to hierarchical superiority.

Critical theory asks that we look not so much at the child or at the school, both of which function well in certain contexts, but at the *relationship* between the child and the school as the primary unit of analysis. Specifically, critical theory looks at the power relationship between the child's culture and the culture of the school in an effort to assess conflicts. Instead of assuming the greater legitimacy of one culture over another, it asks, What is the power relationship among these cultures? When a conflict between child and school is identified, it is therefore treated not as a problem residing in the student but as a mismatch between the culture of the student and the culture of the school, in which the school represents the power of the dominant culture and the child's culture is relatively powerless in this context. A search for solutions to these mismatches is then conducted in such a way that both the needs of the student and the legitimate interests of the larger society are respected.[16]

Cultural Difference Theory   Perhaps nothing has so clarified the inadequacy of traditional social science scholarship as the advance of minority interests in this century. As minority groups have gained power, their self-assertion has compelled the dominant culture to recognize alternative frames of reference. The historical bondage to a single, monolithic cultural perspective runs counter to the dimension of the classical liberal view of education that values understanding and adaptation of multiple perspectives as the key to a fuller and more mature intellect. And it cherishes a diverse and many-sided understanding of perennial issues as the key to human liberty. But modern liberalism has privileged another strain of classical liberalism in which the cultural products of classical societies have become canonized as "culture."

The transition from cultural deficit theories to cultural difference theories marks a significant passage in the social sciences. It represents a transition from a fixed frame of reference to multiple frames of reference. Anthropologists and linguists, disgraced by their willing endorsement of imperialism, nationalism, and cultural jingoism leading up to the world wars, have acquired a respect for human culture in all its splendid variety. This view allows for a richer, more appreciative sense of the human cultural panorama. Other social scientists have followed suit.

Cultural difference theory, then, respects the variety of human cultures and assesses the relationships among various cultural groups. Within education, one of the first tasks of cultural difference theory has been to investigate how the experience of schooling differs for children who grow up in different cultural settings. In the past, educators and others have tended to undervalue the fact that children generally do well when schooled and evaluated within their own culture. It is when children of one culture are schooled by the institutions of another that cultural mismatches result. This is what happens to countless minority children in American society.

Cultural mismatches can occur with respect to subject matter, learning styles, ways of knowing and demonstrating knowledge, attitudes toward authority, modes of behavior, and socialization patterns, among other factors. For example, Native Americans, who as scholars have mastered the dominant culture in addition to their own, point to many discontinuities between the Indian culture and the dominant Anglo culture of the United States. For the most part, Indians are not a competitive people in the ways that the larger society sanctions. Tribal life tends to encourage social cohesion and cooperation rather than competitive individualism.

Also, the Indian worldview does not separate mind and body as Western civilizations have done since the time of Plato. Indians cherish a tribal life quite different from the acquisitive, self-assertive materialism of cosmopolitan Westerners, who have largely tried to subdue nature rather than live in harmony with it.

Learning styles also differ between Anglo and Indian cultures. Whereas White children are accustomed to trying things, to learning new tasks by trial and error, Indian children are often taught to learn by observation. They are taught not to make mistakes but to acquire new skills by watching them being performed.[17] In school, Native American students resist being pushed into public learning tasks they have not yet mastered. Interpreted through Anglo criteria, the hesitant Indian youth seems to lack initiative.

There are other differences between Anglo culture and Indian culture: the interpretation of history, for example, and the criteria for what constitutes excellence in art, literature, and music. And there are extreme differences in how best to interpret and understand nature, human society, and the relation of humanity to nature. American Indians have never fully accepted the notion that the land can be parceled out and sold to the highest bidder. European science and technology, for all its pragmatic success, has had a devastating impact on cultures around the globe through the imperialism, cultural hegemony, and environmental damage it has produced. American Indians have good reasons not to be enamored of the consequences.

The Native American example is simply an illustration. Other cultural groups, too, differ in important ways from the dominant group. Traditional definitions of culture have centered on the formal expressions of a people's common existence—language, art, music, and so forth. If culture is more broadly defined to include such things as ways of knowing, ways of relating to others, ways of negotiating rights and privileges, and modes of conduct, thought, and expression, the term *culture* applies not only to ethnic groups but to people grouped on the basis of gender and social class. Gender identity, then, entails cultural as well as physiological dimensions. And class is characterized by differences of culture as well as differences of socioeconomic status. By expanding the idea of culture to include gender and social class distinctions along with race and ethnicity, we can analyze how different groups experience the world and express themselves and how patterns of dominance and subordination arise between groups.

That schools participate in the subordination of certain social groups is something scholars have resisted examining. The traditional view has held that schools are neutral places where common learning experiences prepare everyone equally well for life in an equitable society. However, critical and radical scholarship of recent decades shows how schools serve as instruments of social policy in which the interests of the dominant group are served at the expense of other groups.

Mechanisms of subordination do not depend on physical duress. Far more effective is the subtle yet systematic reduction of self-confidence—the crippling of personal and group identity that this chapter describes. Castelike minority groups have regularly and deliberately resisted assimilation for the express reason that it would destroy the last vestiges of their group identity and solidarity. And the schools, when faced with such resistance, have tended toward punishment and the withholding of opportunities for status and mobility. Failure to conform to Anglo standards of culture and civility is treated as evidence of an inferior intellect. Our current task, then, is to assess how cultural differences become the basis of cultural subordination.

A common retort is, "If the Irish made it, the Germans made it, and the Asians are making it, then why can't the African Americans, why can't the Indians, and why can't the Mexicans and Puerto Ricans?" The answer is that many of them are making it, but for those who are not, it is necessary to recognize that group status depends on historical circumstances. John Ogbu suggests differentiating among minorities according to whether they have autonomous, voluntary immigrant, or castelike backgrounds.[18] Autonomous minorities, such as the Amish, Jews, and Mormons, differ from African Americans and American Indians, for example, in their histories: The former groups came to North America voluntarily and were able to control some of the terms of their relationship to the dominant culture. Blacks and Indians, however, were enslaved and/or murdered, and those historical legacies remain.

Voluntary immigrant minorities, such as the Irish and the Germans, also have very different historical circumstances from people of color.

Finally, castelike minorities, writes Ogbu, are groups that have been relegated to a subordinate status by legal and extralegal means. As in the traditional caste system of India, the rules of structured inequality are well defined and fairly rigid. African Americans, Mexican Americans, Native Americans, and Puerto Ricans are cited as examples of castelike minority groups that experience forms of institutional racism and bias not generally directed at other minority groups.[19]

Cultural Subordination Theory Cultural subordination theory (the last of the theories summarized in Exhibit 13.1) examines the social processes that lead to lower status for minority groups. It also examines the inequalities that appear to be structured into the social system. Subordination theory followed difference theory when scholars finally realized that discrimination was not an accidental or inevitable consequence of cultural differences. Cultural subordination theory has application not only to relations between dominant and subordinate racial and ethnic groups but to gender relations and social class relations as well.

Exhibit 13.1   Summary of Differences between Various Theories of Inequality

	Genetic Inferiority	Cultural Deficit	Cultural Subordination
Causes of inequality	Inherited	The inferior cultural background of the poor and the superior cultural background of the rich	Power differences embedded in the socioeconomic structure between the rich and the poor
Remedy	None	Force poor to acculturate to the culture of the advantaged class	Change power relationships in the socioeconomic structure
Implications for schooling	Track the poor into less rigorous or vocational programs	Compensatory classes to eliminate the cultural commitments of the poor and provide them with superior culture of the advantaged class; tracking	Critical teaching about power relationships to arm the poor to demand changes and inform the rich that some of their advantages are socially derived and not personal traits

To see what role schools might play in perpetuating social inequalities, Jean Anyon studied five modern elementary schools in New Jersey. In the study, schools serving working-class children were found to be relatively indifferent to academic content beyond "the basics." Teachers rated their students as "lazy" and as not knowing anything. Instruction was by rote and repetition, intended to inculcate basic facts and procedures. Teachers insisted that students follow set ways of doing things. Upon interviewing students, Anyon concluded that most had not developed a very clear sense of how knowledge is created. When asked where knowledge came from, they said it came from "books," "the dictionary," even "The Board of Ed."[20] Anyon documented how students resisted and sabotaged teachers' efforts and, in turn, how teachers resented students.

Anyon then investigated conditions in a school serving "middle class" students, a school serving the children of "affluent professionals," and finally a school in which the children's parents were described as the "executive elite." Throughout this progression up the socioeconomic ladder, the quality of education improves and the nature of instruction changes. The teachers no longer emphasize "the basics" but concentrate on helping students develop advanced intellectual skills. "My goal is to have the children learn from experience. I want them to think for themselves," said one teacher from the affluent professional school.[21] In such schools, students are urged to make decisions, to think things through, to take risks and test hypotheses. Individualism is emphasized, and students understand that knowledge is something people construct from their interaction with the world. They have a good sense of how science operates.

Finally, in the "executive elite" school, teachers frankly confessed that these children of privilege would "go to the best schools, and we have to prepare them." High expectations have been set by parents who are accustomed to having their phone calls answered and their instructions followed. These are educated parents who know how to demand an education for their children. Students in such a school might be asked to debate whether the Athenians were wrong in condemning Socrates for his beliefs.[22] They have a conservative view of knowledge and see it as a store of traditional information that must be mastered. However, most also understand that the knower plays a significant role in knowing. These students are competitive, confident, and relatively sophisticated in their mastery of the school environment.

If the schools Anyon describes are representative, it must be conceded that the processes and outcomes of schooling are not the same for all children in American society. Far from serving as the great equalizer in our society, the schools tend to prepare students for destinies that generally correspond to their social class background. Nor is it any secret how this occurs.

In modern public schools, selection into a given track starts as early as the first grade, when assignments are made to reading groups.[23] Longitudinal studies show very little movement up or down once a student has been assigned to an ability group. But on what basis is this initial selection made? The Coleman Report (1966) showed a high correlation between "achievement" and social class. It also showed that this correlation was not significantly affected by elementary education.[24]

Modern schooling includes testing, tracking, and counseling children into separate destinies. Ability grouping has been criticized as undemocratic because it tends to restrict the entry of many students into opportunities for stimulating higher-order thinking and perpetuates the social class structure of the larger society. John Duffy cites research showing "the numerous advantages for the academic, personal and social development of all students when they learn in cooperative, heterogeneous settings as opposed to homogeneous, competitive settings."[25]

Boards of education, school administrations, and teaching staffs are all composed primarily of White, middle-class professionals with a heavy ideological commitment to the status quo. By the year 2000 minority enrollments in public schools reached 40 percent, yet the percentage of minority college students preparing for roles in education has actually declined in the last 10 years.[26] This cultural imbalance between teachers and students probably will further perpetuate the status quo.

The curriculum also reflects a largely White, male, middle-class worldview. It emphasizes mathematics and science and favors intellectual skills and knowledge over social skills. The literature studied sends a message to minority children that culture is a largely European attainment. The civics, history, and sociology studied tend to vindicate the European experience while devaluing the experience of African Americans, Native Americans, women, Asians, and Latinos.

The structural arrangements of schools and classrooms can also affect how students fare. Large classes may favor socially assertive people. Female and Native American students may, more frequently than their classmates, find a competitive, urgent, and noisy classroom climate uncongenial. And the minority student sitting among self-confident members of the dominant group may feel continuously threatened by the lack of reinforcement for his or her own cultural background. The climate of learning is important because confidence is so necessary to a person's growth and yet so fragile during the years of childhood and adolescence. As Jane Elliott's Discrimination Day exercise demonstrated to dozens of well-off students, it takes very little to shatter that confidence and so turn a potential winner into a second-class citizen.

> ### Thinking Critically about the Issues   #2
>
> While there is a clear contrast between cultural deficit theory and cultural difference theory, cultural subordination theory is presented as flowing conceptually from cultural difference theory. What are the conceptual connections between the latter two theories, in your view, and what difference might these connections make to a classroom teacher?

> ### Thinking Critically about the Issues   #3
>
> A basic assumption underlying American schooling has been that students' success in school and in economic life is based on their learning abilities and attitudes in an equitable educational system. Critically analyze this assumption.

Resistance Theory   One corollary to cultural subordination theory is resistance theory. Researchers have found that students experiencing discriminatory practices soon retreat into a posture of resistance in which they stop working with the school and its agents. Adolescent girls, for example, have been found to act dumb, curtail their efforts, and refrain from demonstrating intellectual prowess because of social pressure and the assumption that as females, they will eventually assume a role subordinate to males in society. Although this is less true of upper- and middle-class girls, some female high school valedictorians lose confidence when they get into college. This rarely happens to male valedictorians, however, since society expects them to continue doing well.

Some African American students, too, exhibit resistance strategies. Cooperation with the schools means capitulation to an alien culture that has long held African Americans in bondage. To take on the cultural attributes of White people is to enter into a client relation with the dominant culture, to engage in "Uncle Tomming." But that is exactly what is required in order to succeed. And so young African Americans, caught between cultures, tend to drop out of school at disproportionate rates and to engage in otherwise self-destructive patterns of resistance. Students with lower socioeconomic backgrounds also engage in resistance strategies. And when they do so, an unsophisticated teaching staff can conclude that they have no interest and no talent for learning.

To better understand how cultural differences can set up patterns of interference with learning, let us examine a topic that has received a great deal of attention in recent decades: the English dialect characteristic of inner-city African American children. The misunderstandings on this topic run deep, and the consequences are severe when a teacher misinterprets why the language of African American children differs from that of the dominant culture. The study of African American English is representative of cultural differences in general and of the consequences that occur when subordinate cultural patterns conflict with those of the dominant group. Let us look first at the basic ideas that most linguists who have studied this problem generally agree on.[27]

First, all of the thousands of languages and dialects that currently exist are capable of supporting complex cognitive processes, and all can adequately express human problems, dreams, and scientific, aesthetic, historical, philosophical, and religious impulses. All these languages can and do generate or borrow new words to express new ideas or relationships. All have a complex grammatical structure. In short, it is not true that one of these languages or dialects is superior or inferior as a means of communication within a culture. "Cockney" is as good as BBC English, African American vernacular is as good as standard American speech, and Spanish is as good as French, English, or German.

Second, the prestige attached to a language or dialect depends not on its intrinsic linguistic characteristics but on the economic and military power of the group that uses it as a primary language. Thus, English is granted higher value than French in Canada. Sometimes a ruling class will decree its language as the official language of the state in order to entrench its own power while making access more difficult for those speaking other languages. For example, after the Norman conquest, French became the official language of England. In Greece the ruling class even created an artificial language to exclude lower-class individuals, who could not afford tutors, from full participation in the civil process.

Third, all people, including children, learn better if they can better comprehend the language of instruction. Thus, instruction in the mother tongue is most effective. *It is necessary, however, for nonstandard speakers eventually to learn to negotiate the standard language if they wish to experience success where that language is dominant.*

Fourth, not all nonstandard speakers have developed their primary language to the same degree. Those who are less proficient in their own native language may need ongoing work in that language in order to acquire the new language. Thus, a bilingual program whose goal of a speedy transition to standard English leads to elimination of instruction in the primary tongue may be less efficient with many students than a program in which primary language instruction is continually developed.

Fifth, the way a child's primary language is valued, especially by teachers and peers, strongly affects the student's self-concept. A positive self-concept is essential for effective learning. Thus, when teachers continually tell students that the use of their primary language is wrong or incorrect, the effect is to diminish the students' confidence as learners and potentially reduce their ability to learn.

Sixth, every language has a variety of linguistic styles. For example, a professor's standard English speech will vary according to whether he or she is lecturing to a class, delivering a paper before professional colleagues, or rehashing the "good old days" with high school friends. It is important to remember that a person's total linguistic capacity cannot be measured through a single linguistic environment. Unfortunately, we frequently make such linguistic generalizations about schoolchildren.

Seventh, a major cause of reading failure is the cultural conflict that occurs between standard-English-speaking teachers and children from nonstandard language backgrounds. The problem is not the difference in cultural or linguistic values but the teacher's ability to recognize and address those differences.

Thinking Critically about the Issues   #4

What sort of classroom practices might follow from cultural subordination theory as opposed to cultural deficit theory? Explain.

A Useful Digression: Bilingual and ESL Instruction as Bridges to English Proficiency

Language and culture are intertwined in complex ways. Since the 1974 *Lau* v. *Nichols* decision, which affirmed the right of language minority students to receive instruction tailored to their needs, the United States has struggled with different approaches to supporting the academic success of limited English proficient (LEP) students, who are more likely to perform poorly in school and to drop out of school than are English proficient students. LEP students are defined by the 1978 Amendments to the Bilingual Education Act as "individuals who come from environments where a language other than English is dominant" or "where a language other than English has had a significant impact on their language proficiency" and who therefore "have sufficient difficulty speaking, reading, writing, or understanding the English language to deny such individuals the opportunity to learn successfully in classrooms where the language of instruction is English or to participate fully in our society."[28]

Because these students are widely distributed throughout the nation, 42 percent of all public school teachers have at least one LEP student in their classes. Only 7 percent of these teachers have classes with over 50 percent LEP students. Of all schools with LEP students, 76 percent provide programs in English as a second language (ESL), while 36 percent offer bilingual education programs.[29] There are very different approaches to instruction for LEP students. Because there are more than 10 times as many Spanish-speaking students in the United States as the next highest language (French), Spanish-speaking students are most likely to receive bilingual instruction (academic instruction in two languages, intended to progress to proficiency in English), though bilingual education may be offered in other languages, too, when the concentration of students is high enough (as it is, for example, in a Polish neighborhood in Chicago). Given the hundreds of thousands of students who speak French, Chinese languages, Korean, Arabic, Portuguese, German, Cambodian, Greek, Italian, Yiddish, Farsi, Russian, and scores of other languages, however, it is not possible to offer instruction to those students in their home language and in English, as bilingual programs do. Therefore, ESL programs are offered so those students can spend concentrated school time making a transition from their language to English.

What might be said at this point is that such programs have been devised for LEP students as a bridge from where they are linguistically to where they need to be to partake fully of the educational and economic benefits of the dominant culture. It was apparently this kind of reasoning that led the Oakland, California, School District to pass a new policy that stirred national controversy, although the basic idea was an admirable one: that many African American students are entitled to a linguistic bridge from their Black English Vernacular (BEV)—or "Ebonics," as the Oakland Board of Education termed it (from ebony phonics)—to standard English. Unfortunately, the policy was unclear enough, and the public (including some African American leaders) hostile enough to the policy, that a great national stir was created, obscuring some of the more interesting educational issues at stake for African American youth who speak a nonstandard form of English.[30] Eventually, the Oakland board revised the policy to make clear that it was not trying to teach Ebonics on an equal footing with standard English but was trying to honor the richness of students' language and culture as a foundation on which to build academic success, including proficiency in standard English.

BEV: Language and Cultural Subordination

Although the Oakland board did not cite this passage from author James Baldwin in their policy, it offers a telling comment on the relations between language and culture. It was written 25 years ago in an essay titled "If Black English Isn't a Language, Then Tell Me What Is?" Baldwin writes:

> The brutal truth is that the bulk of the white people in America never had any interest in educating black people, except as this could serve white purposes. It is not the black child's language that is despised. It is his experience. A child cannot be taught by anyone who despises him, and a child cannot afford to be fooled. A child cannot be taught by anyone whose demand, essentially, is that the child repudiate his experiences, and all that gives him sustenance, and enter a limbo in which he will no longer be black, and in which he knows he can never become white. Black people have lost too many black children that way.[31]

Baldwin concludes that Black English, with its own cultural history and purposes unique to its origins in slavery, is clearly a language. This thought bears further examination.

One of the first difficulties an African American child (not all, but some) might encounter in public school is the well-meaning teacher who tries to correct his or her

Increasingly, it has become recognized that definitions of good teaching must address teachers' abilities to create successful learning environments for children of all ethnic backgrounds.

speech patterns. A child who says "They be mine" or "I ain't got none" is speaking a dialect of American English known as Black English Vernacular (BEV). Bolinger and Sears explain:

> According to one theory, the historical basis for Black English is the African pidgin used in the slave trade, the only language available to blacks sometimes thrown together from different language backgrounds to keep them from communicating effectively with one another. As with all pidgins . . . the nuisance irregularities of morphology were discarded and syntax was simplified. The result was that as blacks gradually rebuilt a speech community in the lands to which they were transported, they had to reconstitute the grammar, which retained certain features of the pidgin even while it was being "relexified" with words taken in constantly from the standard.[32]

The authors quote a passage from Fickett[33] describing verb tenses in BEV: "I do see him." "I did see him." "I done seen him." "I been seen him." These passages lead progressively into the past tense. In the opposite direction, future tenses leading away from the present include these: "I'm a-do it." "I'm a-gonna do it." "I gonna do it."

BEV systematically drops the copula (connective link) "to be" when it is actually superfluous in Standard American English (SAE). "He going" instead of "He *is* going," and "It mine" instead of "It *is* mine" lose nothing in precision or meaning if the convention of usage is understood. Other examples of linguistic differences include "I ask *did he do it*" in place of the "if" construction in SAE: "I asked *if* he did it." The expression "John moves" in SAE becomes a double-subject "John, he move" in BEV. Third-person possessives in BEV drop the "s": "John cousin" instead of "John's cousin." In BEV the present tense of the verb "to be" is rendered "be": "He *be* here." This is a durative (continuing) form of the present tense to indicate ongoing action as distinguished from a fleeting condition in the present. Last in this incomplete list of features is the use of negative concord (double negatives) such as "I don't want none" and "He ain't got none."[34]

Related to the linguistic issue are patterns of thought, ways of knowing the world, that are embedded in the language of African American students. When these ways of knowing and of expression encounter scholastic challenges phrased in standard English, patterns of interference can be set up that result in confusion and nonlearning. In mathematics classes, for example, conflicting ways of employing English prepositions can make word problems difficult for some African American students, as well as LEP students, to understand and solve.[35]

At issue here is neither the presumed inadequacy of African American intellects (genetic inferiority) nor the supposed inadequacy of African American culture as a preparation for school (cultural deprivation) but rather a mismatch between African American culture and the dominant Anglo culture of America. Aware of the long history of racial antipathy, some African American students may resist assimilationist policies designed to "whiten them up" to Anglo standards. The teacher's understanding of cultural differences largely determines whether the uniqueness of African American culture becomes a cause of celebration or a source of discrimination. William Labov writes:

> When the everyday language of black children is stigmatized as "not a language at all" and "not possessing the means for logical thought," the effect of such labelling is repeated many times each day of the school year. Every time that a child uses a form of the BEV without the copula or with negative concord, he will be labelling himself for the teacher's benefit as "illogical," as a "nonconceptual thinker." This notion gives teachers a ready-made, theoretical basis for the prejudice they may already feel against the lower-class black child and his language. When they hear him say *I don't want none* or *They mine,* they will be hearing, through the bias provided by the verbal deprivation theory, not an English dialect different from theirs, but the primitive mentality of the savage mind.[36]

Of course, it must be emphasized that the term *Black English* should not be taken to mean that all African American children speak in that linguistic system. The language one speaks is not biologically determined but is a function of one's cultural background. A great many African Americans grow up in the dominant Anglo culture, speaking standard English. Millions of African American children, however, especially those from poorer families that tend to live in neighborhoods segregated from White communities, speak a language different from that of the larger society and the school because that is the dominant language of their neighborhood and of their home. Theories of cultural subordination show that traits valued in the larger society are those that are also valued and rewarded in the schools. Cultural traits subjected to discrimination in the larger society become the target of subordination in the schools. The question arises, then, of what to do with students whose cultural background is not legitimated by the dominant society in schools, business, and other institutions, though it may be valued in such cultural forms as hip-hop and rap music.

Benign neglect is not the answer. Critical theorists point out that when cultural differences are simply ignored or overlooked by well-meaning teachers, students suffer in the long run because they wind up unequipped to function in the larger society. To leave students as they are is not to empower them to function in the larger society. Characteristics of racial and ethnic minorities, females, and people of lower socioeconomic backgrounds should not be subjected to patterns of censure. But if differences are to be accepted and celebrated, new approaches to education must be found.

Thinking Critically about the Issues   #5

If you do not speak Spanish and therefore cannot offer bilingual instruction, how can you best support the learning of children whose first language is Spanish and who are limited in their English proficiency? How does this relate to the approach you will use with speakers of English as a second language from other language backgrounds, such as those of Asia or Eastern Europe? Finally, is any aspect of your approach relevant to supporting student learning for speakers of Black English Vernacular? Explain your position on all three issues.

Pedagogical Approaches to Pluralism

There appear to be three general strategies for teachers to use with respect to cultural and social group differences. These terms are being used here in the broadest sense to include differences grounded in race and ethnicity, social class, and gender. The three approaches are to (1) ignore differences and to teach to a single standard, (2) seek to eliminate differences by having all students conform to a single standard, and (3) teach in a manner sensitive to differences *without* being biased by group differences, that is, without attributing characteristics to individuals by virtue of their membership in groups. The first two ways tend to be a denial of differences or of the significance of differences. The third approach, based on sensitivity toward differences, rejects the stigma associated with such differences and chooses instead to use these cultural resources as a bridge to the kinds of learning valued by the dominant culture.

Gender Theory: An Illustration of Sensitivity to Differences

Feminist theory has explored these three possibilities with respect to gender issues. In the early phases of modern feminist thinking, scholars asked that girls not be socialized differently from boys or treated in a different manner. While this "gender-free" approach to education overcame some of the grosser policies of sex discrimination, it did not serve to equalize educational results. By ignoring gender-based differences in favor of gender "neutrality," teachers allowed those differences to create a subtle form of social dominance as boys proved more gregarious and forceful in their classroom tactics.

In the second phase of feminist theory, scholars recommended strategies to compensate or equalize the effects of gender differences within the classroom as it was traditionally arranged. This "bias" approach proved less than satisfactory because it still retained a male-oriented framework. It assumed that standards of male performance should be the norm and that through active compensatory measures females could be brought into line with those standards.

In a third phase of thinking, feminist scholars have begun to reconsider all the operational premises of education and society. Instead of looking for ways to overcome the differences between males and females, they have begun a quest to ensure that these differences are recognized, respected, and incorporated into the mainstream of American society and education.

Current research is exploring the extent to which female traits are grounded in socialization and the extent to which they are grounded in biology. The assessment may never be completed because biology and environment interact in inseparable ways, and at present the preference is to see biological determinism as a relatively weak component of genderization. What is significant to the current discussion is not whether nature or nurture is most responsible for gender differences but how those differences are treated by society. When women are relegated to a subordinate status, traits of personality and intellect thought of as female also become devalued. In American society these traits include nurturance, feeling, caring, empathy, social interest, and the capacity to cultivate meaningful and long-range social relationships. Education, designed initially to serve in the preparation of males, emphasizes qualities deemed

In a just society, race and culture would not serve as obstacles to school success.

essentially masculine: rationality, individualism, detachment, commercial productivity, competitiveness, and aggressiveness.

Jane Roland Martin has pointed out that traditional theories of education often took no account of gender and seldom even mentioned females.[37] When females were mentioned, as in Rousseau's *Émile,* the objective was to cultivate a companion for the male, not an interesting, autonomous being. Or in the case of Plato's *Republic,* women were trained as if they were men, without recognition of gender differences. Martin describes the traditional American education as one based on attributes generally associated with males and devoted primarily to the "productive" aspects of society: aspects valued for their production of material well-being. She urges adaptation of a "gender-sensitive" approach that gives equal value to such "reproductive" virtues as caring and nurturance and intimate social connections and in the process helps reconstruct society along more cooperative and humane lines.

A gender-sensitive approach to education requires that schooling be conducted so that traits deemed to be feminine are not stigmatized but are recognized, respected, and cultivated by everyone. In this broadened view, with both men and women freed from gender stereotypes, everyone stands a better chance of developing in accordance with his or her unique nature rather than in accordance with restrictive stereotypes. Martin writes:

"Care, concern, connectedness, nurturance: these are as important for carrying on society's economic, political, and social processes as its reproductive ones. If education is to help all of us acquire them, the ideal of the educated person and the theory of liberal education . . . must be redefined."[38]

Martin's call for gender-sensitive education has a great deal in common with the general pluralistic trend currently emerging in educational theory and practice. This trend does not assume that all performance differences in schools are due to gender, ethnic, or social class differences. Rather, it recognizes that group differences often *can* be important in explaining the relative performance of individuals and that teachers can teach more effectively if they are sensitive to such cultural origins of individual performance. Sophisticated classroom approaches to cultural pluralism, which include consideration of gender and social class, may well become the next major educational reform, one in which teachers will be asked to teach in a way that is "culturally responsive" or "culturally relevant" to their students' diversity (see Exhibit 13.2). Gordon Berry has suggested that "the secondary school pupil has a moral responsibility to learn, understand, and respect values inherent in other races and religions, and to practice behaviors that will ensure dignity and civil rights to males and females of cultural groups different from [his or her] own."[39]

Exhibit 13.2   Culturally Relevant Pedagogy

Culturally relevant pedagogy is an approach to teaching and learning that empowers students intellectually, socially, emotionally, and politically by using cultural referents to impart knowledge, skills, and attitudes (Ladson-Billings, 1994). Unlike sociolinguistically grounded approaches such as *culturally appropriate* (Au & Jordon, 1981), *culturally congruent* (Mohatt & Erickson, 1981), and *culturally responsive* (Cazden & Leggett, 1981; Erickson & Mohatt, 1982), the cultural referents in this pedagogical perspective are not merely vehicles for bridging or explaining the dominant culture; they are aspects of the curriculum in their own right. Three dimensions of culturally relevant pedagogy are its emphases on academic achievement, maintaining and supporting cultural competence, and engendering a sense of sociopolitical critique.

Teachers who might be regarded as *culturally relevant* educators demonstrate broad pedagogical understandings in three areas: conceptions of themselves and others, conceptions of social relations, and conceptions of knowledge. In their conceptions of themselves and others culturally relevant teachers.

- Believe that all students are capable of academic success,
- See their pedagogy as art—unpredictable and always in the process of becoming,
- See themselves as members of the community,
- See teaching as a way to give back to the community, and
- Believe in the Freirean notion of "teaching as mining" or pulling knowledge out, not putting it in.

In their conceptions of social relations, culturally relevant teachers

- Maintain fluid student-teacher relationships,
- Demonstrate a connectedness with all students,
- Develop a community of learners among students, and
- Encourage students to learn collaboratively and be responsible for each other.

In their conceptions of knowledge, culturally relevant teachers

- Understand that knowledge is not static—it is shared, recycled, and reconstructed,
- Understand that knowledge must be viewed critically,
- Recognize the need to be passionate about knowledge and learning,
- *Scaffold* or build bridges to facilitate learning, and
- Believe that assessment must be multifaceted, incorporating multiple forms of excellence.

Multicultural education must address issues of pedagogy. In addition to what we teach students, how we teach them is equally important. Culturally relevant pedagogy attempts to help teachers focus on the totality of the teaching–learning experience. Rather than focus on fragmented pieces, culturally relevant teaching asks teachers to consider their underlying beliefs and ideologies as they attempt to teach all students successfully.

References

Au, K., and Jordan, C. (1981). Teaching Reading to Hawaiian Children: Finding a Culturally Appropriate Solution. In H. Trueba, G. Guthrie, and K. Au (Eds.), *Culture and the Bilingual Classroom: Studies in Classroom Ethnography* (pp. 139–52). Rowley, MA: Newbury House.

Cazden, C., and Leggett, E. (1981). Culturally Responsive Education: Recommendations for Achieving Lau Remedies II. In H. Trueba, G. Guthrie, and K. Au (Eds.), *Culture and the Bilingual Classroom: Studies in Classroom Ethnography* (pp. 69–86). Rowley, MA: Newbury House.

Erickson, F., and Mohatt, G. (1982). Cultural Organization and Participation Structures in Two Classrooms of Indian Students. In G. Spindler (Ed.), *Doing the Ethnography of Schooling* (pp. 131–74). New York: Holt, Rinehart & Winston.

Ladson-Billings, G. (1994). *The Dreamkeepers: Successful Teachers for African American Children.* San Francisco: Jossey-Bass.

Mohatt, G., and Erickson, F. (1981). Cultural Differences in Teaching Styles in an Odawa School: A Sociolinguistic Approach. In H. Trueba, G. Guthrie, and K. Au (Eds.), *Culture and the Bilingual Classroom: Studies in Classroom Ethnography* (pp. 105–19). Rowley, MA: Newbury House.

Vogt, L., Jordan, C., and Tharp, R. (1987). Explaining School Failure, Producing School Success: Two Cases. *Anthropology and Education Quarterly,* 18, pp. 276–86.

Source: Carl A. Grant and Gloria Ladson-Billings, eds., *Dictionary of Multicultural Education* (Phoenix, AZ: Org Press, 1997), pp. 62–63.

Multicultural Education and Democratic Pluralism

The convergence of these several concerns is made explicit in a work by Christine Sleeter and Carl Grant[40] that describes five approaches to achieving a pluralistic education. Sleeter and Grant's categories recall the distinction made between "assimilationist" and "pluralist" approaches to cultural differences described in connection with Native Americans in Chapter 7. Roughly summarized, the assimilationist educational approach seeks to obliterate cultural differences among minority groups so that those groups will have the same cultural knowledge and values as the dominant culture. The pluralist approach seeks ways to preserve and celebrate distinctive cultural heritages as valuable contributions to the vitality and diversity of the wider culture. Applying that distinction to Sleeter and Grant's five approaches to multicultural education reveals some of them to be more assimilationist and others to be more pluralist in orientation.

Thinking Critically about the Issues   #6

What do the authors mean by pluralism and democratic pluralism? How is this relevant to classroom practice?

Teaching the Exceptional and Culturally Different
In the teaching-the-exceptional approach, the goals are to "fit people into the existing social structure and culture." This is done by use of "bilingual education, ESL, remedial classes and special education, all of which are seen as temporary and intensive aids to fill gaps in knowledge." The general strategy is to create bridges between the student's present knowledge and the traditional curricular aims of the school. Because the student must conform to the dominant culture, this approach is favored mainly by "white, middle class teachers who take their own background and culture for granted and are searching for a way to incorporate or deal with those they view as different."[41]

Human Relations   In the human relations approach, the primary goals are to "promote feelings of unity, tolerance, and acceptance within [the] existing social structure" and to "promote positive feelings among students, reduce stereotyping, [and] promote students'

self-concepts."[42] These goals are to be met by teaching lessons about stereotyping and name-calling and to counter such tendencies by teaching positive images of minority groups and teaching about individual differences. This approach, designed to make people feel good about themselves and each other, is criticized on the grounds that the fundamental sources of discrimination and poverty which lead to feelings of inferiority do not reside in human relations but in institutional arrangements that promote inequality.

Single-Group Studies   The goals of single-group studies are to foster social equality, acceptance, and recognition of the identified group and to "promote willingness and knowledge among students to work toward social change that would benefit the identified group."[43] These goals would be addressed by teaching specific units about the identified group, including that group's own perspective, how it has been victimized, and the issues it currently faces. Ethnic studies courses (women's studies, Indian studies, African American studies) are examples. This approach serves a purpose but has limitations. It does not effectively alter the main curriculum, which in the view of many critics only reinforces the very problems a multicultural education attempts to correct. The traditional curriculum derives from the experience of White, middle-class males. Single-group studies convey a sort of add-on approach that lacks incorporation or serious challenge to the status quo.

Multicultural Education   The goals of multicultural education include promotion of "social structural equality and cultural pluralism (the United States as a 'tossed salad')" and promotion of "equal opportunity in the school, cultural pluralism and alternative life styles, respect for those who differ, and support for power equity among groups."[44] Ideas and concepts should be represented as the product of many peoples' contributions, critical thinking and analysis of alternative viewpoints should be taught, and instruction should be allowed to proceed in more than one language. Some critics have argued that an emphasis on different cultures soon decays into a sort of balkanization of culture in which different groups are allowed to develop according to their own ethos and as a result become further disfranchised from participation in the main society. Other critics have argued that in trying to teach a little about every special-interest group, no in-depth learning occurs. Advocates of a particular group are likely to feel slighted when their group gets less attention than they feel it deserves.[45] Finally, critics argue that merely teaching about diversity does little to empower change.

Education That Is Multicultural and Social Reconstructionist Proponents of the reconstructionist approach desire an education that is multicultural, but they also want it to equip students for life "in the real world." The real world, they argue, is not devoted to feel-good pedagogy and the benevolent compensation of inequalities. Instead, the real world is fundamentally sexist, racist, and class-biased. In response to this grim scenario, the goal of multiculturalism is combined with the goal of social reconstructionism—a pedagogy that equips students not only to understand the world but to criticize it effectively and change it.

Advocates of this approach do not loudly and clearly articulate one particular vision of the ideal society. They begin by assuming that resources should be distributed much more equally than they are now and that people should not have to adhere to one model of what is considered "normal" or "right" to enjoy their fair share of wealth, power, or happiness. But advocates believe that it would be another form of elitism for a small group of educators to tell other people what the "right" vision of the better society is. Rather, young people—particularly those who are members of oppressed groups—should understand the nature of oppression in modern society and develop the power and skills to articulate their own goals and vision and to work constructively to achieve that.[46]

Advocates of multicultural and social reconstructionist education argue for (1) practicing democracy, (2) analyzing the circumstances of one's own life, (3) developing social action skills, and (4) forming social coalitions across the boundaries of race, ethnicity, social class, and gender.

Practicing democracy entails a kind of active engagement in the decisions that affect one's own life. Unfortunately, schools often do not encourage such engagement. Relationships in schools are structured hierarchically, and the traditional lecture format from grade school to graduate school encourages passivity and boredom. Practicing democracy means taking

Historical Context

Diversity and Equity Today—Defining the Challenge

Chapter 13 is a companion chapter to Chapter 12. The two have identical timelines because they address the same basic social and educational inequities.

1960s

1960	Six years after the 1954 *Brown* v. *Board of Education* decision against school segregation, the modern "sit-in" movement begins when four Black students from North Carolina A&T College sit at a "Whites-only" Woolworth's lunch counter and refuse to leave when denied service
1960	President Dwight D. Eisenhower signs the Civil Rights Act of 1960, which acknowledges the federal government's responsibility in matters involving civil rights
1961	Michael Harrington publishes *The Other America,* revealing widespread poverty in the United States
1962	The All-African Organization of Women is founded to discuss the right to vote, activity in local and national governments, women in education, and medical services for women
1962	The Supreme Court orders the University of Mississippi to admit James H. Meredith; Ross Barnett, the governor of Mississippi, tries unsuccessfully to block Meredith's admission
1963	More than 200,000 marchers from all over the United States stage the largest protest demonstration in the history of Washington, DC; the "March on Washington" procession moves from the Washington Monument to the Lincoln Memorial; Reverend Dr. Martin Luther King, Jr., delivers his "I Have a Dream" speech
1963	Medgar Evers, field secretary for the NAACP, is killed outside his home in Jackson, Mississippi
1964	Civil Rights Act passes Congress, guaranteeing equal voting rights to African Americans
1964	Head Start, U.S. educational program for low-income preschool children, is established
1964	Civil Rights Act of 1964 is passed
1965	United Farm Workers strike
1966	The Medicare Act, Housing Act, Elementary and Secondary Education Act, a new immigration act, and voting-rights legislation are enacted
1966	Black Panther party founded by Huey P. Newton and Bobby Seale

1968	Dr. Martin Luther King, Jr., and Robert Kennedy are assassinated
1968	Bilingual Education Act passed
1968	American Indian Movement (AIM) launched
1968	Alicia Escalante forms East Los Angeles Welfare Rights Organization, the first Chicano welfare rights group
1969	The Stonewall rebellion in New York City marks the beginning of the gay rights movement

1970s

1971	Busing to achieve racially balanced schools is upheld by the Supreme Court
1972	Title IX Educational Amendment passed, outlawing sex discrimination in educational institutions receiving federal financial assistance
1973	Native Americans defy federal authority at Wounded Knee, South Dakota
1975	Congress passes Education for All Handicapped Children Act (Public Law 94-142)
1978	In *University of California* v. *Bakke,* the Supreme Court disallows a quota system in university admissions but gives limited approval to affirmative action plans

1980s

1980	One million African American students enrolled in colleges and universities in the United States
1980	Ronald Reagan is elected president, promising to reverse the "liberal trends in government"
1982	Equal Rights Amendment fails to win state ratification
1984	Reverend Jesse Jackson becomes first African American to challenge for major party nomination for president
1986	New Hampshire teacher Christa McAulliffe killed along with six astronauts when space shuttle *Challenger* explodes on national TV

1990s

1991	Unemployment rate rises to highest level in a decade
1992	Americans with Disabilities Act, the most sweeping antidiscrimination legislation since the Civil Rights Act of 1964, guarantees equal access for people with disabilities
1993	Pentagon rules "don't ask, don't tell": gays and lesbians may serve in military but may not proclaim or openly practice their sexual orientation
1994	Number of prisoners in state and federal prisons tops 1 million, giving United States the highest incarceration rate in the world
1995	Supreme Court rules against any affirmative action program that is not "narrowly tailored" to accomplish a "compelling government interest"
1996	Census Bureau reports that the gap between the richest 20 percent of Americans and everyone else reached postwar high
1996	Clinton signs welfare reform legislation, ending more than 60 years of federal cash assistance to the poor and replacing it with block grants to states to administer
1996	Clinton signs the Defense of Marriage Act, denying federal recognition to same-sex marriages

2000s

2001	Days after taking office, President Bush announces intent to pass No Child Left Behind law; enacted in January 2002, the bipartisan law reauthorizes the Elementary and Secondary Education Act of 1965 and seeks to raise accountability of local school systems for educating all students
2003	The Supreme Court backs affirmative action in a case involving admissions at the University of Michigan; in a separate decision, a 6–3 vote overrules a Texas sodomy law, legalizing gay conduct
2003	President Bush addresses the nation to request $87 billion for reconstruction of Iraq and Afghanistan, on top of the $79 billion already spent
2006	The U.S. Census Bureau releases data on the most comprehensive survey of immigration in the United States ever performed; the number of immigrants living in American households rose 16 percent in five years, fueled largely by recent arrivals from Mexico, and dispersing to areas across the United States other than traditional centers of immigration
2008	In U.S. presidential primary elections, the last two candidates vying for the Democratic party nomination, for the first time in history, are an African American man (Barack Obama) and a woman (Hillary Clinton); another prominent Democratic contender was former governor Bill Richardson, a Latino; this is hailed as evidence of dramatic progress for women and for minority populations in the United States, but candidates and commentators observe that the campaign repeatedly surfaces issues of race and gender discrimination in the country

Thinking Analytically about the Timeline

What confidence do you have that the conditions of schooling are likely to improve for those portions of our population who are least well served by schools? Why?

active command of one's own life and education, "learning to articulate one's interests, openly debate issues with one's peers, organize and work collectively with others, acquire power, exercise power, and so forth."[47]

Analyzing the circumstances of one's own life means learning to see reality as it is, stripped of the myths that often mask it. Students have to unravel the discrepancies between their commonsense understanding of the world and the ideological explanations they have internalized as truth. Brazilian educator Paulo Freire has long used this approach.

Developing social action skills is a goal incorporated by critical theorists as they watched the repeated failure of earlier protest movements and individual forms of resistance that often proved self-destructive. Stanley Aronowitz and Henry Giroux, for example, argued that "if students are to be empowered by school experiences, one of the key elements of their education must be that they acquire mastery of language as well as the capacity to think conceptually and critically."[48]

Forming social coalitions requires that relatively disempowered social groups, whether defined by race, ethnicity, gender, income, or another shared characteristic, must seek collective influence by working together toward common goals. The question arises, How might schools provide experiences that would help prepare students for such coalition building?

Programs That Work

The view that schools operate as autonomous centers of learning, independent of environing cultural conditions, has proved to be dangerously naive. Schools are institutions embedded in the elaborate context of a society's social, economic, and political structures. What is taught in the schools of any given society and how it is taught depends on the values and views of that society's dominant social group—including that society's values concerning cultural diversity.

Social relations in the larger society tend to be replicated in the schools. For teachers concerned with the fate of disenfranchised children and generally with the future of democracy, the outlook can be discouraging. In the 1960s the language of critique ripened into a language of anger and despair as social critics began to understand the extent to which power and cunning have contributed to social inequalities. These critics lost faith in the axioms that society is fair and that the underprivileged are deserving of their fate.

From the far left came calls for violent overthrow of the corporate capitalist state. Although revolutions are messy and the results are seldom gratifying, there are good moral and ethical as well as social reasons to work for a more equitable society. Even for individuals whose relative prosperity is guaranteed by current social arrangements, there are good reasons to want to see changes made. Moreover, there are strategies that each teacher can employ to promote equity without waiting until someone organizes the revolution. This brings us to the language of possibility. What can be done to provide educational success for those population groups that have succeeded least in our schools?

Many critical theorists now view gradual and localized change as the most reasonable goal, especially for educators, who are among educated society's least empowered people. There are discernible practices that work both to educate students and to empower teachers.

For example, math educator Uri Treisman succeeded in turning around the dismal failure rate of minority students entering freshman calculus courses at the University of California at Berkeley, where the "minority" population now accounts for two-thirds of the total enrollment. The mathematics workshop Treisman established cut the dropout rate among African Americans and Hispanics in calculus classes from 60 to 4 percent, an achievement that has been sustained for several years.[49] The goal was accomplished not by babying students but by challenging them, not by driving them to compete harder but by structuring effective group study sessions that resulted in a professional community of devoted young scholars.

Treisman began by studying the success patterns of another minority group, Asian Americans, who were excelling in calculus. What Treisman found was that Asian students had set up a support network. They studied together, helped one another, and maintained a dialogue by which conceptual understanding was constantly monitored and corrected. African American students, by contrast, were accustomed to a sort of rugged individualism. They socialized together but studied alone and seldom asked for help or acknowledged difficulties. This independent approach had stood them in good stead in high school, where peer influences often were resisted in favor of individual academic success.

Treisman set up a workshop in which African American students were invited to study together. A math department staff member was on hand during study sessions to lend support. The workshop was neither billed nor run as a remedial program for losers but as a professional support group, an honor society having high expectations. Study became a social activity, an accepted and ongoing part of these students' lives.

The success of Treisman's approach has been replicated at several universities, including the University of Illinois by Merit Workshop Program director Paul McCreary. Minority students in McCreary's workshop cut the rate of unsatisfactory performance from 44.5 to 23.8 percent, outscoring all other sections on the final exam. Again, this success has been sustained over each semester of the workshop's existence.

Public schools also may benefit from this sort of commitment to high standards and strategies that work. An article in the *Journal of Negro Education*[50] describes the success of a high school set up by the New York City public school system on the campus of the City College of New York. In a city where the dropout rate runs to 30.7 percent and where an estimated 60 percent of African American students never finish high school, the A. Phillip Randolph High School graduates all but 1.8 percent and sees from 92 to 97 percent of its students accepted into four-year colleges. In this school 44 percent of the students receive some form of public assistance; 76 percent are African American, and 23 percent are Hispanic.

The school succeeds in part because high standards have been set, a clear sense of direction has been provided, curriculum development is ongoing, teachers are directly involved in all stages of planning, and parents, students, staff, and the community are all drawn into the process. Nationwide, these seem to be the characteristics of schools that work. The attitude of the Randolph School is that "every child can learn, must learn, and will learn."[51] The curriculum is rigorous. It emphasizes math and science as well as a mastery of written English and speech. Students are required to devote 80 hours to community service to instill values of civil and social responsibility. Students undergo frequent testing and evaluation to ascertain current academic levels, ensuring correct placement in courses and upward movement when warranted. They are also coached in the skill of test taking so that they will score well on the SAT. Because of concerted, well-managed effort by all involved, Randolph High School has placed in the top 5 percent of all secondary schools in the nation and has sent over 45 percent of its students to Ivy League schools, including Harvard, Yale, Brown, and Columbia.[52]

These few examples reflect some of the principles of a multicultural, reconstructionist education described in the following passage by Sleeter and Grant, leaders in the research on cultural pluralism. They call for an educational approach

that advocates making the school and classroom reflect and celebrate diversity. [The] curriculum, including materials, visual displays, films, guest speakers, and content taught orally, should regularly represent experiences, perspectives, and contributions of diverse groups and should do so in a conceptual rather than a fragmented manner. This should be done all the time, in all subject areas. Nonsexist language should be used, and bilingualism or multilingualism should be endorsed. The curriculum should be equally accessible to all student groups; grouping practices or teaching procedures that enable only certain groups of students access to high-status knowledge or better teaching should be avoided. Teachers should build on students' learning styles rather than assuming that all learn best in the same way, and they should maintain high expectations for all students. Cooperative learning should be used to develop skills and attitudes of cooperation. Sexist possessive behavior should be avoided, and teachers should develop positive self-concepts in all students. Biased evaluation procedures should be avoided; evaluation should be used for improving instruction, not for sorting and ranking students. Home/community-school relations should be developed, and parents should be actively involved, particularly if they are lower-class and/or minority. Staffing patterns should reflect cultural diversity and offer a variety of role models for males and females of different race and class backgrounds. Finally, extracurricular activities should not perpetuate race and sex stereotypes.[53]

Such a vision may be rejected by some as utopian, but there are too many instances to ignore in which American schools serve as successful environments for low-income, African American, and Hispanic students. The late educator Ron Edmonds reminded us that resistance to belief in the academic abilities of students from different cultural backgrounds lies more in prejudice than in the students' abilities to learn. Edmonds wrote in 1979:

How many effective schools would you have to see to be persuaded of the educability of poor children? If your answer is more than one, then I suspect that you have reasons of your own for preferring to believe that basic pupil performance derives from family background instead of the school's response to family background.[54]

Like critical theorists, gender theorists, and cultural pluralism theorists, Edmonds urged that the analysis focus not primarily on the characteristics of the student, not primarily on the characteristics of the school, but on the interaction between the school and the child. Only by examining such relationships can we see how the school culture interacts with the culture and characteristics of the child to support or discourage learning and human development. Edmonds believes that students from all social groups are equally capable of learning and that the duty of the educator is to help create an environment that responds to each child's needs—needs that are importantly conditioned in our culture by social variables such as race, ethnicity, gender, and social class.

It is important to observe that this discussion of approaches that succeed with low-income and minority students is not a discussion about self-esteem. Although strong self-esteem is valuable, it is not a substitute for learning. Educator Lilian Katz drew national media attention in 1993 when she pointed out how many educational programs were focusing on self-esteem as if good feelings were the same as good academic development.[55] Then, in February 1997, an article written by AFT President Albert Shanker was published the day after his death making a similar argument in response to a recent report suggesting that some students, teachers, and the public are still being hoodwinked by a "self-esteem movement" that substitutes big doses of praise for effective instruction. Self-esteem should not be a product of praise, he argued, but of the satisfaction that comes with successful learning.[56]

A recent volume by Michael S. Knapp and associates presents a major nationwide research study of teachers who succeed with children in high-poverty classrooms. As you would expect, these classrooms are disproportionately populated by children of color. Knapp et al. found that teachers who succeed in bringing about measurably strong academic learning with high-poverty children are those who do three things well: maintain classroom order, respond effectively to diverse cultural backgrounds, and *teach for meaning.* By "teaching for meaning," Knapp et al. mean that teachers reject a traditional focus on student deficiencies and the traditional emphasis on learning discrete skills ordered from "basic" to "advanced." Instead, they write, those who teach for meaning use a number of alternative approaches designed to engage students in using higher-order thinking skills to make connections between academic learning and their life experiences. Specifically, teaching for meaning helps students make greater meaning of their studies by maximizing the following:

- First, where they [students] are actively engaged in the attempt to make sense of things they experience in school, they are encouraged to be meaning makers.

- Second, they derive meaning from seeing the relationship of parts to a whole, rather than being left with only parts. Opportunities to connect one concept or one skill to another increase their conceptual grasp of what they are doing, whether it involves communication, problem solving, appreciation of artwork, or carrying out projects.

- Third, they find meaning by connecting new learning experiences to their existing body of knowledge, assumptions, and meanings, many of which are rooted in their upbringing and cultural roots.[57]

This study by Knapp and his associates is particularly meaningful because of its scale; 140 classrooms were studied in diverse school settings in the West, the Midwest, and the East. The findings remind us that the intellectual capacities of low-income children demand our respect and our most challenging—not our most "dumbed down"—instructional strategies.

Thinking Critically about the Issues	**#7**
What would be some examples of "teaching for meaning" in the subject areas and grade levels in which you hope to teach?	

Diversity, Equity, and Special Education

In Chapter 12 we briefly visited the relationship between the growing number of students identified as "learning disabled" and the low academic performance of students from low-income backgrounds. The special education debates that have been ongoing at least since the 1960s have tried to address questions of equity for special-needs students. The very act of labeling students as "special needs" or "disabled" has itself raised equity issues. Recently, Thomas Skrtic argued that the educational and equity needs of students with weak academic skills, many of whom are now labeled learning disabled, cannot be addressed without significant school reforms that place greater decision-making power in the hands of well-trained and educated teachers.[58]

Multicultural education specialist James Banks has offered a definition of multicultural education that is intended to place questions of equity and school reform at the heart of the meaning of multicultural education:

> There is an emerging consensus among specialists that multicultural education is a reform movement designed to bring about educational equity for all students, including those from different races, ethnic groups, social classes, exceptionality, and sexual orientations.[59]

Banks's definition is intended to draw attention to his view that multicultural education is the most equitable way to address the educational needs of all students and that for schools to provide the necessary structure and resources to do so will require reforms in the way schools conduct their business. Banks's definition draws attention to another issue as well: There are many kinds of student diversity, and it might serve students well if we would resist partitioning off some kinds of differences as "special" needs—especially when the educational needs of most children identified as special are the same as the needs of all children. Special educational programs, even under the Education for All Handicapped Students Act of 1975 and in the recent Regular Education Initiative, which is intended to improve on the negative consequences of that act, become another form of tracking. Skrtic writes, "The restructuring debate does not recognize special education as a form of tracking." However, he continues:

> Students whose needs fall on the margins or outside of these standard programs must be either squeezed into them or squeezed out of the classroom. Given the inevitability of human diversity, a professional bureaucracy can do nothing but create students who do not fit the system. In a professional bureaucracy, all forms of tracking—curriculum tracking and in-class ability grouping in general education,

as well as self-contained and resource classrooms in special, compensatory, remedial and gifted education—are organizational pathologies. . . . Students are subjected to—and subjugated by—these practices because, given their structural and cultural contingencies, traditional school organizations cannot accommodate diversity and so must screen it out.[60]

Skrtic's position is underscored by researchers Elizabeth Bondy and Dorene D. Ross, who wrote in 1998:

> The problem of overrepresentation of minority students in special education programs was first called to the attention of the educational community in 1968 . . . [and] this pattern has tenaciously persisted . . . , of all ethnic groups, black students, particularly black males, have the highest overrepresentation in special education placements.[61]

This is not to say that students with carefully diagnosed emotional or physical disabilities should not receive special educational attention. Rather, it reminds us of what Toch pointed out in Chapter 12: The labels on most students may say more about the system than about the students. Skrtic reports that the leading special education advocates of the Regular Education Initiative in special education all agree that "the EHA and mainstreaming are fundamentally flawed, particularly for students who are classified as mildly to moderately handicapped (hereafter mildly handicapped); that is, students classified as learning disabled, emotionally disturbed, and mentally retarded, who make up over two-thirds of the 4.5 million students served under the law."[62]

The challenge to the teacher, then, is to devise an environment that will support learning for students with very different skill levels and interests—so different that some of these students have been traditionally excluded from regular classrooms. Banks and other multicultural education advocates believe that multicultural perspectives are a way to respond to the learning needs of the widest array of students. This is easier said than done, however, when resources are limited. In our Primary Source Reading, for example, we present a discussion of the importance of culture "responsive to students' race and ethnicities and incorporated into curriculum and pedagogy."

Finally, it is important to emphasize the following. Upon completion of their teacher education programs, teachers rarely have the professional maturity to meet the learning needs of students whose learning needs vary widely. Great teachers will attest to this. The development of such expertise requires time, a great deal of further learning, and school organizations that support teacher learning and teacher problem solving. Therefore, all teachers who want their talents and commitments to have impact on their students need to understand how crucial is the organization of the school.

BUILDING A PHILOSOPHY OF EDUCATION

Some schools and teachers have outstanding academic success with low-income and minority students, but most schools do not. What is the difference?

In contrast to Chapter 12, which described some of the dimensions of inequality in contemporary schooling and society, Chapter 13 has focused on how teachers and schools can respond equitably to differences among students. Jane Elliott's classroom experiment with her elementary school students, first conducted over 30 years ago, reminds us that even children can understand that qualities judged as inferior or superior among people are not inherent and permanent but are socially constructed. We see as well that whatever social group is most powerful has the opportunity to define superiority and inferiority in ways that are advantageous to that group.

How human differences are defined and valued in our culture is deeply rooted in ideology. Despite its history-changing positive emphasis on liberty and equality, the history of liberal ideology is marked by racist and sexist assumptions. These assumptions play a role in attempts to explain why one group performs better or is more highly rewarded than another in schooling and in society more generally. Efforts to understand these group differences often become theories of social and educational inequality. Differences among these theories are extremely important because they have very different implications for how to respond to differences among individual students and among groups of students. For example, a theory of genetic inferiority was used in the pre–Civil War era to justify slavery

and the exclusion of African Americans from schooling. Later, genetic inferiority theory was used to justify the tracking of different groups of students into different school experiences and consequently different places in the socioeconomic order.

As the explanation of differences in group performance shifted from genetic deficit theory to cultural deficit theory, a new way of blaming the victim was introduced. In this approach, the problem of low school performance was attributed no longer to the genetic inheritance of the individual but to the individual's home life or cultural inheritance. Such thinking led to efforts to place low-achieving students into remedial programs that would address their supposed cultural deficiencies, protecting the assumption that the performance problem lay with the student, not with the school.

While a great many citizens, including educators, most likely still adhere to a cultural deficit explanation of group and individual differences in school performance, recent years have seen increased attention to cultural difference theory. This approach portrays minority subcultures not as deficient but instead as different from the dominant school culture, leading to a mismatch that advantages students whose home lives most closely resemble the school cultural language, values, and nonverbal communications. Such thinking has led to a questioning of why some cultures' practices are rewarded and honored in the school environment while others' are devalued. The resulting explanation, which recognizes that schools institutionalize the power and ideology of the dominant social group, has led to a cultural subordination theory. The example of Black English Vernacular illustrates how a perfectly complete linguistic system can be devalued in the school culture and how that devaluing can play a role in teachers' expectations of student achievement, advantaging students whose primary language matches the school's.

How to respond to such differences of language and culture so that the needs of every child are served? Is it sensible to assume that the learning needs of all African American children are different from their Hispanic and White non-Hispanic counterparts? Or that the learning needs of all boys are different from the needs of all girls? To make such assumptions is to define individuals only according to group membership, which is clearly a bias to be avoided. Here the differences among bias, neutrality, and sensitivity become important. Treating students neutrally, as if the differences between them did not exist, risks disadvantage to those students whose starting points lag behind, and so neutrality along lines of gender, ethnicity, or social class does not present a solution.

The stance of gender sensitivity, or ethnic sensitivity, or class sensitivity, however, allows teachers to keep before them the question, When is race or gender or class a relevant variable in this student's or group of students' performance, and when is it not? When performance differences originate in group membership, as in the case of language or the different socialization of girls and boys, a teacher's response might well be different than it will be if the origins are idiosyncratic to the child.

To be sensitive to and to respect such differences is a major component of a multicultural approach to teaching. There are several different varieties of multiculturalism, as this chapter has shown, with perhaps the most promising one focusing on James Banks's notion of educational equity for all students. Such an approach honors the importance of group differences, including those identified as physical and mental disabilities, and seeks a pluralistic approach to teaching that benefits all students.

Chapter 12's section on building a philosophy of education placed emphasis on the importance of the teacher's conviction that all children can learn. This section on building a philosophy underscores another conviction: No teacher, especially an early career teacher, knows all that he or she needs to know about how to support the successful learning of all children. The most successful teachers commit themselves to learning from and about their students and their cultures. They commit also to learning from and about other teachers' approaches and techniques, because the community of excellent teachers knows more than any one of them. Finally, teachers who succeed with all kinds of students learn from their own practice by reflecting on what is working, what needs changing, and why. The philosophy of education of the most effective teachers is thus a philosophy of learning as well as a philosophy of teaching.

Primary Source Reading

Teaching Diverse Learners
Culturally Responsive Teaching

Culture is central to learning. It plays a role not only in communicating and receiving information, but also in shaping the thinking process of groups and individuals. A pedagogy that acknowledges, responds to, and celebrates fundamental cultures offers full, equitable access to education for students from all cultures.

Culturally Responsive Teaching is a pedagogy that recognizes the importance of including students' cultural references in all aspects of learning (Ladson-Billings, 1994).

Some of the characteristics of culturally responsive teaching are:

1. Positive perspectives on parents and families
2. Communication of high expectations
3. Learning within the context of culture

4. Student-centered instruction
5. Culturally mediated instruction
6. Reshaping the curriculum
7. Teacher as facilitator

1. Positive Perspectives on Parents and Families

> Whether it's an informal chat as the parent brings the child to school, or in phone conversation or home visits, or through newsletters sent home, teachers can begin a dialogue with family members that can result in learning about each of the families through genuine communication.
>
> —Sonia Nieto

WHAT

Parents are the child's first teacher and are critically important partners to students and teachers. To help parents become aware of how they can be effective partners in the education process, teachers should engage in dialogue with parents as early as possible about parents' hopes and aspirations for their child, their sense of what the child needs, and suggestions about ways teachers can help. Teachers explain their own limitations and invite parents to participate in their child's education in specific ways.

Parent involvement need not be just how parents can participate in school functions. Oftentimes, religious and cultural differences preclude active participation in school activities. However, parental involvement also includes how parents communicate high expectations, pride, and interest in their child's academic life (Nieto, 1996).

WHY

Constant communication with parents is an important aspect of a child's educational progress. Involving parents and families in their child's educational process results in better scholastic achievement. When families share their "funds of knowledge" with the school community, teachers get a better idea of their students' background knowledge and abilities, and how they learn best (Moll, Amanti, Neff, & Gonzalez, 1992).

HOW

1. Seek to understand parents' hopes, concerns and suggestions

   - Conduct needs assessments and surveys (in the parents' first language) of what parents expect of the school community
   - Establish parent-teacher organizations or committees to work collaboratively for the benefit of the students

   - Conduct home visits in which parents are able to speak freely about their expectations and concerns for their children

2. Keep parents apprised of services offered by the school

   - Send weekly/monthly newsletters (in the home language) informing parents of school activities
   - Conduct monthly meeting at parents' homes or community centers to inform parents of school activities
   - Host family nights at school to introduce parents to concepts and ideas children are learning in their classes and to share interactive journals

3. Gain cross-cultural skills necessary for successful exchange and collaboration

   - Research the cultural background of students' families
   - Visit local community centers to find out about the cultural activities and beliefs of the students
   - Tour students' neighborhoods to identify local resources and "funds of knowledge" (Moll et al., 1992)

2. Communication of High Expectations

> When a teacher expresses sympathy over failure, lavishes praise for completing a simple task, or offers unsolicited help, the teacher may send unintended messages of low expectations.
>
> —Kathleen Serverian-Wilmeth

WHAT

All students should receive the consistent message that they are expected to attain high standards in their school work. This message must be delivered by all that are involved in students' academic lives, that is: teachers, guidance counselors, administrators, and other school personnel. Teachers should understand students' behavior in light of the norms of the communities in which they have grown. They should respect all students as learners with valuable knowledge and experience.

WHY

Effective and consistent communication of high expectation helps students develop a healthy self-concept (Rist, 1970). It also provides the structure for intrinsic motivation and fosters an environment in which the student can be successful.

HOW

1. Communicate clear expectations
   - Be specific in what you expect students to know and be able to do

2. Create an environment in which there is genuine respect for students and a belief in their capability
   - Encourage students to meet expectations for a particular task
   - Offer praise when standards are met

3. Learning Within the Context of Culture

   The increasing diversity in our schools, the ongoing demographic changes across the nation and the movement towards globalization dictate that we develop a more in-depth understanding of culture if we want to bring about true understanding among diverse populations.

   —Maria Wilson-Portuondo

WHAT

Children from homes in which the language and culture do not closely correspond to that of the school may be at a disadvantage in the learning process. These children often become alienated and feel disengaged from learning. People from different cultures learn in different ways. Their expectations for learning may be different. For example, students from some cultural groups prefer to learn in cooperation with others, while the learning style of others is to work independently. To maximize learning opportunities, teachers should gain knowledge of the cultures represented in their classrooms and adapt lessons so that they reflect ways of communicating and learning that are familiar to the students.

WHY

Children learn about themselves and the world around them within the context of culture (Northeast and Islands Regional Educational Laboratory at Brown University, 2002). Students from minority cultures may feel pressured to disavow themselves of their cultural beliefs and norms in order to assimilate into the majority culture. This, however, can interfere with their emotional and cognitive development and result in school failure (Sheets, 1999).

HOW

1. Vary teaching strategies
   - Use cooperative learning especially for material new to the students
   - Assign independent work after students are familiar with concept
   - Use role-playing strategies
   - Assign students research projects that focus on issues or concepts that apply to their own community or cultural group
   - Provide various options for completing an assignment

2. Bridge cultural differences through effective communication
   - Teach and talk to students about differences between individuals
   - Show how differences among the students make for better learning
   - Attend community events of the students and discuss the events with the students

4. Student-Centered Instruction

In our multicultural society, culturally responsive teaching reflects democracy at its highest level. [It] means doing whatever it takes to ensure that every child is achieving and ever moving toward realizing her or his potential.

—Joyce Taylor-Gibson

WHAT

Student-centered instruction differs from the traditional teacher-centered instruction. Learning is cooperative, collaborative, and community-oriented. Students are encouraged to direct their own learning and to work with other students on research projects and assignments that are both culturally and socially relevant to them. Students become self-confident, self-directed, and proactive.

WHY

Learning is a socially mediated process (Goldstein, 1999; Vygotsky, 1978). Children develop cognitively by interacting with both adults and more knowledgeable peers. These interactions allow students to hypothesize, experiment with new ideas, and receive feedback (Darling-Hammond, 1997).

HOW

1. Promote student engagement

   - Have students generate lists of topics they wish to study and/or research
   - Allow students to select their own reading material

2. Share responsibility of instruction

   - Initiate cooperative learning groups (Padron, Waxman, & Rivera, 2002)
   - Have students lead discussion groups or reteach concepts

3. Create inquiry based/discovery oriented curriculum

   - Create classroom projects that involve the community

4. Encourage a community of learners

   - Form book clubs or literature circles (Daniels, 2002) for reading discussions
   - Conduct Student-Directed Sharing Time (Brisk & Harrington, 2000)
   - Use cooperative learning strategies such as Jigsaw (Brisk & Harrington, 2000)

5. Culturally Mediated Instruction

   Ongoing multicultural activities within the classroom setting engender a natural awareness of cultural history, values and contributions.

   —Kathleen Serverian-Wilmeth

WHAT

Instruction is culturally mediated when it incorporates and integrates diverse ways of knowing, understanding, and representing information. Instruction and learning take place in an environment that encourages multicultural viewpoints and allows for inclusion of knowledge that is relevant to the students. Learning happens in culturally appropriate social situations; that is, relationships among students and those between teachers and students are congruent with students' cultures.

WHY

Students need to understand that there is more than one way to interpret a statement, event, or action. By being allowed to learn in different ways or to share viewpoints and perspectives in a given situation based on their own cultural and social experiences, students become active participants in their learning (Nieto, 1996). Hollins (1996) believes that culturally mediated instruction provides the best learning conditions for all students. It may help decrease the number of incidences of unacceptable behavior from students who are frustrated with instruction

not meeting their needs. Also, students from cultural groups who are experiencing academic success will be less inclined to form stereotypes about students from other cultures.

HOW

1. Research students' experiences with learning and teaching styles

   - Ask educators who come from the same cultural background as the students about effective ways to teach them
   - Visit the communities of the students to find out how they interact and learn in that environment
   - Ask students about their learning style preferences
   - Interview parents about how and what students learn from them

2. Devise and implement different ways for students to be successful in achieving developmental milestones

   - Ensure success by setting realistic, yet rigorous, goals for individual students
   - Allow students to set their own goals for a project
   - Allow the use of the student's first language to enhance learning

3. Create an environment that encourages and embraces culture

   - Employ patterns of management familiar to students
   - Allow students ample opportunities to share their cultural knowledge
   - Question and challenge students on their beliefs and actions
   - Teach students to question and challenge their own beliefs and actions

6. Reshaping the Curriculum

   [Schools must] take a serious look at their curriculum, pedagogy, retention and tracking policies, testing, hiring practices, and all the other policies and practices that create a school climate that is either empowering or disempowering for those who work and learn there.

   —Sonia Nieto

WHAT

The curriculum should be integrated, interdisciplinary, meaningful, and student-centered. It should include issues and topics related to the students' background and culture. It should challenge the students to develop higher-order knowledge and skills (Villegas, 1991).

WHY

Integrating the various disciplines of a curriculum facilitates the acquisition of new knowledge (Hollins, 1996). Students' strengths in one subject area will support new learning in another. Likewise, by using the students' personal experiences to develop new skills and knowledge, teachers make meaningful connections between school and real-life situations (Padron, Waxman, & Rivera, 2002).

HOW

1. Use resources other than textbooks for study

   - Have students research aspects of a topic within their community
   - Encourage students to interview members of their community who have knowledge of the topic they are studying
   - Provide information to the students on alternative viewpoints or beliefs of a topic

2. Develop learning activities that are more reflective of students' backgrounds

   - Include cooperative learning strategies
   - Allow students the choice of working alone or in groups on certain projects

3. Develop integrated units around universal themes

7. Teacher as Facilitator

A caring adult can make a big difference in the educational outcome of any child that is at risk of experiencing educational failure.
—Maria Wilson-Portuondo

WHAT

Teachers should develop a learning environment that is relevant to and reflective of their students' social, cultural, and linguistic experiences. They act as guides, mediators, consultants, instructors, and advocates for the students, helping to effectively connect their culturally- and community-based knowledge to the classroom learning experiences.

WHY

Ladson-Billings (1995) notes that a key criterion for culturally relevant teaching is nurturing and supporting competence in both home and school cultures. Teachers should use the students' home cultural experiences as a foundation upon which to develop knowledge and skills. Content learned in this way is more significant to the students and facilitates the transfer of what is learned in school to real-life situations (Padron, Waxman, & Rivera, 2002).

HOW

1. Learn about students' cultures

   - Have students share artifacts from home that reflect their culture
   - Have students write about traditions shared by their families
   - Have students research different aspects of their culture

2. Vary teaching approaches to accommodate diverse learning styles and language proficiency

   - Initiate cooperative learning groups (Padron, Waxman, & Rivera, 2002)
   - Have students participate in book clubs or literature circles (Daniels, 2002)
   - Use student-directed discussion groups (Brisk & Harrington, 2000)
   - Speak in ways that meet the comprehension and language development needs of ELLs (Yedlin, 2004)

3. Utilize various resources in the students' communities

   - Have members of the community speak to students on various subjects
   - Ask members of the community to teach a lesson or give a demonstration (in their field of expertise) to the students
   - Invite parents to the classroom to show students alternative ways of approaching a problem (e.g., in math: various ways of dividing numbers, naming decimals, etc.)

References

Brisk, M. E., & Harrington, M. M. (2000). *Literacy and bilingualism: A handbook for all teachers.* Mahwah, NJ: Lawrence Erlbaum Associates.

Daniels, H. (2002). *Literature circles: Voice and choice in book clubs and reading groups.* Portland, ME: Stenhouse.

Darling-Hammond, L. (1997). *The right to learn: A blueprint for creating schools that work.* San Francisco: Jossey-Bass.

Feuerstein, R. (1980). *Instrumental enrichment: An intervention program for cognitive modifiability.* Baltimore: University Park Press.

Goldstein, L. (1999). The relational zone: The role of caring relationships in the co-construction of mind. *American Educational Research Journal, 36*(3), 647–673.

Hollins, E. R. (1996). *Culture in school learning: Revealing the deep meaning.* Mahwah, NJ: Lawrence Erlbaum Associates.

Ladson-Billings, G. (1994). The dreamkeepers. San Francisco: Jossey-Bass.

Ladson-Billings, G. (1995). But that's just good teaching! The case for culturally relevant pedagogy. *Theory into Practice, 34*(3), 159–165.

Moll, L. C., Amanti, C., Neff, D., & Gonzalez, N. (1992). Funds of knowledge for teaching: Using a qualitative approach to connect homes and classrooms. *Theory Into Practice, 31*(2), 132–141.

Nieto, S. (1996). *Affirming diversity: The sociopolitical context of multicultural education* (2nd ed.). White Plains, NY: Longman.

Northeast and Islands Regional Educational Laboratory at Brown University (LAB). (2002). *The diversity kit: An introductory resource for social change in education.* Providence, RI: Brown University. Available: http://www.alliance.brown.edu/tdl/diversitykit.shtml

Padron, Y. N., Waxman, H. C., and Rivera, H. H. (2002). *Educating Hispanic students: Effective instructional practices* (Practitioner Brief #5). Available: http://www.cal.org/crede/Pubs/PracBrief5.htm

Rist, C. (1971). Student social class and teacher expectations: The self-fulfilling prophecy in ghetto education. *Challenging the myth: The schools, the Blacks, and the poor* (Reprint Series No. 5). Cambridge, MA: Harvard Educational Review.

Sheets, R. (1999). Relating competence in an urban classroom to ethnic identity development. In R. Sheets (Ed.), *Racial and ethnic identity in school practices: Aspects of human development.* Mahwah, NJ: Lawrence Erlbaum Associates.

Villegas, A. M. (1991). *Culturally responsive pedagogy for the 1990's and beyond.* Washington, DC: ERIC Clearinghouse on Teacher Education.

Vygotsky, L. S. (1978). *Mind in society: The development of higher psychological processes* (M. Cole, V. John-Steiner, S. Scribner, & E. Souberman, Eds. and Trans.). Cambridge, MA: Harvard University.

Yedlin, J. (2004, January/February). Teacher talk: Enabling ELLs to "grab on" and climb high. *Perspectives.* Available: http://www.mec.edu/mascd/docs/yedlin.htm.

Developing Your Professional Vocabulary

A good understanding of this chapter's content would include an understanding of why each of these terms is important to education.

antiracist education

Black English Vernacular

critical theory

cultural deficit theory

cultural subordination theory

culturally relevant pedagogy

culturally responsive pedagogy

democratic pluralism

ESL instruction

ethnic diversity

gender sensitivity versus gender bias

genetic deficit theory

Head Start project

multicultural education

pedagogy

Plato's myth of the metals

resistance theory

Questions for Discussion and Examination

1. Identify two theories of inquality; discuss how in your experience these played out in your personal school experience, and how they play out in popular culture stereotypes.

2. Identify "resistance" theories of student behavior. Discuss again from your own experience, how these appeared in schooling, and in popular culture or film depictions of schooling.

3. Discuss the issues related to a "gender responsive" schooling. How might this work?

 Online Resources

Go to the Online Learning Center at **www.mhhe.com/ tozer7e** to take chapter quizzes, practice with key terms, access study resources, and link to related websites. Also available on the Online Learning Center are PowerWeb articles and news feeds.

School and Society: Teaching and Teacher Leadership in the 21st Century

Chapter Overview

Chapter 14 situates the study of school and society in the personal choice that people make to become teachers. The chapter first reminds the reader of one of the key messages of the book: that from the early national period to the common-school era; from the progressive era through the cold war to the post–cold war period of contemporary school reform; from agrarianism to industrialism and urbanization; from urbanization to suburbanization and the postindustrial computer age; from classical liberalism to modern liberalism to neoliberalism—the story of public schools in the United States has been marked by a tension between the ideals of democratic equality versus practices of unequal schooling that decade after decade reward power and privilege with educational resources far superior to those of the nonprivileged majority. But this raises the legitimate question: So what? What does this mean for me as a teacher?

What this means for each teacher is partly dependent on why the individual may choose, or has chosen, teaching as a profession. Some people do it for personal reasons having to do mostly with their own individual skills, dispositions, and job opportunities, which may have little to do with goals for students or for society. For others, it's all about student learning, with less regard for themselves and little attention to issues of social structure or political–economic inequality. For others, social issues are paramount, and they see teaching as a political act that can change society.

It might be argued that no teacher can be motivated purely by just one of these perspectives, and that it is always a matter of emphasis. True enough; but this chapter raises the question of how teachers can think about, and how they can accomplish, their professional goals, whatever they might be. For thinking well about achieving one's goals, it is important to understand the connection between how one teaches and what kinds of outcomes such teaching is most likely to achieve. That is, teachers need to have a "theory of impact," or a way to see what their teaching is likely to amount to—for themselves, their students, and for society. And for teachers who wish to increase their impact, it is argued, collective action and leadership are necessary. In this connection, some teachers emerge as leaders—leaders who are much needed if teachers are to achieve their educational goals.

Chapter Objectives

Among the objectives that Chapter 14 seeks to achieve are these:

1. Students should reflect on whether their reading of this book is likely to have any impact on their own practice. To assist in such reflection, students should consider the "theory of impact" that the authors put forward for the value of studying social foundations of education: Those teachers who best understand what this book has to offer are in a better position to help improve student learning because they will understand students, schools, and themselves in the social contexts that affect the meanings and interactions among these three components of educational processes.

2. Students should reflect on their own personal, professional, and political motivations for becoming a teacher, realizing that most teachers have a mix of motives and that motives change over time. For example, a person could start by "just looking for a job," and end up being "all about the students."

3. Readers should also recognize that whatever their motives for teaching, they are more likely to achieve them if they have a clear theory of impact—an explanation of how their practices are likely to lead to the teacher's goals, whether those goals are just keeping a job, maximizing student learning, or contributing to a more just society.

4. Prospective and current teachers should be able to connect their teaching goals to reflect on teaching as an "isolated" versus a "collaborative" profession. That is, some goals may be obtainable without structured collaboration with other teachers, but teachers are increasingly finding that working strategically with other teachers is essential to achieving the most ambitious goals for student learning.

5. Finally, readers should reflect on the changing landscape of "teacher leadership" and what that will mean to teaching and learning. The chapter urges teachers to become willing and able to "step up" to responsibility for school outcomes outside their own classrooms because such teacher leadership can have important consequences for school culture and student learning.

Analytic Framework
The Cultural Contexts of Children and Youth

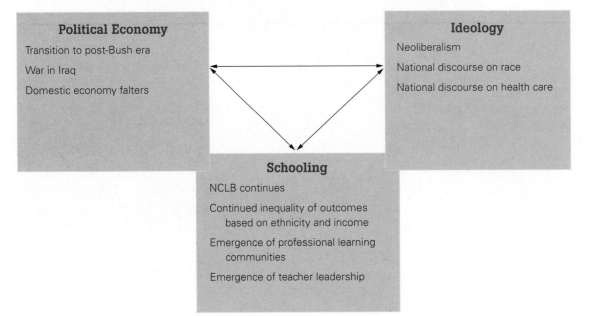

Political Economy

Transition to post-Bush era

War in Iraq

Domestic economy falters

Ideology

Neoliberalism

National discourse on race

National discourse on health care

Schooling

NCLB continues

Continued inequality of outcomes
   based on ethnicity and income

Emergence of professional learning
   communities

Emergence of teacher leadership

Introduction: So What? The Importance of a Theory of Impact

At this point in a textbook such as this, it is fair to ask: What does this all add up to? After thousands of facts and footnotes, and dozens of competing viewpoints, what's the point? Will any of this make a single teacher or school more effective? Will any of it help a single third-grader read better, or a would-be high school dropout stay in school?

To answer that effectively, we need a theory that would explain how a book like this would lead to some kind of results in schools. That is, we cannot simply *assume* that a teacher who reads and understands this book will be more effective; we must have a plausible, even persuasive explanation that shows how one thing is likely to cause another. Such an explanation is often called a "theory of action," or "theory of impact"—an explanation of how something might cause a result. Ideally, the theory of impact should be testable. We should be able to conduct some kind of investigation to find out if the theory really works in practice.

For example, if you assign mathematics homework to elementary school students, you should have an explanation for how assigning such homework will be likely to lead to a specific result—such as learning mathematics, or learning to like mathematics, or learning that a little practice makes you better at something. In fact, researchers have tested that theory, and have shown that mathematics homework can have a positive impact on student learning.[1]

A second example is the conviction embodied in most teacher education programs that if teachers study material in the social foundations of education—something about the social contexts of schooling—they will be more effective as teachers. One way to express a (condensed) theory of impact for study in the social foundations of education is this:

1. Teachers are more likely to teach effectively if they understand their students well. Understanding students well—like understanding a quotation, a book, or a historical event—depends on understanding relevant *context.*

2. Studying the social foundations of education is likely to help teachers understand their students well, because who students are is not simply a

matter of genes; it is also a matter of culture—for students as for all of us, culture is our primary context. Students' language, beliefs about the world, values, habits, and countless other things that are rewarded and punished in schools are shaped by their cultural context. Social foundations study can therefore help teachers understand, for example, what students mean even if they don't say it in standard English; or that students' intelligence manifests itself in many different ways; that students' ways of demonstrating intelligence are affected by cultures that don't always match the school culture; that different students need different kinds of support to succeed academically, depending on their home and community lives; that teachers can effectively partner with parents to help their children succeed in school; or that when teachers and schools fail to act on such understandings, decade after decade, schools can become "sorting machines," in which children from different social groups will have predictably different success experiences in school—and different life outcomes in society.[2] Such social foundations understanding is also likely to provide data and support for the beliefs and dispositions that many teachers have, that all children really are capable of academic success, even if they do not always show it—and that teachers can commit themselves individually and collectively to finding ways for children to succeed academically, whether or not the economic, ethnic, or linguistic background of the students matches that of their teachers.

3. When teachers understand their students well as products of culture just as teachers are a product of their cultures—and when they act individually and collectively to find ways to bridge the cultural gap between the school and the child—low-income and ethnically diverse children can succeed with challenging academic material. Students who were not learning become students who learn well. The evidence for such academic success is overwhelming.[3]

Social Context: Understanding Students, Self, and a Theory of Impact

While the above three points sketch out a theory of impact for how social foundations study can help teachers better support student learning, there are other dimensions to the theory of impact. For example, social foundations study can help teachers understand not just the students in social context, but themselves and their work in social context as well. If schools have been acting too much as "sorting" institutions in which students' socioeconomic status predicts pretty well how they will succeed (or not) in schools, then teachers can examine their own contributions to the sorting functions of the school as opposed to educational functions. Teachers can critically examine their own work to see how they can do more than simply be agents of a mass testing society, for example, and instead become allies of parents who want their children to succeed against the historical odds.

In other words, social context understanding can help teachers better understand their own impact, how to think about the impact they wish to have, and how to achieve that impact in ways that are not reducible to test scores. Social foundations study can help teachers develop their own theories of impact that are consistent with the social contexts in which they find themselves as well as consistent with their own highest aspirations to have a positive influence on the life chances of children and youth. In this connection, you may remember the Ron Edmonds remark from Chapter 13:

> How many effective schools would you have to see to be persuaded of the educability of poor children? If your answer is more than one, then I suspect that you have reasons of your own for preferring to believe that basic pupil performance derives from family background instead of the school response to family background.[4]

Edmonds went on to make what seemed in 1979 like a bold claim:

> We can, whenever and wherever we choose, successfully teach all children whose schooling is of interest to us. We already know more than we need to do that. Whether or not we do it must finally depend on how we feel about the fact that we haven't so far.[5]

Now, 30 years later, Edmonds's claim is no longer so surprising. A significant number of schools throughout the nation have shown what low-income and minority kids are capable of achieving, if the right school conditions are provided.[6] The social foundations theory of impact outlined earlier has been tested and demonstrated many times over since Edmonds's day: If we do not limit student learning solely in the child, but rather in how the culture of the school responds to the child and the child's culture, the child's chances for academic success improve dramatically.

So the theory of impact for this book is this: Those teachers who best understand what this book has to offer are in a better position to help improve student learning because they will understand students, schools, and themselves in the social contexts that affect the meanings and interactions among these three components of educational processes. To frame and execute their purposes well (as Dewey said in *Experience and Education*) teachers will likely have to situate their work in the context of the society as a whole, the specific community in which they work, and their school as an organization of adults who need to work together if the needs of children and youth are to be served. They will also need knowledge of subject matter, techniques for teaching it,

and the dispositions to communicate care and commitment to students.[7]

Notice we did not say "such teachers are likely to have a powerful effect on ending racism, gender bias, and economic discrimination in America." We would like to see such inequities as these come to an end, of course, but we don't think our theory of impact supports such a claim. Although this book documents such inequities, it does so *not* to show that teachers can transform society, but rather to show that despite such social evils, teachers can (and sometimes do) succeed in helping students realize their full potential as learners and as persons. That in itself is a significant social change. But to do this, teachers have to really know what they are doing—and in most instances, they have to know how to do it together.

This position is a disappointment to some people who view the point of teaching primarily as a lever to change an inequitable social structure. We do not reject the idea that teachers can change society, but we think the theory of impact for that view is much less clear than the theory that you as a teacher can teach students effectively regardless of their socioeconomic background. Decades of statistics tell us that it is hard enough to accomplish even that ambitious goal. Teaching to change the world, as one popular textbook is titled, is harder still; and more difficult, too, to support with a plausible theory for how a teacher is likely to have such an impact.[8] But as we will show, it is not unreasonable to believe that teachers can change themselves, change their students, and change society. It's just that a different theory of impact—a different explanation of how one thing leads to another—is needed for each.

You and Your Theory of Impact

So what did the first 13 chapters of this volume tell us about school and society in the United States that a teacher needs to know? These chapters have shown that from the very beginning, the United States has been divided about how much we have wanted to support public education, and certainly divided about how much we believe all children are entitled to equal resources for their education. The Constitution made it a state responsibility, rather than a national priority. And later, states commonly made the funding of schooling a local matter, leading to all manner of inequalities. In the early

1800s, Jefferson couldn't get the state of Virginia to support universal public education. When Massachusetts led the nation in supporting public schools at a state level, the system of private schools continued to serve the wealthy. While state-supported schools eventually took hold in the South, African Americans were prevented from attending them prior to the Civil War, and from the Civil War until the 1950s were not allowed to attend "White only" public schools.

And so the book continues. From the early national period to the common-school era; from the progressive era through the cold war to the post–cold war period of contemporary school reform; from agrarianism to industrialism and urbanization; from urbanization to suburbanization and the postindustrial computer age; from classical liberalism to modern liberalism to neoliberalism—the story of public schools in the United States has been marked by a tension between the ideals of democratic equality versus practices of unequal schooling that decade after decade reward power and privilege with educational resources far superior to those of the nonprivileged majority. (Special note to students: It would not surprise the authors if your professor selected that sprawling sentence as an essay prompt for your final exam. If you can explain every term and the relationships among them to your most tolerant friend or family member, you should be in great shape.) As a consequence, what neighborhood you are born into today—the day we are writing, and the day you read this page—is a powerful predictor of not only what kind of schooling you will experience but where you will end up in the social and economic hierarchy of the United States.

The volume also tells us that it need not be that way. As Rochester, New York, local AFT president Adam Urbanski said, "Socioeconomic status is a powerful predictor of student achievement in school—in the absence of good instruction."[9] In other words, when schools are organized to provide high-quality instruction to low-income youth, high-level learning results. As a number of independent researchers have told us over the past 30 years, and as outstanding schools have repeatedly shown us—we know why kids learn well in some schools and not others, and we know how to produce those kinds of learning environments.

But by and large, we don't produce them. The discussions of political economy and ideology in this volume help us understand why. They help us see, for example, that some people would prefer to spend their local property taxes on their own schools at three times the support level that other schools in their state receive, rather than

on equalizing schools throughout the state. The history of liberalism from classical to neoliberalism helps us understand why people would defend such inequalities as "the American way" by saying that the competitive market should be left to operate, and that it is a violation of freedom to make people use their money for other people's neighborhoods and children. We might not agree with that defense, but we can understand it in the political–economic and ideological context of U.S. history.

And it would be surprising if our current education system did *not* reflect the history of genocide against American Indians, or enslaving African Americans, or progressive era schools that consigned working-class kids to mind-numbing vocationalism. It would be surprising because those days were not so long ago. John Dewey, for example, one of the founders of modern schooling, was alive when the authors of this book were children. Yet Dewey was born before the Civil War, only 33 years after Jefferson's death. Many people today remember clearly when the last of the ex-slaves died in the 1960s.

So on the one hand, the message of this book is that we can understand where we are today by looking at our past. But another message is that, if we are to honor the best of the work that educators have done before us, we have a lot of work to do. If "all men are created equal" was a sentiment that could fuel the civil rights movement, the women's equality movement, for example, and the integration of races, cultures, and sexes in today's schools, it did so only through struggle. People devoted countless hours to strategizing together, protesting together, and politicking together to make our social institutions operate consistently with the ideals of democracy. Many of them were humiliated or lost their livelihoods; some were beaten; some were killed.

Those struggles should remind teachers and administrators today that if we wish to see schools serve all kids' learning needs, and not primarily those fortunate enough to be born into economic privilege, then someone—a lot of someones—will have to work for change. It may be that the most important changes you can bring about are in your own school. And it is almost certain that any important changes you bring about will be the result of your working collectively and strategically with others—parents, teachers, staff, administrators—rather than working alone.

But it's also possible that this is not at all why you got into teaching. Your theory of impact may not be about issues of democracy and equity: It may be about teaching English as well as you can. Or it might be about just getting a job after college. So on the one hand this volume shows how our current schools got to be the way they are, and on the other hand it shows that schools, like other social institutions, can change to better serve the needs of citizens. But that change agenda might not be your agenda.

Why Teach?

There are many different motivations to become a teacher, and to stay in teaching. One is tempted to say that there are as many different reasons to teach as there are teachers—or to get really romantic about it—as many different reasons as there are students. People have career motives, economic motives, "summers-off motives," political motives, psychological motives, and so on. But the reason for examining this question of "why teach" is not to examine human individuality. Rather, it is to theorize a bit about the realities of impact: what you can actually *accomplish* as a teacher, and how what you can accomplish is determined so greatly by what you *want* to accomplish.

Why do people go into teaching, and why do they stay there? For the purposes of this analysis, we might say there are three big reasons, and rarely does a teacher hold only one of them. But they differ enough that different people emphasize different ones in their motives to teach. The many legitimate reasons to be a teacher might be said to fall into these three categories:

- It's mostly about me.

- It's mostly about the kids.

- It's mostly about social change (or democracy, or social justice).

We need to resist the temptation to impose a moral hierarchy on these motives, as if the first one is purely selfish and the third one is selfless and saintly. As individual cases are examined, such judgments may not be valid at all. First of all, people will rarely if ever be motivated by only one of these considerations—generally two or more will operate, with one or two receiving the greatest emphasis.

Second, there may be good and bad reasons to gravitate toward any of these three orientations. If someone is "mostly about social change," for example, he or she may be attracted by playing the role of the social change agent, but not be aware of the real day-to-day work that this requires. Sometimes people leave the profession precisely because their motives don't match the skillset and the opportunities needed to act on them. Some people

choosing to teach could be "mostly about me" because they have vowed to be the first in their families to earn a college degree and because teaching was what they always wanted to do since they were small children—so becoming a teacher is a fulfillment of a dream, rather than primarily being about helping others fulfill their dreams or having a social impact. One would hesitate to say that such an individual was selfish or morally suspect. In fact, one could imagine such an individual becoming a powerful force in kids' lives.

Whether you are making a simple vocational choice because you have to earn a living, or you just want a job that has to do with mathematics because you love it (both "mostly about me"); or you are driven by the learning needs of low-income kids and want to make a difference in their life chances ("mostly about the kids"); or you believe, as George Counts wrote, that "schools can build a new social order," you owe it to yourself to have a clear theory of impact undergirding your work and your goals.[10] Without an explanation of how your work is going to result in certain outcomes and not others, you risk just going through the motions, and you risk being sorely disappointed in what you actually achieve. A theory of impact, quite simply, makes you smarter about what you do.

Orientations to Teaching and Theories of Impact

Given how our teacher preparation programs are set up in colleges and universities, many teachers make their decision to enter the profession at a very young age—some still in their teens—as a vocational decision without much of a theory of impact at all. They are dealing with the more immediate realities of choosing a major and choosing a career track when it would be an exaggeration to say they have a burning desire to choose any one direction over another. Sometimes it's just a process of elimination ("I'm not going to be a doctor or a lawyer, but I am going to do something with the degree"). In other instances, there are more distinct personal reasons, such as liking kids, or liking a particular subject matter. It's often said, rightly or not, that elementary school teachers like to teach kids, while high school teachers like to teach subjects. Sometimes becoming a teacher is about finding a professional identity. In the late teens and early 20s, for example, people are about deciding who they are going to be in life. Increasingly, career-changers are making midcourse corrections in their own professional identities.

None of these examples is unusual. Nor can any of them be said to be a case of a teacher who has clear goals for having an impact on students, or aspirations for changing society in some way. These are examples of teachers who go into teaching for more immediate, personal reasons in which "It's mostly about me." You could say there's nothing wrong with that, but at the same time we would hope that such teachers will come to look beyond their own needs to the needs of their students, and this is usually what happens. However, in 50 years combined experience of working with teachers, we have found that not every teacher develops clear goals; not all teachers have a clear explanation for how their work will have consequences for students. Instead of a theory of impact, such teachers have a hope or a faith. American historian Henry Adams, born during the common-school era and living until well into the progressive era, captured this sentiment well: "A teacher affects eternity; he can never tell where his influence stops."[11]

While this may be a comforting thought, and certainly a famous one, it is not a substitute for a theory of impact. You might call this the "ripple in the pond" theory, if it can be called a theory at all: You disturb the pond's surface and the ripples move on their own beyond your control. But if you want to do more than reassure yourself that you might be having an impact of some unknown kind, then it's a good idea to get clearer about what your theory of impact is. It's useful to get strategic about exactly what impact you are seeking to have on your students' thinking, valuing, understanding, skills, and life chances—and how you could actually achieve those consequences in your classroom and school. Examining teachers for whom "It's mostly about the kids" might be a better place to seek such a theory of impact.

It's Mostly about the Kids

For many teachers, even those who begin their careers with "It's mostly about me" as their orientation, the focus of their work and worry is their students. For such teachers, "It's mostly about the kids." Their primary orientation is to try to make a difference in the lives of their students. The difference might be purely learning-focused, such as awakening as many children as possible to the love of literature, or the belief that they really *can* do algebra. Or it might be about

affecting children's life chances, as in taking whatever steps are necessary to help a child and child's family see college as a real possibility, when they had thought otherwise.

For teachers who measure their own success by their impact on children, having a theory of impact becomes particularly important. Social foundations of education becomes especially relevant, because it helps teachers understand why it is said that "in education, it's never too early and it's never too late." That is, social foundations helps teachers understand that the ability to learn is not simply determined by genetics (except in relatively rare cases of birth defects of certain kinds) but is greatly influenced by the learning experiences that people have in their cultural contexts. This means that no matter how far behind grade level one's students might be, there is strong reason to believe they are capable of learning difficult academic material. That is, *skill* level is not the same as ability to learn—it is more an indicator of the kinds of learning experiences that a student has had in the past, and those experiences are deeply influenced by race, ethnicity, language, and class. Here, too, teachers are in a good position to reflect on how their own cultural experiences are a good "fit" with the students' needs, and whether the school as a whole is sufficiently responsive to the students' ways of learning.

Having a strong theory of impact, for such teachers, may well mean:

- becoming clear about having ambitious learning goals for their students,

- learning about what must be done in their classrooms and in the school more generally to help the students achieve those goals, and

- becoming clear about how they are going to assess whether those goals are being reached.

Having a theory of impact in helping struggling kids reach new heights of learning might require having a theory of *teacher* learning. That is, it may be important to pay attention to the literature on professional learning communities as places where teachers learn together how to meet the needs of their students, because it is rare that any single teacher has all the know-how necessary to help all kids succeed. But together, teachers can share what they know, influence one another's thinking, push each other to new professional levels, and so on. Teacher educator Peter Murrell wrote recently about a particular kind of teacher know-how that we still do not see often enough in schools:

> The "know how" to which I refer is based upon a deep understanding of *what it means to make community*. Obviously, people make communities—and people living in community have to work at maintaining it. But, I refer here to community building as thoughtful, intentional, and collaborative professional action.[12]

Note those words: "thoughtful, intentional, and collaborative professional action." For teachers who are "mostly about the kids," the research and knowledge base are deep and compelling: Teachers who work together to frame and execute common goals, and assess whether those goals are being achieved, have a compelling theory of teacher learning, and this theory of teacher learning is part of a theory of impact. We know a great deal about how kids learn, under what conditions they learn best, and what teachers can do individually and collectively to support them. Teacher learning is an enormous part of this. One of the richest single sources of theory and data on these matters is the work of the Consortium on Chicago School Research (http://ccsr.uchicago.edu/content/index.php). The consortium's work supports the notion of "professional learning communities" (PLCs). One good way to see what is meant by that term is to use the following scoring rubric on a school you are familiar with. The criteria are instructive: They not only describe what a professional learning community looks like; they allow you to assess the degree to which a PLC has developed or is developing in a given school. (See Exhibit 14.1.)

It's Mostly about Social Change (or Democracy, or Social Justice)

It's one thing to say that we know a lot about supporting student learning, regardless of family background; it's another to say we know a lot about how schools can change society. In Part 1 we read an article by John Dewey claiming that schools do not lead social change, but educators can become "allies" of social changes in the making. The idea that there is a direct link between teaching and social change is a popular one. Like Henry Adams mentioned previously, American author Henry James penned a famous statement about the teacher's influence:

> To believe in a child is to believe in the future. Through their aspirations they will save the world. With their combined knowledge the turbulent seas of hate and injustice will be calmed. They will champion the causes of life's underdogs, forging a society without class discrimination. They will supply humanity with music and beauty as it has never been known. They will endure. Towards these ends I pledge my life's work. I will supply the children with tools and knowledge to overcome the obstacles. I will pass on the wisdom of my years and temper it with patience. I shall impact in each child the desire to fulfill his or her dream. I shall teach.[13]

Again we have a viewpoint that sounds appealing, but that is not very useful as a theory of impact. "I shall impact in each child the desire to fulfill his or her dream," and "they will save the world," in part by "forging a society without class discrimination."

One problem with this sort of high-sounding rhetoric is that there is little or no evidence to support it. We don't have a good theory of impact that would lead us to believe that teachers can bring about such changes because, as Dewey pointed out, schools are controlled by those who most benefit from the social order as it is. There is no reason to expect anyone in power to support schools that would overturn that state of affairs, either quickly or slowly. A good theory for how the power structure of the modern world will be dramatically changed by teachers simply has not been put forward in any compelling way—though schools can certainly be shown to have made their contributions to educating students who are less racist and less sexist, once those social movements were under way and supported by legislation.

A second problem is that those who become teachers to make a visible impact on the social order—those who teach to change the world—can easily be disappointed when they see how difficult that is. It's difficult enough to change the behavior of a high school sophomore, let alone Western capitalism as we know it. So teachers who enter teaching without a realistic appraisal of what can actually be accomplished in the teacher's role can be frustrated in their efforts.

At the same time, teachers who are fully committed to student learning often have to lead change in their own schools to achieve it. We do want to encourage such institutional change for the results that can be achieved—for the outcomes that a good theory of impact can support. A low-performing school *CAN* become a high-performing school, as a great deal of research shows.[14] And teachers should not wait for the revolution for this to happen, because teacher leadership can help change the culture of a school in powerful ways. We do not want to deny the spirit of a comment

Exhibit 14.1   Self-Assessment: Professional Learning Community Continuum

School Characteristics	Rating
Rating Scale: 1—Nonexistent; 2—Barely underway; 3—Evidence of progress; 4—A school strength; 5—Truly exemplary, ready to demonstrate to other schools	
1. **Mission:** Evidence that learning for all is school's core purpose. Learning outcomes are clearly articulated to all stakeholders in the school, and each student's attainment of the outcomes is carefully monitored. Practices, programs, and policies of the school are continually assessed on the basis of their impact on student learning.	
2. **Shared Vision:** Do we know what we are trying to create? Staff members routinely articulate the major principles of the shared vision and use those principles to guide their day-to-day efforts and decisions.	
3. **Shared Values:** How must we behave to advance our vision? The values of the school are embedded in the school culture. They are evident to new staff and to others outside the school, and they influence all policies and practices in the school.	
4. **Goals and Priorities:** All staff pursue measurable performance goals as part of their routine responsibilities. Goals are clearly linked to the school's vision. Staff celebrate goal attainment and demonstrate willingness to pursue challenging stretch goals.	
5. **Collaborative Culture—Teachers:** Teachers function as a team (or in teams). They work collaboratively to identify collective goals, develop strategies to achieve those goals, gather relevant data, and learn from one another.	
6. **Collaborative Culture—Administrator-Teacher Relations:** Staff are fully involved in the decision-making processes of the school. Administrators pose questions, delegate authority, create collaborative decision making, and provide staff with the information, training, and parameters they need to make good decisions.	
7. **Parent Partnerships:** The school–parent partnership moves beyond open communication to enabling parents to assist their children in learning. Parents are full partners in the educational decisions that affect their children.	
8. **Action Research:** Topics for action research arise from the shared vision and goals of the school. Staff members regard action research as an important component of their professional responsibilities. Teachers frequently try to learn from their colleagues.	
9. **Continuous Improvement:** Everyone in the school participates in an ongoing cycle of systematically gathering and analyzing data to identify the gap between actual and desired results, setting new goals, developing strategies to achieve them, and monitoring results.	
10. **Focus on Results:** Teams of teachers are hungry for information on results. Teachers themselves gather relevant data and use these data to set goals and monitor progress toward them.	
11. **Overall PLC Development:** This principle is deeply embedded in the school's culture, representing a driving force in the daily work of the school.	

Source: Condensed and adapted from R. DuFour, R. DuFour, R. Eaker, and G. Karhanek, *Whatever It Takes: How Professional Learning Communities Respond When Kids Don't Learn* (Bloomington, IN: Solution Tree, 2004).

typically attributed to anthropologist Margaret Mead: "Never doubt that a small group of thoughtful, committed people can change the world. Indeed it is the only thing that ever has."[15] What is at issue for us as educators is what it means to "change the world." If schools can be changed for the better in this neighborhood and that one, in this city and that one, and thousands and even millions of children are getting the chance to learn who once were not, that's a different world—and an achievable one. But change will likely have to start at home, in one's own school, demonstrating how things can indeed be different. The scholarship on such schools grows year by year.

Teacher Leadership and Professional Learning Communities

We conclude with a brief word about teacher leadership, a theme that is visited again in our Primary Source Reading. It is a truism that leadership is necessary to any organization achieving its goals, whether the leadership is vested in one person or many together. It is also true that your goals as a teacher are most likely going to be achieved, or not, in an organization called "school." Contemporary research is demonstrating that those schools that most succeed "against the odds" of poverty and racism are those in which the principal is not the only leader in the building; teacher leaders are proving to be crucial.

What is teacher leadership? One way to define it is the willingness and ability of teachers to take responsibility for school outcomes outside their own classrooms. Those are the individuals to whom other teachers and administrators turn to help lead a school in new and better directions. What kinds of goals can teacher leadership make it possible to achieve? We now know that teacher leadership can help teachers collaborate to evaluate the effectiveness of their work together, to make decisions about how to make it better, and to implement new approaches in ways that improve student learning. When enough teacher leaders are so engaged, that will be a social change of considerable significance. Teacher leadership can be part of a compelling theory of impact for how schools can better serve populations of students that historically have been ill-served by school and society.

Primary Source Reading

Organizing Schools for Improvement

Research on Chicago school improvement indicates that improving elementary schools requires coherent, orchestrated action across five essential supports.

Anthony S. Bryk

Alexander Elementary School and Hancock Elementary School began the 1990s as two of the worst schools in Chicago in terms of math and reading achievement. Only two miles apart, the schools are in bordering neighborhoods and appear similar in many ways. Both enrolled nearly 100% minority students from families considered low income.

During the 1990s, both launched an array of initiatives aimed at boosting student achievement. Hancock moved impressively forward, while Alexander barely moved the needle on improvement. How did Hancock "beat the odds" while Alexander failed to do so?

This puzzle led us to undertake a systematic longitudinal investigation of hundreds of elementary schools in Chicago, just like Alexander and Hancock. Beginning in 1990, the Consortium on Chicago School Research initiated an intensive longitudinal study of the internal workings and external community conditions that distinguished improving elementary schools from those that failed to improve. That unique 15-year database allowed us to develop, test, and validate a framework of essential supports for school improvement. These data provided an extraordinary window to examine the complex interplay of how schools are organized and interact with the local community to alter dramatically the odds for improving student achievement. The lessons learned offer guidance for teachers, parents, principals, superintendents, and civic leaders in their efforts to improve schools across the country.

Five Essential Supports for School Improvement

Students' academic learning occurs principally in classrooms as students interact with teachers around subject matter. How we organize and operate a school has a major effect on the instructional exchanges in its classrooms. Put simply, whether classroom learning proceeds depends in large measure on how the school as a social context supports teaching and sustains student engagement. Through our research, we identified five organizational features of schools that interact with life inside classrooms and are essential to advancing student achievement.

1. Coherent instructional guidance system. Schools in which student learning improves have coherent instructional guidance systems that articulate the what and how of instruction. The learning tasks posed for students are key here, as are the assessments that make manifest what students actually need to know and provide feedback to inform subsequent instruction. Coordinated with this are the materials, tools, and instructional routines shared across a faculty that scaffold instruction. Although individual teachers may have substantial discretion in how they use these resources, the efficacy of individual teacher efforts depends on the quality of the supports and the local community of practice that forms around their use and refinement.

2. Professional capacity. Schooling is a human resource–intensive enterprise. Schools are only as good as the quality of faculty, the professional development that supports their learning, and the faculty's capacity to work together to improve instruction. This support directs our attention to a school's ability to recruit and retain capable staff, the efficacy of performance feedback and professional development, and the social resources within a staff to work together to solve local problems.

3. Strong parent-community-school ties. The disconnect between local school professionals and the parents and community that a school is intended to serve is a persistent concern in many urban contexts. The absence of vital ties is a problem; their presence is a multifaceted resource for improvement. The quality of these ties links directly to students' motivation and school participation and can provide a critical resource for classrooms.

4. Student-centered learning climate. All adults in a school community forge a climate that enables students to think of themselves as learners. At a minimum, improving schools establish a safe and orderly environment—the most basic prerequisite for learning. They endorse ambitious academic work coupled with support for each student. The combination allows students to believe in themselves, to persist, and ultimately to achieve.

5. Leadership drives change. Principals in improving schools engage in a dynamic interplay of instructional and inclusive facilitative leadership. On the instructional side, school leaders influence local activity around core instructional programs, supplemental academic and social supports, and the hiring and development of staff. They establish strategic priorities for using resources and buffer externalities that might distract from coherent reform. Working in tandem with this, principals build relationships across the school community. Improving teaching and learning places demands on these relationships. In carrying out their daily activities, school leaders advance instrumental objectives while also trying to enlist teachers in the change effort. In the process, principals cultivate a growing cadre of leaders (teachers, parents, and community members) who can help expand the reach of this work and share overall responsibility for improvement.

Using extensive survey data collected by the consortium from teachers, principals, and students, we were able to develop school indicators for each of the five essential supports, chart changes in these indicators over time, and then relate these organizational conditions to subsequent changes in student attendance and learning gains in reading and mathematics. Among our findings:

- Schools with strong indicators on most supports were 10 times more likely to improve than schools with weak supports.

- Half of the schools strong on most supports improved substantially in reading.

- Not a single school weak on most supports improved in mathematics.

- A material weakness in any one support, sustained over several years, undermined other change efforts, and improvement rarely resulted.

This statistical evidence affords a strong warrant that how we organize schools is critical for student achievement. Improving schools entails coherent, orchestrated action across all five essential supports. Put simply, there is no one silver bullet.

Dynamics of Improvement

Schools are complex organizations consisting of multiple interacting subsystems (that is, the five essential organizational supports). Personal and social considerations mix deeply in the day-to-day workings of a school. These interactions are bound by various rules, roles, and prevailing practices that, in combination with technical resources, constitute schools as formal organizations.

In a sense, almost everything interacts with everything else. That means that a true picture of what enables some schools to improve and others to stagnate requires identifying the critical interconnections among the five essential supports: *How do these five essential supports function together to substantially change the odds for enhancing student engagement and academic learning?*

Schools that improved student attendance over time strengthened their ties to parents and community and used these ties as a core resource for enhancing safety and order across the school. This growing sense of routine and security further combined with a better-aligned curriculum that continually exposed students to new tasks and ideas. Engaging pedagogy afforded students active learning roles in the classroom. High-quality professional development aimed to enhance teachers' capacity to orchestrate such activity under the trying circumstances that most confront daily. When this combination of conditions existed, the basic recipe for improving student attendance was activated.

In terms of the organizational mechanisms influencing academic achievement, this can be told in two contrasting stories. Schools that stagnated—no learning improvement over several years—were characterized by clear weaknesses in their instructional guidance system. They had poor curriculum alignment coupled with relatively little emphasis on active student engagement in learning. These instructional weaknesses combined with weak faculty commitments to the school, to innovation, and to working together as a professional community. Undergirding all of this were anemic school-parent community ties.

In contrast, schools in which student learning improved used high-quality professional development as a key instrument for change. They had maximum leverage when these opportunities for teachers occurred in a supportive environment (that is, a school-based professional community) and when teaching was guided by a common, coherent, and aligned instructional system. Undergirding all of this, in turn, was a solid base of parent-community school ties.

There is a logic to reading the five essential organizational supports from left to right—leadership drives change in the four other organizational supports—but the actual execution of improvement is more organic and dynamic. Good teachers advance high-quality instruction, but developing good teachers and retaining them in a particular school depends on supportive school leadership and positive work relations with colleagues.

Meaningful parent and community involvement can be a resource for solving problems of safety and order; but, in a reciprocal fashion, these ties are likely to be stronger in safe and orderly schools. This reciprocity carries over to leadership as the driver for change. While a principal commands formal authority to effect changes in the four other organizational supports, a school with some strengths in these four supports is also easier to lead.

Arguing for the significance of one individual support over another is tempting, but we ultimately came to view the five supports as an organized system of elements in dynamic interaction with one another. As such, primary value lies in their integration and mutual reinforcement. In this sense, school development is much like baking a cake. By analogy, you need an appropriate mix of flour, sugar, eggs, oil, baking powder, and flavoring to produce a light, delicious cake. Without sugar, it will be tasteless. Without eggs or baking powder, the cake will be flat and chewy. Marginal changes in a single ingredient—for example, a bit more flour, large versus extra large eggs—may not have noticeable effects. But, if one ingredient is absent, it is just not a cake.

Similarly, strong local leadership acting on the four other organizational elements constitutes the essential ingredients for spurring school development. Broad-based instructional change and improved student learning entail coordinated action across these various domains. Correspondingly, student outcomes are likely to stagnate if a material weakness persists in any of the supports. The ensemble of supports is what's essential for improvement. Taken together, they constitute the core organizational ingredients for advancing student engagement and achievement.

Building Trust

Effecting a coherent improvement plan across the essential supports can be a daunting challenge. Embracing a coherent improvement plan challenges longstanding norms about teacher autonomy in the classroom and a laissez-faire orientation toward professional development and innovative practice. Not surprisingly, cultivating teacher buy-in and commitment becomes a central concern in promoting the deep cultural changes required for such an initiative to be successful. At this juncture, concerns about building relational trust come forcefully into play.

Some of the most powerful relationships found in our data are associated with relational trust and how it operates as both a lubricant for organizational change and a moral resource for sustaining the hard work of local school improvement. Absent such trust, schools find it nearly impossible to strengthen parent–community ties, build professional capacity, and enable a student-centered learning climate. The reverse is also true: Low trust is linked to weaker developments across these organizational supports.

Given the asymmetry of power in urban school communities, principals play a key role in nurturing trust formation. Principals establish both respect and personal regard when they acknowledge the vulnerabilities of others, actively listen to their concerns, and eschew arbitrary actions. If principals couple this empathy with a compelling school vision, and if teachers see their behavior as advancing this vision, their personal integrity is also affirmed. Then, assuming principals are competent at managing routine school affairs, an overall ethos conducive to building trust is likely to emerge.

Such leadership uses power constructively to jump-start change. In the initial stages, school leaders cultivate low-risk collaborations among faculty members who are predisposed to working together. School-based professional development is designed to advance instructional improvement and enhance a sense of community and shared commitments among faculty. Similarly, principals engage parents and other community members in activities that enable participants to contribute to the school and advance the learning of their own children and thus experience a sense of efficacy. "Small wins" gradually build a school community's capacity for the greater challenges (and higher-risk social exchanges) that may lie ahead.

On balance, as principals seek to initiate change in a school, not everyone is necessarily affirmed or afforded an equal voice. Relational trust can emerge only if participants show their commitment to engage in the hard work of reform and see others doing the same. Principals must take the lead and extend themselves by reaching out to others. On occasion, they may be called on to demonstrate trust in colleagues who may not fully reciprocate, at least initially. But in the end, principals also must be prepared to use their authority to reform the school community through professional norms. Interestingly, such authority may rarely be needed once new norms are firmly established.

Unrecognized Challenges

In many recent discussions about school reform, ideas about parent involvement and school community contexts fade into the background. Some school reform advocates believe only instruction and instructional leadership matter. This perspective assumes that a school's social and personal connections with local families and communities play a small role in reform. Our evidence, however, offers a strong challenge. To be sure, instruction matters—a lot. But social context matters too. We have documented that strength across all five essential supports, including parent–school–community ties, is critical for improvement to occur in all kinds of urban schools. Unfortunately, we have also learned that this organizational development is much harder to initiate and sustain in some community contexts than others.

As data accumulated in Chicago and school-by-school trends in attendance and student learning gains became clear, a complex pattern of results emerged. Improving schools could be found in all kinds of neighborhoods varying by socioeconomic and racial/ethnic composition. Stagnating schools, in contrast, piled up in very poor, racially isolated African-American neighborhoods. We became haunted by the question, "Why? What made reform so much more difficult to advance in some school communities?"

Our analyses led us to two different answers. First, the social capital of a neighborhood is a significant resource for improving its local school. We found that the latter was much more likely in neighborhoods where residents had a history of working together. In contrast, the absence of such collective efficacy in the surrounding community increased the likelihood that a troubled school would continue to stagnate. Correspondingly, communities with strong institutions, especially religious institutions, were more supportive contexts for school improvement. These institutions afford a network of social ties that can be appropriated for other purposes, such as improving schools. They also create connections that can bring new outside resources into isolated neighborhoods.

So, differences among neighborhoods in their bonding and bridging social capital help explain why the essential supports were more likely to develop in some neighborhoods than others. But this was only a partial answer for a subset of the school communities.

A second mechanism was also at work. We found that the proportion of children who were living under extraordinary circumstances—neglect and abuse, homeless, foster care, domestic violence—also created a significant barrier to improvement in some schools. To be clear, these students were learning at about the same rates as their classmates in whatever school they were enrolled. So, the learning gains for these particular students were not depressing the overall results for their schools. But the odds of school stagnation soared when a concentration of these students appeared in the same place. On balance, schools are principally about teaching and learning, not solving all of the social problems of a community. However, when palpable personal and social needs walk through doors every day, school staff can't be expected to ignore those needs. Our evidence suggests that when the proportion of these needs remains high and pressing, the capacity of a school staff to sustain attention to developing the five essential supports falls by the wayside. A few schools managed to succeed under these circumstances, but most did not.

In sum, a nettlesome problem came into focus on improving student learning to truly disadvantaged communities where social capital is scarce and human need sometimes overwhelming. These schools face a "three-strike" problem. Not only are the schools highly stressed organizations, but they exist in challenged communities and confront an extraordinary density of human needs every day.

Our findings about schooling in truly disadvantaged communities offer a sobering antidote to a heady political rhetoric of "beating the odds" and "no excuses." To be sure, we believe that all schools can and must improve. Such claims represent our highest, most noble aspirations for our children, our schools, and systems of schools. They are ideas worthy of our beliefs and action. But there are also facts, sometimes brutal facts. Not all school communities start out in the same place and confront the same problems. Unless we recognize this, unless we understand more deeply the dynamics of school stagnation, especially in our most neglected communities, we seem bound to repeat the failures of the past.

Our concluding point is straightforward—it is hard to improve what we do not understand. We need more attention on how to improve schools in these specific contexts. All plausible ideas for educational improvement deserve serious consideration. Absent systematic analysis of not only where we succeed but also where and why we fail, we will continue to relegate many of our students and their teachers to a similar fate.

Belief and Doubt

Our work has been motivated by a deep belief that schools can and must do much better if we are to revitalize the American dream of opportunity for every child. A good education is now more important than ever in creating the pathway to this opportunity. Unfortunately, for far too many, this pathway is now closed, and opportunity dies early. Thomas Jefferson's observation about America's noble experiment in democracy—"If a nation expects to be ignorant and free, in a state of civilization, it expects what never was and never will be"—is truer today than ever before.

However, a belief in the power of schooling and in our ability to improve this institution must also coexist with a modicum of doubt—a critical perspective—about the wisdom of any particular reform effort. Virtually every initiative involves at least some zone of wishful thinking, and even good designs typically require executing a strategy for which there is no established game plan. We now know, for example, that some schools, especially in poorer African-American neighborhoods, were disproportionately left behind. This is a brutal fact that had to be told; our role as an agent informing reform meant bringing it to light. Absent our inquiry, this result could easily have remained hidden in a more casual accounting of the overall positive test score trends.

But we must also do more than just tell the facts. We must seek to understand, and we must also ask why. To see race and class differences in rates of improvement and to just stop there without probing deeper simply creates more fodder for conflict among critics and apologists of the current state of affairs. This dysfunctional discourse advances no common understandings and helps no children and no families. What is really going on in these school communities, and why are the important tasks of improving schools so difficult to advance? Asking these questions, bringing evidence to bear on them, and in the process advancing public discourse about the improvement of public education is a vital role that applied social inquiry can and should fill in a technically complex and politically diverse democratic society. In the end, melding strong, independent disciplined inquiry with a sustained commitment among civic leaders to improve schooling is the only long-term assurance that an education of value for all may finally emerge.

Notes

Chapter 1

1. S. Tozer, "The Social Foundations of Education: School and Society in a Century of NSSE," in Lyn Corno, ed., *Education across a Century: The Centennial Volume* (Chicago: National Society for the Study of Education, 2001).
2. The term "hidden curriculum" is generally attributed to curriculum theorist Phillip W. Jackson, *Life in Classrooms* (New York: Holt, Rhinehart & Winston, 1968).
3. Abraham Flexner, "The Gates of Excellence," *Journal of Adult Education,* January 1932, p. 5.
4. The material in this section relies heavily on Antony Andrews, *The Greeks* (New York: Norton, 1967).
5. The philosopher Aristotle articulated important purposes for education during this period. David Ross, trans., *Aristotle: The Nicomachean Ethics* (New York: Oxford University Press, 1998), p. 137.
6. Thomas L. Pangle, ed., *The Laws of Plato* (New York: Basic Books, 1980).

Chapter 2

1. Annette Gordon-Reed, *Thomas Jefferson and Sally Hemings: An American Controversy* (Paperback, March 22, 1998); Robert F. Turner, *The Jefferson-Hemings Controversy: Report of …* (Hardcover, 2011)
2. Garry Wills, "Negro President," *Jefferson and the Slave Power* (New York: Houghton Mifflin, 2003).
3. *Historical Statistics of U.S. Colonial Times to 1970,* Part 1 (Washington, DC: Bureau of the Census, 1975), pp. 11–12.
4. Dumas Malone, *Jefferson and His Time* (Boston: Little, Brown, 1948, 1951, 1962, 1963), vol. 2, p. 319.
5. Christopher Hitchens, *Thomas Paine's Rights of Man: A Biography* (New York: Atlantic Monthly Press, 2007).
6. Henri Pierenne, *A History of Europe* (Garden City, NY: Doubleday).
7. Alexander Pope (1730), "Intended for Sir Isaac Newton in Westminster Abbey," in Henry W. Boynton, *The Complete Poetical Words of Pope* (Cambridge, MA: Houghton Mifflin, 1931), p. 135 (emphasis in original).
8. John Chester Miller, *The Wolf by the Ears: Thomas Jefferson and Slavery* (New York: Free Press, 1977), p. 33.
9. See G. H. Koch, *Religion of the American Enlightenment* (New York: Crowell, 1968); H. M. Morris, *Deism in Eighteenth-Century America* (New York: Columbia University Press, 1934).
10. Benjamin Franklin, *Autobiography and Other Writings,* Russell B. Nye, ed. (Boston: Houghton Mifflin, 1958), pp. 163–64.
11. See, as an example, Nancy Cott, *The Bonds of Womanhood: "Woman's Sphere" in New England, 1780–1835* (New Haven, CT: Yale University Press, 1977).
12. Russell B. Nye, *The Cultural Life of the New Nation* (New York: Harper Torchbooks, 1963), pp. 29–30.
13. Julian P. Boyd, ed., *The Papers of Thomas Jefferson* (Princeton, NJ: Princeton University Press, 1965), vol. 10, pp. 244–45.
14. Patrick Henry, quoted in Nye, *The Cultural Life,* pp. 38–39.
15. Isaiah Berlin, *Four Essays on Liberty* (New York: Oxford University Press, 1969).
16. Malone, *Jefferson and His Time*, vol. 2, pp. 222–23.
17. See Ronald Takaki, *Iron Cages: Race and Culture in 19th Century America* (Oxford: Oxford University Press), pp. 36–65. Also see Adrian Koch, *The Philosophy of Thomas Jefferson* (New York: Columbia, University Press, 1943), chap. 1.
18. Boyd, *Papers of Jefferson,* vol. 2, pp. 545–47.
19. Quoted in Faun M. Brodie, *Thomas Jefferson: An Intimate Biography* (New York: Bantam Books, 1974), p. 194.
20. Andrew A. Lipscomb and A. E. Berg, eds., *The Writings of Thomas Jefferson* (Washington, DC: Thomas Jefferson Memorial Association, 1903), vol. 14, p. 284.
21. Boyd, *Papers of Jefferson,* vol. 2, p. 49.
22. Leonard W. Levy, *Jefferson and Civil Liberties: The Darker Side* (Cambridge, MA: Harvard University Press, 1963), chap. 3.
23. Malone, *Jefferson and His Time*, vol. 5, p. 388.
24. Henry A. Washington, ed., *The Writings of Thomas Jefferson* (New York: Riker and Thorne, 1854), vol. 7, pp. 397–99.
25. Boyd, *Papers of Jefferson,* vol. 123, p. 441.
26. Daniel Boorstein, *The Lost World of Thomas Jefferson* (Boston: Beacon Press, 1960), p. 190.
27. Boyd, *Papers of Jefferson,* vol. 12, pp. 14–19.
28. Letter to William C. Jarvis, September 28, 1820, in Paul L. Ford, ed., *The Writings of Thomas Jefferson* (New York: G. P. Putnam Sons, 1899), vol. 10, p. 161.
29. Letter to Edward Everett, March 27, 1824, in Lipscomb and Bergh, *Writings of Jefferson,* vol. 16, p. 22.
30. Boyd, *Papers of Jefferson,* vol. 12, p. 442.
31. Ibid.
32. *Notes on the State of Virginia,* in Saul K. Padover, ed., *The Complete Jefferson* (New York: Tudor, 1943), p. 687.
33. Ford, *Writings of Jefferson,* vol. 9, pp. 424–30.
34. Boyd, *Papers of Jefferson,* vol. 2, pp. 526–33.
35. Ibid., pp. 535–43.
36. Ibid., pp. 544–45.
37. Roy Honeywell, *The Educational Work of Thomas Jefferson* (Cambridge, MA: Harvard University Press, 1931), pp. 233–45.
38. Ibid., pp. 245–60.
39. Ford, *Writings of Jefferson,* vol. 9, pp. 427–38.
40. Boyd, *Papers of Jefferson,* vol. 2, p. 528.
41. Ford, *Writings of Jefferson,* vol. 3, pp. 254–55.

42. *Notes on the State of Virginia,* in Ford, *Writings of Jefferson,* vol. 3, p. 250.

43. Ibid.

44. "Report of the Commission," in Honeywell, *Educational Work,* pp. 248–60; "Notes" in Ford, vol. 3, pp. 250–55.

45. Honeywell, *Educational Work,* pp. 248–60.

46. Ford, *Writings of Jefferson,* vol. 9, p. 465.

47. Lipscomb and Bergh, *Writings of Jefferson,* vol. 15, p. 455.

48. Padover, *Notes on the State,* p. 1108.

49. It was the case that each of the schools had required courses. Thus, while students had free election to choose their schools, they did not have free election among the courses.

50. Honeywell, *Educational Work,* p. 252.

51. Boyd, *Papers of Jefferson,* vol. 2, pp. 544–45.

52. Ford, *Writings of Jefferson,* vol. 10, p. 96.

53. Koch, *Religion,* chap. 9.

54. For a more detailed analysis of Jefferson's views on slavery see Miller, *The Wolf by the Ears.*

55. Brodie, *Thomas Jefferson,* pp. 102–104.

56. Adrienne Koch and William Peden, *The Life and Selected Writings of Thomas Jefferson* (New York: Modern Library, 1944), p. 25.

57. Malone, *Jefferson and His Time,* vol. 1, p. 226, and vol. 6, p. 542; Padover, *Notes on the State,* pp. 661–66; Brodie, *Thomas Jefferson,* pp. 7, 42–48, 103–105, 195–99.

58. Quoted in Miller, *Wolf by the Ears,* p. 276.

59. Brodie, *Thomas Jefferson,* pp. 102–104.

60. Koch, *Religion,* p. 130.

61. Malone, *Jefferson and His Time,* vol. 1, p. 445.

62. Takaki, *Iron Cages,* p. 43–44.

63. Ibid., p. 48.

64. Ibid., p. 50. See also Annette Gordon-Reed's new preface to *Thomas Jefferson and Sally Hemmings: An American Controversy* (Charlottesville: University Press of Virginia), 1998.

65. Ibid., p. 58.

66. Ibid., p. 56. The metaphor Jefferson chose in order to underscore his belief that agriculture was necessary for American democracy while commerce and especially manufacturing were detrimental to its health tells us as much about Jefferson's stereotypical mind-set regarding women as it does about his belief in the potential evils of industry. He indicated that Americans must choose between three potential brides: Agriculture—the "pure damsel"; Commerce—the "vixen"; and Manufacturing—the "diseased harlot." (See Malone, *Jefferson and His Time,* vol. 2, p. 383.)

67. Malone, *Jefferson and His Time,* vol. 3, chap. 8.

68. Letter to N. Burwell, in Padover, *Notes on the States,* p. 1085.

69. Ibid., p. 1086.

Chapter 3

1. Ellwood P. Cubberley, *The History of Education* (Boston: Houghton Mifflin, 1920).

2. Joel Spring, *The American School 1642–1993,* 3rd ed. (New York: McGraw-Hill, 1994), p. 7.

3. Stanley K. Schultz, *The Culture Factory* (New York: Oxford University Press, 1973), pp. 11, 23.

4. Carl F. Kaestle, *Pillars of the Republic* (New York: Hill & Wang, 1983), p. 62; Horace Mann, *First Annual Report* (Boston: Dutton & Wentworth, 1838), p. 32; *Second Annual Report* (Boston: Dutton & Wentworth, 1839), p. 38.

5. Kaestle, *Pillars of the Republic,* p. 62.

6. Calculated from Table 1 in Douglass C. North, *The Economy of the United States 1790–1860* (Englewood Cliffs, NJ: Prentice Hall, 1961), p. 35.

7. Freeman Butts and Lawrence Cremin, *A History of Education in American Culture* (New York: Henry Holt, 1953), pp. 157–60.

8. North, *Economy of the United States,* pp. 48–49.

9. Ibid., pp. 70–71; Kaestle, *Pillers of the Republic,* p. 63.

10. David Montgomery, "The Working Classes of the Pre-Industrial American City, 1780–1830," *Labor History* 9 (Winter 1968), pp. 3–22.

11. Paul Faler, "Cultural Aspects of the Industrial Revolution: Lynn, Massachusetts, Shoemakers and Industrial Morality," *Labor History* 15, no. 3 (Summer 1974), pp. 367–94.

12. E. P. Thompson, "Time, Work, Discipline, and Industrial Capitalism," *Past and Present,* no. 38 (December 1968), pp. 56–97; Herbert G. Gutman, "Work, Culture, and Society in Industrializing America, 1815–1919," *American Historical Review* 78, no. 3 (June 1973), pp. 531–88.

13. Faler, "Cultural Aspects," p. 368; Bruce Laurie, "'Nothing on Compulsion': Life Styles of Philadelphia Artisans, 1820–1850," *Labor History* 15, no. 3 (Summer 1974), pp. 337–66.

14. See Perry Miller, *The New England Mind: From Colony to Province* (Cambridge, MA: Harvard University Press, 1953); and *The New England Mind: The Seventeenth Century* (Cambridge, MA: Harvard University Press, 1954).

15. Irving H. Bartlett, *The American Mind in the Mid-Nineteenth Century* (New York: Thomas Y. Crowell, 1967), pp. 6–18.

16. Jonathan Messerli, *Horace Mann, A Biography* (New York: Alfred A. Knopf, 1972). This is the definitive biography and our source for biographical data; however, Messerli should not be held accountable for our interpretive use of the data he provides.

17. Quoted in ibid., p. 12.

18. Quoted in Lawrence Cremin, ed., *The Republic and the School: Horace Mann on the Education of Free Men* (New York: Teachers College Press, 1957), p. 3.

19. Quoted in Messerli, *Horace Mann,* p. 249.

20. Massachusetts State Board of Education and Secretary Horace Mann, *First Annual Report of the Board of Education Together with the First Annual Report of the Secretary of the Board* (Boston: Dutton & Wentworth, 1838), pp. 5–6. Hereafter referred to as *First Annual Report.*

21. Ibid., p. 21.

22. Horace Mann, *Third Annual Report* (Boston: Dutton & Wentworth, 1840), p. 19.

23. Horace Mann, *Sixth Annual Report* (Boston: Dutton & Wentworth, 1843), p. 51.

24. Mann, *First Annual Report*, pp. 8, 26.

25. Ibid., p. 73.

26. Mann, *Second Annual Report,* pp. 30–31.

27. Horace Mann, *Fifth Annual Report* (Boston: Dutton & Wentworth, 1843), pp. 31–33, 121–35.

28. Carle Kaestle and Maris A. Vinovskis, *Education and Social Change in Nineteenth Century Massachusetts* (Cambridge, MA: Cambridge University Press, 1980), p. 196.

29. For a full discussion see Raymond B. Culver, *Horace Mann and Religion in the Massachusetts Public Schools* (New Haven, CT: Yale University Press, 1929). Also see *The Common School Controversy* (Boston: J. N. Bradley, 1844), and *The Bible, The Rod, and Religion in Common Schools* (Boston: J. M. Whittmore, 1847).

30. See Robert Barger, "John Lancaster Spalding: Catholic Education and Social Emissary," unpublished Ph.D. dissertation, University of Illinois at Champaign, 1976, chap. 4, pp. 78–100.

31. Harold J. Lasky, ed., *Autobiography of J. S. Mill with an Appendix of Hitherto Unpublished Speeches and a Preface by Harold J. Lasky* (London: Oxford University Press, 1924), pp. 327–29.

32. Messerli, *Horace Mann*, p. 251.

33. George Armstrong Kelly, ed., *Johann Gottlieb Fichte, Addresses to the German Nation* (New York: Harper Torchbooks, 1968).

34. Horace Mann, *Seventh Annual Report* (Boston: Dutton & Wentworth, 1844), p. 23.

35. Ibid., p. 133.

36. Kenneth Barkin, "Social Control and the Volkschule in Vormarz Prussia," *Central European History* 16, no. 1 (March 1983), pp. 31–52.

37. Horace Mann, *Lectures on Education* (Boston: Ide & Dutton, 1855), p. 304.

38. Ibid., p. 312.

39. Ibid., pp. 316–17.

40. Ibid., p. 308.

41. Ibid., p. 331.

42. Horace Mann, *Eighth Annual Report* (Boston: Dutton & Wentworth, 1845), pp. 94–97.

43. Ibid., p. 94.

44. Ibid., pp.12, 26, 58–66.

45. Mann, *Fourth Annual Report* (Boston: Dutton & Wentworth, 1841), p. 59.

46. Mann, *First Annual Report,* p. 61; *Fourth Annual Report,* p. 10; *Sixth Annual Report,* p. 31; Horace Mann, *Eleventh Annual Report* (Boston: Dutton & Wentworth, 1848), p. 26.

47. Mann, *Sixth Annual Report,* pp. 31–33; *Eleventh Annual Report,* pp. 26–27.

48. Horace Mann, *Lectures,* pp. vii, 72–73.

49. Mann, *Sixth Annual Report,* pp. 28–30; *Seventh Annual Report,* pp. 140–42; Horace Mann *Ninth Annual Report,* (Boston: Dutton & Wentworth, 1846), pp. 34–35; Mann, *Eleventh Annual Report,* pp. 26–27.

50. Horace Mann, *Twelfth Annual Report (*Boston: Dutton & Wentworth, 1849), calculated from table on p. 21.

51. Ibid., p. 22.

52. D. A. Hollinger and C. Capper, eds., *The American Intellectual Tradition,* vol. 1, 2nd ed. (New York: Oxford University Press, 1993), p. 244.

53. Ibid., p. 245.

54. Substantial portions of this section were taken from Paul C. Violas, "Reflections on Theories of Human Capital, Skills Training, and Vocational Education," *Education Theory* 31, no. 2 (Spring 1981), pp. 137–51.

55. The ideas had first been articulated in England earlier in the 18th century by Robert Owen. Peter Drucker, T. W. Schwartz, and Burton A. Weisbrod are the 20th-century social scientists referred to. See Violas, pp. 137–39.

56. Mann, *Fifth Annual Report,* p. 81.

57. Ibid., p. 83.

58. Ibid., pp. 85–86.

59. Ibid., pp. 93–95.

60. Mann, *Twelfth Annual Report,* pp. 53–76.

61. Ibid., p. 58.

62. Ibid., p. 60.

63. Ibid.

64. Ibid., p. 67.

65. Ibid., p. 68.

66. Maris A. Vinovskis, "Horace Mann on the Economic Productivity of Education," *The New England Quarterly* 43, no. 4 (December 1970), p. 565.

67. Mann, *Seventh Annual Report.*

68. Messerli, *Horace Mann*, pp. 412–21.

69. Orestes Brownson, "Education of the People," *Boston Quarterly Review,* October 1838, p. 403.

70. Ibid., p. 406.

71. Ibid., p. 415.

72. Orestes Brownson, "The School Library," *Boston Quarterly Review,* April 1840, p. 229.

73. Brownson, "Education of the People," p. 412.

74. Messerli, *Horace Mann*, p. 331.

Chapter 4

1. Abraham Flexner and Frank Bachman, *The Gary Schools: A General Account* (New York: General Education Board, 1919).

2. Ibid., p. 17.

3. Leonard Dinnerstein and David M. Reimers, *Ethnic Americans: A History of Immigration,* 3rd ed. (New York: Harper and Row, 1988), p. 54.

4. Paul C. Violas, *The Training of the Urban Working Class* (Chicago: Rand McNally, 1978), p. 2; for example, see Lincoln Steffens, *The Shame of the Cities* (New York: McClure, Philips, 1904). Also, for an introductory overview, see Bruce

M. Stave, ed., *Urban Bosses, Machines, and Progressive Reformers* (Lexington, MA: D. C. Heath, 1972).

5. Barbara Kaye Greenleaf, *American Fever: The Story of American Immigration* (New York: Four Winds Press, 1970), p. 163.

6. Dinnerstein and Reimers, *Ethnic Americans*, pp. 64–65.

7. From the sonnet by Emma Lazarus that appears on the Statue of Liberty.

8. Dinnerstein and Reimers, *Ethnic Americans*, p. 71.

9. Ibid., p. 74.

10. Clarence J. Karier, "Testing for Order and Control in the Corporate Liberal State," in Clarence J. Karier, Paul C. Violas, and Joel Spring, eds., *Roots of Crisis* (Chicago: Rand McNally, 1973), pp. 112–13. See also in that volume, Paul C. Violas, "Progressive Social Philosophy: Charles Horton Cooley and Edward Alsworth Ross," pp. 40–65.

11. Dinnerstein and Reimers, *Ethnic Americans*, p. 76.

12. Ibid., pp. 76–77.

13. Ibid., pp. 50–51; James R. Barrett, *Work and Community in the Jungle* (Urbana: University of Illinois Press, 1987), p. 56; David Brody, "The American Worker in the Progressive Age," in *The Worker in Industrial America: Essays on the Twentieth Century Struggle* (London: Oxford University Press, 1980), p. 15.

14. Joseph G. Raybeck, *A History of American Labor* (New York: Free Press, 1966), p. 52.

15. Robert Reich, *The Next American Frontier* (New York: New York Times Books, 1983), pp. 26–27.

16. Ibid., p. 37.

17. Brody, "The American Worker in the Progressive Age," pp. 11–12.

18. Harry Braverman, *Labor and Monopoly Capital* (New York: Monthly Review Press, 1974), pp. 113, 118.

19. Ibid., p. 106.

20. Ibid., p. 94.

21. Alice Kessler-Harris, *Out of Work: A History of Wage-Earning Women in the United States* (New York: Oxford University Press, 1982).

22. Ibid.

23. Alice Kessler-Harris, "Where Are the Organized Women Workers?" in Linda K. Kerber and Jane De Hart Mathews, eds., *Women's America: Refocusing the Past* (New York: Oxford University Press, 1982), pp. 230–31.

24. Ibid.

25. Leon Litwack, *The American Labor Movement* (New York: Simon and Schuster, 1962), p. 10.

26. Brody, "The American Worker in the Progressive Age," pp. 6–7.

27. Reich, *The Next American Frontier,* p. 64.

28. Ibid., p. 67.

29. Quoted in Jeremy Brecher, *Strike!* (Boston: South End Press, 1977), p. 29.

30. Ibid., p. 28.

31. Raybeck, *History of American Labor*, pp. 167–68.

32. Brecher, *Strike!*, pp. 55–63.

33. Norman Pollack, *The Populist Response to Industrial America* (Cambridge, MA: Harvard University Press, 1962), pp. 11–12.

34. Ibid., p. 18.

35. Ibid., pp. 43–44.

36. Ibid., especially chaps. 5 and 6.

37. The material in this section is based largely on James Weinstein, *The Decline of Socialism in America* (New York: Monthly Review Press, 1967).

38. Gabriel Kolko, *The Triumph of Conservatism* (New York: Free Press, 1963).

39. Ibid., pp. 59ff.

40. Edward A. Krug, *The Shaping of the American High School: 1880–1929* (Madison: University of Wisconsin Press, 1969), pp. 266–67; Lawrence A. Cremin, *The Transformation of the School* (New York: Vintage Books), p. 127.

41. Robert Wiebe, *The Search for Order* (New York: Hill and Wang, 1967).

42. See, for example, Bruce M. Stave, *Urban Bosses, Machines, and Progressive Reformers* (Lexington, MA: D. C. Heath, 1972).

43. Ibid., pp. 11–14.

44. Ibid., p. xvii.

45. Quoted in ibid., pp. 127–29.

46. *Illinois Stage Journal Register,* July 30, 1986, p. 1.

47. See, for example, David Tyack, *The One Best System* (Cambridge, MA: Harvard University Press, 1974); David Tyack, "City Schools: Centralization of Control at the Turn of the Century," in Jerome Karabel and A. H. Halsey, eds., *Power and Ideology in Education* (New York: Oxford University Press, 1977).

48. John Dewey, *Reconstruction in Philosophy* (Boston: Beacon Press, 1984); William James, *The Meaning of Truth* (Cambridge, MA: Harvard University Press, 1975). See also R. J. Wilson, *Darwin and the American Intellectual* (Homewood, IL: Dorsey Press, 1967).

49. John Dewey, *The Public and Its Problems* (Chicago: Swallow Press, 1929).

50. Paul C. Violas, "Progressive Social Philosophy."

51. Clarence J. Karier, "Psychological Conceptions of Man and Society," in Karier, *The Individual, Society, and Education* (Urbana: University of Illinois Press, 1986), pp. 150–83.

52. Quoted in ibid., p. 174.

53. Patricia Albjerg Graham, *Progressive Education: From Arcady to Academe* (New York: Teachers College Press, 1967), p. 8.

54. Ibid., p. 2.

55. David Nasaw, *Schooled to Order* (Oxford: Oxford University Press, 1979).

56. Charles W. Eliot, "Equality of Educational Opportunity," in Marvin Lazerson and W. Norton Grubb, eds., *American Education and Vocationalism* (New York: Teachers College Press, 1974), p. 137. Originally published in 1908 by the

National Society for the Promotion of Industrial Education, Bulletin no. 5.

57. Dewey, *Reconstruction in Philosophy,* p. 186. For a more recent, comprehensive intellectual biography of Dewey that supports this interpretation of his democratic theory, see Robert Westbrook, *John Dewey and American Democracy,* (Ithaca, NY: Cornell University Press, 1991). For a more critical treatment of Dewey's notion of democracy, see Clarence J. Karier, "Liberalism and the Quest for Orderly Change," *History of Education Quarterly* 12 (Spring 1972), pp. 57–80.

58. John Dewey, *The Child and the Curriculum/The School and Society* (Chicago: University of Chicago Press, 1968). Originally published as separate volumes by the University of Chicago Press in 1902 and 1900, respectively.

59. John Dewey, *Democracy and Education* (New York: Macmillan, 1916), pp. 105–16.

60. John Dewey, "Education and Social Change," *The Social Frontier* 3, no. 26 (May 1937), pp. 235–38.

61. John Dewey, *The Child and the Curriculum/The School and Society.*

62. John Dewey, *Experience and Education* (New York: Macmillan 1938), pp. 88–89.

63. Stephen Preskill, "Educating for Democracy: Charles W. Eliot and the Differentiated Curriculum," *Educational Theory* 39, no. 4 (Fall 1989), pp. 353–54.

64. Ibid., p. 352.

65. Ibid., p. 353.

66. Ibid., pp. 354–55.

67. Charles W. Eliot, "The Function of Education in a Democratic Society," *Educational Reform* (New York: Century, 1898), pp. 401–18.

68. Violas, *The Training of the Urban Working Class,* p. 23.

69. Ellwood P. Cubberley, *Public Education in the United States: A Study and Interpretation of American Educational History* (New York: Houghton Mifflin, 1919), p. 490.

70. Preskill, "Educating for Democracy," p. 356.

71. Ibid.

72. Quoted in Samuel Bowles and Herbert Gintis, *Schooling in Capitalist America* (New York: Basic Books, 1976), p. 199.

73. John L. Rury, "Vocationalism for Home and Work: Women's Education in the United States, 1880–1930," in B. Edward McClellan and William J. Reese, eds., *The Social History of American Education* (Urbana: University of Illinois Press, 1988), p. 250. Interestingly, in the 1980s and 1990s, coeducation was questioned again, but for different reasons. It was argued by some that girls are disadvantaged in classes with boys, who receive disproportionate attention and who are socialized to be more confident and aggressive than girls in group settings.

74. *Course of Study 1910–1911* (Beaumont, TX: Beaumont Public Schools, 1910), p. 25.

75. J. F. Bobbitt, *The San Antonio Public School System: A Survey Conducted by J. F. Bobbitt* (San Antonio: San Antonio School Board, 1915), p. 20.

76. Robert S. Lynd and Helen Merrell Lynd, *Middletown* (New York: Harcourt, Brace Jovanovich, 1929), p. 194.

77. *Course of Study* (Lewiston, ID: Board of Education of Lewiston, 1914), p. 91.

78. *Yearbook of the Deerfield-Shields High School, 1912–1913* (Highland Park, IL: Highland Park Board of Education, 1912), p. 37.

79. Rena L. Vassar, *Social History of American Education, Vol. 2: 1860–Present* (Chicago: Rand McNally, 1965), p. 101.

80. Bowles and Gintis, *Schooling in Capitalist America,* p. 191.

81. Charles W. Eliot, "Equality of Educational Opportunity," in Lazerson and Grubb, eds., *American Education and Vocationalism,* p. 137.

82. Eliot, "The Function of Education in a Democratic Society."

83. Cubberley, *Public Education in the United States,* pp. 148, 151–52.

84. Clarence J. Karier, "Testing for Order and Control in the Corporate State," *Educational Theory* 11 (Spring 1971), pp. 159–80.

Chapter 5

1. Mary Wollstonecraft, "A Vindication of the Rights of Woman," in Miriam Schneir, ed., *Feminism: The Essential Historical Writings* (New York: Vintage, 1972), pp. 6–7.

2. Timothy 2:9–15.

3. Elaine Pagels, *Adam, Eve, and the Serpent* (New York: Random House, 1988), chap. 6.

4. Augustine, *City of God* (New York: Penguin Books, 1984), XIV:12, p. 570.

5. Pagels, *Adam, Eve, and the Serpent,* p. 114.

6. It still so informs many contemporary Americans. See, for example, treatments of gender inequity in Shirley Brice Heath and Milbrey W. McLaughlin, eds., *Identity and Inner-City Youth: Beyond Ethnicity and Gender* (New York: Teachers College Press, 1993); and Lois Weis and Michelle Fine, *Beyond Silenced Voices: Class, Race, and Gender in U.S. Schools* (Buffalo, NY: SUNY Press, 1993).

7. Thomas Woody, *A History of Women's Education in the United States* (New York: Science Press, 1929), vol. 1, p. 92.

8. Ibid., p. 142.

9. Carl F. Kaestle, *Pillars of the Republic: Common Schools and American Society 1780–1860* (New York: Hill and Wang, 1983), p. 28.

10. Ibid., pp. 142–46.

11. George Martin, "Early Education of Girls in Massachusetts," *Education* 20 (1899), p. 326.

12. Woody, *History of Women's Education,* pp. 94, 179, 197, 202, 216, 225, 271, 330–33, 339.

13. John Winthrop, "Journal," in Perry Miller, ed., *The American Puritans* (Garden City, NY: Anchor Books, 1956), pp. 44–45.

14. Woody, *History of Women's Education,* pp. 106–7, 128–35.

15. Ibid., pp. 108–10.

16. Ibid., pp. 108, 217–19, 230.

17. Ibid., p. 241.

18. Quoted in Martha Maclear, *A History of the Education of Girls in New York and New England 1800–1870* (Washington, DC: Howard University Press, 1926), p. 6.

19. Woody, *History of Women's Education,* p. 93.

20. See, for example, Benjamin Rush, "Thoughts on Female Education," in Frederick Roudolph, ed., *Essays on Education in the Early Republic* (Cambridge, MA: Harvard University Press, 1965), pp. 25–41.

21. Woody, *History of Women's Education,* pp. 97–104.

22. Nancy Cott, *The Bonds of Womanhood* (New Haven, CT: Yale University Press, 1977).

23. Kaestle, *Pillars of the Republic,* p. 84.

24. Quoted in Elwood P. Cubberly, *The History of Education* (Boston: Houghton Mifflin, 1920), p. 313.

25. Kaestle, *Pillars of the Republic,* p. 28.

26. Maclear, *History of the Educaion of Girls,* pp. 12–26.

27. Quoted in ibid., p. 12.

28. Ibid., pp. 14–23.

29. Rush, *"Thoughts on Female Education,"* pp. 29, 39.

30. *Common School Journal* 2 (1838), p. 100.

31. Quoted in Woody, *History of Women's Education,* p. 318.

32. Quoted in ibid., p. 311.

33. Quoted in Maclear, *History of the Education, of Girls,* p. 18.

34. See Miriam Schneir, ed., *Feminism: The Essential Historical Writings* (New York: Vintage Books), 1972.

35. Sarah M. Grimke, "Letter," in Schneir, *Feminism,* p. 38.

36. Gertrude Martin, "The Education of Women and Sex Equality," *Annals of the American Academy of Political and Social Science,* November 1914, p. 41.

37. The direct quotes in this section on Beecher come from Catharine Beecher, *A Treatise on Domestic Economy* (1841) in D. A. Hollinger and C. Capper, eds., *The American Intellectual Tradition,* 2nd ed. (New York: Oxford University Press, 1993), pp. 244–59. The general approach to interpreting Beecher reflected here is indebted to J. R. Martin, *Reclaiming a Conversation: The Ideal of the Educated Woman* (New Haven, CT: Yale University Press, 1985), pp. 103–38. Both sources rely in turn on K. K. Sklar, *Catharine Beecher: A Study in American Domesticity* (New Haven, CT: Yale University Press, 1973).

38. Martin, *Reclaiming a Conversation,* p. 137.

39. See John Lord, *Mrs. Emma Willard* (New York, 1873); Alma Lutz, *Emma Willard: Pioneer Educator of American Women* (Boston, 1964); Mrs. A. W. Fairbanks, ed., *Mrs. Emma Willard and Her Pupils or Fifty Years of the Troy Female Seminary 1822–1872* (New York, 1898); Henry Fowler, "Educational Services of Mrs. Emma Willard," *American Journal of Education,* vol. 6, 1859, pp. 123–68; Willystine Goodsell, *Pioneers of Women's Education in the United States* (New York, 1931); Anne Firor Scott, "The Ever Widening Circle: The Diffusion of Feminist Values from the Troy Female Seminary, 1822–1870," *History of Education Quarterly* 19 (Spring 1979), pp. 3–27.

40. Fowler, "Educational Services of Mrs Emma Willard," p. 128.

41. Lutz, *Emma Willard: Pioneer Educator,* p. 29; Fowler, "Educational Services of Mrs. Emma Willard," p. 144.

42. Quoted in Goodsell, *Pioneers of Women's Education,* p. 54. This work includes a reprint of the *Plan,* pp. 45-81.

43. Quoted in ibid., p. 57.

44. Quoted in ibid., p. 71.

45. Quoted in ibid., p. 72.

46. Although Willard retired from the principalship of the Troy Female Seminary in 1838, she continued to influence not only the Seminary but American educational thought until her death in 1870.

47. See Goodsell, *Pioneers of Women's Education,* p. 85; Lutz, *Emma Willard: Pioneer Educator,* pp. 40, 93, 97, 113.

48. Fowler, "Educational Services of Mrs. Emma Willard," p. 152.

49. Lutz, *Emma Willard: Pioneer Educator,* p. 47.

50. Ibid., pp. 47–48.

51. Scott, "The Ever Widening Circle," p. 17.

52. Lutz, *Emma Willard: Pioneer Educator,* p. 98; Emma Willard, "Letter Addressed as a Circular to the Members of the Willard Association for the Mutual Improvement of Female Teachers," Troy, 1838.

53. Scott, "The Ever Widening Circle," p. 5. Although Mrs. Willard relinquished the principalship of the Seminary to her daughter-in-law in 1838, she returned to live at the Seminary in 1844 and continued to exercise personal influence on the students until her death in 1870. Lutz, *Emma Willard: Pioneer Educator,* pp. 108-10.

54. Lutz, *Emma Willard: Pioneer Educator,* pp. 49, 115–23.

55. Phillida Bunkle, "Sentimental Womanhood and Domestic Education, 1830–1870," *History of Education Quarterly* 14 (Spring 1974), p. 13.

56. Scott, "The Ever Widening Circle," p. 8.

57. Unless otherwise noted, data and quotations in this section are from A. J. Cooper, "Womanhood a Vital Element in the Regeneration and Progress of a Race" (1886), in H. L. Gates, Jr., and N. Y. McKay, eds., *The Norton Anthology of African American Literature* (New York: Norton), pp. 553–69.

58. Quoted in Renea Henry, "W. E. B. DuBois and the Question of Black Woman Intellectuals," in S. E. Tozer, ed., *Philosophy of Education 1998* (Champaign, IL: Philosophy of Education Society, 1999), pp. 401–03.

59. Ibid.

60. For a fuller description of the academies, see Theodore R. Sizer, ed., *The Age of the Academies.* Classics in Education, no. 22 (New York: Teachers College Press, Columbia University, 1964).

61. Woody, *History of Women's Education,* pp. 341-63; Maclear, *History of the Education of Girls,* pp. 39-46.

62. Maclear, *History of the Education of Girls,* p. 40.

63. Ibid., p. 41.

64. Woody, *History of Women's Education,* p. 519.

65. Ibid., pp. 519–21, 528.

66. Maclear, *History of the Education of Girls,* p. 46.

67. Woody, *History of Women's Education,* pp. 519–24; Maclear, *History of the Education of Girls,* pp. 56–60.
68. Quoted in Woody, *History of Women's Education,* p. 525.
69. Quoted in Kaestle, *Pillars of the Republic,* p. 86.
70. Quoted in Woody, *History of Women's Education,* pp. 527–28.
71. Woody, *History of Women's Education,* pp. 105–6.
72. Ibid., pp. 396, 546.
73. Quoted in Maclear, *History of the Education of Girls,* p. 11.
74. Maclear, *History of the Education of Girls,* p. 69.
75. Ibid., p. 69.
76. Woody, *History of Women's Education,* vol. 2, p. 140.
77. Ibid., pp. 140–47.
78. Maclear, *History of the Education of Girls,* pp. 68–78.
79. Quoted in Maclear, *History of the Education of Girls,* p. 80.
80. Ibid.
81. Maclear, *History of the Education of Girls,* pp. 80–88.
82. Quoted in ibid., p. 82.
83. See, for example, *Report on Vocational Training* (Chicago: City Club of Chicago, 1912), p. 16.
84. John D. Philbrick, "City School Systems in the United States," Bureau of Education, *Circulars of Information* (Washington, DC: Government Printing Office, 1885), p. 89.
85. W. N. Hutt, "The Education of Women for Home-making," *NEA Addresses and Proceedings* (Washington, DC: National Education Association, 1910), p. 513.
86. *New York Annual Report,* 1909, p. 531.
87. *New York Annual Report,* 1910, p. 259.
88. Henry S. Tibbets, "The Progress and Aims of Domestic Science in the Public Schools of Chicago," *NEA Addresses and Proceedings* (Washington, DC: National Education Association, 1901), p. 259.
89. Tibbets, "Progress and Aims of Domestic Science," p. 258.
90. *New York Annual Report,* 1910, p. 131.
91. Both quotations from "Report of the Subcommittee on Industrial and Technical Education in the Secondary Schools,"
Report of the Committee on the Place of Industries in Public Education to the National Council of Education (Washington, DC: National Education Association, 1910), pp. 112, 113.
92. Ibid., p. 11.
93. Ibid., p. 18.
94. John L. Rury, "Vocationalism for Home and Work: Women's Education in the United States, 1880–1930," in B. Edward McClellan and W. J. Reese, eds., *The Social History of American Education* (Urbana: University of Illinois Press, 1988).
95. Ibid., p. 245.
96. Ibid., p. 246.
97. Timothy J. Crimmins, "The Crystal Staircase: A Study of the Effects of Caste and Class on Secondary Education in Late 19th Century Atlanta, Georgia," *Urban Education* 8, no. 4 (January 1974), pp. 401–21.
98. Ibid., p. 13.
99. Ibid., p. 416.
100. Ibid., p. 415.
101. Ibid., pp. 417–18.

Chapter 6

1. For a thorough treatment of the Reconstruction period, see Eric Foner, *Reconstruction: America's Unfinished Revolution, 1863–1877* (New York: Harper and Row, 1988). See also Kenneth M. Stampp, *The Era of Reconstruction, 1865–1877* (New York: Vintage Books, 1965).
2. C. Vann Woodward, "From *Origins of the New South,*" excerpted in Foner, pp. 241ff.
3. Ibid., pp. 241–42.
4. C. Vann Woodward, *The Strange Career of Jim Crow* (New York: Oxford University Press, 1955). Woodward notes that while the origin of the term "Jim Crow" is lost in obscurity, a song and dance named "Jim Crow," written by Thomas D. Rice in 1832, apparently is the source of the term as applied to White supremacy practices in the South. By 1890, Woodward notes, the term was being used in its adjectival form.
5. Louis R. Harlan, *Booker T. Washington: The Wizard of Tuskegee, 1901–1915* (New York: Oxford University Press, 1983), p. viii.
6. The Black belt was the geopolitical area in America in which Blacks constituted a majority of the population and the area in which they demonstrated the greatest political, economic, and cultural solidarity during the life and career of Washington. This area embraced a group of counties in eastern Virginia and North Carolina; a belt of counties extending from the South Carolina coast through South Carolina, central Georgia, and Alabama; and a detached area embracing a portion of the lower Mississippi River Valley. Tuskegee Institute was located in Alabama's Black belt, which extended from the west-central to the southeastern portion of the state where Macon County is located. This portion of Alabama's Black belt contained, in 1910, 21 counties, all with majority Black populations, ranging from a low of 51.7 percent in Pickens County to a high of 88.2 percent in Lowndes County. Alabama's and the South's Black belt populations showed remarkably little change from emancipation to the end of Washington's career in 1915. It was in this context that Washington emerged as the educational diplomat of Black America and sought to apply the Hampton doctrine of economic interdependence, racial separation, and industrial education.
7. Delegates to Alabama's constitutional convention quoted in Horace Mann Bond, *Negro Education in Alabama: A Study in Cotton and Steel* (New York: Atheneum, 1939), 1969 ed., pp. 167–68, 181–82, 192. While the term "freedmen" has a regrettable masculine bias, it is an important historical designation, enshrined by Congress in the Freedmen's Bureau, for ex-slaves.

8. Foner, *Reconstruction: America's Unfinished Revolution,* p. 96; David Tyack, Thomas James, and Aaron Benavot, *Law and the Shaping of Public Education, 1785–1954* (Madison: University of Wisconsin Press, 1987), p. 144.

9. Tyack, James, and Benavot, *Shaping of Public Education,* p. 144.

10. Bond, *Negro Education in Alabama,* pp. 148–49, 156.

11. Robert J. Norrell, *Reaping the Whirlwind: The Civil Rights Movement in Tuskegee* (New York: Knopf, 1985), 1986 Vintage Books ed., pp. 10–11; Bond, *Negro Education in Alabama,* p. 135; and Jonathan M. Wiener, *Social Origins of the New South: Alabama, 1860–1885* (Baton Rouge: Louisiana State University Press, 1978), pp. 93–111.

12. Bond, *Negro Education in Alabama,* pp. 148–49, 156.

13. Ibid., pp. 156, 160.

14. Ibid., p. 161.

15. Ibid., p. 157; Louis R. Harlan, Pete Daniel, Stuart B. Kaufman, Raymond W. Smock, and William M. Welty, *The Booker T. Washington Papers* (Urbana: University of Illinois Press, 1972), vol. 2, p. 443; and Benjamin G. Brawley, *A Social History of the American Negro* (New York: Macmillan, 1921).

16. Louis R. Harlan, *Booker T. Washington: The Making of a Black Leader, 1856–1901* (New York: Oxford University Press, 1972), 1975 paperback ed., in Preface.

17. James D. Anderson, *The Education of Blacks in the South, 1860–1935* (Chapel Hill: University of North Carolina Press, 1988), pp. 148–50.

18. Bond, *Negro Education in Alabama,* pp. 224–25.

19. Booker T. Washington, quoted in Anderson, *The Education of Blacks in the South,* p. 5.

20. Louis R. Harlan, *Booker T. Washington 1856–1901,* pp. 35–36, 44, 228.

21. Booker T. Washington, quoted in Bond, *Negro Education in Alabama,* p. 218, 220–25; Booker T. Washington, *My Larger Education: Being Chapters from My Experience* (Garden City, New York: Doubleday, 1911), p. 305.

22. Raymond Wolters, *The New Negro on Campus: Black College Rebellions of the 1920s* (Princeton, NJ: Princeton University Press, 1975), p. 7.

23. Anderson, *Education of Blacks,* pp. 178–85; Robert A. Margo, *Disenfranchisement, School Finance, and the Economics of Segregated Schools in the United States South, 1890–1910* (New York: Garland, 1985), pp. 6, 16, 24–25, 110–11.

24. Quoted in Louis R. Harlan, *Separate and Unequal: Public School Campaigns and Racism in the Southern Seaboard States 1901–1915* (1958; reprint ed., New York: Atheneum, 1968), and Harlan, *Booker T. Washington: The Wizard of Tuskegee, 1901–1915,* pp. 162, 192–93.

25. Booker T. Washington, "The Successful Training of the Negro," *World's Work* 6 (August 1903), pp. 3731–51.

26. Louis R. Harlan, "Booker T. Washington in Biographical Perspective," *American Historical Review,* October 1970, p. 1589; Harlan, *Booker T. Washington: The Making of a Black Leader, 1856–1901,* p. 58.

27. Booker T. Washington, quoted in Anderson, *Education of Blacks,* p. 39.

28. Harlan, *Booker T. Washington: The Making of a Black Leader, 1856–1901,* p. 61.

29. Anderson, *Education of Blacks,* pp. 51–52; Booker T. Washington and W. E. Burghardt Du Bois, *The Negro in the South: His Economic Progress in Relation to His Moral and Religious Development* (New York: Citadel Press, 1970; also published in 1907 in London by Moring Ltd.), pp. 14, 26, 74.

30. Anderson, *Education of Blacks,* pp. 37, 52; Harlan, "Booker T. Washington in Biographical Perspective," p. 1594; Raymond W. Smock, ed., *Booker T. Washington in Perspective: Essays of Louis R. Harlan* (Jackson: University Press of Mississippi, 1988), p. 113.

31. Anderson, *Education of Blacks,* p. 44.

32. Ibid.

33. Smock, *Booker T. Washington in Perspective,* p. 104; quoted in James D. Anderson, *Education for Servitude: The Social Purpose of Schooling in the Black South,* Ph.D. dissertation, University of Illinois, 1973, p. 175; Washington and Du Bois, *The Negro in the South,* p. 28; quoted in Anderson, *Education of Blacks,* p. 44; Harlan et al., *The Booker T. Washington Papers,* vol. 4, p. 369.

34. Harlan et al., *The Booker T. Washington Papers,* vol. 4, p. 220; Louis R. Harlan and Raymond W. Smock, eds., *The Booker T. Washington Papers* (Urbana: University of Illinois Press, 1976), vol. 5, p. 617.

35. Harlan et al., *The Booker T. Washington Papers,* vol. 4, pp. 197–98, 369–72, 383; Smock, *Booker T. Washington in Perspective,* p. 105.

36. Harlan, "Booker T. Washington in Biographical Perspective," pp. 1593–94.

37. Smock, *Booker T. Washington in Perspective,* p. 106.

38. Anderson, *Education of Blacks,* chap. 2.

39. Ibid.

40. Ibid., p. 75.

41. John Hope Franklin, *Three Negro Classics* (New York: Avon Books, 1965), p. xii. See also the acclaimed biography by David L. Lewis, *W. E. B. Du Bois 1868–1919: Biography of a Race* (New York: Holt, 1993).

42. W. E. B. Du Bois, *The Autobiography of W. E. B. Du Bois* (New York: International, 1968), p. 83.

43. Ibid., p. 236.

44. Ibid., pp. 237–39; also see selection at the end of this chapter.

45. Du Bois, *Autobiography,* p. 262.

46. Lewis, *W. E. B. Du Bois 1868–1919,* p. 2.

47. Margaret Danner and Dudley Randall, *Poem Counterpoem* (Detroit: Broadside Press, 1966), p. 8.

Chapter 7

1. For discussion of Forbes on curriculum, see Susan Lobo and Steve Talbot, eds. *Native American Voice: A Reader* (Boston: Addison-Wesley, 1997).

2. Quoted in Howard Zinn, *A People's History of the United States* (New York: Harper and Row, 1980), p. 515.

3. Brian Dippie, *The Vanishing American: White Attitudes and U.S. Indian Policy* (Middletown, CT: Wesleyan University Press, 1982). See also Virgil Vogel, ed., *This Country Was Ours: A Documentary History of the American Indian* (New York: Harper and Row, 1972); Francis Jennings, *The Invasion of America: Indians, Colonialism and the Cant of Conquest* (Chapel Hill: University of North Carolina Press, 1975); and Alice B. Kehoe, *North American Indians: A Comprehensive Account* (Englewood Cliffs, N.J.: Prentice Hall, 1981), pp. 224–44. Also see Francis P. Prucha, ed., *Documents of U.S. Indian Policy* (Lincoln: University of Nebraska Press, 1975).

4. Dippie, *The Vanishing American,* p. 181.

5. Ibid.

6. Prucha, *Documents of U.S. Indian Policy,* p. 688.

7. See Lawrence Kelly, "John Collier and the Indian New Deal: An Assessment," in Janet Smith and Robert M. Kvasnicka, eds., *Indian-White Relations: A Persistent Paradox* (Washington, DC: Howard University Press, 1976).

8. W. C. Ryan and R. K. Brandt, "Indian Education Today," *Progressive Education* 9, no. 2 (February 1932), p. 81.

9. See Lawrence C. Kelly, *The Assault on Assimilation: John Collier and the Origins of Indian Policy Reform* (Albuquerque: University of New Mexico Press, 1983).

10. Ibid., p. 24.

11. Ibid., p. 36.

12. Ibid., p. 29.

13. R. Lawrence Moore, "Directions of Thought in Progressive America," in Lewis L. Gould, ed., *The Progressive Era* (Syracuse, NY: Syracuse University Press, 1974).

14. Lawrence C. Kelly, *The Navajo Indians and Federal Indian Policy, 1900–1935* (Tucson: University of Arizona Press, 1968). Also see Emily Hahn, *Mabel: A Biography of Mabel Dodge Luhan* (Boston: Houghton Mifflin, 1977).

15. See John Collier, *Indians of the Americas: The Long Hope* (New York: New American Library, 1947).

16. Ibid.

17. Kenneth R. Philp, *John Collier's Crusade for Indian Reform, 1920–1954* (Tucson: University of Arizona Press, 1977).

18. Reports of the Secretary of the Interior (Washington, DC: U.S. Government Printing Office, 1925, 1932).

19. Ibid. (1932).

20. See Arthur Schlesinger, Jr., *The Coming of the New Deal* (Boston: Houghton Mifflin, 1959).

21. M. K. Sniffen, ed., *Indian Truth* (Philadelphia: Indian Rights Association, May 1933), p. 1.

22. Department of the Interior, 1933.

23. Department of the Interior, 1935.

24. See Thomas Weaver, ed., *Indians of Arizona: A Contemporary Perspective* (Tucson: University of Arizona Press, 1974).

25. Oliver LaFarge, ed., *The Changing Indian* (Norman: University of Oklahoma Press, 1942).

26. Ibid.

27. See Laura Thompson, *Personality and Government* (Mexico City: Educaciones Del Instituto Indigenista Interamericano, 1951), foreword by J. Collier, p. xiii.

28. Laura Thompson and Alice Joseph, *The Hopi Way* (Chicago: University of Chicago Press, 1944), foreword by J. Collier.

29. Ibid., p. 9.

30. Laurence M. Hauptman, *The Iroquois and the New Deal* (Syracuse, NY: Syracuse University Press, 1981); Francis Paul Prucha, *The Great Father: The U.S. Government and the American Indians* (Lincoln: University of Nebraska Press, 1984), vol. 2.

31. Willard W. Beatty, *Education for Action: Selected Articles from Indian Education 1936–1943* (Washington, DC: U.S. Indian Service, 1944), p. 24.

32. Willard W. Beatty, *Education for Cultural Change: Selected Articles from Indian Education 1944–51* (Washington, DC: U.S. Indian Service, 1953).

33. Beatty, *Education for Action,* p. 147.

34. U.S. Commission on Civil Rights, *The Navajo Nation: An American Colony,* 1975, p. 41.

35. Ibid., p. 264.

Chapter 8

1. James E. McClellan, *Toward an Effective Critique of American Education* (Philadelphia: J. B. Lippincott, 1968), p. 59.

2. Bernard Bailyn et al., *The Great Republic* (Lexington, MA: D. C. Heath, 1981), pp. 767–72; William Leuchtenberg, *The Perils of Prosperity, 1914–32* (Chicago: University of Chicago Press, 1958), chap. 10; Frederick Lewis Allen, *Only Yesterday* (New York: Harper and Row, 1931), chap. 12.

3. Bailyn et al., *Great Republic,* pp. 779–83, 798–802; David Tyack, Robert Lowe, and Elisabeth Hansot, *Public Schools in Hard Times* (Cambridge, MA: Harvard University Press), pp. 6–27.

4. Tyack et al., *Public Schools in Hard Times,* pp. 13–26, 59–76.

5. Peter Carroll and David Noble, *The Free and the Unfree* (London: Penguin Press, 1977), pp. 348–49.

6. Ibid.; William Appleman Williams, *The Tragedy of American Diplomacy* (New York: Dell, 1959), pp. 268–76; Stephen Ambrose, *Rise to Globalism* (London: Penguin Books, 1980), chap. 5.

7. Harry Truman, quoted in Stephen E. Ambrose, "From Korea to Vietnam: The Failure of a Policy Rooted in Fear," in Blanche Wiesen Cook, Alice Kessler Harris, and Ronald Radosh, eds., *Past Imperfect: Alternative Essays in American History* (New York: Knopf, 1973), vol. 2, p. 205.

8. McGeorge Bundy, Morton H. Halperin, et al., "Back from the Brink," *Atlantic Monthly,* August 1986, pp. 35–41.

9. Ambrose, "From Korea to Vietnam," p. 204.

10. Eric Goldman, *The Crucial Decade* (New York: Vintage Books, 1960), chap. 6.

11. See Harvard Sitkoff, *The Struggle for Black Equality* (New York: Hill and Wang, 1981); John Hope Franklin, *From Slavery to Freedom,* 3rd ed. (New York: Vintage Books, 1969), chaps. 30 and 31; Meyer Weinberg, *A Chance to Learn* (Cambridge, England: Cambridge University Press, 1977), chaps. 2 and 3.

12. Harry Braverman, *Labor and Monopoly Capital* (New York: Monthly Review Press, 1974), chaps. 5 and 6; David Noble, *America by Design* (New York: Oxford University Press, 1977), chap. 7; David Riesman, *The Lonely Crowd* (New Haven, CT: Yale University Press, 1961), chaps. 6 and 7; Joel Spring, *The Sorting Machine* (New York: Longman, 1976), chap. 6; George Santyana, *Character and Opinion in the United States* (New York: Norton, 1934), p. 11.

13. Nicholas Lemann, *The Big Test: The Secret History of the American Meritocracy* (New York: Farrar, Strauss, and Giroux, 1999), chap. 4.

14. James B. Conant, *My Several Lives* (New York: Harper and Row, 1970), p. 49.

15. *The Nation,* May 24, 1933, p. 571.

16. Conant, *My Several Lives,* p. 134.

17. Examples of the use of the Calvinist metaphor include the following: Conant, *Vital Speeches of the Day,* July 15, 1936, p. 638; Feb. 1, 1937, p. 254; *Harvard Annual Report, 1936–37,* pp. 14–15.

18. Quotations in J. G. Hershberg, *James B. Conant: Harvard to Hiroshima and the Making of the Nuclear Age* (New York: Knopf, 1993), p. 11–12.

19. Conant, *My Several Lives,* pp. 428–32.

20. Conant, *Education for a Classless Society* (Cambridge, MA: Harvard University Press, 1940), pp. 1–18.

21. Ibid., pp. 33–35. Also see Thomas Grissom, "Education and the Cold War: James B. Conant," in Clarence Karier, Paul Vicolas, and Joel Spring, eds., *Roots of Crisis* (Chicago: Rand McNally, 1973). Later Conant wrote, "From frustrated individuals with long education and considerable intelligence society has much to fear. From such people come the leaders of antidemocratic movements." Conant, *Ladies Home Journal,* June 1948, p. 107.

22. James B. Conant, *Thomas Jefferson and the Development of American Public Education* (Charlottesville: University of Virginia Press, 1979), pp. 173–82.

23. See especially J. B. Conant, *Public Education and the Structure of American Society* (New York: Teachers College Press, 1946).

24. Lemann, *The Big Test,* p. 47.

25. Conant, *Public Education and the Structure of American Society,* pp. 2–41. Also see Conant, "Selection and Guidance in the Secondary School," *Harvard Educational Review,* Winter 1948, pp. 61–75.

26. Lemann, *The Big Test,* p. 47.

27. Conant, *Education in a Divided World* (Cambridge: Harvard University Press, 1948), pp. viii–ix, 35–37, 104–5; 233; McClellan, *Toward an Effective Critique of American Education,* p. 104.

28. Educational Policies Commission and the American Council on Education, *Education and National Security* (December 1951), pp. 12, 15, 27–28, 38, 45.

29. James B. Conant, *Education and Liberty* (Cambridge, MA: Harvard University Press, 1953), p. 62.

30. Lawrence Cremin, *The Transformation of the School* (New York: Vintage Books, 1961), pp. 334–38; Harold Alberty et al., *Let's Look at the Attacks on the Schools* (Columbus: Ohio State University, 1951), pp. 3–4.

31. Diane Ravitch, *The Troubled Crusade* (New York: Basic Books, 1983), p. 68.

32. Mortimer Smith, *And Madly Teach* (Chicago: Henry Regnery, 1949), pp. 10, 22–23, 37, 43; Arthur Bestor, *Educational Wastelands* (Champaign: University of Illinois Press, 1953), pp. 36–37, 79–80; James D. Koerner, ed., *The Case for Basic Education,* (Boston: Atlantic Monthly Press, 1959), p. v.

33. Hyman G. Rickover, *Education and Freedom* (New York: E. P. Dutton, 1959), p. 38.

34. Henry Chauncey, *Annual Report of the Educational Testing Service, 1957–58* (Princeton, NJ: Educational Testing Service), p. 28. For evidence of how ETS works as a sorting machine, see Allan Nairn, *The Reign of ETS* (Washington, DC: Ralph Nader Report on the Educational Testing Service, 1980).

35. John Gardner, *Annual Report of the Carnegie Corporation of New York,* 1956 (New York: Carnegie Corporation of New York, 1957), p. 25; John Gardner, *Excellence* (New York: Harper and Row, 1961), p. 66.

36. James B. Conant, *The American High School Today* (New York: McGraw-Hill, 1959), p. 15.

37. Ibid., pp. 22, 40; Raymond Callahan, *Education and the Cult of Efficiency* (Chicago: University of Chicago Press, 1962), p. viii; Conant Personal Papers, Box 3, Folder 40, Harvard University Archives.

38. "Report on Dissemination Campaign," March 25, 1959; Tentative Plan for Dissemination Campaign for the Publication of *The American High School Today,* October 28, 1958, both in Conant Personal Papers, Box 2, Folder 34, Harvard University Archives.

39. Conant, *The American High School Today,* pp. 37–38, 40; James B. Conant, *The Child, the Parent, and the State* (New York: McGraw-Hill, 1959), pp. 36–39, 42.

40. Robert Hampel, *The Last Little Citadel* (New York: Houghton Mifflin, 1986), pp. 68–70.

41. Conant, *The Child, the Parent, and the State,* pp. 32–35, 43–44, 191–92.

42. Robert Hampel, *The Last Little Citadel* (Boston: Houghton Mifflin, 1986), p. 69.

43. Quoted in Hershberg, *James B. Conant,* p. 713.

44. James B. Conant, *Slums and Suburbs* (New York: McGraw-Hill, 1961), pp. 31, 96–98, 115, 131–33; Clarence Karier, *Man, Society, and Education* (Glenview, IL: Scott, Foresman, 1967), p. 254.

45. Conant, *Slums and Suburbs,* p. 34.

46. Henry Perkinson, *200 Years of American Educational Thought* (New York: Longman, 1976), pp. 255–56.

47. James B. Conant, *The Comprehensive High School* (New York: McGraw-Hill, 1967), pp. 76–79; Conant, *My Several Lives*, pp. 640–46.

48. Lemann, p. 348.

49. Ibid., p. 350.

50. David Tyack and Larry Cuban, *Tinkering toward Utopia*, Cambridge, MA: Harvard University Press, 1995, pp. 136–37.

51. J. Dewey, *Reconstruction in Philosophy* (New American Library Edition, 1950), p. 147.

Chapter 9

1. Jonathan Kozol, *Shame of the Nation* (New York: Brown, 2005), p. 69; Nicholas Meier, "Reading First?" *Critical Literacy: Theories and Practices* 3, no. 2 (2009), pp. 69–83.

2. International Comparisons in Fourth-Grade Reading Literacy, International Association for the Evaluation of Educational Achievement, Progress in International Reading Literacy Study (PIRLS) 2001.

3. Carl F. Kaestle, "The History of Literacy and the History of Readers," in E. R. Kintgen, B. M. Kroll, and M. Rose, eds., *Perspectives on Literacy* (Carbondale: Southern Illinois University Press, 1988), p. 103.

4. Kaestle, "The History of Literacy and the History of Readers," p. 109.

5. Richard D. Brown, *Knowledge Is Power: The Diffusion of Information in Early America, 1700–1865* (New York: Oxford University Press, 1989), p. 12.

6. Dale Van Every, cited in Howard Zinn, *The People's History of the United States* (New York: Harper and Row, 1980), pp. 135–36.

7. Kaestle, "The History of Literacy and the History of Readers," p. 109; Stanley Schultz, *The Culture Factory: Boston Public School, 1789–1860* (New York: Oxford University Press, 1973), cited in Joel Spring, *The American School, 1642–1990,* 2nd ed. (New York: Longman, 1990), pp. 60–63.

8. Kaestle, "The History of Literacy and the History of Readers," p. 109.

9. This section is partially excerpted from Steven Tozer, "Elite Power and Democratic Ideals," in Kenneth D. Benne and Steven Tozer, eds., *Society as Educator in an Age of Transition,* Eighty-sixth Yearbook of the National Society for the Study of Education (Chicago: The Society, 1987), pp. 186–225.

10. Robert A. Dahl, *Who Governs?* (New Haven, CT: Yale University Press, 1961). President Eisenhower's address is found in Seymour Melman, *Pentagon Capitalism: The Political Economy of War* (New York: McGraw-Hill, 1970), pp. 235–39.

11. Eisenhower, in Melman, *Pentagon Capitalism,* pp. 237–38.

12. C. Wright Mills, *The Power Elite* (New York: Oxford University Press, 1956).

13. Thomas R. Dye, *Who's Running America? The Bush Restoration,* 7th ed. (Englewood Cliffs, NJ: Prentice Hall, 2002), pp. 1–15.

14. John Gaventa, *Power and Powerlessness* (Urbana: University of Illinois Press, 1980), p. vi.

15. T. Jackson Lears, "The Concept of Cultural Hegemony: Problems and Possibilities," *American Historical Review* 90 (June 1985), pp. 567–93.

16. Anup Shah, "Media Conglomerates, Mergers, Concentration of Ownership," www.globalissues.org/humanrights/media/corporations/owners.asp.

17. Robert McChesney, *Rich Media, Poor Democracy: Communications Policy in Dubious Times* (Urbana: University of Illinois Press, 1999), p. xiii.

18. See "Bestriding the World," Granville Williams of Britain's Campaign for Press and Broadcasting Freedom. Prepared for *New Internationalist* magazine, 2002.

19. *International Herald Tribune,* November 30, 2000.

20. GE Workers United, www.geworkersunited.org/news/fast_facts.asp#defense.

21. See www.ge.com/en/company/news/turn_on_light.htm.

22. GE Workers United, www.geworkersunited.org/news/fast_facts.asp#defense.

23. Shah, p. 6.

24. Josh Silver, in the *Huffington Post,* April 26, 2012.

25. See, for example, any of several works by Noam Chomsky, including *On Power and Ideology: The Managua Lectures* (Boston: South End Press, 1987) and *The Culture of Terrorism* (Boston: South End Press, 1988). See also Joshua Cohen and Joel Rogers, *Rules of the Game: American Politics and the Central America Movement* (Boston: South End Press, 1986). Finally, from a more conservative perspective, see *Wall Street Journal* reporter Jonathan Kwitney, *Endless Enemies: The Making of an Unfriendly World* (New York: Penguin Books, 1987).

26. Ben H. Bagdikian, *The Media Monopoly,* 3rd ed. (Boston: Beacon Press, 1980), p. 4.

27. Ibid., pp. 8–9.

28. Ibid., pp. 195–96.

29. Ibid., p. 203. UNESCO data found in Andrew L. Shapiro, *We're Number One* (New York: Vintage Books, 1992), p. 165.

30. Ben H. Bagdikian, *The New Media Monopoly,* rev. ed., http://benbagdikian.net/index.htm.

31. Ben H. Bagdikian, *The Media Monopoly,* 4th ed. (Boston: Beacon Press, 1990), p. 23.

32. Todd Gitlin, "Television Screens: Hegemony in Transition," in Michael W. Apple, ed., *Cultural and Economic Reproduction in Education* (London: Routledge and Kegan Paul, 1982), pp. 206–46.

33. U.S. Department of Education, National Center for Education Statistics, *The Condition of Education 1966* (Washington, DC: National Center for Education Statistics, 1997).

34. Ben H. Bagdikian, *The Media Monopoly,* 5th ed. (Boston: Beacon Press, 1997).

35. Michael Dertouzos, *What Will Be: How the New World of Information Will Change Our Lives* (New York: HarperCollins, 1997), p. 10.

36. U.S. Department of Education, National Center for Educational Statistics, *Digest of Education Statistics 2005,* Table 137, Percentage of High School Sophomores Who Say They Engage in Various Activities, p. 230; Table 416, Public Schools and Instructional Rooms with Access to the Internet, p. 678; Table 420, Student Use of Computers, by Level of Enrollment, Age and Student and School Characteristics, p. 685 (Washington, DC: National Center for Education Statistics, 2005). For a more detailed discussion of the ironic post–*Brown* v. *Board of Education* resegregation and its growth of the digital divide between predominantly White and predominantly Black schools, see Raneta Lawson Mack, *The Digital Divide: Standing at the Intersection of Race and Technology* (Durham, NC: Carolina Academic Press, 2001).

37. Ronald D. Owston, "The World Wide Web: A Technology to Enhance Teaching and Learning?" *Educational Researcher* 26, no. 2 (March 1997), p. 33.

38. Dertouzos, *What Will Be,* p. 241.

39. Ibid., pp. 293–94.

40. Jean Anyon, "Ideology and U.S. History Textbooks," *Harvard Educational Review* 49 (August 1979), pp. 369–70.

41. Michael Apple, "The Political Economy of Textbook Publishing," *Educational Theory* 34 (Fall 1984), pp. 307–20.

42. See, for example, Lears, "The Concept of Cultural Hegemony," p. 569.

43. Jacques Ellul, *Propaganda: The Formation of Men's Attitudes* (New York: Vintage Books, 1963), p. 11. Chomsky argues a similar point in *Media Control: The Spectacular Achievements of Propaganda* (New York: Seven Stories Press, 1997).

44. Peter Bachrach, *The Theory of Democratic Elitism: A Critique* (Boston: Little, Brown, 1967), p. 4.

45. U.S. Bureau of the Census, "Literacy: Current Problems and Current Research," in *Fifth Report of the National Council on Educational Research* (Washington, DC: National Institute of Education, 1979). See also U.S. Bureau of the Census, *The Census of the Population, 1980,* Vol. 1: The Characteristics of Population, Chapter C, General, Social and Economic Characteristics, Table 83, Years of School Completed, Column Years 1940–1980.

46. Shirley Brice Heath, "The Functions and Uses of Literacy," *Journal of Communication* 30 (1980), pp. 123–33.

47. Irwin S. Kirsch, Ann Jungeblut, Lynn Jenkins, and Andrew Kohlstad, *Adult Literacy in America* (Washington, DC: Educational Testing Service and National Center for Educational Statistics, 1993), p. 2.

48. Carmen St. John Hunter and David Harman, *Adult Literacy in the United States: A Report to the Ford Foundation* (New York: McGraw-Hill, 1979).

49. Ibid.

50. Ibid.

51. N. Northcutt, *Adult Performance Level Project: Adult Functional Competency—A Report to the Office of Education Dissemination Review Panel* (Austin: University of Texas, Division of Extension, 1975). The statistics released by the APL study can be potentially misleading. It will help to contextualize the statistics in order to have a better grasp of the information. Specifically, as listed the statistics indicate that all groups are working from a shared baseline of 100. However, more correctly, the percentages should reflect more true population distributions. For example, at that time Euro-Americans composed roughly 76 to 78 percent of the population, African Americans 12 percent, and Hispanic Americans 10 percent. It would be helpful to know the exact numbers represented by the percentage equivalents in the APL study. The numbers as stated offer a potentially false perception of the literacy rates of all groups.

52. Kirsch et al., *Adult Literacy in America,* p. xiv.

53. Northcutt, *Adult Performance Level Project;* Kirsch et al., *Adult Literacy in America,* p. 47.

54. Kozol, *Illiterate America* (Garden City, NY: Anchor Press, Doubleday, 1985), p. 10.

55. Colin Lankshear, "Humanizing Functional Literacy: Beyond Necessity," *Educational Theory* 36 (Fall 1986), pp. 375–87.

56. Kathleen Kennedy Manzo, "Federal Review of Reading First Identifies Serious Problems," *Education Week* 26, no. 5 (September 22, 2006), www.edweek.org.

57. Ibid.

58. Stephen Krashen, editorial, *Education Week* 27, no. 21 (2007), p. 27. See also Elizabeth Jaeger, "Silencing Teachers in an Era of Scripted Reading," *Rethinking Schools* 20, no. 3 (Spring 2006), www.rethinkingschools.org/archive/20_03/sile203.shtml.

59. Larry Rohter, "The Scourge of Adult Illiteracy," *The New York Times: Educational Life,* April 13, 1986, p. 1.

60. Stanley N. Wellborn, "A Nation of Illiterates?" *U.S. News and World Report,* May 17, 1982, p. 53.

61. For example, see Paulo Freire and Donaldo Macedo, *Literacy: Reading the Word and the World* (South Hadley, MA: Bergin and Garvey, 1987). See also Paulo Freire, *Pedagogy of Freedom: Ethics, Democracy and Civic Courage* (Lanham, MD: Rowman and Littlefield, 2001).

62. Henry A. Giroux, *Theory and Resistance in Education: A Pedagogy for the Opposition* (South Hadley, MA: Bergin and Garvey, 1987).

63. Ibid.

64. Freire and Macedo, *Literacy.*

65. Stanley Aronowitz and Henry Giroux, *Education under Siege: The Conservative, Liberal, and Radical Debate over Schooling* (South Hadley, MA: Bergin and Garvey, 1985), p. 132.

66. Giroux, *Theory and Resistance.*

67. Carmel Borg, Joseph Buttigieg, and Peter Mayo, *Gramsci and Education;* E. D. Hirsch, (New York: Rowman and Littlefield, 2002) *The Schools We Need and Why We Don't Have Them* (New York: Doubleday, 1996).

68. Neil Postman, "The Politics of Reading," *Harvard Educational Review* 40, no. 2 (1970), p. 246.

69. Suzanne de Castell, Allan Luke, and David MacLennan, "On Defining Literacy," *Canadian Journal of Education* 6 (1981), pp. 7–18.

70. E. D. Hirsch, Jr., *Cultural Literacy: What Every American Needs to Know* (New York: Vintage Books, 1988).

71. E. D. Hirsch, Jr., Joseph F. Kett, and James Trefil, *The Dictionary of Cultural Literacy*, 2nd ed. (Boston: Houghton Mifflin, 1993), p. xiv.

72. Kwame Anthony Appiah and Henry Louis Gates, Jr., *The Dictionary of Global Culture* (New York: Knopf, 1997).

73. Ibid., pp. 3–7.

74. Hirsch et al., p. xv.

75. Derek Bok, *The State of the Nation* (Cambridge, MA: Harvard University Press, 1996), pp. 366–73.

76. Freire and Macedo, *Literacy.*

77. See, for example, Cameron McCarthy, "After the Canon: Knowledge and Ideological Representation in the Multicultural Discourse on Curriculum Reform," in McCarthy and Crichlow, eds., *Race, Identity, and Representation in Education* (New York: Routledge, 1993), pp. 289–305.

78. Paulo Freire, *Teachers as Cultural Workers: Letters to Those Who Dare Teach* (Boulder, CO: Westview Press, 2003). See also bell hooks, *Teaching to Transgress: Education as the Practice of Freedom* (London: Routledge, 1994).

79. Wayne Au, "From Tourist Hawaii to the 20th Anniversary," *Rethinking Schools* 20, no. 3 (Spring 2006), www.rethinkingschools.org/archive/20_03/hawa203.shtml.

80. Ronald Takaki, *A Different Mirror* (Boston: Little, Brown, 1993), p. 227.

Chapter 10

1. Jonathan Kozol, *Shame of the Nation* (New York: Brown, 2005).

2. Joel Spring, *American Education: An Introduction to Social and Political Aspects,* 5th ed. (White Plains, NY: Longman, 1991), p. 44.

3. John Goodlad, *Teachers for Our Nation's Schools* (San Francisco: Jossey-Bass, 1990), pp. 71–72.

4. William R. Johnson, "Teachers and Teacher Training in the Twentieth Century," in Donald Warren, ed., *American Teachers: History of a Profession at Work* (New York: Macmillan, 1989), pp. 245–47.

5. See Harold Rugg, *The Teacher of Teachers* (New York: Harper and Brothers, 1952). Also, Steven Tozer and Stuart McAninch, "Social Foundations of Education in Historical Perspective," *Educational Foundations* 1, no. 1 (1986).

6. Johnson, "Teachers and Teacher Training," pp. 238–40.

7. Ibid., p. 239.

8. Jurgen Herbst, *And Sadly Teach: Teacher Education and Professionalization in American Culture* (Madison: University of Wisconsin Press, 1989), p. 6.

9. *Tomorrow's Teachers: A Report of the Holmes Group* (East Lansing, MI: Holmes Group, 1986), p. 6.

10. Steve Tozer, Phyllis Burstein, and Carole Bishop O'Connell, "Four Perspectives on Alternate Routes to Teacher Certification," *Success in High-Need Schools* 1, no. 2 (June 2006). Retrieved December 15, 2006, from www.successinhighneedschools.org/journal/issue/2/1/825.

11. C. Emily Feistritzer, *State Policy Trends for Alternative Routes to Teacher Certification,* Conference on Alternative Certification, Washington, DC, September 2005.

12. *Quality Counts,* "A Decade of Standards-Based Education," *Education Week* 25, no. 17 (2006), p. 86.

13. Martin Haberman, "What Makes a Program 'Alternative Certification'? An Operational Definition," *NAAC Online Journal* 1, no. 2 (Spring 2006), pp. 5–6.

14. Ibid.

15. Stockton, Gullat, and Basinger, "Using Comprehensive Needs Assessment to Improve Student Achievement," *Essays in Education* 9. www.usca.edu/essays/archives.html.

16. L. Darling-Hammond, B. Berry, and A. Thoreson, "Does Teacher Certification Matter? Evaluating the Evidence," *Educational Evaluation and Policy Analysis* 23, no. 1 (Spring 2001), pp. 57–77.

17. Louise M. Berman, "The Teacher as Decision Maker," in Frances S. Bolin and Judith McConnell Falk, eds., *Teacher Renewal: Professional Issues, Personal Choices* (New York: Teachers College Press, 1987), p. 202.

18. Goodlad, *Teachers for Our Nation's Schools,* pp. 70–71.

19. Ibid., p. 267.

20. Dee Ann Spencer, *Contemporary Women Teachers: Balancing School and Home* (White Plains, NY: Longman, 1986), p. 5.

21. Herbst, *And Sadly Teach,* p. 6.

22. *National Center for Education Statistics 2008–060 Projects of Education Statistics to 2016,* Section 5. Retrieved April 20, 2008, from http://neds.ed.gov/proams/projections/projections2016/sec5b.asp.

23. *Digest of Educational Statistics* (Washington, DC: Department of Education Statistics, 1988), p. 74.

24. *Occupational Outlook Handbook*, U.S. Department of Labor Bulletin 24000, May 1992, pp. 17, 66, 74, 94, 95, 105. Also, *The Condition of Education 1993,* p. 150.

25. *Digest of Educational Statistics* (Washington, DC: National Center for Education Statitics, 2003).

26. Geraldine Joncich Clifford, "Man/Woman/Teacher: Gender, Family, and Career in American Educational History," in Donald Warren, ed., *American Teachers: Histories of a Profession at Work* (New York: Macmillan, 1989), p. 316.

27. Data from U.S. Bureau of Labor Statistics and Census Bureau cited in "Nine to Five: Profile of Working Women," in *Women's Studies at Parkland College* (Champaign, IL: Summer Newsletter 1989). See also *Statistical Abstract of the United States* (Washington, DC: U.S. Government Printing Office, 1993), p. 426, and U.S. Department of Labor, Highlights of Women's Earnings, Department of Labor Statistics, 2003.

28. Spencer, *Contemporary Women Teachers,* p. 6, citing Grimm and Stern, 1974.

29. National Center for Education Statistics, *Special Analysis: Mobility in the Teacher Workforce,* retrieved April 20, 2008, from http://nces.ed.gov/programs/coe/2005/analysis/sa01.asp.

30. Gerda Lerner, "The Lady and the Mill Girl: Change in the Status of Women in the Age of Teachers," *Journal of American Studies* 10, no. 1 (1969), pp. 5–15.

31. John Rury, "Who Became Teachers? The Social Characteristics of Teachers in American History," in Warren, ed., *American Teachers.*

32. Bill Graves, "School Reform by University Mandate," *The School Administrator* 49, no. 10 (November 1992), pp. 8–13.

33. *Child Welfare Society of Flint* v. *Kennedy School District,* 189 N.W. 1002 (1922).

34. Debra Viadero, " 'Medically Fragile' Students Pose Major Dilemma for School Officials," *Education Week,* March 11, 1987, pp. 1, 14.

35. Michael Apple, "Making Knowledge Legitimate: Power, Profit and the Textbook," in A. Molnar, ed., *Current Thought on Curriculum* (Alexandria, VA: Association for Supervision and Curriculum Development, 1985).

36. Frank C. Nelson, "What Evangelical Parents Expect from Public School Administrators," *Educational Leadership* (May 1988), pp. 40–43.

37. NEA website, www.nea.org/edstats/.

38. Karen Seashore Louis, "Social and Community Values and the Quality of Teachers' Work Life," in Milbrey W. McLaughlin, Joan E. Talbert, and Nina Bascia, eds., *The Contexts of Teaching in Secondary Schools: Teachers' Realities* (New York: Teachers College Press, 1990), pp. 17–39.

39. Louis, "Social and Community Values, pp. 18–19.

40. *Digest of Educational Statistics,* 1988, p. 5.

41. U.S. Department of Education, *Schools and Staffing in the United States: A Statistical Profile, 1993–94.* NCES 96-124 by Robin R. Henke, Susan P. Choy, Sonya Geis, and Stephen P. Broughman (Washington, DC: National Center for Education Statistics, 1996), pp. vi–vii.

42. Ibid.

43. Peter Murrell, *The Community Teacher* (New York: Teachers College Press, 2001).

44. Richard Dufour, *Professional Learning Communities at Work* (Ontario: Solution Tree, 1999).

45. Michael Scriven, "Duties of the Teacher," unpublished manuscript, circulated as "Version Date 9/93" with support of U.S. Department of Education.

46. John Dewey, *Reconstruction in Philosophy* (Boston: Beacon Press, 1984), p. 186.

Chapter 11

1. Edward Krug, *The Shaping of the American High School: 1920–1941* (Madison: University of Wisconsin Press, 1972), p. 181.

2. See, for example, Ray Marshall and Marc Tucker, "Building a Smarter Work Force," *Technology Review,* October 1992; also in *Education 94/95,* 21st ed. (Guilford, CT: Dushkin), pp. 169–73. See also Monika Kosmahl Aring, "What the 'V' Word Is Costing America's Economy," *Phi Delta Kappan,* January 1993; also in *Education 94/95,* pp. 174–81.

3. David Angus and Jeffrey E. Mirel, *The Failed Promise of the American High School 1890–1995* (New York: Teachers College Press, 1995).

4. Ibid., p. 78.

5. Ibid.

6. Mark Ginsburg, ed., *Understanding Educational Reform in Global Context: Economy, Ideology and the State* (New York: Garland, 1991).

7. Angus and Mirel, *The Failed Promise*, p. 84.

8. James Bryant Conant, *The American High School Today* (New York: McGraw-Hill, 1959).

9. Ibid., p. 52.

10. Ibid., pp. 57–60.

11. Arthur G. Wirth, *Education and Work for the Year 2000: Choices We Face* (San Francisco: Jossey-Bass, 1992), p. 159.

12. *Statistical Abstract of the United States, 1993* (Washington, DC: U.S. Government Printing Office, 1993), p. 426.

13. Martha Farnsworth Riche, "America's New Workers," *American Demographics* 9, no. 5 (February 1988), p. 38.

14. William Serrin, "A Great American Job Machine?" *The Nation,* September 18, 1989, p. 270.

15. Ibid.

16. *Statistical Abstract of the United States 1993,* p. 426.

17. Serrin, "Great American Job Machine?" p. 270.

18. *Working Women: A Chartbook,* U.S. Dept. of Labor Bulletin 2385, August 1991, p. 21.

19. This section is adapted from Steven Tozer and Robert Nelson, "Implications of the Holmes Agenda for Emerging Paradigms in Vocational Education," in Mildred Griggs, ed., *Proceedings of the Rupert Evans Symposium on Vocational Education: 1988* (Champaign: University of Illinois Press, 1989).

20. John Dewey, "Vocational Aspects of Education," *Democracy and Education* (New York: Free Press, 1966), p. 310.

21. Ibid.

22. Ibid.

23. Allen Weisberg, "What Research Has to Say about Vocational Education in High Schools," *Phi Delta Kappan* 64, no. 5 (January 1983), p. 359.

24. Dewey, *Democracy and Education,* p. 162.

25. W. Norton Grubb, ed., *Education through Occupations in American High Schools,* vol. 1 and 2 (New York: Teachers College Press, 1995).

26. The material in this section is adapted from a portion of Steven Tozer, "The Liberal Education of Teachers: Remarks on the Holmes Agenda," *Visual Arts Research* 14, no. 1 (Spring 1988), pp. 17–31.

27. Ernest Barker, ed., *The Politics of Aristotle* (London: Oxford University Press, 1980), p. 322.

28. Ibid., pp. 317–23.

29. Ibid., p. 323.

30. Ibid., p. 318.

31. W. H. Woodward, *Vittorino DeFeltre and Other Humanist Educators* (New York: Teachers College Press, 1963), p. 102.

32. Alfred North Whitehead, "The Study of the Past—Its Uses and Its Dangers," in Whitehead, *Essays in Science and Philosophy* (New York: Philosophical Library, 1948), p. 112.

33. Gene V. Glass, *Fertilizers, Pills and Magentic Strips: The Fate of Public Education in America* (Charlotte, NC: Information Age, 2008), p. 20.

34. Ernest L. Boyer, "Elementary and Secondary Education," in D. W. Hornbeck and L. M. Salamon, eds., *Human Capital and America's Future* (Baltimore: Johns Hopkins University Press, 1991), pp. 172–75.

35. Ibid., pp. 176–77.

36. Ibid., p. 173.

37. Mark G. Yudof, "Educational Policy Research and the New Consensus of the 1980s," *Phi Delta Kappan,* March 1984, pp. 456–59.

38. Christine M. Shea, "Pentagon vs. Multinational Capitalism: The Political Economy of the 1980s School Reform Movement," in Christine M. Shea, Ernest Kahane, and Peter Sola, eds., *The New Servants of Power: A Critique of the 1980s School Reform Movement* (New York: Praeger, 1989), p. 20.

39. Ibid.

40. William A. Firestone, Susan H. Fuhrman, and Michael W. Kirst, *The Progress of Reform: An Appraisal of State Education Initiatives* (Palo Alto, CA: Center for Policy Research in Education, 1990), p. 13.

41. David Tyack, "Restructuring in Historical Perspective: Tinkering toward Utopia," *Teachers College Record* 92 (Winter 1990), pp. 170–91.

42. Ibid., p. 170.

43. Ibid., p. 171.

44. William Ayers, "Perestroika in Chicago Schools," *Educational Leadership* 48 (May 1991), p. 71.

45. Frank Margonis, "What Is the Meaning of Contemporary Educational Nationalism?" in *Philosophy of Education 1988* (Normal, IL: Philosophy of Education Society), pp. 343–52.

46. Ibid., pp. 349–50.

47. Ibid., p. 351.

48. Shea, "Pentagon vs. Multinational Capitalism," pp. 32–33.

49. Larry Cuban, "Techno-Reformers and Classroom Teachers," *Education Week* 16, no. 6 (October 9, 1996), p. 39.

50. David C. Berliner and Bruce J. Biddle, *The Manufactured Crisis: Myths, Fraud, and the Attack on America's Public Schools* (White Plains, NY: Longman, 1997), p 26.

51. Quoted in Berliner and Biddle, *Manufactured Crisis*, p. 173.

52. Ibid., p. 179.

53. Bob Chase, "Which Charters Are Smarter?" *Education Week* 16, no. 14 (December 14, 1996), p. 52.

54. Mark Walsh, "Voucher Plan in Cleveland Is Overturned," *Education Week* 16, no. 32 (May 7, 1997), p. 1.

55. Chase, "Which Charters Are Smarter?" p. 52.

56. Paul T. Hill, Lawrence C. Pierce, and James W. Guthrie, "How Contracting Can Transform America's Schools," *Education Week* 16, no. 33 (May 14, 1997), p. 60.

57. Gerald Tirozzi, "Vouchers: A Questionable Answer to an Unasked Question," *Education Week* 16, no. 30 (April 23, 1997), p. 64.

58. John F. Witte, "Politics, Markets, or Money? The Political Economy of School Choice." Presented at American Political Science Association Annual Meeting, San Francisco, August 29–September 1, 1996, p. 27.

59. Melissa Roderick, *Researching College Attendance Rates*, November 15, 2007, Educated Nation website, retrieved at www.educatednation.com/2007/11/15/researching-college-attendance-rates/. See also the Consortium on Chicago School Research website, http://ccsr.uchicago.edu/content/index.php.

Chapter 12

1. R. H. Tawney, *Equality,* 4th ed. (London: Allen and Unwin, 1952), pp. 49–50.

2. See Clarence J. Karier, Paul Violas, and Joel Spring, *The Roots of Crisis* (Chicago: Rand McNally, 1973), esp. chaps. 3, 5, and 6.

3. See Paul C. Violas, *The Training of the Urban Working-Class* (Chicago: Rand McNally, 1978).

4. "Brown et al. v. Board of Education at Topeka et al." August 1952, 1953, 1954, 347 US 483(1954). U.S. Supreme Court decision written by Chief Justice Earl Warren.

5. Michael Harrington, *The Other America: Poverty in the United States* (New York: Macmillan, 1962).

6. Hyman Rickover, *Education and Freedom* (New York: Dutton, 1959).

7. Arthur Bestor, *Educational Wastelands: The Retreat from Learning in Our Public Schools* (Urbana: University of Illinois Press, 1953).

8. Nat Hentoff, *Our Children Are Dying* (New York: Viking Press, 1966).

9. Samuel Bowles and Henry Levin, "The Determinants of Scholastic Achievement," *Journal of Human Resources* 2 (Winter 1968), pp. 3–25.

10. Frederick Mosteller and Daniel P. Moynihan, *On Equality of Educational Opportunity: Papers Deriving from the Harvard University Faculty Seminar on the Coleman Report* (New York: Random House, 1972).

11. It is not without interest that Daniel Moynihan had five years earlier paved the way for such an argument with his work *The Negro Family* (Cambridge: Harvard University Press, 1967). In it he argued that a major reason for African American inequality was structural defects in the Black family. This conclusion was soundly criticized by historians Herbert G. Gutman, *The Black Family in Slavery and Freedom, 1750–1925* (New York: Pantheon Books, 1976); and James D. Anderson, "Black Conjugations," *The American Scholar* 46, no. 3 (Summer 1977), pp. 384–93.

12. C. Jencks et al., *Inequality: A Reassessment of the Effect of Family and Schooling in America* (New York: Harper and Row, 1973). A summary of the conclusions of *Inequality* was published under the title "The Schools and Equal Opportunity," *Saturday Review Education* 55, no. 38 (October 1972), pp. 37–42.

13. Jencks et al. also suggested that since schools could not improve economic inequality, the government should institute a guaranteed-income program to ensure everyone an income equal to one-half the national average. In assuming that economic inequality is both natural and functional, Jencks again showed his modern liberal moorings. The concern of modern liberal reform has always been simply to reduce the gap between the extremes of wealth and poverty.

14. H. M. Levin, "Schooling and Inequality: The Social Science Objective Gap," *Saturday Review Education* (December 1972), pp. 49–51.

15. Ibid., p. 2.

16. Success and Culture.net. Per Capita Income Around the World. Retrieved April 25, 2008, from www.success-and-culture.net/articles/percapitaincome.shtml.

17. M. A. Rebell, "The Need for Comprehensive Educational Inquiry," C. R. Belfield and H. M. Levin, eds., *The Price We Pay* (Washington, DC: Brookings Institution Press, 2007), p. 262.

18. *U.S. Census Bureau News,* August 28, 2007. Retrieved April 28, 2008, from www.census.gov/Press-Release/www/releases/archives/income_wealth/010583.html.

19. Ellis Cashmore, *Dictionary of Race and Ethnic Relations,* 4th ed. (London and New York: Routledge, 1996).

20. Paul Salopek, "We Are All the Same," *Chicago Tribune,* April 27, 1997, p. 1.

21. Cornel West, *Race Matters* (Boston: Beacon Press, 1993).

22. Vladimire Herard, "Schools Failing Minorities," *The Chicago Defender* (December 4, 1996), p. 1; and *The American Almanac 1996–97: Statistical Abstract of the United States* (Austin, TX: Hoover's, 1997), pp. 159, 204, 219.

23. Sheldon Danzinger, "The Poor," in David W. Hornbeck and Lester M. Salamon, eds., *Human Capital and America's Future* (Baltimore: Johns Hopkins Press, 1991), p. 153.

24. Andrew Hacker, *Two Nations: Separate, Hostile, Unequal* (New York: Scribner, 1992), p. 94.

25. Harold Hodgkinson, "Reform versus Reality," in Fred Schultz, ed., *Education 9394* (Guilford, CT: Dushkin, 1993), p. 39.

26. U.S. Census 2000: Annual Demographic Survey, March supplement.

27. Ibid.

28. Census 2003, March supplement.

29. Ibid.

30. U.S. Census 2000.

31. Ibid.

32. The 2008 Statistical Abstract: Education. Mean Earnings by Highest Degree Earned. Table 220. Retrieved April 25, 2008, from www.census.gov/compendia/statab/cats/education.html.

33. Hacker, *Two Nations,* pp. 103–4.

34. U.S. Department of Labor.

35. U.S. Census Bureau. Stark Contrasts Found Among Asian Americans. Retrieved April 25, 2008, from API%20Heritage%20Month%20May%2007_files.

36. Capital Times online, February 17, 1994, www.hist.umn.edu/~rugglescaptimes.html; and National Center for Children in Poverty (NCCP), Columbia University Mailman School of Public Health, www.nccp.org.

37. Hodgkinson, "Reform versus Reality," p. 37.

38. *The American Almanac,* p. 469.

39. Hodgkinson, "Reform versus Reality," p. 36.

40. Andrew L. Shapiro, *We're Number One* (New York: Vintage Books, 1992), pp. 17–18.

41. These comparisons are found in Marian Wright Edelman, *Families in Peril—An Agenda for Social Change* (Cambridge, MA: Harvard University Press, 1987).

42. Gary Orfield, "Separate Societies: Have the Kerner Warnings Come True?" in F. R. Harris and R. W. Wilkins, eds., *Quiet Riots—Race and Poverty in the United States* (New York: Pantheon, 1988), pp. 106–10; Hacker, *Two Nations,* p. 162.

43. Marian Wright Edelman, *The Measure of Our Success: A Letter to My Children and Yours* (Boston: Beacon Press, 1992), pp. 23, 24.

44. All statistics in this paragraph are from *Digest of Education Statistics 1988* (Washington, DC: U.S. Department of Education, Office of Educational Research and Improvement, September 1988).

45. The 2008 Statistical Abstract: Education. Educational Attainment by Race, Hispanic Origin, and Sex: 1960 to 2006. Table 218. Retrieved April 25, 2008, from www.census.gov/compendia/statab/cats/education.html.

46. U.S. Census Bureau, 2006 American Community Survey Table 7. Retrieved April 25, 2008, from www.census.gov/prod/2007pubs/acs-08.pdf:Table7.MedianEarningsinthePast12MonthsofWorkersbySexandWomen'sEarningsasaPercentageofMen'sEarningsbySelectedCharacteristicsfortheUnitedStates:2006.

47. Ibid.

48. *1992 Information Please Almanac,* pp. 54, 56; Shapiro, *We're Number One,* pp. 10–11.

49. U.S. stands apart from other nations on maternity leave. The Associated PressUSATODAY.com. (Posted 7/26/2005)

50. Maternity Leave in the United State. Institute for Women's Policy Research #A131. August 2007, p. 1.

51. Clarence Karier, "Testing for Order and Control in the Corporate Liberal State," *Educational Theory* 22 (Spring 1972), pp. 154–80. Also see Paul Violas, "Progressive Social Philosophy: Charles Horton Cooley and Edward Alsworth Ross," in Karier et al., eds., *The Roots of Crisis,* pp. 40–65.

52. *The American Almanac,* p. 470.

53. Ibid., p. 153.

54. "Who Is the Middle Class?" *Now with Bill Moyers,* June 25, 2004, www.pbs.org/now/politics/middleclassoverview.html.

55. S. Tozer, "Class," In David Gabbard, ed., *Power, Knowledge, and the Politics of Educational Meaning* (New York: Erlbaum, 1999), pp. 149–159.

56. Some figures in this paragraph come from *New York Times,* September 22, 1988, and the National Center for Education Statistics, Announcement 92-129a, October 1992. The 1998 figures are from Manhattan Institute for Policy Research, report written by Senior Fellow Jay P. Greene, *High School Graduation Rates in the U.S.*

57. "The Persisting Racial Gap in College Student Graduation Rates," *Journal of Blacks in Higher Education,* 2004, www.jbhe.com/features.

58. R. Wilson and S. C. Melendez, *Second Annual Report on the Status of Minorities in Higher Education* (Washington, DC: Office of Minority Concerns, American Council on Education, 1983). Also, *Statistical Abstract of the United States 1993,* p. 153.

59. Robert Pool, "Who Will Do Science in the 1990s?" *News & Comment,* April 27, 1990, pp. 433–35.

60. David Owen, *None of the Above* (Boston: Houghton Mifflin, 1985); Myra Sadker and David Sadker, *Failing at Fairness: How America's Schools Cheat Girls* (New York: Scribner, 1994).

61. US School Segregation Rises. BBC News, Wednesday, 18 July, 2001, news.bbc.co.uk/default.stm.

62. Profile of Teachers in the U.S. 2005. National Center for Educational Information. Retrieved April 24, 2008, from www.ncei.com/POT05PRESSREL3.htm.

63. Nation's Population One-Third Minority. *U.S. Census Bureau News,* May 10, 2006. Retrieved April 24, 2008, from www.census.gov/Press-Release/www/releases/archives/population/006808.html.

64. "Linguistic Diversity in the USA," *USA Today,* December 15, 1993, p. 9A.

65. Ronald Takaki, *Strangers from a Different Shore* (New York: Penguin Books, 1998), p. 475.

66. Ibid., p. 49.

67. Ibid.

68. Valerie Ooka Pang, "Asian-American Children: A Diverse Population," *Educational Forum* 55, no. 1, pp. 49–66.

69. Irwin S. Kirsch, Ann Jungeblut, Lynn Jenkins, and Andrew Kolstad, *Adult Literacy in America* (Washington, DC: Educational Testing Service, 1993), p. 33.

70. Sucheng Chan, *Asian Americans: An Interpretive History.* (New York: Twayne, 1991), p. 3.

71. Ibid., p. 145.

72. *The State of Asian Pacific America: Policy Issues of the Year 2020* (Los Angeles: LEAP Asian Pacific American Public Policy Institute and UCLA Asian American Studies Center, 1993), p. 26.

73. Chan, *Asian Americans,* pp. 187–88.

74. Asian/Pacific American Heritage Month. *U.S. Census Bureau News,* May 2007. Retrieved April 24, 2008, from www.census.gov/Press-Release/www/releases/

75. Melvin G. Holli and Peter d' A. Jones (eds.), *Ethnic Chicago: A Multicultural Portrait* (Grand Rapids, MI: Eerdmans, 1995), p. 346.

76. Angela L. Carrasquillo, *Hispanic Children and Youth in the U.S.* (New York: Garland, 1991), p. 24.

77. Ibid., p. 4.

78. *U.S. Census Bureau News.* U.S. Hispanic Population Surpasses 45 Million, Now 15% of Total. Retrieved April 23, 2008, from www.census.gov/Press-Release/www/releases/archives/population/011910.html.

79. U.S. Census Bureau Reveals 16% Immigration Increase in 5 Years. August 17, 2006. Retrieved April 23, 2008, from www.workpermit.com/news/2006_08_17/us/census_data_increase.htm.

80. Holli and Jones, *Ethnic Chicago,* p. 346.

81. Laura E. Perez, "Opposition and the Education of Chicanaos," in Cameron McCarthy and Warren Crichlow, eds., *Race Identity and Representation in Education* (New York: Routledge, 1993), p. 276.

82. Ibid.

83. Thomas Toch, *In the Name of Excellence* (New York: Oxford University Press, 1991), p. 127.

84. These conclusions are drawn from a study by Jean Anyon, "Social Class and School Knowledge," in *Curriculum Inquiry* 2, no. 1 (1981), pp. 3–42.

85. This issue is explored in a nicely detailed account by Annette Lareau of Southern Illinois University in "Social Class Differences in Family-School Relationships: The Importance of Cultural Capital," *Sociology of Education* 60 (April 1987), pp. 73–85.

86. The last conclusion relates to the field of sociolinguistics. Exemplars include the works of William Labov, Basil Bernstein, and Michael Stubbs.

87. Judith D. Singer and John A. Butler, "The Education for All Handicapped Children Act: Schools as Agents of Social Reform," *Harvard Educational Review* 57, no. 2 (May 1987), p. 125.

88. *The American Almanac,* p. 166; and National Center for Education Statistics, 2003, Tables 54 and 52.

89. Toch, *In the Name of Excellence,* p. 125.

90. Ibid., p. 126.

91. Ibid., pp. 126–27.

92. Ibid., p. 127.

93. Ibid.

94. Peggy Orenstein, *School Girls: Young Women, Self Esteem, and the Confidence Gap* (New York: Doubleday, 1994); Myra Sadker and David Sadker, *Failing at Fairness: How America's Schools Cheat Girls* (New York: Scribner, 1994).

95. Barbara Sinclair Deckard, "The Self-Fulfilling Prophecy: Sex Role Socialization," in Barbara Sinclair Deckard, ed., *The Women's Movement: Political, Socioeconomic and Psychological Issues,* 2nd ed. (New York: Harper and Row, 1979), p. 29.

96. Ibid., p. 30.

97. AAUW report, *How Schools Shortchange Girls* (Wellesley, MA: American Association of University Women Educational Foundation and National Education Association, 1992), p. 10.

98. Lawrence Kohlberg, "A Cognitive-Developmental Analysis of Children's Sex-Role Concepts and Attitudes," quoted in Deckard, "The Self-Fulfilling Prophecy," p. 32.

99. Kirsten Amundsen, *The Silenced Majority* (Englewood Cliffs, NJ: Prentice Hall, 1971), pp. 116–17.

100. L. Serbin et al., "A Comparison of Teacher Responses to Pre-Academic and Problem Behavior of Boys and Girls," *Child Development* 44 (1973), pp. 796–804; M. Ebbeck, "Equity for Boys and Girls: Some Important Issues," *Early Child Development and Care* 18 (1984), pp. 119–31.

101. Myra P. Sadker and David M. Sadker, *Sex Equity Handbook for Schools* (New York: Longman, 1982), pp. 107–9; Carol S. Dweck et al., "Sex Differences in Learned Helplessness. II: The Contingencies of Evaluative Feedback in the Classroom" and "III: An Experimental Analysis," *Development Psychology* 14, no. 3 (1978), pp. 268–76; Judith M. Bardwick, *Psychology of Women* (New York: Harper and Row, 1971), p. 113.

102. M. Sadker and D. Sadker, "Sex Equity and Special Education," *The Pointer* 26 (1981), pp. 33–38.

103. D. Sadker and M. Sadker, "Is the Classroom OK?," *Phi Delta Kappan* 55 (1985), pp. 358–67.

104. Veronica F. Nieva and Barbara A. Gutek, "Sex Effects on Evaluation," *Academy of Management Review* 5, no. 2 (1980), pp. 267–76.

105. Phillip Goldberg, "Are Women Prejudiced against Women?" *Trans-Action* 5 (1968), pp. 28–30.

106. Angele M. Parker, "Sex Differences in Classroom Intellectual Argumentation," unpublished master's thesis, Pennsylvania State University, 1973; R. Simmons and D. Blyth, *Moving into Adolescence: The Impact of Pubertal Change and the School Context* (New York: Aldine de Gruyter Press, 1978), p. 227.

107. P. Arnow and C. Froschl, "Textbook Analysis," in F. Howe, ed., *High School Feminists Studies* (Old Westbury, NY: Feminist Press, 1976); Kathryn P. Scott and Candace Garrett Shau, "Sex Equity and Sex Bias in Instructional Materials," in S. Klien, ed., *Handbook for Achieving Sex Equity through Education* (Baltimore: Johns Hopkins Press, 1985), pp. 218–36; G. Britton and M. Lumpkin, *A Consumer's Guide to Sex, Race, and Career Bias in Public School Textbooks* (Corvallis, OR: Britton Associates, 1977); M. Hulme, "Mirror, Mirror on the Wall: Biased Reflections in Textbooks and Instructional Materials," in A. Carelli, ed., *Sex Equity in Education: Readings and Strategies* (Springfield, IL: Charles C Thomas, 1988), pp. 187–208; Marjorie B. U'Ren, "The Image of Women in Textbooks," in Vivian Gornick and Barbara K. Morgan, eds., *Women in Sexist Society* (New York: Signet, 1971); L. Weitzman and D. Russi, *Biased Textbooks and Images in Elementary School Textbooks* (Washington, DC: Resource Center on Sex Roles in Education, 1976).

108. *Dick and Jane as Victims* (Princeton, NJ: Women on Words and Images, 1972), pp. 6–27.

109. J. Trecker, "Women in U.S. History High School Textbooks," *Social Education* 35, no. 3 (1971), pp. 249–60, 338.

110. AAUW report, *How Schools Shortchange Girls*, p. 62.

111. Ibid., p. 62.

112. Ibid., p. 63.

113. In Lois Weis and Michelle Fine, eds., *Beyond Silenced Voices: Race, Class, and Gender in United States Schools* (Albany: State University of New York Press, 1993), pp. 169–90.

114. Ibid., pp. 170–71.

115. Ibid., p. 176.

116. Ibid., p. 187.

117. Ibid., pp. 169–70.

118. Carl A. Grant and Christine E. Sleeter, "Race, Class and Gender and Abandoned Dreams," *Teachers College Record* 90, no. 1 (Fall 1988), pp. 19–40.

119. Linda K. Christian-Smith, "Voices of Resistance: Young Women Readers of Romance Fiction," in Weis and Fine, *Beyond Silenced Voices,* pp. 183–84.

120. AAUW report, p. 12. Because comparable data are not available for boys, it is not clear what portion of the "unhappiness" is due to adolescence and what portion is due to gender and its interaction with adolescence.

121. Deckard, "The Self-Fulfilling Prophecy," p. 43.

122. AAUW report, p. 16.

123. AAUW report, pp. 48, 67, 70; Sumru Erkit, "Expectancy, Attribution, and Academic Achievement: Exploring Implications of Sex-Role Orientation," Working Paper No. 27, Wellesley College Center for Research on Women, 1979.

124. Ibid., p. 45. This still represents only one-half of the male participation.

125. AAUW report, pp. 6–8.

126. Ibid., pp. 6, 90–91.

127. Ibid., p. 7.

128. "Wanted: School Supt.: But Women Need Not Apply," *Aggie Daily,* Texas A&M University, August 2, 2001.

129. Kathleen D. Lyman and Jeanne J. Spieler, "Advancing in School Administration," *Harvard Educational Review* 50, no. 1 (February 1980), p. 25.

130. Suzanne E. Estler, "Women as Leaders in Public Education," *Signs* 1 (1975), pp. 363–85.

131. Ibid., p. 29.

Chapter 13

1. Katharine Q. Seelye, "Group Seeks to Alter S.A.T. to Raise Girls' Scores," *The New York Times,* March 14, 1997, p. A25.

2. Peter Applebome, "Minorities Falling Behind in Student Achievement," *The New York Times*, December 29, 1996, p. Y9.

3. Steven A. Holmes, "For Hispanic Poor, No Silver Lining," *The New York Times,* October 13, 1996, p. E5.

4. Cornel West, *Race Matters* (Boston: Beacon Press, 1993); Michelle Campbell, "Hate Crimes in Illinois: 1.4 per Day," *Chicago Sun Times,* November 24, 1996.

5. Jeannie Oakes, Amy Stuart Wells, Makeba Jones, and Amanda Datnow, "Detracking: the Social Construction of Ability, Cultural Politics, and Resistance to Reform," *Teachers College Record* 98, no. 3 (Spring 1997), pp. 482–510.

6. The following account and all quotes are taken from William Peters, *A Class Divided—Then and Now* (New Haven, CT: Yale University Press, 1987).

7. Videocassettes and 16-mm print films of this documentary are available from Guidance Associates, The Center for Humanities, Communications Park, Box 3000, Mount Kisco, NY, 10549. The follow-up documentary is available from PBS Video.

8. In an August 1988 poll taken by Media General-Associated Press, 53 percent of White Americans and 68 percent of African Americans surveyed said the society is racist.

9. Peters, *A Class Divided*, pp. 37–38.

10. The topic is covered extensively in Henry Giroux, *Teachers as Intellectuals* (Granby, MA: Bergin and Garvey, 1988).

11. Lewis M. Terman, *Intelligence Tests and School Reorganization* (New York: World, 1923). We have taken this quote from Clarence Karier, "Testing for Order and Control in the Corporate Liberal State," *Educational Theory* 22 (Spring 1972), pp. 154–80.

12. Quoted in Karier, "Testing for Order and Control."

13. See, for example, Arthur R. Jensen, *Bias in Mental Testing* (New York: Free Press, 1980).

14. R. Herrnstein and C. Murray, *The Bell Curve* (New York: Free Press, 1994).

15. See, for example, William Deutsch (ed.), *The Child's Construction of Language Behavioral Development* (San Diego: Academic Press, 1982); Basil Bernstein, *Class Codes and Control,* 2nd revised ed. (London: Routledge and Kegan. Paul, 1974).

16. Lisa Delpit, *Other People's Children* (New York: New Press, 1995).

17. Longstreet conducted a study of learning style among Navajo children. Mentioned by Karen Swisher, "Styles of Learning and Learning of Styles: Educational Conflicts for American Indian/Alaskan Native Youth," *Multilingual and Multicultural Development* 8, no. 4 (1987), p. 348.

18. John U. Ogbu, "Minority Status and Schooling in Plural Societies," *Comparative Educational Review* 27, no. 2, pp. 168–90.

19. John U. Ogbu, "Understanding Diversity," *Education and Urban Society* 22, no. 4 (1990), pp. 425–29.

20. Jean Anyon, "Social Class and School Knowledge," *Curriculum Inquiry* 2, no. 1 (1987), pp. 3–42.

21. Ibid, p. 17.

22. Ibid., p. 26. This was one of the questions found in a text used by the executive elite school.

23. In recent decades, the competition for elite preschools has grown.

24. Ray C. Rist, "Student Social Class and Teacher Expectations," *Harvard Review* 40, no. 3 (August 1970).

25. John Duffy, "Getting Off Track: The Challenge and Potential of the Mixed Ability Classroom," *Democracy and Education,* Fall 1988, pp. 11–19. Duffy is citing the 1987 research by David and Roger Johnson.

26. P. A. Graham, "Black Teachers: A Drastically Scarce Resource," *Phi Delta Kappan,* April 1987. Also, *The Condition of Education 2000,* National Center for Education Statistics, U.S. Department of Education, 2000, p. 9.

27. William Labov, *Sociolinguistic Patterns* (Philadelphia: University of Pennsylvania Press, 1972); Michael Stubbs, *Language Schools and Classrooms,* 2nd ed. (London and New York: Methuen, 1983); Peter Trudgill, *Sociolinguistics* (New York: Penguin Books, 1983); J. B. Pride and J. Holmes (eds.), *Sociolinguistics: Selected Readings* (Harmondsworth, England: Penguin Modern Linguistics Readings, 1972).

28. Ursula Casanova and M. Beatriz Arias, "Contextualizing Bilingual Education," in *Bilingual Education: Politics, Practice, and Research,* Ninety-second Yearbook of the National Society for the Study of Education Part II (Chicago: NSSE, 1993), p. 13.

29. *A Profile of Policies and Practices for Limited English Proficient Students: Screening Methods, Program Support, and Teacher Training* (SASS 1993–94). U.S. Department of Education Office of Educational Research and Improvement NCES 97-472 (Washington, DC, January 1977), p. 5.

30. Lynn Schnaiberg, "Ebonics Vote Puts Oakland in Maelstrom," *Education Week* 16 (January 15, 1997), pp. 1, 32. The story was carried by all major national and big-city news outlets as well.

31. James Baldwin, "If Black English Isn't a Language, Then Tell Me What Is?" in *The Price of the Ticket: Collected Nonfiction 1948–1985* (New York: St. Martin's Press, 1985), p. 652.

32. D. Bolinger and D. A. Sears, *Aspects of Language* (New York: Harcourt Brace Jovanovich, 1981), p. 198.

33. Joan G. Fickett, "Tense and Aspect in Black English," *Journal of English Linguistics* 6 (1972), p. 19. The quote referred to appears in Bolinger and Sears, *Aspects of Language,* p. 198.

34. Most of these examples are taken from Bolinger and Sears, *Aspects of Language,* Table 9–1, p. 199.

35. Eleanor Wilson Orr, *Twice as Less* (New York: Norton, 1987).

36. William Labov, "Academic Ignorance and Black Intelligence," *The Atlantic* 229, no. 6 (June 1972), pp. 59–67.

37. Jane Roland Martin, *Reclaiming a Conversation* (New Haven, CT: Yale University Press, 1985).

38. Jane Roland Martin, "Bringing Women into Educational Thought," *Educational Theory* 34, no. 4 (Fall 1984), p. 349.

39. Gordon L. Berry, "The Multicultural Principle: Missing from the Seven Cardinal Principles of 1918 and 1978," *Phi Delta Kappan,* June 1978, p. 745. For an extended account of one approach to culturally responsive teaching, see C. A. Bowers and David J. Flinders, *Responsive Teaching* (New York: Teachers College Press, 1990).

40. Christine Sleeter and Carl A. Grant, *Making Choices for Multicultural Education: Five Approaches to Race, Class, and Gender* (Columbus, OH: Merrill, 1988).

41. Ibid., p. 66.

42. Ibid., p. 100.

43. Ibid., p. 131.

44. Ibid., p. 168.

45. Ibid., p. 166.

46. Ibid., p. 166.

47. Ibid., p. 187.

48. Ibid., p. 190.

49. Cited in Allyn Jackson, "Minorities in Mathematics: A Focus on Excellence, Not Remediation," *American Educator* (Spring 1989).

50. Lottie L. Taylor and Joan R. Pinard, "Success Against the Odds: Effective Education of Inner-City Youth in a New York City Public High School," *Journal of Negro Education* 57, no. 3 (1988), pp. 347–61.

51. Ibid., p. 351.

52. Ibid., p. 361.

53. Sleeter and Grant, *Making Choices,* pp. 193–94.

54. Quoted in The Committee on Policy for Racial Justice, *Visions of a Better Way: A Black Appraisal of Public Schooling* (Washington, DC: Joint Center for Political Studies Press, 1989), p. 1.

55. Lilian Katz, "All About Me," *American Educator* (Summer 1993), pp. 18–23.

56. Albert Shanker, "Love Ya!" *The New York Times,* February 23, 1997, p. E7.

57. Michael S. Knapp and Associates, *Teaching for Meaning in High Poverty Classrooms* (New York: Teachers College Press, 1995), pp. 3, 7–8.

58. Thomas M. Skrtic, "The Special Education Paradox: Equity as the Way to Excellence," *Harvard Educational Review* 61, no. 2 (May 1991), pp. 148–206.

59. James Banks, "It's Up to Us," *Teaching Tolerance* (Fall 1992), p. 21.

60. Skrtic, "The Special Education Paradox," p. 177.

61. Elizabeth Bondy and Dorene D. Ross, "Confronting Myths about Teaching Black Children: A Challenge for Teacher Educators," *Teacher Education and Special Education* 21, no. 4 (1998), p. 241.

62. Skrtic, "The Special Education Paradox," p. 177.

Chapter 14

1. See, for example, H. Cooper, "Synthesis of Research on Homework," *Educational Leadership* 47, no. 3 (November 1989), pp. 85–91.

2. J. Spring, *The Sorting Machine: National Educational Policy Since 1945* (New York: McKay, 1976).

3. S. C. Carter, *No Excuses: Lessons from 21 High Performing, High Poverty Schools* (Washington DC: The Heritage Foundation, 2000); P. Davenport and G. Anderson, *Closing the Achievement Gap: No Excuses* (Houston, TX: American Productivity and Quality Center); R. DuFour et al., *Whatever It Takes: How Professional Learning Communities Respond When Kids Don't Learn* (Bloomington, IN: National Education Service, 2004); C. C. Yeakey and R. Henderson, *Surmounting All Odds* (Greenwich CT: Information Age). See also Education Trust website: www2.edtrust.org/edtrust/.

4. R. Edmonds (1979). Quoted in Committee on Racial Justice, *Visions of a Better Way: A Black Appraisal of Public Schooling* (Washington, DC: Joint Center for Political Studies Press, 1989), p. 1.

5. Ibid.

6. See, for example, sources in note 3; also websites for Education Trust (www2.edtrust.org/edtrust/) and Consortium on Chicago School Research (ccsr.uchicago.edu/content/index.php).

7. J. Dewey, *Experience and Education* (New York: Macmillan, 1938, 1959) p. 77; L. S. Shulman, "Those Who Understand: Knowledge Growth in Teaching," *Educational Researcher* (February 1986), 4–14.

8. J. Oakes and M. Lipton, *Teaching to Save the World* (New York: McGraw-Hill, 2002).

9. A. Urbanski, Presentation on "Improving Results" to Civic Committee of the Chicago Commercial Club, Chicago, IL, 2003.

10. G. Counts, *Dare the Schools Build a New Social Order?* (Carbondale: Southern Illinois University Press, 1932).

11. H. Adams, *The Education of Henry Adams: An Autobiography* (London: Oxford Press, 1907), p. 244.

12. Peter Murrell, *Just Like Stone Soup* (Washington, DC: AACTE, 1998), p. 55.

13. H. James, From a letter to Henri Berson, in *Letters of Henry James*. Retrieved on April 28, 2008, from www.quoteland.com/author.asp?AUTHOR_ID=1462.

14. Carter, *No Excuses.*

15. Although it is not clear that Margaret Mead wrote this, it is widely attributed to her. See discussion in Mary Bowman Kruhm, *Margaret Mead: A Biography* (Westport, CT: Greenwood Press, 2003).

Glossary

The American High School Today a book published by James B. Conant in 1958; popularized the modern conception of the large comprehensive high school and helped shape policies to make such schools the norm in urban and rural communities.

antiracist education an educational approach preferred by some people to multicultural education because it emphasizes the importance of combating racist ideology through educational processes.

assimilation the process in which an individual or group is absorbed into a new social context through a process of acculturation that results in the individual or group's original culture being replaced by the new culture.

Athenian citizenship in classical Athens the status granted to Athenian-born males not of the slave or the metic class; a status that granted civil liberties as well as the right to participate in the governance of Athens.

Athenian slavery an institution of bondage and servitude to Athenian citizens that was an important part of the political and economic system on which Athenian democracy was built.

Beatty, Willard Walcott (1891–1961) president of the Progressive Education superintendent of a model school system in Bronxville, NY. Director of Indian Education under John Collier.

Beecher, Catharine (1800–1878) an advocate of women's education who remained prominent through most of the 19th century and who argued that women's education should develop their intellectual capacities for better execution of responsibilities in the woman's sphere.

Bill for the More General Diffusion of Knowledge a bill for the public funding of locally controlled schools that Thomas Jefferson twice tried to push through the Virginia legislature (1779 and 1817) but which failed to pass.

Black Codes after Reconstruction, local laws passed throughout the South that restricted African Americans' civil and political rights.

Black English Vernacular linguists' term for the grammatical and phonemic variant of English used today in many African American communities; its origins lie in slaves' success in developing a common language from an amalgam of different African languages and English.

boarding school schools designed to house and teach children away from their home communities. Especially problematic for Native American children because boarding schools were used to replace native culture and language with European culture.

bourgeoisie originally, European city dwellers who were members of the new middle class that emerged after the breakdown of feudalism; neither nobility nor serfs nor clergy, they were part of the new classes that formed as a result of capitalism and commerce.

Brown v. *Board of Education* Supreme Court case of 1954 in which the Court ruled that racially segregated schools are, by definition, unequal in terms of the educational experiences they provide.

Bureau of Ethnology a bureau of social science active during the New Deal; used experts to create a greater awareness of tribal cultural and potential cultural obstacles to administration.

Bureau of Indian Affairs an agency of the Department of the Interior charged with the administration of American Indian lands and goods.

capitalism the "free market" economic system in which money and credit are exchanged for goods and services according to the laws of supply and demand in an attempt not only to make a living but also to secure financial profits that can be invested to generate further income and wealth; although known as a "free market" system, capitalism can be regulated heavily by governments.

character education the effort to shape young people's moral and ethical dimensions; took different forms in different historical periods; grounded in religious instruction in the 17th and 18th centuries; more secular and nonsectarian in the common-school era and increasingly secular thereafter.

charter schools an idea popularized in the 1990s to encourage teachers, parents, and others to develop new approaches to schools and obtain from the state a "charter," or a contract permitting a school to depart from certain state regulations to create an innovative schooling environment.

Cherokee Nation v. *Georgia* 19th-century Supreme Court case that, with leadership from Justice John Marshall, established the doctrine of Native peoples as "domestic dependent wards" of the federal government.

civic freedom in Aristotle's formulation, the aspect of liberty that emphasizes limitations on the government's power to interfere with the right of the individual to live as he or she chooses; the basis of the notion of civil liberties and civil rights today.

classical liberal historians' term for an array of beliefs and values that emerged in about the 16th century after the breakdown of feudalism, emphasizing individual rights and liberties, social progress, human reason, and scientific inquiry; "classical" denotes links to classical Athenian roots and differentiates it from the "modern" liberalism of the 20th century.

college education of women historically restricted to males, college-level education of women began to be more common in the 19th century as women's colleges were founded, of which several exist today, though some have merged with historically male colleges; most women throughout the 20th century were educated in coeducational institutions, though for most of the century women's professional options were concentrated in teaching, nursing, social work, and other female-dominated occupations.

Collier, John (1884–1968) a social reformer who advocated for Native Americans. Commissioner for the Bureau of Indian Affairs in the President Franklin D. Roosevelt administration, from 1933-1945.

colonial education of women generally available only to middle-class White girls and women, usually provided at home by parents and tutors, and often justified by the need for women to be able to read the Bible and teach their sons.

community college a two-year college developed to provide local postsecondary education, largely for vocational purposes but also equipping some students to transfer to four-year institutions.

community control emphasis on community democratic decision making in contrast to state or federal government control of social and educational programs.

containment U.S. foreign policy that used multiple strategies (military, economic, and political) to keep communism and socialism from power in foreign nations, former colonies, and the developing world in general.

conventional literacy an account of literacy that accepts a minimal criterion, such as the ability to sign one's name, as evidence of the ability to read and write and that results in estimates of literacy rates in contemporary society from 97 to 99 percent.

The Crisis a journal founded and edited by W. E. B. Du Bois shortly after the founding of the NAACP in 1910; dedicated to educating people about racial discrimination; reached a peak circulation of 100,000 in 1918.

critical literacy an account of literacy that emphasizes not merely the ability to read and write but the ability to use reading and writing as the basis of higher-order thinking skills that allow a person to analyze and critically evaluate that which is read and written.

critical theory an educational perspective that focuses on the problem of how power is unequally distributed in contemporary society. This perspective focuses on the educational consequences of antidemocratic social arrangements, as well as ways to educate people to live more democratic lives. This critical perspective analyzes inequalities based on many social factors, including class, race, ethnicity, gender, and sexual orientation.

cult of domesticity emphasized in the 18th and 19th centuries; the general view that a woman's place is in the home, with the corollary view that women should be educated to execute the responsibilities of home and hearth.

cultural deficit theory explanations that find that the cultural backgrounds of different ethnic groups are the source of low-income and minority children's relatively weaker academic performance in schools.

cultural deprivation studies sociological studies conducted in the 1960s that appeared to prove that the source of low-income and minority children's relative lack of success in public schools was insufficient cultural and linguistic stimuli at home, dooming to failure efforts to teach such children in schools.

cultural literacy a conception of literacy that emphasizes not the ability simply to read and write but the ability to make sense of what is read through familiarity with a wide range of cultural references and allusions.

culturally relevant pedagogy (see *culturally responsive pedagogy*)

culturally responsive pedagogy approaches to and methods of teaching that seek to respond to and incorporate the cultural knowledge of students, with an eye toward building new learning on respect for what students already know from their own cultural experiences.

cultural pluralism a condition in which social and educational values encourage a variety of ethnic and cultural perspectives, languages, and values that enrich one another through their harmonious coexistence.

cultural subordination theory an explanation for the learning gap between the haves and the have-nots that emphasizes that the primary thing the haves possess is the power to reward their cultural knowledge, skills, and styles though institutions that favor those factors over other forms of cultural capital.

Dawes Allotment Act a statute of 1887 that enabled American Indian tribal members to claim private ownership of tribal land.

decentralization in the context of school governance, the shift from a single authority for all schools in a region or district to more local forms of authority.

democracy usually understood as government by informed popular consent rather than by a monarch or an elite group; defined more specifically by Jefferson, Du Bois, and Dewey, among others, who emphasize democracy as a mode of government that educates citizens through participation in decision making (see developmental democracy).

democratic ethics in the context of teaching as a profession, the commitment to democratic values, including the view that all people should be educated toward having an effective voice in the decisions that affect their lives.

democratic localism an emphasis on the value of people making shared decisions in their immediate circumstances as much as possible so that they have genuine influence on the decisions that affect their lives in local contexts.

democratic pluralism related to cultural pluralism; values cultural differences and seeks to preserve them in processes of self-governance.

developmental democracy a political and educational view that values popular participation in decision making in part because such participation educates or develops the capacities of those who participate in it.

Dewey, John (1859–1952) a philosopher of democratic life and democratic education who founded the University of Chicago Laboratory School to test and develop his progressive educational theories.

discipline and a "pedagogy of love" disciplinary approach which exploits the child's emotions and need for love and acceptance, to effect desired behavior.

"divine right" of the nobility a late feudal period justification for the absolute authority of the monarchy in which it was claimed that the authority of the monarch derived from God's will and therefore could not be questioned.

dominant culture that culture which is most strongly represented in a society's power structure and institutions such as government and schooling; may be a numerical minority in the culture as a whole but exerts disproportionate power.

Du Bois, W. E. B. (1868–1963) a scholar and political activist; author of Souls of Black Folk and numerous other books; founded and edited the Crisis, an early NAACP publication.

due process protection in schools grounded in the Fourteenth Amendment to the Constitution; equal protection under the law is granted to students and teachers just as it is to citizens in the larger society.

educational excellence a term popularized in the 1980s when the report *A Nation at Risk* drew public attention to the mediocrity of schooling in the United States.

Educational Testing Service considerably influenced by James B. Conant; established in 1947 by the College Entrance Examination Board, the Carnegie Corporation, and the American Council on Education as a nonprofit center for administering the Scholastic Aptitude Examination and other higher education exams.

Education for All Handicapped Children Act passed by Congress in 1975 as Bill 94-142; required school districts to educate special education students in the "least restrictive environment" possible so that they would be educated as much as possible with the general population of students, with accommodations made to support the learning of students with special needs.

education through participation (see *democracy* and *democratic localism*) in government, an emphasis on democracy as a system of government that develops people's capacity for decision making and self-rule while engaging them in processes of democratic decision making; in education, applies to the philosophy of learning by doing.

elementary schools a local school for teaching the basics of literacy, mathematics, and social knowledge and skills, with origins in colonial America and with a prominent role in Jefferson's efforts and later efforts to provide public education in the United States.

Eliot, Charles (1834–1926) perhaps the most influential educator of his era; Harvard University president from 1869 to 1909; represented many of the social efficiency dimensions of progressive education.

equality sameness of treatment or condition, as distinct from equity, which emphasizes fairness of treatment or condition.

equity fairness of treatment or condition among two or more parties; does not entail equality of treatment or condition; sometimes requires differential treatment.

ESL instruction techniques of teaching English as a second language; differs from bilingual instruction in that little or no effort is made to teach in the student's native language; often used when speakers of several languages are instructed at the same time in English.

ethnic diversity a condition in which people from two or more different cultural backgrounds share a common social or institutional space.

ethnicity a person's cultural inheritance, including language, values, customs, beliefs, and usually cultural identity.

eugenics a view emerging in the latter half of the 19th century that the human gene pool should be controlled by social policy that discourages reproduction of some populations of people while encouraging reproduction among other, more desired groups.

expert management an element of modern liberal ideology that seeks to place institutional decision making as much as possible in the hands of a few people who have been trained to have specialized knowledge and skills.

faculty psychology a theory of learning, popular in the 18th and 19th centuries, asserting that the mind is a collection of separate faculties (such as memory, reasoning, and aesthetic taste) that can be developed through vigorous exercise and that learning in some areas transfers to increased learning in other areas; at its most extreme, led to the nonscience of phrenology, which measured the human skull to draw conclusions about a person's character and mental faculties.

faith in human reason a prominent element of classical liberal ideology; asserts that if individuals and groups are free from government oppression, their inherent ability to reason will be the most effective authority for their actions, especially if that reason is informed by education.

feminization of teaching a change in the profession of teaching that came about in the 19th century; the majority of schoolteachers were male at the beginning of the 1800s but were female by the end of the Civil War.

feudalism a system of political and economic organization prevailing in Europe from about the 9th to the 15th centuries; based on the holding of lands by the nobility and clergy, with serfs bound to the land and the landholder by birth and a system of tenant farming and without a voice in government.

Fifteenth Amendment to the U.S. Constitution adopted on March 30, 1870; reads in part, "The right of citizens of the United States to vote shall not be denied or abridged by the United States or by any State on account of race, color, or previous condition of servitude."

Fourteenth Amendment to the U.S. Constitution adopted on July 28, 1868; reads in part, "All persons born or naturalized in the United States, and subject to the jurisdiction thereof, are citizens of the United States and of the State wherein they reside . . . nor shall any State deprive any person of life, liberty or property, without due process of law; nor deny any person within its jurisdiction the equal protection of such laws."

Freedman's Bureau formed by Congress in 1867 under the first Reconstruction act; a U.S. government agency designed to help ex-slaves exercise new economic, civil, and political rights and freedoms in the post–Civil War United States.

freedom one of the basic components of classical liberal ideology; committed to preventing government interference with individuals and groups in their personal, intellectual, and economic lives.

Freire, Paulo (1921–1997) author of *Pedagogy of the Oppressed* (1972); a Brazilian educator whose work was translated throughout the world in the 1970s and 1980s and after his death in the 1990s; seminal theorist in critical, liberationist pedagogy.

functional literacy a conception of literacy that emphasizes the level of ability to read and write necessary to function well in a particular society.

gender sensitivity versus gender bias a distinction based on the difference between awareness of when differences in gender may contribute to differences in how life and learning are experienced and the assumption that characteristics in individuals are based on their membership in a sex group.

general academic track the "middle" ability group or "track" that emerged in 20th-century schools between the academic or college preparatory track and the vocational track.

general education broad education across the major domains of mathematics and science, social sciences, and humanities to produce a well-educated person in a nonspecialized sense.

genetic deficit theory the view that differences in group achievement among different ethnic groups can be explained by a different genetic endowment of intellegence in those groups.

GI Bill of Rights an act of Congress passed after World War II that allowed military veterans to attend colleges and universities at government expense.

glass ceiling for women an invisible barrier in the workplace and government above which it is supposedly difficult for women to rise; explains the very low percentage, for example, of women in CEO positions in Fortune 500 companies and of women in the U.S. Senate.

Goals 2000: Educate America Act: a congressional act to implement a set of far-reaching goals for public education to be reached by the year 2000; outlined by the first Bush administration as *America 2000* and continued in the Clinton administration as *Goals 2000*.

grammar schools in Jefferson's proposal for public schooling in the state of Virginia, the tier of schooling after elementary school; reserved for those who could afford it and those meriting scholarships; formal academic work would include the study of Latin, Greek, composition, mathematics, and other liberal studies.

Grimke, Sarah M. (1792–1873) a radical feminist political activist and author who was prominent in the first half of the 19th century.

happiness a term Jefferson borrowed from Aristotle to designate the fundamental importance of the satisfaction of the individual as a measure of the goodness of the social order, as in "life, liberty, and the pursuit of happiness."

Head Start project a federal government–funded program that started in the Great Society years of the early 1960s; supported preschool education for low-income children.

heterogeneous grouping the practice of placing children with different academic skill levels in the same group for purposes of instruction (as opposed to *homogeneous grouping*).

hidden curriculum a term coined by the educational researcher Philip Jackson in the 1960s to describe the socializing processes of schooling that are not described in the formal or academic curriculum.

Hispanic versus Latino terms debated among the descendants of Spanish-speaking Americans because each of these identity names has its own history and political significance and because different Americans identify more with one of those political histories than with the other; similarly, some Americans of Mexican descent prefer the designation Chicano to either Hispanic or Latino.

historically Black colleges: colleges (some of which have become universities) that were founded for the higher education of African Americans after the Civil War.

Holmes Report named after the former dean of the Harvard School of Education and published by representatives of about a hundred leading research universities in the United States in 1985; the first Holmes Report presented a blueprint for the education of the nation's teachers; later reports focused on reform of schools of education of the teaching profession.

homogeneous grouping the practice of placing children with similar academic skill levels in the same group for purposes of instruction (as opposed to *heterogeneous grouping*).

humanitarian reform in the context of 19th-century reform movements in the United States, refers to various efforts to address social problems such as alcoholism, slavery, prison cruelty, urban poverty, and discrimination against women.

ideological hegemony an explanation of social harmony in the presence of deep social inequality; emphasizes the domination of public discourse by such a limited range of explanations that the disadvantaged lack access to alternative explanations of the social order that might mobilize resistance to powerlessness.

ideology as used in this book, the constellation of beliefs, values, and habits of thought shared by people in a large or small social group; a society's explanations of and justifications for the prevailing social order or an envisioned ideal order.

information marketplace versus marketplace of ideas a distinction designed to draw attention to the difference between the Jeffersonian ideal of an unfettered exchange of ideas in search of the truth and contemporary practices that package new ideas as products to be sold to the consumer.

intellectual freedom one of the basic components of classical liberal ideology; emphasizes the right of the individual to believe as he or she chooses, uncoerced by government power; closely related to religious freedom.

John Birch Society an extreme right-wing group particularly active in southern and southwestern states in the middle of the 20th century.

labor market the totality of jobs for which people may offer themselves for employment; the labor market for physicians is typically more limited than the labor market for fast-food workers.

Lau* v. *Nichols Supreme Court decision that Chinese-language students were not receiving sufficient support for learning in schools; led to legislation mandating bilingual instruction in public schools when non–native English speakers needed bilingual instruction to be able to learn subject-matter material.

liberal education historically, the education appropriate to a free person; typically construed today as a broad, general education that equips a person to think well in a wide range of domains and to know at least one discipline in depth.

life-adjustment education an approach to public education popularized by Charles Prosser and others in the 1940s who thought that for students who were not college-bound, an education preparing them for their life roles as family members and consumers was appropriate; criticized as a "soft" curriculum in the 1950s and 1960s.

literacy as a social construction a concept emphasizing that what counts as literate, like how important it is to be literate, varies with the cultural context.

Mann, Horace (1796–1859) a prominent Massachusetts legislator and advocate of humanitarian reforms who became executive secretary of the Massachusetts Board of Education and took a leadership role in establishing a system of public common schools and normal schools that would become models for the nation.

mass media broadcast, electronic, and print media that reach large proportions of the population nationally and internationally in the contemporary world.

McCarthy, Senator Joseph (1908–1957) a rabid anticommunist congressman during the 1940s and 1950s; his vicious attacks on "communist sympathizers" and "fellow travelers" who were prominent in entertainment and the arts destroyed many careers and eventually his own.

meritocracy a term for the view popularized by Jefferson, Conant, and others in different times and places that a society's institutions should be led by those who merit it by their talent and character.

Merriam Report "The Problem of Indian Administration"; a report that increased the awareness of social and educational problems on tribal lands during the 1920s.

Mississippi Plan a system of codes and laws instituted by the state of Mississippi to deprive African Americans of their civil and political rights after Reconstruction; the eventual basis for Jim Crow laws throughout the South until the 1954 Supreme Court decision *Brown* v. *Board of Education.*

model minority a term wrongly applied to Asian Americans to show that Asian American immigrant groups have adjusted successfully to U.S. mainstream culture.

monopoly capitalism in contrast to simple capitalism, a 19th-century development that consolidated control of the market for particular goods or services in one or a few companies.

multicultural education an educational reform initiative to improve learning for all children by emphasizing the cultural contexts of learning and helping schools respond better to children of different ethnic backgrounds by using those differences as a foundation on which to build new learning.

NAACP the National Association for the Advancement of Colored People; an advocacy group formed in 1910 to fight for the legal, civil, and political rights of African Americans.

NAEP (National Assessment of Educational Progress) an ongoing longitudinal study of student learning in schools; sometimes referred to as "the nation's report card" because it is informative about educational progress across the United States.

National Board for Professional Teaching Standards (NBPTS) founded with philanthropic funds as a direct result of the school reform movement that began in the 1980s; began assessing teacher quality by using a portfolio assessment method in the mid-1990s; has assessed thousands of teachers who have applied voluntarily for certification.

nationalism one of the basic components of classical liberal ideology, emerging from and in contrast to feudalism; the emphasis is not on the tribe, estate, or city-state but on the nation as the basic political unit and source of political identity.

A Nation at Risk a 1983 report by the Presidential Commission on Excellence in Education; declared the United States "at risk" in the competitive world marketplace and compared the educational system of the nation to an "act of war" by a foreign power; received a great

deal of publicity and launched public dialogue on school reform lasting almost two decades.

natural aristocracy (meritocracy) classical liberal term used by Jefferson to indicate the need for a system that granted leadership to those with talent and character as opposed to those with inherited wealth and power, whom Jefferson termed the "false" aristocracy.

natural law one of the basic components of the classical liberal ideology that emerged in the Enlightenment era; committed to the view that the universe (nature) operates according to scientific principles or laws that are understandable by human reason.

negative freedom freedom achieved through a *lack* of government interference.

new immigration the 19th-century shift in immigration to the United States from northern and western European immigrants to southern and eastern European immigrants.

new psychology a loose constellation of approaches to studying the psyche and human learning; emerged around the beginning of the 20th century and emphasized nonrational, subconscious, behavioral sources of human actions rather than rational and consciously chosen sources.

No Child Left Behind Act of 2001 controversial centerpiece of the George W. Bush education platform, emphasizing educational accountability for school systems, high-stakes testing for all students, and an increased requirement for "highly qualified" teachers.

normal school initiated in the United States by Horace Mann; a post-secondary or college-level school for the preparation of teachers.

On the Origin of Species Charles Darwin's (1809–1882) revolutionary 1859 scientific study of how species evolve over time to adapt to their environment.

pedagogy approaches to and methods of teaching.

pedagogy of love (discipline and a pedagogy of love.) Horace Mann's view that teachers could be more effective by developing relationships with their students based on affection rather than relationships based on authoritarianism and punishment.

Plato's myth of the metals the "noble lie" or "necessary fiction" that people are born with gold, silver, or bronze in their systems and thus are destined to be in one of three levels of society: at the apex, in the second leadership tier, or among the broad masses.

political economy according to Webster, "a modern social science dealing with the relationship of political and economic processes"; more generally, a society's institutional arrangements and processes.

political freedom a distinction first made by Aristotle, identifying the freedom to exercise political, as distinct from civil, liberties. Whereas civil liberties emphasize the right to live as one chooses, political freedom emphasizes the right to participate in government.

populism a 19th-century movement in the United States that had its origins in rural life and advocated "industrial democracy," or greater local and popular control of industrial production rather than factory production organized and controlled through corporate and governmental collaboration.

profession typically, a "white-collar" occupation characterized by a specialized body of knowledge, requiring college education or beyond, and rewarded with special status and prestige.

professional autonomy the expectation that the members of a profession, such as teaching, will be free to exercise independent judgment based on their expertise.

professional ethics codes of conduct typically meant to ensure that professionals will exercise their expertise in the service of the interests of their clients.

professionalization versus professionalism a distinction intended to emphasize the difference between an occupation taking on the external characteristics of a profession and a commitment among its members to professional conduct, expertise, and ethics.

progress one of the basic components of classical liberal ideology; emphasizes the inevitability of social improvement through the ability of people to reason about how to achieve their best interests together.

progressive educational reform various and sometimes conflicting policies and practices that changed education in the late 19th and early 20th centuries from traditional, academically oriented studies for all students to different schooling experiences for different children, depending on the perceived needs of the child in the context of the perceived needs of the social order; changed the governance of schooling from local to more centralized forms of decision making.

provisional freedom a notion of freedom that is not absolute, but subject to change, even temporary, depending on changing political contexts.

Prussian model the educational system of 19th-century Prussia, which provided free public education, well-educated teachers, and different school experiences for different positions in the social order.

race a term used to identify supposed biological differences among human beings; does not stand up to scientific scrutiny based on biology; based more on social perceptions of human difference and often used to sustain and justify unequal power relations among cultural groups.

racism the practice of treating people unequally and inequitably because of their membership in an ethnic group.

Reconstruction the period mandated by Congress after the Civil War in which the political, social, and economic structure of the South would be rebuilt without slavery; lasted from 1865 to 1877.

redemption the period after Reconstruction when the South would be "redeemed" from the federal interference with state autonomy and White rule.

religious revelation truth revealed through religious texts and authority rather than through the processes of science or reasoning, which could create a basis of opposition to religiously "revealed" truth (revelation).

resistance theory an effort to explain the school performance of low-income and minority children and youth in terms of their noncompliance with school norms that seem "stacked" against them; noncompliance, or resistance expressed in antiacademic and antisocial behaviors, may be seen as an assertion of self in a cultural environment that may not seem to value each child's identity equally.

Scholastic Aptitude Test (SAT) founded in the early 20th century to provide a fair predictive tool for college success across secondary schools with different academic standards; has been shown to be of limited predictive value but remains in wide use in the United States.

school choice an educational policy that supports the right of parents to choose whatever public school they want for their children; justified by the view that students perform better if they attend a school chosen for its compatibility with the beliefs and values of the family.

schooling versus education a distinction intended to point out that whatever takes place in schools (schooling) may or may not help develop the individual's qualities of mind and body (education).

school restructuring a general term for any of a number of approaches to school reform that emphasize changing such organizational features of schooling as how decisions are made, the length of the school day, and the allocation of time during the school day.

scientific administration the application of social science research to social policy.

scientific reason one of the basic components of classical liberal ideology; emphasizes the human ability to understand the world through agreed-on, systematic processes of discovery of truth as opposed to understanding the world through revealed truth or on the authority of others.

sectarianism in organized religion, the strong focus on differences among various orders (or sects) of the same religion, even to the point of conflict among them.

Seneca Falls Convention of 1848 historically important conference on women's political and civil rights held in Seneca Falls, New York, featuring notable activists such as Elizabeth Cady Stanton and the abolitionist Frederick Douglass.

service occupations the fastest-growing sector in the late 20th-century and early 21st-century labor market in terms of the total number of jobs; usually refers to relatively low-skill, low-pay jobs providing services to others, such as domestic labor and food service.

sex-role socialization the shaping of beliefs, values, and behaviors in accordance with gendered social expectations about differences between the sexes.

sex versus gender a distinction between the biological differences between males and females and the social meanings attached to those differences; "gendered" occupations are grounded not in biological differences between the sexes but in social beliefs about what is appropriate for men and women to do.

skilled artisanship in contrast to low-skill factory labor, a mode of production of goods that emphasized highly skilled labor producing and marketing uniquely individual products one piece at a time, whether in textiles, leather, wood, or another type of conversion of natural resources to handcrafted products.

Slums and Suburbs written in the early 1960s by James B. Conant after the success of *The American High School Today* to address educational differences between low-income urban neighborhoods and middle-income, largely White suburbs.

social efficiency a philosophy of centralized public policy or educational policy formation that places the good of the larger social order ahead of a commitment to full participation by all individuals in shaping that order.

social foundations of education the cultural contexts within which human learning takes place; the study of those cultural contexts.

social meliorism the belief that society can be improved slowly over time through organized human effort.

social theory efforts to explain data about humans living together in groups of various kinds; perspectives on human association used to guide the search for information about social groups as well as to explain that information.

socioeconomic class term derived from sociology, which describes a status level in society derived from income, occupation, and family economic history.

Sputnik the Soviet Union's first human-made vehicle to orbit the earth in space (1957); preceded a similar effort by the United States and caused national concern over Soviet technological superiority.

standardized achievement testing for accountability a 1990s emphasis of the contemporary school reform movement, continuing into the new century, that seeks to hold school districts, schools, administrators, teachers, and students accountable for learning through frequent and systematic use of achievement tests to measure student learning.

Taylorization named after the efficiency expert Frederick W. Taylor; a process of factory production developed in the late 19th century and early 20th century that broke complex production skills into the simplest component parts so that each worker would repeat a simple activity over and over to achieve increased productivity.

Thirteenth Amendment to the U.S. Constitution adopted on December 18, 1865; reads in part, "Neither slavery nor involuntary servitude, except as a punishment for crime whereof the party shall have been duly convicted, shall exist within the United States, or any place subject to their jurisdiction."

Title IX a federal act passed in 1972 that prohibits inequitable treatment of students in schools on the basis of sex, including in extracurricular and sports activities; has been credited for U.S. women's successes in world athletic competitions since the mid-1990s.

tracking and detracking tracking refers to the practice of "ability grouping" students by skill differences in schools for the purposes of instruction and preparation for different academic and occupational futures; detracking is the effort to resist such grouping of students.

training versus education a distinction intended to point out the difference between being prepared for the reliable performance of skills for a particular role (such as in medical training or musical training) and being prepared for a variety of social roles that may require a wide range of knowledge, skills, and critical perspectives (such as a liberal education).

tribal self-determination a term that developed during the 1960s to describe the desire of Indian tribes and communities for self-government.

Troy Female Seminary founded by Emma Hart Willard in 1821 in Troy, New York; a school for young women that prepared hundreds of schoolteachers for eastern schools before the normal school system was developed by Horace Mann.

Tuskegee Institute founded by Booker T. Washington in 1881; an institution for the vocational training of African American youth that later became a major university and is now counted prominently among the nation's historically Black colleges and universities.

university in the United States today, a higher education institution that typically has undergraduate and graduate degree programs in multiple fields in the sciences, social sciences, and humanities; has its origins in 17th- and 18th-century colleges and academies as well as in 19th-century normal schools, historically Black institutions of higher education, and the European research university.

urbanization growth in the size and/or number of cities as a society's population shifts from rural to urban life.

virtue one of the basic components of classical liberal ideology; emphasizes the good character of the individual as demonstrated in good works for others and visible religious devotion or piety.

vocational education the policy and practice of providing experiences that prepare people for specific occupational futures; historically implemented at the expense of a more general or liberal education that develops a range of intellectual capacities for a wide variety of political, personal, and occupational possibilities.

voucher system for schools a proposed approach to public schooling that would provide government money to the family, not to the school system, so that the family could spend that educational allocation (voucher) in any school it chose, public or private, religious or secular.

Washington, Booker T. (1856–1915) founder of the Tuskegee Institute and a high-profile leader of African Americans at the end of the 19th century and the first 15 years of the 20th; the author of *Up from Slavery*.

Willard, Emma Hart (1787–1870) the founder of the Troy Female Seminary in Troy, New York, and a prominent advocate of women's education.

Wollstonecraft, Mary (1759–1797) an 18th-century British feminist who argued for political and civil rights and equality for women and wrote that marriage was an ingenious device for enslaving women; author of *A Vindication of the Rights of Woman* (1792).

Worcester v. *Georgia* a Supreme Court case that strengthened the federal status of tribes and excluded them from state control.

Photo Credits

Part 1

Opener: Courtesy of The University of Pittsburgh, Digital Research Library

Chapter 1

Opener: © Look and Learn/The Bridgeman Art Library; p. 8: © Design Pics/Ron Nickel RF; p. 12: © Bettman/Corbis

Chapter 2

Opener: Courtesy of The University of Pittsburgh, Digital Research Library; p. 26: North Wind Picture Archives; p. 29: Library of Congress; p. 31: © Pixtal/age Fotostock RF; p. 33: The Granger Collection, NYC; p. 41: © Stock Montage; p. 42: © Bettman/Corbis

Chapter 3

Opener: Courtesy of The University of Pittsburgh, Digital Research Library; p. 53: Culver Pictures; p. 59: © National Portrait Gallery, Smithsonian Institution/Art Resource, NY; p. 62: Culver Pictures; p. 63: Culver Pictures; p. 67: Culver Pictures; p. 69: Library of Congress; p. 70: North Wind Picture Archives; p. 72: © National Portrait Gallery, Smithsonian Institution/Art Resource, NY

Chapter 4

Opener: Courtesy of The University of Pittsburgh, Digital Research Library; p. 88: © Bettman/Corbis; p. 94: Courtesy Everett Collection; p. 95: © Carl Linde/AP Photo; p. 99: © AP Photo; p. 102: The Granger Collection, NYC; p. 108: Library of Congress; p. 111: © Bettman/Corbis

Chapter 5

Opener: Courtesy of The University of Pittsburgh, Digital Research Library; p. 127: © UPI/Bettman/Corbis; p. 129: © Bettman/Corbis; p. 131: © Getty Images; p. 133 (top): © Bettman/Corbis; p. 133 (bottom): © Corbis RF; p. 138: The Granger Collection, NYC; p. 143: Library of Congress; p. 145: © Bettman/Corbis

Chapter 6

Opener: Courtesy of McGraw-Hill Companies; p. 160: USDA Photograph Archives; p. 166: © Bettman/Corbis; p. 170: Library of Congress; p. 172: Library of Congress; p. 175: Library of Congress; p. 179: Library of Congress; p. 180: McGraw-Hill Higher Education wishes to thank the Crisis Publishing Co., Inc., the publisher of the magazine of the National Association for the Advancement of Colored People, for the use of the "Crisis" magazine cover first published in the April 1936 issue of Crisis Magazine

Chapter 7

Opener: Courtesy of The University of Pittsburgh, Digital Research Library; p. 199: © Hulton Collection/Getty Images; p. 201 (left): Culver Pictures; p. 201 (right): Culver Pictures; p. 203: © Bettman/Corbis; p. 207: Culver Pictures; p. 211: © Bettman/Corbis

Chapter 8

Opener: American Book Company; p. 226: © Bettman/Corbis; p. 228: © akg-images/Newscom; p. 230: © Bettman/Corbis; p. 233: © UPI/Bettman/Corbis; p. 236: © Chris Ryan/Getty Images RF

Part 2

Opener: © PhotoAlto/Alamy RF

Chapter 9

Opener: Courtesy of McGraw-Hill School Division; p. 258: © Digital Vision RF; p. 259: © Mark Edward Atkinson/Blend Images RF; p. 265: © AP Photo; p. 273: © Susan See Photography RF; p. 280: © Design Pics/Ron Nickel RF

Chapter 10

Opener: Courtesy of McGraw-Hill Companies; p. 296: The Granger Collection, NYC; p. 299: © McGraw-Hill Companies, Inc. Mark Dierker, photographer; p. 305: © Tetra Images/Getty Images RF; p. 312: © Digital Vision/Getty Images RF; p. 314: © Ruth Dixon/Stock Boston; p. 317: © AP Photo

Chapter 11

Opener: Courtesy of McGraw-Hill Companies; p. 334: © Lifesize/Getty Images RF; p. 335: © Zero Creatives/Getty Images RF; p. 346: © Yann Layma/Getty Images

Chapter 12

Opener: Courtesy of McGraw-Hill Higher Education; p. 360: © AP Photo; p. 370: © Nick White/Getty Images RF; p. 374: © Fancy Photography/Veer RF; p. 377: © Bob Daemmrich/Stock Boston

Chapter 13

Opener: © Jack Kurtz/The Image Works; p. 400: © LWA/Dann Tardif//Blend Images/Corbis RF; p. 404: © BananaStock/PunchStock RF; p. 405: © Elizabeth Crews; p. 411: © Hill Street Studios/Blend Images RF; p. 414: © Hill Street Studios/Blend Images RF

Chapter 14

Opener: © Hazel Hankin/Stock Boston; p. 435: © Rudi Von Briel/PhotoEdit

Index